FROM GRACE TO GLORY . . .

FROM GRACE TO GLORY . . .

A Little Bit About A Lot of Things

Naomi Ruth Jones Kilpatrick

Library of Congress Control Number:		2017903858
ISBN:	Hardcover	978-1-5245-9115-1
	Softcover	978-1-5245-9113-7
	eBook	978-1-5245-9114-4

Print information available on the last page.

Rev. date: 03/31/2017

To order additional copies of this book, contact:
Xlibris
1-888-795-4274
www.Xlibris.com
Orders@Xlibris.com
543275

CONTENTS

Dedicated to
Lenzo, Sharon, Kevin
My Future

In Memory of
My Parents
Cora Virginia Shockley Jones
James Thurlo Jones

&
My Three Angels
Lenard, Katrina, Linda

for

showing me the Mosaic of Life

PREFACE

I have wanted to write a brief history of our church for a number of years; too many years. It seems that I've thought about it for so many years instead of just doing it. It took confidence in my skills, which I felt I lacked, namely words. Time was a factor for it seems I always had something else to do, something more important. Materials, records, information, facts were not a real problem because when I got this vision, I began collecting "stuff". My dream was a church history, but I knew that would be my history as well, so I gathered and kept everything that seemed pertinent. There was no place for writing; no quiet, lonely place of beauty, no environment of silence. I needed to be able to think, to reflect, and to pray. There was much encouragement from the brethren years ago to write. As a matter of fact, they were enthusiastic and excited about my attempt at "searching the roots" of the little place that we love, Grace & Glory Gospel Chapel. I sought to honor the assembly, not as though it is above all others, but to show that we are, indeed, one together with them; to show that a little church family of believers can make a difference in this world of ours. Grace & Glory is a testament to, not only our surrounding neighbors, but to my family, my progenies, my descendents.

I now have the confidence to begin this writing journey, knowing that God will give me the words that are needed to write a clear, precise, and hopefully, enjoyable account.

My "kick-off" date was June 10, 2011.

The next day began with prayer and scripture reading: I Timothy 1:1, 12-17; Proverbs 10; and Psalm 10. I fed my cat, "Myles", and began writing. Each day of the process was a struggle, a struggle with having enough time to write with all of the things I have to do to run my household. At home, I am in constant motion, doing "first one thing and then another."

A typical day begins at around 5:30 A.M., washing and drying the kids clothes, fixing breakfast, and getting the kids up and ready for school. Like most kids, they hug those covers as long as they can. They shower and eat breakfast and then off to school – 4th grade for him, 2nd grade for her. At 3:06, school ends and I pick them up. They eat a snack, watch a little TV or computer, and then its time to help with their homework. Dinner is prepared and we sit down at the table together, all 4 of us – Lenzo, Le Shawn, Kyonna, and me. The children and I go to bed between 9:30-10:00 PM. Sometimes, I read to them the "Do You See What I See?" books. They have hidden pictures and hidden messages that you have to find. The kids absolutely love this. The 3 of us are very competitive; we each try to find the pictures first.

On March 27, 2012 at 4:47 P.M., I had my little cat, Myles, put to sleep. The cancer, yes, pets have this dredded disease, had caused him to lose weight, so much so that he was "skin & bones. He seemed to be eating more and drinking water continuously, yet still losing weight. I knew something was drastically wrong. When I took him to the "Vet", he said he had a tumor in his kidneys and was in a lot of pain. Lenzo and I had him euthanized at the animal hospital. "Myles" had lived a long life as a cat, 17 years old in human years; not sure what that is in animal years. He had been my son, Lenard's, cat and he lived 8 years after Lenard's death. Myles had a good life because he was a member of the family, and especially loved by Kyonna. He brought us much happiness; now we will go on with our lives having been made richer by his life.

On June 5, 2012, I did some writing, but it seems to be going slowly. Tomorrow is the last day of school so that will free me up to spend a couple of hours more in the morning to write. This morning, I noticed how much I am reliving all the wonderful memories of my loved ones – family and friends. When doing research, it is so exhilirating to see so many historical black events, and so many black contributors . . .

On July 22, 2012, I wrote, "Today is Sunday, July 22, 2012, at 2:00 P.M. Natia and Joe are having their little baby son, Joe, Jr. christened today at Grace & Glory. It is a momentous occasion. There are approximately 30 people in attendance here for the ceremony. A small dinner will be served afterwards.

I wrote a little on my book today. What I'm finding is that I need to write at least 2 hours per day to reach my tentative deadline of November 1, 2012. I'm adding much to it, but I wanted it to be truly historical. My dilemma is having it flow smoothly as it is read. This book is my perception, my recollection of facts, my understanding of its principles, its traditions, and its people. As I look back, this account of my experiences should answer questions:

> **"What did my life really mean?"**
> **"What is my legacy that I leave to my children, grand children, and great-grandchildren?"**
> **"What impact did a small church, a small congregation of believers, have on my legacy?"**

Therefore, I continue on my journey to write this book, and to keep writing until it is finished. And at its completion, hopefully, I would have answered my questions. I will enjoy the ride!

INTRODUCTION

This journey I've partaken, this goal I'm pursuing, this vision I'm fulfilling has been some kind of a joy ride. I started to actually write the manuscript about 3 years ago, but I've collected material over several years. The process of reading to better understand, the process of reading to get knowledge, the process of reading to get a sense of history, and the process of reading for pleasure is the epitome of joy. I have been fascinated to learn the roots of our church, and to learn of the "Brethren Movement." It is affirmation to look at what Grace & Glory's ministry is all about and to check that with the Word of God. The church leadership over these 50 plus years have sought to present the Word of God without "adding to," or "taking away from" its message. They have sought to not "sugar coat" the Word, no fanfare, no show. They are not perfect by any means, but they serve a perfect God.

It has been an awesome experience searching the scriptures more fully. It has given me a renewed joy for the Word. I've been in a "praise mode" as I think of our God and how much He loves us. He loves me through all my mistakes, through all my doubt, through all my discouragements, through all my pain, and, He loves me through all my joys, my "mountain top" experiences, through my "giddiness", through my immaturity, and through all that is "me". My dream has not "dried up like a raisin in the sun", on the contrary, I'm on my way to the realization of my dream. I've begun that process.

My research included the civil rights movement, which was stimulating because I "lived" it as well. The great sacrifices that were made to move this country forward, to move it away from racism and discrimination and disenfranchisement elicited a myriad of emotions. Also, I have watched the evolvement of the Black Church and its' involvement with its community. Some have preached the gospel, some have not, but they have changed their communities by providing food and clothing, by providing financial support, and by giving counseling and other services for families. Churches do make a difference. In this age of social media with so many of our young people disconnected from the values and mores and beliefs of our generation, it gives me hope when I look at the dedication of the Black Church.

As I continued on my journey, doing the research and the collecting, I began to actually put down on paper a brief history of my assembly, Grace & Glory Gospel Chapel, as it relates to my own history. I wanted to tell the truth, as I know it, and to tell the facts as they occurred. However, I can only relate what I have experienced and heard by word of mouth (oral history) and what I have read over the years.

I write to leave a legacy of exploration and discovery; a legacy of honesty and transparency; and a legacy of pride and cultural awareness. God exhorts us in Deuteronomy 6 to instruct our children on their history. The Israelites were to teach their history to their children, day and night. It was important that they know what God had done for them. So it is today. It is important that our children know and remember and understand from whence they came. Only then can they look to the future with hope and anticipation. Only then can they "shape" their future and move in the direction of making a difference in this ever changing, ever shrinking world that we live in.

The title of my book, "From Grace to Glory" – A Little Bit About a Lot of Things – speaks to the legacy I leave my children, my grand children, and my great grand children. As I look back upon my childhood, I see God's grace bringing me through horrible accidents. At a very young age, I burnt my left arm on the face of one of those ancient, heavy black irons. In those days, the women put the iron on the stove to let it get hot to iron the clothes. I don't remember how it happened, but it must have been life –threatening because, for years, the scar covered my whole arm – the outer side. The scar is still there but as I have aged, it has gotten smaller and thinner. Also, when I was two or three years old, I fell into the fire place and burnt my other arm, my right arm. It also covered a large part of my arm. Down south, they lit the small fire place for warmth, as well as, for putting sweet potatoes in it to cook. We ate sweet potatoes for lunch. I developed a dislike for sweet potatoes at an early age, but I had to eat them, or else. I don't know who took care of my burns – it was either my mother or my Aunt Hattie – but I survived. God's grace sustained me. Psychological scars, as well as physical scars remain until this day.

During my teen years, 1947-1951, life was pleasant. I had boyfriends and we did things like – go for a walk around the block, holding hands; go to the show (movies), which I truly enjoyed, and watched the movie intently, remembering every scene. I knew every movie star (it seems) and every movie, which I usually saw over and over. "Gone With the Wind" was an example of that. We'd sit on my front porch, and talk. My friends, Susan Benson, Jean Jones, and Georgia Stewart and their friends would join us. We'd sit for a long time until my mother came to the door and told me to come inside. Very simple living. Kids tried to smoke cigarettes, but no alcohol, no drugs. I remember seeing a boy who died of an apparent drug over dose in the late 1940's. We found him, in the back of our apartment building, in an alley. He was laying on his back with one leg folded underneath the other one. It was an image that stayed with me, even unto this day.

When I met Lenzo and we started to date, he took me riding in someone's car, along with his friends, Robert Davis and his girlfriend and Maurice Waters and his friend. We hung out on the far east side of Chicago, south of Commercial on 91st Street over by the New Friendship Baptist Church. Lenzo's cousin, Willie Joe, lived around that neighborhood back then. Lenzo and I married when I was 17 years old and he was 19 years old. God's grace and mercy sustained me and took me through those years. My young adult life was filled with having babies, raising children, going to undergrad school and studying, day and night it seems. Wherever I went with my children, I had a book. Attending junior college and then graduate school was challenging and stimulating. I met my life long friends – Jackie Crook, Annette Campbell, Lillie Clinton, Nancy Mitchell, Joanie Redus, and Gussie Rose. We studied together and supported each other through the personal ups and downs of weddings, births, losses, and celebrations. God's grace and mercy took us through. My later years included a stellar career that went beyond my wildest dreams. My retirement years are the busiest ever and as I look back at my past years fraught with bad choices and mistakes followed by good choices and forgiveness, it is all good. My days are filled with thanksgiving and praise for "one more day." My "Little Bit

About a Lot of Things" is all about my favorite things, people, and places. My life has developed and mellowed because of these facts.

Being a part of the Jones/Thompson family and the Brockman/ Shockley family is a source of pride. My dad and my mom left a legacy of strength, love, and commitment. The cliches "never give up" and "stick-to-it-tive-ness" came directly from them and permeates my whole being. My dad was an overcomer. Even though he was only 7 years old, he was already plowing the cotton fields in Fitzhugh, Ark. He could barely touch the handles of the plow. While his sisters could attend school, he could not because he had to help out at home. He was the oldest boy, so much of the responsibility of work fell on him. Nothing seemed to dampen his spirit. He was a happy-go-lucky guy, always joking, always laughing, and always fooling around with everybody. He flipped his finger at adversity. He proudly served his country in World War II like other young black men living through the cruel racism and discrimination, but never complaining. When he came home on furlough, he was upbeat, joking and laughing with us. I remember he said to my mother on one of his visits, "You still love me like you used to didn't?" He always brought cheer and laughter with him.

My Aunt Mabel, my mom's sister, had a stroke at a relatively young age, probably in her 50's,. It was a massive stroke that left her partially paralyzed and unable to speak. It was "touch and go" for weeks. The doctors predicted that she was going to be disabled, unable to walk or communicate. However, with therapy, and love and support, Aunt Mabel learned to walk again and to communicate beautifully. She lived alone for years after her husband died and took very good care of herself and her big, German Shepherd dog. She loved going to church on Sundays. She wore fashionable outfits with dress, hat, gloves, and shoes matching. She was very sociable and personable. She loved to talk, always with a smile, and a joke. God's grace and mercy took her through her illness and blessed her with good health and prosperity until she passed away.

It was a blistering, hot early afternoon on a Sunday. The sun was beaming down on us, so much so that it felt like being inside an oven. Lenzo, Le Shawn and Kyonna and I were attending my granddaughter, Keveesha's church to witness her baptism ceremony. We were so happy to see her take this step in her spiritual development. She had accepted the Lord as her savior at an earlier time. After we arrived, other members of our family started showing up to support Veechie - Veech. Kevin's ex-wife,

Veleese, Veechie's mom, was there as well. We had to stand outside in the heat, along with a long line of worshippers waiting for the first session to be over, and the second session to begin. When we finally got inside the church, and started to take our seat toward the front, my husband fell ill. He suffers from diabetes and hypertension and standing in that hot sun caused him to lose consciousness. He collapsed in his seat and the whole church came to a stand still, but the emergency team at the church immediately went into action. The paramedics were called, but the moments before they got there, the team performed CPR on him. Everyone in the church started praying out loud. They continued to work on Lenzo, and at first, he did not respond. They kept working on him, and we anxiously prayed, as well. Finally, his breathing resumed. They shouted, "he's breathing, he's breathing!" There was a loud cheer, en masse, and individual praising God for His mercy. The paramedics came and took him to the hospital.

It was a life – threatening moment, but God's grace and mercy pulled him through.

In the early hours on May 20, 2010, my friend and sorority sister, Carolyn Wortham, lost her beloved son, Tommy, to gun violence. He was victim of a foiled, deadly robbery attempt. His dad, Thomas Wortham, III, a retired policeman shot 2 of the 4 men involved, killing one. Tommy had served two terms in Afghanistan/Iraq and was currently serving the Army National Guard. He was also a Chicago Police Officer. He was only 30 years old. There was an outcry in the media in Chicago when this happened. For days, the newspapers and radio, and television, as well as, other media ran front page coverage. The funeral was held at the Trinity United Church of Christ on Friday, May 28, 2010. For more than four hours, family, friends, and loved ones, and colleagues celebrated the life of Thomas, IV. The church was filled with more than 3000 mourners and more than 1,000 more mourned outside. It was a poignant occasion as different ones paid tribute to his life. His dad, Thomas Wortham, III said after his son's death, "I don't intend to let my son's death be in vain. I intend to start a movement to stop this violence." He and Carolyn have started a movement. There are scholarship programs for young men in Tommy's honor, and the Cole Park has been dedicated in his name. Carolyn and her husband, and her daughter, Sandra have been all over the country, speaking, to help families who have experienced similar tragedies, making a difference in Tommy's name. And now, according to the Chicago Sun – Times, Nov. 14, 2014 Edition, two of the men involved were found guilty of murder and face mandatory life in prison. God's grace and mercy saw the Wortham Family through the most painful period in their lives and He is keeping them on a day by day basis.

Some years ago, my daughter, Sharon, experienced domestic violence in the worst possible way. It was shortly after her marriage to Alex – some 25 years – had ended. She was stabbed, beaten, and douced with gasoline by this absolutely "crazy" man who was insanely jealous and very controlling. She escaped and was taken to the hospital. She made a police report; the man was punished, according to the laws at that time, and Sharon slowly recovered physically. She decided to try and help other women of domestic violence, so she went to several places speaking of her experience, places like Westside Holistic Center, etc. (after her healing and after her own counseling) Sharon went on to serve God in a mighty way, using skills and gifts that God blessed her with to create programs, write messages of comfort for the bereaved, serving as financial officer for 4 organizations – CCWC, Circle Y Ranch, Iota Phi Lambda Sorority, Inc., and Grace & Glory Gospel Chapel. To God be the glory for her life.

In 1994, my granddaughter, La Shundra, and Tierra's dad, Genoit suffered an invasion of men with guns in their apartment. It was late night/ early morning. Tierra was three years old. The thugs started shooting; Shundra shielded Tierra with her body from the gun shots, but took a bullet to her neck. Geno and Tierra were not shot; but Shundra was rushed to the hospital in critical condition. I went into "caniptions", hollering and screaming when I got the news. My mother was with me when I went to the hospital. I thought she was going to die, but the bullet had passed through her neck without hitting arteries or vital tissue. The doctor later said she was very lucky. God saved her life. The doctor had done a wonderful job of working on her and keeping her alive. It was a miracle because I thought we had lost our granddaughter. God's grace and mercy pulled her through. I took my first retirement from my job as principal at Carver Middle School in Altgeld Gardens after that incident. I felt a need to spend more time with my family. I had promised myself, years before, that if I could not give my all to my very demanding position, I would give it up. God helped me through that whole process and it was a great decision, and what was needed at the time.

On December 17, 2011, on a Saturday, I had a life – threatening, death – defying experience. I was on my way to my daughter's home to take her a mac & cheese casserole. I had baked especially for her. It had snowed earlier and the roads were slippery and dangerous. As I entered the expressway, I accelerated too quickly and went into a virtual spin. It was the most frightening thing I had ever experienced. I could see myself losing my life. In that split second when trucks and cars could have slammed into me, my thoughts went to my two little great-grandchildren and I didn't want them to experience another loss in their young lives. I had lost all control of my car. When the car stopped, it was close to the guard rail and headed in the opposite direction on the Bishop Ford expressway. My car was partially in the first lane. A lady approaching my car, slowed down and put her hand out to stop the traffic in the next lane. Through my tears, and through my total disbelief, I thanked her with my mouth and my hands . . . after the manner of Jane Wyman in the movie "Johnny Belinda". I started my car again, turned it around and drove in the right direction. I was crying, uncontrollably, thanking the Lord for His divine protection. It was like the Lord sent an angel to watch over me; it was God who had kept all those trucks and cars from slamming into me. It was an "out of body" experience. I am still in disbelief and in "praise mode" each day, thankful for each day, each moment with my family. I proceeded to my daughter, Sharon's home and she immediately knew that something was wrong. It was role – reversal as she consoled me, instead of the other way around. She calmed me down, giving words of encouragement. I had been angry when I left home and having unkind thoughts. The Lord permitted that experience to teach me a lesson of forgiveness. I asked the Lord's forgiveness for being angry and unkind. And when I returned home, I apologized and had sweet fellowship with my family. I was thankful for many things, but the most important thing was that I was alone in the car. Thank God, for my life. Psalm 91:11 spoke out to me . . . "He will give His angels charge concerning you, to guard you in all your ways."

My grandson, Charles "Bub" Levy, was traumatized as a young man, when he saw his best friend shot point blank in front of his eyes, right next to him. Bub never got over Anthony's death and how he died. A few months later, he was chased and caught by a gang of thugs who almost killed him. That was enough for us to do something to save our grandsons. He and his brother, Tremaine, then went to Harrisburg, Pennsylvania to live with their dad, my son-in-law, Charles "Butch" Levy. Life is simpler there and things move at a much slower pace. They both have families now and are progressing. God's grace and mercy prompted that move.

There was a period in my marriage, during the early years, where we saw much "rain", "dark clouds", and "whirlwinds". There were problems with the way we were raising our kids; there were financial problems; and there were social problems. My husband and I were going in different directions. We were both seeking happiness in our own way. We wanted to control the pursuit of happiness, not only for our personal selves, but for each other. There was conflict and resentment and vindictiveness. It was a very stressful, very painful time for me. I was crying a lot. I was trying to juggle raising the children, managing my household – cooking, cleaning, washing, ironing, and working on a job, and going to school as well. After I finished school with a degree and a teaching certificate, I started teaching. My youngest son, Lenard, was born in Dec., 1968. I had been teaching for about 1½ years, so I took a maternity leave from my first school, Reavis Elem. School. When I returned, I went to work at Fort Dearborn Elementary School in September, 1969. It was a second grade class. I taught there and really enjoyed it until August, 1972. Those years from 1967 through the early 1970's were difficult in our marriage. I asked God to harden my heart so that I would not feel so much pain, thinking if I could shield my heart, it would give me some relief. I thought of ending my marriage, but I thought of my children and somehow remained. It was difficult for us all. The children were in their teen years and my youngest child was just starting school. The marriage survived because we discovered at that time that we still loved each other very much. We started taking it one day at a time, and remarkably we have been married some 60 plus years. God's grace and mercy took us through that period in our lives.

This story, my story, is like anyone else's story with its ups and downs and highs and lows. It clearly shows that into every life some rain must fall. The "rain" in my history caused the "flowers" of blessings to grow and flourish. My story is about many things, not least of all about my relationship with a gracious and merciful God.

- This story is about an ordinary person, who survived extraordinary experiences, surrounded by extraordinary people.
- This story is about the sheer joy of living each day doing something, being totally engaged in something, in contant motion, every moment doing something pertinent.

This story is about decades of dreaming, and then finally putting pen to paper to make that dream come true.

This story is about two families, my dad's and my mom's, that provided the roots of love and kindness and strength.

This story is about a church that represents integrity and honesty and commitment.

The scripture verse that says, " . . . For where two or three are gathered together in my name, there am I in the midst of them.," has special meaning to us as we sometimes meet in such small numbers. Regardless of the small numbers, this congregation of believers have overcome obstacles and difficulties to keep the ministry going. God's blessings to this ministry is truly a "monument of grace."

This story is about great friends, who love children and are dedicated to making a difference in their lives; friends who are involved in helping other women, teaching them to "know Christ and to make Him known"; friends who enjoy giving to charitable causes; friends who serve as shepherds of the money God has blessed us with. And finally, friends who are actively involved in providing scholarships to help young people further their education.

So, as others read these words of my historical account, sharing my amazing journey, and comparing it to theirs, it is my hope that they too will tell their story. Hopefully, they will tell their children about our generation. Let them know that we didn't just "go through" the civil rights era. We lived the civil rights. We gathered around a little black & white TV and watched white police put water hoses on black marchers as they peacefully protested. Share with them the raw emotions of sadness and anger as we watched them put vicious dogs on black civil rights marchers and beat them with police sticks. Ask for their reaction to our seeing and hearing the deep hatred of white people taunting a little black girl as she enters an all – white school. Tell the children how you felt when President John F. Kennedy was assassinated, and how that whole weekend of events with his death, and then the killing of the man, Lee Harvey Oswald, by Jack Ruby; the funeral of the President with all the pageantry, precision, and ceremonial honor given to a great leader who lost his life partly because he was trying to help African – Americans have a place in America. Let them know that we, as a people, have helped to build this great country, from the beginning, with our blood, sweat, and tears. My generation remembers the day that Dr. Martin Luther King, Jr. was shot and killed. I was at school, teaching my class, when the news came over the radio. The news spread through the country like wild fire. The children and the staff at my school, and at all of the schools in the city, were dismissed early in anticipation of trouble. We drove home (black teachers) with our headlights on to signal solidarity and to pay tribute to a great leader, a great man. People in cities across the country protested, rioted, looted, and proceeded to burn and plunder their own communities. It was all part of the "turbulent 60's." Also, in the 60's, we were shocked and saddened by the deaths of Nat King Cole and Sam Cooke. There was hope as well, as we applauded President Lyndon Baines Johnson for signing the Civil Rights Act and the Voting Rights Act, 1965 and 1968. Our generation went to the movies in the 1940's and 1950's to see some of the greatest movies ever made; we listened on the radio to the blues, jazz, pop music, rock & roll, and to our chagrin, "country music," and it fit us just fine.

As a kid, in the 1940's, I began my love affair with books and it hasn't dissipated in all these years. Reading is my passion, my escape, my make-believe world, and my refuge.

The horror of September 11, 2001 (911) hit us all, very hard, and changed our country into something very different. The tragic event took away freedoms we enjoyed and took for granted as Americans. We felt the grief of each family who lost a loved one. By the grace of God we survived as a nation. Share with the kids what it felt like to elect our very first African-American President, and he is truly African and truly American, with a black African father and a white American mother. Ask them to share their feelings, as well.

So, when I began writing this book, I thought about all of these things; about what my life had been as a kid, as a young person, and as an adult; about my patriarchs and matriarchs who came before me, and how far I have come, and how far I still have to go. As I reflected on everything I've been able to remember, I made a new commitment to see "life with new, clear, and focused eyes."

Additionally, as I listened to voices from the past – voices from my generation – it implored me to tell my story. Now, let that story begin.

Naomi Ruth Kilpatrick

CHAPTER ONE

The History

The history of the Assembly, named Grace & Glory Gospel Chapel, began many years ago with Talbot Burton Nottage (affectionately called T.B.) and his brothers Berlin Martin (affectionately called B.M.) and Whitfield Nottage. These three brothers had been in service for the Lord some 60 years. They were sons of Clementine Nottage and were born on the island of Eluthera in the Bahamas. They were discipled by gifted bible scholars, and they became "street preachers" and evangelists throughout the world.

The Nottage Brothers were avid students of the bible, and dedicated themselves early to the task of planting churches wherever they preached the gospel.

T.B. was the first to travel to the U.S. to seek employment. The others followed shortly afterwards. Like the Apostle Paul in the New Testament; the Nottage Brothers had a passion for spreading the Gospel to the lost all over the world.

When the Brothers arrived in the U.S., they were alarmed to discover a dearth of gospel preaching and a lack of sound bible teaching in the communities in which they settled. This then became their pioneering effort and finally their full time life work.

Sis. Lucy Lewis, one of the charter members of Grace & Glory, said that T.B. and B.M. Nottage came to her home to invite her and her siblings to attend their little church they were starting at 47th and Langley in Chicago. It was a little "store front" church. T.B. would normally preach first and then B.M. would preach. They were "Plymouth Brethren" and helped to establish that at the church. They had a tent and got people interested. The people who got saved in the tent meeting were sent to the store front church.

The Nottage brothers walked the neighborhoods, going from house to house asking people to send their children to Sunday School. This is how Sis. Lucy met Sis. Nola Hicks. They had asked Sis. Hicks' mother to send her to their Sunday School. Sis. Hicks' mother was very "particular" about where she sent her children, and she did not want to send her to this church. She eventually permitted her to attend. Sis. Nola Hicks was a fast learner and enjoyed reciting scripture verses. She never forgot those verses and continued to recite them over the years.

It is not recorded what year this occurred, but the Nottage Brothers made the trip from the Bahamas to Key West, Florida, first by T.B. and then B.M. and Whitfield later. They all found gainful employment in the U.S. By 1913, they were evangelizing in the Black Districts of New York City. They were holding "open air" meetings with hundreds being saved or restored to the Lord Jesus Christ. "Unbeknownst" to the New York Christians, a testimony of "colored" believers had already been established in 1912, in Richmond Heights, Missouri. This assembly was the outgrowth of a home bible study taught by a sister from the nearby Maplewood Bible Chapel. Therefore, this assembly probably has the distinction of truly being the first "Assembly" established among African-American believers in the U.S.

Branching out, Whitfield Nottage moved to Richmond, Virginia where he pioneered with tent meeting ministries. He was blind for his last 20 years of faithful ministry. For the next 20 years, T.B. and B.M. traveled widely throughout the United States. They traveled primarily by trailer, using a P.A. system and distributing bibles and testaments. It was called the "Gospel Trailer". The Gospel Trailer went from New York to Florida, Wisconsin to Kansas, Texas to Mississippi, and from Iowa to Michigan preaching the gospel of deliverance through the shed blood of Jesus Christ. Besides tracts, posters were erected on highways. Bibles were given out in churches and in the streets, in homes, and left on porches.

Everywhere and to everyone was the message shared, the only message of salvation, that glorious gospel of Christ that is still the "power of God unto salvation to everyone that believeth." By 1936, T.B. Nottage and his wife, Josephine and family moved to Cleveland, Ohio evangelizing until 1941. Many inner city assemblies began building buildings instead of using store fronts. A heart attack took his life on April 27, 1972 at the age of 87.

In the meantime, while pastoring the First Baptist Church of Detroit, Rev. Theodore Williams happened to hear a radio broadcast by B.M. Nottage. He was impressed by the message. Mr. Nottage heard Rev. Williams speak on the same station at a different time. B.M. offered Rev. Williams the free use of his gospel tent and on June 2, 1936, Mr. Williams raised the 60 x 40 foot tent. This began an association that would eventually result in the church plantings in Chicago.

Believing firmly that God was calling them to work in Chicago, the two preachers left Detroit. They arrived in Chicago in 1945 after nine years of ministry in Detroit. They found a company of eight believers meeting in a small store front at Langley and 47th Street. Brothers Edwards, Moseley, Stephens, Wooten and others were among these believers.

Earlier visits of the Nottage Brothers were responsible for the Southside Gospel Church Assembly. The present church building was erected in 1947. On July 1, 1947 this assembly was incorporated. It was called Grace Gospel Hall. The original trustees were Brothers Hoy, Mullin, and Williams. For six years, T.B. commuted from New York, coming four (4) to six (6) weeks at a time to help in the work in Chicago. Grace & Glory Gospel Chapel branched out from Grace Gospel Hall under the eldership of Brothers Gall, Mullin, and McCray. Bro. Gall chose the name "Grace & Glory" from the scripture, Psalm 84:11 which reads: "For the Lord God is a sun and shield; the Lord will give grace and glory. No good thing will be withhold from them that walk uprightly."

The late Sis. Nola Hicks remembers going to that little store front church to the Sunday School class. Bro. Mullin was the Superintendent; Sis. Lucy and Sis. Mullin were there also. Bro. Gall and Bro. Talley attended the same church in New York. Bro. Williams came from Detroit and joined Mullin and Gall at the assembly and they were the "Elders". Sis. Lucy and Sis. Mullin were the Sunday School teachers and Sis. Elizabeth, Sis. Lucy's and Sis. Mullin's sister, donated large sums of money to the church. It was still known then as Grace Gospel Hall.

The church then moved to 92nd and State in the back of a funeral home."

Sis. Hicks remembers the whole church having big treats where everyone got presents – everyone got treats during this big celebration. There was one male teacher. Sis. Lucy taught scripture verses and beautiful poems, skits, and plays and children had to memorize every line. You had to be articulate and enunciate each word. Mrs. Lois Davis, a friend of Sis. Hicks left Grace Gospel Hall and went to West Point Baptist Church after the split from 92nd St. There was much "turmoil" and the church split. It became Grace & Glory Gospel Chapel. Bro. Harvey Rollerson stated that he knew Bro. Gall, Bro. Williams, and Bro. Mullin before they incorporated Grace & Glory. He used to meet with them when they were holding meetings at the funeral home.

Bro. Williams was strong in his position and quite controlling at that time. Bro. Gall left and started Grace & Glory Gospel Chapel along with Sis. Lucy, Sis. Mullin, and Bro. Mullin. They started meeting at the YMCA on 51st and Indiana on the lower level and the believers sat in a circle to worship. Communion was conducted each Sunday with <u>one loaf</u>, <u>one cup</u>, and the same two pouches for collection that are currently used.

Inez Douglas was one of the early believers, when they started meeting at the "Y". She brought in Naomi Kilpatrick to the church. Adine Douglas, Inez's mother, Agnes Williams, Agnes Wilson, along with Lucy Lewis, Marian Mullin, and others become part of the believers that were gathered there.

Edward Watkins, who had been led to the Lord by B.M. Nottage, started at Grace & Glory at a later time. Clifford Larkin, from Wheaton, wanted Bro. Watkins to attend a fundamentalist church. Bro. Watkins first attended the Southside Gospel Chapel in the early 1950's where Melvin Banks, Leroy Yates, Bill Pannell, and Bro. Edwards were Elders. Bro. Watkins was mentored by Bro. Moseley and Southside became his "Mother" church. He began to attend Grace & Glory so that he could be close to his job and his home. Bro. Watkins worked 2 jobs to support his family. He remembered at that time, there were very few fundamental churches – where the gospel was preached and where believers worshipped according to the New Testament churches.

Bro. Owbridge Fay Gall established Grace & Glory along with Bro. Frank Mullin, and Bro. Lucius McCray in 1947. The assembly moved to its present location – 7708 South Indiana in 1960 after meeting as a church, with Steward's Foundation in 1957. Steward's Foundation funded the property after having each believer, sitting in a circle, agree to paying off the loan over time. The congregation of believers were all dedicated to keeping that commitment.

The Learning Center of Jesus Christ in Harvey, Illinois was a branch from the Grace & Glory Gospel Chapel with the original leadership of Bro. James Fair and Bro. Ceolia Henry.

Laflin Gospel Chapel and the 86th and Bishop Gospel Hall provided baptismal pools for the newly emerging assemblies in the early days.

Changing ethnic patterns however, resulted in some movement within these churches. Laflin Gospel Chapel remained, however, under the leadership of Bro. Jack Mostert and Bro. McDonald.

The Westlawn Gospel Chapel branched out from the Southside Gospel Church in the 1960's under the leadership of Bro. Leroy Yates, Bro. Melvin Banks, and Bro. Harvey Rollerson.

The Lighthouse Gospel Chapel was another branch out from the Southside Gospel Church Assembly. From the Westlawn Gospel Chapel the following branches emerged; the Roseland Chapel, the Christ Community Church and the Family Gospel Chapel in Bangor, Michigan.

B.M. Nottage continued to reside in Detroit, Michigan where he had founded the Bethany Tabernacle in 1932. He continued to be well known throughout the country. In Chicago, he spoke at the Moody Founders' Week Conferences and on the WMBI Radio Station. B.M. continued his ministry at Bethany Tabernacle until his death, May 3, 1966 at the age of 76.

Much was happening in the United States and throughout the world in the 1940's, 1950's, and the 1960's when Grace & Glory was conceived. These happenings, events provide a backdrop as to what God was doing in this little body of believers.

In 1945, on August 14th World War II ended and that same year, the beloved President Franklin Delano Roosevelt died suddenly on April 12th.

The whole country was in mourning. In 1947, many things happened that affected the thoughts of the believers at Grace & Glory:

- On behalf of the NAACP, W.E.B. DuBois edits and presents to the United Nations an appeal against racism in the U.S.
- Ralph J. Bunche is appointed to the United Nations' Palestine Commission and works with Count Folke Bernadette on the Arab-Israeli dispute; after Bernadette is assassinated, Bunche carries on the negotiations and arranges an armistice in 1949.
- The Presidents' Commission on Civil Rights attacks racial injustice in US in a formal report, "To Secure These Rights." and

In the 1950's, history continued to make a difference in the lives of believers:

- Brown vs. Board of Education had a big impact upon our nation.
- Montgomery Bus Boycott inspired others to get involved in the civil rights' movement.
- In 1955, the Selma to Montgomery March raised awareness of voting discrimination against blacks.
- Jackie Robinson, baseball player, becomes the first black to appear on the cover of "Life" magazine.
- Marian Anderson becomes the first black to sing in the Metropolitan Opera House in New York City In Verdi's "The Masked Ball".

And, of course, the turbulent 60's was a test of resilience and survival for the entire nation. Believers and their families relied on their faith in a loving and caring God as year after year brought tragedy and trials to the black community:

1960 • Fifty blacks, among them Rev. Martin Luther King, Jr. are arrested for sitting in at the Magnolia Room of Rich's Department Store in Atlanta, Georgia. The others are released, but King is sentenced to four months of hard labor at the Reidsville State Prison. Senator John F. Kennedy (D. MA), Democratic presidential candidate, calls Coretta Scott King to express his sympathy. Kennedy's campaign manager and brother, Robert, calls the Georgia judge who sentenced King and pleads for his release. King is released the following day.

1961 • Thirteen CORE sponsored Freedom Riders begin a bus trip throughout the South to force desegregation of terminals. The bus is bombed ten days later, and its passengers are attacked by whites near Anniston, Alabama.

1962 • The US Supreme Court orders the University of Mississippi to admit student James H. Meredith. The governor, Ross Barnett, tries unsuccessfully to block Meredith's admission.

• President John F. Kennedy prohibits racial discrimination in federally financed housing.

1963 • More than 200,000 marchers from all over the US stage the largest protest demonstration in the history of Washington, D.C. The "March on Washington" procession moves from the Washington Movement to the Lincoln Memorial. Rev. Dr. Martin Luther King, Jr. delivers his celebrated "I Have A Dream" speech.

• In a televised address, Pres. John F. Kennedy made an impassioned plea for an end to discrimination in the nation. The US Congress continues to take no action on the presidents' civil rights proposals.

• Four girls – Addie Mae Collins, Denise McNair, Carole Robertson, and Cynthia Wesley – are killed during Sunday School service when the Sixteenth Street Baptist Church is bombed by a group of white men in Birmingham, Alabama.

• Medgar Evers, field secretary for the NAACP is killed outside his home in Jackson, Mississippi.

• President John F. Kennedy is shot and killed while campaigning in Dallas, Texas.

1964 • The bodies of three slain civil rights workers – James E. Cheney, Michael Schwerner, and Andrew Goodman, a college student – are discovered in a shallow grave on a farm outside Philadelphia, Mississippi. The FBI accuses nearly two dozen white segregationists of complicity in the murders.

- The US Congress passes the Civil Rights Act of 1964. The Act gives the US attorney general additional power to protect citizens against discrimination and segregation; forbids discrimination in most places of public accommodation; establishes a federal Equal Employment Opportunity Commission (EEOC); requires the elimination of discrimination in federally assisted programs, authorizing termination of programs or withdrawal of federal funds upon failure to comply; and authorizes the US Office of Education to provide technical and financial aid to assist communities in the desegregation of schools.

- Rev. Martin Luther King, Jr. receives the Nobel Peace Prize in Oslo, Norway. Most African-Americans are unaware of the fact that Dr. King divided his winnings among the Southern Christian Leadership Conference, the Student Non-Violent Coordinating committee, the Congress on Racial Equality, the National Association for the Advancement of Colored People, the National Council of Negro Women, and the American Foundation on Non-violence.

1965 • Malcolm X is assassinated at an Organization of Afro-American Unity meeting at the Audubon Ballroom, New York. Actor Ossie Davis delivered the eulogy at his funeral six days later.

- A clash between black residents and white police officers triggers the Watts rebellion, the most serious single racial disturbance in US history, Los Angeles, California.

- Pres. Lyndon Baines Johnson organizes the Council on Equal Opportunity, composed of cabinet officers and heads of agencies with overall civil rights responsibilities, and appoints Vice-President Hubert Humphrey chair.

1966 • Rev. Joseph H. Jackson, president of the National Baptist Convention, issues a statement disassociating himself from Martin Luther King's movement.

- A dispute between police and black children over the use of a fire hydrant for recreation results in rioting, in Chicago, Il. Chicago Mayor Richard J. Daley and Rev. Martin Luther King, Jr. announce new recreational programs for Chicago's youth.

- The "Black Power" concept – which is generally thought to mean that African Americans should take a more aggressive posture toward obtaining civil rights – is adopted by CORE and the SNCC, while the Southern Christian Leadership Conference shies away from the idea and the NAACP disassociates itself from the concept entirely.

- Senator Edward W. Brooke is the first black since Reconstruction to be elected to the US Senate.

- Barbara Jordan becomes the first black to serve in the Texas senate since 1883.

1967
- The worst summer of racial disturbances in US history occurs in major urban areas throughout the country, including Newark, N.J., Detroit, MI, and Chicago, Il.

- Pres. Johnson appoints US Solicitor General Thurgood Marshall associate justice of the U.S. Supreme Court. Marshall is the first black US Supreme Court justice.

- Richard B. Hatcher is elected mayor of Gary, IN.

1968
- Rev. Dr. Martin Luther King, Jr. is assassinated in Memphis, TN. During his funeral service in Atlanta, GA, over 30,000 people form a procession behind the coffin. Rev. Benjamin E. Mays delivers the eulogy. Pres. Johnson decrees a day of national mourning. Widespread violence occurs in 125 cities, and 50,000 federal and state troops are called to duty all over the country.

- Pres. Lyndon Baines Johnson signs what will be known as the 1968 Housing Act, which outlaws discrimination in the sale, rental, or leasing of 80% of US housing. The bill also protects civil rights workers and makes it a federal crime to cross state lines for the purpose of inciting a riot.

- James Brown releases the song "Black is Beautiful, Say It Loud, I'm Black and I'm Proud", and begins a tour of military bases in the Pacific for the USO.

- Arthur Ashe wins the US Open Tennis Championships at Forest Hills, N.Y. and is ranked the number one player in the world.

- Following riots in major US cities, Pres. Johnson convenes the National Advisory Commission on Civil Disorders. The Kerner Commission Report concludes that white racism is one of the fundamental causes of rioting in the U.S.

<u>1969</u> • James Earl Ray pleads guilty to the charge of first degree murder in the assassination of the Rev. Martin Luther King, Jr. and is sentenced to 99 years in prison.

• Gwendolyn Brooks is named Poet Laureate of Illinois.

• The Jackson Five, a family consisting of brothers Marlon, Michael, Jackie, Jermaine, and Tito, performs at a campaign benefit for the mayor of Gary, IN.

• Among the guests at the benefit is singer Diana Ross, who is so taken with the boys' talent that she immediately introduces them to Berry Gordy of Motown Records.

• Under instruction from Edward V. Hamahan, Cook County state attorney, fifteen Chicago, Il policemen fire at and destroy the home of several Black Panther members, killing Panther leaders Mark Clark and Fred Hampton.

These events and people made a big impact on the growth and progress of, not only Grace & Glory, but other churches, as well. Over the years, through the "turbulent 60's" and beyond, much movement occurred in the churches.

Grace & Glory Gospel Chapel started as a small group of believers assembled on Sundays at a neighborhood YWCA. They met on the lower level in a medium sized room. The chairs were arranged in a circle so everyone saw the face of each believer. The service usually began with a song from "The Believers Hymnal Book". That same book is still being used today by the assembly. The songs were led by Bro. Gall, who loved singing. His voice had volume, like a professional singer, and he sang loud and clear and with "zest". He loved singing those hymns and sometimes, it seemed as if he was "alone" offering worship and praise to his God. The "Breaking of Bread"/Communion/Lord's Supper was shared each Sunday morning. Collection of donations, tithes, and building funds were made each Sunday among believers, only. The same two pouches used then for collections are still used today. Visitors were not included as the pouch was passed around, however, a small box was provided for those who wanted to give. Then the message was preached, mostly by Bro. Gall, and then the service ended. The names of some of the early members of Grace & Glory were: along with Bro. Gall, Bro. Mullin, and Bro. McCray, Ruby Gall, Marian Mullin, Roberta McCray, Adine Douglas, Inez Douglas, Agnes

Wilson, Agnes Williams, Nola Hicks, Lloyd and Lois Colar, Ruth Davis, Annie Allen, Alexander Allen, and Naomi Kilpatrick.

The current building was completed in 1960, with the land having been purchased in 1957 through the Steward's Foundation. Through the years, during the 1960's, the country was in turmoil with so much violence occurring. But somehow, with God's help, Grace & Glory prospered and grew. The little assembly has remained and has survived, like so many other churches, in spite of the times. It has managed to bring the gospel message to those that are lost.

For many years during the 1960's and 1970's, many visitors passed through the doors of Grace & Glory. Some of them were students from Moody Bible Institute, from Emmaus Bible School, from Wheaton College, and from other places. The students were sometimes part of the service; sometimes they ministered in the Sunday School; and sometimes they were just there to share in the Breaking of Bread and to enjoy the message. Bro. Gall delivered a powerful gospel message each week. One of the most memorable families to visit and minister to us was the Bolt – Digby family.

Ansel and Stella Bolt were the parents back then, Joyce Bolt Knol-Digby was the daughter and a college student at the time. Joyce wrote this narrative regarding her history with Grace & Glory:

> "My father came to know about the assemblies through the testimony of a Christian co-worker at the Wilson meat packing plant in the 1940's, and he, my mother, and I began fellowshipping at the Laflin Street Assembly until we moved to Iowa in 1948. There my father and two of his brothers started an assembly in Ames. I was in fellowship there until I left Iowa to attend Emmaus Bible School in Oak Park, Illinois, in 1963. While there, I attended the Sunshine Mission and taught a Sunday School class. But on one occasion I was invited to go with some fellow students to Grace and Glory. I never forgot the wonderful time I had there and the warm welcome I received from all I met. In 1968, having completed my college education, I moved to the south side of Chicago and taught English at the Canterbury Junior High School in Markham. I had an apartment mate named Ginny Tillery who had been

a friend during our college days together. On our first Sunday I told Ginny I was going to go to Grace and Glory and invited her to go with me, which she did. She had been raised in a free Methodist orphanage in Kansas City but attended the Assembly in Greenville, Illinois, with me when we were in college. We both felt so welcome and at home at Grace and Glory and enjoyed the fellowship there so much that we decided that would be our home assembly while we lived in that area. We were in fellowship during the five years we taught in Markham. Whenever my father came for a visit, he came with us. This time at Grace and Glory was definitely the highlight of his visits in the Chicago area! In 1973 Ginny and I moved to Ames, Iowa, and have been in that area ever since. Ginny's last name is now Khan, and she is the mother of two young adults, Jaleel and Sherri. David and I married in 1987. He had five children, three of them special needs adopted children, and so I became an instant mother at the time of our marriage. My time at Grace and Glory was a wonderful experience! I especially remember Bro. and Sister Gall; Bro. and Sister Mullins and her sister Lucy; Bro. and Sister Chambers; Bro. and Sister Watkins; Bro. and Sister Ferguson; Sister Hatch; and many, many others whose lives and testimonies were such an encouragement to me. I hope and pray that the work continues there and that I will have more opportunities to meet with you whenever I can!" This narrative was sent to me by e-mail on August 11, 2011 by Joyce Bolt.

Grace & Glory has enriched the lives of many who have sought spiritual guidance and Christian fellowship. And as the members of Grace and Glory continue the ministry, they realize that they stand on the shoulders of those who have gone before. They, not only, continue God's work, but continue to "stand by the stuff," as Bro. Gall used to say.

"History, despite its wrenching pain, cannot be unlived, but if faced with courage, need not be lived again". Maya Angelou

Grace & Glory's history has some unpleasantness that is sad and shocking. But this history cannot be changed because it happened.

Sis. Lucy did not want me to know of this history, and told me not to write of the church because of it. But I was not deterred. Writing the history was a burning desire, so I proceeded to do the research in preparation for that task.

Below is a brief description of the legal conflict between Brethren at the Grace & Glory Gospel Hall.

UNPLEASANT CHURCH HISTORY

"On March 12, 1957, the Appellants brought suit against the Appellees in the Illinois Appellate Court, First District, First Division.

"The Appellants attacked the right of the three defendants to the office of trustee and of the fourth defendant to the office of trustee and secretary of the Grace Gospel Hall, a member church of the Plymouth Brethren.

The complaint alleges that the realtors were elected trustees of the church on or about January 15, 1951; that the church has no by-laws or rules; that no meetings of the members of the church or of the trustees were held at any time and no trustees or other officers were elected after January 15, 1951.

In testimony given on pretrial depositions each defendant stated that he was appointed to his respective office. Before the beginning of the trial and before the selection of the jury the defendants filed their joint verified second amended and supplemental answer in which they deny the election of the relators as trustees, alleging that the relators were appointed trustees by the Elders of Grace Gospel Hall on or about June 15, 1951 and announcement of the appointment made to the congregation, who made no objection thereto, and that the defendants were likewise appointed to their respective offices by the Elders and announcement thereof made to the congregation, who made no objection thereto; admit that the church has no by-laws and allege that according to the doctrine, faith, and religious belief of the Plymouth Brethren and the congregation of Grace Gospel Hall, all rules necessary for the government and regulation of the church are found in the Holy Scriptures; deny that Grace Gospel Hall has members and allege that the individuals of the congregation are in fellowship with each other, and that according to the doctrine, faith, and religious belief of the congregation and the usages and customs of the church, trustees and other officers are not elected by the "members" but are appointed by the Elders, and announcement of the action of the Elders made at the following Sunday meeting of the congregation; that each defendant was appointed to the respective office held by him by the Elders of the Grace Gospel Hall and announcement thereof made to the congregation at the following Sunday meeting in accordance with the doctrine faith, religious belief, customs and usages of the Grace Gospel Hall; that relators vacated their respective offices by failure to act as such trustees, and that the vacancies thus created were filled on or about June 23, 1952.

All of these issues were submitted to the jury. A verdict finding the issues for defendants was returned and judgement entered thereon. Relators moved for judgement notwithstanding the verdict for a new trial. The motion was denied and the relators appealed.

The steps taken in selecting defendants as trustees, whether by election or appointment, the authority of the persons acting and the effect of the action taken under the customs and usages of the church, are not peculiarly or exclusively within the knowledge of defendants. The trial court properly allowed the statements of the defendants to be used for impeaching purposes. It did not err in refusing to direct a verdict for relators or enter judgement for them notwithstanding the verdict.

Minutes of meetings corroborating defendants' claims were received in evidence. There is testimony that relators did not attend to the duties of a trustee and that their offices were declared vacated. Relators do not argue in the alternative that the verdict is against the manifest weight of the evidence if their contention as to judicial admissions is not sustained.

No objections to the giving or refusing of instructions are argued on appeal. Relators state in their brief that the court erred in refusing to permit the jury to take with them the complaint, the original answer of the defendants and their answers to the relators interrogatories, received in evidence as relators exhibits, but do not point out wherein this was error. In like manner relators call our attention to certain incidents occurring on the trial, but do not show wherein relators were harmed as a result of such incidents. We find no reversible error in the record. The judgment is affirmed." This incident split the Brethren and Grace & Glory was then founded by Bro. Gall and others.

Plymouth Brethren

Grace & Glory Gospel Chapel, was founded under the auspices, and after the tradition of the Plymouth Brethren. Bro. Owbridge Gall and other founders desired a church that would not only spread the gospel, but would practice and worship and serve after the manner of the churches in the New Testament. They believed in reading the Bible and gathering in the same simple manner as Christians did in the New Testament. The characteristics of a "Brethren" assembly are:

- Avoidance of traditional symbols
- Fellowship, not membership
- No clergy
- Weekly "Remembrance" meeting
- Other Sunday meetings
- Low key offerings taken
- Separate roles of men and women.

The church is a conservative, Evangelical Christian Assembly. And though we have no official clergy or liturgy, the title "Brethren" is "official" enough.

The actual Plymouth Brethren Movement started in Dublin, Ireland in the 1820's and then spread to Britain. The first English Assembly was in Plymouth, where the movement became well-known. Brethren assemblies began growing throughout Europe and other countries. According to some accounts, Leonard Strong led the formation of assemblies in the year 1836 in the British Guiana among slaves. In the early years, those involved were largely unknown to one another, with no direct contact between the various groups. The movement started mainly because some Christians began to feel uncomfortable about denominationalism, a clerical hierarchy, and certain "compromises" coming into their churches. They decided to simply read their bibles and to try to gather in the same simple manner as Christians did in the New Testament.

One of the influential figures among the original "Plymouth Brethren", and the founder of the "Exclusive Brethren was John Nelson Darby (November 18, 1800-April 29, 1882). He produced a translation of the Bible based on the Hebrew and Greek texts.

Over the years, Darby developed the principles of his mature theology – most notably his conviction that the very notion of a clergyman was a sin against the Holy Spirit, because it limited the recognition that the Holy Spirit could speak through any member of the church. During this time he joined an interdenominational meeting of believers who met to "break bread" together in Dublin as a symbol of their unity in Christ. By 1832, this group had grown and began to identify themselves as a distinct Christian Assembly. As they traveled and began new assemblies in Ireland and England, they formed the movement now known as the "Plymouth Brethren."

Darby gave 11 significant lectures in Geneva in 1840 on the hope of the church. These established his reputation as a leading interpreter of biblical prophecy. The beliefs he disseminated then are still being propagated, in various forms, at such places as Dallas Theological Seminary and by authors and preachers such as Hal Lindsey and Tim LeHaye.

In 1848, Darby became involved in a complex dispute over the proper method for maintaining shared standards of discipline in different assemblies that resulted in a split between Open Brethren and Exclusive Brethren. After that time, he was recognized as the dominant figure among the Exclusives, who also came to be known as "Darbyite" Brethren. He used his classical skills to translate the Bible from Hebrew and Greek texts into several languages. In English he wrote a Synopsis of the Bible and many other scholarly religious articles. He wrote hymns and poems, the most famous being, "Man of Sorrows". He is noted in the theological world as the father of "dispensationalism", later made popular in the United States by Cyrus I. Scofield's "Scofield Reference Bible."

The Nottage Brothers had an almost legendary impact, both within the Plymouth Brethren Assemblies and outside. After many years as a traveling evangelist and church planter, B. M. Nottage moved to Detroit and founded the Bethany Tabernacle, which was base for his ministry and radio work for the rest of his life. His preaching and in-depth Bible teaching were powerful influences on the nurturing of thousands in the Christian faith. B.M. was gifted in evangelism and church planting. He also had a passion for lost souls, particularly Afro-Americans, whom he found to be very churchy and religious, and very lost. B.M. Nottage wanted black people to know what it meant to be saved according to the Scriptures, and to have a clear bible testimony, and to know the importance of gathering to the person of the Lord Jesus Christ, and Him alone, and an understanding of how to witness to the lost, and to know the importance of the family altar. He was or among the first, to introduce the unadulterated gospel, without religious hype and ritual, to the black communities in the United States.

The Black Church

During the 1990's, the Black Church saw many changes as activism and new denominations appeared.

The ending of World War II, caused the African-American religious community to share fully in the dramatic changes that have occurred in the larger society. As in the aftermath of every war in which African-Americans have participated, the surrender of Japan "triggered on intensification of historic struggle for full civil rights and non-discriminatory practices in all aspects of national life." Many Black ministers and their congregations were participants in this time of history. In this, they continued a long-established tradition of being concerned with the salvation of souls as well as with issues relating to equal justice for all people.

By the mid - 1960's, it had become clear that access to establishments serving the public and even to the ballot box was of little effect unless the economic circumstances of African Americans were improved. As a consequence, the struggle was intensified for enhanced employment opportunities, for improved education and training, for affordable housing, and for equal access to political office and power. This social upheaval, fueled by riots and unrest, was particularly turbulent in cities in the North. The news media referred to it as the "crisis in the city."

The role of the churches began to change as well. They became places where government - funded programs such as Headstart, child-care and feeding were housed. The Church has also become the sponsors of housing and after-school tutorial programs for children, as well as a variety of other services for the community.

The election of Richard Nixon in 1968 was the beginning of a shift in the body politic which resulted in a reordering of national priorities toward the "benign neglect" of issues central to the civil rights struggle. During the presidency of Ronald Reagan the country completed a 180-degree turn away from concern for the poor and underserved persons in the society. Consequently, the inner cities were besieged with crime, violence, substance abuse, deteriorating schools, high population of homeless and hungry persons, and substandard and insufficient housing. To this was added the onslaught of AIDS, crumbling family structures, high levels of incarceration of young Black males, increasing numbers of single parent households, and a rapidly increasing population of teenage parents. Contributing to the diminished quality of life in the inner cities had been the continuing emigration of middle-class families. Only the churches have not emigrated. In creative and sacrificial ways, the churches sought to address this critical array of problems. They organized parochial schools, established feeding centers, created family life centers, built and rehabilitated housing, built nursing homes, and developed a wide range of economic development programs.

While the social outreach of African-American congregations had been expanding, internal changes, were taking place within the churches themselves. Since the 1960's, the unchallenged "hegemony of Protestantism" in African-American communities had been challenged by Roman Catholicism and by the Nation of Islam. Many nominal Christians were attracted to the Catholic Church in the 1960's by its egalitarian worship and its parochial schools. The Muslims, under the leadership of Elijah Muhammad and Malcolm X, attracted many Protestants with their aggressive social and political agenda, the clarity of their beliefs and the discipline required of members. Additionally, African-Americans were adopting some of the more "exotic" religious, including Buddhism, Yoruba, Orthodox Islam, Voudan, and a host of religions of African origin by way of Latin America.

In the meantime, social, political and moral changes were taking place in some African American congregations. A subtle decline in membership was occurring. Among the reasons cited for this decline was the changing demography of the cities, the aging of the congregations and the unchanged leadership styles and programs. By contrast, the churches that were growing by "leaps and bounds" were characterized by vibrant worship, relevant preaching and warm evangelical preaching, systematic Bible study, aggressive social ministries, and by trained, informed leadership that had "implemented appropriate staff structures" and "efficient management practices."

Circle Y Ranch

Circle Y Ranch is a summer youth Bible camp, for ages 8-17, situated on 80 acres of land beside beautiful School Section Lake in Van Buren

Country in Bangor, Michigan. It is a place where youth have enjoyable experiences in a wholesome, safe, and healthy environment.

Circle Y Ranch Bible Camp and Conference Grounds is owned by African-American Christians through the support of interested donors, friends and participating churches. Most of its campers are drawn from the inner cities of Detroit and Chicago. It is uniquely equipped to ministerto urban youth through its adults, modeleing balanced lives, and well planned programs. Young people are assisted in their physical, social and spiritual development while surrounded by the natural rustic environment with support systems that prepare them for places in their community. Circle Y Ranch is an equal opportunity camping facility in regards to race, sec, or religious belief. The motto is "The Camp where kids have "Fun in the Son".

In the early 1950's, a group of people from the African-American Christian Brethren Assemblies in Detroit, Michigan developed a Christian camp for boys and girls in their respective churches. A few years later, they united with their Brethren counterparts in Chicago and expanded their vision to reach children throughout the Midwest. Mr. James Humphrey, of Chicago, was led to purchase an eighty-acre farm outside the town of Bangor, Michigan and donated the land specifically for the camp. With the sacrificial giving of many individuals to build the initial facilities, Circle Y Ranch was incorporated in January 1964, and held its first week of camp that July with 58 campers and 26 volunteers staff persons.

Bro. Jim Humphrey designed the logo for Circle Y Ranch and drew it by hand himself. Ironically and surprisingly, Bro. Humphrey was the great uncle of Bro. Mark Soderquist of Westlawn Gospel Chapel.

Berean Chapel of Detroit

Rev. Theodore Williams, Sr. accepted a call to the pulpit of First Baptist Church of Eight Mile Road then located in Wisconsin, with his wife, Eunice, in 1931. The congregation was not really prepared for the preaching fire, dedication, and determination of this young preacher, as he preached fervently, and as he sought to win many in the community to personal assurance of salvation in Jesus Christ as he had, rather than to hold on to an empty profession of faith in religion.

Brother Williams began a radio broadcast over station WEXL, Royal Oak, to reach out to others with the Gospel, beyond the walls of First Baptist. Bro. Williams heard of Bro. BM Nottage (since he also had a weekly program on the same radio station on Sunday afternoon) through another theological classmate, Jessie McGruder, and had opportunity to evaluate his positions on scriptural teaching and preaching. Bro. Nottage was invited to the pulpit at First Baptist for several Bible classes in a study series, and Bro. Williams found an ally with a similarity of desires and goals to reach African-Americans with the simple Gospel of Jesus Christ, and to worship in a New Testament form. Bro. Williams accepted the Word as taught by Bro. Nottage. He felt the Word was so clear that he could no longer stay at First Baptist Church, so he gave the congregation his resignation to set out to preach the Word according to the leading of God. Several members of First Baptist followed his call to begin a New Testament assembly. On June 2, 1936, Bro. B.M. Nottage, Joseph P. Anderson, David Jones, Lucious Minter, Major Q. Holley, Revo Pattmon, Joe Nottage, and Theodore Williams, Sr. assisted in raising a 60 by 40 foot tent in Royal Oak Township on Westview Avenue near Eight Mile Road next to the Bowden family home. It remained there through late October to early November, 1936, while the building on Reimanville was being constructed. The first Breaking of Bread was held in September, 1936 in the tent with Joe Nottage (possibly E. Jerome Nottage, a nephew of B. M. Nottage) and another brother from Bethany Tabernacle assisting with the order of the service and the elements. In attendance were: Joseph and Ruth Anderson, Lucious and Alyce Minter, Major and Ethel Holley, David and Lu Quido Jones, Theodore and Eunice Williams, Revo and Mary Pattmon, Maggie Washington, Gertrude Williams, Emma Williams, and Richard and Adeline McNeal. With a $10.00 down payment on a $600.00 lumber bill, Mr. Leach agreed to match the requirement of $10.00 each month from his own pocket. The amount for the lumber and the lot was eventually paid off by a Mr. Marion. The exterior construction was concrete block, built on the foundation without a basement. The meeting area was on the first floor, and family quarters on the second floor.

The Williams' had five children at that time: Theodore, Jr., Ruth, Hiram, Curtis and Naomi. They moved into the upstairs on December 18, 1936. They experienced the Lord's Supper for the first time in their new building led by Bro. Nottage and Bro. John Ollivere. On December 19, 1936 around a $10 tin tub as a source of heat since there was no furnace or heater for the first floor as yet.

During World War II, when additional housing for defense factory workers (African-Americans) was built in Royal Oak Township beyond Wyoming Avenue, a bus was purchased by Brother Minter, and he used it to pick up boys and girls for Sunday School, youth meetings, etc. and in the fifties to Smith Creek Bible Camp. The families of the Jones, Minters, Holleys, Pattmons, Williams (Theodore and Eunice, and Emma's children) were joined by the Love's, Rich bow's, Hamilton's and Saddler's, Rice's, Riley's and Conners' children along with Grannie Maggie Washington's grand children and many others.

Bro. Williams later felt the call to plant an assembly in Chicago, Illinois which was realized when Grace Gospel Hall began there in 1945. Bro. Williams was followed in leadership on the first Sunday in January, 1945 when Grant Love became the pastor of Berean Tabernacle. Grant, Oretha, and their three children, Elaine, Gwendolyn and Norman came to the assembly in 1940. Bro. & Sis. Love assisted in the continued growth of the meetings as the Eight Mile Road community grew. The increase in the community population due to World War II provided additional opportunities for service. Many young people were involved in music ministry, and exposure to citywide youth and assembly rallies which was encouraged by Bro. Nottage who furthered the development of Berean young people. Several of the sisters (Minter, Jones, Holley) were involved in public school Bible Clubs for boys and girls. Several men assisted Bro. Nottage in music ministry, jail ministry, and Bible classes at Detroit Public Works garages, etc.

The youth meetings at the assembly would provide the seed-bed for being part of the ministries, such as the United Youth Retreat, and Smith's Creek Bible Camp, for it exposed many of the young men and women to leadership roles and ministry, Under the leadership of Brother Love during the mid-fifties relocation was sought. The present building was entered for use on December 8, 1961. The name of the assembly was changed after the relocation to Berean Bible Assembly and then to Berean Chapel of Detroit. The new sanctuary was completed for use in February 1973 and is where worship is still going on today.

Bro. Love ministered faithfully and fed the flock for almost forty years until October, 1980 when the Lord called him home. His love for the Lord's work is still expressed today in the many dedicated services that are a part of Berean Chapel. Even his choosing of Bro. Gore to minister to the congregation was a blessing to Berean Chapel. "We thank the Lord for lending us Brother Love, and sending us Brother Gore. In 1980, Bro. Barney Gore resigned and Brother William E. Perry became Berean's Interim Pastor. Bro. Perry accepted the challenge with compassion and enthusiasm. Under the leadership of Bro. Perry, Berean experienced continued spiritual growth in the local assembly and its outreach ministries. Bro. Perry increased the ministerial staff by adding two additional men of faith to be developed. Additional programs were added: Man's Prayer and Fellowship, Pure and Godly Treasures, Fasting and Prayer, Youth Seminars, Fifth Sunday as Youth Day, and Singles' Ministries among a few. In 2003, the church building was improved with the addition of these additional classrooms and state of the art restrooms with handicapped accessibility. Bro. Perry ministered faithfully and fed the flock for almost twenty-five years until June 8, 2005 when the Lord called him home. His love for the Lord's work is still expressed today in the many dedicated services that are a part of Berean Chapel.

On November 19, 2006, he was installed as pastor/teacher of Berean Chapel of Detroit.

The growth and outreach of Berean Chapel must still be that original trust that Bro. Theodore Williams and the initial group of pioneers from Eight Mile Road envisioned for their community when they began meeting in the tent in June, 1936; to worship simply, to live honestly, and to be true to the Word of God. They are continuing to worship and are carrying on the work of Christ. Alton Minter, Charles Minter, Carol Minter, Jacqueline Gresham, and others represent the continuity of their prayers.

Bethel Gospel Chapel

In the early years of the twentieth century a number of immigrants arriving from the United Kingdom who had met in simple fashion to worship the Lord in the "Old Country," started to meet in the same way in the store front of a building situated at 2481 St. Antoine St; Montreal. They were known as "Plymouth Brethren" and their meeting place as the 'Gospel Hall'. This was actually one of the first assemblies in the province of Quebec. They met for breaking of bread and gospel preaching and over a period of time their numbers increased. They started a Sunday School on Sunday afternoons which attracted some of the children of the neighborhood. Just as believers came to Montreal from Britain, so too did some arrive from the West Indies, via Nova Scotia, and joined the testimony. Over time other Afro-Canadians became Christians and came into the fellowship of the assembly. A good number of the British brethren soon set up another testimony in another part of the city. The name of "Bethel" was added and Bethel Gospel Hall became predominantly West Indian. The numbers were small, but the brethren were faithful. It was not their practice to meet during bitterly cold winter months. In the 1940's and 1950's, through person to person witnessing and special gospel efforts, many folks of African descent were saved, baptized and added to the assembly.

One outstanding evangelist who held meetings at Bethel was Bro. B. M. Nottage, one of the four well-known Nottage Brothers from the Bahamas. The brothers were instrumental in building up many assemblies in the USA. Bro. Nottage's labors bore much fruit; many professed faith in Christ under his ministry. The late 1950's brought many more young believers from the West Indian islands augmenting the numbers in the assembly. Youth activities also drew many to the testimony.

The city of Westmount, within Montreal has been the place where many prominent businessmen and politicians lived. A little church building was erected there by a group of Baptists well over a hundred years ago for their meetings. They sold it to another group and the building changed hands a few times by groups whose numbers had grown too large for the building. Bethel had been looking for a building of its own for a long time. In the spring of 1972 this church building, located at 4250 de Maisonneuve Boulevard, West in Westmount, became available. Bethel purchased it and it became Bethel Gospel Chapel; the change of name had to do with government dealings.

The Lord richly blessed the assembly throughout the years. The present leadership continues to follow the New Testament pattern and trust this will continue unto the appearing of our blessed Lord.

Grace Bible Church

The "Open Bible Church" was established in 1940 by Edward and Emily Stahnke. In 1960, the "Open Bible Church" was turned over to five Christian faith families to spread the grace message and was named Grace Bible Church of Riverdale. Over the years, the church leadership and congregation changed from an all white church to six white families and one African American family sharing the Word of the Lord. The Henrys' were the first African American family to settle and hear the Word of the Lord through the teaching of Apostle Paul.

Bro. Ceolia Henry, his wife Ann and all eleven of their children became members of Grace Bible Church of Riverdale in the early 1990's and remained faithful to the church throughout the years. However, before Bro. Ceolia and his family became members, he first started studying the word with several other families in the 1970's. Bro. Ceolia Henry, Bro. James Fair, Bro. Curtis Davis, and Bro. Waddell Johnson studied the book of Daniel and Revelation at Bro. Charlie Knox' home. In 1972, Bro. Waddell Johnson searched for a home church where the families could attend. He was blessed to find a small family oriented Bible teaching church located in Chatham at 7708 South Indiana called "Grace & Glory Gospel Chapel". At that time, it was under the pastoral leadership of Brother Frank Mullin, along with several other families already attending. The families were welcomed with open arms to further their studies of the Lord through worship on Sundays, Thursdays, and every first Friday for young people's night. Grace & Glory Gospel Chapel became the spiritual corner stone for many families sharing the Salvation of Jesus Christ who died on the cross to save our souls.

After years of studying the Word and establishing themselves as Bible leaders, Bro. Fair and Bro. Henry moved on to start a food pantry church in Harvey, Illinois called the Learning Center Gospel Chapel. Not only did this church feed the community, it also fed their souls. Bro. Fair and Bro. Henry, as well as, their families, worked hard for the Lord by teaching not only those in the Harvey community, but also to the surrounding ones as well. Bro. Ceolia Henry was on his way to work when he passed a church in Riverdale that he wanted to visit and that Sunday, he and his family attended their first Sunday service at Grace Bible Church of Riverdale.

At that time, Grace Bible Church of Riverdale was under the leadership of Bro. Giron, Bro. Gobrah, and Bro. Smith. After a few years of attending service, Bro. Ceolia Henry became the Pastor of Grace Bible Church promising to keep the doors open and spreading the good news of Jesus Christ. Bro. Henry served the Lord faithfully, until he was called home to glory. The church underwent several pastors including the last pastor, Bro. Davis, who also passed away. By the grace of God, Bro. Henry's children continue to praise and worship the Lord at Grace Bible Church.

Currently, there are six families spreading the Word to the Riverdale community every Sunday for Sunday School and Morning Worship service, community outreach program and monthly free giveaways. The youth participate diligently in serving the Lord through scripture reading, bringing the message on youth Sundays, various holiday programs or leading the service in order to get practice to become future spiritual leaders.

<u>Grace Conservative Baptist Church</u>.

When Grace Conservative Church first opened, I was there briefly. I attended the bible classes that Bro. and Sis. Ranney conducted. They had classes that were designed to prepare us to be Sunday School teachers to children. I attended along with Fay Spooner, Annie Allen, Ruth Davis, and Sis. Eleanor Agins. In addition to the bible classes, we held all-night prayer meetings. Sis. & Bro. Ranney were very gentle people but strong advocates of the Word of God. They were patient and understanding as I struggled to learn "the meat of the Word". I was a new Christian and anxious to succeed with children. Sis. Ranney had a "nervous condition" that caused her hands to shake noticeably. She never let it bother her or prevent her from her mission. After they left the ministry, I kept up with them for a short time. I inquired a few years ago about them and was told that Sis. Ranney was in a nursing facility with Alzheimers, and Bro. Ranney was in poor health. Below is a summary of the church which I took from a brochure on October 20, 2013:

Fifty-three years ago, Eleanor Agins, a young dedicated Christian woman, carried a deep personal burden for what was then called the Negro people, and like the Apostle Paul, she knew that many of her people had a sincere zeal for God. Many were active church members but had not accepted the Lord as their personal Savior, in accordance with scripture. Unknown to her at the time, in the soverign will of God, Robert (Bob) and Freida Ranney were appointed to the Conservative Baptist Home Missions Society (CBHMS) in January, 1955. At that time he was a student at Bethel Seminary, in St. Paul Minnesota. After graduation, he and his wife moved to Belvidere in Northern Illinois.

Pastor Ranney, much like Sis. Agins, shared a deep love and affection for humanity, and strongly felt the call of God to minister to the rapidly growing Negro population in the city of Chicago.

The church started as Bible class. Under the leadership of Bob and Freida the small Bible study moved into a storefront at 3453 S. Indiana Avenue and established a mission in the neighborhood – sharing the good news of Jesus Christ.

The little mission was a humble beginning. Pastor Ranney and the organizers prayed that God would send faithful workers and members. Soon the attendance began to grow and the faithful held fast to the cause of reaching others with the Gospel. Carl Bailey, Victoria Bradford, and Dorman Smith who came to know the Lord joined Eleanor Agins.

Velma Elam, one of Grace's founders, was introduced to the mission through her sister, Marie Taylor. Marie walked in one Sunday and said, "I hear you preach the Gospel here!" The response was "we sure do!" The following Sunday, Sister Elam came. Shortly thereafter other faithful members like Charmaine Horney, Mary Jane Thomas and Jessie Mae Johnson followed.

While still meeting in the rented storefront, the group organized the Grace Conservative Baptist Church of Chicago, Illinois on March 30, 1960. The charter was signed by the original eight members, and ratified March 10, 1961. Most of the other workers became members of the church.

Another member was won into the family of God during an evangelistic meeting at Grace. Rev. Warren Mattox was preaching the Word of God and Vesta Miller lead by the Holy Spirit, was convicted of her sin and became a believer in Jesus Christ. She shared her experience with her husband, James Miller, who was already a believer. They both became members and have served the Lord faithfully ever since.

Slowly, the congregation of Grace began to grow. Most of the new members were women, Doris Coleman, Frankie Preyear, Edna Caldwell and others. Men came but soon left. As a result the church depended on its "faithful four", Bob Ranney, Carl Bailey, James Miller, and Virgil Amos.

As the converts/membership grew, Grace began to pray and look for a larger building in which to house the ministry. A Building Fund was established. It grew steadily as the members prayed and gave. Within four years the members had a building fund totaling $3,500.00 (which was a sizable amount at that time). With the assistance of a realtor the church examined and considered several pieces of property before deciding upon the current location 1002 East 75th Street (75th and Ellis).

In October 1964 the congregation of Grace moved into its current facility. A city clinic occupied the first floor paying $400.00 per month rent. The church auditorium, offices and extra rooms were on the second floor and the fellowship hall and kitchen took up the third floor area.

As time progressed, the church paid its mortgage with the rent from the clinic. This arrangement worked well since the congregation needed the income. However, the church was one day informed that the clinic had intentions of moving. This brought much prayer and consideration to the small church family. Again the members began to pray and ask God for direction as to how they could meet their monthly mortgage obligations.

In answer to prayer, God allowed the church to meet its total financial burden before the clinic moved out! This was a special blessing to the church because, in addition to the needed income, the church needed more space in which to teach its growing number of new members. As it turned out, God met both the financial and space need all with perfect timing. The congregation praised God's name realizing what a mighty God they served!

The Ranney's worked tirelessly until March 6, 1970, when they were led of the Lord to resign the position for which they had worked so hard. The entire Grace family was saddened to receive the resignation letter of its founder and leader, Pastor Ranney. A farewell dinner and gift was given on September 13, 1970. The Ranney's later moved from Illinois to Nebraska and finally relocated to Minneapolis, Minnesota. Pastor Ranney went home to be with the Lord on December 2, 2006. Mrs. Ranney went home to be with the Lord in April, 2010.

Over the past 53 years, God has been truly gracious and merciful to Grace. He has done exceedingly; abundantly above all we could ask or think. Our faith in our struggles always rested on his power and in His ability to help us not to get weary in doing what was right, because He said, "We would reap if we did not faint." We are in our season of reaping as we enter into a merger with Christ Bible Church. The merger was finalized on September 27, 2013. We have a new name which is Christ Bible Church #3 and a new opportunity to once again reach out to this community with the message of the Gospel. Pastor James Ford, Jr. is the Pastor and Leader of the merger.

Laflin Gospel Chapel

Laflin Street Gospel Hall – 6617 So. Laflin – had as its early leading brethren Jim Humphrey, Ken Widener, and Messengers Miller, Arnot and Parker. As the demographics of the neighborhood changed, most of the assembly moved to Oak Lawn in 1959. However, a few stayed, notably Jack & Charlotte Mostert. They invited the black people in the neighborhood to join with them and a few did so. Steve Thompson, saved while in prison in Japan, came to work with the Mosterts. He and Jack Mostert were the leading men in the integrated assembly, which at the time was the most integrated assembly in Chicago.

"New Life Christian Fellowship"

The New Life Christian Fellowship was founded in July, 2012 by Christopher Salley, along with his wife, Kimberly, and others. New Life branched off from the Westlawn Gospel Chapel on Chicago's west side. The church was housed at the Grace & Glory Gospel Chapel for a few years as their numbers grew and until the Lord blessed them with a new location at 1645 Wilson Avenue, Chicago Heights, Illinois – a south side suburb.

Pastor Christopher Salley serves as the Senior Pastor and his involvement in ministry to the body of Christ began when he preached his first sermon at 17 years of age. He has affiliated with various ministries including "Challenge Ministries" as a board member and conference speaker, "Circle Y Ranch Bible Camp" as Camp Director, and "Trinity Christian College as a member of the Board of Trustees. He also is one of the contributors to the "Men of Color Study Bible".

God has gifted Pastor Salley with a powerful gift to preach and teach the Word of God, speaking at several churches and conferences around the country.

He was ordained as a minister of the gospel in 1993 at Westlawn Gospel Chapel and served as an Elder and Associate Pastor until he moved to Stamford, Connecticut in 1997. While in the New York area, he helped to establish the New York Covenant Church in 1998. Pastor Salley served as its assistant Pastor alongside his longtime friend, Pastor David R. Holder until God opened the door for him to return to the Chicago area. Shortly after his return, he began to move upon the vision that the Lord gave him to establish NLCF as a church that would target the needs and speak to the concerns of his generation.

Pastor Salley also maintained a successful 19-year business career and retired in 2007 as a Senior Vice President and Principal at Greenfield Partners, a real estate investment management firm to pursue the pastorate full-time. He has a B.S. in Economics from the University of Pennsylvania as well as a Masters in Management from the Kellogg School Northwestern University. He has also completed course work at Trinity Evangelical Divinity School.

Pastor Salley has been married to the lovely Kimberly for some 25 years and they have four wonderful children Kendall, Courtney, Christin, and Kyle.

Roseland Bible Church

The history of Roseland Bible Church is connected to the history of Grace & Glory Gospel Chapel for Bro. Walter Anderson was a member of Grace & Glory during the early years. He served as an elder brother preaching the Word of God, teaching Bible studies, and ministering and admonishing the young men. Bro. Anderson, along with his wife, Margaret, an excellent Bible teacher in her own right, left an indelible mark of integrity and commitment on Grace & Glory. He left the church in 1968 to found the Roseland Bible Church. Bro. Anderson is quite an historical icon. He shared a few things about himself that are noteworthy:

- his middle name is "Roland", named after Roland Hayes, born in the 1800's. He was the first African American male concert artist to receive wide acclaim nationally and internationally. He sang in French, German, and Italian. So, it is no surprise that Bro. Anderson is a soloist as well.
- In 1943, Bro. Anderson was a naval petty officer, stationed at Camp Robert Smalls, in Great Lakes, Illinois. It was a black, segregated camp, named after Robert Smalls. Robert Smalls was an enslaved African American who during and after the American Civil War, became a ship's pilot, sea captain, and politician. He

freed himself, his crew, and their families from slavery on May 13, 1862. He did this by commandeering a Confederate transport ship, the CSS Planter, in Charleston Harbor and sailing it to freedom beyond the Federal blockade. Robert Smalls' example and persuasion helped convince President Abraham Lincoln to accept black soldiers into the Union Army. After the Civil War, Smalls became a politician, elected to the South Carolina State legislature and the United States House of Representatives.

- While serving at Camp Robert Smalls, Bro. Anderson was asked to sing the National Anthem with Marian Anderson (no relation). As we all know, Marian Anderson, in 1939, sang on the steps of the Lincoln Memorial to thousands of people. The Daughters of the American Revolution would not permit her to sing in the Auditorium in Constitution Hall in Washington, D.C. A mural had been drawn, in honor of Marian Anderson, to capture the performance. Harold Ickles who was the Secretary of the Interior, got permission from Eleanor Roosevelt to commemorate the mural at the Interior Department Auditorium, Washington, D.C. on January 6, 1943.

- Bro. Anderson, along with seven other officers, 2nd class, sang, first bass, the National Anthem with Marian Anderson. He still has the actual program from the event. This was a once in a lifetime experience to sing with the greatest singer in the world.

The Roseland Bible Church was founded on the First Sunday in January, 1968 in the home of the Anderson Family, at 8023 So. Bennett Avenue in Chicago, Illinois 60617. It was founded by Pastor Walter Anderson, his wife, Margaret, his daughter, Sharon, and his son, Steven. His son, Richard was in the army in Vietnam at the time. It was initially named South East Bible Church and renamed later.

Special Prayer meetings were held at the home of Sis. Marie Griffith in July, 1968 and again in July, 1969 - to November, 1969 along with Bro. Anderson and his wife, Margaret before going to work.

At Sunday morning worship, about the first Sunday in October, 1969, Pastor Walter Anderson told the church he believed that the Lord wanted them to move out of the house and to seek a place for the believers to worship in the community. The church agreed and made it a matter of urgent prayer for the Lord to lead him to such a place. They began searching Monday morning and Wednesday of the same week. Pastor Anderson found a place at the YWCA on 83rd & Ellis. The rent was approximately $10 per hour and so they rented it for three hours per Sunday for three Sundays. Meanwhile, without Bro. Anderson's knowledge, a group of concerned Elders, of which he was affiliated, had recommended the group to Steward's Foundation as a worthy Christian Assembly to receive a building from them at 233 West 111th St., Chicago, Illinois 60628 at a very low price. Only a small improvement loan required. Through the Elders of Southside Gospel Church, Laflin Gospel Church and with close relationship with Westlawn Gospel Chapel, they acquired the building.

The membership on the First Sunday, October, 1969 was:

- Pastor Walter Anderson, his wife, Margaret, daughter, Sharon, and son, Steven.
- Doris Walker, her daughter, Lynn, and son, Reggie.
- Marie Griffith, daughter, Nona Brown, son Ricky Griffith, and daughter, Deborah Griffith.
- Mary White, son, Larry.

Others in membership: Mabel Smith, Barbara Jefferson Mattie Robertson, Mary Blanchard, Maxine Miller, Johnnie Mae George, Sandy Campbell, and Eva Springfield.

Roseland Bible Church continues to service its' community with the spreading of the gospel. They currently meet for the Breaking of Bread and Sunday School. The Worship Service starts at 11:15 AM. and on Tuesdays from October through April, they conduct the Awana Clubs for the youth. Roseland's Awana Club is extremely popular and a big part of the ministry. Prayer Meeting and Bible Study is still held on Wednesday evenings and Fridays are especially planned for teens and young people.

The current Pastoral Leadership is:

James "Jim" Albright
Hubert Jackson, Jr.
Robert E. Adams

Sharing in the ministry are their wives and their families and other believers who have been called to further the work of the Lord.

South Side Gospel Chapel

South Side Gospel Assembly church was founded and incorporated in 1947. The founders were Brother and Sister Burley Edwards, Brother Samuel Stephens, Brother Martin, and Sister Agnes Williams, and Brother A. Antoine.

In 1949, about ten (10) people purchased the building located at 863 East 64th Street in Chicago, Illinois, which would be the home of South Side Gospel Assembly Church. Among those were Brother Frank and Sister Estelle Wooten and family, (Willie and Juanita Johnson), Brother Frank Pagnes and later came Captain Luegemes Bratton and Family, Brother Hamlin Moseley.

Elder Leroy Yates and Sister Beverly Yates, Elder Melvin and Sister Olive Banks, Elder Harvey Rollerson came in 1950 and his wife Doris Rollerson came in 1954 after their union of marriage. These few moved to the west side of Chicago, Il and founded the Westlawn Gospel Chapel. The Davis' also from the South Side went to Wisconsin to form the Lighthouse Gospel Chapel.

In 1958, the Morgan Family moved in the neighborhood. They brought a great spiritual and physical joy to the South Side Family. In the 1980's, the Peak Family, Johnsons and the Millers come. In the 1990's, the Waddells' joined the church and the late James and Pat Martin sponsored a very successful Vacation Bible School program.

In 1995, under the leadership of Bro. Hamlin A. Moseley, Brother Roosevelt Morgan, Sr. was ordained as an elder. In 2011, his son Roosevelt Morgan, Jr. became an ordained deacon.

In 1999, Pastor Harvey L. Rollerson(Monte) was appointed by the late Elder and Pastor Hamlin Moseley of South Side Gospel to be the senior pastor. Later that same year, Pastor Monte Rollerson was ordained as an elder along with the blessing from the Chicago United Bible Conference.

Members of South Side Gospel Chapel are:
Deaconess Ruby Peak and family; Deacon Allen Waddell; Sister Brenda Johnson; Brother George Edwards; Deacon Matthew Milam II; Sister Katrina White (through baptism); Sister Lynette Lee; Brother

Jimmie Dickerson; Brother Patrick Tramble; Sister Maxine Miller; Brother William Johnson and family; Brother Willie Seldon; and a strong supporter Sister Edna McCoy; Demarean Foster, and Nashon White. The church has a background and legacy of people whose service is commendable:

- Samuel Stephens – an Elder/Pastor of South Side for many years. Not only did he teach the Word of God through his "Spiritual Assignments", but through his medical assessments as well, for he was a successful pharmacist.
- Pastor Hamlin Moseley, Pastor Harvey L. Rollerson and wife, Doris used their gifts through education within the Chicago Public School System.
- Pastor Leroy Yates used his gifts through counseling and his wife, Beverly, through nursing.
- Pastor Melvin and wife, Olive Banks used their gifts through a very successful business of Spiritual Learning and Teaching through Urban Ministries Communications.
- Elder Gibson spreads the Good News through sales; Elder Coco Jackson founded the "Door of Hope Mission" for men in whom families were able to come and get counseling.

South Side Gospel Church has grown in ministries. They have a strong Out-Reach ministry. They have an "Open Door" policy for all children where they can find a Safe Haven in the Church.

The Outreach to children has brought the following new additions: By baptism – Jerome White, Dariana Murphy, and Aaliyah Murphy. Dedicated were Olivia Waddell, Kaleb Mayfield, and Joshua Tramble.

South Side Gospel Church has opened its' doors for the Community to use the facilities for meetings, tutoring, and social gatherings. Presently, South Side is sponsoring ministries designed to reach out to others on a local and global scale such as: "Families in the Chicago Area" and "The West African Christian Ministry". They have answered the call to reach out beyond its local community to make disciples of all nations.

Westlawn Gospel Chapel

Brother B. M. Nottage, along with his brothers, came to the United States and began house to house ministry which resulted in Bible classes and small churches springing up in New York City; Washington, D.C.; Detroit, Michigan; Chicago, Illinois; Cleveland, Ohio; and St. Louis, Missouri. Southside Gospel Church in Chicago grew out of this move of the Holy Spirit in 1947.

B. M. Nottage had taught and challenged Elders Burley Edwards, Samuel Stephens, Frank Wooten, Luegemes Bratton, and Martin Williams, along with their wives, to start a church. They bought a building at 863 East 64th Street in Chicago. These men and women worked diligently to bring people to a saving knowledge of Jesus Christ through teaching God's Holy Word.

By 1955, Southside Gospel Church was blessed with many young families, and some of the men and women were students at Moody Bible Institute and Wheaton College. Ruth Lewis-Bentley, Yvonne Rollerson-Abatso, Lessie Merriweather-Farmer, Melvin and Olive Banks, Harvey and Doris Rollerson, and Leroy and Beverly Yates were among those earnest about their studies and their personal witness for Christ.

The Elders of Southside Gospel Church were encouraged to open up a Bible teaching mission on the west side of the city. They put a down payment on a church building and a two flat apartment building that was being vacated by white Christians at the Lawndale Bible Church. Members of Lawndale Bible Church sold the property at a reasonable price because it was their desire to leave a "witness for Christ" in the changing neighborhood.

Melvin Banks, Harvey Rollerson and Le Roy Yates accepted the call to be involved in the ministry at Westlawn Gospel Chapel. They immediately began touching the lives of men, women, boys and girls in the North Lawndale community.

Settling there in the spring of 1956, the three men began home visitation and Bible classes. With the assistance of young students from Weston College, an afternoon Sunday School began filling the buildings at 2115 and 2120 South St. Louis Avenue.

While they held full time jobs, these three young men succeeded in meeting several families in the neighborhood who desired to attend Sunday services at Westlawn Gospel Chapel. The first member of the church from the neighborhood was Betty Dixon-Mallory. Among the children in Sunday School were Donna McConney-Ray and her brother Eric McConney, and Dudley Tatem.

LeRoy Yates, Harvey Rollerson and Melvin Banks were ordained by the Elders of Southside Gospel Church. Thereafter, Westlawn Gospel Chapel was legally established as a New Testament Assembly. The Senior Elders have, along with Elder Max Dansbie and for a while James Johnson, worked tirelessly meeting the needs of many people in North Lawndale and the greater Chicago community. They have also used their talents and resources to assist in the establishment of other ministries. Lighthouse Gospel Chapel in Milwaukee, Wisconsin, Roseland Gospel Chapel, Christ Community Church in Chicago, Circle Y Ranch and Family Bible Chapel in Bangor, Michigan and New Life Christian Fellowship in Chicago Heights, Illinois are trophies of their labors. The Chicagoland Christian Women's Conference began by the women of Westlawn in 1962 and is still reaching many women for Christ.

In recent years Elders Tyrone Lawrence, Derrick Rollerson, Forrest Stampley, and Mark Soderquist have been mentored and ordained to continue the ministry of Westlawn Gospel Chapel that began over fifty years ago, teaching women, men, boys and girls that "Jesus Christ is the way, the truth and the life." Their goal is to take Westlawn into the future for His Glory. The newly constructed Westlawn Youth Center will serve as a needed facility for ministry into the future.

Currently, Derrick Rollerson serves as Pastor of Westlawn Gospel Chapel.

Bro. B.M. Nottage
Established several
churches in the Chicago
area, in Detroit, St. Louis,
Cleveland, and other cities.

Bro. T. M. Nottage & Wife
Established several churches along with
his brothers in the 1940's & 1950's.

The Nottage Brothers

Sis. Ruby Gall,
Wife of Founder, O.F. Gall

Bro. Owbridge Fay Gall Founder &
Elder of Grace & Glory Gospel Chapel.
He named the church after Psalm 84

Sis. Lucy Lewis, Founder

Sis. Lucy & Sis. Mullin, Founders
Allison McClean, Daughter of
Bro. Gall, Founder
Naomi Kilpatrick, Charter Member

Mrs. McCray

Bro. Lucious McCray
Founder

Bro. Frank Mullin, Founder
Sis. Marion Mullin, Founder
Bro. Edward Watkins, Elder

Elder George Ferguson & Wife, Mildred

Adine Douglas
Charter Member

Amber McNulty, Connie & Cheryl McNulty, Edwina
Reckley, Elizabeth Reckley, Edwina Reckley

Annie Mae Allen, Naomi, Lois & Lloyd, founded the land for Grace & Glory.

Elder Edward Watkins,
Daughter, Suzette

Cathlyn Hatch

Chef Stephen Watkins

Bro. Hamlin Mosely
Southside Gospel

Larry & Inez Clayton

Bro. Pershing Hatch

Sis. Adine Douglas, Mother of Inez
Historian

Mrs. Gall on the steps
Bro. Chambers
Bro. O. F. Fall & Sis. Comer

Sis. Nola Hicks, Historian
First Lady, Juanita Stem

The Bolt Family

Ansel & Stella Bolt
1991

Jack & Charlotte Mostert
Laflin Gospel Chapel

Lenard & Zita

Natasha & Charlton Jelks

Sisters Carter, Morgan & Watkins, Faithful
Cooks of Circle Y Ranch Camp

Brenda Johnson, Vivian Morgan, & Ruby Peak

Vernice & Pershing Hatch & Valoree & Charles Harrington

Grace & Glory Members, Past & Present

The Henry Family/Grace Bible Church

The Elders and their Wives

Westlawn Gospel Chapel

Mrs. Olive Banks, Dr. Leroy & Beverly Yates, Willie & Barbara Horton,
Bro. Anderson, Steve & Felecia Thompson, Rev. Dr. Joseph Rhoiney

Sis. Vernice Hatch

CHAPTER TWO

Challenge of the Times

Hope for a Better World

"We cannot hope to build

a better world

without improving

the individual . . .

each of us must work

toward his own

highest development,

Marie Curie

Changes of our Times

While Grace & Glory continued to grow spiritually and as people sought to bring the "lost" to the kingdom of God; as people developed and carried out plans for their families; as families grew and presented greater responsibilities; and as each individual Christian at Grace & Glory pursued their own personal goals, much was happening in our city, in our state, in our nation, and yes in the world.

On December 1, 1955, after a long day at work, a forty-two-year-old seamstress named Rosa Parks boarded the Cleveland Avenue bus in Montgomery, Alabama, and, being a "Negro", took her place at the back. Montgomery, like most southern cities in the 50's, had segregated buses. The first rows were for whites, the remaining rows for blacks. Rosa Parks sat at the front of the black section. But when the bus reached the next stop, enough whites got on to fill the white seats, leaving one white man standing, where upon the driver turned around to request that Parks and three other blacks give up their seats, as was the practice when the white area was filled. The three others complied, but Parks refused, sitting stone-faced. The driver asked her again, but she said "No."

He called the police and had her arrested. After her bond had been posted, she was released, but within hours, an elaborate network of civil rights leaders in Montgomery had met and determined that they would use Park's arrest to both challenge the constitutionality of the city's segregation laws and rally black commuters to a boycott of the city's bus system.

To lead them, the Montgomery organizers chose a twenty-six-year-old minister named Martin Luther King, Jr. Born Michael King, Jr., his name had been changed at age five by his preacher father, who changed his own, at the same time in order to pay respect to the Protestant religion's most powerful leader of reform and defiance. Dr. King had been in Montgomery less than a year when the boycott began. He seized the opportunity to put into practice the principles of non-violent protest he had learned from the writings of Mahandas K. Gandhi, the Hindu leader whose fasts had brought the era of British rule in India to an end.

King joined Gandhi's method of passive resistance with the Christian doctrine of love to create a form of nonviolent protest he referred to as "Christianity in action." The Montgomery demonstrators would force their opponents to justice not by confrontation, nor by submission, but by embrace. They would court their own arrests, and, if convicted, said King, they would "enter jail as a bridegroom enters the bride's chamber." He told his followers that they must commit no violence, raise no fist, no matter how powerful the provocation. "Blood may flow . . . before we receive our freedom, but it must be our blood."

To keep the Montgomery boycott going, more than twenty thousand black citizens formed car pools, drove bicycles, hired taxis, or simply walked to work. Their cars were stopped regularly by police in search of a violation, any violation, so much so that most car pool drivers crept along the roads at a snail's pace, signaling turns well in advance, so that police would have no reason to ticket them.

During the boycott, Montgomery's black citizens relied on an efficient car pool system that ferried people between more than forty pickup stations. Support for the protest came from within the black community – workers donated one fifth of their weekly salaries – as well as from outside groups such as the NAACP, the United Auto Workers, Montgomery's Jewish community, and sympathetic white southerners.

The protest went on for over a year, and always with the same dependable rhythm: the white establishment would challenge the protesters, the protesters would stand firm. Dr. King and his followers were on trial for another infraction – this time it was for "running a business without a franchise" (the "business" was the boycott car pool) – when news came that the Supreme Court had ruled in the protesters favor. Soon after, Martin Luther King, Jr. boarded a Montgomery bus, accompanied by Reverend Ralph Abernathy, Inez Jessie Baskin, and Reverend Glenn Smiley, a white minister from New York. After depositing fifteen cents into the coin slot, Dr. King then sat down in what had only recently been a "whites only" seat. The boycott had lasted 381 days.

At the same time African-American parents across the nation in the states of Delaware, South Carolina, Virginia, and the District of Columbia, were also challenging local school boards in their communities. Directed by the National Association for the Advancement of Colored People (NAACP), its local chapters, and its lawyers, these cases were brought before the United States Supreme Court. In 1954, these parents won their cases when the court decided:

> " . . . that in the field of public education the doctrine
> of separate but equal has no place. Separate educational
> facilities are inherently unequal . . . therefore plaintiffs
> and others . . . are deprived of the equal protection of the
> laws guaranteed by the Fourteenth Amendment of the
> Constitution."

Those who organized and argued the Brown case helped to change American history. Thurgood Marshall who was the director-counsel of the N.A.A.C.P. Legal Defense Fund, Inc. led the team of attorneys for the case. One of the attorneys who worked alongside Marshall was Robert L. Carter who recently passed away on January 3, 2012 at 94 years old. He provided the strategy for the case using the research of Kenneth and Mamie Clark, whose doll test demonstrated the impact that segregation had on Black children.

The Brown et al. vs. Board of Education of Topeka, Kansas, United States Supreme Court, May 17, 1954 was an important moment in American History that set the stage for dismantling decades of Jim Crow laws.

The battle to end legal segregation in America, which the Rev. King and others fought so hard for, had mostly been won by the end of the 1960's. Voting restrictions were abolished in the mid-1960's. Black leaders then began to concentrate on getting more and more African-Americans registered to vote. And beginning in the late 1960's and early 70's, an ever increasing number of Blacks did begin to win election to positions of power in government. By the 1980's, many of America's largest cities were being led by Black mayors. In 1984, It seemed that the civil rights movement had finally "arrived" with the presidential campaign of the Reverend Jesse Jackson, once a close aide to the Rev. Martin Luther King, Jr. His strong showings in both the 1984 and 1988 primary elections proved that millions of Americans, both Black and White, were now ready to take an African – American candidate for president seriously. Still, big problems continue to challenge African-Americans. Family breakdown, drugs and crime, a lack of jobs, and continuing racial prejudice have created a mood of deep despair among many Blacks left behind in the nation's run-down inner cities. The long struggle for racial justice is not over. But some things have improved in the lives of African Americans and in overcoming the nation's tragic legacy of racial strife and injustice.

Facts About The 1970's

Population	-	204,879,000
Unemployed in 1970	-	4,088,000
National Debt	-	$382 billion

Average Salary   - $7,564

Food prices: milk, 33 cents a qt; bread: 24 cents a loaf; round steak, $1.30 a pound

Life Expectancy - male, 67.1; female 74.8

The chaotic events of the 60's, including war and social change, seemed destined to continue in the 70's. Major trends included a growing disillusionment of government, advances in civil rights, increased influence of the women's movement, a heightened concern for the environment, and increased space exploration. Many of the "radical" ideas of the 60's gained wider acceptance in the new decade, and were mainstreamed into American life and culture. Amid war, social realignment and presidential impeachment proceedings, American culture flourished.

Two trends not directly related to education nonetheless heavily impacted the nation's schools and campuses during the seventies. Social movements, particularly the anti-war movement, were highly visible on college and university campuses. The Kent State massacre was the most devastating event, with four students gunned down by Ohio National Guardsmen attempting to stem the anti-war demonstration. In the lower grades, forced busing to achieve racial integration, particularly in Boston and other Northeastern cities, often led to violence and a disruption of the educational process. On a positive educational note, Congress guaranteed equal educational access to the handicapped with the Education of all Handicapped Children Act of 1975.

Houston's U.S. Representative Barbara Jordan gained national prominence with her eloquence during the Watergate investigation and hearings which resulted in impeachment proceedings against Nixon.

This decade saw the break up of the Beatles and the death of Elvis Presley, robbing rock of two major influences. Among the top names in music were: Aerosmith, Bee Gees, David Bowie, Alice Cooper, Fleetwood Mac, Billy Joel, Elton John, Led Zeppelin, John Lennon, Bruce Springstein, Rod Stewart, and the Who. "Easy listening" regained popularity with groups such as the Carpenters, and Bob Marley gained a huge core of fans in the U.S. performing Jamaican reggae music.

The Seventies was the decade of the big comeback for the movies. After years of box office erosion caused by the popularity of television, a combination of blockbuster movies and new technologies such as Panavision and Dolby sound brought the masses back to the movies. The sci-fic adventure and spectacular special effects of George Lucas' Star Wars made it one of the highest grossing films ever. Other memorable movies were the disaster movies, Towering Inferno, Earthquake, Poseidon Adventure, and Airport. Sylvester Stallone's Rocky reaffirmed the American dream and gave people a hero with a "little guy comes out on top" plot. The Godfather spawned multiple sequels. There also was the terror of Steven Spielberg's Jaws, the chilling Exorcist, and the moving Kramer vs. Kramer. There was a definite public yearning for simpler, more innocent times as evidenced by the popularity of the movies, American Graffiti and Grease, which both presented a romanticized view of the fifties. Saturday Night Fever with John Travolta fueled the "disco fever" already sweeping the music and dance club scenes; and the nation's experience in the Vietnam War and its aftermath influenced the theme of several movies, including Coming Home, The Deer Hunter, and Apocalypse Now.

Television came of age in the Seventies as topics once considered taboo were broached on the airwaves for the first time. Shows like, All in the Family had plots on many controversial issues such as abortion, race, and homosexuality. Saturday Night Live also satirized topics and people once thought of as off limits for such treatment, such as sex and religion. Nothing was considered sacred. Television satellite news broadcasts from the frontlines of the conflict in Vietnam continued to bring the honors of war into the homes of millions of Americans and intensified anti-war sentiment in the country. The immensely popular TV miniseries "Roots" fostered an interest in genealogy, a greater appreciation of whites for the plight of blacks, and an increased interest in African American history. "Happy Days", which followed the lives of a group of fifties-era teenagers, was TV's primary nod to nostalgia, while "The Brady Bunch" comically presented the contemporary family. The relatively new publically funded Corporation for Public Broadcasting gained viewers and statue with such fare as Sesame Street for children, and live broadcasts of the Senate Watergate hearings.

Facts About The 1980's

- Population – 226,546,000
- Unemployed in 1980 –
- National Debt – 1980 $914,000,000,000

- National Debt – 1986 $2,000,000,000,000
- Average salary – $15,757
- Life Expectancy – Male, 69.9, Female 77.6
- Minimum Wage – $3.10
- BMW was $12,000; Mercedes 280 E. was $14,800
- Attendance – at movies 20 million per week.

The 1980's became the Me! Me! Me! generation of status seekers. During the 1980's, hostile takeovers, leveraged buyouts, and mega-mergers spawned a new breed of billionaire. Donald Trump, Leona Helmsley, and Ivan Boesky iconed the meteoric rise and fall of the rich and famous. If you've got it, flaunt it and you can have it all! were watchwords. Binge buying and credit became a way of life and "Shop Til You Drop" was the watch word. Video games, aerobics, minivans, camcorders, and talk shows became part of our lives. The decade began with double-digit inflation, Reagan declared a war on drugs, Kermit didn't find it easy to be green, hospital costs rose, we lost many, many of our finest talents to AIDS which before the decade ended spread to black and hispanic women, and unemployment rose. Jesse Jackson was the first black man to run for president. The stock market tripled in 7 years yet survived the 1987 crash. Televangelist Jim Bakker was sentenced to 45 years for selling bogus lifetime vacations. Rock Hudson, movie star, died of AIDS in 1985. Prisons overflowed and violent crime rates which, in 1980, had tripled since 1960, continued to climb with the appearance of crack in 1985. From 1985 to 1990, the use of cocain addiction was up 35 percent, though the number of users had declined. Nancy Reagan's "Just Say No" campaign had great influence. Toward the end of the decade, President George H. W. Bush called for a kinder, gentler, nation and volunteerism and contribution reached an all time high.

The 80's continued the trends of the 1960's and 1970's – more divorces, more unmarrieds living together, more single parent families. The two-earner family was even more common than in previous decades, more women earned college and advanced degrees, married, and had fewer children.

Materialism and self-indulgence characterized the atmosphere of the 1980's as yuppie culture emerged, and for an elite few value was judged in houses, cars, and gadgets. President Ronald Reagan's economic policies left countless auto workers and farmers searching for jobs. The personal computer age began in the eighties when two guys named Steve introduced the Apple Computer to the world. Sadly, in 1980, a crazed gunman murdered John Lennon. In 1984, the music video became a staple in popular culture when MTV hit the airwaves. In 1986, tragedy struck when the space shuttle "Challenger" exploded shortly after take-off killing all seven crew members including a schoolteacher. Headway in international relations occurred in 1989 when out of the blue the Cold War ended with the collapse of the Soviet Union and the fall of the Berlin Wall.

In education, in 1980, college freshmen were more interested in status, power, and money than at any time during the past 15 years. Conservatives advocated a return to the classics for college students and back to the basic skills for public school students. An attempt was made to improve the teacher quality by slightly raising salaries. Columbia University, the last all male, Ivy League School, began accepting women in 1983. President Reagan endorsed a constitutional amendment to permit school prayer. It was defeated.

Team sports were popular with kids and their mothers ran car pool after work. Kids had after school, weekend cheerleading, baseball, football, soccer, gym, dance, and jazz.

Food of the 80's included fast food places like Taco Bell and McDonald's. Kids loved Sweet arts, Skittles, Nerds, Roots, Hubba Bubba Chewing Gum, and Five Alive.

The "Flashdance" look had young and old in tank tops, tight-fitting pants, and leg warmers. Teens wore Michael Jackson's glove and Madonna's fishnet stockings, leather, and chains. Older women wore the "Out of Africa" look. Sneakers were so popular and so expensive that shoe companies were accused of cashing in on the easy drug money picked up by inner city kids.

Cable was born and MTV, originally intended to be promos for albums, had an enormous impact on music and young people. The digital compact disc (Cd) revolutionized the music industry. Pop, rock, country and especially rap music became popular in the 80's. Rap music had started in prison 20 years earlier by jailed black inmates who, in the absence of instruments, turned poetic meter into musical rhythm. The early rap heard on ghetto streets was abrasive and laced with hostility toward society.

Important names during this time were Milli Vanilli, M. C. Hammer, and L. L. Cool J. Michael Jackson's album, "Thiller", became the best selling album of all time. Also big during this decade were: Stevie Wonder, Kenny Rogers, Paul McCartney, Rolling Stones, David Bowie, Julio Iglesias, Willie Nelson, Billie Joel, The Commodores, Bruce Springsteen, Whitney Houston, and Bonnie Raitt.

T.V. innovations and trends included anti-family sitcoms like Roseanne, Married With Children, Geraldo, Phil Donahue, Sally, Oprah, Bill Cosby, and Jerry Seinfeld. Infotainment included: Nightline with Ted Koppel, CNN Cable News, and 20/20 with Hugh Downs and Barbara Walters.

Facts About the 1990's

- Population – 281,421,906
- Unemployment – 5.8 million, 4.2%
- National Debt – $3.830 Trillion
- Average Salary – $13.37 hr.
- Teacher's Salary – $39,347
- Minimum Wage – $5.15/hr.
- Life Expectancy – Male 73.1, Female 79.1

The 1990's was the electronic age. The World Wide Web was born in 1992, changing the way we communicate (e-mail), spend our money (online stores), and do business (e-commerce). In 1989, 15% of American households had a computer. And by 2000, it increased to 51%, with 41.5% online. Internet lingo like plug-ins, BTW (by the way), GOK (God only knows) IMHO (In my humble opinion), FAQs, SPAM, FTP, ISP, and phrases like "See you online", or "The server's down" or "Bill Gates" became part of our everyday vocabulary. And everyone had a cell phone.

During this decade, theme restaurants like Planet Hollywood and casinos like New York-New York in Las Vegas proliferated. Health care and elder care homes were big business for builders and architects during these ten years. Martha Stewart became the guru of home crafts and design.

Reading entire books online became available and audio books became the rage. If you were taking a trip, you could listen to a book in the car. The biggest trend in book selling during the 1990's included online bookstores and publishers like amazon.com. Mega-bookstores like <u>Borders</u> or <u>Barnes</u> and <u>Noble</u> drove the small specialized bookstores out of business. The price of books skyrocketed and half-priced books (used books) became popular. Oprah Winfrey's picks encouraged a new readership and culminated in <u>Oprah's</u> <u>Book</u> <u>Club</u>. Some of the best selling authors were Toni Morrison, Danielle Steele, and Tom Clancy.

In the 1990's, the United States played the role of world policemen, sometimes alone but more often in alliances. The decade began with Saddam Hussein's invasion of Kuwait and the resultant <u>Gulf</u> <u>War</u>. The decade was to end much as it began with U.S. forces deployed in many countries, and the U.S. playing arbitrator, enforcer, and peace keeper throughout the world.

Violence seemed a part of life. In 1992 South-Central Los Angeles rioted after four white policemen were acquitted of video-taped assault charges for beating a black motorist, Rodney King. In 1993, terrorism came to the American shores as a bomb was detonated in the garage beneath the World Trade Center in New York City. Americans were glued to their TV sets in 1995 as the football hero, O. J. Simpson, was tried for the murder of his ex-wife, Nicole, and her male friend, Ron Goldman. This trial pointed out the continued racial division in the country as most blacks applauded the not guilty verdict while most whites thought an obviously guilty man had gotten away with murder. In the months between February, 1996 and April, 1999, there were at least fourteen incidents of school shootings with the most lethal being on April 20, 1999 when 14 students and 1 teacher were killed and 23 wounded at Columbine High School in Littleton, Colorado.

There was good news, also. The booming economy led to record low unemployment. Minimum wage was increased to $5.15 an hour. The stock market reached an all-time high as individuals learned to buy and trade by way of the internet. Americans enjoyed the country's affluence by traveling more by reveling in sporting events such as the Atlanta Summer Olympics – 1996, and by "consuming" as never before. America faced the new millennium with an open, diversified society, a functioning democracy, a healthy economy, and the means and will to face and overcome its problems.

On December 31, 1999, at noon, the United States returned management and control of the Panama Canal and the Canal Zone to Panama. This ended a remarkable period of 85 years in which the United States' control over the waterway served as a powerful reminder of the strength of the U.S. in the Western Hemisphere.

Beginning with Ronald Reagan, the stage was set for performers to become more publicly involved in government. Business men felt they had the abilities which made them natural leaders and viable candidates for public office. Secretary of State, Madeline Albright provided an American presence abroad. Military leader, Colin Powell was popular and was considered to be a strong candidate for the presidency, but he chose not to run for office. Sally Ride was the first woman to explore space.

Dominating the world of technology were Steve Jobs and Bill Gates. Successful women included Oprah Winfrey and Martha Stewart. Michael Jordan and Tiger Woods were heroes for all young athletes. Two important losses were Jackie Kennedy O'Nassis to cancer, and later her son, John F. Kennedy, Jr. in a plane crash.

Television graced 98% of the households in the U.S. in 1998 with the average viewer spending seven hours a day watching T.V. CNN had live coverage of the Gulf War in 1991. I was at a Leadership Conference in Arizona during the first night of the war and we were in awe to actually be witnessing the bombs being dropped and the lights from the explosions right there on a big, big screen. We were all very sad, and those of us that were there in that room had prayer and a moment of silence. It was a moment that was similar to when John F. Kennedy was assassinated. You remember what you were doing at the time that it happened.

The Academy Award Winning Movies of the decade were:

- 1990 Dances With Wolves
- 1991 Silence of the Lambs
- 1992 Unforgiven
- 1993 Schindler's List
- 1994 Forrest Gump
- 1995 Braveheart
- 1996 The English Patient
- 1997 Titanic

- 1998 Shakespeare in Love
- 1999 American Beauty

- 1990 Hubble Telescope Launched Into Space
  Nelson Mandela Freed

- 1991 Collapse of the Soviet Union
  Operation Desert Storm
  South Africa Repeals Apartheid Laws

- 1992 Official end of the Cold War
  Riots in Los Angeles after the Rodney
  King verdict

- 1993 Cult Compound in Waco, Texas Raided
  World Trade Center Bombed

- 1994 Nelson Mandela Elected President of South Africa
  O. J. Simpson Arrested for Double Murder

- 1995 Oklahoma City Bombing

- 1996 Two Royal Divorces

- 1997 Hale-Bopp Comet Visible
  Hong Kong Returned to China
  Princess Diana Dies in Car Crash
  Scientists Clone Sheep
  Tiger Woods Wins Masters

- 1998   India and Pakistan Test Nuclear Weapons
         "Titanic" Most Successful Movie Ever
         U.S. President Clinton Impeached

- 1999   JFK, Jr. Dies in Plane Crash
         Killing Spree at Columbine High School

- 2000   Elian Gonzalez Goes Home
         Russian Submarine Sunk in Barents Sea
         Unclear Winner in U.S. Presidential Election

Chapter Three

The People

Grace & Glory Gospel Chapel
Church Family

1946 – 2014

"For by grace are ye saved through faith; and that not of yourselves: it is the gift of God; not of works, lest any man should boast." Ephesians 2:8-9

"Ye are of God, little children, and have over come them; for greater is He that is in you, than he that is in the world." I John 4:4

Bro. Owbridge Fay Gall, Founder

Bro. Owbridge Fay Gall was born on the island of Barbados probably around 1900' or 1901. The island of Barbados is the eastern most island in the Lesser Antilles. When Bro. Gall talked to us about his birthplace, I was fascinated. It seemed like an exotic place to visit (this was before I saw the Caribbean islands on 4 cruises). Barbados is situated in the Atlantic Ocean, east of the other West Indian Islands. I don't really know which city Bro. Gall lived in, but it could have been the capital and main city, Bridgetown. Barbados became an independent country in November, 1966 with Queen Elizabeth II as head of state. The 1780 hurricane killed over 4,000 people on the island and in 1854, a cholera epidemic killed over 20,000 inhabitants. At emancipation in 1833, the size of the slave population was approximately 83,000. Between 1946-1980, Barbados' rate of population growth was diminished by one-third because of emigration to Britain and the U.S. Grammy Award winner, Rihanna, is a native of the island, having been born in the city of Saint Michael. The Merrymen are a well-known Calypso band that is based in Barbados, performing from the 1960's to the 2010's.

Bro. Gall left the island and settled into the state of New York, the city of Brooklyn. He joined the congregation of the Grace Gospel Chapel where he remained until he came to Chicago, Illinois. He joined with Bro. Theodore Williams at the Grace Gospel Hall. There was a deep split among the Brethren, with Bro. Williams remaining and Bro. Gall, Bro. Lucius McCray, and Bro. William Frank Mullin leaving and forming another assembly, Grace & Glory Gospel Chapel. Bro. Owbridge Fay Gall was very strict, very "straight-laced" and he "took no prisoners" for what he believed to be true, he stood by that. He did not "give in" to criticism of his beliefs, his policies; he did not give in to "whims" and other ideas of others; he did not bend, not even a little, when it came to the doctrines practiced at Grace & Glory. He taught us to:

(1) Wear a covering on your head for worship service and communion each Sunday. Communion was observed each Sunday; not once per month like some other churches.
(2) Be on time – don't practice CPT (Colored Peoples' Time)
(3) Women may not wear pants (not to church, not at home, not outside, not anywhere, not anytime).
(4) Study the Word of God daily. Bro. Gall believed in bringing your bible to the Assembly each Lord's Day (Sunday) and for Bible Class (Thursday). He believed in saints <u>knowing</u> the Word of God. He wanted us to be knowledgeable about Jesus and the promises in His Word.
(5) Grace & Glory was an "Assembly" of believers, not "Church". The believers are the church; the church building is an "Assembly".

The believers sought to abide by those principles. Bro. Gall was married to Sis. Ruby Gall in 1926 in New York and they both attended Grace Gospel Chapel. Sis. Gall was the one person that Bro. Gall responded to. She had a strong will and was truly Bro. Gall's partner. She had a "voice" and made her point clearly, whatever it happened to be. Sis. Gall told us (as young mothers, still having babies) to go to the drugstore to get birth control if needed. She was bold and fearless, and she was like a mother, or grandmother to us. She and Bro. Gall had one daughter, Allison McClean, and she had one son, "Joseph" or "Jesus" McClean. I spoke to Allison, over the years, about once a year to see how she was doing. One day, about 2 years ago, I tried to get her on the phone and the phone was no longer in service. I called her church, Grace Gospel Chapel in New York and was informed that Allison had passed away. She lived in Brooklyn, New York for decades. When Bro. Gall went to be with the Lord in May, 1971, his body was shipped to New York for a second funeral and for burial. Sis. Lucy Lewis, Lois Colar, and I went to New York for Bro. Gall's services. We spent the night at Allison's home in Brooklyn.

The last time I talked to Allison, she was going through a difficult time; her husband was ill and suffering from dementia and it was very stressful for her; and she had concerns about her son. If I'm not mistaken, Sis. Ruby Gall went to be with the Lord in June, 1990.

Bro. Lucius McCray

Bro. Lucius McCray was one of the brothers, along with Bro. Owbridge Fay Gall, and Bro. William Frank Mullin, who founded Grace & Glory Gospel Chapel. He was part of the deep and bitter split between Bro. Gall and Bro. Theodore Williams, Sr. At that time, they were all members of Grace Gospel Hall on the south side of Chicago. Bro. Gall, Bro. Mullin, and Bro. McCray left Grace Gospel Hall and founded Grace & Glory in 1947.

Bro. McCray was of medium height, and medium size, with a upright stance and a proud demeanor. He was a very strong man, with very strong convictions. He was opinionated and was not shy in telling others what he believed to be true. He was at Grace & Glory for many years before moving to a beautiful little place called Altadena, California. It's located between Los Angeles and San Diego, close to Perris, California where Inez Clayton and Sis. Adine Douglas lived. My husband, Lenzo, and our children (& me) visited the McCrays one year after they moved there. I was fascinated by the place – the street they lived on was lined, on both sides, with homes that resembled showplaces of the "rich and famous." When we walked into the McCray's home, it was no different. It was elegant and beautiful, with furniture and walls in colors of white, and blue, and silver. They were gracious hosts and I remember Sis. McCray holding one of the children on her lap. We had a wonderful visit.

I remember Sis. Roberta McCray, as a small lady, very fair complexioned (like Bro. McCray) with silver, white hair like silk. She wore thick eye glasses and was always impeccably dressed. She wore dresses of silk and lace and chiffon and fine cotton. She had a soft voice and everyone who came to Grace & Glory was questioned by her. She'd ask, "Are you saved? Do you know the Lord?" "You can be saved right now!" She did this every Sunday, without fail. Sis. McCray prepared delicious meals at her home and on some Sundays, she graciously invited me and my children to her home for dinner. It was always enjoyable because in addition to the food, she loved conversation. She was a great talker and had strong feelings about people and about the current news of the day. She led an interesting life. Bro. McCray was her second husband and she simply adored him. Some Christians frowned on her having gotten a divorce and getting married again, but she was not offended by it. She kept being her "spread the gospel" self.

After they moved to California, they found a bible teaching church there in Altadena and contributed much to its ministry.

Years later, after Sis. McCray died, Bro. Lucius McCray married again. He remained there until his death. He and Sis. Roberta McCray were wonderful believers and contributed much to the culture and tradition of the little assembly called Grace & Glory Gospel Chapel.

William Frank Mullin
Founder

William Frank Mullin, along with Owbridge Fay Gall, founded Grace & Glory Gospel Chapel. He was known, and was mostly called, "Frank Mullin." He was born in Marietta, Georgia on October 14, 1904. Bro. Mullin came to Chicago during his early childhood years. He was prominent during his adult life and one wonders what it must have been like, as a kid, in Marietta, Georgia. Like so many other black families, he migrated north to seek a better future and to seek more freedom in another city, Chicago.

Bro. Mullin accepted the Lord as his savior as a young man through the ministry of Bro. B. M. Nottage at the dinner table of his future wife, Marion. He later helped to establish Grace & Glory Gospel Chapel along with Bro. Gall. He loved Grace & Glory and served as the elder brother until his death on July 19, 1986. His duties as Elder included preaching the gospel of the Lord Jesus Christ, visiting the sick and shut-in, picking up Christians to take them to the Assembly, and planning conferences and programs.

Bro. Mullin was strict, wanting to have believers understand the sanctity of the "Breaking of Bread," Communion Service. It was very important to him. He was also a stickler for time. Promptness to the meetings were essential and if you served as a Sunday School teacher, you could not just come for Sunday School. You had to also attend the Communion Service and the Sunday Morning Worship Service. Although he was stern and really committed to spiritual correctness and tradition, he had a warm, personable, and friendly side. He cared about the believers at Grace & Glory and sought to meet their spiritual needs in a loving, Christ-like way.

Bro. Mullin was hard-working; and having worked at the American Maize Products Company for years until his retirement.

He met and fell in love with Marion Lewis, and they later married. They were completely devoted to each other. They never had children, just the two of them. He was a doting and caring husband for his wife during her years of illness. He unceasingly cared for her in a loving, tender manner, seeking to make her as comfortable as possible. Sis. Mullin looked on him as a precious man.

Bro. Mullin's favorite scripture verse was I Timothy 1:15, which he recited almost every Sunday:

"This is a faithful saying, and worthy of all acceptation, that Christ Jesus came into the world to save sinners, of whom I am chief."

The saints at Grace & Glory really missed him when he died, suddenly, in July, 1986. His funeral was held at the church, and Bro. Willie Horton preached the Eulogy; Inez played the piano; Bro. Anderson and Sis. Reckley and Sis. Mayola Fain sang solos.

Marian Harland Lewis Mullin was Bro. Frank Mullins wife. She was born in Chicago, Illinois to John Lewis and Lucy Morgan. She was the sister of Sis. Lucy Lewis, of Grace & Glory. Marian accepted the Lord Jesus Christ as a young girl and attended the Portage Park Gospel Hall Sunday School class on the North Side, for several years. When Grace & Glory Gospel Chapel was established, Sis. Mullin was a faithful member. She remained faithful until she became ill in 1983.

She was an outstanding primary teacher, with excellent diction and a strong intimidating voice. She stressed excellence from her students and also the children at Grace & Glory. She received her B.A. Degree from Northwestern University, serving as a teacher in the Chicago Public School System for many years.

Sis. Mullin passed away in November, 1986, four months after her husband, William Frank Mullin, died. Pastor Leroy Yates preached the Eulogy. Sis. Mayola Fain and Sis. Beverly Yates sang solos. She was sorely missed by the believers at Grace & Glory.

Sis. Lucy

Sis. Lucy was such an important person in the history of Grace & Glory Gospel Chapel. She was there, at the beginning, with Bro. & Sis. Mullin (her sister) and Bro. Gall. She was instrumental in our Sunday School where she taught the children portions of scripture in her own special way. She was a teacher by profession and she absolutely loved to teach the bible to children. Sis. Lucy also enjoyed prepping children to do their parts perfectly on the Easter Program and the Christmas Program. She, along with Sis. Mullin, stressed boldness, projection, diction, and grammar. She demanded that children (and adults) memorize their parts. Her influence is still felt at Grace & Glory. She was loved and respected by us all.

Sis. Lucy had an interesting family history which was the first attempt I made to write it. I wanted to share with others, on paper, the life story of Lucy Lewis. Her father, John Lewis, wanted the best for all seven of his children, Henry Willis, Elizabeth E., Lucy Ann, John Walter, Jr. Edward Oliver, Marvin, and Frederick. He expected them to obey and if they did not, they would get a spanking (mostly the boys!) The girls "pleased" him, but the boys did not.

John Walter Lewis, Sr., Sis. Lucy's father was born in a little place called Crewe, Virginia probably around the time of the Civil War. He was an only child raised in a strict household of very proud parents. As an adult, he walked with his shoulders back, and carried himself as a statesman. Sis. Lucy's mother, Lucy Jane Morgan Lewis, was of medium build, medium complexion and a very distinct voice. She met John and they fell instantly in love. She was also from Crewe, Virginia and had 4 siblings – three sisters – Frances, Cammie, and Laura, and one brother, Baker.

John Walter Lewis, Sr. was of average height with an intellectual appearance and also was very intelligent, with a very intellectual demeanor. He had a fair-skinned complexion and was of medium build. He read a lot and read a lot to his children, with all the dramatics. Sis. Lucy loved to listen to him read the stories. He worked in City Hall, in the Comptroller's Office in Chicago, the only black in the office. John, Sr. was very congenial, very likable, very personable.

The year he died (unknown), he died suddenly, it was in February. It was a bad snowstorm. He got off the street car at Irving Park & Central and he had to trudge through the snow to their house which was several blocks away. He was very tired when he got home. He died soon after getting home of a massive heart attack. He was a super father! exclaimed Sis. Lucy.

I imagined that Mr. Lewis was like the character, Henry Townsend, in the book, "The Known World". The book depicts the 1850's and the 1860's (and beyond), right before the Civil War between the States. In 1855, in Manchester County, Virginia there were thirty-four free black families, with a mother and father and one child or more, and eight of those free families owned slaves, and all eight knew one another's business. Like Henry Townsend, John Lewis was an only child and undoubtedly came into wealth for when he and his wife migrated to Chicago, they bought property and built a modest and attractive home. The property was like a prairie for when he built his house there were no other houses around. Years later, a "bustling" and "thriving", white neighborhood grew up around his family. Mr. Lewis sent his children to the white, public schools within their neighborhood. His daughters, Elizabeth, Lucy, and Marion would later become teachers and they taught in all-white schools.

Mr. John Walter Lewis was indeed a remarkable man. Sis. Lucy's mother, Lucy Jane Morgan Lewis, was kindhearted, but stern; not as stern as the father, but stern, non the less. She was light-complexioned, of average height, somewhat heavy weight, and very stately-looking. She used to teach school in the south, but after moving to Chicago, she remained a housewife.

She was an excellent cook and enjoyed it. She created her own recipes, or she got some from magazines or papers. She tried them on her family and if they didn't like it, she never fixed it again. Mrs. Lewis could sew, but she never knitted or crocheted.

Sis. Lucy stated that they lived in that house (5621 Berenice) and in that neighborhood all by themselves. She said there were houses 6 or 7 blocks away. The family used to go to a Swedish Church and they spoke Swedish along with the members, although they did not know what they were saying. Mrs. Lewis tried to teach her children to be good housekeepers, good cooks, keep everything nice and clean, remember their allegiance to the Lord, go to church, and keep themselves nice and neat and clean. She died in 1923 of cancer of the breast. She called her children in to her to say "Goodbye". Sis. Lucy and Johnny came, but the others did not respond. She suffered for about 2 months before she passed away.

Sis. Lucy attended the William Perry Gray School located at 3730 No. Laramie, near Kilpatrick Av. & Irving Park Road. She was the only black face there. Elizabeth and Marvin went to another school. I was completely mesmerized by Sis. Lucy's story. Her childhood was so interesting.

Her and her family lived on this prairie type land with nothing around except this little shack. It had a pump and Sis. Lucy and her siblings used to go there to get water from that old pump. As I mentioned the school was located between Kilpatrick Av. and Irving Park Road and the kids called it the "Tin Can School". There was one teacher, Ms. Dignum, who taught all the grades. A janitor came to the school each day to put coal in the little potbelly stove. He stayed all day to tend to the fire. He was irritable, and the kids teased him. Ms. Dignum, on the other hand, was nice to the kids; So motherly, so sweet and kind. She had to take the streetcar to the school to teach the children and she used to get very cold on her way. Ms. Dignum opened the class with the Pledge of Allegiance to the flag and a quotation. After the "Tin Can School", they built a big school on Laramie & Grace called the William Perry Gray School. Sis. Lucy graduated from that school and she later became a teacher in her own right. During her teaching career, where she taught almost all white children, she used quotations that she wrote on the board, every day. The students would memorize them and recite them in chorus at the end of the week. After graduating from the Gray School, Sis. Lucy attended the Schurz H. A. Then she went to the Normal College (now Chicago State University) at 69th and Stewart. She went there for two years and then they assigned her to Peabody School, located at 1444 W. Augusta. Her classroom was right on the stairway, and the children used to call her "coony-bug". She was very upset. They stopped after a while. The Principal encouraged her to stay in spite of the problem. The problem was worked out and the children would grow to like her a lot. Sis. Lucy remained at that school for 25 years. She loved it. She taught mostly white, polish children with the exception of one or two black children.

Previously at the Schurz School, Sis. Lucy and her siblings went to different rooms; each room was a different grade. They were the only black kids there, but it was no problem because the kids treated them as white and they felt like they were white. The teachers never made any difference with them, whether black or white. If the teachers were prejudiced, she never recognized it. Their subjects were: algebra, English, zoology, chemistry, physics, gym, and music. Sis. Lucy was taught to play the piano, but she hated it; she did not do well with it. She never learned to be a proficient player. Her sister, Sis. Marian Mullin, however became an accomplished pianist. She later taught a mixed choir that included 3 black students.

Sis. Lucy encountered many principals and assistant principals over a 25 year period, as they came in and out at the Peabody School. She got along with all of them. She enjoyed teaching there. She met her best friend there, Esther Yost. They were inseparable, so they were known as the "Gold Dust Twins". I received a letter from Ms. Yost in February, 1982 after she, and Sis. Lucy had lunch together. Sis. Lucy loved going to Marshall Fields downtown, to shop and to have lunch. She had gone to Fields because I had given her a gift card. She had invited Esther Yost to join her. She came and they enjoyed the time together. She said she was lucky to have been invited to share in Sis. Lucy's birthday. They had a delicious lunch and enjoyed their time together. Ms. Yost commended Sis. Lucy for influence with her students and was amazed at her "deep devotion to God." I have treasured that letter from her all these many years.

Sis. Lucy retired from the Chicago Public Schools and was asked how she spends her day? She works in her yard, doing things around the house, helping with the cooking, and doing other things. She thought about her teaching a lot but she couldn't say that she missed it.

The Sisters of Grace & Glory visited Sis. Lucy often after her retirement. She loved having us visit and would always fix something special for our enjoyment. At Christmas time, she made cookies, all different kinds of delicious cookies – including her famous lemon bars – and put them in little "tins" and gave each one of us a "tin" (that held a lot of cookies) to take to our families.

Sis. Lucy never married and never spoke of it, and never seemed bothered by it. She told me that she was engaged once to a gentleman named Richard Shirley. He was a West Indian. He was insanely jealous and they eventually broke up. She never had another romantic relationship after that.

During her later years, as she began to age, after losing her sisters, and her brothers, and finding herself with no one except adopted relatives, her quality of life changed. Sis. Vernice Hatch often spent the night (sometimes 2 and 3 nights) with her to "keep her company" and to keep her from being alone in that big house. It was the same house that her father had built. She lived in the house with Sis. Marian Mullin, her sister, and Bro. Frank Mullin, her brother-in-law until their deaths. Her brothers had each passed away, as well. The ladies from Grace & Glory and also from some of the other assemblies continued to visit her. She gave us beautiful pieces of jewelry. She had tons of pieces that she had purchased over the years, mainly from Marshall Fields (now Macy's). She picked out special pieces and gave to each one of us. We were all delighted. Sis. Lucy's "cousins", put her in a nursing facility where she later died at 91 years old.

As I think of her, I am reminded that this unusual, outstanding Christian woman, lived a wonderful life before God and man, and God blessed her tremendously. It is also interesting to note that Sis. Lucy was born on Christmas Day, December 25, 1900. She was a special gift from God and she, in turn, gave many gifts to mankind.

Sis. Lucy loved Ecclesiastes 9:10 and shared it over and over with her Sunday School Class. *"Whatsoever thy hand findeth to do, do it with thy might; for there is no work, nor device, nor knowledge, nor wisdom in the grave, whether thou goest."*

Willie James Horton

Willie James Horton currently serves as Elder, teacher, and preacher at Grace & Glory Gospel Chapel. He has led the congregation for some 40 plus years from the pulpit. Bro. Willie has an insatiable thirst for knowledge of the Word of God which causes him to spend countless hours searching the scriptures. He reads extensively and shares his gift of expository teaching enthusiastically. He's been at Grace & Glory since his teen years, where he attended the Sunday School classes. Bro. Howard Wood picked up him and his future wife, Barbara Looney, along with other students and took them to the Sunday School on the west side of Chicago. Eventually classes were held at Grace & Glory.

Bro. Horton conducts the worship service, beginning with the Breaking of Bread ceremony, and concludes with the Gospel message.

Bro. Horton worked for Sears, Roebuck, & Co. for over 30 years, like his dad, never missing a day, and never late, always prompt and hard-working. He never ran away from a difficult task. He accepted every responsibility given to him. Bro. Horton's responsibilities as Elder of Grace & Glory have been difficult at times, and exhausting, but rewarding as he continues to "stand by the stuff." in the ministry. Through the grace of God, Bro. Horton continues to serve the congregation of Grace & Glory – and the surrounding community – preaching the gospel of Jesus Christ, our Lord.

Bro. Horton is uncompromising in his beliefs. On November 14, 1999, he preached a sermon on "The Fall and the Promise of Redemption" (biblical title), Genesis 3. He said, "Satan is attacking (1) the family, (2) the government, and (3) the church – all three which is the "core of society." Satan's weapon – deception; losing respect for the Word of God; he mentioned that, after the fall, – Eve's spirit died; her soul died, and her body died. God, however, reversed it."

Further evidence of his uncompromising belief – on August 17, 2003, he stated during his message: "In the beginning, God created man in His own image. Today, men are trying to create a "god" in their own imagination". On September 28, 2003, Bro. Horton stated:

"If it's new, it's not true – If its true, it's not new, it's old."

Although Bro. Horton is very strict and very disciplined, he has a soft side, and a realistic view of his responsibility as the leader at Grace & Glory.

He preached a powerful message on October 31, 2010 at the morning worship service. His text was from Exodus 17:1-16. He talked about the

Amaleks and how they were Israel's first enemy in the wilderness. The Amaleks killed the first king, Saul.

Bro. Horton expounded on each verse, going verse by verse in scripture. It brought back memories of Bro. Gall, who founded Grace & Glory.

Elder Willie Horton was born in Chicago, Illinois on February 19, 1944. His wife, Barbara, was born in 1946. Willie is the oldest of 6 children, 4 boys and 2 girls. His three brothers are George, Jr., Harold, and Larry. George, Jr. passed away; Harold lives here in Chicago, and Larry lives in Sacramento, California. His two sisters are Jeardean Horton and Onedia Thomas. Jeardean died in 1993.

Bro. Horton and his wife, Barbara, married in 1969. They had 5 children – Randy, Timothy, Aaron, Priscilla, and Rachel; and 5 grand children.

When asked what he enjoys doing, he stated that he loves worshipping and serving God, and he loves music. He sings beautifully well and plays a "mean" guitar. Actually, Bro. Horton plays softly and precisely. When asked if we are showing love to one another, he stated, "I believe we are meeting the spiritual needs of our members. I believe we are showing love, and I believe a lot of times its' based on what we believe showing love is and includes, showing love to a sister is different than showing love to a brother. Children and adults differ also." Bro. Horton's ministry continues.

Bro. Tyrone Stem

Bro. Tyrone Stem served as Elder of Grace & Glory Gospel Chapel for many years. He brought the gospel message every other Sunday, sharing the pulpit with Elder Willie Horton. Bro. Stem brought many memorable moments to his messages. He brought the message on Sunday, February 11, 2007. It was a beautiful Sunday with a lot of things going on. Can goods and clothing were donated and given to Pacific Garden Mission to give to the homeless. The gospel message that Bro. Stem preached was also an invitation to the congregation to give to the Excellent Way House for Homeless Women & Children. At the time of Bro. Stem's message, four other Elders were still serving and were still here. They were: Bro. George Ferguson, Bro. Timothy Horton, Bro. Willie Horton, and Bro. Edward Watkins.

On November 18, 2012, Bro. Stem's "invite," Rev. Ferlander N. Lewis, served as Guest Speaker. It was Grace & Glory's 52nd Anniversary with many guests in attendance. Bro. Lewis "rocked the house." He brought a wonderful message that was interspersed with humor and power designed to grab your attention. The next month on December 23, 2012, Bro. Stem brought a powerful Christmas message; and again the next year on Sunday, December 22, 2013. On Sunday, July 22, 2012, Bro. Stem conducted a Christening Ceremony for his little grandson, Joseph L. Brownlee, III at G & G. The parents are Natia and Joseph Brownlee, Jr.

Bro. Stem showed his bravery, his talent, his dignity, his great faith in the Lord, his courage, and his determination by his service at Grace & Glory. He sought to have others look at the way they behave as Christians and sometimes, there was disagreement. When there was dissention, we all looked for resolution and harmony. The same thing is done in our families. When there is discord, we seek to correct it right away. We realize that angry words and bruised egos may arise from time to time, but we try not to let it harm the integral fellowship of our Assembly. By the grace of God, we seek to strengthen, encourage and restore brothers and sisters in difficulty, being mindful of our responsibility for maintaining peace and fellowship.

Bro. Tyrone Stem is a Viet Nam and Gulf War veteran as a member of both the Air Force and the Army. Tyrone's military experience spans 19 years, which includes him being part of the 928th Tactical Airlift that was deemed the safest flying unit in the Air Force. He was introduced to "trucking" by his brother and after earning his degree and being a mechanic in the Air Force; he earned his CDL from Prairie State College.

When Bro. Stem went to Schneider National as a company driver, his plan was to take the Schneider career path to becoming a Small Business Owner Operator. After 5 years of being a company driver, he contacted Schneider Finance, Inc. (Small Business Owner Operator Development) and is now the owner of his own business and a new Freightliner Cascadia.

Bro. Tyrone Stem is blessed to have his parents, Mr. and Mrs. Stem, with him. He has been married for some 30 years to Juanita Hatch Stem and they have 2 adult children, Natia Stem Brownlee and Akil Stem. Natia is married to Joseph Brownlee, Jr. and they have 3 boys – Isaac, Joseph, III & Josiah.

Bro. Stem continues to be in active ministry for the Lord and enjoys spending time with his wife, kids, and grandkids.

Timothy J. Horton

Timothy Horton is an occupational therapist and enjoys making a difference in the lives of people. He is responsible for helping people exercise to stay healthy and fit on their jobs.

Timothy was married to Katina Horton for several years, and they had two children, Timothy, Jr. and Hanna. The children are very bright and talented. Timothy, Jr. plays the guitar and Hannah plays the piano and I think, the violin.

Tim served at Grace & Glory Gospel Chapel as Elder for several years. He came to the church as a baby for he is the son of Willie and Barbara Horton. He sat under the teaching and leadership of his father from a child.

Timothy preached sermons that always dealt with our everyday practical lives. He taught that the Word of God should guide us in every minute detail of our experiences.

During one of his sermons, Bro. Timothy stressed these three points:

(1) Sin will take you farther than you want to go
(2) Sin will keep you longer than you want to stay
(3) Sin will have you paying more than you want to pay.

Bro. Timothy Horton preached a sermon on Dec. 2, 2001 stating that there is a building ladder between earth to heaven; Christ is the ladder; angels are descending and ascending, but you can't get angels without the ladder. You can't pray for something you can't see unless you have faith in God. Faith is essential:

(1) Take the Word of God seriously.
(2) Have faith in God's Word
(3) Have faith in God's Son.

On another occasion, January 2, 2000 he preached about the "dry" Christian:

1) love of God not growing strong
2) "boredom" instead of opportunity
3) If I don't hear from God

4) if things of God don't excite you
5) not witnessing to the lost
6) if you don't remember the Lord in "breaking of bread"
7) if you don't have a genuine desire to come to God's house
8) if you only read your bible on Sunday.
9) if I pray only on Sunday or less than twice a day
10) if "self" always comes before the things of God ("I" all the time)

He said that if you are guilty of these things, you are a "rusty", "dusty" Christian. God can restore you, He loves you, He cares about you. He will forgive you.

Bro. Timothy J. Horton was sorely missed when he left to attend another church. They lived out of the city and it became increasingly more difficult to make it to Grace & Glory.

Bro. Azariah Wallace

Bro. Azariah Wallace attended Grace & Glory for many years. He lived on the north side of Chicago and of course, G & G is on the south side of Chicago in the Chatham area. He would take the "L" train from up north, get off at 79ᵗʰ Street and State and walk those blocks to Grace & Glory, hot or cold weather, rain or shine. He came every Sunday, without fail, to worship and participate in the Gospel Service. He, on occasion, brought the message from the Word of God. He was very strong in his beliefs and like some of the other brethren from the "Islands", he was critical of some of the traditions observed at Grace & Glory.

Bro. Wallace was very impatient with the progress and changes being made at the Assembly because of the "changes of the times" and changes in membership. He was a very "learned" brother who brought sound, fundamental messages from the Word of God. He brought a message on November 29, 1992. The scriptures he expounded were: II Timothy 3: 1-7 and II Timothy 4:4. He said, "In the last days, there will be more sin, more violence, no regard for the law – perilous times will come, children will be disobedient to parents." (II Tim. 3:1-7) "Children are bringing weapons to school these days as well, – "men, lovers of themselves, covetous, boasting of status in life, boasters of themselves. Men have a form of Godliness, but they creep into houses and lead captive silly women –" II Tim. 4:4 He said there will be destruction – fire, flood. Make preparations when you see these things happening; they are signs of His coming; make all the necessary preparations – accept the Lord Jesus Christ as your Savior and Lord.

Bro. Azariah Wallace left a legacy of discipline and discernment at Grace & Glory. He left after a while and did not return. I've tried calling the last phone number we had on record without success. Only the Lord knows his whereabouts, but we will remember, and will rejoice for his service to this ministry.

Bro. Elder George Ferguson

Bro. George Ferguson served as Elder of Grace & Glory Gospel Chapel for many years until his death in December, 2010.

He was beloved for his positive attitude, his warm smile and greetings, his wit and humor, and his dedication and commitment to the work of the Lord. He in turn, loved Grace & Glory Gospel Chapel and its' people.

Bro. Ferguson was "steadfast, unmovable, always abounding in the work of the Lord.
George Rayful Ferguson was born on January 4, 1925 in Wrightsville, Georgia to the loving union of Leola and Oliver Ferguson. After the passing of his father, his mother moved the family to Miami, Florida. His junior high school years were spent there, and he received his high school diploma from Central Y School in Chicago, Illinois.

He served in the United States Army as a sergeant and received an honorable discharge in 1946. In 1950, George met and fell in love with Mildred Isabelle. Their marriage produced two beautiful daughters, Pamela and Karen, and they were married for 60 loving, committed years together. It was very seldom that they were apart from each other.

Bro. Ferguson resumed his education by attending De Paul University for two years and Worsham College of Mortuary Science, where he graduated in 1951. While he had started an apprenticeship as a mortician, the Chicago Transit Authority lured him away with an employment offer which he accepted and held until he retired in 1986. During his 36 years of devoted service, he never used a single sick day. He loved photography; it was his favorite past-time and he loved family-oriented activities, such as cooking and relaxing in the kitchen with his beloved wife, "Mil". He was an integral part of the superb after-school care that his granddaughters, Tiffany and Tracey enjoyed when they were youngsters. Each day after school, their "Grandpa" was there to pick them up, wisk them home to "Grandma's" good, home-cooked meals and then get them started on their homework until their parents' workday ended. Bro. Ferguson's spiritual journey began at Carey Temple, A.M.E. Church in Chicago, and continued at Grace & Glory Gospel Chapel where we called him "Brother Fergie". He was an active brother, making sure that everything was handled graciously and in order. He loved it and was supportive of its' doctrine, its' traditions and its' programs.

As an Elder, he shared sweet fellowship for many years with Elder Willie Horton and the late Elder Edward Watkins, who was his closest friend. He was loyal and faithful, attending regularly until his health started to fail.

Bro. Ferguson was also friends with Sis. Kilpatrick's husband, Lenzo. They were both born in the state of Georgia; they both shared the same doctor for a number of years; and they both got a kick out of talking sports, especially the Bulls.

Bro. George Ferguson was a remarkable man of God who led a stellar life of commitment, dedication, and love for his fellowman. His legacy continues at Grace & Glory Gospel Chapel.

<u>Sis. Vernice Hatch & Bro. Pershing Hatch</u>

Sis. Vernice Hatch, now deceased, was a faithful and loving believer at Grace & Glory Gospel Chapel. She was brought to the Assembly by Emily Donahue and the date is unclear, but she left a lasting and indelible mark upon this Assembly. Emily Donahue held bible classes at her home, and Sis. Hatch attended those classes. Emily encouraged her to visit Grace & Glory. Sis. Hatch remained for 41 years until her death in November, 2003.

Vernice Hatch was born in Chicago, Illinois on July 20, 1928. She met Pershing B. Hatch and they had a beautiful wedding, and a strong, God-fearing marriage. Their lives were built on love of God, teaching their children using discipline, firmness, and a lot of love. They taught their children to go to church, religiously, and to love and serve God in the beauty of holiness. They raised 6 beautiful, wonderful, prominent children: Theresa Ivery, Juanita Stem, Valoree Harrington, Timothy Hatch, Tony Hatch, and Paul J. Hatch. Four of their children – Theresa, Juanita, Valoree, and "P.J." – are still faithfully attending and serving the Lord at Grace & Glory Gospel Chapel.

Juanita is on the Board of Trustees, serving as Secretary, Valoree serves as primary Sunday School teacher, and P.J. serves as Deacon and Assistant to the Elder. Theresa serves as Co-Teacher for the adult women's Sunday School class, when needed.

Tony Hatch and Timothy Hatch have built their own families and are living very prominent lives with God being at the head of their households.

Bro. Pershing B. Hatch, before his health issues, was the co-teacher for the Thursday evening bible class. He loved telling the students to live Godly lives. It was important to him that we live chaste, sinless lives before an awesome God.

Sis. Vernice Hatch was such a "tireless spirit," who always gave her best. With a drive to have things done decently and in order, she accomplished much for the work of the Lord. She was sensitive to the needs of the sick and shut-in. When interviewed back in 2001 she said, "I like to help people and try to do all that I can as a Christian – to let Christ be seen in me every way." When asked about the doctrine at Grace & Glory, she said, "it is "Brethren" and that means that women are to keep silent and still do the work of the Lord." When asked what she wanted to be included in the telling of our history, she said, "How it is rooted and grounded in the Word; kept by the older brothers." She recognized that Bro. Gall started the Assembly, and that Bro. Mullin was also a founder. She felt that we are not as effective as we should be as a ministry; we are trying to reach the lost. She also felt that there was a responsibility on the part of the people, as well. People must hear and receive with a spiritual ear. Sis. Hatch said, "we are trying to show love as much as we can."

Sis. Hatch was a faithful and loving believer at Grace & Glory. She was in turn well loved and respected by the church family. Although she had health issues toward the end of her life, she was always a source of inspiration to all who watched her maintain her spiritual integrity in the face of a devastating surgery. Her faith in the true and living God never wavered, but instead caused her to say with Job, "though he slay me yet will

I trust in Him." She loved sewing and crocheting and she was a licensed Poodle Groomer. She was a great cook and enjoyed cooking for the many special occasions like the anniversary, the Christmas programs, the Easter programs and other special days at church. She entertained at home, as well. Sis. Hatch taught her children to cook, as well. Her service at Grace & Glory, her love of the believers, and her great loyalty is very much a part of what Grace & Glory has become as a ministry. She will always be remembered. Bro. Pershing B. Hatch's ministry and service continues.

Elizabeth Reckley

Elizabeth went to be with the Lord some 17 years ago. Her death was sudden and totally unexpected. She had had a massive stroke and was in a coma. I continued to believe that she would recover. I just thought to myself, "Elizabeth can't leave the "girls" (Edwina & Zerlina – her twins). But I had to yield to God's sovereign because He makes no mistakes.

Elizabeth was one of my closest friends. She was an encourager, not only to me, but also to the women in our adult Sunday School class. She was a beautiful role model – for the younger women at Grace & Glory for she lived a chaste and Godly lifestyle. She followed Christ in the beauty of holiness. Her twin daughters, still, after all these years love reading the Word of God; love memorizing the Word of God; love attending church and taking communion each Sunday; and they simply love being with the saints of God. This is the result of Elizabeth's teaching and bringing them up in the admonition of the Lord.

Elizabeth loved to sing and often blessed us with her songs at our services. She was an accomplished soloist, singing old Negro spirituals with a melodious and "clear as a bell" voice. Elizabeth, Inez, and I had been close friends for over 40 years. Under the tutelage of Inez and her mother, Sister Adine Douglas, Elizabeth and I grew together spiritually.

I can never forget Elizabeth's integrity, her strength of character, her uniqueness of spirit, and her moral of character.

The three of us worked together as educators at Michele E. Clark Middle School; we served together on the Board of Directors of Chicagoland Christian Women's Conference (CCWC); and over the years, we shared our difficulties, our joys, and our blessings as we tried to raise our children and build our families.

Shakespeare said "Friendship is constant in all things" and truly Elizabeth had been a friend that "sticketh closer than a brother".

I admired Elizabeth especially as I watched her with her girls. She taught them to appreciate culture, language, the arts, and literature. She taught them also how to manage their finances and how to be adept shoppers. She took them on trips every year and took them to church and to musicals and to plays and to movies and to every other place that she visited. We still call them "girls" because even though they are adults, they still look like teenagers. Elizabeth Reckley will always be remembered as one who helped in the culture of Grace & Glory.

Bro. Elder Edward Watkins

Bro. Watkins brought his family to Grace & Glory Gospel Chapel after attending Southside Gospel Chapel for a short time. He had been led to the Lord by B. M. Nottage some time earlier, and he wanted to go to an Assembly closer to his home and his job. He often worked two and three jobs to care for his family. He and his wife, Orlee Watkins had 6 children, 3 boys and three girls, with Suzette Watkins being the first born. Bro. Watkins served as Elder for decades at Grace & Glory, bonding with Elder Willie Horton, and Elder George Ferguson.

Edward Pope Watkins was born on January 1, 1927 in Memphis, Tennessee to the loving union of Fredrick and Mozella Watkins. He had 6 siblings – Fredrick, Jr., Alphonzo, Irene, Inez, Noble, and Lawrence. He graduated from Booker T. Washington High School in Memphis, Tennessee in 1945. After high school, he worked as a porter on a Mississippi River steamboat. After a year, he relocated to Chicago and stayed with his Uncle Ray. Uncle Ray got him a job at the Pullman Railroad Company. It was there he met Robert Conner. Robert introduced him to Orlee. Mr. Conner told Edward "I have a daughter that's "courting age". I want you to meet her. "Their courtship started and they married on March 23, 1946 on her birthday.

Bro. Watkins worked for the railroad 24 years, in addition to working as a security guard. He held two full time jobs at once to care for his family. He accepted the Lord in his early twenties and he and Sis. Watkins joined Southside Gospel Chapel where they met many friends – Mel Banks, Leroy Yates, Bill Pannell, and Bro. Edwards; and Sis. Payne. They enjoyed the fellowship of the believers there. However, the family later moved to 70th and Michigan which was a short walk to Grace & Glory Gospel Chapel. They left Southside in the late 1950's and joined Grace & Glory to be close to his home and close to his job, as well. Bro. Watkins remembered that Bro. Gall, Bro. Wood, Bro. Mullin, and Bro. McCray were at G & G at that time. He said that Bro. Gall was, "a man who was for real, always lifting up Jesus; he was a true minister, very dedicated, and "could do it all." Bro. Watkins found him to be a spiritual-minded person who lived the life that he preached.

Bro. Watkins talked about the split between Bro. Gall and Bro. Williams. He said both men were strong, opinionated, and stubborn. Bro. Gall established Grace & Glory Gospel Chapel.

Bro. Watkins stated that at that time, there were very few fundamental churches that had qualified teachers and preachers. He mentioned Moody Bible Institute, Emmaus, and Wheaton College as the places where one could go to be rooted and grounded in fundamental teaching. He mentioned Bro. Banks, Bro. Gall, and the Nottage Brothers as preachers of the fundamental Word of God.

He talked about attending the Billy Graham Crusade here in Chicago, with Ethel Waters as the singer, and of course, George Beverly Shay. Many people came to the Lord from Billy Graham's ministry.

Bro. and Sis. Watkins had six beautiful children, 3 girls and 3 boys – Suzette, Chara, Zita and Gregory, Norman, and Stephen. They're all adults and living prosperous lives. Gregory is recently deceased and is greatly missed by his family and friends.

Bro. & Sis. Watkins volunteered during the summer to help meet the needs of Circle Y Ranch Bible Camp. Suzette, Chara, and Stephen worked tirelessly during the summers also in various roles at the camp. They enjoyed this service, and along with the other workers at camp, did it as unto the Lord.

Bro. Watkins was extremely devoted to his family. He had a very strong work ethic and he was a stern disciplinarian. He had a big heart, especially for children. After he retired, in his later years, he was referred to as, "Porsha's grand-daddy" and the "bike mechanic." He was always putting air in someone's tires or buying all the kids popsicles. He was a very giving person. His door was always open to family and friends. He never turned family down if they needed a place to stay or if they needed a hearty meal. Friends and family knew they would always be welcome at the Watkins home.

Bro. Edward Watkins brought the message at Grace & Glory's morning worship service on September 21, 1997. He spoke on II Timothy 2 about being a faithful servant, and the mportance of commitment, dedication; and hard work for the Lord's work in the church. Bro. Watkins' legacy lives on at Grace & Glory.

Johnnia Kirk Greene

Johnnia Kirk Greene is Grace & Glory's newest member. She lives in the neighborhood of the church, just a block away. She has been in the Chatham community for many years.

Johnnia enjoys walking and greeting her neighbors. She reaches out to the poor and disenfranchised by giving food, by giving an encouraging word.

Johnnia's husband is deceased, gone but not forgotten, for she speaks of him often. They had a loving relationship that produced 2 sons, Joseph, now 27 years old and Robert "Bobbie," now 31 years old. Johnnia's sense of humor comes through as she talks about her sons. She adores them, but she "takes no prisoners" where they are concerned.

Johnnia has a number of family members that she sometimes talks about, and is very proud of her heritage and her roots. She attended a prestigious college in Mississippi and received her teaching degree there. Now retired, she taught in the Chicago Public School System (CPS) for several years. She had a deep impact on her students, teaching them, not only subject matter, but teaching them how to be a better person and how to reach their goals in life.

Johnnia came to Grace & Glory because she was looking for a new place of worship. She came into our doors, and "the rest is history". She has been here since November 4, 2012, and has been a blessing ever since.

She enjoys attending the worship service, the gospel service, and the adult women's Sunday School class. She greatly contributes with her words of wisdom and her keen sense of humor. Johnnia really enjoys "prepping" the church for special occasions like the anniversary, the Easter program, and the Christmas decorations. Johnnia is a wonderful, God sent believer who adds to the culture, and class, of Grace & Glory.

Johnnia Kirk Greene's service continues.

<u>Valoree</u> <u>Hatch Harrington</u>

Valoree has been a member of Grace & Glory Gospel Chapel since her childhood. She is the third daughter of Vernice and Pershing Hatch. The Hatch family came to the church in the late 1960's. Valoree, along with her siblings, and the other children that were there, participated in the Easter Programs, the Christmas Plays at Christmas, and was an active part in the Sunday School Classes. She currently serves as the Primary teacher for the younger children. She prepares Easter Programs and Christmas Programs – getting special presentations together so that children can perform.

Valoree was baptized at Grace & Glory and she raised her three children there. She wanted to make sure that their mental and spiritual needs were being met. Her husband, Charles Harrington, was a member at Grace & Glory, as well. He attended regularly until his untimely death. Their three children are Shakiya, (KiKi) Charles, Jr. (Chuckie), and Shantae (Sha-Sha).

Valoree has remained here at the church because the gospel is preached and the winning of souls is taught by "God-filled" Elders. She is excited about the history of our church and is a big part of our vision for the future. She is proud of the ministry of the brethren assembly and feels that it is God-centered. She longs for more effective support and encouragement to the surrounding community. Valoree feels that the relationship between elders, pastors, and their congregation is vital to effectively deal with issues and concerns plaguing people today. Our ability to be sensitive to our members has a definite impact on our ability to reach the lost. It's wonderful to see the gifts within our church exercised to meet the needs of others, as well as, using those gifts to praise and glorify the Lord Jesus Christ.

Valoree would like for the history of the church to include, not only past history, but our vision/goals for the future. Keeping our youth as part of our ministry is one thing that is so important to Valoree.

She attends Grace & Glory each Sunday, without fail, seeking to worship the Lord and to offer the sacrifice of praise and adoration.

Valoree wrote and presented an emotional tribute to Linda Kilpatrick on the occasion of her death on January 31, 2008. Valoree read it to our grieving family to comfort and console us. Her words brought much comfort and peace knowing it came from our church family.

Valoree is an Assistant Principal in the Chicago Public School System, serving for many years at the Beethoven Elementary School. She's an awesome administrator who tries to effect change in children and she leads staff members as they sharpen their skills to work directly with children.

Meanwhile, the ministry of Valoree here at Grace & Glory Gospel Chapel continues.

Paul "P.J." Hatch

P. J. Hatch is a beloved brother at Grace & Glory Gospel Chapel. He is just a nice guy, to everyone. He must be the most gentle person on the planet. He shows a special love, a special respect, a special concern for others. P. J. is very kind, always has a smile and a hug for us; although he "walks softly," he has a strength that is displayed by his promptness, his loyalty, his love of the Word of God, and by his attention to protocol, tradition, and rules and regulations. He is a "banker", as he is affectionately called, who has been employed by banks most of his adult life. He carries himself in a very upright manner, just like a person who understands finances and management of finances. P.J. is the Assistant to the Treasurer at Grace & Glory.

The thing that stands out about P.J. is his great love for his family. His mother, Vernice Hatch, and his dad, Pershing Hatch taught him and his siblings, the value and blessing of family. It has been ingrained into the fabric of the Hatch family and into the Grace & Glory family, as well.

P.J. has strong opinions about the Word of God. He's serious about studying the Bible and "getting it right." He believes in being a doer of the Word, as well as, a hearer. A few years ago, a controversy arose about "head coverings for women in the church. There was misunderstanding and some dissention about it. It bothered P.J., so he did research from the Bible to find the answer. Although he had not been a part of the controversy, he wanted to have the issue resolved. Below is what he discovered: "Should Christian Women wear head coverings?"

Answer: I Corinthians 11:3-16 addresses the issue of women and head coverings. The context of the entire passage of I Cor. 11:3-16 is submission to the God-given order and "chain of command". A "covering" on a woman's head is used as an illustration of the order, headship, and the authority of God. The key verse of this passage is I Cor. 11:3 – "But I want you to know that the head of every man is Christ, the head of woman is man, and the head of Christ is God." The implications of this verse are found in the rest of the passage. The order is: God the Father, God the Son, the man or husband, and the woman or wife. The veil or covering on the head of a believing Corinthian wife showed that she was under the authority of her husband, and therefore under submission to God. Within this passage is also verse 10: "For this reason the women ought to have a symbol of authority on her head, because of the angels."

The relationship of God with men is something that angels watch and learn from (I Peter 1:12). Therefore, a woman's submission to God's delegated authority over her is an example to angels. The holy angels, who are in perfect and total submission to God, expect that we, as followers of Christ, be the same.

This covering not only means a cloth but also can refer to a woman's hair length. "Does not even nature itself teach you that if a man has long hair, it is a dishonor to him? But if a woman has long hair, it is a glory to her; for her hair is given to her for a covering (I Cor. 11:14-15). Therefore, in the context of this passage, a woman who is wearing her hair longer marks herself out distinctively as a woman and not a man. The Apostle Paul is saying that in the Corinthian culture, when a wife's hair was longer than her husband's, it showed her submission to his headship. The roles of the male and female are designed by God to portray a profound spiritual lesson, that is of submission to the will and the order of God. Paul is addressing something in the Corinthian culture that was being allowed to disrupt the church. Women in service in the pagan temples had their heads shaved. Paul says in this passage that a woman who is shorn or shaved should be covered (I Cor. 11:6), for a woman shorn or shaved of her hair had lost her "glory", and she was not under the protection of her husband. Paul is teaching that hair length or the wearing of a "covering" by the woman was an outward indication of a heart attitude of submission to

God and His authority. God's order is that the husband is the head of the wife as God is the head of Christ, but there is no inequality or inferiority implied. God and Christ are equal and united, just as the husband and wife are one. It does not teach that the woman is inferior to man or that she should be submissive to every man. In the Corinthian culture, a woman who covered her head during worship or when she was in public displayed her submission to authority.

In today's culture, we no longer view a woman's wearing of a head covering as a sign of submission. Today, scarves and hats are fashion accessories. A woman has the choice to wear a head covering if she views it as a sign of her submission to the authority of her husband. However, it is a personal choice and not something that should be used to judge spirituality. The real issue is the heart attitude of obedience to God's authority and submission to His established order "as to the Lord" (Ephesians 5:22). God is far more concerned with an attitude of submission than an outward display of submission by way of a head covering.

First Timothy 2:9-10 states, "I also want women to dress modestly, with decency and propriety, not with braided hair or gold or pearls or expensive clothes, but with good deeds, appropriate for women who profess to worship God."

After doing that research, and finding that information, P.J. had this to say:

> "I agree with this wholeheartedly and I for one agree that a woman's hair is her covering before God. I can see if her hair was cut real short then yes a covering would be in order. My opinion. We shouldn't have to let this be a form of turning others away. Search the scriptures and make your decisions from them and it will be between you and God. But if the Brethren churches want women to cover their head then the women should follow their rules. I'm sure God is not going to hold this against you if you decide not to cover your head."

P.J. is an asset to Grace & Glory. He is part of the "fabric," the culture that is ours, and ours alone. His service as Assistant to the Elder continues.

Theresa Hatch Ivery

Theresa Hatch Ivery has been at Grace & Glory since her childhood. Like her siblings, her mom, Vernice Hatch brought the family here when the children were young. Theresa is the oldest girl and proud to be looked up to as the leader, and the one who got to make the decisions.

Theresa was stunningly beautiful as a young adult woman, with long, flowing hair and a complexion that was the image of Vernice, and a poise that caused her to walk straight and tall. She took pride in her appearance, wearing beautifully crafted clothes and jewelry. In addition to her outer beauty, she has an inner beauty as well. Theresa is quiet and unassuming, but very strong in her beliefs. She is serious about Grace & Glory and has very little patience with tardiness and disorganization. She's a stickler for time. Time is important and Theresa takes it seriously.

She is a big part of the Adult Women's Sunday School Class where discussions take place of personal experiences, and current events, and issues & concerns. The Sunday School Class is a close-knit group that cares deeply about each sister and supports and loves them unconditionally. Theresa is a leader in that group and takes the lessons that God teaches seriously.

Theresa is very committed to the community and to charity work. She also enjoyed taking the "girls"– Zerlina & Edwina – home on occasions. She works with her organization, Sickle Cell Anemia, to help victims. Not only does the organization have a big fundraiser every year, but they work with doctors and nurses at the Michael Reese Hospital, and others, to help those affected on a daily basis. They publicize the big affair, but behind the scenes, the organization is actually changing lives. Theresa has been a member for several years. Charles Dickens had her in mind when he said,

"Have a heart that never hardens, a temper that never tires, a heart that never hurts."

Theresa has two adult children, Natasha Ivery and Fred Fletcher. "Tasha" was at Grace & Glory until she went off to college. She was an excellent student and earned her Bachelors' degree. Tasha lived in New York, New York for a while before returning to Chicago. She absolutely enjoyed being in "New Yawk, New Yawk"! Tasha is now pursuing her career goal in finances. She is a member of Trinity Church, a bible-based church successfully reaching the African American community and beyond. Tasha served as Director of the Praise Team Ministry for years. She continues to serve the Trinity Church family, using her talents and skills to make a difference in the lives of young people and others. She is now married and has a beautiful baby girl!

Fred went off to college and finished with a Bachelor's degree in music production. He is pursuing a career in music, as a manager and as a producer, and also as a director. He attends Apostolic Church of Christ, where Dr. Byron Brazier is Pastor.

Theresa lives the legacy left by her wonderful mother, Sis. Vernice Hatch. That legacy teaches that families that bond together overcome adversity and they help the next generation accomplish more than the one that came before it. Our mothers and fathers before us fought for civil rights and they fought to give their children a better life. Our responsibility is to continue that legacy. Theresa is committed to doing just that as she continues to serve at Grace & Glory.

<u>Naomi Ruth Jones Kilpatrick</u>
(Author)

I've been a member of Grace & Glory Gospel Chapel since 1956. It was the year that I accepted the Lord Jesus Christ as my Lord and Savior. It was the year my youngest daughter was born, and was a few months old when I came to the church. Inez invited me to attend with her and her mother, Sis. Adine Douglas. The service for G & G was being held at the YMCA on 51st & Indiana on the south side of Chicago. My family and I lived in the Ida B. Wells Housing Projects on 36th St. in an apartment on the 3rd floor. When the current building was built, I walked to So. Park (now King Dr.) with my three girls and later with my baby, Kevin, in tow and took a "Jitney" cab to 77th St. and walked to Indiana where the church is located.

When I first joined the fellowship, we met at the "Y", on the lower level in a large room. We sat in a circle as we sang songs, had communion, gave our tithes and donations, and heard a powerful message, usually given by Bro. Gall. I felt "out of place" at first because the ladies wore no makeup, not even lipstick, and dressed plainly. Everyone seemed quiet and very spiritual. I thought, "I'm not holy enough to be here." As I began to grow in grace and in the knowledge of the Lord and His Word, I started to understand what was truly going on at Grace & Glory. We were there until 1961 when we moved to 7708 So. Indiana Avenue. I have enjoyed teaching Sunday School classes over several decades; children, teens, and lastly, adult women. My life at Grace & Glory has been one of constant, ongoing exposure to the Word of God. The Bible is taught each week, and the Lord is present each week in the midst of the small congregation. The size of the congregation does not matter if the Word of God is being preached. Mr. Joshua Du Bois has a word of encouragement for those of us who have experienced "toiling all night and caught nothing." He said: ". . . Like Peter in the fishing boat, and Pastor Collins, God is doing something behind the scenes. And one day, if we continue to be faithful and follow his word, we'll throw down our nets and bring up a catch for the ages."

Inez Clayton had a big impact on my life and the life of my family. She became ill after moving to Perris, California. She suffered from many health issues and was being cared for by her husband, Larry Clayton. On April 29th, 2013, Beverly Yates and I went to visit Inez in California. She was in a nursing facility in Orange, California located in the University of California, Irvine Healthcare. The doctors there had recently removed the dialysis from her. They felt that her body was no longer responding to the treatments and felt that it was not helping her condition. Beverly and I prayed that God would give her peace and comfort through this crisis. Inez's face had a quiet, serene, and peaceful look when we saw her. Her eyes were piercing, seeming to look right through me. I think she recognized us and was glad to see us. We talked to her, we talked to each other, we sang songs to her, and tried to get her to smile. She did smile once at us and tried to speak. Later that day, we watched the paramedics take her to the nursing facility, from the hospital, where she would be staying. Beverly and I then went on to visit Larry, Inez's husband, in another hospital, AHMC Anaheim Regional Medical Center. He had undergone minor surgery earlier in the day and was recuperating overnight in the hospital. He said he was feeling okay. The next day he went back home to Perris, California.

I was anxious to see Inez to encourage her and to especially say some things to her. I wanted her to know how she had blessed so many people over many years. I was especially blessed when she:

- brought me to Grace & Glory
- encouraged me spiritually
- encouraged me to go back to school
- asked me to be a bridesmaid in her weddings – first to Joe Washington and then to Larry Clayton
- touched many women through her CCWC ministry and through her music, as well
- contributed to Westlawn Gospel Chapel through her music as pianist, director, and group formation

- joined Iota Phi Lambda Sorority, Inc. and affected the lives of many women by encouraging them to accept the Lord as their Savior
- donated an exhibit display of her grandmother's "WAC" experiences – WWII – to Du Sable Museum. It remained on display for a long time. She did this while she was a Soror.

Inez and I had been friends for many years, creating a trio of friendship with Elizabeth Reckley, Inez and myself. We worked together at Michele E. Clark Middle School; Inez and Elizabeth as guidance counselors and me as a team leader; we worshipped together at Grace & Glory Gospel Chapel; we prayed together at Sis. Douglas' all night prayer meetings and weekly bible studies; we planned together at CCWC meetings; we laughed and talked together as "bosom buddies" friends sharing our secrets and our dreams; and lastly, we shared a love of Jesus Christ, our Savior.

Beverly and I left the next couple of days, May 2, 2013 for home. We spent one day with my awesome cousins, Sandra, Venita, Wilma, Dessola, and Shelva who treated us to dinner; and one day with Beverly's wonderful brother, Bill Pannell, who treated us to lunch. That was the last time we saw Inez alive. She went to be with the Lord in December, seven months later. I praise God for her life. My journey down through the years has been a true "from grace to glory" experience. God has blessed me in every way possible and even if I had a "thousand tongues" to sing His praise, it would not be enough. I'm still here after 58 years, and looking forward to more years. Like everyone on the planet, my life has been one of ups and downs, through losses that are too painful to articulate, and some mountain top experiences that took months to dissipate, and have remained on a pretty even keel daily. I enjoy being the "elder sister", where I hear such "accolades" as, "I didn't know she was that old!", and "she used to run up & down those stairs!", and "she's slowed down quite a bit!", and "she's the oldest one at our church!". Seriously, it's a joy to continue my service at Grace & Glory. To God be the glory!

Juanita Hatch Stem

Juanita is currently the Assistant Principal at the Carnegie Elementary School. She taught the Gifted Program and the Baccalaureate Program for several years before her promotion. She directed the total program. She is considered to be a teacher "extraordinaire" at her school. Juanita has served the Chicago Public School System (CPS) for a number of years and holds several degrees.

She has attended Grace & Glory Gospel Chapel since her childhood. She currently serves on the Board of Directors/Trustees as the Secretary. She also serves as youth Sunday School teacher.

Juanita is intelligent, smart, with outstanding skills in Language Arts; very creative and extremely helpful – never saying "No" to a need. Very resourceful and task-oriented. If Juanita says she will do something, she does it, without fail. She is deeply committed to Grace & Glory and works toward maintaining and enhancing the ministry of spreading the gospel and supporting its' programs. Like her siblings, she is deeply committed to living by those principles taught by her mother, Mrs. Vernice Hatch, and her father, Pershing Hatch. She is very devoted to the memory of her beloved mom, who passed away, suddenly, in November, 2003. She treated her mother with the utmost respect and dignity, showing a special warmth and tenderness for her. Juanita, again, along with her siblings, sought to meet each need of her parents. She is part of the very close-knit family unit that is the "Hatch Family". They seek to do things in an excellent way as they raise their own families and while they are pursuing their dreams. I believe God is pleased.

Juanita is married to Elder Tyrone Stem for over 30 years and they have two adult children, Natia and Akil. Her daughter, Natia, is married to Joseph Brownlee, Jr. and they have 3 little beautiful and bright boys – Isaac, Joseph, III and Josiah.

Some years ago, Juanita wrote a beautiful tribute to the Women of Grace & Glory. Below are her very touching, and very loving words of recognition:

"A Grace & Glory Legacy of Sisterly Love"

"There have been many godly women who have crossed the thresholds of the doors of Grace & Glory Gospel Chapel. Take a trip with me as I try to paint a picture of how each of these women and their love for God was manifested in their lives. This legacy began many years ago with God fearing, spirit filled women like Sisters Gall and Mullin; sisters who encouraged the younger women to read our Bibles to study and show ourselves approved of God so we could grow in grace and knowledge of Him.

Psalm 119:10 Thy word have I hid in my heart that I might not sin against thee. Sister Lucy, who faithfully, every Sunday captured the attention of every child in Sunday School with her dramatic interpretation of scripture verses that we so diligently committed to our memory.

Psalm 100:1-2 Make a joyful noise unto the Lord all ye lands; serve the Lord with gladness, come before his presence with singing. Sisters Fain and Reckley, whose melodious voices ministered to us during Sunday morning worship services still echoing within the halls of the sanctuary.

I Peter 4:7 Use hospitality one to another without grudging. Sisters Watkins and Ferguson warmly opened their homes and ensured you had a place at the table, no matter what time of day it was.

Matthew 5:5 Blessed are the meek for they shall inherit the earth. Sisters Comer and McNulty sat in their same spots every Sunday as they worshipped and praised God in their still, quiet spirits.

Psalm 122:1 I was glad when they said unto me; let us go into the house of the Lord. Out of their love for the Lord, Sisters Carter and Hicks never let their infirmities stop them from coming to church.

Psalm 1:1-2 Blessed is the man that walketh not in the counsel of the ungodly, nor standeth in the way of sinners, nor sitteth in the seat of the scornful. But his delight is in the law of the Lord, and in his law doeth he meditate day and night. Sister Hatch, my mother, who modeled her life after these verses set the example of how a godly woman should live.

Titus 2:4 The aged women likewise, teachers of good things, teach the younger women to be discreet, keepers at home and that the word of God be not blasphemed. Sister Kilpatrick, our elder sister of the church, who faithfully teaches the women's adult class every Sunday sharing her knowledge of the Lord.

All of these sisters, those who are in the presence of the Lord and those who are still with us today have devoted their lives to Christ and have allowed his love to show through them. I thank God for each of them and how they have influenced my life. And as Grace & Glory celebrates 51 years of ministry and as this legacy continues in the lives of Sisters Suzette, Theresa, Joyce, Sharon, Valoree, Elaine, Edwina, Zerlina, Tamir, Shanta, and myself, my prayer is that we experience the words of the song; Oh Love of God, how rich and pure! How measureless and strong. It shall forever more endure the saints and angels song." Her words say as much about her as the ones she wrote about.

Juanita Hatch Stem continues with her service and love to Grace & Glory.

Joyce Mosely

Joyce M. Mosely has been at Grace & Glory Gospel Chapel for many years. She's endearing to the believers because of her quiet strength. She came from Rev. Clay Evans' church, Fellowship Missionary Baptist Church to Grace & Glory to be closer to her home. She's well versed in the Word of God and enjoys sharing her experiences in the Adult Women's Sunday School Class.

Joyce works for the Ada S. McKinley Day Care Center. She's been there for years, helping to serve the children and their families in our community. She uses her talents and skills, which are many, to assure excellence in the lives of children. She brings leadership and confidence to McKinley, as well as, valuable experience with child development.

Joyce is an excellent mother. Her children show forth her parenting skills. First, her daughter, Katina, is a bright, intelligent adult who has her own family. Katina, along with her husband, Timothy, raised 2 children – Timothy, Jr. and Hannah – beautifully. Katina home schooled her kids for years, and now they each play instruments and excel in their studies. The two children are actively involved in their church, Faith Church of Grayslake. They are part of the mission team, spreading the gospel to the lost, feeding the homeless, and participating in "free prayer stations." Timothy, Jr. and Hannah are two awesome kids.

Joyce has two other children, Ivan and Tamir. Tamir is away at college, in her junior year, at the Middlebury College in Vermont. Currently, she's in Paris, France on some kind of special exchange project at Middlebury. At an early age, Tamir displayed interest in the arts. She would often try to mimic the way her father drew the cartoon characters that were found in the daily newspaper. Tamir's father is Othabert Williams, Jr. She attended Alexandre Dumas Elementary School, graduating in 2008. She was accepted to Dr. Martin Luther King Jr. College Preparatory High School. During her four wonderful years at King, Tamir became a part of numerous clubs and organizations such as the National Honor Society, Philosophy Club, Debate Team, Big Sister Little Sister, and Jaguar Peer Leaders. Tamir continued to pursue her love of the arts at King and was awarded various awards for her artwork. She participated in two E.F. Educational Tours at King, allowing her to travel overseas to five different countries. As her senior year at King approached, Tamir started to research the college that would be the best fit for her. She decided upon Middlebury College in Vermont, and was accepted after winning the Posse Full-Tuition Leadership Scholarship. She was also awarded the Gates Millennium Scholarship. The Gates Millennium Scholars (GMS) Program selects 1,000 talented students each year to receive a good-through-graduation scholarship to use at any college or university of their choice. Tamir graduated from King College Prep in June, 2012 as valedictorian of her class.

Joyce has a son, Ivan, and Ivan is "holding his own" in prominence. He continues to pursue his dreams and goals on his ladder of success.

Joyce Mosely is a big part of the ministry at Grace & Glory. In her personal life, she is a wonderful caregiver to her friend, Tony Love who has a serious illness. She continues to be a role model to others, not only as a parent, but as a caring, dedicated, and loyal Christian woman. Her service at Grace & Glory continues.

Zerlina & Edwina Reckley

Zerlina & Edwina Reckley are twin daughters of Elizabeth and Edwin Reckley, both now deceased. They are adults now, but we still call them "the girls" because they still look very young. They came to Grace & Glory as babies brought here by their mom, Elizabeth. Zerlina & Edwina, along with Carolyn Carter were baptized at Laflin Gospel Chapel.

Elizabeth took the girls every where she went. They, all three, loved to sing. Elizabeth took them to sing in the Wooten Ensemble Choir at Beth Eden Church. The three of them went to Westlawn Gospel Chapel to sing in the choir, along with Sis. Mary Golsby. Elizabeth sang solo at Grace & Glory on a regular basis. Zerlina always desired to sing solo like her mom.

Zerlina and Edwina remember the people that were there when they were young. Some of the people they admired were: Marjorie Brooks, Emily Donahue, Betty Abbott, Gloria McDonald, Bro. & Sis. Gall, Bro. & Sis. Mullin, Sis. Lucy, and Ramona Susberry.

Zerlina still remembers going to the CCWC Retreats every year with her sister, Edwina and her mom, Elizabeth, from 1963 or 1964 when the Annual Retreats were held at the Hyatt Regency O'Hare Hotel in Rosemont, Il. Also, in 1964, they went to Perris, California to visit Sis. Douglas' mom, Irene Hunter. While there they saw Betty Abbott, Clara & Earl Hampton, and Bro. & Sis. McCray.

The girls enjoyed Bible Class & Prayer at Emily Donahue's home, and going to Friday Night Youth Meetings at Grace & Glory. Usually, Bro. Howard Wood picked up children for Youth Meetings.

Zerlina said Elizabeth and Genevieve Carter went on a Norwegian Cruise in July, 1978. Elizabeth & Genevieve took several trips together.

Elizabeth used to take Zerlina & Edwina to Moody Bible Institute to hear, listen, and enjoy the Moody Gospel Concert Choir and other activities. They went to Moody Church, up north, to hear the choir. Along with Inez Washington, they all joined the choir at Moody Church in 1992, 1993, 1994, and 1995. It was called the All Chicago Choir. They have never given their mother up since her death. For all of their lives, they had been a team of 3, so when they lost their mother, it was a devastating blow. They, about 3 years ago, lost their dad, Edwin Reckley. She writes again," I miss my mother, I remember her, and I love her. They also mentioned the deaths of Genevieve, Destalear, Sis. Ayers, Sis. Agins, and Sis. Lucy. They gave the year when each one died. They then wrote Deuteronomy 4:1-10. They started with verse 3 which reads: "Your eyes have seen what the Lord did because of Baal-peor; for all the men who followed Baal-peor; the Lord thy God hath destroyed them from among you." Zerlina then talked about their childhood. She said she and Edwina used to spend the night sometimes at Aunt Rossie's (Campbell) home. She kept them during the day while Elizabeth went to work. She baby sat the girls for a while until she passed away. Ms. Pace baby sat them for a while. There was a problem trying to find an excellent person to baby sit the girls while Elizabeth worked. Ms. Pace came to Elizabeth's house to keep the girls.

I sought to tell Zerlina's & Edwina's story in their own words. They led an interesting life while their mother lived. Elizabeth was determined to teach her twins to walk, talk, read, and do everything that other people were doing. She taught them how to manage their money; she taught them how to shop; she taught them how to keep and find rare coins; and she taught them the basic rules of taking care of body, mind and spirit. Because Elizabeth was my very own friend, I made a silent vow to her (that she could not hear) to do what I could to help the girls get to church and home and to take them on social outings as well. They are still attending Grace & Glory Gospel Chapel on a regular basis thanks to their cousins, Cheryl and "Pee Wee" McNulty.

Elaine Shaw

Sis. Elaine Shaw has been at Grace & Glory Gospel Chapel for decades. She was here when Sis. Lucy and Genevieve Carter and Elizabeth Reckley and Etta Holmes were alive and well. Elaine enjoyed going to visit Sis. Lucy in her home, along with the other sisters. Sis. Lucy fixed a nice meal; we ate, often delicious desserts, and then had sweet fellowship together.

Elaine is very "low key," but is very strong in her beliefs. She is a born leader, and exhibits great confidence and poise. She loves Grace & Glory and can always be found helping with serving and preparing for our big events, like the Anniversary, the Christmas Program, and the Easter program. Elaine is also a great cook.

Elaine' has a stellar career, being employed at the Chicago's Kent School of Law. She is responsible for helping students qualify for the courses and classes at the University. She has a special concern for these students who come seeking to further their education. Some are the infranchised, who have had traumatic experiences and have only seen the underside of life. Some are eager and excited about "climbing the ladder of success". Some students are merely there to be compensated for their education. Whatever their intent, Elaine is there to help them transition through the process, through the system.

Elaine Shaw possesses many skills and talents. She is a de facto interior designer. She is excellent in matching color and fabric and design. She loves finding and purchasing things for Grace & Glory, things that add to the beauty of our church. The plush, red leather piece in the corridor was purchased by Elaine. No fanfare about it, no mention of it, she just does it. Elaine decorated and put in the necessary pieces in the Ladies Washroom & Lounge. This is part of her ministry as unto the Lord.

Elaine enjoys helping others. When called upon to help with a task, she's always there. Sharon Tang relies on her to help her on several occasions. She never says "No". Elaine is very close to Suzette Watkins; they have been close friends for decades, and together they have done countless projects for Grace & Glory. Elaine loves doing outreach projects, as well. Doing more work for women shelters is her vision and goal.

Elaine Shaws' service is continuous and noteworthy.

Sharon Marie Kilpatrick Tang

Sharon Marie Kilpatrick Tang came to Grace & Glory when she was a child. Her sister, Katrina, was just a baby, and her sister, Linda, was one year younger than her. Sharon's two brothers, Kevin and Lenard, were not born as yet. Her mother, Naomi Kilpatrick, brought her to the Assembly each Sunday with her and her sisters holding hands and holding on to their mother's skirt tail. The family lived in Ida B. Wells Projects – the new, high rise buildings – on 36th St. The address was 540 E. 36th St., Apt. 304. The apartment was brand new and very nice.

Sharon's mom walked to South Park and took the "Jitney" cab to 77th Street. It cost about 15¢. The Jitney cabs ran north & south on South Park (now Martin Luther King, Dr.). After getting off on 77th Street, Sharon and her family walked to Indiana Avenue where Grace & Glory was located. This ritual was followed for years until the family purchased a small car.

Sharon was a model child for her parents. She was always obedient and respectful, never causing a moment of trouble. She always did her chores, voluntarily, without having to be reminded. She took pride in doing an excellent job, no matter the task.

Sharon attended elementary school and high school in the Chicago Public School System, excelling in her classes. She was very competitive, seeking to be at the top in extra curricula activities, as well. Her major in undergrad school was business, taking accounting and typing. Sharon could type very fast, so many words per minute, without errors. She graduated from Chicago State University with honors.

Sharon taught classes at National Lewis University (Adjunct Faculty), and later taught in CPS. She served as a Substitute Teacher at several schools before coming to work at her mom's school, Carver Middle School. She served until 1994, and then started teaching at Lake View H.S. She taught computer, accounting, entrepreneurship, and Business English classes. She taught there for 19 years before taking an early retirement. She currently serves as Substitute Teacher at the Percy L. Julian H.S. Sharon is like the old "cadres" in the school where they just call them when someone is absent. They at Julian trust Sharon to do an excellent job with the children, so they call her on a daily basis. She has the option of saying "No", which gives her the freedom of "retirement", and extra compensation to buy some wonderful things or to just save for a rainy day.

Sharon married Alex Tang, her high school sweetheart, on November 14, 1970. Pastor Leroy Yates performed the wedding ceremony held at Inez Washington's home. Inez prepared her famous seafood gumbo for the reception of family and friends. She cooked fluffy, white Uncle Ben's rice, and had a big green salad with several kinds of salad dressing. And of course, the big cake and ice cream, were the icing on the cake. Sharon's sister, Linda, was her maid of honor and Adolph, Alex's brother was best man.

Sharon and Alex had three children, Shatese, Alexis, and Sean. Shatese "Tesa", has one son, Derek who is a good kid (adult), doesn't do drugs or alcohol or smoke cigarettes. Derek has a cute little boy, Macari, (who Shatese calls her grandmonster) with Marciara Mitchell. Macari says he wants to "give his pennies to Jesus." He likes going to church.

Alexis has one son, Anthony, with her husband, Anthony, Sr. Anthony, Jr. who is in 8th grade, has been a straight A student since 1st grade. Sean, who Sharon named after Sean Connery (007, Bond, James Bond), with his wife, Karisha, has 3 sons, Tyrone, Sean, Jr., and Jaden. Tyrone is in 8th grade, looking to go to an excellent high school; Sean, Jr. is an excellent student, plays sports, and (to my amazement) plays the trombone; and Jaden, who is a bright, smart kid with great curiosity, and a really funny sense of humor. Sharon absolutely loves her kids and talks to each one, every day. She texts quite a bit, but she hears their voice every day. She adores her 5 grandsons and looks for occasions to spend time with them.

As already mentioned, Sharon has been at Grace & Glory since her childhood. She has not, over all these years, affiliated with any other assembly or church. When her siblings reached adulthood, they left G & G and went to other places, but Sharon continued to "stand by the stuff" as Bro. Gall used to say. Not that it has always been easy for her. There was a big "bump in the road" in her late teens, and over the years, things have not looked bright for the ministry, but she continued to attend, continued to come every Sunday, faithfully, and every Thursday for bible class, faithfully. So now, decades later, she still attends church service every Sunday, and bible class, on Thursdays.

Sharon is a member of Grace & Glory's Board of Trustees serving as the Treasurer. Grace & Glory has remained solvent over all these years because of the tithing and donations of the members and her management of those funds.

Sharon serves as an important asset to our church and our church family. Her commitment is apparent and greatly appreciated by the believers.

Sharon M. Tang's ministry continues.

Suzette Watkins

Suzette Watkins came to Grace & Glory when her family left the Southside Gospel Chapel. The family had moved, and Bro. Edward Watkins, Suzette's dad, wanted to attend church close to his home. Suzette brought elegance, dignity, and passion to Grace & Glory. She was saved when she was 12 years old, accepting Christ as her Savior when the Wheaton students came to teach Sunday School. She mentioned the names, "Sherman", and "Clifford Larkins" from Wheaton College. Suzette and the family, at one time, lived in the Dearborn Homes' Projects. She said Sherman and Clifford wanted them to attend a fundamentalist church where the gospel was preached and where the invitation was given to accept the Lord. Bro. Watkins mentioned later that at the time he was saved (when he was in his 20's), there were very few fundamental churches that actually preached the "unadulterated Gospel", the Word of God. Bro. Watkins stated that they came to Grace & Glory in the late 50's.

Suzette remembers the early years at Grace & Glory when we had strong youth groups that met on Friday nights, and Bro. Howard Wood is remembered fondly. He was a very positive man who used to pick up the children and take them to the Sunday School classes. Suzette had very positive experiences at the weekly teenage meetings.

Suzette would love to see a youth director at Grace & Glory; someone with training from a Christian facility like Moody Bible Institute, or Wheaton College, or Trinity College, or Emmaus Bible Institute. The schools could send students to help with recruitment, and help with the music, and other things involving young people. It would also help to get young men off the street. The youth director would do those things that young people like to do e.g., bowling, skating, movies, etc.

Suzette is such an asset to our church. She has a passion for and a compassion for it. She plans, enthusiastically, for events that will attract people and make people happy. Her plans always involve food, whether it's Easter, where she prepares 100 baskets to be given out to highlight the resurrection of our Lord and Savior, Jesus Christ, or other events. In addition to the baskets, dinner for Grace & Glory families has also been prepared by Suzette in the past. She is a gourmet cook, having been taught by her mother and ultimately by her dad, as well. She had been trained to help, not only in the kitchen, but she had been taught to help her mother with her siblings – Gregory, Stephen, Norman, Zita and Chara. So the meals that Suzette prepared were always "gourmet", and delicious – filled with wonderful spices and a whole lot of love.

At Christmas time, Suzette also prepares baskets to be given to the children and to adults. It's for families. In addition to the fruit and nuts and candy, there's always a tract, urging people to accept the Lord. PJ and Valoree and Johnnia are her faithful supporters, helping her to fill the baskets. Sometimes, everybody helps her, not only with the baskets, but with decorating the tables, as well. Often, pot luck lunch is served and we get a chance to sample many delicious dishes because the Hatch family members are also gourmet cooks.

Suzette is absolutely estatic to plan and carry out with Stephen's help, her "Mexican Fiesta" every year. She plans a program around delicious Mexican cuisine. The program included lots of music, and sing-a-longs directed by Tanya Hicks; a pianist, a speaker; and prayer.

Decorating the church, seasonally, is another expertise of Suzette's. Bro. Willie is usually there by her side helping her with the table decorations. She has beautiful plastic table cloths (rolled), with all kinds of designs and colors; and she uses plain cloths as well. She mixes the two or three kinds of tablecloths to get a certain look. Each table is perfectly fitted and measured; each table has to be the same pattern, and she has her own way of doing it to make them especially beautiful. She is the "boss" at this, completely controlling the process; we all follow her rules to get it done because we know it will be beautiful when completed.

In addition to the tables, she decorates the entire lower level of the church; including the walls, the "beams," and the windows. The place is transformed into whatever the season is, with Christmas being the most impressive. Suzette's friend, "Soli" helps her make everything outstanding. When entering the church, one gets the feeling of peace, love, and warmth. (We have all benefitted and enjoyed the aura and atmosphere of the ediface, Grace & Glory, created out of love of church and of God) Psalm 2:11 speaks to Suzette's heart. It says: "Serve the Lord with fear, and rejoice with trembling."

Stephen Watkins

Stephen, Suzette's brother, is the Master Chef of the family. Professionally, Stephen is not only a gourmet chef, but he teaches others had to cater, how to create a meal for 5 people or 500 people. He serves the Chicago Public School System (CPS) as Instructor, a realization of a dream he has had for some time. Stephen has helped serve churches, over the years, when they have needed elegance, experience in service, and delicious food for their big events. Whether it is an anniversary, wedding, birthday, or a celebration, he can be counted on to give you excellence and class when he serves at your event. Stephen has served as Grace & Glory Gospel Chapel's chef for its' anniversary for many years.

Zita Watkins

Zita is Suzette's sister. She came up as a youngster in Grace & Glory. She participated in the Sunday School class, and performed on the Easter programs and the Christmas programs, as well. Like her siblings, Zita has developed into an excellent cook. She cooks gourmet meals, and enjoys making people happy through their stomach! Zita recently cooked a multi course dinner meal and invited the entire Grace & Glory church family to attend. It was at the church and no cost, out of the goodness of her heart and because of her love for the Lord Jesus Christ.

Zita continues her service at Grace & Glory through the Adult Women's Sunday School class, encouraging her friend and former Grace & Glory member, Melody Jones to attend.

Suzette and her family are a huge part of the culture that is Grace & Glory. She adored her mother, and revered her father. That legacy and her legacy lives on with gusto.

Very Important People To Mention

Lois Colar – Lois found the land on which Grace & Glory was built - it's actually 3 lots. (7708 Indiana). Lois and her husband, Lloyd, and I were baptised together at the YMCA on 50th & Indiana by Bro. Owbridge Faye Gall. Lois attended Bro. Gall's funeral in Brooklyn, New York in May, 1971.

Howard Wood – Howard was a big part of the growth of Grace & Glory. He used to pick the neighborhood kids up and take them to the Sunday School, which was located on the west side of Chicago. Barbara Horton (Looney, then) and Willie Horton were 2 teens that he picked up. They later married and had 5 children. Howard used to pick children up and bring them to the Friday night activities. He would drive the bus (acquired by Grace & Glory) and pick people up to attend church.

Howard built the Women's Lounge at Grace & Glory.

He also worked hard to get Circle Y Bible Camp started.

He worked with others in building and maintaining the camp.

He later moved to Bangor, Michigan on the Camp grounds.

He met his wife there and they had a daughter. They lived in that little house there for years.

Emily Donahue – born in 1924 (90 years old) still driving each day, still in her same home, still conducts her weekly bible class, still visits Africa, once per year, to minister to a village there.

Emily used to ride the bus with the attendees to CCWC Annual Retreats. She would meet the bus at Grace & Glory Gospel Chapel and ride the bus to the Retreat at the Hyatt Regency – O'Hare Hotel. She served as a volunteer chaperone for the ladies.

She rode back to the church, as well.

She had the key to the church, so that she could let people in the church to use the phone, use the washroom, or wait on their rides, etc.

She was a valuable asset to the Chicagoland Christian Women's Conference (CCWC).

Emily Donahue was very animated as a Christian. She came to Grace & Glory, years ago, right after she was saved. She simply loved sharing the good news of the Gospel – at G & G and outside of G & G. She was an "on fire" kind of witness for the Lord. Emily was a member for a number of years. She was responsible for bringing her aunt to the Assembly, Sis. Jimmie Comer. Sis. Comer was a sweet, gentle Christian woman who loved coming to Sunday services. She almost never missed church. She demonstrated God's love of the brethren. She attended until her death.

Emily also brought Sis. Vernice Hatch and her family to Grace & Glory. Emily took special care to mentor Ramona Susberry, who had recently accepted the Lord as her Savior. They developed a beautiful relationship over the years which also included Sis. Henrietta Broussard, Ramona's mom, now deceased.

Emily is currently involved with Ambassador Fellowship. It is a missionary group that takes trips to Benin, West Africa to minister to children and adults. It involves adopting a village and encouraging them to accept the Lord as Savior. The missionaries are able to give them money to buy more bibles printed in their language; they have a tutoring program to teach the people how to read so that they can read their bibles. They take the trip to Africa each year, usually around September, to again share the Gospel with the village people, knowing that God is not willing that any one should perish, but, that all should come to the knowledge of Christ.

Cora Latson, CCWC Board member, has been accompanying Emily on these annual trips serving as a missionary to the village people, as well. She has committed to building a well to provide fresh water to the village.

Eva Lowe

Eva Lowe is no longer at Grace & Glory, but because she had such a positive, powerful impact upon our ministry, I wanted to mention her. By profession, she was a technician, with three children and four grandchildren. Eva was born in Louisiana and moved to Chicago in 1962, where she met and married her husband, Horace Lowe. She attended Grace & Glory for several years having started there because she was looking for a church "where His Word was being taught, so that I may be edified." In her words she told what the doctrine was: "The doctrine of Grace & Glory is to teach His Word from the Holy Bible and that you must be born again."

Her sister, Flora Stubblefield, had the same impact upon us. She was positive, funny, loving, and outgoing. She's married and has four children. Eva was responsible for bringing "Flo" to Grace & Glory. Flo liked the idea of writing a history of the church.

Jean Fair, Mildred Ferguson, & Ann Henry

Jean Fair, Mildred Ferguson, and Ann Henry have the distinction of all having served as "First Lady" of Grace & Glory Gospel Chapel some years ago. Their husbands – Bro. James Fair, Bro. George Ferguson, and Bro. Ceolia Henry were all leaders in the service of the Lord at Grace & Glory.

Jean and Bro. Fair came to Grace & Glory when their family was young and growing. Their two daughters are Felicia Fair Thompson and Jamie Fair. Jean was an absolute mom to many, sometimes her family members, sometimes friends. She took in and cared for those children in need and did it "naturally", without fuss or fan fare. Career wise, Jean is an educator, having taught in the Chicago Public School System for decades. She retired some years ago after making a difference in so many children's lives. She and Bro. Fair spend their time between serving the Lord Jesus Christ and spending time with their beloved grand children. Bro. Fair and Jean left Grace & Glory decades ago to start a new church, a new ministry. Bro. James Fair and Sis. Jean Fair continue to serve the Lord, continue to serve their family, and continue to serve their community, in a big way. Their ministry is at the Learning Center Gospel Chapel.

Mildred and Bro. Ferguson came to Grace & Glory when their family was young and growing. Their two daughters are Pamela Ferguson - Thomas and Karen Ferguson and they were youngsters when they came to Grace & Glory. They enjoyed being in the Sunday School class and they were good friends with Tanya Hicks, Carolyn Carter Thaxton, Sharon Kilpatrick Tang, and Felicia Fair Thompson. Bro. George Ferguson was an Elder at Grace & Glory and he was a sheer joy to be around. He had this keen sense of humor and gentle teasing of different ones like Connie McNulty, Vernice Hatch, and Elaine Shaw. He adored his wife, "Mil", and talked incessantly of his children and (later) his grand kids. Bro. Ferguson took his responsibility as Elder seriously, not only his duties with the services, but also his mentoring of the young men. He encouraged Bro. Tyrone Stem to become an Elder at Grace & Glory, and he became an Elder and served for several years. Mildred left a legacy of love, kindness, and generosity at the church. She prepared delicious meals at her home and invited Grace & Glory's church family and others to feast with her and her family. Her ministry is sharing the love of Christ though her meals and her hospitality. She cares so deeply for others and as a result, God has richly blessed her and her beautiful family. Bro. George Ferguson went to be with the Lord several years ago. Sis. Mildred Ferguson's ministry of love continues.

Bro. Ceolia Henry and Ann came to Grace & Glory as a very young married couple and a fast growing family. Ann loved having her beautiful little babies, in spite of being under the watchful, critical eye of Sis. Ruby Gall at the church. Ann had 10 little children and she and "Hank" were deliriously happy. They quoted scripture several times to describe their close-knit family: Psalm 128:3 "Thy wife shall be as a fruitful vine by the sides of thine house; thy children like olive plants round about thy table." and Psalm 27:3-5: "Lo, children are an heritage from the Lord; and the fruit of the womb is his reward. As arrows are in the hand of a mighty man, so are children of one's youth. Happy is the man who hath his quiver full of them; they shall not be ashamed, but they shall speak with the enemies in the gate." The children are all adults now, with their own families, and prominent and blessed. They make their mom proud and are at her "beck & call" to meet her needs and to keep her happy. Bro. Ceolia Henry went to be with the Lord years ago; he's looking down on his kids and just "bursting with pride". Sis. Ann Henry and her family continue their great ministry, serving the Lord Jesus Christ, at Grace Bible Church in Riverdale, Illinois.

<u>Lastly</u> . . .

The Grace & Glory church family has shaped me into the kind of person I have become.

I have tried to "love" people into loving other people; I have tried too hard. Oftentimes, people are not interested. Everyone has their own way as it relates to other people.

I also thought, as a little kid, that if you love someone, they will love you back. Boy, was I wrong about that one!

When I have been discouraged, my church family has given me encouragement; when I cried, they were a "shoulder to cry on;" instead of haste and rush to judgement, they showed me patience; instead of gossip, they gave me the sweet hand of friendship; instead of receiving God's wrath, God showed me mercy; instead of disdain, God showed His understanding; and lastly, a backward view of myself in the rear view window, shows that I have gone from "grace to glory."

CHAPTER FOUR

Events & Happenings

"We are what we repeatedly do. Excellence, then, is not an act but a habit."
Aristotle (384-322 B.C.)

"Happiness lies in the joy of achievement and the thrill of creative effort."
Franklin Delano Roosevelt

"Don't judge each day by the harvest you reap, but by the seeds that you plant."
Robert Louis Stevenson

"Service is the rent we pay for living. It is the very purpose of life and not something you do in your spare time."
Marian Wright Edelman

When someone looks for a church family, they inadvertently look for, not only a place of worship, but they seek a "haven", a place of shelter and safety; a place of refuge. There is a need to feel comfortable and affirmed. The people there have an attitude of support and love and concern.

It is a place where you readily share your concerns, reluctantly share your sorrows, and respectfully share your fears and issues.

Such a church is a place where they celebrate each other's joy, celebrate each other's success, and celebrate fulfilled dreams.

Grace & Glory Gospel Chapel is that kind of place. The bond that runs through our little church, the bond that runs through our services is the Spirit of Jesus Christ. He is lifted up inside the church, as well as, outside the church, at our homes, at social events, and at all times and places.

We follow a program on Sundays beginning with the "Breaking of Bread" and ending with Sunday School classes and on Thursdays, prayer is offered, scripture is read, and a Bible lesson is taught.

In addition to regular services, other events have taken place over the years.

- During the 2012-2013 year, a Book Club was started with the book, "What's In the Water", by Velma Wilson (Soror Dorothy White's Sister-in-law)
- Little Joseph L. Brownlee, III was christened on July 22, 2012. The ceremony was conducted at Grace & Glory by his grandfather, Elder Tyrone Stem. <u>Parents</u>: Natia Stem Brownlee & Joseph Brownlee, Jr.
- Grace & Glory Presented, "The Passion of the Christ" – a film detailing the crucifixion of our Lord & Savior, Jesus Christ. Saturday, April 7, 2012.
- Grace & Glory Vacation Bible School - Monday - Friday July 16 - July 20, 2012, 4:00 PM - 6:00 P.M.
- Bro. David Foster, Westlawn Gospel Chapel, was the Guest Speaker at Grace & Glory on Sunday, August 19, 2012. The theme was "Purpose and Power of God" - John 3:16-21.

  - Bro. Lawrence Perkins, author of "Transcending Greatness", was the guest speaker on Sunday, March 11, 2012. His message was from the scripture, Matthew 14:22-31. The message was clear, precise, thought-provoking, and humorous. Bro. Lawrence said at the beginning of his message, "It looks like Grace & Glory is empty, but with a telescope, I can see others that are already here. He asked, "What do we see?" He also brought a compass with him. He gave many illustrations and told some interesting stories. Lawrence told the story of the man who was trying to sell vacuum cleaners, but was unsuccessful because this one woman told him," I need a kidney not a vacuum cleaner!

After spending a year in New Orleans, Louisiana in 2005, initiating a charter school there after the Katrina crisis, Bro. Perkins came back to Chicago where he serves as the Associate Pastor of the Redeeming World Church located in Hammond, IN. He was featured in the Chicago SunTimes for leading the charge of iniating the Uno Charter School in New Orleans.

He concluded his message by exhorting the congregation to "stay focused, and keep the faith." Bro. Lawrence Perkins is a close friend of Sis. Valoree Harrington.

- On Friday, August 10, 2012, at G & G, an "Honorarium and Trunk Party" was held for Tamir N. Williams, daughter of Joyce Mosely. Tamir graduated from King College Prep in June, 2012 as valedictorian of her class. She won the prestigious Gates Millennium Scholarship and attended Middleburg College. On that same evening, tribute was paid to:

  Isaac Bibbs - Graduated from Kindergarten
  Pamela Thomas-Ferguson - Masters' degree
  Anthony Jones - 1 B Program - 6th Grade
  Juanita Stem - Masters Degree/Assistant Principal
  Sharon Tang - Masters Degree/Type 75 Certificate

The celebration ended with a Mexican Fiesta Dinner prepared by Suzette Watkins.

- Dr. Ben Carson was the Keynote Speaker at the 1995 Annual Circle Y Ranch Banquet. He was invited by Dr. Leroy (Butch) Yates. This fundraiser raised $17,000 for the camp.
- Stephen Watkins, assisted by Suzette Watkins sponsored a program entitled "The Real Meaning of Christmas" (Charlie Brown) at Grace & Glory on Friday, December 14, 2012 at 6:00 P.M. Music was provided by Tanya Hicks and Prof. Frank Morrison.

Pastor Derrick Rollerson presented the message, "The Meaning of Christmas." Dinner was prepared by Stephen & Suzette.

- The United Bible Conference was held from May 16-19, 2013 at the Roseland Bible Church located at 233 West 111th St., Chicago, Illinois 60643. The Pastoral Leadership is James Albright and Hubert Jackson, Jr. and Walter Anderson, Founder. The United Bible Conference consists of the Brethren Churches on the South Side of Chicago and beyond.

  - Family Gospel Chapel
  - Grace Bible Church
  - Grace & Glory Gospel Chapel
  - Laflin Gospel Chapel
  - Southside Gospel Chapel
  - Roseland Bible Church
  - The Learning Center Gospel Chapel
  - Westlawn Gospel Chapel

The Conference meets once per year, usually in May, and the churches take turns hosting. It usually lasts for 4 days – Thursday through Sunday.

The Community News around G & G during the 2007 year read like this:

- Olive Harvey College
  February 27, 2007

"Come Home To Gospel Festival"
6:30 - 8:30 P.M.

- Symphony Center Presents
  Sunday, March 11, 2007
  Grace & Glory Food &
  Clothe the Homeless Drive

- Reach out to someone all year round.
  Every Sunday, Grace & Glory will collect can goods and clothing.
  These items will be given to:
  Pacific Garden Mission

- Excellent Way House for Homeless Women & Children Special Needs

"Formula, Diapers, Children's Clothes
Note: Clothes must be clean or new

On December 9, 2007 at Grace & Glory Gospel Chapel, Bro. Derrick Rollerson served as Guest Speaker, Bro. Rollerson is from Westlawn Gospel Chapel. His theme was: "Believe This" – Luke 1:26-38

His 6 points were: (1) Faith - object → God

(2) Faith - evidence of things not seen

(3) Faith - we all have some

(4) Faith - doesn't take a lot of faith

(5) Faith - our victory

(6) Faith - by hearing the Word of God.

It was a powerful message of encouragement.

On November 25, 2001, The Adult Women's Sunday School Class honored Sister Vernice Hatch. It was held at Grace & Glory with all her family participating. The Scripture passage used was Proverbs 3: verses 10, 11, 20, & 25-30. It was a fitting backdrop to the character and service of Sis. Hatch at the church and beyond. Naomi R. Kilpatrick coordinated the event, planning with Sharon Tang, Valoree Harrington, Juanita Stem, Theresa Ivery, and the other Grace & Glory sisters. The food was prepared by Melvin Jones, a friend of the Kilpatrick Family.

There was other scripture read, poetry was rendered, prayer was offered, and tributes were made. There were tributes from a number of people and then a special tribute and a special presentation of gifts were given to Sis. Hatch. Sis. Hatch gave a beautiful response to the honor and left everyone laughing and happy. It was a wonderful affair and important, for Sis. Hatch was "given her flowers while she could yet smell them."

"Events & Happenings" are at the heart of the ministry that is Grace & Glory Gospel Chapel. I view it as a mission to help others; and as we help others, it has a "boomerang" effect. We get it all back! Like Abraham when God told him: "I will bless you . . . and you shall be a blessing. He was blessed by God so that he could bless others. What Abraham received was not for his own selfish enjoyment, but for the welfare and betterment of others. The same is true for us here at G & G. Although our "events and happenings" bring us personal satisfaction, God redeems us that we may go out and "preach the gospel to every creature." (Mark 16:15)

And so, our ministry continues.

Statement of Faith

1.) We believe the Bible to be the inspired, the only infallible authoritative Word of God.

2.) We believe that there is one God, eternally existent in the three persons:

Father
Son
Holy Spirit

3.) We believe in the deity of our Lord Jesus Christ,

in His virgin birth,
in His sinless life,
in His miracles,
in His vicarious atonement through His shed blood,
in His bodily resurrection,
in His ascension to the right hand of the Father,
in His personal premillenial return in power & glory.

4.) We believe that man is totally depraved and sinful, by virtue of choice, practice, and scriptural teaching, and that regeneration is absolutely necessary for his salvation.

5.) We believe that salvation is possible only by faith in the atoning work of Christ at Calvary, that this faith includes repentance of one's sinfulness, receiving Jesus Christ as personal Savior, and commitment of one's life to Jesus Christ, as Lord and Master

6.) We believe that the two ordinances enjoined upon believers are baptism and the Lord's Supper

7.) We believe in the Holy Spirit as the third Person of the Holy Trinity, whose ministry is to indwell the believer, convicting him of sin, enabling him to live a victorious and godly life.

8.) We believe in the resurrection of both the saved and the lost – they that are saved unto the resurrection of life

– they that are lost unto the resurrection of damnation.

9.) We believe that Satan exists as a personal being, seeking to control the minds and deeds of men, opposing all works of righteousness; that he is the arch enemy of God, under sentence to be destroyed by Him.

10.) We believe in the spiritual unity of all believers in Christ, constituting the true church; that though God has, in spite of divisions, seen fit to work within limitations; denominationalism tends to constitute a direct denial of this divine principle.

These 10 Beliefs that make up my "Statement of Faith" are taken from Grace & Glory Gospel Chapel's Constitution & Bylaws.

CHAPTER FIVE

My Early Years

Me at 2 years old

In 1935, the year of my birth, things were not easy for black families in the south. In Arkansas, my birth state, the Federal Emergency Relief Administration and the Resettlement Administration was in place to help people in need. Black families were not aware of this assistance for the poor and needy. At that time, black people were picked up, sometimes in wagons to pick cotton on white plantations. They were known as "sharecroppers." They stayed on the land and were responsible for taking care of the land and its crops. In the summer, they picked cotton, trying to pick as fast as they could and trying to fill as many cotton "sacks" as possible, from sun up to sun down. They congregated at the start of the day, some in groups, maybe one or two by themselves. A mother may be among the group, sitting there nursing her baby in full view of everyone. She gives everyone a penetrating glare with no shame or shyness. The ones who came to pick cotton had on loose - fitting, big, unattractive clothing. They all had on hats to protect themselves from the scorching sun. It gets extremely hot in Arkansas during the summer. In the fall, they chop cotton. You take a "hoe," with a wooden handle and a flat, steel bottom. I don't know which is more unpleasant, picking cotton or chopping cotton. I experienced both when I visited my cousins, Dorce, Sonny, and Irene in Auvergne, Arkansas when I was a young kid.

Beginning in 1933, the Agricultural Adjustment Administration had tried to counteract a badly depressed cotton market by paging planters not to grow cotton. This federal program benefitted large landowners and displaced small farmers, tenants, farm laborers, and share croppers, forcing many of them to take less-secure and lower paying work as wage hands. No state suffered more than Arkansas, where, by the spring of 1935, conditions were so bad that the newly formed Southern Tenant Farmers Union called a strike. The entire issue focused attention on the need for rural assistance and rehabilitation, paving the way for Franklin Delano Roosevelt's establishment of the Resettlement Administration. There was an association between the crop and the blacks who worked it since the time of slavery. Although times were hard, the poor were rich in spirit, amidst hopeless prejudice, bigotry and ignorance.

When picking cotton, you pick a row, with a long, white cotton sack around your shoulder. You'd pick cotton until that sack was too heavy to pull. Schools for black children did not open until January 1st so as not to interfere with cotton picking.

I was born in Fitzhugh, Arkansas on February 6, 1935. Fitzhugh is located in Woodruff County. I was delivered by a midwife at my mothers' home. I've been told that the midwife remarked, "what a black little baby this is!" My mom was fair-skinned and beautiful, but my dad was medium brown complexioned. I looked more like him than her. I must have been an ugly little baby for her to make that remark. I was from "pillar to post" when I was a kid. My mother was trying to "find herself", trying to see who she was as a person. She did not like being tied down with a kid. Aunt Hattie and her family and mama and me stayed at the same house – like my cousin, Dorce, used to say – we were born in the same bed, in the same house. Dorce had been born six months earlier and Aunt Hattie still had milk in her breasts, so she nursed me right along with her kids. The little town of Fitzhugh, where we lived was so small, sometimes it doesn't show up on a map. I'm sure at some point, there was beautiful green grass, and beautiful bushes, and trees that produced luscious fruit and vines that grow pecans; but what I remember is dirt, dirt, dirt. Dust settled on our hair, as kids, and kept our clothes dirty. Mama and Aunt Hattie use to wash clothes once per week in that big iron kettle that sat on hot coals to heat the water. Aunt Hattie would put that "lye" soap in there and beat the clothes up and down to make sure they were clean. She rinsed them out with clear water and hung them on a line with wooden clothespins and hung them on the one fence we had. The sun would soon dry the clothes and they smelled so fresh and clean. During that week, the clothes were "sprinkled" with clear water, ball them up, and iron them with a "smoothing" iron that had been put on the kitchen stove to get hot. This was a process, because when the iron cooled off, it had to be heated again, so you ironed a little then put the iron on the stove again. The kitchen stove was a big monster that had 4 plates on it. Sometimes, it had 2 if it was not a big stove. First thing in the morning, Aunt Hattie would put wood in the one side of the stove and light the fire.

We would walk to school from our home. It was a long distance where we walked each day past a graveyard, walking on the side of the road. When we saw a car coming, (there were not a lot of cars on the road during that time – 1940-1946), we would walk in the ditch. We walked in the cold, as well as, in hot weather. The school house was a two story, "shot gun" frame house - first floor with about 2 rooms and the second floor was basically, an attic. The house was typical of that period – 1930's, 1940's; one door for entry and four windows in the front, two windows in the top level and and two windows on the first level; two windows on each side of the school house. The color was an ugly gray or dark "charcoal" gray. The students were all ages, all taught together in one room. It was usually 30 or 40 students; the "instructor" was Professor Page assisted by his wife, Mrs. Page. He rang a small hand bell and the children ran promptly to class. The furniture was a few desks, stationery, with seats attached. The desks were worn and in bad shape. Each desk had an ink well to dip your pen and a grooved place to place a pencil or pen. Professor Page always began with devotion which was a moral lesson and singing. The lessons were usually reading, using "Dick & Jane" books, arithmetic (math), and penmanship, and geography. We learned by rote, memorization, and recitation. We were taught spelling and your hand was smacked if you misspelled a word. We were taught "times tables" (multiplication facts) and you had to learn them and recite them. We were taught sayings and poetry (Paul Laurence Dunbar, Frederick Douglass, George Washington Carver, and others) and we had to memorize and recite the material. For recreation, we played basketball and the guys played a version of football. Everything we used in that little school house came from used, worn and hand me downs from white schools.

I experienced the school part on a visit to my cousins because my mother and father took me to St. Louis, Missouri when I was two years old. However, we would visit, like every few months. After a while, and when I was older, my mother sent me on the train from St. Louis to Auvergne to visit my cousins. The train station was in Newport, AR.

I attended school in St. Louis during my early years, but we moved to Chicago when I was eleven years old and I attended the Doolittle School while I was in the 5th Grade. The 6th through 8th grades were spent at Douglas Elementary where I graduated from 8th grade in 1950. Although I was "quiet" and "shy" and "introverted", I did extremely well in school. I was an avid reader and loved learning new things. My high school career started right away at Wendell Phillips H. S., located on the south side of Chicago. I attended my 9th and 10th grades there, where I was on the honor role and a participant in the National Honor Society for the 2 years. I left in 1952 and got married before finishing my entire 4 years. I went on to have 4 children before continuing my education. It was bittersweet leaving high school because my childhood dream, my burning desire was to become a teacher. I never gave up on that dream; it was only "deferred". I was determined that my dream would not dry up like a "raisin in the sun." I went back to school in 1962 when my baby, Kevin was 2 years old. I enrolled in a special program at the junior college level. If I could take courses and maintain a "C" average, I could take an exam and be placed into a four year program at one of the local universities. And of course, my grades were never lower than a B.

I was elated at going back to school! I studied with a vengeance. I was determined to make it and was confident that I would succeed. By God's grace, my family's support, my mentor's encouragement, and my hard work and determination, I received my Bachelor of Science in Education in December, 1966 from Illinois Teachers' College - South, now Chicago

State University. I began my teaching career at the Reavis Elementary School in January, 1967, with a 2nd grade class. As the cliche goes, "the rest is history." My career was interrupted in 1968 as I left to have my fifth and last child, Lenard. I went back to work in September, 1969 at the Fort Dearborn Elementary School. I taught there until 1972, when I left to go to a "spanking, brand new" school, Michele E. Clark Middle School on Chicago's west side.

Before I married, my mother and I lived at 4730 S. Prairie Ave. We lived in a basement apartment and shared the bathroom with two other apartments. We had the front apartment where we could look out the window. The view wasn't fabulous because our "gaze" was street level and we saw people walking back and forth all through the day. Billy Reed lived in the middle apartment, next to us, and he was the first openly gay man I had ever met. He was a beautician and he used to do my hair to perfection. Billy was hilarious from his "walk", always fast, to his "talk"! He was always joking and teasing and he always had a funny story to tell us. We listened intently, wanting more and more of his funny "tales". We laughed at his mannerisms and his boldness. He talked about all of us, but his harshest words, in jest, were for my Aunt Mabel. As a beautician, he was hair stylist "extraordinaire", who loved his craft. Aunt Mabel, also a beautician, perfected her craft under Billie's mentorship. He showed her many "tricks of the trade", tips of successful hair styling, and tips on keeping the customers coming back, e.g. "people skills." Aunt Mabel had a few tricks up her sleeve, as well, to share with Billie. She could "zing" him back, in a second, and then burst out laughing! It was a pleasant atmosphere for me, so I enjoyed going to the shop. Billy's Beauty Shop was a pretty nice place when you take in to account that it was the 1950's. It was a small, three room place. He had a small kitchen in the back room; the middle room held the bowls for washing customers' hair, and 2 chairs; and the front room had a floor length hair dryer, some chairs, a big juke box, and a wall telephone (rotary). I have a picture of Billy with him wearing a pair of white pants and a knee length white smock (top). Of course, he has a cigarette in his left hand. When he left the shop to go other places, he put on his beige trench coat, pulling the belt tightly around him, walking fast, with the air of a "queen". He had no inhibition and he had no shame about who he was. We loved him and treated him like one of the family.

As mentioned, the building we lived in at 4730 So. Prairie, had 3 apartments in the basement. I remember the hallway being cold when I had to use the bathroom at night. My Aunt Mabel came to live with us for a while until she "got on her feet."

My mother, Cora Virginia Shockley Jones, and her two sisters, Mabel Kidd and Hattie Egeston, were born in a little place called Newport, Arkansas. They were part of the Shockley family. There was Uncle Frank, (Frank Shockley), Mama's brother born to Gilbert Shockley and Virginia Brockman Shockley. My grandfather had 3 other sons with other women; he was a "rolling stone" from the Temptations' hit song, "Papa was a Rolling Stone, wherever he laid his head was his home . . .," etc. The names of the three sons were: Wayman Shockley of Auvergne, Arkansas; "Sonny Boy" Shockley, Little Rock, Arkansas, and Oliver Shockley, Chicago, Illinois. My grandmother, Virginia, had one other son with another man and his name was Charlie Brown. He drowned when he was relatively young, but fathered three children with Aunt Lois Egeston. The children were my cousins: Mildred Viola Brown; Jack Brown, and Franklin Brown, now deceased. I've only seen one picture of my Uncle Charlie. It was a dark, unsmiling, sad, troubled young man that looked back at me from the photo. He might have been thinking about being a black man and how difficult that was, how especially hard that was to live in the heart of the deep south where black men (and black women) endured racism, discrimination, and disrespect on a daily basis. The black man had to carry himself in such a way that was demeaning to them in order to stay alive, in order to survive. I remember having to hide under the bed at Grandpa's house, and having to darken all the lamps in fear of the Ku Klux Klan coming to our grand father's home. We, as children, had heard about these white men who wore white robes and white hoods over their heads, riding on horses to your house and burning a white cross in your front yard. My grandfather, Gilbert "Gillie" Shockley, was one who did not "cowtow" to the white man; he was fearless. He left Arkansas after many years because it became too dangerous for him and the family.

My mother and I lived with Uncle Oliver when we came to Chicago in 1946. I was 11 years old. I remember Uncle Oliver as an unsmiling man, but he was kind and generous. He opened his apartment to us, which was a nice, comfortable place on the first floor. I don't remember the address, but it was on the south side of Chicago. He had beautiful furniture and a big lamp in his living room. Uncle Oliver lived alone at the time and seems to have made a nice life for himself after leaving Arkansas many years earlier. He had no children, to my knowledge, and he lived in Chicago until his death. I remember breaking one of his nice lamps and I was devastated, felt really bad about it. I don't remember how I broke it, but I do remember how bad I felt. My mother was very upset with me. I seemed to always be "getting into" something.

Uncle Wayman lived in either Shoffner or Weldon, Arkansas and raised his family. He had several kids but I don't remember meeting them. Uncle Wayman was the "spitting image" of Grandpa and was always upbeat and funny, laughing and smiling a lot.

Uncle Sonny Boy lived in Little Rock, Arkansas and fathered my cousin, Maxine Gillerson. I met him only once. My mother and Maxine attended his funeral when he passed away years later.

I remember Uncle Frank well and spent a lot of time with him after he came to St. Louis and again when he came to Chicago. He followed my mother to whatever city she happened to move to. Uncle Frank got married in St. Louis and had 3 children, 2 girls and a boy, Frank, Jr. His children looked so much like him. Aunt Hattie tried to bond with his children after Uncle Frank's death, but they did not want to have anything to do with the family. Uncle Frank loved us – Dorce, Sonny, Irene, and me – and we loved him back, as well. He'd come to see us, no matter where we were. He died at 47 years old and spent his whole life chasing dreams in the pursuit of some measure of happiness. I don't think he ever found it. He died before Grandpa and Mama and her sisters kept his death secret from Grandpa because he was ill at the time. They told him later.

As a kid, I lived in St. Louis, "off and on", between visits back down south. I spent a lot of time with my cousins, Dorce, Sonny, and Irene. When I was 11 years old, Daddy took me to Chicago to live with him briefly. My mother soon followed and we lived with Uncle Oliver. We later moved to 4730 Prairie. I used to walk from my apartment to 47th and Indiana where I caught the streetcar to Phillips High School which was located at 39th (Pershing Rd.) and Prairie. Lenzo, in the meantime, was working at Sam's Fish Market on 47th Street, between Prairie and Indiana. Lenzo's uncle, Tommy Edwards had gotten him a job working with him. "Unbeknownth" to me, Lenzo watched me every day as I came from school. He also saw me at Phillips because he attended the same school. There were only 3 high schools, at the time, where black kids could attend: Phillips, Dusable, and Inglewood. Lenzo watched me for a while before he finally introduced himself to me. He was a pretty "cool" guy, with lots of friends. The guys wore dress pants, shirts, with no tie, and hats. Lenzo was persistent in his pursuit of my favor, even though I already had a "boyfriend," literally, not taking "No" as an answer. We became a couple and spent a lot of time with his friends and their girlfriends.

We went on car rides, going to the movies, some times visiting friends in South Chicago, east of Dorchester, spending a lot of time together. Lenzo and I were inseparable during those early years, usually holding hands. In the end, Lenzo beat out the competition and we have shared 60+ years and counting!

After we got married in 1952, we lived with Lenzo's uncle, R. B. Edwards and his wife Lucy, at 37th and Giles. We had our own room, but shared the apartment with them. We then moved to 46th St. (1024 E. 46th St.), just past Drexel, where we had an apartment, but shared the kitchen and the bathroom with Ira Teague and her daughters, Peggy and Kay. My daughters Sharon and Linda were babies. I remember sitting on the side of the bed, in the middle of the night, and crying my eyes out, because I had to change their diapers (cloth) and give them their bottles. They were only 11 months apart, so they were babies together, so to speak. I remember washing those diapers, in the middle of the night, and hanging them on a little, portable line. I was so frustrated trying to take care of my precious babies, trying to keep the little place clean, and trying to learn to cook meals. By His grace, I made it and my daughters were healthy and beautiful.

We later moved into Chicago Public Housing Projects, the Ida B. Wells Projects. We lived in a brand new apartment in the high rise buildings, on the 3rd floor, located at 540 E. 36th St. It was the year, 1954 and we stayed there until we moved into our own home at 7429 So. Sangamon. It was 1962, when my baby, Kevin, was 2 years old.

I remember reading an article a few years back about public housing. There was a picture of a family – a mother and her two kids - just moving into a housing complex in the Ida B. Wells. It was from the 1940's when public housing was a very nice place to live. It was the Ida B. Wells project that were built like town houses. They were attractive and well kept. It could have been us because we were happy to be in such a beautiful apartment with a nice kitchen and our very own bathroom. At the time we lived in the projects, it was different from the visions of crime, decay and extreme poverty that dominated some public housing in the later years. At the new Ida B. Wells high rise buildings, residents were fined if caught cutting across the grass, two-parent, working families were the norm and most residents viewed the projects as a major step up from the cramped ghettos of Chicago's "black belt". When we moved into the new apartment, it was like I "died and went to heaven."

The projects afforded us the opportunity to spread out, to have some form of privacy, and to live together as a family, truly as a family. Lenzo went to the army in 1953, just months before my daughter, Linda, was born, and he served for two years. When we lived in Ida B. Wells, the buildings were maintained, the elevators were promptly repaired if something went wrong, we had been screened through the application process, and there were rules that we had to follow to remain a tenant. The system worked well for us as a family and it gave us shelter and protection as we planned for moving higher toward owning our own home. It was a lofty dream of ours and we realized that dream in 1962. When we moved to our first home at 7429 So. Sangamon, we integrated that block and soon after, the white families began to move out of the neighborhood.

I came to Grace & Glory Gospel Chapel in 1956 when my little daughter, Trina, was about 6 months old. Inez Douglas brought me into the Assembly. I don't remember the occasion for inviting me, but I remember feeling strange in their midst because the women wore no lipstick, no other kind of makeup. Everyone seemed "holy" and "chaste"; everyone seemed so "serious". Very little laughter or joking; except that Inez was always "zinging" people in jest. She was a teacher in the Chicago Public Schools, later to become a guidance counselor. I considered her to be excellent with children. She was witty and bright. Elizabeth Reckley was also an educator. Inez brought her to Grace & Glory after I came along. Sis. Lucy, my mentor, was there and dear Sis. Adine Douglas was there as well. She was an excellent bible teacher. Sis. Lucy served as the Sunday School teacher to the children. Sis. Mullin, Bro. Mullin's wife and Sis Lucy's sister, was there and chided the children to "speak up and pronounce the words correctly". Bro. Gall was our leader and he was "bigger than life" to me. He was such a strong personality, like a stern father or grandfather. He was very opinionated, very knowledgeable in the Word of God, and he "took no prisoners". Bro. Gall loved to teach from the book of Revelation and the book of Daniel. He personally drew a map/time line of Armageddon, the

Rapture, the Millennium, the New Heaven and the New Earth, the Lake of Fire, the Judgement Seat of Christ, the Great White Throne Judgement, Satan, the Anti-Christ, and so on. In spite of Bro. Gall's strictness, he was a kind man and personable. Lenzo, my husband, enjoyed talking to him. He used to visit our home on 74th and Sangamon and he often shopped at our little grocery store on 74th and Peoria.

None the less, Bro. Gall was serious (as a heart attack) about the ministry of Grace & Glory. He set up the work after the doctrine, tradition, and practice of the Plymouth Brethren, Scotland, England. He was born in Barbados, but got his training and his calling to the ministry in New York City. He and his wife, Sis. Ruby Gall had one daughter, Allison Gall McClean, and she and her husband had one son, named after Bro. Gall. When Bro. Gall passed away in May, 1971, we held a funeral service here, but Sis. Gall took his body to New York for another funeral there and that's where he is buried. Sis. Gall soon moved to Brooklyn, New York to live with Allison and her family. She died several years later. I continued to communicate with Sis. Gall long after Bro. Gall's death.

During Bro. Gall's ministry, a young, shy, unassuming, and quiet man named Willie Horton was sitting under the "wings" of Bro. Gall. Willie would come to service, sit in the very back row, and scoot down in the seat, as if he was hiding from someone. He was so reluctant to talk that he very seldom said "Hello". However, the Lord loosened his tongue because he later became the spiritual leader, the Elder of Grace & Glory Gospel Chapel.

When looking back on my early years, I am amazed at the amount of living I've done! How thankful I am for the grace of God that has "brought me through".

CHAPTER SIX

Daddy

Daddy

The History of Our Family

The Black Family in our country has been and is "magnificently durable and amazingly creative. The continued existence of us, as a people, has confounded the world. We remember always how our ancestors were torn from Africa and sold into bondage in a land that was alien to them in every way: the climate, the people, the language and, most importantly and most devastating, the unimaginable inhuman brutality to which they were subjected.

Families were created to give and receive affection, compassion and comfort. Our ancestors were not allowed to legally marry, and often children and mates were sold away. But even this terrible system sustained our ancestors, making it possible for us to be here today. The tradition of extended families continued even after slavery was abolished. The greatest and largest migration of our people in the history of our nation succeeded because of this kinship of blood and bond. "From the early 1900's through the 1970's, some six million African Americans left the agrarian South for the industrialized North for better paying jobs and a life relatively free from racist oppression and violence."

Today, we are still the vital force of our people. As families, we take in and care for the children of our relatives and "extended family" when they experience hardships. As a great-grandmother, and as a grandmother, I share my resources to assist when it is needed. Lenzo and I have shared our home when unemployment, illness, or death leaves a relative homeless or in dire straits. Additionally, we commemorate . . . family graduations, weddings, new jobs, new babies, and "home-goings".

Our family looks forward to the reunion which occurs every two years. We go from state to state and usually plan for four days. The first day, we "meet and greet" and get the t-shirts, roster, and "goody bag", and the Itinerary. The second day is spent doing fun activities, touring, and more eating and the banquet. The third day is usually the all day picnic, and the fourth and last day is the church where we remember our departed loved ones and one of my cousins gives a message. At the last family reunion which was held in St. Louis, my cousin Herbert (Junior) gave an excellent inspiring message on the "Beatitudes". The reunion keeps us all connected and we, the older ones, pray that our children and grand children keep it going. We meet during the month of July or August. Our relatives come from all over to celebrate each other and give thanks for our ancestors and acknowledge their accomplishments as well as ours. We have come this far because of loyalty, courage and sacrifice. We will go forward with the continuing devotion and support of our loving, creative and resilient and beautiful family.

Daddy

My father, James Thurlo "Buddy" Jones, was born on March 16, 1916, in a little town called Fitzhugh, Arkansas. Daddy had two children with my mother, Cora Virginia Shockley Jones,. I was born on February 6, 1935 and my little brother, James Thurlo Jones, Jr. was born in early 1937. He lived 6 days. My father grieved for him a very long time. I don't know that he ever really "got over" his death (according to my mother and my aunts). It reminds me of how David lamented for his newborn, sick child who died at 7 days old. The Lord took the child; then "David arose from the earth, and washed, and anointed himself, and changed his apparel, and came into the house of the Lord, and worshipped." (II Samuel 12:18-20) I was the oldest, so when my little brother died, I was left to be an only child. In spite of his grief and sorrow for my brother, Daddy loved me and doted on me all the days of his life.

Daddy was the third child, behind Aunt Alma and Aunt Thelma, but the oldest boy, so he had a very difficult, hard life as a child. He started "plowing the field" on their land at the age of 7. His sisters were able to go to school, but Daddy seldom went to school. He had to do the hard work on the farm that men and boys had to do. The women did the work in the house, e.g. cooking, cleaning, washing, ironing and taking care of the babies (there was, seemingly, always a baby to care for). My grandmother, Dessie Anna, had twelve children, one of them died in early childhood. My grandmother was dark complexioned, skin smooth as chocolate, a slightly "plump" figure, and big pretty legs. She was known for her shape and her legs and her strength of character. She had a deep love for and an unswerving commitment to her children. She prayed daily for her children. My grandmother, I'm told, raised 11 children with a strong hand of discipline, teaching them how to take care of each other. She taught them the tenets of teamwork – compete against each other internally, within the group, but stand strong against the outside forces; stand with each other and protect each other. The "Jones" family was known as a close-knit family that was tough and intimidating when met with danger. They fought many little fights as children that solidified their commitment to their brothers and sisters. It was 8 sisters and 3 brothers. The girls were known as the "Jones' girls", and after a while, no one messed with them.

My grand mother, Dessie, as I said, taught them to sew, to cook, and to take care of babies. All eight of those girls learned those lessons well going into their adult lives being excellent seamstresses and excellent cooks. They cooked gourmet meals that could put Rachel Ray and Paula Deen out of business, starting with Aunt Alma, who cooked delicious meals "in bulk". She always cooked large amounts and everyone was welcome in her house.

James Thurlo Jones was affectionately called "Buddy", but to me he was just "Daddy. He grew up to be a handsome young man, a "ladies man". He met my mother and they fell "head over heels" in love, they were childhood sweethearts. After my birth and the death of their son, and as they tried to build a life together, things started to fall apart. My mother didn't have a job, although she sought jobs as a waitress, and selling drinks in a small bar. Daddy was an auto mechanic, so his work depended upon how many cars he could repair. Money and other issues loomed large in their relationship, so they started to drift apart.

My grandfather was James Knox Polk Jones, affectionately called "Polk Jones". His grandkids called him "Papa". We looked up to him as if he was royalty. We were in awe of his proud, stern, uncompromising demeanor. We hung on to his every word as if it was law. When we grew into adulthood, the grandkids recognized his warmth, his acceptance, and yes, his love. During Daddy's childhood, Papa was in and out of the home, but when he was there, he ruled with a strong hand. Daddy received his formal education, what there was of it, from the Fitzhugh Public Schools. His education as a youngster was precious for from the age of 7, he had to learn to do a "man's job" around the farm. He was "behind the plow" when he could hardly reach the handlebars; plowing the field, helping to plant and harvest the crop. Daddy grew up during a time of oppression and discrimination of black people, especially black men. He was sustained and he survived because of a strong family structure which included his twin sister, Thelma, and the rest of his siblings. He worked hard and prospered by the "sweat of his brow." He served proudly and valiantly in World War II. He loved serving his country and everyone was proud of him. I remember his coming home, on furlough, in his crisp, beige uniform and shined to the max shoes. He served during the years, 1943-1945. My mother received a check from the government during his time in the service, and I remember having to "ration" everything. We were on a fixed allowance of provisions and food. There was an allotted amount of food and money. My mother managed and we happily went about living our lives, never complaining, content with the blessings of food, clothing, and shelter.

Daddy was an auto mechanic by trade, and after being honorably discharged from the army, he set up a little alley shop to work on cars. In 1946, we moved from St. Louis to Chicago, and Daddy had an alley shop there as well. People brought their cars to his shop for repairs, and

I remember seeing several cars and people waiting as he worked to fix their problems. He loved working and experimenting on cars. He got hurt, several times, while doing this work. He spent countless hours at his shop, working on cars. Daddy continued pursuing his dream of being the ultimate, master auto mechanic making money to care for his family.

Daddy was "a rolling stone", like the Temptations' "Papa Was a Rolling Stone", – "wherever he laid his hat, was his home . . ." He loved women and the pursuit of women. He was looking for love in all the wrong places. He was living life in the "fast lane" – "women, wine, & song." He drank excessively; he smoked Camel cigarettes – one after the other, a chain-smoker; he absolutely loved to dance; and he used to get the biggest kick out of "singing the blues". And then, he had a massive stroke . . . He recovered, but it left him with paralysis on one side. Slowly, his life started to change. He moved to San Diego, California where his sister, Rutha, and his two brothers, Wiley and Theodore (Sonny) lived. He enjoyed his life in San Diego. He got a cute little house with 2 bedrooms, a small kitchen, and a living room with one bathroom. He had a flower garden in the front yard and a vegetable garden in the back yard. There was a large avocado tree in the back and Aunt Rutha would go get those avocados off the tree and take them home to enjoy. Daddy had two big dogs and a cat and for a short time, he had a few chickens. I guess he was trying to bring farm life to San Diego.

His life in San Diego was pleasant, given the beautiful California weather – warm during the day, cool at night. Daddy especially enjoyed playing dominoes with his brother-in-law, Uncle Jenkins, Aunt Rutha's husband. Daddy was a skillful player and very competitive. Uncle Jenkins visited him every day to play dominoes. Daddy's health started to decline during his later years, but Aunt Rutha and Uncle Jenkins were always at his "beck and call", when he needed them.

Daddy had a special bond, a special love for his twin sister, Thelma, who lived in St. Louis. They had a keen sense when something was not going right. They talked frequently by phone, and Aunt Thelma visited him several times. She said she was his "better-half". Daddy lived in San Diego for over 20 years and then he developed cancer. He needed special care, so I brought him back to Chicago, to my home to care for him. Lenzo and I had just bought our home in South Holland in March of 1996. Daddy came in January of 1997. He lived with us for nine months before he passed away in October, 1997. We put him under the care of Dr. Cheryl Woodson, and the care of home makers and nurses who visited him at home on a weekly basis. It was a very difficult time for me. It took a while for me to realize that my father was dying, slowly slipping away each day. It was hard being a care giver for him because it was a 24/7 experience. Secondly, I felt badly about having to take him away from his little home that he loved so dearly in San Diego. It took away his freedom, his independence, and sometimes, his dignity. It was a time where I experienced a myriad of emotions that kept me depressed most of the time. You might ask, where was my faith in the Lord? My church, Grace & Glory Gospel Chapel was supporting me, praying for my family; my mother and my husband were helping; my friends lifted me up in prayer; my friend, Beverly Yates, came over from time to time to help turn my father over in the bed; and I was praying and searching the scriptures each day for encouragement and affirmation. And yet, it continued to be a very difficult time. Daddy lived for nine months after we brought him from San Diego. I remember I had made plans to go on a cruise with Erse (my aunt, his baby sister and the same age as me) and her social club. It was planned for August, 1997. The trip had been paid for several months earlier and I was really looking forward to going, but Daddy's illness caused me to wonder whether I should go. I was concerned that he might die while I was away. I talked to my mother and my daughter, Sharon, and of course, to my husband, Lenzo, about my concerns. They all insisted that I should go. They promised to take care of Daddy. I then called my cousin, Delores in St. Louis and talked to her (Delores is Aunt Thelma's daughter). She enthusiastically encouraged me to go. She affirmed what my family had already said, so I went on the cruise to the Caribbean. I forgot to mention that I told Daddy that I was going and he said, "You go on "Poochie", and enjoy yourself. I'll be okay." Needless to say, I had a wonderful time. It was relaxing at times, and at other times on the ship, it was exciting and exhilarating. I especially enjoyed the food; the "dressing up" for dinner; watching the sun rise in the morning; going to the top deck and watching the ship pull away from the port; and the shopping at each port. Although I totally enjoyed the experience, I was happy to arrive back home after 7 days. My family was happy to see me and Daddy's condition seemed to be about the same.

Daddy had come to know the Lord while he was in San Diego. He attended church there and enjoyed having his minister as a neighbor. And although he lived his life in the "fast lane", he did it his way, like Frank Sinatra. As Gwendolyn Brooks says in one of her poems, he "scraped life with a fine toothed comb." He enjoyed people and being with his sisters and making them laugh. Daddy had a keen sense of humor, always with a ready joke and a big laugh. He gave his nieces and nephews "bear hugs" and kisses.

During the nine months of illness in South Holland at our home, he got reacquainted with his grandchildren, his great grandchildren and his great great grandchildren. They surrounded him with love and attention and he "ate it all up" – a typical granddad. His sisters and his brother, Sonny, came to visit him during his illness. Aunt Thelma was the last one to visit him before he died, but she had come to see him more than once. He loved seeing her; it lifted his spirits just being with her. Daddy smoked his Camel cigarettes almost to the end. When he stopped a few days before, I knew he was quickly slipping away. He told me on his death bed (in my back room, right off the family room), right before his passing, "I'm happy. I'm in God's hands." I believed him. He died on a Thursday morning, at about 4:05 on October 16, 1997. Mama, Lenzo and I watched him as he passed from this life into eternity. Daddy lived to be 81 years old, so Psalm 90:10 says: "The days of our years are threescore years and ten; and if by reason of strength they be fourscore years, yet is their strength labor and sorrow; for it is soon cut off; and we fly away." Amen.

Daddy's funeral service was held at Grace & Glory Gospel Chapel with Elder Bro. Willie Horton doing the Eulogy. His sisters and the "slew" of the rest of the family attended. It was a dark time in my life, but God took me through.

My Uncle Wiley wrote a long letter to his siblings that cited the Jones' history. Below are excerpts from that letter:

"It was said that our grandfather's mother was Black and his father White. When you look at the various tones in the family and the eye coloring of some it is very evident of the mixture. It's also said that our grandfather did not want his sons to marry Black women and that he sent his son James Polk Jones (my father) away to keep him from marrying my mother, Dessie Thompson! Well, he came back and married her anyway! He loved our beautiful mother, thinking of my mother's beauty is seen in the eight Jones sisters. Those eight ladies show that we had a very beautiful mother.

Up till this day, August, 1986, "This Jones Family" strives to give their children and their offspring a better life than we had in our young days.

I guess you are wondering why I am not saying much about our Grandmother. I don't know much about her. My sister, Alma, spent more time with her than any of us. Alma went to live with Grandma as a young child because my mother's second pregnancy just happened to be with twins! (James Thurlo and Thelma)

"Some people wonder what drives "This Jones Family." How we can go on and on, year after year, and still have the love and feeling of family that we were raised with. We have had very little sickness. All eleven of us seem to be in pretty good shape. God drives us and shines a bright light of hope and faith upon "This Jones Family". It frightens me when I look back and see that we are all still here. Sometimes I stop and think, who will be first and how strongly it will touch the ones who are left.

As "This Jones Family" gazes into the sunset of our lives, it makes me proud to see our children and their offspring progress on past big goals in life. Our grandfather did not go to church as this family does today, but we feel strongly that God was watching over our family. This Jones Family still has strong faith in prayer.

Jim Jones had road blocks as we have today. Our grandfather loved his children and grandchildren. He gave all of his sons land to use anyway they wanted to use as long as they remember one thing, they could never sell it or pass it on to their wives. It was willed to the third generation of Jones and that's how This Jones Family got the Jones farm. Our dad and uncles did not like that but, this was our grandfather's wish and will. Our uncles tried to break the will but the will was written in the twenties and could not be broken.

Our grandfather knew that when he passed on his sons would sell the farm. Jim Jones wanted his farm to remain in "This Jones Family" for years to come. So he willed it to his grandchildren. So you can see why we are proud to be Jones.

Our dad, James Polk Jones had his faults like his dad did, and we loved him. Dad always told me he did not want us to sell the farm. He was a proud man just like his dad was. He enjoyed his children and his grandchildren.

He looked forward to the Father's Day picnic in Detroit at Plymouth Park. We enjoyed it too. That's how "This Jones Family" reunions got started.

James Polk Jones like his dad was a very skillful man. He was good at almost anything he wanted to do. He was an auto mechanic, carpenter, electrician, plumber and painter.

Our house was the the first Black house in the rural area to have electric lights. Our dad tried to get the light company to install lights in our house. They said no, so he got the church Oscar vong Bagwell before they would bring the line one hundred feet with a pole outside our house. Our dad wired all these houses complete from reading a book. He could listen to a car run and tell what was wrong with it. We had lamp lights for so long we were amazed at the electric lights. We were in a rural area so this was something new for everyone. We all worked for our dad.

Our mother passed away in the late thirties. Our strongest family ties come from our mother, Dessie Anna Thompson Jones. She always told us to love one another and stay together as a family. Our mother was a beautiful brown woman, as you can see from these Jones sisters.

James Allen Jones and Millie Elizabeth Butler are our foundation. You can't penalize our nationality, because we are so many nationalities rolled up in one neat little bundle. This what makes us special people. The blood that ran through the veins of Jim and Millie Jones is the blood that makes us think right; blood that will make you get a good education and make you take good care of your family.

They thought enough about education, to build a school. They thought enough about community, to build a store. They thought enough about family to own some property.

Jim Jones was an un-learned man, who didn't know the Lord. But he had a heart of gold, and a mind like a computer, and he worked like a beaver day and night that he might inherit the joys of his labor. We are grateful for our heritage from Jim and Millie Butler Jones.

So all that you are, and all that you can be, and all that you will be, you owe it all to James Allen Jones and Millie Elizabeth Butler."

This letter was written by Uncle Wiley, my dad's brother. It appeared in my cousin, Floyd Boykin's book entitled, "The Family Tree of Thelma Jones Boykin".

To God be the glory. Great things He has done for "This Jones Family".

Millie & Jim Jones/Great-Grandparents
{Date unknown}

Roots of our Family Tree
My Paternal Great-Grand Parents

(Father)   James Allen "Jim" Jones
<u>Born</u> - July 4, 1857 in
Griffin, Georgia - Spaulding County
<u>Died</u> - March 3, 1936 79 years old

(Mother)   Millie Elizabeth "Buttler" Jones
Born - January 10, 1863
Westpoint - White County – West Point, Arkansas
<u>Died</u> - May 24, 1933 70-years old

(Children) All born in Augusta, Arkansas - Woodruff County

lived 42 years	1. Elgirta Jones	10/7/1880-2/8/1922
lived 85 years	2. Edward T. Jones	1/29/1882-12/8/67
lived 34 years	3. Penola Jones	1/22/1889-6/2/23
(80 yrs) my grandfather	4. James Knox Polk Jones	9/3/1891-11/20/71
lived 60 years	5. Floyd K. Jones	3/17/1894-3/25/54
lived 86 years	6. Charles H. Jones	8/16/1897-6/21/83
lived 52 years	7. Alice S. Jones	2/4/1899-5/5/51
lived 86 years	8. Samuel O. Jones	11/30/1902-10/20/88
lived 56 years	9. Walter H. Jones	2/27/1904 – 12/27/60

Jim Jones and Millie E. Buttler Jones were married on January 8, 1880 Their first child, <u>Elgirta</u>, was born on October 7, 1880. She was the first child to die at age 42. Millie was 59 years old.

The next year, 1923, her child Penola, passed away. Penola was 34 years old when she died. Her mother, Millie, was 60 years old. She would live 10 more years after losing her second daughter.

Millie had nine children over a period of 24 years. She had 3 daughters and 6 sons. Two of her sons left the home, left the south, and went north. Seeking a better life, they decided to "pass" as white men. All of Jim Jones' kids looked "white". Like him, they were all fair skinned and "nice" hair (white folks' hair) Three of the sons, James K. and Floyd K. and Samuel O. ended up in Detroit, Michigan. Charles H. "Chuck", ended up in Chicago, Illinois. They all spent some time in Arkansas where they built families, but eventually they all left to seek a better life by pursuing their dreams and by climbing up that ladder of success. They were all prominent and excellent in their own right.

The 3 girls, Elgirta, Penola, and Alice lived less years than their parents and their brothers. The boys; Edward, James (my grandfather), Charles, and Samuel (Uncle Sam) lived to be 80+ years.

Millie, their mother, was a strong woman, giving birth to nine children during a very difficult time for black families.

My Great - Grand Parents -:

The Descendants of: James Allen Jones & Millie Elizabeth Butler Jones

1. Emma Elgertha Jones Mitchell
2. Penola Jones Thompson
3. Edward Taylor "Chuck Jones
4. James Knox Polk Jones (my grandfather)
5. Floyd Kenneth Jones
6. Charlie Hayes Jones
7. Alice Sephronia Jones
8. Samuel Otis Jones
9. Walter Huey Jones

(1) Their descendants: Emma Elgertha Jones Mitchell and James "Foot" Mitchell (Papa's sister)

1. Emerson Mitchell
2. James Mitchell - Spouse: Arnell Mitchell
3. Millie Mitchell West, Son - Robert West
4. Beatrice Mitchell Moore

   Spouse: Edgar Moore, Sr.

Sons: Edgar Moore, Jr.

James Herman Moore

Donald Moore

5. Odell Mitchell Swanson
Spouse - Corby Swanson
Son - William "Billy" Swanson
Grandson - William Harold Swanson
                Eric Swanson

(2) Penola Jones Thompson and Edward Thompson (Papa's Sister)
Their Descendants

1. Daisy Thompson Gillespie
Spouse: Virval Gillespie
2. Walter Henry Thompson
Spouse: Mable Murray Thompson
3. Edward Taylor "T-Boy" Thompson
Spouse: Alma Thompson

(3) James Knox Polk Jones and Dessie "Bunch" Jones
    (Papa)   (1st Wife)

Their Descendants

1. Alma Jacqueline Jones
Spouse: Sent Clair Stevenson
2. Thelma Jones
Spouse: Herbert Boykin, Sr.
3. James Thurlo Jones
Spouse: Cora Virginia Jones
4. Willie Louise Jones
Spouse James "J.M." Moore
5. Rutha Mae Jones
Spouse: Willie Jenkins
6. Elgirta Eugenia Jones
Spouse: Chester Lee "CL" West
7. Nesha Jones
First Husband: Ernest White
2nd Husband: Durie Bailey

8. Wiley Jones
   Spouse: Argel Jones
9. Deborah Ernestine Jones
   First Husband: Vincent Atteberry
   Second Husband: Willie Lyons
10. Theodore Roosevelt "Sonny" Jones
    Spouse: Shirley Jones
11. Earselean Estella Jones
    Spouse: Alvin West

On the Thompson side of the family – I remember seeing Aunt Nesha, Aunt Pearl, Uncle Buddy, and Uncle Ebbie – These are my dad's aunts and uncles. Uncle Buddy was daddy's "jug buddy" – pun intended – Daddy was "Buddy", too, so they – made a great team! I used to go to Fitzhugh, Arkansas with Daddy and Uncle Buddy. They laughed all the way there, while they were there, and on the way back home. Uncle Buddy's son was Rufus, one of the 4 Step Brothers (see info on another sheet).

Uncle Buddy had another son, Donald Thompson who lives in Chicago, Illinois and is married to the very beautiful Rosa Thompson.

Aunt Alma Jones Stevenson

Aunt Alma, my dad's oldest sister, was born on February 5, 1915 in Fitzhugh, Arkansas. She was the first child born to my grandparents, James Knox Polk Jones and Dessie Anna Thompson Jones. Aunt Alma was always considered kind of special because she was the only one that got a chance to spend time with her grandparents Jim Jones and Millie Thompson Jones. She went to stay with them because the next year, 1916, the twins were born (James & Thelma), making it very difficult to care for 3 "babies" in such a short period of time. We were told that her grandparents doted on her and spoiled her, giving her pretty little dresses, and showering attention on her. I can believe it because Aunt Alma did the same, and showed the same love and attention to her own children.

Aunt Alma went to school in Weldon, Arkansas for a while. She met and married Sentclair Stevenson in 1935 and had six children – Dorothy, Gwen, Deborah, Tommy, Richard, and Stanley. The family moved to St. Louis where they stayed for several years. I remember visiting Aunt Alma and my cousins Dorothy and Gwen on "Finney". We played and played in the neighborhood and at a park where there was a pool. I enjoyed visiting my cousins and Aunt Alma never minded having her brother's child join her own children and others.

Aunt Alma's home was always full of children and people. Everyone loved being at her house where there was always plenty of delicious food. Aunt Alma was the ultimate, gourmet cook. She always cooked big meals, and everyone was welcome to eat. I think Aunt Alma holds the honor of being the best cook of her sisters. I heard, several times, "Alma can cook!"

Aunt Alma and Uncle Sentclair moved their family to Chicago in 1961. Some of her adult children came to Chicago later. Aunt Alma worked for the Rudin Grai's Company for many years, and was known for her dedication to her job and for her love for her many friends.

Aunt Alma and Uncle Sentclair celebrated their 50th Wedding Anniversary in 1985. It was a beautiful affair, with her sisters and her brothers there en masse.

Aunt Alma was God-fearing, having accepted the Lord as her Savior while in Weldon, Arkansas. She joined the Mary Magdalene Church and remained there until her death. She was the sweetest aunt and the sweetest person on earth, helping everyone who crossed her path. She loved her six kids and their spouses and absolutely loved and enjoyed her grandchildren. Her nieces and nephews simply loved her for her sweetness and love.

Aunt Alma died on May 11, 1996 surrounded by her doting sisters, by her beloved children, and other family members, me included. Uncle Sentclair had passed away six years earlier on July 1, 1990 after a long illness. Their legacy lives on in their six children.

Dorothy – is Aunt Alma's first born. She was born in 1937, two years after me, the second grand child to James Polk and Dessie Anna. She is energetic with a special passion for life. Dorothy loves discovering new things and is not afraid of challenges. She loves traveling and seeing new places. I took my grandkids to Disney World/Florida in 1988. Dorothy arranged the trip, made the reservations, and acquired all tickets through her travel agency. Needless to say, we had a great trip.

Dorothy's husband passed away some years ago. She has three children Patti, Derek, and Toni, three grandchildren, Teneka, Shanima, and Kesha, and one great-grandchild, Darion.

Dorothy lives in St. Louis where she enjoys her big beautiful sprawling house and going to church and visiting our Aunt Dee in the nursing facility.

Gwen: is Aunt Alma's second child and second daughter. Gwen, Dorothy, and I played together as kids and have been close as adults, as well. Gwen seeks excellence in everything she does. She was a sharp dresser in her teen years and early adult years, wearing her hair very short with perfectly coiffed bangs in front. She started a "trend" in short hairdos, but no one was able to get that special look like Gwen. When she moved to Chicago, her career was Executive Secretary to a group of doctors at the University of Chicago. She took much pride in that position, and while there, she received many honors for her work.

Gwen married Lawrence Thomas after moving to Chicago and they have remained married for decades.

Gwen and Dorothy were part of the Chi-Town family reunion committee, along with our cousins on the Thompson side. We carried out successful reunions over the years.

Gwen & Lawrence moved to Arizona several years ago for the warm climate. After moving there, Gwen demonstrated her love and her big heart to some of her cousins, by sending a box of big, yellow juicy lemons. She had picked them from a tree in her own backyard. Gwen and Lawrence packed them up nicely and shipped them to us. The lemons were fresh and large and they made delicious lemonade. I appreciate that Gwen was very thoughtful and caring to do such a beautiful thing.

Deborah – Deborah Stevenson Dawson, was the youngest daughter of Aunt Alma. She was born on November 2, 1948. Deborah loved going to her church, Mary Magdalene Baptist Church, after accepting the Lord early on, when she was very young. Deborah contracted polio when she was only one year old. She was a treasured and well-loved baby. Her siblings doted on her, and "spoiled her rotten." Throughout her life, Deborah was strong in her belief and love of God, and strong in her relationships with people. She and my daughter, Linda, were close buddies before her death. Deborah "took no prisoners," for she told it like she saw it, and "pulled no punches" with people. She loved writing and was in the process of writing her story when she passed away. She loved to read, also, and was excellent at solving crossword puzzles. She loved and adored her two kids, Karmen and Diondre. Deborah died on August 14, 2014.

"TeeDee" – Richard Stevenson – we all affectionately called him "TeeDee" – was Aunt Alma's second son, and was born on April 6, 1943 in St. Louis Missouri. He was married twice; his first wife was Paulette Stevenson and they had a daughter, Michelle. He married his second wife, Elfreda Nelson Stevenson on June 5, 1981. They remained together until his death. Tee Dee accepted the Lord as his Savior in 1982. He was a welder by trade, receiving his training in St. Louis. He had a great sense of humor, always looking on the bright side of life. He loved making people laugh and he loved to laugh. Teedee usually had a bubbly spirit, and he absolutely loved to dance. He was a pretty "cool cat" on the dance floor. Teedee was known for his impeccable attire and he was admired for his intellect and knowledge. Sadly, he died in January, 2004. Lenard, my beloved son, would be dead a month later.

"Bubby" – Tommy Stevenson, was Aunt Alma's oldest son. He was born in St. Louis, Missouri in 1941. Bubby is a genuinely nice guy who is a great family man. He married Annie several decades ago, and they have remained a loving couple ever since. They cherish their three kids, Tommy, Jr., Bridgett and Randall. They lost Randall a few years ago and they have never gotten over the pain of losing him. They have five grandchildren and three great-grand children. Bubby and Annie lived in Chicago for several years and then they relocated to Blytheville, Arkansas. Bubby and Annie enjoy living a quiet, peaceful life surrounded by their children and grandchildren and other family members.

Stanley – Stanley Stevenson, was Aunt Alma's youngest son, and her youngest child. He was born in St. Louis, Missouri in 1951. Stanley, "Stan the man", was/is a guy that marches to a different drummer. He's a very intelligent guy, and he has a stellar work record at the Chicago Transit Authority for a number of years until his retirement. He has a strong sense of how he wants his life to evolve, and he is about the business of making that happen.

Stanley moved to Chicago with the family and happily started building his own family. He met and married Rollinda and they had a beautiful daughter, Autumn. Stanley has another beautiful daughter, La Tonya, from another relationship.

Stanley is very committed to his siblings and his nieces and nephews. He, like his other siblings, was hit hard by the recent death of Deborah, his youngest sister.

Stanley is dedicated to continuing the legacy that Deborah left, the legacy of writing her story. He has promised to take on the task of writing a family history.

Stanley currently lives on the north side of Chicago in a gorgeous home with his wife, Rollinda, enjoying the fruits of his labor; traveling; and spending time with his sisters and brother.

To God be the glory for Aunt Alma's family.

Aunt Thelma

Aunt Thelma, my dad's twin sister, was born on March 16, 1916, in Fitzhugh, Arkansas to the union of my grandparents,-James Knox Polk Jones and Dessie Anna Thompson Jones. She was the second daughter born to them and she was the first to be born of the twins, ahead of James, my father. It was only fitting because she was the leader of the two. She always said she was his "better half". He adored her and "looked up to her" until he passed away.

Aunt Thelma was special to me, and all my cousins will say the same thing, as well, but she was special to me because of her relationship to Daddy. She was like a second mom to me. I literally "sat at her feet" as she taught me many things. She shared her wisdom with me, as a child and adult, to make my life better.

She taught her children the value of hard work; the value of honesty and integrity; the value of strong discipline and high expectations. My aunt was tough. She expected great things from her children and she got it. Aunt Thelma was a nurse and she, for years, worked the night shift. She expected her children to act responsibly to keep them safe and secure. As a nurse, Aunt Thelma wore those crisp, white uniforms; a pert little nurse's white cap; and white shoes polished to perfection with white polish. She took special care to go to her hospital looking very professional. She took pride in helping people who were ill; people who were depressed and seeking medical treatment. Her daughter, my cousin, Delores, followed in her footsteps and became a nurse, as well. However, Delores was at the supervisory position when she retired.

Aunt Thelma married Uncle Herbert Boykin in the late 1930's. They remained happily married until his death in January of 1992. They raised their children together, having the same high expectations, and the same goals for building their family. Uncle Herbert was affectionate and loving to us, his nieces and nephews. He gave us "bear hugs" and spoke to us gently with his "booming" voice. I enjoyed pleasant conversations with Uncle Herbert, listening to him and appreciating every word. He projected a strong wisdom, and his strong, black man image that he had was projected into his 5 sons. Uncle Herbert loved to cook, and as a matter of fact, he did most of the cooking for his family. The thing that I remember most about him was his love for and his pride in his beautiful family.

Aunt Thelma lived a long, productive, and beautiful life. As her health started to fail, her daughter, Delores took special care of her (along with her brothers). She made outfits for the two of them, so that everywhere they went, they looked like "twins". Delores took her to church, every Sunday, which pleased Aunt Thelma, for she took pride in attending her church. She met all of Aunt Thelma's needs, small or big, physical or emotional; never complaining about it, but savoring every moment with her precious mother. My six cousins are known and revered in our family for the outstanding love and care shown to their parents.

Aunt Thelma died in September, 2010 at the age of 94, leaving a legacy of strength, tenacity, dignity, and grace. She loved her children, her church, and all of us with a passion.

Herbert Boykin, Jr.

"Junior", is about the best you will ever find. He learned those lessons well that were taught him by his parents. He was the oldest and the responsibility of that position in his family, with his siblings, rested heavily on his shoulders as a kid. We played together as kids (he was 3 years younger) and we might have gotten into trouble once or twice, but we played well together. He was a nice guy – he didn't get into fights, and he didn't look for mischief to get in to. (His siblings might differ)

When Junior grew up, after his schooling, he joined the U.S. Navy and he was stationed at Great Lakes, Illinois Naval Base. I was married at that time, and Junior would come and visit Lenzo and I at our home. I remember trying to get a nice meal together when he came, and he always waited patiently for me to cook dinner. It seems, I was just so slow with everything, being a young wife and a young mother. Junior didn't mind the wait. He and Lenzo enjoyed talking and we enjoyed seeing him in his impeccable, white uniform. He was pleasant and friendly, like Uncle Herbert.

Junior married his beautiful wife, Helen, and they began to build a family and to build a life together. They had two children, Wanda and Christopher, and now have two grandchildren, Michael and Christopher, Jr. They have remained together through "thick & thin", through losses and through many wonderful, delightful experiences.

Junior teaches an adult bible class at his church. He was entrusted with this responsibility because of his love of God, his knowledge of the Bible, and his impeccable character. (He's just simply the "best" in my opinion:) One of our family reunions was held in St. Louis in August, 2012. On Sunday, the Sermon and Candlelight Service was held. Kenneth, Junior's brother, did the Candlelight Service where a candle was lit to remember those who had passed away since the last reunion. The family heads were honored as well. Herbert Boykin, Jr., "Junior", brought the message from Matthew 5:1-12, the "Beatitudes" or as he said the attitudes of Christians; to be blessed (happy); Junior said Matthew 5 spoke to the poor in spirit; those that mourn; the meek; they that hunger and thirst; the pure in heart; merciful; the peace makers; shaft and wheat together – don't judge; don't gossip; for those who are persecuted. Jesus went into the mountains to be alone, some followed Him, but there were those who left Him; He was not on the road alone; they followed Him for different reasons. Jesus wants us to rejoice and be glad. Junior gave a wonderful, inspiring, and encouraging lesson.

Junior has been retired for several years. He and Helen are living beautifully and comfortably in an elegant home, in a St. Louis suburb, that they had built "from the ground up".

<u>Kenneth Boykin</u> –Kenneth, was Aunt Thelma's second son, and her second child. Like the rest of Aunt Thelma's children, Kenneth and I had a special bond because of his mom and my dad. Kenneth was born on October 23, 1939 in St. Louis, Missouri. He attended the St. Louis Public School System for his education, going to Simmons Grade School and the Summer High School. Kenneth was highly motivated to go to the highest levels in education, earning a Bachelor's Degree in Industrial Electronics and a Master's Degree in Business Administration. He proudly worked at the Chrysler Motor Company, in management, for 32 years. After those many years of service, he retired and enjoyed many good years before his recent death.

I remember Kenneth as a kid, and as a young man, he was a pretty "cool" guy. He loved dressing to the "10's" and he definitely loved "putting his best foot forward!"

Aunt Thelma and Uncle Herbert made sure that Kenneth (and the rest of the kids) was always in church. He was baptized at the Newstead Baptist Church as a child. Later, after he got married, he joined the Central Baptist Church. He was a deacon there for over ten years. He loved working with the "Feed the Hungry Program" which was held on every Tuesday morning at the church. Kenneth absolutely loved his church. The last service that he attended was on New Year's Eve to bring in the year of 2015. He passed away on January 22, 2015.

Kenneth's service to his country was in the United States Army.

Kenneth met his wife, Shirlene, and God blessed them to be married for 51 years. They had a son, Earl, who preceded him in death, and a daughter, Angela, who has always been a "Daddy's girl". I remember Kenneth's great love for his wife. They had a love and chemistry that was a joy to watch. They were in sinct with whatever they were involved in, whether it was her antiques or his lodge and his service to others. And of course, they cooked and cooked and cooked together. They made us all happy with their delicious meals and the service that accompanied that.

He was an active Prince Hall Mason and Shriner. He received his 33rd Degree under the Eureka Consistory. He served for over 39 years and was very devoted to his Lodge. Kenneth served as a Motor Patrol Marshall for the Gateway Classics and the Annie Malone Parade. He was a proud member of the Omega Psi Phi Fraternity, and a loyal member of his fraternity. He enjoyed working with the youth Mentoring Program with his frat brothers.

Kenneth had a concern and compassion for others. He took John 13:34 to heart for God said, "A new commandment I give unto you, that ye love one another; as I have loved you, that ye also love one another." Kenneth tried to make the world a better place. He heard the voice of the writer who said, "Go within every day and find the inner strength so that the world will not blow your candle out."

Kenneth left a great legacy for his family and now he is with Aunt Thelma & Uncle Herbert in heaven. We thank God for his life.

Floyd Boykin, Sr. is a multitalented guy with great social skills. He is a "jack of all trades", and master of each one he pursues. He is Aunt Thelma's third child and third son. Floyd, extremely handsome, is a smart guy but down to earth and pleasant to be around. He loves to laugh and he wears a smile everywhere he goes.

Floyd was born on March 1, 1942 in St. Louis, Missouri. Like his siblings, he was taught valuable lessons by his parents. He learned to tirelessly seek higher education and training to have a successful and fulfilling life. He pursued several dreams and goals for himself, taking pride in accomplishing them. He owned and operated a karate school for several years. Floyd didn't smile much there . . . he was as serious as a heart attack when it came to his business.

Floyd, in his early years, was a "ladies man". Unlike his siblings, he married several times. His wives were beautiful and they all simply adored him. He had wonderful, precious children from these unions: Kimberly, Wyuon, Floyd, Jr., Keisha, Camron, and Bayron.

Floyd worked in the U.S. Postal Service for 42 years. Currently, Floyd is enjoying the fruits of his labor. He and his children are into music, having a band, writing and recording music. They are writers – Floyd recently finished his book entitled, "The Family Tree of Thelma Jones Boykin".

Robert Boykin, Robert, is "mysterious". He's mysterious because I know very little about him. He lives in Columbia, South Carolina and is happy and content. He has lived there for years, working and "marching to a different drummer." He is strong and independent, answering to no one, and never, ever seeking advice from anyone (but our God!). And yet, he is kind and considerate and loved Aunt Thelma, his mom, with a passion. He used to come home to St. Louis every two or three weeks to visit her and shower her with gifts. He helped to meet her needs, taking special care during her later years as her health started to fail. He absolutely loved his brothers and sister.

When his brother, Kenneth, passed away, everyone was concerned about Robert and how he would deal with his death. They were all so close-knit as a family unit. Robert arrived for the services and his siblings surrounded him with their arms of comfort, as they also sought to deal with the devastating loss of Kenneth.

I admired Robert, as a young man, for his kindness and generosity. When he came to the family reunions, he seemed bigger than life. He loved joking and kidding around with his brothers and cousins. He lived (and still does) a life of wealth and privilege; wearing the most expensive clothes and traveling extensively to other countries and all over our country, as well. And yet, he was kind and decent and caring.

Robert, called "Spike", is the owner of Spike Boykin Productions, in Columbia, South Carolina. He is the Promoter, Producer, Booking Agent, Artist Management, head of Recording Studio, Photo Studio, and Sound Equipment Rental.

I remember, years ago, at our family reunion in Los Angeles, Robert and my cousin, Venita and her husband, Al, and I went shopping. We had a great time. I saw this beautiful black & white chiffon dress, and thought "I would love to have this dress!", but I couldn't afford it. Robert saw that

I liked the dress, so he bought it for me. I kept that dress for over 30 years and whenever I wore it, I thought fondly of my cousin, Robert.

<u>Delores</u> "<u>Dee Dee</u>" <u>Boykin</u> <u>Ware</u>, is the only girl, and the fifth child of Aunt Thelma. She is the undisputed, de facto leader of her brothers. The rest of the cousins in our family admire Delores and her brothers because of the great care they have given Aunt Thelma during her aging process and ensuing decline in her health. Delores set up a "schedule of care" and served as the "watchman" in making it happen; as if she had to. They all adored Aunt Thelma and readily and enthusiastically took turns in meeting Aunt Thelma's needs. When Aunt Thelma died, Delores served as executor of her estate, handling everything, down to the minutest detail with compassion, fairness, and extreme care. Her brothers look up to her for her wisdom, her integrity, and her honesty.

Delores is tall and stately, with the manner of the ultimate professional. Her husband, Lee Ware is even taller, and has an air of leadership, confidence, and control. He worked for Union Electric in St. Louis, for decades before he retired. He served as a business administrator for that company. Delores followed Aunt Thelma in the nursing profession. After her retirement, she supervised nurses in hospitals in St. Louis and went all over the states training nurses in the field of nursing. Her official title was F.N.P. for B.J.C. Hospitals and Walgreen's Stores. She worked for the Missouri Bd. of Nursing – LPN, ADN, BSN, & MSN. Delores and Lee both serve in the Masonic Order; Delores as I.D., and Lee as a P.M., 32* degree Mason. Lee served in the military, and Delores is a member of the Sigma Theta Tau Sorority.

They have two adult children, Darryl Ware and Patricia Ware Wilson; a daughter-in-law, Lerietha; and a son-in-law, Cleveland Wilson. They have four grand children: Darius Ware and Tyra Ware, Jasmine Christine Perkins, and a brand new little girl. Patricia is an elementary school principal. Darryl is prominent and takes pride in caring for his family.

Delores, like her siblings, is hard working, never stopping to "come up for air". She is always in the pursuit of another project to help someone. Although she is retired, Delores continues to travel to other states training hospital workers (mostly nurses) to help those who are sick and hurting.

Delores and Lee have been married for more than 50 years. They are enjoying their kids and grandkids in St. Louis, Missouri; as well as, serving faithfully in their church and participating in several outreach programs.

Gregory Boykin, is Aunt Thelma's fifth son and sixth child. Greg is the baby of the family, and I was told years ago that everyone spoiled him because he was simply adorable, as well as, being the baby. He is extremely handsome with a beautiful, elegant wife, Barbara. Gregory, like his siblings, was born and raised in St. Louis, Missouri. He attended elementary and high school there and went on to pursue his college degree. In high school, Greg was a member of the Memorial Lancers marching band. He was smart and aggressive as he tried out for these athletic programs and competition. Greg loved baseball as a kid. He was the star catcher for the O'Fallon Tech. baseball team.

He served his country in the U.S. Army proudly and notably. Both Greg and his wife, Barbara belong to the Masonic Order; he as a degree mason, and she as an O.E.S. They serve beautifully together in their organizations, as they do in their marriage.

Greg's career choice was to be a security officer. His education was in that area. It was only fitting, for he is the strong, silent type with excellent discipline and organization skills. Hard working and conscientious, Greg stayed true to his upbringing. He was serious as a heart attack about his job, and he "took no prisoners" - so to speak - pun intended. Greg was the Head of Security for B.J.C. Hospitals for 21 years. He is now retired and enjoying his life with Barbara and their three kids – Gregory Lamont, Matthew, and Tamara. – and their grand kids – Justin, Justine, Tamia, and Jordan.

To God be the glory for His mercy and His grace to Aunt Thelma's family.

My dad, James Thurlo Jones, was next in line of his siblings, right after Aunt Thelma, his twin. She was born first.

Daddy's story is at the beginning of this chapter.

Willie Jones Moore

Aunt Willie

Aunt Willie married James "J.M." Moore in 1939, and they moved to St. Louis, Missouri to raise their family and to seek a better life. They both were prominent in their respective careers and pursuits. They both belonged to the Masonic Order, he was a 32° mason and she was in the Medival Court #15, Illustrious Commandress. Uncle J.M., as we called him, and Aunt Willie were married more than 50 years, and they raised their children with a strong, tough love discipline.

Uncle J.M. developed cancer and was sick for a long time, but Aunt Willie, being an (L.P.N.) nurse, took wonderful care of him. She kept him so clean and neat and met his every need. She gave him tender loving care until he passed away in May, 1987. Aunt Willie's health started to fail soon after his death.

Aunt Willie loved to travel, sometimes with her organizations and sometimes with just Uncle J.M. and sometimes with the family. She loved fashions and was always beautifully dressed and hair beautifully done and in place. I remember her showing me pictures and gifts and souvenirs from some of her travels. She told me to go places and always take your children with you. Give them the same pleasure of travel that we get.

Aunt Willie loved taking care of her grand daughter, Shannon, who was her son, Thurman's daughter. She loved her sisters and enjoyed spending time with them; sometimes she visited them and at other times, they came to see her. They would talk and laugh out loud, for hours, talking about their family and friends. Those "Jones girls" just loved being together.

Aunt Willie's influence, her ideas, her vision, and her opinions have left an indelible imprint on my own life. I will remember her always for her feistiness and her strength. She was bold and strong in her experiences with us, her nieces and nephews. Aunt Willie taught us to appreciate culture and language and the Arts and literature. She encouraged us to do things and go places and enjoy life to the fullest.

Aunt Willie was Daddy's third sister, and fourth child of James Knox Polk Jones and Dessie Thompson Jones, and she was one strong, black woman.

Aunt Willie had a strong, commanding voice; when she spoke you listened; when she told you to do something, you did it – like right away. She had a big laugh, one of those "laugh out loud", "real" laughs. Her hands were strong and sure (we all have unique looking hands and unattractive feet). When she use to whip her sons – Thurman, Alfred, and Jerome – I felt for them, and tried to stay out of trouble myself. I don't remember getting a whipping from Aunt Willie, and I don't think she whipped Juanita, her only daughter, either. Maybe she had a soft spot for us girls.

I remember Aunt Willie putting Juanita on her kitchen table to wash her up. She kept "Nita" squeaky clean, hair beautifully braided every day, and with the prettiest little dresses one could only dream of. Aunt Willie loved her sons, but was especially fond of her only daughter, "Nita".

Juanita Moore Brown, is Aunt Willie's first born child, and only daughter. She was born on November 23, 1939 in St. Louis, Missouri. Juanita, or "Nita" as her cousins called her, went to elementary school in the St. Louis Public School System, graduating from the Soldan high school in 1958. Right after high school, Nita began working at Southwestern Bell Telephone Company, and was there for ten years. In 1969, after leaving Southwestern Bell, Nita was employed at TWA - Trans World Airlines. I remember when she worked for the TWA. She was tall and very poised and was the ultimate professional young woman. I admired her demeanor and the manner in which she carried herself at work. She looked absolutely beautiful in her uniform.

While she was employed at TWA, she went to Poro Beauty School and graduated in 1970 as a licensed cosmetologist. At TWA, Nita started in reservations working her way up to The Ambassadors' Club as a manager until she retired July 30, 1999.

Juanita married Walter Brown, the love of her life, in 1961. They were married 52 years before her untimely death. They had one son, Walter Anthony "Bobby" Brown, who died accidently while serving in the military. She and Walter were devastated. Nita never really recovered from the loss of Bobby.

Nita and our cousin, Gwen, were very close as teenagers and young women. They were inseparable and were as close as sisters. They remained close until Gwen and Aunt Alma's family moved to Chicago. Even afterwards, they remained close with a special bond.

Juanita was a fun loving person who loved to laugh; she loved to dance; and she loved to travel. She loved being around people, very social. She was a member of the Sippers Social Club for several years. She entertained at her beautiful home and traveled extensively with them. I went on 2 cruises to the Caribbean with Nita and my Aunt Erse with their Sippers' Club. Nita also loved to bowl.

Juanita died on July 15, 2013 leaving a void in the heart of her husband and leaving her family and loved ones to cherish her memories.

And yet, her life was rich and full. Her husband, Walter, honored her memory with a profound saying, entitled "Life With You". It spoke of his love for her, and served as a fitting tribute to their loving life together.

Thurman Moore, is Aunt Willie's oldest son, and second child. Thurman, a great guy, was born in St. Louis in 1944. He attended school there, completing grammar school and high school with excellent grades. He was a typical boy at that time, playing outside for hours with his brother, Alfred, and his friends. I don't know for sure, but he probably played a lot of sports. When he got into fights, he fought with his fists and his wit, growing up to be tough and fearless. I don't remember Thurman ever running away from confrontation, physical or verbal. Like his parents, he met life, "head on" and "in your face".

Thurman is the historian of our family. He relentlessly searches for people who might be a "Jones" or "Thompson". He spends hours looking through records and uses his imagination to recreate our history and distant past. He's responsible for locating our cousin, Arthur Sanders, III, whose mother was Rosa Mae Jones Hamilton. He was also instrumental in locating our cousins in Atlanta, Georgia, the Collins' Family, whose ancestors were Robert and Katie Belle Jones.

Thurman served in the Marines from 1965 - 1969. His time spent as a marine was exemplary, as well as, a learning experience. It caused him to view life through a different lense. It was a reality check for him. He came to Chicago several times, after leaving the service, and usually stayed at my daughter Sharon's home. He was great friends with Sharon and her husband, Alex.

Thurman would sometimes stop in Chicago on his way to Detroit to visit Aunt Dee. She had a computer at the time, and Thurman was always at her "beck & call" when she needed help with it. Sometimes, he stayed overnight, sometimes longer. He seemed to be in the pursuit of always helping people in need, starting with our family members.

Thurman met and married the lovely Beverly after his military service. I'm sure he was "smitten" because she was "drop dead" gorgeous. Beverly is beautiful "inside" as well. She and Thurman have been married now for some 40+ years. Beverly is such a help and support system for my aunt, Ersé. Erse has health issues, so Beverly is there to take her shopping; to take her to events; and to be "company" when Erse needs it.

Thurman considers himself a connoisseur at cooking. He has a summer home in a rural area in Illinois, about an hour's drive from St. Louis. He would invite his cousins up there every year for a big "fish fry". The food was delicious; so, I have to admit that Thurman really is an excellent cook.

Thurman had a lucrative career that provided an excellent life for his family. He retired after several decades and they gave him a big retirement party. I did not attend, but I remember writing a nice tribute to him, sending it by my daughter, Sharon. It was a fitting end to one phase of his life, and the beginning of another phase.

He lives quietly with his wife, Beverly, never ceasing to research and study the Jones/Thompson family. He and Beverly have two adult children, Shannon who is married to Donny and Bryan who is married to Kyeshia. They have three grand children – Nyla, Jayla, and Bryan, Jr.

<u>Alfred</u> <u>Moore</u>, is Aunt Willie's second son, and third child. Alfred is a very handsome guy, resembling the rest of the Jones' cousins. He has an olive complexion, nice hair, and is of medium height. Alfred has always "marched to a different drummer"; definitely living life on his own terms. He's a "cultural" guy, loving, with a passion for music. He's from the old school of music lovers e.g. blues, and pop, and rock & roll. Alfred collected the old records - "33" and the "45" - over many years, so he has quite an impressive collection.

Alfred contacted me recently to remind me that Daddy loved to listen to the blues. He had the records and he wanted to share them with me. He absolutely loves sharing his knowledge, his music, and his pictures. Alfred, like my other cousins, spent time with my dad. He admired Daddy for his humor and his playfulness with his nephews. His nephews were the "sons" he always wanted.

Alfred is also an accomplished photographer, taking hundreds of, not only, family pictures, but "life" photos as well. He captured people, places, and things naturally and beautifully, and sometimes humorously. He absolutely loves taking pictures and collecting pictures, as well. He has sent me several pictures of Daddy, over the years; Daddy with his siblings and with his many lady friends.

Alfred served in the military, mostly overseas, for four years, and then he returned home to St. Louis. Several years later, he met his lovely wife, Barbara. Barbara is classy and elegant as she interacts with others. She is thoughtful and conscientious. In 2012, Barbara sent a beautiful card congratulating Lenzo and I on 60 years of marriage. She sent it on behalf of Alfred, as well. Barbara & Alfred have been married for decades and recently bought another fabulous home.

Alfred has one child, a daughter, Keisha Lynn Moore, who lives in Florissant, Missouri and owns and runs her own business.

Jerome Moore, is Aunt Willie's third son, and youngest child. He was born in 1952, in St. Louis, Missouri. Jerome was a tough kid, having grown up with two older brothers and an older sister. During his childhood and teen years, he lived on the edge of life, trying to fit in and find his ladder of success.

As an adult, Jerome did fairly well, trying to find work that would pay a decent salary so that he could be independent and prosperous. He married a very nice girl who loved him and cared for him. They remained together for years, but eventually separated.

I've lost touch with Jerome over the years, but like his siblings, he has been blessed beyond measure. His parents, Willie & J.M. Moore left him a legacy of strength, love of family, and a commitment to seek a better life through service and dedication to others.

To God be the glory for the family of my Aunt Willie.

Aunt Ruthie

Rutha Mae "Dumpy" Jones Jenkins, was the fourth daughter, and fifth child of James Knox Polk Jones and Dessie Thompson Jones. Aunt Ruthie is my namesake and we share the same birth date – February 6th. She was one of the prettiest of the "Jones" girls. She had a light, olive complexion with a beautiful crop of black hair. A picture of her in her early 20's, holding her daughter, "Brenda Joyce" is a family treasure because that picture was taken in St. Louis by a photographer and remained in his shop window for years. It caught everyone's eye as they passed the shop. – Aunt Ruthie had on a black dress with a bold white strip over her shoulder, pearls around her neck, and her hair done in an upsweep, called a "pompador" at the time. Brenda had on a tiny white, silk dress with the cutest little white bow in her hair.

Aunt Ruthie was born on February 6, 1919 in Fitzhugh, Arkansas. She went to school in the Fitzhugh Public School and continued to learn to do numerous things, excelling in everything she attempted to do. In her adult life, she was involved in service oriented professions and many business endeavors as well. Aunt Ruthie later became a licensed nurse (LVN), a phlebotomist for Cutter Lab, a seamstress and a cosmetologist, receiving her license at age 50. She was also an entrepreneur who had the vision to obtain property in order to have the Bronze Beauty Salon built from the ground up in 1967 for her daughter, Brenda.

Aunt Ruthie married Willie Lawrence Jenkins in November, 1942. They had a beautiful, made-in heaven marriage and remained together until her death in 2006. In August, 1991, they renewed their vows to celebrate their 50th wedding anniversary. They said their vows on a Carnival Cruise to the Caribbean, and were celebrated by the Captain, family and friends. They were totally devoted to each other. He called her "Dumpy", and she called him "Daddy". We, my cousins and I, called him Uncle Jenkins. He was a Naval Officer, making the navy military service his career. He enlisted in 1934 and served continuous active duty until he was honorably discharged in 1964. Uncle Jenkins received numerous medals and awards: National Defense Service Medal; Korean Service Medal; and a United Nations Service Medal. He had the privilege to prepare a meal for First Lady Eleanor Roosevelt for which she was highly complementary. He also served as Second Chef Cook for the Senior Citizens Federal Food Program in 1976. Uncle Jenkins, like Uncle Herbert, was a great cook.

Aunt Ruthie and Uncle Jenkins had two beautiful daughters, Venita and Brenda. The family lived in Charleston, SC for a while and then San Francisco, California. They relocated to San Diego, California in 1948.

Aunt Ruthie and Uncle Jenkins made a great couple. She enjoyed working in her church, Bethel Baptist Church in San Diego, where she was a member of the Bethel Baptist Missionary Society, the Altar Guild and the Nurses' Ministry. Aunt Ruthie was very social and had many friends. She was a member of the Agnes Knight Social Club, Les Grandmeres Moderne of Los Angeles, California and the Ladies Auxiliary of the Fleet Reserve Branch 62 of San Diego. Uncle Jenkins, on the other hand, was just as impressive. We all loved him and use to admire him in his sharp white uniform, white shoes, and white navy cap. He was one handsome man, but he was nice, personable, and loving, and generous. Whatever task he had to do, no matter how "bad the pain, or hard the strain," he completed it with a cheerful and giving heart. He was a happy man and managed to make everyone around him laugh and smile by finding something good in everything. Uncle Jenkins loved to dance, and I found out later that he had a beautiful tenor voice.

We, cousins, always felt beautiful and special around Uncle Jenkins because he always made you feel like the "Belle of the Ball."

Aunt Ruthie loved her "sisters" and her brothers, and they loved her. She and Uncle Jenkins took such good care of Daddy after he moved to San Diego and began having health issues. They checked on him on a daily basis. And when I visited my dad which was fairly often, Aunt Ruthie took great care of me. She prepared my own special room in her beautiful home; prepared wonderful meals for me; and took me on stimulating walks in the mountains, then she & Uncle Jenkins took me on the military base in San Diego and treated me to breakfast. It was absolutely wonderful experiences for me with her and I will never, ever forget those times. She and Uncle Jenkins were solid gold, and I honor both of them with accolades and praise.

Robin Adams Loving and Rhonda Adams, Aunt Ruthie's two granddaughters, paid tribute to Aunt Ruthie on the occasion of her death. They absolutely adored their grandmother, and they continue to live out her legacy each day.

Venita Jenkins Strange, was Aunt Ruthie's oldest daughter, and was the pride and joy of Aunt Ruthie and Uncle Jenkins. Venita was born in 1940, a year full of happenings and profound change. The whole world was in turmoil, bracing for World War II, and here in our country, Franklin Delano Roosevelt had just been elected President for the third time; Richard Wright had just published his "Native Son", and the movies "Grapes of Wrath" and "Rebecca" were playing in theatres; that year, Duke Ellington became known as a composer and jazz pianist; popular songs were: "You are my Sunshine", "How High the Moon", "The Last Time I Saw Paris", "When you Wish Upon A Star", "It's a Big, Wide, Wonderful World", "Blueberry Hill" and the "Woodpecker Song." Black people were on the move, making history and changing the world in all kinds of ways:

- The U.S. Postal service issues the first stamp honoring a black American, Booker T. Washington
- Abram Hill, Frederick O'Neal, and others found the American Negro Theater in New York City, where the careers of Harry Belafonte, Ruby Dee, and Sidney Poitier are launched.
- The Virginia legislature chooses James Bland's "Carry Me Back to Ole Virginny" as Virginia state song; the state legislators are not aware of Bland's race.
- Hattie McDaniel becomes the first black American to win an Oscar when she receives the Academy of Motion Pictures Arts and Sciences' Award for best supporting actress for her role in "Gone With the Wind".

And while all this history was being made in the world, and in our nation, a smaller, but yet significant, history was happening in the Jones/Thompson family. Aunt Ruthie, in that year 1940, gave birth to a beautiful baby girl named "Venita". Venita was the spitting image of Aunt Ruthie: light olive complexion, bright eyes, and an infectious smile. Venita, as far back as I can remember, is very independent. She has always strived for total control of her own life. She has a strong will, a strong commitment, and a strong determination to get the job done, whatever it is. When I think of Venita, I think of the word "ultimate", and "thorough". My memories of Venita are always prefaced with admiration and amazement at the beautiful things she has accomplished in her lifetime.

Venita and her husband, Al, have been married for decades, and they live a life full of service and "movement". Recently, and during the "Obama" era, they have become politically active. They participated in President Obama's campaign and are proud of his success, realizing that they played a role in it.

Venita and Al live in Los Angeles, California. She lived in San Diego with her parents and her sister, Brenda for her early years. As a young adult, Venita moved to L.A., where she and Al married. They have been married for over 30 years. They live there, still today, becoming a part of that culture of the "elite", with a house in the mountains with the gorgeous view of the city below.

I love Venita for a number of reasons:

- she's my cousin
- she spent so much time, energy and love on our double-cousin, Elva. Elva was like our aunt, and we treated her as such. She and her husband, James Reynolds also lived in Los Angeles for years. When their health started to wain, Venita cared for them with tenderness and great concern. Elva loved her like a daughter. When Elva passed away here in South Holland, Illinois, Venita came to pay last respects to her beloved Elva.
- she, along with my other beautiful cousins in L.A. – Wilma, Dessola, Shelva, and Sandra – came to see me and my friend, Beverly Yates at our hotel in Los Angeles. Beverly and I had gone to see Inez Clayton who was gravely ill. Venita and my other cousins treated us to dinner and we had a great time of fellowship together. Also, Venita brought me some epsom salt, lavender scented especially for my "soaking" pleasure.
- Years ago, I spent the night with Venita and Al in that home in the mountains. I remember thinking "it's like a "maze" going to her home. They were gracious hosts.
- Venita's handwriting is beautiful, unique and unusual. She "creates" as she writes. No one in the family comes even close.
- When going to family reunions, Venita and Brenda would take the plane to the city where it's being held, rent a car, and find their way around without any help from anyone. Years ago when we stayed at each other's home instead of at a hotel, Venita and Brenda always stayed at a hotel instead of "being a bother" to the host family.
- The Summer Olympics were held in Los Angeles in August, 1971 (I think that's the year), and Venita got one of the prestigious jobs at the Olympics, uniform and all. It was an exciting time to be there and experience some of the activities that were going on.
- When my Aunt Neshie passed away in August, 2013, Venita and Al, my cousin Thea and I stayed at our cousin Jackie Boys' ranch in Celina, Texas. Jackie Boy is Aunt Neshie's third son and he invited us to stay at his beautiful ranch to attend Aunt Neshie's funeral. Jackie Boy, along with his special friend, was the perfect host. Lenzo and I used to visit him and his beautiful wife, Eileen (now deceased) when they lived in West Covina, California. Meanwhile, back at the ranch . . . Venita, Thea, and I just enjoyed being together. We went shopping and we had a really delicious

lunch together there in Celina, Texas. We tried to go to a wine-tasting orchard, but it was closed at the time. We were there to mourn the death of our aunt, and the memories we shared helped to ease the pain of her loss.

Venita and Al's two sons are Alton Christopher Strange and Brandon Collins Strange, both medical doctors, and they have two granddaughters, Sofia and Simone.

<u>Brenda</u> <u>Joyce</u> <u>Jenkins</u> <u>Adams</u>, was Aunt Ruthie's second daughter born two years after Venita in 1942. She was the "apple of the eye" of her parents. The four of them – Aunt Ruthie, Uncle Jenkins, Venita, and Brenda – made up a tight-knit family unit. They were very attractive, as well, with Uncle Jenkins in his white uniform, Aunt Ruthie dressed to the "nines" whether casual or dress-up, and the two girls, always in the prettiest dresses or "sun-suits", shiny little shoes, and white socks.

Brenda attended school in San Diego, California and as a teenager in high school, she met "Chuck" Adams. He fell "head over heels" in love with Brenda and later after she finished school, they married. They remained together, through thick and thin, through good and bad until Chuck's death. They had two daughters, Robin and Rhonda. Aunt Ruthie loved and cherished her two granddaughters. Like all grandchildren, Robin and Rhonda were the "center of the universe" to Aunt Ruthie.

Brenda and I spent a lot of time together back in the 1980's and the early 1990's. Daddy had health issues and myriad problems during those years. His life in the "fast lane" were beginning to take a toll on him. I was concerned about him, and even though he lived in San Diego and I lived in Chicago, I visited him often. It also gave me an opportunity to be with my aunt and my cousin, Brenda. Brenda would pick me up from Daddy's house, or Aunt Ruthie's, or sometimes I was spending the night at her beautiful, beautiful home. She and Chuck were prominent and successful and her home reflected that. We would go shopping and then we'd have lunch. Brenda took me to the big malls, but sometimes she took me to small boutiques and outlet stores where we bought things for a bargain. She loved designer shoes, so we shopped and shopped, till we "dropped". I still have some of those clothes in my closet. I "downsized" the shoes over the years.

Not only did Brenda take me shopping, but she cut my hair; I was wearing it short at the time. She owned a Beauty Shop, "Bronze Beauty Salon", that was built from the ground up - especially for her –, and she did my hair whenever I visited San Diego. I looked forward to that each time. Brenda's "Bronze Beauty Salon" is well known in San Diego. In November, 1999, Brenda and her shop appeared in the USA Today, on the front page, with then presidential candidate, Bill Bradley's wife, Ernestine Bradley visited her shop. Venita sent me a copy of the article.

Mrs. Bradley was campaigning for her husband and she visited Brenda's Bronze Salon while she was in San Diego. Mrs. Bradley, a cancer survivor, had come to Brenda's to hear about a breast cancer education program. At the time, Black beauty - shop operators were trained to teach breast self-examination and hand out literature. Brenda said, "Black women have lower risk of breast cancer, but their death rate is high because they don't get in early enough for screening." The article was written by Richard Benedetto, and it highlighted the plight of women and children and a lack of health care. Mrs. Bradley, a native of Germany who spoke with a slight accent, asked whether there were any breast cancer survivors in the crowd. Two women came forward. She hugged them, whispered encouragement to them and posed for pictures with them. She got so caught up in the wonderful exchange that she forgot to ask the women to vote for her husband, Bill Bradley. Al Gore was running for president, also, at the time.

In August, 1993 while visiting, I went to church with Brenda. Typically, the day was bright with sunshine and warmth. As we got out of Brenda's car, I again noticed how beautiful Brenda looked with her elegant skirt suit and sharp designer shoes.

We walked briskly to the entrance of the church, and I immediately felt the Spirit of the Lord in that place. The church was Bethel Baptist Church located at Clay and 29th Street, San Diego, (2885 Clay Avenue). We were right on time for the morning worship which started at 10:55 A.M. on that Sunday. The pastor was Dr. John W. Ringgold.

Brenda has a strong work ethic; she rises early and is in "constant motion". She has important work that has to be done on a daily basis. She is deeply committed to pursuing a goal each day. Her goal is always the pursuit of excellence. She is super organized and goes about her duties with calm, confidence, and "cool". To top it all, she is an outstanding gourmet cook. Brenda doesn't talk a lot, but we used to share with each other as we talked about our husbands, our children, and our jobs.

One night, I spent the night with Brenda. We got up early and Brenda prepared breakfast. Uncle Jenkins, in his nineties, was at a nursing facility and she took me with her to visit him. He was doing wonderfully well, still had that great smile. Going to see her dad was a daily thing with Brenda. She went each day to feed him and to monitor his care. I will never forget the experience of visiting Uncle Jenkins before his death in 2009; it was a part of history that keeps us humble and grateful.

Brenda lives prominently and peacefully surrounded by her family and friends. Her daughter, Robin, has three children: Damontey Durham, Preaujanae Loving-Washington, and D'Aire Loving; and two grand children: Symone Washington and Cameron Khyree Rogers. Brenda's daughter, Rhonda lives near by and forms a team trio of mom and two beautiful daughters. They adore each other.

Thank God, and to Him be the glory for Aunt Ruthie's family.

Aunt Sugar

Elgirta Eugena Jones West, known as Aunt "Sugar", was the sixth child born to James Knox Polk Jones and Dessie Thompson Jones. She was born on April 7, 1920 in Fitzhugh, Arkansas. She was educated in the Arkansas School System learning on a fast pace and developed a strong work ethic. Like her siblings, Aunt Sugar worked hard and managed her money well and lived a great life. Aunt Sugar was deeply spiritual and dedicated to the Word of God. She met Uncle C. L. West in Arkansas and he told her that she was the "apple of his eye." They married in 1939, and remained married for over 60 years until her death in 2005.

Aunt Sugar and Uncle C. L. raised their six children in Arkansas and migrated to Los Angeles, California in the 1960's. They had 3 girls and 3 boys – Wilma, Dessola, and Shelva, and Harold, Jamie, and Mack Ray. Wilma is the oldest child, then Dessola; Harold and Jamie came next; and then Shelva and Mack Ray. They raised their children with a strong hand of discipline, teaching their children to love God, work hard, and love the family.

Both Aunt Sugar and Uncle C. L. were hard working and involved in many causes. They loved God, they loved serving him, and they loved serving others, in their church, First Bethany Baptist Church and in other civic organizations. She was a Deaconess, a Sunday School Teacher, a choir member, and she was also President of the Missonary Society. Aunt Sugar was a life member of the Los Angeles Chapter of the Arkansas Association; a member of the Los Angeles District Association; and a member of the Western Baptist State Convention. She was committed to worthy civic causes that served mankind.

Aunt Sugar was outstanding in upholstery and decorating. She worked for the giant Woolworth Company as a Supervisor in Human Resources and retired after 17 years of enjoyable and dedicated service.

My memories of Aunt Sugar are of her being proud and feisty and humorous. She had a proud walk with her head held high, always dressed in beautiful suits and dresses, with high heels and beautiful costume jewelry. She loved red. She had a wonderful sense of humor, telling jokes (laugh out loud jokes) and laughing with you at the "punch line". At our family reunions, she was the "life of the party." We loved seeing her model in our fashion shows; and we loved seeing her and Uncle CL dance. They could really "cut a rug", bringing the house down with their dancing.

Before Lenard passed away, Aunt Sugar visited me in my home in South Holland. I was so honored to have her visit. Lenard had washed and dried a load of his clothes and Aunt Sugar taught him how to fold his clothes. We were amazed at how she folded those clothes, like a professional. Her mantra was always "whatever you do, do it in an outstanding manner." She internalized and lived the verse in the Bible that says "whatever your hands find to do, do it with thy might". (Ecclesiastes 9:10)

Aunt Sugar wrote me a letter right before she passed away. She was very ill toward the end of her life, but she kept right on fighting until she took her last breath. In the letter she greeted me with "Hi "Poochie" & Family." She was teasing me because "Poochie" was the nickname that Daddy gave me. In the letter, she talked about Dorothy moving to St. Louis and Gwen moving to Arizona. She said, "Well I guess it is time for some of us to explore," and she put "smiles" on that. She said Pamela (her granddaughter) had come over and wanted to finish a roll of film that she had, so she took pictures of Aunt Sugar with her long hair. She sent me 6 of those pictures with her long hair in her bathroom and in her living room, a picture of her blue flower/floral arrangement, and a picture of Pamela. I cherish the letter and the pictures.

Aunt Sugar was known for her culinary skills, as a gourmet cook specializing in down-home soul food and other foods, as well. She believed in eating with elegance and style.

Uncle C. L., like Aunt Sugar, was born in 1920 in Fitzhugh, Arkansas. He was an only child and was raised and educated in Fitzhugh. He was taught about the Lord Jesus Christ when he was very young by his parents, Arnella and Alex West and his grandmother, Sarah Anthony, and at an early age, he accepted Jesus Christ as his Savior. As a young man, Uncle C. L. showed great leadership as a deacon and Superintendent of Sunday School at the Mount Olive Baptist Church. After moving to Los Angeles, he became a member of Bethany Missionary Baptist Church where he continued to be a great steward and leader. He served as deacon, Member of the Board of Trustees, President of Lamen Ministries and a member of the Bethany Missionary Baptist Church Men's Choir. Uncle C. L. was employed with the Hughes Aircraft Company for twenty-five years.

In January of 1998, Uncle C. L. and Aunt Sugar renewed their love and vows for each other during their 50th Wedding Anniversary at their church, Bethany Missionary Baptist Church.

I'm told that Uncle C. L.'s favorite song was "He's Leaving on the Midnight Train to Georgia" by Gladys Knight and the Pips. I will always remember Uncle C. L. as a loving, humble man who had a great sense of humor; an infectious laugh; a beautiful smile and a Christ centered forgiving spirit.

Aunt Sugar and Uncle C. L. prospered and became prominent in spite of enduring the hard rigors of life. They raised their children and built a beautiful family unit known for their honesty and their integrity.

Wilma West Rideout, was Aunt Sugar's first born child. She is the sweetest among us cousins with a heart of pure gold. She has a quiet, confident spirit, never raising her voice, although I know she must get angry at times. She might, but I've never seen it or heard it. She's a tough mother so I would characterize her as "walking softly, carrying a big stick".

Wilma was born in 1939, in Fitzhugh, Arkansas and being the oldest, she had to help with her younger siblings and do a lot of work in the house. She was taught how to cook, how to clean, how to help with the children, and most importantly how to work hard at everything she attempted to do – a strong work ethic. Life was a struggle and if you are to survive and prosper, you have to work hard. Wilma learned that lesson well having gone on to not only to prosper, but to become prominent and quite successful.

Wilma was 18 years old when she married Richard Frank Rideout. Wilma is one of our tallest cousins, and Richard was tall as well, hovering over Wilma. It was August, 1957 when they married and remained together until his death over 50 years later. Their love story is fascinating and funny: Richard was born in Augusta, Arkansas in 1939, the same year as Wilma. He attended Carver High School in Augusta, Arkansas. While attending there, he saw and met for the first time Wilma West and wrote in her autograph book.

During his lifetime, Richard would affectionately explain how they met. He said, "I pointed my finger at her and said 'She's mine. One day I'm going to marry her.' And he did, of course, and again, they remained together for 55 years. They were blessed with three beautiful children: Valerie Rideout Handy, Richard Frank Rideout, Jr. and D'Mitri La Mar Rideout. Valerie grew up to be a beautiful young woman who always looked like a model, and carried herself in a graceful manner like a model. Richard is a policeman, strong and soft-spoken, with a lovely family; and D'Mitri is a young "Idris Elba" muscles and all, who is a sought after ladies' man.

Wilma and Richard moved to Los Angeles, California with their family in tow and Wilma lives in L.A. today in an elegant, big house, with big furniture, beautiful art pieces and, of course, many family pictures of happy times and fond memories. They became members of First Bethany Missionary Baptist Church where Richard served as Deacon, Member of the Trustee Board and Sunday School Superintendent. Wilma and Richard cared about others deeply and they served with humility and love. Richard began having health issues, but continued to serve showing a Christian example for others to follow. After many years, Richard became a member of Central Baptist Church in Carson, California where he attended Sunday School on a regular basis and served as a Deacon. Richard attended the L.A. Trade Technical College and the Southwest College in

L. A. earning degrees in both. Professionally, he worked in Logistics at Simmons Mattress Company for twenty years. He continued his career at the L.A. Police Department (LAPD) for approximately two years and then after eighteen years, he retired from Chromalloy Company as Vice President of Logistics.

Richard enjoyed music, both dancing and singing. Family Reunions were always fun because we got a chance to see, not only, Uncle C. L. and Aunt Sugar dance, but we enjoyed watching Richard and Wilma, as well. He loved dancing and singing to the songs of Sam Cooke, Smokey Robinson, and Luther Van Dross and he loved "My Girl" by the Temptations.

Richard always spoke with words of wisdom, whether he used a metaphor, a poem, or a prayer, or a story, to uplift and encourage others, especially his children.

He told them: "You can do anything you put your mind to. Don't ever allow anyone to tell you different. Just stick to it and don't ever give up." He had other words of wisdom: "Prior preparation prevents poor performance." "To thine own self be true."

- "Don't ever think you are more important than others, and don't ever think others are more important than you."
- "Always bring your money home. Take care of home first."
- "Family is always better than friends. A lot of people give up family for friends and find out sooner or later that the friendship was skin deep. Friends will abandon you but family will stick with you until the end."

His stories were always funny and thought-provoking:

- "We used to get on our bikes and run the front wheel of the bicycle up the old people's butt! My momma used to whip me so hard."
- "The old people would say, 'don't point at no graveyard, or your finger will fall off."
- "Me and Itema would walk behind Mr. Riley and make sounds at him and he would start jumpin cuz he was so goosey!"
- "Back in the day, Mama Lula would tell me to go and get a chicken. So I would get a rock and hit it upside the head and knock it out.

Then she would take the chicken by the leg and pull the head off and throw the chicken back in the yard. And the chicken would walk around out there and sooner or later he would realize . . . he ain't got no head. And he would fall out."

Wilma is my own special cousin. We share a similar way of "looking at life". We talk a few times a year, and we're always "there" for each other during the times of trouble and loss. We pray each other through the grief and sorrow, and celebrate when good things happen. We laughed together recently because when our uncle, Sonny, called us once, he talked to me and thought I was Wilma and talked to Wilma and thought it was me. He laughed with us. Both Wilma and I love talking to Sonny. He is one crazy, funny guy. Like Daddy, Sonny has a great sense of humor and loves making his nieces laugh.

Wilma still misses Richard in her life, but she is comfortable and happy in her beloved Los Angeles. Her kids shower her with love and attention, and her two lovely, tall, granddaughters, Ashley and Taylyn, make sure she has everything she needs and wants. She has two other grandchildren, Ricky and Idallys who are just as precious. Life is good for Wilma.

<u>Dessola</u> <u>West</u> <u>Johnson</u>, is the second child of Aunt Sugar. Dessola is our most religious and spiritually minded cousin. Dessola was born in 1942 in Fitzhugh, Arkansas where she grew up and where she went to school. She was smart, learning her lessons well, and she was tough. If you messed with her, you would probably get "beat up". Like Wilma, she had many chores around the house. Dessola learned how to run her own household by working hard as a child and as a young person.

The year 1942, when Dessola was born, it was full of military history, with Franklin Delano Roosevelt as President of the United States; the 93rd Infantry, the first black division formed during WWII, is activated at Fort Huachura, AZ; the U.S. Marine Corps begins the enlistment of blacks, Camp Le Jeune, NC; the Women's Army Auxillary Corps is formed and accepts both blacks and whites. African-Americans were contributing much to our nation all over the states: Margaret Walker's first book of poetry, "<u>For</u> <u>My</u> <u>People</u>" is published; John H. Johnson begins publishing "<u>Negro</u> <u>Digest</u>"; Aretha Franklin was born on March 25, and would go on to earn 21 gold records; Lena Horne makes her film debut in "Panama Hattie;" Baseball pitcher, Leroy "Satchel" Paige leads the Kansas City

Monarchs to victory in the Negro World Series; Charity Earley is the first black commissioned officer in the Women's Army Auxiliary Corps; and Congressman William Dawson, a black Democrat from Illinois is elected to the U.S. Congress.

The things that were happening in the world that year pose the backdrop of Dessola's life choices: she loves black history; she loves music; she loves the arts; and she loves the Lord. She, along with her younger sister, Shelva, is part of an acting group in Los Angeles. Dessola is absolutely a "comedian" in my book. She makes me laugh out loud at her jokes and her stories.

Dessola was one of my cousins who a couple of years ago, came to see me and my friend Beverly at our hotel in Los Angeles. We were there to see our friend, Inez who was ill. Dessola kept us laughing. I enjoyed it so much, both the stories and just being with my cousins. I love Dessola for her humor and positive outlook and I love her because she has a kind heart and a passion for others. She is very close to my cousins Gwen and Dorothy and when they need her, she jumps on a plane to be there for them. She doesn't hesitate to help when needed.

Dessola left Fitzhugh, Arkansas and moved to Los Angeles, California where she married and started a family. She had four children: Pamela Mosby, Ernest "Red" Mosby, Dennetta Mosby, and Anthony "Tony" Stitt. I remember Pamela as a little girl – Aunt Sugar used to baby sit her years and years ago. Pamela resembled Dessola a lot. She was always devoted to her grandmother and spent a lot of time with her.

Dessola loved the family reunions. She enjoyed being with her aunts, uncles, and cousins. She learned the lessons well that her parents taught her: integrity, hard work, and love of family. Also, like Aunt Sugar and Uncle C. L., she had a keen sense of humor and a deep love of Jesus Christ. Her commitment to her church and to her community is well known in the family and she is greatly admired by her cousins.

God has blessed Dessola with many spiritual blessings and with many physical blessings and she is thankful for being a wife, mother, grandmother, and great-grandmother.

Harold Gene West, is Aunt Sugar's third child and oldest son. Harold is married to the beautiful, Josie West, and they live, prominently, in St. Louis,

Missouri. Harold, like his siblings, was taught how to be successful in his adult life: independence; responsibility, honesty, seriousness; maturity; hard work; money management; dedication to a cause; love of family; and love of God. He learned those lessons well and continues to carry on the legacy of his parents.

When I think of Harold, I think professional, business-like, dressed to the "nines", and dignified. He takes "dignity" to another whole level. His posture is excellent and straight, and he is an impeccable dresser-dressed appropriately for every occasion. When his dad passed away, Harold was quick to acknowledge the great impact Uncle C. L. had on his life. Among other things, he wrote: "Dad, I thank you for being there in our younger years of decision-making."

Harold and Josie have four adult children, Harold, Jr; Marylan; Meshawn, and Nicci Barbara, and he enjoys spending time with his grandchildren: Aaron, Keshara, Tylan, Kymiah, Ahyries, Desorie, and Destiny, who live in Los Angeles and in Jennings, Missouri.

James "Jamie" West, is Aunt Sugar's fourth child and second son. He is one of my favorite cousins because of his kind heart and generous nature. He and his lovely wife, Joanne, live in St. Louis, Missouri in one of those big, beautiful homes surrounded by big trees, lush bushes, and colorful flowers. Joanne is more like "cousin" than cousin-in-law; when we greet one another, we say in unison, "Hi, pretty lady!" Jamie and Joanne have been married, happily, for decades. I don't remember how many, but enough to have had five children and several grand children.

Jamie is a big support for his cousins. Wherever and whenever he's needed, he's right there, whether it's picking someone up, or dropping someone off, or just providing a shoulder to cry on. When my cousin, Deborah, passed away recently, Jamie was a big support to Dorothy and Gwen, Deborah's sisters. He and Joanne had driven up from St. Louis to be with the family at the funeral. He was very helpful at that very sad and grievous time.

When I look at Jamie, I am reminded of Uncle C. L. (the resemblance is striking). Like his father, Jamie is committed to serving others and making life a little easier for those he comes in contact with.

Shelva "Shelvie" West Quinine, is the fifth child and third daughter of Aunt Sugar and Uncle C. L: She is the undisputed star of our family.

Shelvie was born in 1948 in Fitzhugh, Arkansas and like her siblings, she learned valuable life lessons that she never forgot; lessons of hard work; dedication to a task; honesty; love of God; and commitment to family.

I call Shelvie a star because we realized early on that she was especially beautiful. She is light brown, olive complexioned; bright, grey eyes; medium height; thin, shapely built; and confidence and boldness "through the roof." Years ago, when Bob Barker was host, Shelvie was a contestant on "The Price Is Right". She won all the top prizes, including a car. We were all in awe of her for it was unusual for "us" to go that far on a game show at that time. Shelvie went on to do some modeling, some acting, and much singing. Some of her music has been recorded.

She moved to L.A. with her parents and got married. She married a great guy, Don Curtis Quinine and they had four beautiful adult children: Don, Jr.; Darwin Phillip; Dannon; and Monica. Their precious little grandchild, Arianna, is Don, Jr.'s daughter.

Shelvie and Don had a beautiful life together for decades before he passed away suddenly. It was a devastating and grievous loss to her and her family. She said, "Naomi, my husband was alive when I went off to work that morning, and he was dead by the time I got home from work." His legacy lives on in his children; they make sure we don't forget Don because Monica keeps us informed on Facebook. She mentions her dad on his birthday anniversary and at special holidays like Christmas.

When Uncle C.L., Shelvie's dad, passed away, She wrote: "I love you, Daddy. We'll always remember that special smile, that caring heart, that warm embrace you always gave us. You being there for Mom and us through good and bad times, no matter what. We'll always remember you, Dad, because there will never be another one to replace you in our hearts, and the love we will always have for you." Her words, along with her siblings, say much about her dad, but they also give us a little peek into her heart and the kind of person Shelvie is.

Mac Ray West, was Aunt Sugar's sixth child, the third son, and the "baby" of his siblings. He was his parents' "pride & joy" and the last child of their union. Mac Ray was born in 1950 in Fitzhugh, Arkansas. Although he was the youngest sibling, he never the less had chores and responsibilities, and consequences when he failed to carry out his duties.

He took his jobs seriously and when his dad passed away, he had this to say as a tribute to him: "Dad, thank you for your caring love and training in the work ethics of life." He learned those wonderful lessons well. The year he was born was a year of history and events:

- Dr. Ralph J. Bunche was awarded the Nobel Peace Prize
- Gwendolyn Brooks was awarded the Pulitzer Prize for Poetry, "Annie Allen"
- The films (and 2 of my favorites) "Sunset Boulevard" and "All About Eve" were playing; "All About Eve" received the Academy Award.
- Songs that were popular that year were: "If I Knew You Were Comin' I'd Baked a Cake", "Ragg Mopp", "A Bushel and a Peck," C'est Si Bon", "Good Night, Irene", "Music! Music! Music!", and "Mona Lisa".
- Racial quotas are abolished in the U.S. Army.
- Steveland Morris (Stevie Wonder) was born that year in Saginaw, Michigan, and will become a musical and singing sensation winning 12 Grammy Awards and an Oscar for best song.

All of these significant happenings were not lost on Mac Ray. He went on to be prominent and successful, as well. He married the very lovely Dorris and together they built a beautiful family.

Mac Ray and Dorris had six kids: Mac Ray, Jr; Renina; Cathy Eugena; Lisa Mosely; Cynthia Harris; and Della Michelle West. Some of the children moved to Los Angeles, California and started their own families. Mac Ray has a slew of grandchildren while Dorris continues to look like a teenager herself.

Mac Ray and Dorris live in Little Rock, Arkansas in a big house, enjoying the fruits of hard work, excellent financial management, and a great family structure.

Aunt Nesha

Nesha "Neshie" Jones White, was the 7th child, and the 6th daughter of James Knox Polk Jones and Dessie Anna Thompson Jones. She was born on October 10, 1921 in Weldon, Arkansas and was destined to be the example of strength and courage. Aunt Neshie spent her school years in the Fitzhugh, Arkansas school system and reached the 8th grade. Her mother passed away when she was fifteen leaving her and four younger siblings at home with her father. Aunt Neshie quickly took the reins as cook and managing the household. She did not complete her schooling but she became a great money manager. Her youngest sister, Ersé, said that Neshie could always stretch a dollar; she said, "when nobody else had money, Neshie always did."

Aunt Neshie, at eighteen, met and married Ernest White in Fitzhugh, Arkansas. They built a big, tight-knit family of ten children: Edward, Elbert, Jimmy, Herman, Jo Ann, Sandra, Phillip, and Patricia. Two of the children were still born, and Jo Ann and Patty died as infants. They were then left with six children to nurture and love. Aunt Neshie told me that when Ed was a baby, she was carrying him on her hip to someplace. She was walking on one of those little 'country roads, and Ed kept crying and crying and crying; apparently for no reason. Aunt Neshie was comforting him, trying to calm him down, but he kept crying, so Aunt Nesha put him down and left him on the side of the road, still crying. Uncle Ernest went back and got him. It was a much different world back then and we laughed when Aunt Neshie told us about it. We could picture it because we knew Ed; he always seemed to be in trouble with his mom for something or other. When he became an adult, married and had his own kids (7 of them) he understood Aunt Neshie's experiences with him. We laughed at the story; it shows Aunt Neshie's humor, but also her wisdom.

While in Arkansas, Aunt Neshie worked as a cotton picker to help support the family, but she promised her children that they would not have to pick cotton like she did. She kept that promise when she moved her family to St. Louis, Missouri. Aunt Neshie got a job as a Nurse's Aide in the Pediatric Department of the big hospital there in St. Louis. Later, Aunt Neshie got her training and worked as a nurse for most of her working career. She felt so proud of the fact that she did not retire until she was a young 80 years.

Aunt Neshie loved her "sisters"; (and of course, her three brothers) they were extremely close - knit as siblings. The sisters spent time together at our family reunions and outside the reunions. They visited each other often, whether it was for illness or just to visit for a good time together. When Daddy was gravely ill in 1997, Aunt Neshie came to visit him at my home to help care for him. It brought tears to his eyes to see his sister, all the way from West Covina, California, come to comfort him in his illness.

Aunt Neshie and her sisters would stay up for hours talking, laughing, and gossiping during our family reunions. I always hung with my aunts rather than with my younger cousins for I wanted to hear their history and their dreams for the future. I felt honored to be in their midst. My aunts were such interesting women who were not shy or quiet or "laid back". They all had such great confidence and poise. Aunt Neshie loved to travel with her siblings and their spouses; all over the states and to other countries, as well.

Aunt Neshie was an excellent seamstress and made many of her clothes in her younger years.

She was so proud of the fact that she did not look her age. She lived to be 91 years old, but she looked like a much younger woman. Aunt Neshie adopted a healthy lifestyle by eating healthy (fruits and vegetables), getting proper rest and sleep, and loving and serving her children and her grandchildren. She got up early each morning, at the exact same time; she fixed her bowl of oatmeal and ate it, each morning, without fail; and she went to bed each night at 8:30, without fail. She prayed constantly for God to bless her with health and strength – she said: "If you have your health and strength you can get some money." She was proud of the fact that she was 80 years old when she retired. Aunt Neshie remained the same size, basically, over 50 years, still able to wear the same clothes.

Aunt Neshie accepted the Lord Jesus Christ as her Savior at an early age at the Lake Grove Church in Arkansas. She later joined the St. Stephens Baptist Church in La Puente, California. Her grandchildren were her pride and joy and would do whatever it took to help them but always after a long lecture. She was a strong disciplinarian.

I remember Aunt Neshie's compassion and love for her children when they had to drive cross - country for a special occasion. She was over come with tears as she worried about the safety of her kids as they tried to do all that driving. She felt grateful and was relieved when they arrived safely.

Aunt Neshie went to be with the Lord on August 15, 2013 after a long life of strength and honor. Her hands were always busy helping, serving, and giving. When I was a young mother, she taught me how to properly change diapers, and how to pin the diapers (we had cloth diapers for our babies back then); how to wash clothes and hang them on a line; and how to iron clothes and properly fold them. Her hands made the best caramel cake I have ever tasted; and her hands made the most delicious corn bread, hush puppies and fried fish. Aunt Neshie's legacy lives on in her children & grandchildren.

Edward "Ed" White, is Aunt Neshie's oldest child, the first born and the first son. He was born in 1940 in Fitzhugh, Arkansas. Ed grew up and went to school in Fitzhugh. He was a typical "boy", mischievous and getting into trouble all the time; but Ed had a big, loving heart for other people. He was fun-loving and funny with a big smile and a "gift for gab".

Ed married a beautiful girl, Joyce, as a young man and they had seven children – 5 boys and 2 girls: Edward "Pooh" White, Mark White, Danny White, Keith White, Sean White, Nina White-Butler, and Angela White. Joyce was a good mother to her kids, taking special care of them, meeting their every need. Ed and Joyce loved each other and proceeded to build their family, looking forward to a bright future. And then Joyce developed Leukemia, a terrible disease in which the body produces too many white blood cells. It was fatal. Joyce died from the disease and her loss devastated the whole family. Aunt Neshie and Ed, while still grieving, began trying to keep the large family of children together. The children survived that tragedy, but never really got over the loss of their mother.

Ed lives in Augusta, Arkansas. Some of his children live in California, some in Missouri, and one in Oregon.

Elbert "Bubble" White is Aunt Neshie's second child and second son. Like Brenda, Floyd, and Dessola, he was born in 1942, in Fitzhugh, Arkansas. Bubble was raised under the hard discipline of Aunt Neshie. Uncle Ernest, his dad, loved his kids and nurtured his sons with tenderness and care, showing them and modeling for them how to be strong men. Bubble, like his siblings, loved his parents and tried to do those things he was instructed to do. He learned tough lessons growing up on that farm, in the big house on the hill. The chores that he had to do prepared him for the world outside of Fitzhugh, Arkansas; it prepared him for the economic condition at the time; it gave him the necessary work ethic for being successful; and it taught him the value of completing a task after setting goals. He knew what his job was and he did it well.

As a young, adult man, Bubble made his mom proud. He was "cool", "suave", and self-assured, very confident. He was the ultimate "ladies man". Not only was Bubble handsome, but he brought girlfriends to the family reunions that were absolutely "drop dead" gorgeous as well. He was always "in control", a downright confident guy.

Bubble settled down and later married Victoria "Vickie" White. They built their life together, not only for the two of them, but for their families, as well. Aunt Neshie, his mom, was getting older and experiencing health issues. Vickie's dad was also having difficulty as he aged. Bubble and Vickie decided to spend time with both parents by alternating – they would spend weeks in Texas with Aunt Neshie and then spend several weeks caring for her dad in St. Louis.

Bubble simply adored his mother and eventually stayed with her during the last years of her life. He lovingly became a care giver for her along with his other siblings.

Bubble lives in McKinney, Texas enjoying the fruits of his labor. He has one son, Justin White.

Jimmy "Jackie Boy" White, was Aunt Neshie's third child and third son. He was born in 1943 in Fitzhugh, Arkansas. He went to school, like his siblings before him, in the Arkansas school district. Jackie Boy was smart and enjoyed going to school; always eager to learn as much as he could. He grew up under strict rules and he learned early that discipline is important. Discipline meant that you were loved and cared for, but you had to pay a price; the price was obedience and respect. Jackie Boy learned those rules for his adult life was evident of this. He was very successful career wise and other wise.

Jackie Boy moved to St. Louis, Missouri where he met his beautiful wife, Eileen. She was truly the "love of his life." They had four lovely children together: Karen, Phyllis, Candace, and Jimmy, Jr. Jackie Boy and Eileen built a loving and a closely tight - knit family unit. They lived in St. Louis for many years and then relocated to West Covina, California. They bought a beautiful home there where they proceeded to be a "perfect" mom and dad. They believed in doing things "right" and "correct" and proper. It was a joy to spend time with them. Lenzo and I would visit them in West Covina. They treated us like royalty e.g. cooking the meals, taking us out to dinner, and to events. And then just to sit and fellowship together was wonderful. I will always remember those times. Eileen passed away a few years ago, but I will always remember her and the beauty of her character. Eileen had such a close relationship with Aunt Neshie, her mother in law, which was hard to do because Aunt Neshie doted on her sons. Somehow Eileen had that "magic touch" with Aunt Neshie; they simply adored each other. They cooked together and shared recipes for big family gatherings, each one known for a special dish.

Later, Jackie Boy and Eileen relocated to Celina, Texas. He bought a ranch with a big house. It has become his retreat, his ultimate comfort and pleasure. He has remained there after Eileen's death. He's more of a "home body" now; just going out for necessities. Candace, his daughter; who also lives in Texas, cooks delicious meals and she makes sure Dad has plenty of it. Karen, his oldest child, lives in Shreveport, Louisiana. Phyllis and Jimmy, Jr. live in California. Jackie Boy has six grand kids and enjoys spending time with them.

<u>Herman</u> <u>White</u> is Aunt Neshie's fourth child and fourth son. Herman was born in 1948 in Fitzhugh, Arkansas. He was born the same year as my cousins Deborah and Shelva. Herman is a very special guy to me because he is so nice, so unassuming, so helpful, and so down to earth. Herman is my drop-dead handsome cousin who doesn't even know he's good looking. He's tall, light-complexioned, with an infectious smile, and eyes that are bright and warm, and a friendly personality. Herman has three sons – Derrick, Darrell, and Damian – with his equally drop dead gorgeous wife, Brenda, and those three sons are the spitting image of their dad.

Brenda, Herman's wife, is beautiful physically and spiritually. She is a cancer survivor and when she was cancer free, in remission, she launched a campaign to help other women who were suffering from the disease. When my daughter, Linda, got cancer, Non Hodgkin's Lymphoma, Brenda encouraged her and supported her through that very dark period in her life. Brenda wrote letters, sent cards, sent valuable information, and made calls to check up on Linda and to keep her motivated.

Herman and Brenda live in Melissa, Texas surrounded by their children & grandchildren.

Sandra Rae White Moseley, was Aunt Neshie's only girl; two other little baby girls died in infancy. "San" as we affectionately call her was born in 1951 in Fitzhugh, Arkansas. To all my aunts and uncles, "San" always said she was their "favorite". She always introduced herself as the favorite, jokingly. But in reality, she really is a favorite and a special cousin with multiple skills and talents and a great love for our family. Recently, when we learned that our cousin, Gwen was ill, San set up a conference prayer vigil on the phone for all our cousins to participate in. We had a wonderful time in prayer, not only for Gwen and her husband, Lawrence, but for all our families and loved ones. San is an ordained, licensed minister. She has a special love and concern for not only her immediate family, but for her cousins in particular. Although there are many cousins, we are a pretty close - knit group. San is always "there" for us when we are in need, whatever the need. A big hug from San means a lot. San continually praises God for His faithfulness and for His mercy.

San was raised in Fitzhugh, Arkansas just like her brothers, going through the hard times of growing up, learning to cook and clean and wash and iron. She always wanted to do excellently and wanted to be the best she could be. Even then, as a child, there was something special about the way she tackled her chores. She grew up and began right away to pursue her life's goal. San excelled in school, eager to do well, eager to make her mom and dad proud. They had high expectations for her, being the only girl, and she did not disappoint them.

San met Harold James Mosley, her soul mate, and they married in 1991. We all call him "James". They built a beautiful family unit with Dy Nesha, Jabary, and Kim. James was a genuinely nice guy, with a cool, calm, confident demeanor. He was a private guy who kind of kept everything "close to the vest". Their home they purchased was in the mountains in a place called Covina Hills, California. My son, Kevin, and I visited San and James in this fabulous home back in 2004. I had just lost my youngest son, Lenard, and was still grieving. They comforted Kevin and I with love and concern and sympathy. The home reminded me of one of those layouts in a celebrity magazine. The windows were from the floor to the ceiling, no blinds, no shades. The furniture was ultra modern with some antiques; pillows and accessories unusual and so beautiful. It was truly what I would call a "dream house". It was no big deal to San; she was "free and easy" and the best host in the world. She and Kevin had great fun together, joking and teasing and "roasting" each other. Kevin teased her the whole time we were there because she didn't have a microwave. She bought a smaller house later, after James' death, and she still has no microwave.

San and James took us to a quaint little town about an hour away, a place where the "elite meet," to treat us to lunch. It was an elegant restaurant where we enjoyed a delicious meal, and then headed back to Covina Hills and San's beautiful home. Five years later, James was dead from cancer, at age 64 leaving San a grieving widow. His body lay in state in their home for two days in a casket where the wake was held. It was a trying and traumatic time for San, but the Lord brought her through it.

San wrote the very first family newsletter in 2001. We had had a wonderful family reunion here in Chicago in August, 2000, the new millennium.

We had over 100 family members and friends in attendance and we had a similated show with my great grandchildren – Tierra and Derek – performing as Ike & Tina Turner at the banquet. Tierra was 9 yrs. old and Derek was 8 yrs. old. They brought the house down. It was hilarious! My granddaughters, Shatese and Shundra and their friend, Lutrice, performed as Diana Ross and the Supremes, and my cousin, Dorothy, did a great Aretha Franklin. Patti, Dorothy's daughter, and her friends – performed as the Emotions. In the newsletter, we read that the room was filled with excitement as Ike & Tina took center stage and rocked the house with "Proud Mary". The picnic was held at the park and the food was delicious. The weather was great and the memories were, of course, unforgettable!

In the newsletter, San encouraged everyone to attend the 2002 Family Reunion which was to be held in Atlanta, Georgia. She mentioned and highlighted our own "Denzel Washington", my cousin Thea's husband, Dennis Tate. Dennis is a United Airlines pilot. Dennis was selected to represent thousands of United Airlines employees in a commercial aimed at getting the company flying again. We were all so proud and congratulated him on doing a great job. Jokingly, San said to him when he reaches the silver screen, not to forget us "little people."

Before the 2000 Family Reunion, San and her brothers lost their father, Uncle Ernest. It was a devastating loss for them. In the newsletter, San expressed their gratitude for those who attended the funeral and those who sent flowers, and cards, and those who prayed, those who called, those who sent food, and those who gave many hugs. It helped them during their time of bereavement.

She gave suggestions as to how to live a happy life:

- Watch a sunrise at least once per year
- Treat everyone you meet like you want to be treated
- Tape record your parents & kids' laughter
- Spend more time with Jesus.
- For beautiful eyes look for the good in other people.

She ended the newsletter with this scripture verse:

"The Lord is the strength of His people."
Psalm 28:8

At our July, 2006 Family Reunion which was held in Los Angeles, California, San and the L.A. cousins presented a "Tee-licious Breakfast" entitled "These Are the Women We Come From." It was on a Saturday morning, and it was one of the most impressive, most beautiful events I've attended.

The room where it was held was decorated like a wedding reception with beautiful covered chairs and cloth tablecloths. The tea cups on each table, at each setting were small, colorful, elegant, with a unique design. Everyone eagerly waited for what was coming next. Most of us, cousins and aunts (women only), had not experienced such a "tea" event. We all had to wear white attire and colorful hats. The program included poetry, scripture verses, entertainment, tributes, and great food. On the flip side of the program were pictures of some of our family members (women) interspersed with women of history like Sojourner Truth. At the bottom of the pictures was the theme "These Are The Women We Come From". My great granddaughter, Tierra, was there and I was proud and happy that she shared such a beautiful moment in our family history. Tierra signed my program, "Lady Tierra Kilpatrick". Others who signed my program were: "Love, Gwen Thomas", "Love, Dorothy", "Lady Brenda Adams", "Valerie Handy," and my aunt, "Dee Lyons". A story was told at the Tea, and we were all mesmerized.

I remember thinking at the time that all our lives tell a story; in every situation – good or bad – and people around us are watching and listening to the story we are telling.

"You are an epistle of Christ . . . written not with ink but by the Spirit of the living God."
II Corinthians 3:3

By San's request, I made a presentation entitled "Tea History" which I truly enjoyed doing. It was well received for our history of women on the Jones side and Thompson side is truly rich and interesting.

Sandra has worked hard over the years, as is her tradition and God has truly blessed her and her family. She works for the County of Los Angeles as the Communications' Services Analyst. She is well liked and respected by her co-workers. San has traveled and has seen a lot of fascinating places, has met a lot of wonderful people, and has done a lot of exciting things, e.g., Great Wall of China; Nile River High Tea Cruise; Red Sea – Egypt; Safari, Kenya, Tanzania, Nairobi, Massai, Mara; Big Bear, Germany, Budapest, Cairo, Munich, Shanghai; the Danube River and other places. After seeing all these places (she sent me a card with her pictures in these places), San said that she has come to realize that there is no place like home and nothing like family and friends. She lives in Walnut Grove, California surrounded by her daughter, Dy Nesha, her granddaughter, Cheyenne, her son, Jabary, and her two dogs, Minnie and Honey.

Phillip White, was Aunt Neshie's last child, and fifth son, the baby of his siblings. They teased him sometimes for being the youngest, and being able to get what he wanted. Phillip was born in Fitzhugh, Arkansas in 1953. In that year, a loaf of bread cost 16¢, a gallon of gas was 20¢, a pound of coffee was 76¢, a new car was about $1,651, and you could buy a new house for $9,525. The President was Dwight Eisenhower and the Vice-President was Richard Nixon. The Salk Polio Vaccine was used successfully, the best motion picture of the year was "From Here To Eternity"; the best actor was William Holden for "Stalag 17"; the beast actress was Audrey Hepburn for "Roman Holiday"; the popular songs were Ebb Tide, How Much Is That Doggie In The Window, Rock Around The Clock, and Dragnet; the Lakers were the NBA champions, the Detroit Lions were the professional football champions, and the New York Yankees were the AL champions.

Phillip is one of my younger cousins, next generation cousin, having been born in the same year as my daughter, Linda. He's a product of that era – fun - loving, fast moving, and energetic.

Phillip, like his siblings, loved his dad and loved and adored his mom. When Aunt Neshie passed away in 2013, he along with Ed, Bubble, Jim, Herman, and San, wrote a tribute to her. Her children wanted to show their appreciation for the life she provided for them.

Phillip married the love of his life, Robin, many years ago. They are a loving and devoted couple who have been together through trials and tribulations, and through joys and good times. They live in a town called "Cabazon", California.

Phillip has one son, Phillip Allen White, Jr.

Praise God for the legacy of Aunt Neshie and Uncle Ernest, and for the lives of their children.

Uncle Wiley

My uncle, Wiley Jones, was the son of James Knox Polk Jones and Dessie Thompson Jones. He was the second son and the eighth child who was born in Fitzhugh, Arkansas on February 8, 1923. As a kid growing up in the deep south, Uncle Wiley experienced the rigors of living on a farm. He had many chores that he did on a daily basis; these responsibilities taught him tough life lessons. His parents had high expectations for him as a young man, and he didn't disappoint in that area. Uncle Wiley faced every challenge thrown at him with gusto and bravado; he was fearless. Uncle Wiley was feisty, strong-willed, and could be confrontational, if prompted. He had a strong work ethic that he passed on to his three children later on. He gladly worked hard to achieve his goals, and he eagerly pursued his dreams and aspirations.

When he was not quite twenty years old, Uncle Wiley enlisted in the United States Army, serving in the 24th Infantry in the Pacific Theater. He was honorably discharged nearly three years later in December, 1945.

Over the next few years, Uncle Wiley lived in St. Louis, Missouri, and Chicago, Illinois where he met Argel Henry. They married in 1952 in Chicago. Together, they raised three children, Darrell, Marcia, and Angela on the south side of Chicago. They lived in Chicago for many years with Uncle Wiley working at General Electric and Argel working at Cromwell Paper Company.

In late 1971, Uncle Wiley moved his family to San Diego, California where his sister Rutha Jenkins lived and where his younger brother, Theodore had moved with his wife, Shirley, and their family. The weather was so pleasant there and there were many opportunities for employment. He continued to work for General Electric, Hotpoint Division in San Diego. They both enjoyed life there and developed beautiful relationships with family and friends. His sisters visited him often and he started an automotive repair business in partnership with his brother, Theodore.

Argel (all of us called her Argel), Uncle Wiley's beloved wife was one of my favorite aunts. She was articulate, with perfect diction and intonation; she was bright and smart and hardworking. She loved Uncle Wiley with a passion and they built a beautiful family together. Argel was a wonderful housewife, keeping her home neat and clean. She loved cooking delicious meals. Lenzo and I visited them often when they were in Chicago, and we sat at her table and enjoyed her cooking. They visited us, as well. We kept in close touch with each other; Argel and I always had so much to talk about. She was warm and friendly, with a big smile and a pleasant demeanor. We were devastated when she passed away in San Diego in 1995.

Uncle Wiley loved us, his nieces and nephews. We saw his softer, more tender side. When he moved to San Diego, he attended St. Rita's Catholic Church and invited me to attend on one of my visits to the city. I had a beautiful time on that Sunday morning. Uncle Wiley, dressed in a suit, performed his duty as usher, also responsible for counting the offering, in a quiet, dignified manner. He stood tall and proud as I watched him, and I, in turn, felt pride and joy in the Lord for that precious experience in my Uncle's place of worship.

Both Uncle Wiley and Argel loved to bowl. They were avid bowlers, with Argel winning two city championships. Uncle Wiley and I shared many similarities: both of us born in February; him and Argel married the same year, 1952, as Lenzo & I; and his son, Darrell, was born in the same year as my daughter, Katrina, 1956. I admired my uncle for his strength, for his leadership skills, for his intelligence, and for his love for his heritage, his family. Uncle Wiley did the research and wrote the beautiful historical document, "This Jones Family". He died on April 7, 2004 – two months after Lenard died. He called me after Lenard's death to give his condolences and comfort. Then he, too was gone. He leaves a rich legacy that lives on in his children and his grandchildren.

Darrell Jones, is Uncle Wiley's first born, and only son. He was born in 1956, in Chicago, Illinois. He and my cousin, Theodore "Teddy" Jones, Jr. were born in the same year. It was a signature year for sports: Floyd Patterson knocked out Archie Moore in five rounds, becoming the youngest heavy weight champion at 21 years old; President Dwight Eisenhower personally asks Bill Russell to play basketball for the US Olympic team, he plays and becomes the most popular one on an all-American team; Charles Dumas, freshman at Compton College, CA is the first high jumper to top seven feet; and Ann Gregory becomes the first black American to play in an integrated women's amateur golf championship. African American talent was observed and appreciated thoughout the black community.

Darrell, having been born in that signature year, proceeded to exhibit his own talents and God given gifts. As a young man and into his adulthood, he made his dad and mom very proud. He excelled in his studies and he worked hard to achieve and succeed. He developed strong leadership skills and excellent communication skills. Darrell possesses great speaking skills, talking confidently and always with a ready smile and a hearty laugh.

Darrell, some years ago, had an occasion to come to Chicago on business. He had lived in Chicago as a kid and then moved to San Diego with Uncle Wiley and Argel. He met and married his lovely wife, Donna, and they had two kids, Darrell, Jr. and Joshua. They moved to another California City and continued to build their family. In San Ramon, California, Darrell was a Fire Inspector, having moved up to that position of prominence. He came back to Chicago and he visited Lenzo and I in South Holland, and I took him over to visit our double cousin, Elva. She was living in a Senior Citizens Complex in Dolton, Illinois which was about 10 minutes from my home. (My mom lived in that same building for years until her death. She lived on the 3rd floor. Elva lived on the 8th floor.) Elva was delighted to see Darrell and we had a wonderful time talking about the family, as well as, the current events. He audio-taped Elva as she gave the beautiful chronology of the Jones/Thompson family, which she presented at the following family reunion banquet.

Darrell brought us up to date on Donna and his two sons, proudly stating their accomplishments. His son, Joshua and his wife Monica now have 2 beautiful daughters, Jocelyn and Milana. They live in Sacramento, California. Darrell, Jr. and his wife Sarai live in Livermore, California, the same city as Darrell and Donna. They all live happy lives surrounded by family, friends, and church family. Darrell takes pride in being a Jehovah Witness for decades, assuming a leadership position there, always sharing the good news of the Kingdom of God with others.

Marcia (Jones) Jones, was the second child and first daughter of Uncle Wiley. Her last name is "Jones" because she was born a Jones and then she married her husband whose name was Isaac Jones. Thus we label her Marcia Jones Jones. Marcia was born in Chicago, Illinois in 1957, a year after Darrell.

During that signature year, some good things were happening for African Americans:

- Rev. Martin Luther King, Jr., the NAACP, and other groups organize the Prayer Pilgrimage that was held on the steps of the Lincoln Memorial in Washington, DC to a gathering of over 30,000 people
- Dwight D. Eisenhower was President and he signed the first Civil Rights' Act (since 1875) of 1957; he elevated the civil rights section of the Department of Justice to the status of a division; and he created the U.S. Commission on Civil Rights
- Although Gov. Orval Faubus ordered units of the Arkansas National Guard to Central High School, Little Rock on the first day of school, to block the nine black youths who were chosen to integrate the school – known as the "Little Rock Nine", Pres. Dwight Eisenhower sent 1,000 paratroopers from the 101st Airborne Division to Little Rock to enforce the Brown us Bd of Educ public school desegregation decision.

Those historical facts provide the "back drop" for Marcia's own successful life. She spent her early years in Chicago, attending elementary school and high school here. Marcia was an excellent student, wanting to get the highest grades in each of her subjects. I imagine her highest grades were in the language arts for she is a prolific writer. Marcia wrote me a long letter some years ago. She described her children, her home, and the land surrounding her home with such words that gave me a clear picture in my mind. The phrase "one picture is like a thousand words" comes to mind when I think of Marcia. It was a joy to read and also to imagine her reality, her experience, and her pride. She lived in California at the time with her husband, Isaac and her children. Marcia possesses a strength of character that comes straight from the heart of her father, Uncle Wiley. When she had her children, she had natural child birth. I saw the video tape of the birth of one of her precious babies. I was in awe because I have experienced child birth, and it is the most excruciating pain a woman can have, but Marcia went through it and brought her babies into the world with very little help from anyone. She accepted the help after delivery, but she bore the pain alone, in her own home. She was her own "mid wife". She, along with Isaac, had three beautiful children, Noland, Myhin, and Bethany. Marcia is living the legacy left by Argel and Uncle Wiley; one of love, courage, determination, resolve, integrity, and great pride. She and Isaac continue to live, happily, with her family in that same beautifully described home in El Cajon, California. Her oldest son, Noland, is now married to Jessalyn and they live in Farmington, New Mexico.

Angela "Angie" Jones, is Uncle Wiley's third child, and second daughter. She was born in Chicago, Illinois in 1964, and has the distinction of being the youngest cousin of the 41 of us. Angela was born in the same generation as my own children, making her especially precious and special in my sight. In the year that Angie was born, things were happening too quickly, and it was right in the middle of the "turbulent sixties". President John F. Kennedy had been assassinated the year before, 1963. The country was still stunned and struggling to set things right again. During the sixties, there was the Cuban Missile Crisis; and in addition to Pres. Kennedy's assassination, there was the assassinations of Dr. Martin Luther King, Jr. (1968), and Senator Robert F. Kennedy (1968), and Malcolm X (1965). In 1964, the year of Angie's birth, the bodies of three slain civil rights workers are discovered in a shallow grave in Philadelphia, Mississippi – the FBI accuses several white segregationists of committing the murders. President Lyndon Baines Johnson signs the Civil Rights Act of 1964 that gave the U.S. Attorney General additional power to protect citizens against discrimination and segregation. On a lighter note, also that year, Louis "Satchmo" Armstrong's song, "Hello Dolly" becomes the number one record on Billboard's Top 40 charts, replacing the Beatles' "I Want to Hold Your Hand"; "Hello Dolly" was Armstrong's first and only number one record.

Angie, I think, invented the word "nice". She is one of the nicest cousins among us; always pleasant, with a bright smile and a sparkle in her eyes. She enjoyed going to the family reunions and marveled at our family's history. Uncle Wiley shared with his children how he grew up in the deep south and the hardship he endured, but he proudly talked of "Papa," our grandfather, his dad. Angie was amazed at the story of "Jim Jones", our patriarch; how he shrewdly negotiated the purchase of acres of land; and how he started a business and a school, and yet could not read or write. Angie then contributed to that history, that legacy by entering the field of education, working for the state of California School System. She enjoyed working with kids and making their lives better.

Angie adored her mom, Argel, who loved to travel. Angie accompanied her on almost all of her wonderful trips. They enjoyed being together and Angie learned about each interesting place; learning about the culture and mores; and experiencing the joy and happiness of a world that got smaller and smaller with each trip.

Aunt Dee

My Aunt, Deborah Jones Attyberry Lyons, is the ninth child and seventh daughter of James Knox Polk Jones and Dessie Anna Thompson Jones. "Aunt Dee", as we affectionately call her, was born on February 28, 1925, in Fitzhugh, Arkansas. She spent her childhood in Fitzhugh, but moved to St. Louis, Missouri in her teen years. Like her sisters, she was strikingly beautiful. She met and married Vincent Fernandez Attyberry in St Louis. They married on December 24, 1946 and remained happily together until his sudden, and untimely death on January 21, 1958. Aunt Dee and Uncle Vincent did not have children of their own, but they loved us, their nieces and nephews. They kept up with each of us, checking on our families and making sure we were okay. After Lenzo and I married, Aunt Dee and Uncle Vincent visited us in Chicago often. They lived in St. Louis, but they came to Chicago to visit, not only Aunt Dee's relatives, but Uncle Vincent's, as well. I remember Uncle Vincent had a deep, articulate voice and a big laugh. He was kind and gentle and had a great sense of humor. When he died suddenly of a heart attack at 34 years old, we were devastated. The family rallied around Aunt Dee, with Papa and all ten of her siblings in attendance at the funeral services. I attended with my little baby, Trina, who was 2 years old. There is a picture of all of us together at Aunt Dee's house after the funeral that I treasure.

Aunt Dee kept up with all her nieces and nephews. She never had any children of her own, even with her second husband, Willie Lyons. Uncle Bill, as we called him, was equally wonderful. He loved Aunt Dee and they had a wonderful 43 years together before his death. They married, with the blessings of Papa, in Detroit, and Aunt Willie, her sister. They married in St. Louis, but lived in Detroit, Michigan for all those years, in the same nice, modest bungalow home. Aunt Dee cared for her home with a special care, keeping it clean and neat, with everything in its place and in perfect order.

From a child, I've watched Aunt Dee and admired her, not only because she's Daddy's sister, but because of her impeccable character - a strong sense of right & wrong; because of her sense of humor; her feistiness, and her elegant beauty. She wore her beautiful, jet black hair (that resembled black fur) in a short hair cut with cropped bangs. Aunt Dee wore expensive dresses, suits, and shoes. She worked at the Bon Ton fashion clothing store in Detroit and she dressed up each day going to work. She always looked elegant.

Aunt Dee was the ultimate role model for us all, never saying "no" to a need. When we were in trouble, or had a problem, or just depressed, she was always there to help. She was like a "bridge over troubled waters" as she supported me through my grief and sorrow and pain when Lenard died. She came in from Detroit and was here from the start of the sad, sad funeral until the end, staying a few days to comfort my family. Whenever there was a hint of trouble, in any of our families, Aunt Dee was there, on the phone checking on us.

Her sense of family was obvious and her love for all of us was genuine and sincere.

She taught us to be strong and steadfast and to be unintimidated by people or circumstances. She demonstrated this by her own life, by her integrity; her strength of character; her uniqueness of spirit; and by her moral of character.

Aunt Dee loved writing letters, beautiful letters full of family news and interesting things she was experiencing. She wrote to me in March, 2001 and April, 2001 where she talked about Tiger Woods and his decision to get married. She loved watching him play golf and she loved watching Venus and Serena play tennis. In the other letter she talked about our cousin, Jeanette's funeral. Jeanette, our Uncle Floyd's daughter, lived in Detroit before her death. She also mentioned our uncle, Sunny, her brother, had been called to the ministry and was getting ready to preach his first sermon on Men's Day. Also, she mentioned that she was getting ready to go to the bowling alley. She loved bowling and also loved watching the soaps.

Uncle Bill, Aunt Dee's second husband, died on November 17, 2004. He was a quiet man, easy going and kind. He was classy and the perfect gentleman. He sang, lovingly, at his church as a soloist, and also as part of the choir. No one could sing like Uncle Bill. He brought joy to all who heard his voice. He enjoyed the family reunions where he hung out with the uncles and nephews, laughing and joking and just having a great time.

Aunt Dee and Uncle Bill shared a deep love for each other, being together some 43 years. They lived their lives simply, plainly, and with dignity until he passed away at 82 years old.

Aunt Dee's legacy lives on through her nieces and nephews even though she is in a realm of existence that we can not enter. Sometimes when I have visited her, and I looked in her eyes, I imagined that, for a split second she recognized who I was. On the last visit to her, taken there by my cousin, Herbert, I became emotional when I left her. I was thinking of the past, reminiscing of her in her prime, and when she was in her right mind. She seems happy and content, always smiling and laughing to herself.

To God be the glory for He has done great and marvelous things in the life of my precious Aunt Dee.

Uncle Sunny

My uncle, Theodore Roosevelt "Sunny" Jones, was the tenth child and the fourth son of James Knox Polk Jones and Dessie Anna Thompson Jones. There was another son, Floyd, that was born in July, 1928 and died in October, 1929. Floyd was born three years after Aunt Dee and four years before Sunny. Sunny was born on April 10, 1932 in Fitzhugh, Arkansas. Like his older brothers, he was handsome and a typical, goes without saying, "ladies' man." He has a winning smile, and a friendly, joking manner. He enjoys "horsing around" with everybody. As a young man, in his teens, he kept me in "stitches." He used to draw cartoons, with funny looking characters and I would laugh until my jaws hurt. He was offended by my laughter because he was trying to be serious. He was really good at doing those cartoons; he could have made a living being a cartoonist, a journalist if he had wanted to go in that direction. Sunny had many skills and began to think about what he wanted to do with his life. We were very close at that time, more like a brother - sister, than uncle - niece relationship. I looked forward to his many visits to Chicago when he lived in Detroit with Papa.

In the year of Sunny's birth, 1932, Franklin Delano Roosevelt was elected President, promising to bring a "New Deal" for everyone. It brought hope to Black families who were experiencing agricultural distress and also racial oppression in the South. A second major wave of black migration began as they sought better lives for their families. They moved to the cities in the North that were rumored to be booming industrial centers. Cultural changes were taking place that brought pride and encouragement, like Bill "Bojangles" Robinson starring in the first all-black talking movie, "Harlem Is Heaven", and "Fats" Waller recorded "Ain't Misbehaving", his biggest hit.

Sunny spent his early childhood in Fitzhugh. He was 5 years old when his mother passed away, so his older sisters cared for him. As a young man, he moved to Detroit, where his dad migrated to, and married a new wife, Sally Evans. He attended high school there where he met Shirley Allison, fell in love, and married, and had five children. Shirley was drop-dead gorgeous and Sunny was smitten.

Sunny and Shirley lived in Detroit for a while and then moved to San Diego, California where they continued to build their family. Their children are Renee, Theodore Bradford, Danny Eric, Beaurette Michael, and Donna. They all live in California, with the exception of "Teddy". He moved to San Antonio, Texas years ago, where he built his life and pursued his dreams.

Shirley and I were close as young mothers. We were having our kids around the same time, so we had a lot to talk about. She, along with my aunt, Erse and me, spent time together talking about our husbands, our kids, and our life's dream. Shirley was always moving, making things happen. She was a real "go-getter", striving to make a beautiful life for her kids.

Sunny and Shirley bought their home there on Bonita Drive in San Diego many years ago. They continue to live in that beautiful home to this day, surrounded by their grandchildren and their great grandchildren.

Sunny has two children from another union, Denita Harris and Andre T. Harris.

Renee Jones Goring is the oldest child and first daughter of Theodore Jones and Shirley Allison Jones. She was born on July 20, 1951 in Detroit, Michigan. She was born in the same year as Stanley and Sandra, our cousins, and one year before my oldest daughter, Sharon.

I remember that year well because some of my favorite songs and movies came out, like "Hello Young Lovers," "Getting To Know You", "Come On-a My House", "In the Cool, Cool, Cool of the Evening", "Cry," and "Kisses Sweeter Than Wine". Some of the movies were "From Here To Eternity", "The Rose Tattoo", "The End of the Affair," and "The Caine Mutiny".

Renee is very beautiful, light complexioned like her mom, with a wonderful smile that shows sparkling white teeth, a friendly personality, and a bright intelligence. She simply adores her mom and dad and is totally "there for them" to meet their every need. She loves to laugh and is always looking for the positive in every situation.

Renee lives in San Diego where her only child, Kimberly Goring Anderson also lives with her husband, Mark and her son, Jordan Rene Goring.

Theodore Bradford "Teddy" Jones, was the second child and first son born to Sunny and Shirley Jones. He was born on May 23, 1956 in San Diego, California, the same year as our cousin, Darrell and my youngest daughter, Katrina.

Teddy spent his childhood and his teen years in the California School System's elementary and high school. He was an eager student, trying to learn all he could. Teddy wanted to be his own person, he wanted to be independent and "go his own way". He was handsome and personable, so having girls pursue him was almost "second nature". Even with all the attention, Teddy kept his eye on the "goal", the "prize". He continued to pursue his goals, alone, as he moved to San Antonio, Texas. He lived there for several years and had one son, Theodore Bradford, Jr.

After a while, Teddy longed for his mother and father. He went back to San Diego to visit them and tragically in 2013, he was involved in a terrible accident while riding his bike. He did not have on a helmet, suffered brain trauma to the head and remained in a coma for several days before passing away. My uncle, Sunny, and my aunt, Shirley have not gotten over the loss of Teddy. His brothers and sisters were devastated, stunned by such a grievous thing as losing their oldest brother.

A little more than a year after Teddy's death, his only son, died as well. Such a tragedy, but we believe they are together in heaven in the loving arms of our Lord and Savior Jesus Christ.

We yield to the sovereignty of our God. To Him be the glory.

Danny Eric Jones was the third child and second son born to Theodore Roosevelt Jones and Shirley Allison Jones. He was born on April 30, 1957, in San Diego, California, the same year as our cousin, Marcia. He is a genuinely nice guy; a nice person to be around. Danny loved the family reunions. I remember one year in particular when it was held in Chicago, and Danny came. He had been so excited about coming and when he got to Chicago, he enjoyed the activities that were presented. He stayed with my daughter, Katrina and Butch, her husband.

Trina stayed at the building at 8201 South Peoria and enjoyed hosting her cousin, Danny, from California.

Danny lives in San Diego with his wife, Roselle,. They have three children, Juliette Nicole Jones, Danny Eric Jones, Jr., and De 'Ondre Southall Jones. I was amazed when Danny had two grandkids. How time flies.

Beaurette Michael "Snoopy" Jones, was the fourth child and the third son of Theodore Roosevelt Jones and Shirley Allison Jones. He was born on June 25, 1958 in San Diego, California. We call him "Snoopy," a nickname he hates. He prefers to be called "Michael", but he will always be Snoopy to me. The year in which he was born was significant. Dwight D. Eisenhower was President of the United States at the time. National

Black leaders called a summit meeting and demanded that the President address full civil and voting rights. Pres. Eisenhower said, "Be patient". Also that year, the Rev. Martin Luther King, Jr. was stabbed by a deranged black woman while he autographed copies of his book, "Stride Toward Freedom". The book was about the Montgomery bus boycott. Dr. King was in Harlem, New York at the time, and he did recover from his wounds. Artistically, "Little Richard" Penniman recorded his record "Tutti Frutti" and it sold over 3 million copies. And choreographer Alvin Ailey founded the Alvin Ailey Dance Theater, which premiered in New York City.

Michael, like his brothers and sisters, absolutely adores his parents. He makes countless sacrifices to make sure they are being taken care of. As their needs increase in their older age, Snoopy lovingly meets those needs. He brought them to the last family reunion in Las Vegas, Nevada. It was a great reunion, each one more precious than the one before. We have 3 of our 11 patriarchs and matriarchs left, so we treasure each moment with them.

Beaurette Michael Jones and his wife, Tina Jones live in California with their daughters, Jacqueline Annette Jones and Jennifer Ashley Jones. Their prominence is proof of a beautiful family trying to bring happiness and contentment to others.

<u>Donna</u> <u>Annette</u> <u>Jones</u> <u>Duniver</u>, is the fifth child and second daughter of Theodore Roosevelt Jones and Shirley Allison Jones. She is the baby of the family and the next to the last of our 41 cousins. Donna was born in 1960 in San Diego, California. She is our most energetic, animated and bubbly one ever. She just loves life and wants to make sure she savors every moment. Donna enjoys not only, the family reunions but she loves a great party. At our last reunion, Donna did food and had an additional gathering of family members, making sure no one got "bored". Just kidding. We were in Vegas so no way were we going to be bored, but the family members enjoyed another occasion to be together.

Donna absolutely loves being on Facebook. She communicates beautifully on social media with great pictures, great meals, and again, great parties at Christmas, at Thanksgiving and other holidays. She does a lot of swimming, sometimes at a pool, and sometimes on the beach. She uses it to exercise and also as pleasure, as well. Donna loves to dance which makes her the life of the party.

Donna made her parents happy very early on. She has always been beautiful, a combination of her mom and dad, and resembling her dad's sisters, as well. The guys take a second look, as well as a backward glance when Donna is around. She met her husband, Calvin Ray Duniver, and they fell in love and married in San Diego. They had three sons from their union, Jermaine Anthony Duniver, Jason Adam Duniver, and Walter Ray Duniver. These guys are three drop dead gorgeous men who look more like mom than dad. Just kidding, they are really handsome displaying resemblance to both parents. Donna is an outstanding mother. When her son developed life threatening kidney problems and needed a new kidney, she made the ultimate sacrifice for her son and gave him one of her kidneys. There were healing concerns and medical adjustments that had to be made, but he survived and is doing well. Donna had some problems, but is doing quite well.

Donna lives in San Diego with her husband surrounded by her beloved four grand kids. She visits her mom and dad often, hovering over them and fussing over them, making sure they go to the doctor, and making sure they are comfortable, content, and happy. To God be the glory for His mercy and His grace.

Aunt Ersé

My aunt, Earselean Estella Jones West, was the eleventh child and eighth daughter born to James Knox Polk Jones and Dessie Anna Thompson Jones. She was born on January 13, 1935 in Fitzhugh, Arkansas. Her precious mother died two years later in April, 1937. "Ersé," affectionately called by everyone who knows her, was then nurtured and loved by her older sisters, Thelma and Willie. Her early childhood was spent in Fitzhugh, but when her sisters married and migrated to other cities and states, she moved with them in St. Louis. She was 4 years old. Aunt Ruthie took Erse to San Diego and she lived with her for about 1½ years. She lived most of those years with Aunt Willie. Erse lived with her father and his new wife, Sally Evans Jones, in Detroit, Michigan for about 5 years. Those were not happy years for her so she moved back to St. Louis, Missouri where she finished her schooling, got married, and built her family.

Erse is one of the most intelligent persons I have met in my lifetime. She "soared" through her studies, making excellent grades and learning wonderful life skills. She was beautifully educated in the St. Louis Public

School System and then attended the Lincoln University Jefferson City, Missouri, where she received her Bachelors' Degree in Education. She began teaching elementary school children in the St. Louis Public School System in the late 1960's.

Erse became, as I describe her, the teacher's teacher. She not only instructed, directed, and nurtured children, but she taught them how to think and how to "discover" things, "discover" the hidden jewels of life. I remember visiting her in St. Louis when my three girls, Sharon, Linda, and Trina were little. I remember her taking them outside and showing them the flowers and plants and explaining to them how things grow in the earth. She showed them how the "circle of life" works with animals, and teaching these things with such patience and gentleness.

She visited me in South Holland a few years back and she spent such a wonderful time with Kyonna and Le Shawn, especially LeShawn. They had a similar bond like my son, Lenard, had with Erse. She was drawn to his "quirkiness" and his great reading skills. The children were mesmerized, not only by her knowledge, but by her patience, her understanding, and her interest in them. She asked thought-provoking questions and listened to their answers, sometimes countering with another question. When she returned home, she sent them monetary gifts and 2 big books (500 pages) for Le Shawn to read.

Erse has been the closest aunt to my heart because we are more like sisters. We are only 3 weeks apart; she was born January 13, 1935 and I was born February 6, 1935. Erse lost her mom and I lost both my grandmothers, a few months apart, in 1937. We share a lot. She ended up being the sister I never had.

Although we have taken similar paths and we share so many experiences, our personalities are almost opposite. Ersé is feisty, brutally honest, very outspoken, and very articulate. She sews beautifully, like her sisters, and is an excellent cook. In her younger days, she possessed a "green thumb", creating gardens of beautiful flowers and plants.

Erse married her husband, Alvin Lewis "Nibbles" West in 1953, and they remained together until his death on March 2, 2011. His friends and some of our relatives called him "Nibbles," but he was always "Alvin" to me. Like Erse, he attended Lincoln University in Jefferson City, Missouri where he received his Bachelor's Degree. His graduate studies were done at Webster University. During his tenure at Lincoln, Alvin pledged into the Omega Psi Phi Fraternity. He loved the fraternity and faithfully served the Upsilon Omega Chapter in St. Louis for over 50 years.

Alvin was extremely intelligent, very bright, "oozing" confidence and assurance. He was a genuinely nice guy underneath his "suave", "smooth", knowledgeable demeanor. He loved to read, reading several newspapers each day. He absolutely loved traveling and snapping picture after picture, as he did on one of the cruises I went on. He and Erse had two children together, Ursula Thea and Adrian. Alvin was a proud dad who enjoyed talking about "Thea" and "Agy" and their many accomplishments. He encouraged his children to go higher and higher in pursuit of their dreams. He and Erse built a strong family unit around love, trust, discipline, and much humor.

Alvin retired from the Defense Mapping Agency in the Aeronautical Charts Division (DMAAC) of the Federal Government, where he led a fulfilling career as a cartographer in the Chart Research Division.

He loved life and he lived it to the fullest until his health started to fail. He was fun - loving with a wonderful smile and a hearty laugh. He was fearless and enjoyed doing things in his own way. I, along with Erse and his family celebrated his life, thanking God that he touched our lives in such a wonderful way.

Erse has been with me through my grief, and through my sorrow, and through my pain but also she has shared in my joys and my good times. When I lost my son, Lenard, I was in such a dark place, in such distress and sadness, but Erse comforted me with words of encouragement and peace.

Both, Erse and Alvin, traveled extensively over the years. On one of her trips, she went to Juneau, Alaska. While there, she purchased a beautiful, sparkly piece of jewelry to send to me. The piece of jewelry is a small gold bee with the front of it covered with Swarovski crystals. I cherish it and each time I wear it, I think of my aunt, Erse.

Recently, Erse's family honored her with a big, fabulous birthday party at a "sidity" banquet hall in St. Louis. It was her 80th birthday and a wonderful tribute to her longevity. I did my own little tribute to her and sent it to Thea to read at the Party. My cousin, "San" read it in my absence. In addition to the tribute, I included parts of chapter 3 of Ecclesiastes because Erse said she loved the book of Ecclesiastes. I mentioned that the book from the Bible, God's Word was written by Solomon, David's son, in the 10th century, B.C. Included was Chapter 3 verses 1-8.

Erse enjoyed the honor bestowed upon her by her family. She said she will never forget all the wonderful words of people who heaped praise and adoration on her. She said she didn't remember doing some of things, but she felt proud and thankful. It was a great night. I did not attend because it was held on the same night as my "photo shoot".

Erse and I share a love of reading and a love of service to kids and a love of family. She has never, to my knowledge, missed a family reunion.

Ursula Thea West Tate, was born in 1954 in St. Louis, Missouri to the union of Earselean Estella Jones West and Alvin Lewis West. She is the first born child, and the only daughter of Erse. All of her cousins call her "Thea", including me, but I always thought "Ursula Thea" was a beautiful name. Thea was, and is extremely bright. Even as a kid, she excelled in her studies and her extra curricula activities. She was very well educated in the St. Louis Public School System at the elementary and high school level. Thea later completed her college degree and went on to graduate courses and degrees.

I still have the newspaper article and picture when Thea was awarded second place honors as part of the court of the Illustrious Commandress Queen Coronation and Dinner Dance at the St. Louis Gateway Hotel. It was in the early 1970's. Thea has on a beautiful sleeveless white, long dress, decorated with a big white corsage, white shoes, long white gloves, and a huge afro. It's a picture of all six ladies in the court. It has gotten "brown" and faded with age, but I keep it because Thea is highlighted. In the same newspaper and on a related picture is my Aunt Willie pinning a corsage on an honoree at a Queen Coronation ceremony. Aunt Willie was the co-chairman of the Ways and Means Committee.

Thea married the love of her life, John Dennis Tate, around 1974 or 1975. They had a beautiful, elegant wedding that made the society page in the newspaper in St. Louis, Missouri. They have 2 beautiful daughters: Kristen Leigh Tate and Karyn Elizabeth Tate. They lived in St. Louis for several years building their family and pursuing their careers. "Dennis" as we all call him became a pilot with United Airlines. They later relocated to Atlanta, Georgia where they purchased their home that looks like a page out of a movie magazine. Their daughters traveled all over the world, sometimes alone, sometimes with their parents, and sometimes just the two of them. They are global-minded and absolutely fearless. Kristen and Karyn did their undergraduate studies in different states, attending graduate school later. Kristen settled in New York City where she married Morten Friis Olsen from Denmark. They have one little precious daughter, Vega, who is a little more than a year old.

Thea is an Operations Manager at Turner Broadcasting in Atlanta. She is admired and highly respected at TMC. I can imagine working for Turner Movie Classics' empire company must be interesting, if not downright exciting. Dennis has the distinction of being our family's first pilot. I discovered in my reading that it's a "glamorous" job, piloting large aircraft packed with passengers from all over the world. It takes a lot of training just to get licensed to fly these planes, let alone getting hired by a major airline. Pilots have a tremendous amount of responsibility and must make critical decisions in seconds, as the U.S. Airways crash on the Hudson River demonstrated. Dennis safely flies the plane, but he does much more than just fly. He checks weather and flight plans, and has to make sure the plane has been pre-flighted and all logs have been reviewed. When he's ready to take off on a flight, he oversees the "push-back" and then taxis to the runway. While he's flying, Dennis monitors aircraft systems and communicates with FAA and the company. In his early years with United Airlines, Dennis had to work long hours and strange shifts, often being away from home for several days. Dennis has been a pilot for several decades; his demeanor is always "calm, cool and collected".

Thea, Dennis, Adrian, Veronica, and our cousins, The Collins' Family, hosted the August, 2010 family reunion in Atlanta. We had a wonderful time. It went from August 5th, Thursday to Sunday, August 8th. We were greeted on Thursday with a cleverly crafted, homemade card entitled "Greetings from Georgia". It had a little sprig of rosemary on the cover; inside was this message: "Rememberance" by Peggy Cathay

"Reunions are for families reuniting
Together again, laughing and crying
Remembering all the times that we had
Most of them happy, some of them sad

But you know the fun just doesn't begin
'Till somebody says, "Hey, remember when . . .?"

They told us: In the language of flowers Rosemary is for Rememberence.

Take this sprig of Rosemary and rub it between your hands. Then cup your hands over your face and take a few deep breaths. Now sit back, relax, close your eyes and remember . . ."

On Friday, the Banquet was held at an upscale, elegant restaurant where we enjoyed the fellowship of each other, as well as, a delicious meal.

On Saturday, the picnic was held at the Piedmont Park. The menu was mouth watering: baby back ribs, barbeque chicken, beef brisket, baked beans, potato salad, cole slaw, corn, bread, brownies, cookies, iced tea, soft drinks, and water.

And then on Sunday, the traditional church service was held at the hotel in Suite #1424 on August 8, 2010 from 8:00 AM to 9:00 AM. Adrian served as the master of ceremony and Dennis brought the opening prayer. Our cousin, Cheryl Collins read the scripture, Psalm 96; and Minister L. Crawford, Skatavia Crawford, Joe Crawford, Jr., and Cheetara Crawford did the "Praise & Worship." The speaker for the morning was Rev. Crawford, Sr., who spoke from II Corinthians 13:11. He spoke wonderfully about family – that the "cord is not easily broken". Adrian and Kristen led the audience into "A Libation Ceremony". This was held in the place of the Candle lighting Ceremony, which is usually the tradition at our reunions. A libation is a prayer used in traditional African life. It is performed at significant events, such as the birth of a child, a wedding or in this case, a family reunion. According to Morris F. X. Jeff, Jr., founder of Sankafa Communiversity, an African-centered University in New Orleans, the pouring of libations is a long standing African tradition born of the knowledge that life never dies. "Everything that lives returns to its source. The source of life – our ancestral heritage – is revealed again and over again to the world. Thus life is a circle. In that circle there is no distinction between past, present and future.

Bryant Hedgeman read poetry entitled "He Only Takes the Best", and the family/audience sang together "What A Fellowship". Thea offered the last prayer for a safe journey home, and we all left, happy that we had had another beautiful family reunion.

Thea and Dennis reside in Alpharetta, Georgia where they have lived for a number of years. They have a beautiful family life, now centered around their first grandchild, Vega. Kristen and Mortan live in Brooklyn, New York and Karyn lives in Washington, D. C.

Adrian Douglas West, is the second child and only son of Earselean Estella Jones West and Alvin Louis West. Adrian, also known as "Agy", was born in 1955 in St. Louis, Missouri. He is the only one of our cousins born in 1955. Adrian, like his dad, is extremely good looking, down to earth, and really into healthy living. He's a happy go lucky guy who treats everyone like he wants to be treated. Like the others in the West family, he is smart, bright and intelligent. I guess you would characterize him as your typical "nerd", the kind like Bill Gates or Steve Jobs. He's an air traffic controller, for decades now, as a result of his highly specialized knowledge, his skills, and his abilities. He has been trained to maintain the safe, orderly and "expeditious flow of air traffic in the global air traffic control system." I read that air traffic controllers must apply "separation rules" to keep planes at a safe distance from each other in their area of responsibility and to move all planes safely and efficiently through their assigned sector of airspace, as well as, on the ground. Like pilots, controllers have an incredibly big responsibility while on duty and they have to make countless split-second decisions on a daily basis. Although Adrian is now a specialist in his field, he experiences "stress and strain" dealing with equipment, configurations, weather, traffic volume, human factors, and who knows what else.

Adrian, as I look at him and remember him as a young man, was kind of a "natural" for that kind of career. He was super organized, quick with numeric computations and mathematics; he had assertive and firm decision making skills; he was always a pretty "cool" guy; and had an excellent memory. Like his mom, he has excellent speaking skills; and he was in excellent physical and medical condition. He made an excellent Air Traffic Control Officer.

Adrian moved from St. Louis to the state of Georgia to complete his undergraduate and graduate studies. He met his beautiful wife, Veronica Denise Thompkins West in Atlanta, Georgia. Veronica is so prominent in her own right, having served in the military, having served her community as a licensed, certified nurse, all while pursuing and completing her academic career. She and Adrian have built their family in a place called Fayetteville, Georgia. They have two sons, Adrian, Jr. and Jonathan Michael, who were born in Georgia and got their elementary, high school, and undergraduate diplomas and degrees from the school system there.

Adrian is a genuinely nice guy, who is special to me because he was great friends with my youngest son, Lenard. I admire him for the wonderful balance in his personality. In spite of his prominence, and his growth as a person, he remains the same, he's always "Agy".

To God be the glory, great things he has done in the family of my aunt, Ersé.

Mattie Louise Evans Hall

Mattie Louise Evans Hall was born to Sally Evans, probably in Detroit, Michigan. Sally Evans was the 2nd wife of my grandfather, James Knox Polk Jones. Sally Evans Jones died in Detroit, Michigan. Mattie married Dolphus Frank Hall in Detroit. We all called him "Frank," and he absolutely adored his wife, Mattie. Whatever she wanted or needed, he was there to get it for her. There was nothing too big or too small, if she wanted it, tried his best to get it. Mattie enjoyed being the step-sister of the children of James Knox Polk Jones. They got along well together, laughing a lot and talking a lot together. Most of the time spent with Mattie was in Detroit where the family reunions started. The family met there at Papa's big house and Mattie and Frank were always there. They had five children: Bonita Roberts, Tommy Lee McIntire (died on April 2, 2003), Delora Hall, Dolphus Frank Hall, Jr., and Michael Anthony Hall. Mattie has grandchildren and great grandchildren.

To God be the glory for the rich legacy of Mattie and Frank Hall.

Jeanette Rosemay Jones Smith

Jeanette Rosemay Jones Smith was born on May 30, 1923 in Chicago, Illinois to the union of Floyd Kenneth Jones and Minnie Roberta Jones. Jeanette is Daddy's first cousin, the oldest daughter and first child to Uncle Floyd and Aunt Minnie. When Jeanette was 8 years old the family moved to Kansas City, Kansas where she attended public school - graduating from Summer High School in 1940. She also obtained a cosmetologist license in 1941. Lincoln University in Jefferson City, Missouri was her college of choice. There she met and married Julius M. Smith. Later, she attended Wayne State University for her graduate studies.

Jeanette and her husband, Julius both developed warm relationships with their Lincoln University alumni members and with Kappa Alpha Psi Fraternity members through the years. As a result, their home was a "beehive" of social, civic and family activities.

Jeanie and Joe – as they were affectionately referred to, had no children of their own, but they were always there to "help raise" nieces, nephews, god - children and any young friend who needed advice or just someone to listen.

For many years, Jeanette was a legal secretary in the Law Offices of Morris & Senator Cora M. Brown in downtown Detroit. Later, she was appointed auditor - comptroller at Home Federal Savings & Loan where she worked until her retirement. She was baptized into Christian fellowship at Strangers Rest Baptist Church in Kansas City.

Jeanette's husband passed away some years ago. Jeanette died on February 9, 2001 in Detroit, Michigan surrounded by those who loved and cared for her.

I thank God for the wonderful life of Jeanette. May her legacy live on in her nieces and nephews.

Alice Estella Jones Morris

Alice Estella Jones Morris was born on December 13, 1925 in Chicago, Illinois to the union of Floyd Kennedy Jones and Minnie Roberts Jones. She was the second child and second daughter born to them. Uncle Floyd was my grandfather's younger brother. He died at 60 years old in Detroit, Michigan on March 25, 1954. Uncle Floyd and Aunt Minnie moved their family first to Kansas City, Kansas where Alice and her sisters, Jeanette and Dorothy attended public school. The family moved to Detroit, Michigan and that became the city where the girls married and raised their own families.

Alice married Norman Julius Morris on April 21, 1950 in Detroit. Their only child, Jill Morris, was born in Detroit on April 9, 1963. Jill later moved to Forest Park, Georgia where she currently resides. Alice and Jill have a very special closeness and a beautiful love for each other, possibly because Jill is an only child. I know something about that kind of love, for I experienced that with my own mother.

Alice chose law as her profession and as such, she was the one that executed the Jones estate and the Jones' Brothers' property management and sales. She, legally, over saw the distribution, as well as the record keeping for such a big responsibility. She took the responsibility of making sure that the heirs from James Knox Polk Jones and Floyd Kennedy Jones shared in the property sales from the land owned in Fitzhugh, Arkansas; land originally acquired by Jim Jones back in the late 1800's and early 1900's. I received documents from Alice (on behalf of Daddy) dated June, 1998 concerning the sale of some of the Jones property in Fitzhugh, Arkansas. It was the F. K. Jones and the J.P. Jones Trust for the sale of the Charles Jones farm. There were 14 heirs of Jones' children to distribute to: Papa and Uncle Floyd's children.

Alice now lives in Southfield, Michigan. She lives in a senior citizens' assisted living facility that she just loves. I talked to her by phone a couple of years ago. She said she sold her house and gave most of her furnishings to her daughter, Jill, and her nieces and nephews. She said she "did not look back". She still has her independence in the facility and her beloved nieces and nephews check on her regularly. Jill lives in Atlanta and keeps "tabs" on her. Recently, Alice sent me birth and death records of my grandfather's mom and dad, and his sisters and brothers. I learned valuable info from those records.

Alice is 90 years young this year; to God be the glory.

Dorothy Charline Jones Carter

Dorothy Charline Jones Carter was born on September 15, 1930 in Pine Bluff, Arkansas to the union of Floyd Kennedy Jones and Minnie Roberta Jones. She was the third daughter and youngest child of Uncle Floyd and Aunt Minnie. Dorothy spent her younger years in Kansas City, Kansas where she attended elementary school. She later moved to Toledo, Ohio where she met and married her husband Otis Carter. They married on July 26, 1947. Dorothy and Otis later moved to Detroit, Michigan where they had together seven children, all of them born in Detroit. Her children were: Pamela Lenora Carter who was born on June 23, 1947. Tragically, Pamela died less than 20 years later on April 23, 1967.

- Michael Anthony Carter was born on November 21, 1950 and married his wife Pamela Lynn Fanning on August 26, 1972 in Indianapolis, Indiana. They now reside in Franklin, Tennessee. They have 2 children
- Patricia Carter was born on January 7, 1954. She married Clinton Brackett, and they reside in Detroit, Mich. They have 3 children.
- Paula Jean Carter was born on April 28, 1956 and married Ralph King on August 29, 1980. She married a second time to Kenneth Bunch on August 4, 1992 in Detroit, Michigan.
- Peggy Eleanor Carter was born on March 30, 1958 in Detroit and currently resides there. She has 2 children.
- Mark Clayton Carter was born on June 3, 1959 in Detroit and went on to marry Carolyn Haliburton on August 29, 1989. They have 3 children.
- Marvin Kennedy Carter was born on February 26, 1962 in Detroit and tragically, he died on October 15, 2004. Marvin and my youngest son, Lenard were good friends. They always hung out together at the family reunions. Marvin had a beautiful voice, singing professionally, as well as, in his church and at special events. Marvin and Lenard died within months of each other in the year 2004.

Dorothy was such a nice, warm, friendly person. She absolutely loved her big family and took pride in all their successes and their pursuits. She enjoyed the family reunions and wrote us to let us know how she felt.

Dorothy, Alice, and Jeanette, all three, came to one of our reunions and we were honored and happy to see them there together. They were wonderful – Dorothy was "bubbly", Alice was warm and sweet, and Jeanette was reserved and elegant, but so appreciative of all her cousins. To God be glory for the great legacy of these 3 sisters.

Sally O'Connor Taylor

Sally O'Connor Taylor was born in 1927 in Fitzhugh, Arkansas to the union of Jennie "Sissy" Thompson and Thomas O'Connor. Jennie Thompson O'Connor was my grandmother's, Dessie Anna Thompson Jones sister. Sally is always reminding us that we have Thompson blood in our veins, as well as, Jones blood. I don't remember Sally ever missing a family reunion. She loves the family and it shows. With her quiet, unassuming manner, Sally has managed to encourage her nieces and nephews and her own children and grandchildren to attend the family reunions. Not only did they come for every reunion, but they came en masse - Gloria's children and grandchildren and Barbara's children and grands. Her niece, Barbara, Gloria's sister, has gone on to be with the Lord, but her spirit is still with us.

Sally married D. L. Taylor and they had two children, Valerie Jenkins Taylor and Gerald D. Taylor. Sally currently lives in Milwaukee, Wisconsin with her daughter, who is the caregiver for her. Sally lived most of her life in Chicago, over east in an apartment building that she loved, until her health started to fail. Sally's children Valerie and Gerald now have children and grandchildren and they simply adore Sally. Although she has some health issues, she is happy and content, surrounded by her beloved children, grandchildren, and great grandchildren.

Gloria O'Connor Felt

Gloria O'Connor Felt, my cousin, was born on May 14, 1938, in Chicago, Illinois to the union of James O'Connor and Althea Vinson O'Connor. She is Sally O'Connor Taylor's niece, and the granddaughter of Jennie "Sissy" Thompson. Aunt Jennie was my grandmother's (Dessie Anna Thompson) sister. Gloria has no memory of her grandparents having been born in Chicago. Some of our ancestors remained in Fitzhugh, Arkansas. They seemed to be content to raise their children and build their homes with much less comfort and resources than our generation.

Gloria was born in the same year as our cousin, Herbert "Junior" Boykin. Her nickname growing up was "Boots". She was called that because she had very small feet; so small until sometimes her mom had trouble finding shoes to fit her. Both her parents, James and Althea were artists. They loved making art pieces using images, colors, paints, and other materials; anything to create art. Gloria has beautiful, pleasant memories of her parents.

Gloria has 4 siblings: James, Jr. who was born one year after her in 1939; Thomas "Tommy" O'Connor was born in 1941; Vincent O'Connor, who was born in 1942; and Barbara Jean O'Connor Mayberry who was born in 1945. They were all born in Chicago, Illinois. Thomas was married to Flora O'Connor and they had three children – Anthony, Barbara, and Althea. Thomas and James, Jr. are both deceased. Vincent is married to Kathy O'Connor and they have no children. Barbara Jean was the youngest child, and Gloria's only sister. She married Elijah Mayberry on May 2, 1966. They had four children, Victor, Latrice, Elijah, Jr., and Shawn. Barbara and her family lived in Chicago for many years, but moved to Maywood, Illinois in 1977 and there, they raised their children and built their family. Barbara was employed at the "Phillip 66" on 9th Avenue in Maywood for more than twenty years. She was considered "a bright ray of sunshine" by her customers. Barbara was not only a cashier, but she was a teacher, advisor, and a friend. She passed away, suddenly, in August, 2005 (around the same time my daughter, Trina, passed away). When Barbara died, Mary Mitchell, columnist with the Chicago Sun-Times, mentioned Barbara's passing in her column. She had beautiful, glowing, warm words for Barbara in the article, praising her for making a difference and bringing so much joy in the lives of others.

Barbara really enjoyed her life to the fullest, living each day as if it was her last. She enjoyed going on family vacations, spending time with her kids especially. She was an avid card player and looked forward to her weekend trips to the casino with her daughter, Latrice "Tricy". Barbara loved her ten grandchildren and gave them special love and special attention on a daily basis.

Gloria was devastated at the loss of her sister, and has fond and sweet memories of the times they spent together.

Gloria has three children, and several grand children, and one great grand child. Her children are: Yolanda Tillis Swanson who is married to Leon Swanson who has three children – Ricardo Johnson, Andre Swanson, and James Swanson. Gloria's second daughter is Renea Primous who is married to Vada Primous and they have three children – Jerome, Tyrone, and Daniel; and one grandchild, Jerome, Jr. Gloria's only son, Theophilus "Theo" Tillis is married to Cara Tillis. They have three kids – Karisma, Amir, and Kiara.

To God be the glory for the O'Connor family and the rich legacy that is carried on, daily, in the lives of their descendants.

Cousins That I Remember From Years Ago

- Beatrice "Bea" Mitchell Moore and Edgar Moore I remember Bea and Edgar when I was a kid in St. Louis, Missouri. They lived close to Aunt Alma when she lived on "Finney". They visited Aunt Alma and Uncle Sentclair often. Bea and Edgar are the parents of our cousins:
  Edgar Moore, Jr., James Herman Moore, and Donald Moore.
- Odell Mitchell Swanson
  Odell was Bea's sister and I remember her well. She had one son, William Harold Swanson, who was called "Billie." Odell loved Billie with the passion of a mom for her only child.
- Daisy Thompson Gillespie
  Daisy was my very dear cousin who was more like my aunt because of her love and care for me during my early teen years and beyond. She, along with Elva, mentored me when I came to Chicago from St. Louis. Daisy did not have biological children of her own but she showered her attention and special love to, not only me, but to her nieces and nephews. She was my dad's "double first cousin" for her dad, Edward "Ebbie" Thompson, was his mom's brother; and her mother, Penola Jones Thompson, was his father's sister. Daisy had one sister, Sally Thompson, and two brothers, Walter Henry Thompson and Edward Taylor "T-Boy" Thompson. Sally died at a very young age so I never got to see her. Walter Henry remained in Arkansas mostly so I can't quite remember him, but his children lived here in Chicago, so I got to meet them. He named his oldest child and only daughter, Henri Mable. Henri Mable was later diagnosed with cancer. She died

after much suffering. Henri Mable's three brothers were Edward Thompson, Floyd Thompson, and Harry Thompson. Daisy was very close to Henri Mable, treating her like her very own daughter. T-Boy, Daisy's youngest brother, was born in Weldon, Arkansas, but moved to St. Louis where he married Alma Thompson. They had four children, Velma "Val", Donald, Willard, and Douglas. I saw T-Boy when I visited St. Louis. He and Alma were such nice people. Alma, his wife, was very close friends with my Aunt Alma, working at the same place for years. T-Boy died on August 20, 1986 in St. Louis.

Daisy married Virve "Virval" Gillespie when she was a young woman. Daisy was tall, fair-skinned and striking. She had the kind of smile that was contagious and she had a soft, warm, friendly demeanor. Daisy loved her husband and did everything that she could to be a good wife and to make his life pleasant, but he seemed "cool" to her. He did not show warmth to her, in my opinion (on the outside looking in). Daisy had the most expensive taste when it came to her house; the most elegant sheets and matching pillow cases, beautiful, unusual quilts, and the prettiest bed spreads. She loved fluffy towels and wash cloths, the fluffier, the better. She had pretty "doilies" on her dresser and chest of drawers. Her China and crystal were the most elegant. She knew where everything belonged and made sure everything was in place. She gave me nice gifts for my little small apartment after Lenzo and I married. I remember when she died. I had talked to her on the phone in the hospital 2 days before she passed away. She was so weak, I couldn't understand her words. Her death left me devastated and sad. And yet, as time passed, her teachings, her admonitions, her lessons on being a lady, her high expectations for me, and her affection for me has helped me realize the value of family.

• Tommy "Hughey" Huggins.
Tommy Hughey as we called him was born on December 17, 1913 in Fitzhugh, Arkansas, the only child of Oscar and Nesh "Neshi" Thompson Huggins. He was my dad's first cousin for Aunt Nesh was my grandmother's sister. I remember seeing Aunt Nesh when I visited down south in Fitzhugh. She lived there most of her life until she came to Chicago to be with Tommy Huey, her beloved son. She absolutely idolized her son, putting her hopes and dreams on his shoulders.

Tommy Huey used to visit Lenzo and I when we lived in the Ida B. Wells Projects. He'd come over for dinner and we enjoyed his company.

Tommy Huey died on September 6, 1980 at the Veteran's Medical Center Hospital in Chicago. He had served faithfully as a Sargeant in World War II from 1942 to 1945.

He moved to Chicago in 1950 where he met his wife, Mable. When he passed away, he had 14 children and 11 grandchildren.

Arthur Charles Sanders, III

We met "Art" in Chicago (through my cousin, Thurman) at one of our family reunions. He was one of our "long lost" cousins on my dad's side; the Jones side of the family. Art wrote us a letter explaining his connection to the family. The letter was dated July 1998 from Oak Park IL. Art is the great grandson of Walter Jones, who is the youngest son of my great grandfather, James Allen Jones. Art's mother's name is Dorothy Nelle Hamilton Sanders and her brother's name is William Jones Hamilton. His other uncle is Walter Larkin Hamilton (Uncle W.L.). His two children, Scarlett R. Lea and Billy Hamilton are Art's only 1st cousins. He says the three of them are the Jones brothers great grandchildren. Art says that James Allen Jones and Walter Jones had 2 sisters, one of them lived in Cleveland and then moved to California.

Carol Jones Collins

Carol Jones Collins was born to the union of Robert and Katie Belle Jones. Carol and her family were our "long lost" cousins, as well. But they have been attending the family reunions for years now and participate with our other cousins in Georgia when they are hosting the reunion. Carol married Curtis Collins and they settled in Atlanta, Georgia to raise their children. Their children and their spouses and their grandchildren all reside in the state of Georgia. They are:

1.) Nicole Collins Blair and David Blair
   Their children are: Clifford Curtis Butler, Colin Butler, and James Seamster.
2.) Joe Lee and Latanya Collins Crawford

Their children are: Chee Tara Crawford, Joe Lee Crawford, Jr., and Shatavia Crawford.

3.) Timothy and Valerie Collins Bailey

4.) Belinda Yvette Collins Collier and her children Keary Dalton, Jr. and Alexis Collier

5.) Roger E. and Tawanna Collins Grant

Their children are: Bryant Hedgeman and Roger E. Grant, Jr.

6.) Cheryl Collins

- Rufus McDonald

Rufus "Flash" McDonald was born on March 6, 1919 in Fitzhugh, Arkansas to the union of my great uncle, Walter Henry "Buddy" Thompson and Commie McDonald. Commie was Uncle Buddy's first wife; he married several times after that.

Uncle Buddy was a "rolling stone" who had several children, but Rufus was his oldest child. His second child, I believe, was Theopolis "Sugar Nun" McDonald, a boy who was crippled; and again, several children were blamed on him.

Rufus was an original member of the famed Four Step Brothers of the 1940's. They helped break the color barrier in the world of entertainment. Rufus moved to St. Louis with his family during his childhood. It has long been said that he started dancing on the local street corners in St. Louis to keep warm. He soon became known throughout the city as a top young dancer. Around 1940, he convinced his mother to let him go to Chicago to mix with some "real performers". His agent signed him up with the Louis Jourdan Show where he worked consistently up to his big break at the "Apollo Theater" in New York City.

After a two year stint in New York, Rufus left for Hollywood where he met and joined the "Four Step Brothers", also referred to as the "Eight Feet of Rhythm". After dazzling the nation, the group left for its first European Tour in 1947. In the years to come, the group performed before Royalty and Heads of State, and in over 30 countries. In doing so, they danced their way through racial barriers in America and Europe and opened doors for other black entertainers.

Returning triumphant to the states, the "Four Step Brothers" starred on stage and screen, performing in over 20 movies and on stage with Bob Hope, Milton Berle, Jerry Lewis, Donald O'Connor, Frank Sinatra, and others. I have several pictures of Rufus with not only some of those stars, but others like Peter Lorre, and Don Ameche. There are others in the picture whose names I've forgotten, black & white shiny pictures.

In 1989, in Hollywood, California the group became the first tap dancing act to have a star placed on the Hollywood Walk of Fame. At the ceremonial dinner commemorating the event the group was commended and praised for their contributions by Mayor Tom Bradley, Milton Berle, Sammy Davis, Jr., Danny Glover, and a host of other dignitaries and stars.

The Four Step Brothers nearly lost out on a chance to appear on the Texaco Star Theater because of racial prejudice. But the show's star, Milton Berle, stood up for the group. When Milton Berle wanted to book the tap dance group for the show, they did not want black acts on the show. Berle replied he would not appear if the Four Step Brothers did not. Milton Berle held out until 10 minutes before the show was scheduled to air live – at which time, Texaco relented and the show went on with The Four Step Brothers. I read Berle's words of this account on Wikipedia' biography on Milton Berle. I still have (acquired from my cousin, Elva) some newspaper articles on their tours and in 1989 when they unveiled the star on the Walk of Fame. The other members of the group were Maceo Anderson, Al Williams, and Prince Spencer. Rufus, "Flash," was married to Beatrice McCaine and they had one daughter, Debra McDonald Moore in St. Louis. He absolutely adored his daughter and after he retired from dancing, he spent much time with her and her son Christopher Moore. I remember seeing Rufus once at Uncle Buddy's house. My dad and his siblings were really proud of "Flash" and his fame.

Rufus "Flash" McDonald died on March 20, 1991 in St. Louis, Missouri at the age of 72 years. Another one of Uncle Buddy's sons, my "long lost" cousin, Donald Thomas Thompson, contacted me recently to reconnect to the family. He had been in contact with my cousin Wilma. We had a wonderful time of reminiscing. He used to visit Lenzo and I when we lived at 7429 So. Sangamon. He married the very lovely Rosa M. Thompson and they live here in Chicago on the south west side of the city.

Elva Gene Reynolds

Elva Gene Watson Reynolds was born in Fitzhugh, Arkansas on May 5, 1915. Her mother was Estelle "Stella" Thompson who was my grandmother's sister. Stella married Escue Watson who was born in Augusta, Arkansas. They later moved to Chicago, Illinois. It was always rumored in the family that Floyd Jones (my grandfather's brother) was Elva's father. Elva said she did not accept him as her father because he shunned her as a child. She said her mother loved her and cherished her as her only child and that was enough for her. Elva loved "Uncle Polk", my grandfather because he always treated her so beautifully well as his niece. Elva loved her mother and was especially devoted to her. She had this large picture of her mom that hung prominently on her wall and she took it wherever she moved and displayed it proudly. Elva admired her mother for instilling self-confidence, independence, and a strong determination to live and survive. Elva lived long after we had initially thought she was on her death bed. She survived that illness and outlived her husband, her stepson, and his wife.

Elva attended school in the state of Arkansas and was always a bright student who learned fast and well. She did not complete her schooling, but she was ever learning, citing and reciting poetry and working hard to reach her life's goals and aspirations. She particularly enjoyed one very long poem that had several stanzas. She memorized every line articulating each word. Elva was the family historian, reciting each matriarch and patriarch of the Jones family in perfect order, in the correct year of their birth. She delighted the family at the Family Reunion of 2000 in Chicago with her historical presentation. Although Elva was legally blind, she took care of herself and her affairs until a year before her death. Elva had a keen sense of fashion, wearing things that depicted her unique style and taste. She selected elegant clothes and she wore them with sophistication and class. She walked upright, shoulders straight and head up, with confidence and boldness. Her aura was one of dignity and pride. Elva was a great conversationalist and a good listener.

Elva was married twice. She married Willard Wilson Woodward and they remained together for 5 years. On December 29, 1945, she married James Ernest Reynolds, and their holy matrimony lasted almost 54 years. They had a wonderful life together. Elva absolutely adored her husband and sought to do those things that pleased him. She was a loving and faithful wife, meeting his needs willingly. James was born in Newport, Arkansas but like Elva, he went to school in Fitzhugh, Arkansas. At some point they moved to Chicago where James found work at the Wilson Meat Packing Company where he remained for fourteen years. They then moved to Los Angeles, California where he worked for the Luer's Meat Packing Company for some eighteen years. His son, Edward and his daughter-in-law, Annie persuaded Elva and James to move from Los Angeles to South Holland, Illinois to be with them, where they provided loving care and medical attention.

James was always pleasant, with a beautiful smile for everyone he met. He loved the lively art of conversation. He and Elva had a special love for each other and their marriage remained strong and beautiful until his death on May 20, 1999 in Chicago.

Elva enjoyed "doing hair". In 1951, in Chicago, she attended the Lillias Cosmetology School of Beauty Culture. She completed the course and thus began her career of beauty culture and hair design.

Elva expressed strong faith in the Lord Jesus Christ and prayed each day. She enjoyed the ministry of Rev. James Meeks and Bishop Arthur M. Brazier. She relied on God's mercy and grace for her measure of health and strength. She was well-blessed, giving God the glory for 91 years of life and breath and being. Her mind was sharp and clear as a bell. She was feisty and opinionated and exhibited a strength of will that amazed all of us.

Along with Daisy, Elva represented both the Jones and Thompson side of the family. She was close to Sally and all of my aunts who were her double first-cousins, but she called them all her "sisters." They spent a lot of time together. During Elva's illness, Sally visited her, often traveling by public transportation.

Elva passed away quietly and peacefully on a Thursday morning, December 28, 2006 in a nursing facility, surrounded by those who took special care of her at the end. God blessed Elva whereof we are glad. To Him be honor and glory and majesty and dominion.

The Years of Loved Ones' Death

<u>1996</u>   Aunt Alma

<u>1997</u>   (Daddy) Uncle Buddy

<u>2004</u>   Uncle Wiley

<u>2004</u>   Aunt Willie

<u>2005</u>   Aunt Sugar

<u>2006</u>   Aunt Ruthie

<u>2010</u>   Aunt Thelma

<u>2013</u>   Aunt Neshie

<u>My</u> <u>Paternal</u> <u>Cousins'</u> <u>Birthdates</u>

		<u>Year</u> <u>of</u> <u>Birth</u>
	1. Naomi Kilpatrick	1935
	2. Dorothy Johnson	1937
	3. Herbert Boykin, Jr.	1938
	4. Gwendolyn Thomas	1939
*	5. Kenneth Boykin	1939-2015
	6. Wilma Rideout	1939
*	7. Juanita Brown	1939-2013
	8. Edward White	1940
	9. Venita Strange	1940
	10. Tommy "Bubby" Stevenson	1941

	11. Brenda Adams	1942
	12. Floyd Boykin	1942
	13. Dessola Johnson	1942
	14. Elbert "Bubble" White	1942
*	15. Richard Stevenson	1943-2004
	16. Robert Boykin	1943
	17. Jimmy "Jackie Boy" White	1943
	18. Thurman Moore	1944
	19. Harold Gene West	1944
	20. Delores Ware	1945
	21. Alfred Moore	1946
	22. James West	1946
	23. Herman White	1948
*	24. Deborah Dawson	1948-2014
	25. Shelva Quinine	1948
	26. Gregory Boykin	1949
	27. Mac Ray West	1950
	28. Stanley Stevenson	1951
	29 Sandra Mosley	1951
	30. Renee Jones	1951
	31. Jerome Moore	1952
	32. Phillip White	1953
	33. Thea Ursula Tate	1954
	34. Adrian West	1955
*	35. Theodore "Ted" Bradford Jones	1956-2012
	36. Darrell Jones	1956
	37. Danny Eric Jones	1957
	38. Marcia Jones	1957
	39. Beaurette Michael Jones	1958
	40. Donna Jones Duniver	1960
	41. Angela Jones	1964

*deceased

My uncle Sonny had two children from another union:

- Danita Harris
- Andre T. Harris

I was told by my Aunt Thelma, Daddy's twin sister, that my grandmother, her mother, Dessie said on her "death bed":

> "Lord, I'm dying – please take care of my children."
> – The Lord heard her and answered her cry affirmatively.
> She had lost one of her children, as a baby, several years
> before, but her surviving 11 children all lived to be 81
> years or older. There are three that are still living –

- Earselean – 78 yrs.
- Theodore – 82 yrs.
- Deborah – 88 yrs.

They lived and raised their children and made their mark in the world. All the 8 girls were great cooks, great semstresses, and great leaders. The 3 boys were all hard workers and had great responsibilities in raising their families.

The legacy for our children has been respect, loyalty, dignity, love, and compassion. Our children have little or no knowledge of the awesome strength, courage, and resilience of our ancestors. It was those attributes that enabled our family to survive the physical and psychic atrocities and traumas which characterized the Black existence in America.

We will continue to remind our children that except for the endurance of our ancestors, we surely would not be enjoying today's opportunities.

James & Elva Reynolds, Daisy & Virval Gillespie **(Double Cousins)**

Cousin Gloria Felt

Cousin Sally Taylor

Aunt Dee & her nieces & nephews

Daddy In Uniform - WWII

Daddy, Tierra, & Aunt Thelma

Naomi, Aunt Thelma, Aunt Willie, Aunt Alma, Aunt Dee, & Argel

My Precious Cousins

Stanley, Bubby, Greg & Thurman

My cousins in Arkansas in the 1940's

Papa (sitting) Daddy (standing) Aunt Willie, Aunt Ruthie

CHAPTER SEVEN

"Fine As Wine in the Summertime"!

My Mom, Cora V. Jones

My Dad –James T. Jones

"How you doin', Miz Jones?"

"Fine as wine in the summertime!"

Whenever anyone asked my mother about her health, or if they just wanted to see how she was doing, she inadvertently would say, "Fine as wine in the summer time!" She was positive thinking and very seldom complained when she was "under the weather."

My mother, Cora Virginia Shockley Jones Lyons, was born on July 25, 1918 in Newport, Arkansas. Her dad was Gilbert "Gillie". Shockley and her mom was Mary Virginia Brockman Shockley. Mama had two sisters, Hattie and Mabel and one brother, Frank. Her mother had one son, Charlie Brown, from another marriage, and her dad had three sons from other unions, Wayman, Oliver, and Gilbert "Sonny Boy" Shockley.

Mama went to elementary school in Weldon, Arkansas, a little school that housed a few black children. She then went to another school when the family moved to Fitzhugh, Arkansas. My mother did not finish her formal schooling, but she was ever learning, forever reading her bible and working hard to reach her life's goals and aspirations. I remember my mother, sitting at her table, reading a big family bible. She put information in there, but it has been lost over the many years. The church that my grandfather attended and took his children was called "Church of Christ", a denomination that Mama and Aunt Hattie and Aunt Mabel attended all of their lives.

My mother accepted the Lord into her life when she was very young, and in later years, she attended the Church of Christ in Harvey, Illinois. Bro. Eddie McMillan was the minister. She loved the church and attended regularly until her health started to diminish. Mama received several Certificates of Completion over the years for bible correspondence courses.

The year my mother was born, 1918, was a signature year: Woodrow Wilson was President and the country was going through a terrible war against Germany. A postage stamp cost 3 cents, a loaf of bread was 10 cents, a quart of milk was 13 cents, and you could purchase a house for $4,821.00.

It was a time of hardship and pain for the black families in the little town of Fitzhugh, Arkansas. It was a struggle to survive, and it was an era, a time in history where they started to migrate to northern cities, seeking better jobs, and a better life for their kids. This was the back drop, the root of my mother's legacy. Her legacy was one of love of family – unconditionally; loyalty to one another – unconditionally; and a legacy of commitment to a goal – regardless of hardship. My mother grew up to be feisty and full of "witticisms" and humor.

She married Daddy in 1935, the year of my birth. James Thurlo Jones was part of the Jones Family, who were prominent in Arkansas, with a brood of 11 children and lucrative land and property holdings. In 1937, a boy was born to Mama and Daddy. My little brother only lived 6 days. His name was James Jones, Jr. I'm told that my father never got over losing his son. He loved and cherished me, calling me "Poochie" all my life, he wanted more children. My mother wasn't "having it" for she never had more children.

They migrated to St. Louis, Missouri, with me in tow, in the late 1930's. My mom and my dad were very social, having many friends. They soon separated, leaving me devastated. Well into my teen years, I hoped my mother and father would get back together. They tried to make it work several times over the years, but it was not to be because they were like "oil and water" together – no mix. They loved each other, ironically, but they couldn't "get along." My mother loved to talk, loved asking questions and always demanded answers. Daddy "met no strangers," but had his own way of making friends. One of my mother's closest' friends was Louise Green, who lived in St. Louis. Louise had three handsome sons and one daughter, Yvonne. Yvonne was very close with my daughter Sharon in the early years. Louise and Yvonne visited us in Chicago several times, sometimes staying for weeks. My mother would go back to St. Louis, as well, to visit Louise.

Mama was quick with words and never backed down from an argument. She and her sisters, Aunt Hattie and Aunt Mabel interacted with each other constantly. My son, Lenard, used to get the biggest kick out of listening to them "zing" one another with one-liners, seeing who could win the "one-up-man-ship," friendly battle. they were hilarious and Aunt Mabel would laugh the hardest. After telling her joke or one-liner, she would burst out laughing. Those sisters were something else together.

Mama taught me the "Ten Commandments" and made me go to Sunday School and church, every Sunday. If no Sunday School, then no going to the movies (which I absolutely loved) or to the "show" as we called it when I was a kid. She read her bible for hours, trying to learn as much as she could about the Lord and His statues. She encouraged me to fear no one, and to meet life's challenge, head on, with courage, and dignity, and determination.

I will always remember how my mother and I stayed up all night every Thanksgiving and every Christmas, preparing meals for the family dinners. She made delicious lemon meringue pies, caramel cakes – making the caramel on top of the stove using brown sugar, white sugar, butter, etc. (the old-fashioned way), and her special peach cobbler. She taught me how to cook a turkey and corn bread dressing, and potato salad.

She was devoted to her family. She loved her grandchildren like only a proud grandmother can. There was nothing she had that she withheld from them. And although she "doted" on them, she still used discipline with them which included spankings and strong reprimands, and stern warnings. She warned them of the dangers of cigarettes and alcohol and drugs. Mama encouraged them, as well, telling them about the Lord and how important it is to keep Him in their lives. The grandchildren can attest to the fact that mama didn't "spare the rod."

Mama became a foster parent in the early 1970's. There were children on the block at 74th & Sangamon who were in dire need of care. She stepped in to help these children. She also devoted many years to being a homemaker for families who resided in the suburbs of Chicago. Again, my mother was feisty, fearless and witty, with a funny sense of humor. She was very friendly and loved to sit and just talk. She was also a good listener. She wanted her grandchildren to be strong and tough to deal with life's challenges.

I have such fond memories of my mother and our life together. Because I was an only child, our relationship was very special.

During her declining years, she showed her family how to gracefully accept physical challenges. Even though she was ill, Mama kept a positive attitude. Whenever anyone asked her how she was doing, she would reply, "Fine as wine, in the Summertime!"

Cora Virginia Jones Lyons died on October 10, 2004 at her apartment that she shared with her husband of 6 years, Raymond Lyons. Mr. Lyons, Sharon, and I were with her when she took her last breath here on earth. She left and entered into the open arms of our Savior, Jesus Christ.

•   •   •   •   •

Mama's family roots as I know them:

Lemuel Brockman   Eliza Wilson Brockman

Eliza had brothers and sisters, namely Lula Wilson, Stella Wilson, Albert Wilson, and Newton Wilson. Stella's children and grandchildren settled in Columbus, Ohio.

Lemuel and Eliza had thirteen children:

1. Mary Virginia (my grandmother)
2. Lemuel, Jr.
3. & 4. Herbert & Rosie Lee (twins)
5. Irene
6. Lucille
7. Isabel
8. Johnny
9. Viola
10. Annie
11. & 12. Eva & Erie (twins)
13. one "still" birth

These children were born in Arkansas.

Gilbert "Gillie" Shockley & Mary Virginia Brockman Shockley

A.) Oliver
B.) Gilbert "Sonny Boy," Jr.
C.) Wayman
D.) Frank
E.) Cora
F.) Hattie
G.) Mabel
H.) Charlie Brown

A.) Oliver – family Unknown (Chicago)

B.) "Sonny Boy" Shockley & Irma "Dee" Shockley

   1. Maxine Shockley Gillerson & Albert Gillerson

      a.) Pamela
      b.) Rhonda
      c.) Ronald
      d.) Reginald

C.) Wayman Shockley – Wife & children unknown (Arkansas)

D.) Frank Shockley – Wife & 3 children (St. Louis, MO) youngest son and youngest child born to Gilbert & Mary Virginia

E.) Cora Virginia Shockley Jones & James Thurlo Jones

   1. Naomi Ruth Jones Kilpatrick & Lenzo Kilpatrick

      a. Sharon Marie Kilpatrick Tang & Alex Tang, Jr.

         1. Shatese Tang Jenkins – Steve Jenkins

            a. Derek Rylon & Marciara

               1. Macari Rylon

         2. Alexis Tang Jones & Anthony Jones

            a. Anthony Jones, Jr.

         3. Sean Tang & Annette Karisha Tang

            a. Tyrone Brantley
            b. Sean, Jr.
            c. Jaden

      b. Linda Susan Kilpatrick Stevens & Willie Stevens

      c. Katrina Rae Kilpatrick Levy & Charles "Butch" Levy

1. La Shundra Kilpatrick Levy & Jenoit Cameron

   a. Tierra Kilpatrick Cameron

2. Charles "Bub" Levy & Tihiese Levy

   a. Yasmin

3. Tremaine Kilpatrick Levy & Shavonne

   a. Tremaine, Jr.
   b. Trina
   c. Travonne

4. Latrina Rae Kilpatrick Levy

   a. Le Shawn
   b. Kyonna

d. Kevin Lamont Kilpatrick & Veleese Smith Kilpatrick

   1. Keveesha Kilpatrick

      a. Kevin Lenard Kilpatrick

   2. Veleesha Mia Kilpatrick
   3. Kelley Kilpatrick

d. Kevin Lamont Kilpatrick & Twanda Taylor Kilpatrick

   1. Twan Taylor

      a. Malani Taylor

   2. Gerald Rowan
   3. Gordon Thornton

e. L. Lenard Kilpatrick –

F.) <u>Hattie Dorce Shockley Lott</u> & Eddie Lott

   1. Dorce Lott Hines & Jack Hines

      a. Jack Hines, Jr.

         1. Ten children, many grandchildren

   2. Charles Donald "Sonny" Lott & Mary Frye Lott

      a. Nina Faye Lott
      b. Charles Lott, Jr. "Chuck", Spouse, Delores
      c. Carmen A. Lott
      d. Mary Carol Lott Johnson – Spouse, Eddie
      e. Reginald Lott

         30 Grandchildren, 45 Great-Grandchildren

   2. Charles Donald "Sonny" Lott & Partner Maggie Mabey for
      over 30 years. Maggie has two daughters, Rita & DOrene.

   3. Earica Irene Lott Brown & Alfred Brown

      a. Alfred Brown, Jr. & Marie Brown

         1. Alfred Brown, III, Spouse, Children
         2. Alicia, Spouse, children

      b. Frederick Brown, Spouse, Children

F.) Hattie Dorce Shockley Egeston & Zollie Egeston

   1. Zollie Egeston, Jr.

G.) Mabel Shockley Magness,
Spouse, R.H. Magness, 2ⁿᵈ Spouse, Robert "Van" Kidd

   No Children

H.) Charlie Brown & Lois Egeston Brown

    1.) Mildred Viola Brown Miller & Roy Miller

        a. Gary Martel
        b. Kelvin Leuell

    2.) Jack Brown

        a. Floyd
        b. Son

    3.) Franklin Brown

        a. Donna
        b. Debra
        c. Kim
        d. Eric

Aunt Lois had nine children with husbands Uncle Charlie, & Uncle Nathan. She later married Udell Hyde and they remained married until his death.

My grandfather, "Gillie" Shockley, Mama's dad was one strong, fearless man, "fearless" in the heart of the South where black families were surpressed and discriminated against, and sometimes terrorized. Grandpa is what we called him, had a shotgun, and he'd carry it on his hip at times. Grandpa had horses, mules, hogs, chickens and other things found on a farm. He had a wagon, with a wooden plank in the middle to sit on. My cousins – Dorce, Sonny, and Irene – used to ride in this wagon to go to church and sometimes Grandpa took us to pick cotton. We made about $3.50 per day picking cotton.

My grandfather and my grandmother, "Virginia" as she was called, must have married around 1915 or 1916. My grandmother already had one son, Charlie, when they married, from another marriage or relationship. My mother, Cora, was the next to be born and the first one from that union. Everyone called Grandpa "Gillie", both black and white. He did not "kowtow" to the white man and years later, he left Arkansas because his life was in danger.

I have no remembrance of my grandmother at all; I was 2 years old when she died in 1937. She and my paternal grandmother, "Dessie," died within a few months of each other in 1937.

I'm told she was tall, and stately, head held high with a proud walk. She was very light – complexioned, like her siblings and very attractive. There is a certain "mystery" about her that I conjured up in my own mind. After the experiences with her four siblings – Irene, Belle, Viola, and Erie – I wondered what her personality was like. I wondered if she was "uppity" like them. I tend to think that she was proud but sensitive; strict but loving; could have been "high-classed" but chose to be down to earth. She could have shunned my grandfather, because he was a "rolling stone" (many women) but she embraced him and clung to him as the ultimate devoted wife. I often wondered why she didn't leave the south like her sisters. I know she had her children by then, for her sisters left in 1923. Why didn't she take her children and move to St. Louis where life might have been easier? Was it because of her love for her husband? She raised her children in the deep heart of the south and they all turned out well, except my Uncle Charlie (Viola's dad), who drowned years later.

I concluded that my grandmother was a remarkable woman who chose to stay because she loved her children with a passion and was a devoted wife who constantly prayed and looked to the Lord to guide her life. She died, much too soon (for me) in 1937, but to God be the glory for "great things He has done" for our family.

Grandpa had several siblings, but I only got to spend time with Aunt Ina and Aunt Madie. He married several times, I'm told. I don't know how long he was married to my grandmother before she passed away. In June, 1937, Grandpa married yet again. Her name was "Rose" Brown and she was 23 years to my grandfather's 57 years. They married in Newport, Arkansas, but they stayed in a little town called Weldon, Arkansas. She is the only grandmother I remember. We called her "grandma", and were very fond of her. She was a "difficult" person to my mother and Aunt Hattie and Aunt Mabel. She was "suspicious" of everyone and "superstitious," as well, but she treated us, the kids, with warmth and humor. "Grandma" was not attractive to us kids and we often wondered what Grandpa "saw in her," that we didn't. She loved Grandpa and catered to his every need, from their time in Arkansas to the years spent in Chicago until Grandpa died in July, 1974.

The 1920's had a big impact on my great aunts, my grandmother's siblings. Anti segregation riots had occurred in Chicago, Knoxville, Omaha, and Washington, D.C. in 1919. It signalled the emergence of a more militant "New Negro" who would dare to pursue economic opportunities and a better life. During the 1920's, one million African Americans left the South for northern cities to follow the promise of better jobs. They were destined to be disappointed for only the most precarious, dirtiest industrial jobs were opened to black men, and black women were excluded entirely from industrial work and left with only traditional domestic labor.

Nonetheless, my grandmother's sisters decided to leave Arkansas and become part of that great migration by moving to St. Louis, Missouri in 1923. They, like many others, were seeking a better life and a more dignified, elegant lifestyle. They had lived with racism and discrimination and Jim Crow and disrespect which promised a very dark future. They saw no future of dignified work or financial security in Arkansas. My aunts were beautiful women who were characterized as "uppity", "sidity", and seemed to prefer living like "white folks". The four of them – Aunt Irene, Aunt Belle, Aunt Viola, and Aunt Erie - left and settled in St. Louis. They found housing in the same complex, a big, sprawling building with sculptured lawns and beautiful flower gardens; a definite "step up" from their prior existence. They absolutely loved it and stayed there for decades.

Aunt Irene found work with the very rich, very prominent white people in St. Louis. She cleaned, cooked, served and did other tasks required of her. She brought home gifts, expensive gifts from them and of course, she talked about it a lot. She was extremely proud of her work.

Aunt Irene had been born on April 7, 1903 in White Plains, Alabama. Her parents were Lem and Eliza Brockman. She was one of thirteen children and she ironically, was the last surviving sibling when she passed away on March 27, 1991. She was 88 and still resided in St. Louis. She had married Frank Nolan in 1940 and they remained together until his death. They had no children. Aunt Irene, Aunt Belle, Aunt Viola, and Aunt Erie helped my grandmother, financially, with her children.

Aunt Irene was a floor delegate in her senior citizens complex for many years. She belonged to several clubs and organizations, enjoying the interaction and serving her community, as well. When she passed away in 1991, it was the end of an era.

<u>Aunt Belle</u> had one son, "Bud", who as an adult lived in Indianapolis, Indiana. He married and had a happy life, working and taking life slowly. He and his wife came to Chicago for several years, attending our annual family reunions.

Aunt Belle was very particular with everything. She tried to do everything perfectly, everything "decent and in order." She'd fix breakfast for us and we enjoyed watching her prepare it. She did the prettiest, yellow scrambled eggs, and she gave us ½ piece of toast and grape fruit. She cut the grape fruit in half and cut each little section to make it easy to eat. I think Aunt Hattie was more like Aunt Belle than the other aunts. I don't think my mother was like any of them. She "marched to a different drummer"; she had her own way of doing things. Aunt Belle looked more white, than black, and even though she was "uppity", she was kind and gentle with us. I've never forgotten her face or her mannerisms.

I did not spend a lot of time with <u>Aunt Viola</u>. She lived upstairs in the complex and I remember climbing those steep stairs from Aunt Belle's or Aunt Irene's apartment. Aunt Viola was very kind and very soft-spoken. Her voice was almost a whisper and she moved slowly. Aunt Mabel resembled Aunt Viola, although there was nothing "slow" about Aunt Mabel.

My Aunt Erie had a beautiful face and the confidence of a movie star. She had the smoothest complexion, beautiful bright eyes, and her hair was always beautifully coiffed. Her clothes were immaculate and stylish. I felt blessed to be with her in the same room. When we came to visit her, she looked to see if we had clean underwear and socks with no holes in them. Aunt Erie developed a kidney problem early on in her life and of course, at that time, there was no dialysis center. She had a terminal illness and she knew it, but she always kept that smile and kept on living her life, as usual. She died from kidney failure at a relatively young age.

All four of these aunts had their own apartments in the same complex, each with nice furniture and very elegant china and dishes. I still have 5 beautiful dishes that Aunt Irene gave me some thirty years ago. The pieces have no chips on them; they are basically in the same condition as when she gave them to me. They are a pale color that is pink or beige; all glass and crystal. I treasure them, but I use them often when my family comes over for dinner. I wash them by hand and carefully put them back in my china cabinet.

They all left the South and found a better life in a "northern" state, Missouri. They left my grandmother there and she raised her children and died in her forties. I don't remember her, but she was remarkable to have raised her family well. I look at her siblings and I can imagine her through them. They all worked, earned money, and managed it well. They learned to appreciate the value of money and the freedom it gives you in life.

Aunt Hattie, Mama's sister, used to "can" vegetables, fruits - like okra, tomatoes, peaches; and something she called "chou chou" which was hot with peppers. She canned just about everything she grew in her garden. And she made some kind of soap, as well. She used to cook delicious, mouth-watering fried pies – usually peach, sometimes apple. I loved those pies. Haven't had any fried pies like them since the old days at Aunt Hattie's house.

Aunt Hattie was born in Newport, Arkansas on June 7, 1919 when Woodrow Wilson was President. It was the same year as the riots in Chicago were happening. She was the 2nd child born to Mary Virginia and "Gillie" Shockley. Her older sister, Cora, was born a year earlier, on July 25, 1918. Her younger sister, Mabel, was born one year after her on July 6, 1920. They grew up to be very close, although there was that "sibling rivalry" thing from time to time. This rivalry acted as a motivator, driving each one to seek their own place in the world, and to pursue their own dreams. Aunt Hattie was energetic and hardworking, as a child, as a teen, and as an adult.

She married George Eddie Lott and they had three children together - Dorce, Sonny, and Irene. Uncle Eddie was an attractive man of short statue, light - complexion, and a wonderful smile. Perhaps she met him at school or just knew him from the town of Fitzhugh, Arkansas. I don't know, but Aunt Hattie went to the little school in Weldon, Arkansas, and then to the school in Fitzhugh. She loved learning, always studious, taking classes for one thing and then another, as an adult. She attended South Suburban College in South Holland, Illinois after she moved her family to Chicago.

Aunt Hattie, (getting back to Uncle Eddie) married Eddie Lott in 1933 and their oldest child, Dorce Virginia, was born the next year 1934, September 20th. Two years later, Charles Donald (Sonny) was born, December 26, 1936. The youngest child, Earica Irene, was born 2 years later on June 1, 1938. Uncle Eddie died young, leaving Aunt Hattie to raise her children alone, as a single parent. She was up to the challenge, with God's help. She raised them well and in the interim, she managed her meager finances by stretching each dollar as far as she could, and living a chaste, disciplined life style. She taught her children to work hard and how to survive and "flourish" in spite of hardship. Aunt Hattie made sure her kids went to school every day, no matter what the weather was like. And we had to walk to school every day which was a long way at that. We passed a grave yard on the way to the little school house that had one big room for all the students to assemble together for devotion. Our teacher was "Professor Page". He was over the whole school; the "whole school" consisting of about 2 or 3 classrooms. We opened with devotion, and then we broke up into the classes. We did not get into trouble at school, because if we did, we would be in more trouble at home.

It sounds as if I lived with Aunt Hattie all the time, but actually, I lived in St. Louis with Mama, and then Chicago, but during the summer, I'd visit Dorce and Sonny and Irene. I looked forward to the visits, but by the end of summer, it was time to go home. My cousins thought I must have been the dumbest "city" girl ever. They taught me the "ropes," e.g. how to pick cotton; how to wash dishes; how to make corn bread; how to milk a cow (I never learned); they taught me how to churn butter (I loved doing that); and I watched, wide-eyed, as they canned fruits and vegetables and stored them.

I watched as Aunt Hattie made biscuits for breakfast. I watched as Sonny chased the chickens and wrung their necks. They had to be feathered and then cut up and fried. I didn't enjoy eating that fried chicken.

I watched Aunt Hattie fry rabbits, and to this day, I can't stand "rabbit".
And I remember baked sweet potatoes. It seemed that every day, for lunch, we'd have baked sweet potatoes.

On Saturdays, we took baths in a tin tub having to heat the water on the stove. And then we went "to town", which was Newport, Arkansas. When we got there, we ate "chili dogs" that were so delicious. I haven't tasted any, since then, that taste like Newport's chili dogs. The other thing we did, which I just loved, was going to the "show" which was the movies. We had to sit in the balcony, blacks were not permitted on the first floor where the "white folk" sat.

It was during the 1940's up to 1951 when I was visiting. Right in the midst of Jim Crow laws and segregation – 2 separate races – black and white. The 2nd World War started with the attack on Pearl Harbor in December, 1941. The 93rd Infantry - the first black division formed during the war - was activated. The Congress of Racial Equality was staging sit-ins at restaurants in Chicago. The U.S. Navy admitted blacks to all branches of the services. The first black marine unit was sent overseas during the war – a lot of black history was taking place at this time, but Aunt Hattie continued to take care of her kids. On Sundays, we went to church. We went on a wagon drawn by a horse. Our history in the making.

As I reflect on that time, it was a valuable experience for my development into adulthood. Those things that were shared with me by my cousins meant a lot to me and I'm thankful. I'm proud to have Aunt Hattie's blood in my veins and I'm grateful for the lessons she taught.

Aunt Hattie taught her children to fear no one; and to meet life's challenges, head on, with courage, with dignity, and with determination.

Aunt Hattie married Zollie Egeston in 1960, and they had one son, Zollie, Jr. who died at a few months old. They had a full life together, having been together for (30+) years until his death. They both attended the Ogden Avenue Church of Christ until she moved to Harvey, Illinois and joined the Harvey Church of Christ. She enjoyed going to church and served on many committees. She received Certification of Completion for her work that she did at the church. Uncle Zollie was a friendly man who loved to talk and loved to laugh and "joke around". He loved his family and his friends.

Aunt Hattie lived to be 91 and even during her years of decline and difficulty, she kept a pleasant and positive attitude. She left a legacy for her children and for future generations; a legacy of frankness, and boldness, and toughness; and a legacy of hard work.

She went to be with the Lord on January 13, 2011. I'm thankful to God for the life of Aunt Hattie.

Mabel E. Shockley Magness Kidd, was my mother's youngest sister. She was born on July 6, 1920 when Woodrow Wilson was President. Like her sisters, the family, and the country was going through hard times because it was during the terrible war against Germany. Things were rough for everyone, but especially black families. And yet, Aunt Mabel and the family survived. When she was nine years old, the country went through yet another crisis, the Great Depression of 1929. Again, the family survived and "thrived", in a way.

Aunt Mabel attended school first in Weldon, Arkansas before going on to Fitzhugh, Arkansas to continue her grammar school education. After moving to St. Louis and ultimately, Chicago, she attended cosmetology school and became a beautician. She loved straightening and curling hair to perfection. Aunt Mabel never stopped learning; always seeking a better life; always reaching to the next rung on the ladder of success.

Aunt Mabel married Uncle R.H. Magness and they remained together until his death. Uncle R.H. was a fun-loving, jovial kind of person. He loved to keep you laughing. I remember he had a very distinct voice with deep overtones.

Aunt Mabel married Robert "Van" Kidd several years later. Van was more of a somber kind of guy, very serious and very studious. He enjoyed reading big books, like "War and Peace," "Moby Dick", and Machiavelli's "Prince." Aunt Mabel and Van remained together until his untimely death, building a couple of businesses together. They enjoyed their life which included owning 2 big dogs, cooking, going fishing, and spending time with their neighbors.

Aunt Mabel lived in Belleville, Illinois at 1000 High St., Apt. 12 for several years. She had previously lived in East St. Louis with her husband, Van. After he passed away, she moved to Belleville and it was a new building. Aunt Mabel was happy and felt blessed to get it. She fixed it up a little bit at a time. Mama and Aunt Hattie visited her often, frequently going to her church with her, Centreville Church of Christ. Aunt Mabel had a massive stroke in 1972 and another one in 1983, so Mama and Aunt Hattie encouraged her to go and find a church of Christ to serve the Lord for giving her a second chance at life. Aunt Mabel joined the Centreville Church of Christ and they became her church family. She loved wearing her "Sunday go to meeting" clothes to church. She always wore a hat, a dress or suit, and shoes to match, each Sunday. She absolutely loved costume jewelry and she wore beautiful pieces to match each outfit. Then she would ask, "How do I look?". After having accepted the Lord at an early age, she felt a deep commitment and dedication to the Lord for His grace and His mercy. At the Centreville Church, she enjoyed the teaching of Bro. Ralph Smith. He encouraged the congregation to go directly to the Bible to learn, instead of just going by what Bro. Smith said. Aunt Mabel went to church religiously each Sunday where she said she "serves the Lord." She only missed service when weather conditions prevented her.

When Aunt Mabel came to live with me in 2004, she attended the Harvey Church of Christ with Aunt Hattie.

She was devoted to her two sisters, Cora and Hattie. She loved her nieces and nephews and bragged about them to her neighbors, her church family, and to anyone who would listen.

Aunt Mabel loved sports; she loved having her friends over; she loved going out to dinner, and she loved to shop. She, not only, leaves a legacy of "strength and toughness", but also one of warmth and friendliness.

I am thankful for her life and to God be the glory for His grace and His mercy.

Frank R. Shockley, my uncle, my mom's youngest brother, died in Chicago, Illinois at the young age of 48 years old. He was born on October 11, 1921 in Newport, Arkansas. Warren G. Harding was President and across the country, other events were happening that added to the richness of African-American history:

- Jesse Binga founded the Binga State Bank in Chicago, Il; the bank flourished in the 1920's.
- Georgiana Simpson at the University of Chicago, Sadie Tanner Mossell Alexander at the University of Pennsylvania, and Eva Dykes at Redcliff College are the first black women in the US to receive PhD's.

- Harry Pace establishes Pace Phonograph Company to produce records on the Black Swan label; it is the first blacl-owned and operated record company and will record blues, jazz, spirituals, and operatic arias.

His year of birth was significant with these, and other events, happening. However, Uncle Frank's life was troubled. His early years were spent in school and growing up in the deep south enduring racism, discrimination and humiliating experiences. He was demeaned as a black man, but he still managed to squeeze out a few years of contentment when he was with his sisters. He started to drink at an early age, trying to drown his sorrows at the bottom of a liquor bottle.

Uncle Frank moved to St. Louis, Missouri in the late 1940's, and remained there several years. He got married in St. Louis and had three children with his wife – 2 girls and one boy, Frank Shockley, Jr. His marriage was troubled, and after several years together, he and his wife separated. He moved to Chicago in the 1960's and lived at 4744 So. Dorchester. I used to visit him when I could catch him home. He loved spending time with Sonny, Dorce & Irene and me, and we loved him very much. Sadly, Uncle Frank died on June 18, 1969. I remember it well and I remember being so sad. My youngest son, Lenard, was 6 months old, and I remember the walk on the moon occurred that same year, 1969.

To God be the glory for sending Uncle Frank in my life.

My maternal grandfather, Gilbert "Gillie" Shockley, had a large family with many siblings, both sisters and brothers. Grandpa was so precious to us as kids. When I was born, I am told he named me from the book of "Ruth": naming me Naomi Ruth. I don't remember having ever seen any of his brothers. I was told that they left home, seeking a better world. My grandfather was estranged from them, never really speaking fondly of any of them. Two of his sisters lived in Weldon or Shoffner, Arkansas – two towns real close in proximity to Auvergne, Arkansas where Aunt Hattie lived. Those two great aunts were, Aunt Ina and Aunt Madie. They had "strong genes" because they looked so much alike, and so much "akin" to grandpa; they were definitely part of the Shockley family. I remember Aunt Ina; my cousins Bobbie Shepherd and "Tootsie" are her descendants. Tootsie use to visit me when she was on her way to St. Louis. She was very friendly and loved her family. Tootsie passed away at a very early age.

Bobbie Shepherd Woodruff is Aunt Ina's granddaughter. I remember her parents who were the most caring, most loving people I have ever known. Bobbie's sister, "Bidi", was born severely handicapped, and yet, they all loved her and doted on her and tried to meet her every need. Like other parents of disabled children, Mr. & Mrs. Shepherd received special love from God to shower on Bidi.

My cousin, Bobbie, and the rest of my cousins on Mama's side would see each other at school. We loved playing. Bobbie was an excellent sports' person; she played basketball very well and she exhibited strength and stamina as we had gym classes, and as she played other sports. I remember her from a picture that was taken of the team at the school in Auvergne. Bobbie remained in Arkansas after all of us left with our families to go to different places "up north". She married and had several children. She also has several grandchildren. Although she has done her share of traveling, she remains in Arkansas, in Newport, surrounded by her beautiful family.

Maxine Shockley Gillerson, is Uncle Sonny Boy's daughter. She lived in Little Rock, Arkansas for many years with her parents until she moved to Kansas City, Missouri and then she settled in Chicago with her husband, Albert and her four children. Her mother's name was Irma "Dee" Shockley. Maxine lived in Chicago, with Albert, and her family for several years. She lived a few blocks from us when we lived at 8201 So. Peoria. She lived at 80th and Morgan and we saw each other often and remained close until Albert passed away and she moved to Grandview, Missouri. She lost 3 of her 4 children - Pamela, Rhonda, and Ronald. Only Reginald is left of her children. Ronald passed away on December 30, 2010. Lenzo and I attended the services and that's the last time I saw Maxine, although we keep in touch by phone. While we were at Ronnie's funeral, I met more Shockleys - Hinton "Sam" Shockley, Eddie Hinton Shockley, and Tiny-Young Shockley. They were relatives of Uncle Sonny Boy and Maxine and I didn't learn exactly who was who. They came up from Little Rock to comfort Maxine during her loss. Years ago, my mother attended Uncle Sonny Boys' funeral in Little Rock with Maxine.

While living in Chicago, Maxine joined Commonwealth Community Church, which was located at 140 West 81st St., Chicago. She was devoted to that Church. Below is a newspaper article and picture from the churchs' newsletter, dated Saturday, October 20, 2001 depicting Maxine and others planning for their Annual Usher Vesper Scheduled for November 11,

2001. She worked tirelessly for the church. I wanted to know what she was taught; what are her beliefs? Below is a brief description:

> "Commonwealth Church?
> What is that . . . a Baptist Church?
> No . . . it is a church for the community. The West Chatham Improvement Association meets here . . .
> "The Boys To Men Choir meets here . . . Royce Glamour's T.V. show meets here . . . Piano lessons for the Church Musicians meet here . . . The Community Basketball team meets here . . . We offer counseling here . . . We build homes here . . . Senior Citizens dance here.
> But not only that - we worship God here - not according to any particular denomination - but according to where you are. We believe that Jesus Christ is Lord - and if you don't believe it - we have some people here who will try to convince you of that fact. We are tolerant here and we don't rule anybody out - We include all who seek God!!"

May God continue to bless Maxine. She is still in Grandview, still making a difference in the lives of her grandchildren, who, like me, took care of them after the deaths of her two daughters.

My mother's oldest brother, Charlie Brown, was her half-brother who was born to the union of my grandmother, Mary Virginia and her first husband. Uncle Charlie fathered my three cousins, Mildred Viola, Jack, and Franklin Brown. Aunt Lois was their mother. When I was visiting Fitzhugh as a kid, I enjoyed going to Aunt Lois' home. She lived "down the road" from my paternal grandfather's home, from Aunt Sugar and Aunt Nesha. Aunt Lois always had something delicious on her stove; something was always smelling good (as a kid it seems I was always hungry) and she was always glad to see me. I don't remember my Uncle Charlie, he had drowned some years ago. Aunt Lois, not only had my three cousins with Uncle Charlie, but she raised six other children with her husband, Nathan Howard. She also raised Viola's two sons, Gary and Kelvin.

My cousin's name is Mildred Viola, but we called her "Viola"; she prefers Mildred, but she'll always be Viola to me. She is drop-dead gorgeous, with dimples in each cheek, a flawless complexion, and a winning smile. She has two sons, and currently lives in St. Louis, Missouri with her husband, Roy Miller. Her life is filled with service to her church and service to her community. As a cancer survivor, she considers it a blessing to spend her life helping others.

Jack Brown, Viola's brother, is prominently living with his wife, Regina, in Syracuse, New York. He has two sons.

Franklin "Frank" Brown, Viola's youngest brother, is now passed away, but he leaves four beautiful, adult children – Debra, Donna, Eric, and Kim. They live in St. Louis. My cousin, Frank, was a nice guy, friendly and pleasant, and "low key". He looked like Uncle Charlie with his piercing eyes and thick eye brows.

Aunt Lois died at the ripe old age of 99 years. She lived a life full of love and care for her children and grandchildren. She absolutely adored her children and their needs, and wants, and desires were her top concern. She lost three children, Frank Brown, Rylin Robinson, and Charles Howard, but she left six adult children – Mildred (Viola) Miller; Jack Brown, Joe Louis Robinson, Kenneth Howard, Lois Clark, and Acie Howard.

My three cousins, Dorce, Sonny, and Irene, were Aunt Hattie's children. They were born in Fitzhugh, Arkansas, my place of birth. I used to brag that Dorce and I were born 6 months apart, in the same house, in the same bed.

As children, we were very close, like siblings. They resembled my mother much more than me. I looked more like Daddy, and the "Jones'es". Dorce is the oldest, and then Sonny, who is 2 years younger, and then Irene, who is 2 years younger than Sonny. Their mother, Aunt Hattie, was my mother's sister. Mama was the oldest of the "whole" siblings – Cora, Hattie, Mabel, and Frank.

My cousins' dad, and Aunt Hattie's first husband was Eddie Lott. He was fair-skinned and handsome and short. He died at an early age, but his mother, Ollie Lott Doyle lived to be about 100 years old. She lived in St. Louis, Missouri and Dorce and Irene used to go visit her every year. Sonny gave me names of some of his relatives in the Lott family that he did not know: Montgomery Lott; Arthur Lott; Ethan Lott; and Henry and Luke Lott.

I grew up, to a degree, in Fitzhugh. My parents took me to St. Louis when I was about 2 or 3 years old, but I visited my cousins every summer and even between summers. I spent months at a time "down south". I had a "normal" childhood, meaning that like the rest of the black children in my generation, we grew up and experienced things that taught us how to survive in this world. I did not have a lot, but I didn't know that at the time because we always had food. We had no luxurious meals or foods; we ate biscuits, molasses, corn bread, greens, beans, black-eyed peas, and a lot of baked sweet potatoes. We ate foods that Aunt Hattie canned, fruits and vegetables in abundance. We never lacked food. Aunt Hattie had a smoke house where the meat was stored and prepared. My grandfather had one, too. Aunt Hattie saved the meager dollars and cents that she earned, and encouraged us to save and sacrifice. My mother and father took me to St. Louis when I was 2 or 3, but we came back year after year during my youth. The house I was born in burned down. It caught fire while Dorce and Sonny were there. No one else was home, but they escaped the fire without harm. It's not known what caused the fire. Aunt Hattie and her family ended up in the little town of Auvergne, Arkansas which was not that far away from Fitzhugh. Grandpa and his new wife, Rose, moved to Weldon, Arkansas. Rosie Lee Shockley was born on June 3, 1914 in Augusta, Arkansas. She was raised by Clarinda and Felix Brown of Augusta. She married Grandpa in 1937 after the death of my grandmother, Mary Virginia. She became a member of Ogden Avenue Church of Christ after she and Grandpa moved to Chicago. Grandma Rose accepted the Lord when she was very young. She died on November 4, 1977 in Chicago.

She was the only grandmother I remember. Dorce remembers our biological grandmother, Virginia. Dorce said she walked very straight, like Aunt Hattie, with her head held high. She was, no doubt, like her siblings who also "carried themselves" in a dignified, elegant manner.

As a kid, living in St. Louis, I would take the train to Newport, Arkansas and Aunt Hattie or Grandpa would pick me up at the train station. There were restrooms that said "Colored Only" and "White Only". I also remember water fountains that had signs that said the same thing. You dare not drink from the wrong fountain or attempt to use the wrong restroom. I enjoyed these visits with my three cousins, Dorce, Sonny, and

Irene. When I visited them, I did whatever they did. Dorce and I played together most of the time and Sonny and Irene played together. We all got into trouble sometimes, but I don't remember getting any whippings. According to Dorce, Sonny and Irene got whippings every day! They were "jug buddies" and when other kids messed with Sonny at school, Irene would "beat 'em up." Irene was a tiny little kid, but tough as "shoe leather". The kids knew not to mess with Lil' Irene.

The school had one big room and 2 smaller ones. We were summoned to class by the ringing of a big hand bell. We all went into the big room for the morning devotion to start our day. The classes included penmanship, recitation, reading from "Dick & Jane" primers; arithmetic and geography. In the interim Professor Page (and his wife) taught Black History, e.g. facts about George Washington Carver and Frederick Douglass and Harriet Tubman, and Mary McLeod Bethune, and others. He told us about President Abraham Lincoln and President Franklin Delano Roosevelt. We each took a little brown bag for our lunch which mostly included a small baked sweet potato. At the end of the day, we headed home.

<u>Dorce</u> <u>Lott</u> <u>Hines</u> is Aunt Hattie's oldest daughter and oldest child. Sonny was the middle kid and the only boy, and Irene was the youngest. Dorce learned to cook great meals; and to clean house; and to manage a household; and to take responsibility of caring for her younger siblings. Aunt Hattie liked everything "in place" and organized, so Dorce learned these things at an early age. She was always shy, but that never stopped her from being excellent in everything she attempted to do.

Dorce got married after she came to Chicago. She married Jack Hines, a Chicago Police Officer, and they had one son, Jack, Jr., who I still call Lil' Jack, although he has ten children. Jack was a premature baby, having to stay in the hospital for months until he weighed enough to come home. Dorce was at the hospital with him every day, for most of the day. She loved him and doted on him and gave him the care that only a mother can give. He came home and of course, thrived, and grew up to be 6 feet tall. He has beautiful, beautiful daughters; the oldest being "Zakiyah", who has a daughter and a baby boy of her own, now – as well as, being happily married for several years.

Dorce worked for the National Screen Theater in Chicago on 13th St. for 18½ years. She worked for the Chicago Public School System for years and retired in 2003. She lives prominently well surrounded by her husband, her son, and her grandchildren.

Charles Donald "Sonny" Lott, was Aunt Hattie's second child and only boy. He was born the day after Christmas, 1936 in Cape Girardeau, Missouri. "Sonny," as we all called him, was a typical boy who sometimes got into trouble as he grew and matured as a young man. He was always fun - loving, laughing, and joking, and kidding around. As a kid, he experienced what we experienced on the farm. He had to get the eggs under the hens in the hen house. He didn't have to help can fruit (mostly peaches) or the pickles, but he sure helped us eat a lot of them. I was amazed that one year Aunt Hattie canned some kind of meat. Sonny had to go to the smoke house to get ham and other meat that she smoked. Usually, he had to catch a chicken, wring his neck; she would then pour scalding hot water on the chicken and pluck the feathers. We'd have fried chicken and gravy for breakfast. I had a hard time trying to eat chicken while visiting my cousins. I saw what happened to the chicken and it "turned my stomach".

In 1950, when Sonny was 14, Dorce was about 15 or 16, and Irene was 12, the family moved to Chicago. They stayed with Aunt Mabel for a while until the family got their own apartment.

In 1956, Sonny met Mary Frye and they married in 1958. They remained married for 17 years and had 5 children together – Faye, Chuckie, Jr., Carmen, Carol, and Reggie. He taught his children to walk and then to fish. Persuant to his dream, Sonny became a truck driver. He enjoyed driving his truck and traveling all over the U.S. He was excellent in giving directions; he was the family's GPS.

Sonny met Maggie Mabry in January, 1980. In September of that year, they decided to become life long partners. With his five children and Maggie's two daughters, Rita and Dorene, a blended family was formed. Sonny and Maggie shared many "firsts" together: Sonny's first airplane trip; Maggie's first ride in an 18 wheeler; first fishing trip where Sonny caught no fish and Maggie caught several; and finally Sonny becoming self-employed as an independent owner/operator of Lott Trucking, a life-long dream of his. One of his greatest accomplishments was merging two families and uniting them into one with new sisters, brothers, aunts, uncles and cousins, not all by blood, but all out of love.

My beloved cousin, Sonny, passed away in August, 2012. He had kidney failure and complication from the dialysis process. He died one year and a half after his mother, Aunt Hattie. Aunt Mabel died in February, 2010; and my mother died in October, 2004. They are all gone now. Thank God for the lives they lived, their legacies live on.

Earica Irene Lott Brown, is Aunt Hattie's youngest child and youngest daughter. Aunt Hattie had a baby boy shortly after she and Uncle Zollie married. He died as a baby. "Irene", as I continue to call her, grew up in Auvergne, Arkansas. She was smart and energetic, going about her chores dutifully and obediently. She eagerly participated in the school activities. She was on the basketball team and played pretty good basketball.

Irene finished her education after moving to Chicago. She attended Dunbar Vocational High School, graduating with an excellent grade point average, and dreams of a bright future.

She married Alfred Brown in the 1950's and they were together for 18 years until his untimely death from a heart attack. They had two sons, Al, Jr. and Frederick Brown. They are both happily married with their own children and families. After Al's death, Irene went to work and she went back to school. She then got a position as a Social Worker in the Chicago Public School System. She worked there until she and her family moved to Wyoming, Michigan in 1994. She wanted a life for her family that was at a slower pace and at a quiet, peaceful existence. She achieved that in that little city, Wyoming. Irene did well there having worked at B.A. Blodgett – a Social Service Center – until her retirement. She received the "Lifetime Child Advocate Award" from the Child and Family Resource Council in 2009. She made a big difference in the lives of children and their families and she received that award/reward in appreciation of her service.

Irene serves the Lord in the "beauty of holiness" at her small church in Wyoming. The way she described it reminded me of my own little church, Grace & Glory Gospel Chapel, where there are few members, but lots of love and caring for the community. She attends faithfully and is greatly admired by her church family.

I have wonderful pictures of Irene and her family:

- picture of her with her two sons, Al, Jr. and Frederick. They adore their mom and they are there to make her life as pleasant as possible. Their wives follow suit, as well. They are doting daughters-in-law.
- picture of Irene at the gym of the little school in Auvergne, Arkansas with the basketball team, and the coach (holding the basketball).
- picture of Irene, as a kid, in the elementary school year book in Auvergne.
- picture of Irene and her husband Al, the father of her two sons, affectionately with hand and arm entwined, at a bar. It was during the early years of their marriage. "Al" was a dapper and smart dresser. Whenever he went out, he was dressed to the "nines"; usually in a suit jacket and tie. He was very handsome and he loved Irene very much.

Irene celebrated her 75th birthday on June 1, 2013. We were invited to the celebration which was held at the Wedgewood Christian Services, 3300 36th St., S.E., Kentwood, Michigan which is about 3 hours drive from Chicago. Nine of my family members and I made the trip on that Saturday, on June 1st, which was her actual birthday. Lenzo, Kevin, Twanda, Sharon, Alexis, Lil' Kevin, Lil' Anthony, Le Shawn, and Kyonna (and me) attended and we had a great time. The food was simply delicious, but the fellowship with Dorce and Irene and her family was most precious. Sonny had passed the year before and he was greatly missed.

Irene currently lives a beautiful life surrounded by her sons, her daughters-in-law, her grandchildren and her other family members.

To God be the glory. Great things He has done.

I thank God for my precious mother, for whom this chapter is dedicated. Mama was from the "old school" of strong black women and she did not "half-step" through life. She lived it fully, without regrets and without excuses and without explanations. She lived true to herself, doing it "her way".

The legacy that Mama left me was one of survival; a legacy of strength, determination, and unity; and a love of family. I am living that legacy now and I proudly pass it on to my children, my grandchildren, my great-grandchildren, and yes, to my great-great grandchild, as well.

Tierra, my oldest great granddaughter, wrote a tribute to my mother – Cora Jones Lyons – on the occasion of her death: (she was 13 at the time)

"Everything that happens is for a reason and the day my grandmother left us was for a reason. The reason was because it was her time to go and be with our Lord and Savior Jesus Christ. Now she is in a better place, she's home for good, and now better off. Although she will be missed by all of our family, I was relieved to hear that she had passed away. Why? Because the days before she passed, she was in so much pain. It made me uncomfortable to see her like this because she was so weak she could barely open her eyes to see all of her family there for her. As we sat there, we reminisced about all the good "OLE" days we spent together. I loved "Cora" very much. All of her grandchildren called her "Cora" because that's what she wanted to be called. For the 13 years of my life, I can tell you about her very well.

She wasn't the silent person that kept her feelings bottled up, believe me, whatever she thought came out and when it came out I mean she let it go. She made everyone smile on the worst day. Cora brought joy to all who surrounded her. So when you leave here today, don't you ever think to feel bad or sorry for us because my grandmother was loved and she knew it! When you leave, tell us how you loved her and that you're glad we were able to spend time with her. I am so proud to be the great-great granddaughter of Cora Virginia Jones Lyons.

God bless you!

Mary Lott with her family (Sonny's family)

Irene, Naomi, Dorce

Frederick Brown & his family

Irene & Al Brown

Cousin Mildred V. Miller & Husband

Charlie Brown, Mama's brother

Aunt Hattie, Mama

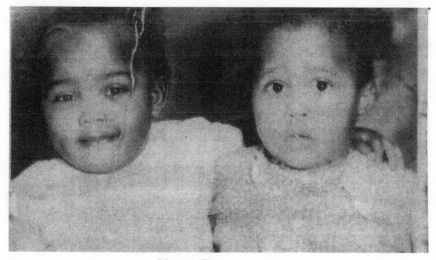

Naomi, Dorce, cousins

Dorce, Jack & Family

Al, Marie & Family

Sonny, Maggie, Kevin & Veleese

Mama & her BFF

Mama with Derek, Tierra, Kelley

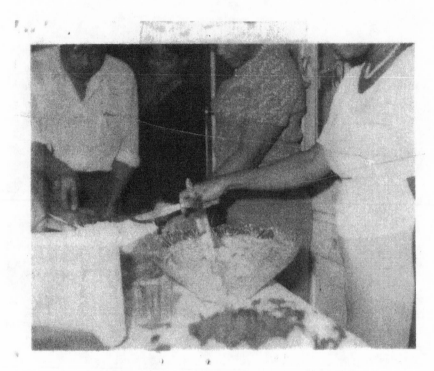

Grandpa, Dorce, Mama

Sonny & his family

Aunt Hattie, Uncle Sonny Boy, Maxine

Chapter Eight

Marriage, Children, Family

In the "beginning", God created marriage. It was between Adam and Eve. The Apostle Paul talks about marriage extensively in I Corinthians, Chapter 7. With all the controversy about the institution of marriage, one thing is certain in my own mind and that is, to put God first in our lives, in our homes, and in our families. As we grow in/with the Lord, our marriage relationship will grow as well.

The marriage relationship is important to God although problems will come – financial problems, social problems, and spiritual problems, and sexual problems. Sometimes children in a marriage cause big problems. However, God exhorts us to love each other and to respect each other. Another exhortation is that every man is to have his own wife and every woman is to have her own husband.

I thought of something a little comical about marriage. It came from Langston Hughes where he says:

> "Looks like what drives me crazy
> Don't have no effect on you –
> But I'm gonna keep on at it
> Till it drives you crazy too."

Marriage

Lenzo and I were both teenagers when we got married. It was on May 17, 1952, at a pastor's home with his wife, my mother, and my sister-in-law, Pearl as witnesses. We had a small, very nice wedding reception at Lenzo's Uncle R. B.'s home. It seems so long ago. We both attended Wendell Phillips High School in Chicago, on Pershing Rd. and Prairie Avenue. I lived at 4730 So. Prairie and Lenzo worked at Sam's Fish Market on 47th St. between Prairie and Indiana Streets. He used to watch me each day as I passed by going to and from school and other places. He met me at school and introduced himself; and the rest is history. I had two other boyfriends at the time, but Lenzo was the "coolest," and of course, the most aggressive in his pursuit. Like the other guys, he wore jackets, usually suit jackets, pants, a white shirt, open at the collar, and a hat, and of course dress shoes. It was important in the 1950's that young men be "cool" and "sharp". Lenzo was both. He was a strong personality, always wanting to control whatever happened to be going on at the time. He had a slew of friends – Maurice, Robert, Dave, Jack, Frank, Leroy, Thierry, Leonard, Larry, Bass and others – and they were all in the process of meeting the girl of their dreams. We did a lot of riding around and visiting the few places we could go to eat, drink soft drinks, and laugh and talk. We did a lot of hanging out together. Although Lenzo and his friends bonded together like a fraternity, and though they were young, they did clean fun things. I don't remember alcohol or drugs being abused at that time. Lenzo and his friends did not smoke cigarettes at the time. Later on, everyone went their own way and ended up doing a lot of those things, but while we were together as a group, we did (almost) innocent fun things. After Lenzo and I got married, I tried to smoke a cigarette, just once. We were at a little "joint" (as they called some of those places where Muddy Waters and the blues singers performed) and I lit the thing and tried to "inhale". First of all, I couldn't do it, and secondly, when I looked at my little snubby fingers (I used to bite my nails), I thought 'this is not cool nor attractive.' I never tried again. Lenzo has never smoked or drank alcohol over all these years. To this day, he doesn't like to be around people who smoke and he has had confrontations with people who have consumed too much alcohol.

We had a small wedding, and we were both nervous, but happy with the prospect of being together. We have remained together all these years because of an unspoken standard of compromise and patience. We love each other, we love our children, we love our families, and the Lord directs our path daily.

Lenzo is a very thoughtful, careful, resourceful man who takes much time before making a decision. He takes great care in trying to meet my needs and is always considerate of my work ethic and the way in which I try to care for Le Shawn and Kyonna.

Like most marriages, ours has had many obstacles and challenges and losses, but somehow we work to smooth the rough places and to keep our sanity in the meantime. Instead of it driving us apart, the problems have brought us closer together. We have sought to weather the storms together, drawing on the strength of each other.

Lenzo was born on July 30, 1933 in a little town called Eastman, Georgia. It's located about 80 miles south of Atlanta. Eastman is a busy, fast paced, interesting place full of many friendly faces and full of very proud people. They go about their business with heads held high and with a brisk step and a ready story to tell. Everyone knows every one and every one is related.

Lenzo is the youngest of seven children – two boys and five girls. His sister, Pearl, lives in Chicago and the two of them are the last survivors of the siblings.

He had a rough time as a kid having lost his mother at 4 years old. Life was extremely hard for black families in the 1930's and 1940's, but his maternal grandmother kept the family together. When he became a young teenager, he moved to Chicago to live with his aunt, Helen Johnson. After he started school, his uncle, Tommy Edwards, got him a job at Sam's Fish Market where he worked alongside him. While working there, Lenzo acquired an excellent skill of properly cutting all kinds of fish. He was very adept at his job and took it seriously.

After we were married, we had five children with Sharon being the "first-born". Then came Linda, who was born in Great Lakes, Illinois at the naval base there while Lenzo served in the Army; then came Katrina (Trina). We had these three beautiful girls and I thought my family was complete. Then four years later, Kevin was born, our first son. His birth brought us such joy to have this little boy after 3 girls. And then, 8 years later, our last child, our second son, Lenard, was born. The family grew as the children began having children of their own, and their children had their own. Lenzo and I built a tightly knit family unit. They love each other, they support each other, and they celebrate each other's successes. Lenzo is the ultimate father, for when our daughters were young, he protected them with a critical eye. Any boy who was interested in his daughters were carefully scrutinized. They had to come through him first. He wanted only the best for his children.

During his early years as a married man, Lenzo pursued an aggressive business career. He owned and operated several business ventures including a restaurant, a service station/gas station, a grocery store, and co-owned a beverage company with Jerry "Iceman" Butler, Ice Man Beverages. He was an entrepreneur, providing jobs for young men and women.

He has gone through many hardships, health issues, grievous losses, disappointments, and many ups and downs. But through it all, he has been able, with God's help, to stand tall. He has been able to hold his head up and look to the hills from whence cometh our help. God has been the strength of his life as he has tried to care for our family and keep them together. As he looks to the future, he seeks to leave a legacy of strength, courage, dignity, respect, a great love for family and friends and a reverence for our God.

On June 15, 2008, a friend of our daughter, Trina, Rev. Lucius Farmer gave a stunning, very beautiful tribute to Lenzo at his church. As pastor and founder of his church, he sought to honor Lenzo H. Kilpatrick as an example of how men should raise their families. Lucius was a special friend of Trina. He grew up in our old neighborhood, so he knew Lenzo quite well and had always admired him. He named Lenzo the "Outstanding Father of the Year" on that day in June. It was a great honor bestowed upon him and it was deeply appreciated by our family.

Lenzo's Family Roots

Mattie Lou Madison Edwards
Spouse - Elbert Edwards

Children
I.) Beulah Edwards Searcy

A. Willie Jo Searcy
    1. Lewis B. "L. B." Searcy
    2. Richard Searcy
    3. Melvin Searcy
    4. Gloria Searcy
    5. Patricia Searcy
B. Elizabeth Searcy Smith
C. Eddie Lewis Searcy

II.) <u>Dessie</u> <u>Mae</u> <u>Edwards</u> Kilpatrick (Lenzo's Mom)
Spouse – Howard Kilpatrick
    A. Mary Jean Edwards Brown
        Spouse – Sidney "Sid" Brown
    B. Mattie Mae Kilpatrick Jackson
        1. Mary Fluellin Plunkett
           Spouse – Steve Plunkett
        2. Charlton "Charles" Kilpatrick
           Spouse – Brenda Kilpatrick
           2nd – Kathryn Kilpatrick
        3. Dorothy Lee Jackson
        4. John "Jack" Jackson
           Spouse – Elayne Jackson
        5. Oletha Jackson
        6. Claretha Jackson
        7. David Jackson
        8. Bobby Jackson
           Spouse – Verdell Jackson
    C. Clara Kilpatrick Lewis
    D. Pearl Kilpatrick Harper
        Spouse – Jimmy Harper
    E. Harry Kilpatrick
        Spouse – Odie Bell Howard Kilpatrick
        1. Solomon Kilpatrick
           Spouse – Rosemary Kilpatrick
        2. Harrison Kilpatrick
           Spouse – Sally Kilpatrick
        3. Lonzo Kilpatrick
        4. Earl Kilpatrick
        5. Wayne Kilpatrick
           Spouse – Carolyn Diane Kilpatrick

6. Leon Kilpatrick
7. Mary Ann Kilpatrick Brown
    Spouse – Reginald Brown
8. Gail Kilpatrick
9. Debra DeLaine Tuff Dixon
F. Ilean Kilpatrick Fruitree
  1. Alonza Fruitree
G. Lenzo H. Kilpatrick
  Spouse – Naomi Jones Kilpatrick
  1.) Sharon Marie Kilpatrick Tang
    Spouse – Alex Tang
    a. Shatese Tang Jenkins
      Spouse – Steven Jenkins
      1. Derek Rylon
        a. Macari Rylon
    b. Alexis Tang Jones
      Spouse – Anthony Jones
      1. Anthony Jones, Jr.
    c. Sean Tang
      Spouse – Annette Karisha Tang
      1. Tyrone
      2. Sean Tang, Jr.
      3. Jayden Tang
  2.) Linda Susan Kilpatrick Stevens
    Spouse – Willie Stevens
  3.) Katrina Rae Kilpatrick Levy
    Spouse – Charles "Butch" Levy
    a. La Shundra Kilpatrick Levy
      1. Tierra Kilpatrick Cameron
    b. Charles Ray "Bub" Levy
      Spouse – Tihiese Levy
      1. Yasmin
    c. Tremaine Rayneal Kilpatrick Levy
      1. Tremaine
      2. Travon
      3. Trina
    d. Latrina Rae Kilpatrick Levy
      1. Le Shawn Lamarr Kilpatrick
      2. Kyonna Rena Kilpatrick

4.) Kevin Lamont Kilpatrick
    Spouse – Twanda Taylor Kilpatrick
        1st – Veleese Smith Kilpatrick
    a. Keveesha Kilpatrick
        1. Kevin Kilpatrick
    b. Veleesha Mia Kilpatrick
    c. Kelley Kilpatrick
5.) L. Lenard Kilpatrick

III.) <u>Callie Edwards Padget</u>

IV.) <u>Queen Edwards McClain Jones</u>
    Spouse – Mann Jones
    A. Elmore McClain
    B. Herman Lampkin

V.) <u>Ernest Edwards</u>
    A. Vernon Edwards
    B. William Edwards
        Spouse – Patricia "Pat" Edwards
        1. Anthony "Tony" Edwards

VI.) <u>Russell Edwards</u>
    A. Russell, Jr.

VII.) <u>Otis "Uncle Buddy" Edwards</u>
    Spouse – 2nd Rochelle Edwards
        1st Queen Edwards

VIII.) <u>Willie Edwards</u>
    A. Dorothy "Billie" Branch

IX.) <u>Robert Bennett "RB" Edwards</u>
    Spouse Lucy Edwards
    A. Mildred Edwards

X.) <u>Clemmie T. "Tommy" Edwards</u>
    A. Tommy, Jr.

XI.) <u>Cora Belle Edwards Gibbs</u>
   A. Joyce Lee "Joie Lee" Young
    1. Jo Ann Young Coley

XII.) Helen Edwards Johnson
   Spouse – Frank Johnson
   A. Robert Johnson

I was fortunate enough to meet many of Lenzo's family members since we have been married some 60 plus years. I met his beloved grandmother, "Ms. Mattie" in Eastman, Ga. on our visits to his hometown. She was always so happy to see him and treated him like a celebrity, fixing his favorite meals, and bragging about him to neighbors who dropped by. We visited Aunt Queen and Aunt Belle in Eastman where they lived all their lives. I adored Belle; she talked all the time and cooked delicious food, 3 times a day, while we were there.

Uncle Buddy lived in Winter Park, Florida with his wife, Aunt Rochelle and we used to visit them with the children during the summer months. It was so very hot there, we had to pick times to take the children to the swimming pool there. Lenzo's first cousin, Elizabeth Smith, lived across the street from Uncle Buddy and we were great friends.

Uncle Willie moved to Chicago for a few years, but then moved back to Eastman where he died on February 23, 1980. He had moved to Chicago seeking a better life.

Tommy, the youngest uncle, lived in Chicago and became a mentor of Lenzo. he looked out for him and taught him how to be a man. He was partial to him and taught him the "tricks of the trade." Tommy died at an early age. I remember going to the hospital to see him when he was near death. I went alone because I wanted to witness to him about the Lord, about how Jesus died on the cross for our sins, and how he rose again on the third day, and how He is "not willing that any should perish". I asked him to receive the Lord into his heart. He was too weak to respond to me, but I believe he responded to God.

Aunt Callie and Aunt Helen lived in Chicago, as well. Aunt Callie lived at 3403 So. Calumet for years. I remember she was a kind woman, very proud and very devoted to her siblings. Aunt Helen was Robert's mother and she loved him as her only son. They had a close relationship and when she passed away, Robert relied on Lenzo to be his confidant and his friend. Aunt Helen never warmed up to me. She opposed our marriage, and although she was not overt in her criticism, she let me know, in subtle ways, how she felt.

Lenzo's uncle, "R.B.", and sometimes he was just called "B", was my absolute favorite. He was a strong, strong man who took no "crap" from anyone. He very seldom smiled, but he was a kind man. He and his wonderful wife, Lucy, treated us like we were their own kids. After we got married, we lived with RB and Lucy. In those days, apartments were broken down into separate rooms that were rented out and you shared a kitchen and the bathroom. Lenzo and I had a room in their apartment. It was on 34th & Giles. RB loved playing cards, mostly "whist", and he was a master of the game. He played against his nephews and against his friends. He enjoyed beating everyone. Lucy, his wife was tall and attractive. She must have been at least 6 feet tall. She loved driving their car and loved helping RB's family. After a while, Lenzo and I got our own apartment and Lucy would come over and help me with my chores. I remember her coming over one day to help me iron my children's clothes. She stayed a long time and we got a lot done. A few days later, she was dead. Her death stunned and shocked us all and I grieved for her for months. She was very special to me.

Lenzo's cousin, Elmore McClain was the son of Aunt Queen McClain Jones, his mother's sister. Elmore was quite a character. He was funny, always talking, and always laughing when he was a younger man. He had the funniest laugh and got a real kick out of teasing and joking around. He especially enjoyed playing cards with his uncle R.B. They lived down the street from one another in Chicago. Elmore was a hard-worker at the steel mill foundry and he was known for having amassed a fortune because he was extremely "tight" with his money. He spent 30 years with his companion, Cleona Maddox. Cleona died, suddenly, on December 27, 1995. We used to go to their home every New Year's Day. Cleona cooked a big meal and invited the whole family. I remember she always cooked a "coon", and it just turned my stomach. I ate her other delicious food, but I could not touch that "coon".

Elmore united with his companion, Priscilla Hardy, and they produced four children – Glen, Yolanda, Latory, and Natasha. Elmore had a strong will, a deep determination, and an unswerving commitment to his children. He lost his sight over the final years of his life. He died on September 24, 2003 after alerting everyone else to vacate the building during a fire. He saved their lives, but lost his. His heroics and the event of the fire appeared in the Chicago Sun - Times newspaper. Glen Pierson visits us occasionally to keep in touch. Glen is married to the very beautiful Cheryl and they have three beautiful girls. – They just celebrated 10 years of marriage on April 20, 2013. We attended the renewal ceremony. Cheryl's colors were yellow & white; everything was just beautiful, and we had a ball.

Lenzo's oldest sister, Mary Jean Brown was born on May 12, 1921 in Eastman, Georgia. She moved to Cincinnati, Ohio about 1940 seeking a better life and more opportunities. This is where she met and married her husband, Sidney A. Brown. "Sid" as he was called was a genuinely nice man; classy, mature, and wise.

She was an excellent, honest, and dependable housekeeper for several Cincinnati families. She enjoyed her work and took much pride in how she performed her duties. She attended the Bond Hill Christian church where she enjoyed participating in the church projects, helping out wherever she could.

Lenzo and I visited Mary jean in Cincinnati a number of times over the years; driving there in a few hours and usually staying one or two days. Lenzo enjoyed it for not only did we see Mary Jean and Sid, but he saw some of his other relatives there, as well. Mary Jean visited us in Chicago as well. We were then living at 7429 So. Sangamon. Mary Jean went to be with the Lord on March 24, 1988.

Lenzo's sister, Clara K. Lewis was born on November 25, 1925 in Eastman, Georgia to the union of Dessie Mae Edwards Kilpatrick and Howard Kilpatrick. I loved Clara very much because she was the nicest, most gentle person one could meet. She made me her delicious biscuits whenever I visited her in Eastman. Her biscuits would literally melt in your mouth. Although Clara was gentle and kind, they told me that she could be extremely violent when provoked. Clara died in Eastman on November 21, 1980, during the same year as her Uncle Willie.

My dear sister-in-law, Mattie Mae, was born on February 28, 1922 to the union of Dessie Mae Edwards Kilpatrick and Howard Kilpatrick.

She spent her childhood in Eastman, Georgia where she was born and in 1942 she married Ocie Lee Jackson. They had eight children together. The family then moved to Miami, Florida and raised their children there. They built a beautiful family there and enjoyed life in that historic, fast paced city. Mattie Mae's daughter, Dorothy Lee, was tragically shot and killed while working at a bar there, and the family was devastated. After her husband passed away, Mattie Mae moved to Chicago and lived with her son, Jack and his wife, Elayne. She eagerly joined her son's church, the Faith Tabernacle No. 1 Apostolic Church of God and was baptized in 1982.

Mattie Mae was a wonderful mother and loved being surrounded by them and her grandchildren. She had a softness and a gentleness about herself, with a warm heart toward others. In her younger years, she enjoyed fixing delicious meals (she was a great cook) and inviting her friends and family over to share it. She always tried to give her guests a nice little gift "to remember her by". On July 15, 1988, Mattie Mae went to be with the Lord, leaving her family and loved ones thankful for the beautiful way in which she touched their lives.

There are three children still living, and still thriving out of Mattie Mae's eight children. Her oldest daughter, Mary, was Lenzo's favorite niece, by far. She was born in Eastman, but moved to Chicago during her early years. She met and married her husband, Steve Plunkett, and they raised 5 children in Chicago. She was very close to her Aunt Pearl. They spent each day cooking together and talking and sharing the latest news about the children and other things that were happening in the world. Mary raised her children to be tough, to be strong, to be independent, but most of all, to be a family. They were to take care and love all the babies, no matter what, take care of the children. Her children are Cynthia Metcalf, Mitchell Fluellen, Jay Plunkett, Rodney Plunkett and Cherie Plunkett. Mary, like her Mom, was a great cook, always preparing meals especially for her family, but welcoming friends who might stop in, as well.

She experienced many health problems over the years, but she continued on through pain and suffering. Even though she was in and out of the hospital, and even though her body was weakened, her spirit was not. She continued to have a "smile" in her voice over the phone. Lenzo and Pearl talked to her frequently, keeping up with her, checking on her health. They both talked to Mary the day she died and she was in pain. On the other hand, Mary called them often also, checking on Linda's health.

Mary passed away in April, 2007 leaving the family to try and cope with such a great loss. I think of her almost daily and thank God that she touched my life in a beautiful way.

Charton "Charles" Kilpatrick was Mattie Mae's first son and second child. He was born on July 17, 1941 in Eastman, Georgia. He moved to Chicago as a teenager and stayed with Lenzo and me until his adulthood. He became like one of our own kids. He attended Wendell Phillips High School. We were living in the Ida B. Wells Projects at the time.

Charles was never any trouble for us. He was cooperative and pleasant, and always tried to abide by the house rules.

Charles met and married Brenda Kilpatrick in Chicago and they had one son, Charlton Lee Kilpatrick. Over the ensuing years more children were born, Charles Love, Omarr Williams, Latoya Appling, and Deontra Appling. Later, Charles was united in holy matrimony to Kathryn Kilpatrick, but no children were born to this union.

He attended my church, Grace & Glory Gospel Chapel in Chicago where he accepted the Lord as His Savior. He was a teenager at the time under the leadership of Elder Owbridge Fay Gall. The current Elders are Willie Horton and Tyrone Stem.

Charles was tall and muscular, making him an excellent player in sports. He loved playing basketball, sometimes with his brothers. He enjoyed all kinds of sports on T.V. He shared time with his siblings and they watched the "Bears", the "Bulls" (in their glory years) and the "Cubs" and the "White Sox".

Charles was hard-working in every job he had. He served for many years as a retail shoe salesman, which he absolutely enjoyed. He loved being in "sales", also serving as an insurance salesman for many years until his health started to fail.

He loved his family which included his children and his brothers and sisters. He doted on his children and talked about them proudly with anyone who would listen. He was proud of the fact that they were each prominent and successful in their own right. He always felt that it doesn't get much better than that.

Charles made many friends, one of them being Odell "Bye Bye". They were very close friends, along with his wife Brenda, "Nyema". Charles was a genuinely nice guy who loved to sit and just talk and "chew the fat". He had a ready smile and a firm handshake. He was a good listener which is rare these days.

During his years of decline and difficulty, Charles kept a positive attitude. When he was in the nursing facility, his Aunt Pearl went to see him almost daily. She brought him food, delicious meals each time – greens and corn bread; sweet potatoes; and chicken, fish or beef as the meat. Needless to say, he loved seeing her. Charles never liked mayonnaise, but when Aunt Pearl brought her potato salad, he ate it heartily.

Charles died on a Saturday, October 6, 2012 at 71 years old. My daughter, Sharon and I attended a prayer breakfast on that same day. The prayer breakfast was held at the Bellevue Baptist Church, which is an annual event. Minister Gloria Randolph was the dynamic speaker. Pastor Lucius Fullwood was the senior pastor. Sharon and I were the guests of our Sorors Eartha Campbell and Zellner Barry. We received the call of Charles' death at that breakfast. The theme was apropo and ironic as we struggled to accept the great loss of Charles. It was comforting for Sharon and I to know that we were "under the shadow of the Almighty."

Dorothy Lee "Dot" Jackson was the second daughter and the third child born to the union of Mattie Mae Kilpatrick Jackson and Osie Jackson. She was born on April 4, 1946. She spent her childhood and early adulthood in Miami. Dorothy was a beautiful young woman whose life was cut short, tragically, by a senseless shooting on April 9, 1973. Her mother and her siblings mourned for her as David mourned for his son, Absolom in the Old Testament. They never really recovered from her loss.

John Lee "Jack" Jackson was born in Miami, Florida to the union of Mattie Mae Jackson and Osie Jackson. He spent his childhood and teen years there, excelling in school, seeking excellence and success, even then. As a young adult, Jack met and married Sylvia Jackson. They had two children together, Johnnie Jackson and Sabrina Jackson. He later moved his family to Chicago, Illinois. He prospered and succeeded in Chicago because of his wonderful work - ethic and his conscientiousness. He is a "people person," using his social skills to draw them to the Lord. His career of choice was sales and he was a master salesman. He quickly moved up to the manager, supervisor status at the jobs that he chose to serve. He took everything seriously, always seeking excellence in everything he touched.

After some time, Jack and Sylvia's marriage unraveled. He then met and married Elayne Jackson. They have two sons together, Jonathan and Bryan. They remain together even unto this day, continuing to grow spiritually, as they serve together and pray together in the ministry. Jack and Elayne have been married for several decades.

Jack is one of my favorite nephews because of his dedication to his church, and its' ministry. He travels from city to city and from state to state carrying out the duties of his office. He has worked hard to earn credentials and qualifications to officiate at functions. We know who to call when we need a minister, and Jack never says "No" to a need or to a family request, whether it is just participating; whether it is for "overseeing"; or whether it is for officiating at funerals, . . . weddings, anniversaries, and other events. He is a born leader, knowing how to guide people in the right direction. It has been difficult for him at times when he had to preside over his siblings' and other loved ones' home - going services, but he stands tall (he's about 6'7" or 6'8") through it all.

Jack and Elayne reside in Chicago where they are content to live quietly and peacefully in their beloved community.

<u>Oletha Jackson</u> was born in Miami, Florida on May 15, 1949 to the union of Mattie Mae Kilpatrick Jackson and Ocie Lee Jackson. She was one of four girls and the fifth child of eight children. She attended elementary school in Miami and went to the Northwestern High School there. Oletha relocated, with her family, to Chicago, Illinois in 1975. She became a caseworker for children at the Lutheran Social Services. She enjoyed her work because she loved kids.

Oletha raised five boys – Jeffrey (died on December 11, 2003 suddenly from a heart attack), Steve, Jerome, Dwight, and Lance. She was tough and used tough love to raise them. They, in turn, were tough, as well. I don't think they come any tougher than those guys. Oletha was serious about discipline. She taught her kids respect for others and hard work.

She attended her brother's church, the Full Gospel A.O.H. Church at 6633 So. Normal Blvd in Chicago, and was baptized in 2001. Her brother, John L. Jackson, was the Pastor, Overseer of the Church. She was a faithful member and enjoyed working on the Pastor's Aid Committee, the usher board, and the nurses' board.

It was sheer delight knowing Oletha. We used to have long talks on the telephone, where we exchanged witticisms and health news. She was extremely wise, using her past experiences as a mom, and her knowledge of the Word of God. She was a sweet woman with a wonderful "listening ear" and great culinary skills. She was a great cook.

Oletha shared with me that she had health issues. She suffered from heart problems for years. And then suddenly, on July 26, 2005, Oletha passed from this life in to the one prepared by her Lord. It was less than two years after the death of her oldest son, Jeffrey.

Claretha Jackson was born in 1951 in Miami, Florida to the union of Mattie Mae Jackson and Ocie Lee Jackson. She is the fourth daughter and the sixth child of eight children. Claretha attended elementary school and high school in Miami. Her undergraduate work was done in the local colleges and universities. Claretha has spent her whole life in Miami, but she has traveled extensively. In her young adult life, she enjoyed coming to Chicago to visit her siblings. And now that she has two brothers left, she comes every year to Bobby's annual cookout in Chicago where she gets a chance to see Jack, also. She adores her older brother, Jack and dotes on Bobby, her youngest brother.

Claretha is tall and stately, carrying herself like an African queen or a royal princess. She "oozes" confidence and class. Claretha gets her height from her mom, Mattie Mae, her great Aunt Helen, and her great Aunt Queen. And yet, Claretha is kind and helpful and always seeking to please.

Like her siblings, she is tough and street-savvy, knowing how to survive and prosper in this culture and environment. We live in a dangerous world, but Claretha knows and believes that God sustains her and her family. She relies on Him for her strength and wisdom. She has taught her kids to look life squarely in the eye and say, "I got this!" "God will take me through the valleys, and through the storms; sometimes over the mountains, and when

I've gone through the rain, He shows me the rainbow over the clouds." Praise God.

Claretha has three beautiful children (now adults), Corey Hinton, Mark Arm brester, and Cathy Armbrester.

<u>David</u> <u>Earl</u> <u>Jackson</u> was born on December 13, 1952 in Miami, Florida to the union of Mattie Mae Kilpatrick Jackson and Ocie Lee Jackson. He spent his early years in Miami where he attended elementary school and high school. David relocated to Chicago, Illinois in 1974 to join some of his siblings.

David was a great guy, nice and kind and would do anything to help others. He always said "yes" to his uncle, Lenzo, when we needed repairs done around the house. David was skilled and talented in many things. He came over every holiday season to hang our Christmas lights to decorate the outside as well as the inside of our house. He loved helping Le Shawn and Kyonna put up the Christmas tree. He was a mentor to Le Shawn having taken him on the train to the city and then taking him on the "L" train, showing him how to get from place to place on public transportation. David had a real soft spot for children.

He worked on cars with gifted hands, buying "beater" cars and refurbishing them. David was a master chef in the kitchen, cooking those "down home meals" like his mom. He loved fishing, and playing basketball with his brothers. He was skilled in handicrafts, as well. David had a very humble spirit, willing to help everybody he could.

David died on a Friday morning, June 8, 2012. He had been living in Danville, Illinois for a few years prior to his death. His friend, Cary, called me at 2:20 A.M. to tell me that David was not breathing, and his eyes were "fixed". He had come over to her house complaining of not feeling well. She fixed some food for him, he took a shower, and laid down on her bed. She awoke because of his loud breathing. She called 911; the paramedics came and worked on him a long time, in Cary's home, and then outside in the ambulance. They took him to the Danville Provena Hospital. I later called the hospital, and identified myself and they told me he had passed away. I prayed for Lenzo and Pearl and David's surviving brothers and sister. At the time, Charles, his brother was in the hospital here in Chicago in the

ICU. He was very ill and we were praying for his recovery. Sadly, in a few months, he would be gone also.

The family struggled to deal with the loss of these two brothers, these two precious family members that were loved and treasured. Somehow, and by the grace of God, we as a family survived. To God be the glory for the lives of David Jackson and Charles Kilpatrick. Their legacy lives on in the lives of their loved ones.

Bobby Jackson was born on January 27, 1956 in Miami, Florida to the union of Mattie Mae Kilpatrick Jackson and Ocie Jackson. Bobby was the fourth son and the eighth child of eight children. He was the baby of the family and enjoyed all the "privileges" it brought. His siblings doted on him and protected him from many hurts and downfalls. His brother, Jack, especially looked after his little brother. Bobby got his elementary and high school education in Miami, always working hard to not only be a good student, but to learn as much as he could. He had dreams and aspirations to be successful. His plan was to move up in the world and to make the world a better place.

When he became an adult, Bobby relocated to Chicago where some of his siblings lived. That was in 1976. He quickly began to pursue his dreams, starting with a job. He worked at Lefton's and learned many things about employment: how to interact with and get along with co-workers; and how to manage your pay e.g. how much to save and how much to spend; and how to pay your bills. Bobby learned those lessons well and now lives prominently with his family in Chicago.

Bobby left Lefton's after 5 years, and went to work with his brother Jack at Chernins' Shoes. He worked there, in sales, for approximately 6 or 7 years. He worked at Whole Foods for about a year before going to Roscoe Company. He has been employed there for the last 15 years, and counting. He drives a truck for the company which he totally enjoys.

Bobby met his wife, Verdell in Chicago and they married on December 24, 1981. They immediately started to build a tight-knit family unit which included three children: Ronnie Heard, Ecola "Coco" Ann Jackson Knox, and Bobby Jackson Jr. Bobby, Jr. just recently got married to the lovely Kiyona. The wedding ceremony was conducted by his Uncle Jack. "Coco" married a few years ago and had a beautiful, elegant wedding.

Bobby and Vernell live quietly, peacefully, and gracefully in their lovely home on the South Side of Chicago enjoying the many blessings God has bestowed upon them.

Pearl Kilpatrick Harper was born on February 5, 1927 in Eastman, Georgia to the union of Howard Kilpatrick and Dessie Mae Edwards Kilpatrick. Pearl is the fourth daughter and the fourth child of seven children. Pearl told me that she had a really happy childhood spending a lot of time with her beloved mother. She was ten years old when her mother passed away in 1937. Pearl remembers her mother told her that the records say she was born February 3rd, but it was February 5th instead.

She remembers her mother dressing she and her sister, Clara alike, like twins. Pearl's memories of her mother are pleasant and so precious. She would sit on the porch with her; she would help her with her chores; and she enjoyed just being with her as she did whatever. She said her mother worked hard at everything she did.

Pearl remembers her and Clara going to this little school, which in her mind, that was a private school. They got snacks and small meals at the school when they attended. Those were good memories of learning and growing up with her sister, Clara.

When her mother got sick, she told Pearl that she wanted her kids to stay together; don't give her kids away. She did not want another woman "over her kids." Dessie Mae Kilpatrick Edwards died in the year 1937 and her mother, Mattie Lou Edwards and their father, Howard Kilpatrick cared for her beloved children and tried to keep them together.

Pearl spent her young adult years in Eastman where she met and married Jimmy Harper. They later relocated to Chicago, Illinois where Pearl still resides. Jimmy died years ago, but he and Pearl were together for decades. Pearl and Jimmy had no children which meant that they lived for each other, always looking for ways to please. However, Pearl had many nieces and nephews that she helped along the way, just as if they were her own biological children.

She worked for many years at the Lutheran Family Services, making a difference in the lives of children. She loved those kids, going beyond the call of duty to meet their needs. Those needs included academic, emotional, and social needs. The children responded well to her service. She also bonded with the rest of the staff, developing life long friendships along the way.

Pearl was especially close to her niece, Mary. She visited her every day. They would chat and cook. There was always food around or waiting to be prepared. It was easy to bond together for Pearl and Mary lived only a few blocks away from each other on the south side of Chicago, so they enjoyed preparing those meals together daily. I especially loved the fried catfish and fried chicken; both Pearl and Mary were excellent cooks.

Pearl mentored Mary's oldest daughter, Cynthia, and helped her raise her son, Joe. She took special care of him as a baby and as a kid and as a young man.

Pearl was devastated when Mary passed away, and then again when David and Charles passed away. She was close to each one and was "there for them" through difficulties, hard times and good times, as well.

Pearl is Lenzo's only surviving sibling and is like my very own sister whom I never had. She has remained strong over these sixty plus years of our marriage. Pearl is strong in her love for the Lord and Christian values; strong in her commitment to her brother, nieces, and nephews; and strong in her belief to "do the right thing". Pearl's birthday is February 5th and mine is February 6th so we are alike in temperment and demeanor. She has a quiet nature, but when you "push her buttons", she'll get you straight.

Pearl is well past 85 now, but you would never know it. She goes out every day, sometimes walking across the street to Lake Meadows, and sometimes driving there, but she gets out to see her buddies at Dunkin' Donuts or just to "stretch her legs". She wants to stay animated and moving. She and Lenzo talk on the phone daily. Pearl enjoys giving monetary gifts to her nieces and nephews.

She resides on the south side of Chicago in a very nice, high rise building occupied by seniors, and in some cases, their families, as well. God has blessed her with a good, quiet life surrounded by pleasant memories and nice neighbors. To God be the glory for His mercy and His grace.

Harry Kilpatrick was born on June 13, 1929 in Eastman, Georgia to the union of Dessie Mae Edwards Kilpatrick and Howard Kilpatrick. He was the fifth child and the first son of seven children. Harry attended school in the Dodge County School System. He was a fast learner and a born rebel in his thinking. He followed the rules in the confines of his creativity and in his own way. His teachers adored him because of his leadership qualities and because he was a "charmer".

He was drafted into the United States Army on November 15, 1950 and served valiantly for 2 years. He was honorably discharged on August 14, 1952. He was awarded the Combat Infantry Badge, the United Nations Service Medal, the Korean Service Medal with 3 bronze stars and the Purple Heart. After his military career, he worked for many years and retired from the Piggly Wiggly Food Chain.

Harry married Odie Bell Howard Kilpatrick in the early 1950's and they had eight children together: Solomon, Mary Ann, Wayne, Leon, Harrison, Lonzo, Earl, and Gail. They met and married in Eastman, Georgia and they remained there most of their lives. I used to encourage Odie Bell to visit us in Chicago; she would say "maybe I will", but she never wanted to leave her children or her husband. All of her attention was focused on her family.

Harry was gentle and loving to his wife, to match her gentle, kind nature. He loved and cherished her in his own special way.

He loved his kids and dealt with them in a firm, but kind way always encouraging them to be strong and to work hard. He seemed to have understood each of his kids, and encouraged them to keep pursuing their dreams. He was so proud of their accomplishments and successes in life.

Harry was truly remarkable, being known as somewhat of an "icon" in that little town of Eastman. He had his followers who looked to him for advice and wisdom. He was affectionately called "Kil" and "Kilroy". I was amazed at his skills in playing checkers. He was a master. He loved shooting pool and was excellent at that, as well. Harry was "fearless" and enjoyed doing things in his own way. Like Frank Sinatra, Harry must have thought at the end of his life, "I did it my way". He lived his life with a vengeance in the pursuit of his own happiness and his own dreams. When I think of my brother-in-law, Harry, I think of him with dignity and respect for everyone has a right to pursue happiness in their own way.

Odie Bell, Harry's wife died on September 3, 2001. Lenzo and I went to Eastman to attend the funeral. I was devastated, as was her family, at the loss of this beautiful woman who lived her life with unselfishness, and humility, and trust. The sweetness of her character demonstrated to me what God can do through the meek and lowly of heart. The example of her peace and courage have filled me with hope. I am so fortunate to have had her life touch mine in such a beautiful way.

I will never forget her death, because we flew home right after the services. It was September 10, 2001. The next morning while I was looking at Channel 5 TV, I saw that first plane fly into one of the Twin Towers. I was shocked and thought someone accidently hit the building in a plane. I was terribly wrong, and we all know it was a terrorist attack on our homeland. Lenzo and I sat in front of the TV all that day in total shock and sadness and grief. It is an image that is seared on my heart and mind, never to be forgotten.

Harry died on October 24, 2008 at the Carl Vinson Veterans' Administration Center in Dublin, Georgia, some seven years after the death of his beloved, Odie Bell. He left a legacy for his children of love of family, hard work, and utter toughness to face the challenges of life "head on" and "fearless".

Solomon Kilpatrick is the oldest son of Harry and Odie Bell. He resides in Eastman with his wife, Rose Mary. Solomon is tall, thin, with a complexion like Hershey's dark chocolate, and a head of hair that resembles black fur. He's about the nicest guy you could meet with a nice smile and a ready laugh. As a young man, before he married his wife, Solomon stayed with us in Chicago. Lenzo got him a job at Burger King and he was quite content. He was great friends with my sons, Kevin and Lenard. After a while, Solomon started thinking about home, and parents, and siblings and decided to return to Eastman. We tried to talk him out of it because we thought he had a bright future in Chicago. It fell on "deaf ears", but he promised to come back and visit us often. He came back in February of 2004 to attend Lenard's funeral.

Solomon married Rose Mary when he returned to Eastman and they had one daughter, Shatese, who they named after my oldest granddaughter, Shatese Tang Jenkins. Solomon bought property where he and his wife lives in Eastman that is extremely valuable with acres of trees. He works extremely hard to maintain that property. Rosemary pastors her own church and serves the surrounding community. Like so many others in the family, she's a great cook.

Mary Ann Kilpatrick Brown is Harry and Odie Bell's oldest daughter. She resides in Eastman, Georgia with her husband, Reginald Brown, and their four children. Mary Ann has a lucrative job in Eastman where she works for the State Health and Human Services. She takes pride in helping people who are disenfranchised and suffering.

Wayne Kilpatrick is the second son of Harry and Odie Bell. He was born in Eastman, but moved to the state of Texas as a young adult. He served in the military courageously. Wayne is tall and handsome with poise and dignity, and disciplined resolve which decries his training in the military. I visited his church, Church of Christ at Cedar Valley in Lancaster, Texas in October, 2011. I had gone to Texas to celebrate my Aunt Nesha's 90th birthday who lived in a nearby city, McKinney, in Texas. Wayne and Carolyn (Diane) his wife, opened up their home to me for four days and it was wonderful. They treated me like royalty. On the Sunday before I left to come home, Wayne and Carolyn took me to their church. I was inspired by the message and the obvious love of the members for each other. When I got home, I e-mailed the minister a message of encouragement. The minister responded in kind.

That ended our communication, but he made my day, as well. I had been impressed because the church was large, not quite a "mega church", but large. And yet, he along with his congregation seemed to be like what, I imagine, the New Testament churches were like.

I was impressed with Wayne because like his brothers, he stood tall and straight as he directed guests to their seats. He had been an usher for a long time and had been trained well. I felt pride and admiration. His mom and dad were looking down on him, from heaven, and were proud. His wife, Carolyn (Diane) has health issues, waiting for a heart transplant, and Wayne cares for her with love and tenderness. He cooks the meals, takes her for her doctor appointments, and takes her wherever she needs to go. He is exceptional in that he exists to meet her every need, if possible.

Harrison Kilpatrick was born in Eastman to the union of Harry and Odie Bell Kilpatrick. Most of his life has been spent in Eastman, but he came and stayed with us for a short time in Chicago. He did not enjoy that time away from his beloved home town. He soon went back to Eastman where he married his wife, Sally, and they then began to build their family. Harrison continues to live in Eastman and enjoys a pleasant and prosperous life.

Earl Kilpatrick, Leon Kilpatrick, and Lonzo Kilpatrick were all born to the union of Harry and Odie Bell Kilpatrick. Earl continues to live in Eastman, working and spending time with his family and friends. Leon spent his childhood in Eastman and went to school there. In his early adult life, he moved to Atlanta, Georgia where he lives privately, and prominently. Sadly, Lonzo recently passed away after a long illness. He had experienced health problems for a number of years.

His death was a devastating blow to his siblings and the rest of the family. It caused them to stop and to ponder the sanctity of life, but also, the brevity of life. In Psalm 90:10, the Word says "The days of our years are three-score years and ten; and if, by reason of strength, they be fourscore years, yet is their strength labor and sorrow; for it is soon cut off, and we fly away." Life is fleeting, as verse 12 of the same chapter says: "So, teach us to number our days, that we may apply our hearts unto wisdom."

Gail Kilpatrick is the second and the youngest daughter born to the union of Harry and Odie Bell Kilpatrick. She was born in Eastman and has spent most of her life there. Gail has always been bright and energetic, as well as, animated – constantly on the move. Gail was great friends with Lenard, my son, her cousin. They always hung out together when we visited Eastman. As a young person, she knew where the fun places were. She was devastated when Lenard passed away. Gail continues to reside in Eastman to this day, spending valuable time with her siblings and her friends.

Debra Delaine Tuff Dixon was born on February 21, 1957 in Eastman, Georgia to the union of Harry Kilpatrick and Martha Tuff Jones. She attended the Peabody High School and graduated from the Job Corps.

Debra worked at the Dodge County Hospital for several years, but later was employed with the Dodge County Board of Education at the High School. She was very hard working and conscientious in everything she attempted to do. She went beyond the call of duty on her job and she always sought to have an immaculately clean home. She was serious about her relationship to her siblings. Although they had a different mother, she sought to spend time with them, showing them how much she loved them.

Debra came to Chicago to visit her Aunt Pearl and Uncle Lenzo once, some years ago. She was so gracious and kind and considerate. When we visited her in Eastman, she was the same. She would drive Lenzo around to visit different relatives and friends that he was concerned about. She also loved taking pictures; we still have one very nice picture that she took of us at Lenzo's high school reunion. She was a concerned and loving person and related to everyone. She always had a smile; she was always pleasant; and she was always in "good spirits".

Sadly, Debra died suddenly of a heart attack on October 19, 2008. It was five days before her beloved dad, Harry Kilpatrick, passed away. He died on October 24, 2008. Her funeral service was held on October 25, 2008, one day after Harry's passing. I thought how sadly ironic is her death, but our God is sovereign and He never makes a mistake. I yielded to His sovereignty.

Debra left a daughter, Jasmine Dixon, and a son, Christopher Cofield. She also left her devoted companion Winston Cofield, and her "slew" of siblings from her mother's side and her dad's side. To God be the glory for the legacy, and the memories, that Debra left to her family and friends.

Ilean Kilpatrick Fruitree was born on December 16, 1930 in Eastman, Georgia to the union of Howard Kilpatrick and Dessie Mae Edwards Kilpatrick. She was the youngest daughter and the sixth child of seven children. Ilean spent her childhood years in Eastman where she attended elementary school and high school. She, similar to her brother Harry, was a rebel, marching to a different drummer.

Ilean's son, Alonza, was born on April 9, 1947, and while she was pregnant, she moved to Miami, Florida where she gave birth. After the birth of her son, she took him back to Eastman to be raised by the family there. Ilean had recently married Winston Fruitree, and began sharing her life with him.

Ilean loved living in Miami. Her sister, Mattie Mae was already there and they spent just about every day together. She had many life changing experiences there. She absolutely ruled the space she happened to enter. Ilean was innovative and creative, passing those skills down to her son.

Lenzo and I used to visit Ilean (and Mattie Mae) in Miami and she was always glad to see us. She simply adored her brother and urged us to stay longer. When she became gravely ill, Lenzo visited her in the hospital. She was laughing and talking and so glad to see her brother from Chicago. Sadly, soon after that visit, she passed away. Ilean died of cancer at the young age of 38 years. The service was held in Miami, but her body was shipped back to Eastman for burial. The family was devastated, never quite getting over it. Her name is mentioned so often in family gatherings. Her legacy lives on in her son and his family who reside now in Chicago, Illinois.

Alonza "Junior" Fruitree was born in Miami, Florida to the union of Ilean Kilpatrick Fruitree and Robert Henry Hamilton, Sr. "Junior" was the only child of his mother, but one of five children of his father. He spent some of his early childhood in Eastman, but spent a few years with his mother in Miami. At the age of 15, Lenzo brought him to Chicago to live with us. He lived with us and became part of our family as another one of our kids. He attended high school and had the unique experience of working in our first business venture, a little corner store on 74th and Peoria. Junior had a kind of certain persona that he brought to the store. He took no prisoners; he was tough with the kids (and adults) who thought they could "get over" you with foolishness. Junior wasn't having it. He honed his professional skills at the store. He developed many relationships with the people who came to the store and appreciated having a neighborhood store and the ones that noticed that Junior was a really nice guy trying to do a great job. And he did a great job, not only at the store but at anything he attempted to do. He has been a construction worker as a career, which is apropo for he can build anything, fix anything, or create anything. He's smart, bright, and hard working; always seeking to perfect every project down to the minuest detail.

Junior married the very lovely Betty Chavers Fruitree on June 8, 1968, the same year he went to serve in the United States Army. Junior and Betty built their family on the south side of Chicago. They have been married for over 40 years and counting. Betty takes such pride in maintaining an orderly, beautiful home. Additionally, Betty is a great cook - skills she learned from her mom, Ella Chavers. She prepares big, big meals and invites family and friends over to enjoy. They love to dance, so her parties are sheer fun and excitement.

Junior served in the military from 1968-1970, being deployed on the Okinawa Island in Japan for most of that time. He did not enjoy that period of his life. He wrote us letters that told of his frustration and his longing for home. He told me about the time of his mother, Ilean's passing in 1969. The Red Cross made it possible for him to fly home to attend her funeral. He had to pay them back for the cost of airfare.

Junior bares a striking resemblance to his dad, Robert Henry Hamilton, Sr. Mr. Hamilton was quite prominent in Eastman. He graduated from the Peabody High School in 1944 at the age of 16, and went on to Morehouse College in Atlanta where he received a Bachelor of Arts degree in Business Administration. Mr. Hamilton joined the Phi Beta Sigma Fraternity and as a young man entered the military at Fort Jackson South Carolina, earning the rank of Sargeant and receiving the National Defense Service Medal. He instructed illiterate young inductees in reading, enabling them to meet the military standards of that day and time.

Mr. Hamilton had an insatiable thirst for the psychology of learning and human behavior. After his stint in the military, these factors motivated him to enter the field of Education. He received a Masters of Arts degree in School Administration, Guidance & Counseling from Atlanta University in 1955. In 1956, at the tender age of 28, he became principal of the William James Elementary & High School in Bulloch County, Statesboro, Georgia.

He went on to become a very innovative and successful principal; he continued to pursue higher education and training; and received numerous honors and rewards for the things that he did to advance, not only education, but to advance science experiments and research, as well. One of the most prestigious honors he received was to be appointed a Southern Foundation Fellow at George Peabody Teachers' College by Governor Carl E. Sanders.

He was named to the 1990 Dream Team by the Board of Commissioners of Fulton County. This reflects Mr. Hamilton's wonderful work ethic and also describes his son, Alonza "Junior" Fruitree.

Junior and Betty reside in their beautiful home in Chicago, Illinois. They have one daughter, Sharniece and one son, Lonza, and two grandsons, Christopher and Matthew. Sharniece "Niece" is a renowed poet and Lonza is an educator in the Chicago Public School System (CPS).

David Kea, Lenzo's nephew, lives in Detroit, Michigan where his ancestors settled after leaving the state of Georgia. David's grandfather, Alton Kea was Lenzo's half-brother, both having Howard Kilpatrick as their father. David is one of Lenzo's favorite because of his intelligence, his confidence and "in your face" conversations, his "gift for gab," and his great sense of charity, wanting to help others, always looking for ways to make someone happy. When my Aunt Dee lived in Detroit, and before her illness, David would visit her, doing repairs, running errands, and doing other things to assist her, and then sometimes just to visit her and "keep her company" for a few minutes. Because she was my special aunt, he treated her as such. On occasion, when I visited Detroit, David would bring me the best corned beef sandwiches I had ever tasted (and still the best).

David was married to Gale, and they had two sons together De Juan and David, Jr. When the kids were younger, David and Gale brought them to our family reunions (Jones/Thompson Reunions), no matter what city. David brought his family to wherever we celebrated our family gatherings. He met "no strangers". He loved talking and he could elaborate on any subject, as a matter of fact, he could talk "every body under the table", including my cousin, Thurman.

David and Gale have continued to visit us over the years, sometimes spending a night or two; sometimes spending just a few hours. David loves to travel. He rides a motorcycle, going from city to city on his bike.

His youngest son, De Juan, recently got married. It was the most elegant (and most expensive) wedding I have ever attended. Of course, Lenzo and I were treated like royalty. We used his hotel suite to house our grandkids, Le Shawn & Kyonna. De Juan provided everything for their stay, including pizza and other treats. It was on the top floor of the hotel, and the kids had a ball. De Juan married Bukola, who is African, and the wedding and the fabulous reception was traditional American and culturally African. De Juan invited our whole family, so my sister in-law, Pearl (his great aunt), my children, my grandchildren and my great grandchildren were all there. It was an experience that we will never forget. De Juan is a lobbyist in Springfield, Illinois and Bukola is a lobbyist for the RTAC. They are both prominent and successful in their own right.

David, Jr., the oldest son is a career military man. He lives prominently in Newport News, Virginia with his wonderful wife and beautiful little son.

Lenzo's father, Howard Kilpatrick, was born on March 16, 1899 in a small town called Newnan, Georgia. His mother was Mae Lou Kilpatrick and his father's name was Andrew Kilpatrick. Mr. Howard had siblings, but their names and their families are unknown, with the exception of his sister, Aunt Glenn Willis who lived in Helena, Georgia. We went to visit Aunt Glenn once, many years ago, and I remember how excited we were to be going to see Mr. Howard's only sister. She however was not excited to see us; she was not pleasant and had very little to say. We never went again. There was talk that Mr. Howard had a sister named Marie who left home and was never seen again. He had a brother in Eastman named "Uncle Jeff". He was said to be a "fortune teller," and kept people entertained and amazed on a daily basis.

Mr. Howard was an interesting man who loved his children and enjoyed checking on them, keeping up with what was happening in their lives with their growing families and various problems. He tried to be very helpful to his children when they encountered difficulties. Lenzo bares a striking resemblance to his father. He feels very happy about that, because he really loved and admired Mr. Howard. He passed away on May 11, 1975 at the age of 76 years. His legacy lives on in Pearl and in Lenzo and his children and grandchildren.

One of Mr. Howard's brothers was <u>Dwelley</u> <u>Kilpatrick</u>. He married Henrietta Kilpatrick in Eastman and their children were the ones who relocated to Detroit. <u>Willie</u> <u>Kilpatrick</u> was the oldest son, and was my absolute favorite. He was the nicest guy. When we visited Detroit, Willie dropped everything and came to pick Lenzo and me up. He and Lenzo were very close. He died at a young age after years of alcohol abuse. Although he suffered from that disease, he remained kind and thoughtful and helpful. He tried to help his family and friends. I respected him and admired him for the good things he did in his life. He was genuine.

Willie and the rest of his siblings were fair complexioned, with light brown skin tones. Lenzo and his siblings, on the other hand, were dark complexioned like Hershey's chocolates. Mr. Howard and his brother, Dwelley were different hues, and their children reflected that. It's like with all African American families, we are of all hues & colors of blackness.

Willie's sister, Jessie M. Kilpatrick Bailey, was the oldest girl born to Dwelley Kilpatrick and Henrietta Kilpatrick. Everyone affectionately called her "Sister." She was born in Eastman, Georgia on November 13, 1925. Jessie went to elementary school and high school in Eastman, but attended beauty school in Macon, Georgia. She was a member of the Parkinsongille Baptist Church in Eastman. She married John W. Bailey. Jessie moved to Detroit, Michigan in 1945 when she was twenty years old. She lived at 3333 Northwestern for decades. She died there on February 28, 1976 at 11:20 A.M. Along with her family, Jessie left two sisters, Christine and Irene to mourn her passing.

Christine Kilpatrick Whitaker was the second oldest daughter born to Dwelley Kilpatrick and Henrietta Wilson Kilpatrick. She was born on October 11, 1932 in Eastman, Georgia. She spent her very young years in Eastman, but as a young girl she moved to Detroit, Michigan to live with her oldest brother, Willie. She was educated in Eastman and graduated from the Pershing High School in 1952. Christine married Felton Whitaker in 1963 and instead of seeking a career of employment, she decided to stay home and be a homemaker for her husband. She was well known for her baked goods, and for making beautiful ceramics that she gave to her relatives and friends. Christine and Felton visited us in Chicago a couple of times, and we visited them in Detroit. She sent me a beautiful ceramic piece for my mantle years ago. It still sits on the entertainment center in our family room. Christine was a "colorful", interesting person, and I was stunned and devastated when she died on March 5, 2003. She had diabetes and accidentally cut her foot. She tried home remedies to deal with it instead of getting medical attention. It steadily got worse and by the time she went to the doctor, it was too late. She was hospitalized and days later, she slipped into a coma, and never woke up. Christine left her husband, Felton, and other family members and friends to mourn her loss. All of her siblings preceded her in death.

Irene Kilpatrick Burns was born on October 10, 1937 to the union of Dwelley Kilpatrick and Henrietta Wilson Kilpatrick in Eastman, Georgia. She was the youngest daughter among seven children. Irene went to school in Eastman where she was an eager and energetic learner. She learned quickly and was eager to put those skills in doing many creative tasks. She enjoyed knitting, and crocheting, and sewing on a sewing machine. Her hands were quick and nimble. I'm told she accepted the Lord as Savior at a very early age. During her adult years, she moved to Detroit to join her siblings who were already there. On April 18, 1961, Irene married Freeman Burns. Irene and her husband used to visit us quite often when we lived at 7429 So. Sangamon in Chicago. Irene was fine because she enjoyed being with us, but her husband posed a problem for me. I did not like him, and tried to avoid him at all times. He was not a pleasant man. Irene, on the other hand, loved being with us and the kids. The visits were usually short, and that was a good thing.

Irene was a member of the Pilgrim Star Baptist Church in Detroit. She loved to sing, so she joined the Golden Harps singing group and was with them for years. She later joined the Tones of Faith group.

Irene had one son, Ralph, and he came to visit us, as well. He spent time trying to find his way in the world; just trying to find happiness. I'm not sure if he found it, but God knows. Ralph died at a very young age. I remember he used to wear a little hat on his head most of the time. I pray that he is with the Lord. Like so many of our fine young men, he died much too soon.

Irene Kilpatrick Burns died on December 14, 1985 in Detroit, Michigan at the age of 48 years. She and her siblings are all gone now, leaving their grandkids and other family members, the legacy of the Dwelley Kilpatrick family. To God be the glory for His mercy and His grace.

Another cousin on the Edwards' side of the family was Willie Joe Searcy. Willie Joe Searcy was born on March 7, 1920 in Eastman, Georgia to Beulah Edwards Searcy who was the oldest child of Mattie Lou Madison Edwards and Elbert Edwards. Willie Joe attended elementary school and high school in Eastman. He expressed an interest and faith in God at an early age, joining the Mount Zion C.M.E. Methodist Church in Eastman during his youth.

He later moved to Chicago, Illinois where he met and married Emma Kate Jeffries and began building his family. They had three children together and there were two children born to other unions. His oldest, and first born son was Lewis B. "L.B." Searcy and he was born on July 4, 1938 in Eastman, Georgia when Willie Joe was about 18 years old. He moved to Chicago in 1956 to be close to his dad. L.B. served in the Armed Forces shortly afterwards. He met Gloria Perkins, and they married on June 27, 1962. They had three children together, Archie, Terry, and Sina. L.B. used to visit us often after he moved to Chicago. He enjoyed hanging out with his cousins and the rest of the guys from Eastman. He always seemed to have a "nervous energy", always rushing, always in a hurry. Tragically, L.B. died on July 20, 1975. His body was found floating in Lake Michigan, off 31st St. They found him right away because someone saw him jump in the water. L.B. was a good swimmer, but we never found out why he jumped in or what happened afterwards.

Willie Joe's other children are Richard Searcy, Patricia Searcy, and Melvin Searcy, all of Chicago; and Gloria Searcy Cooper who lived in Benton Harbor, Michigan. Willie Joe was devoted to his family. He worked hard to provide for them, and to bring some happiness in their life. He was a genuinely nice guy who suffered, for years with health issues. He spent the later years of his life in a wheelchair. Willie Joe died on May 3, 1982 at Cook County Hospital in Chicago, following a long illness. His family described him as a very kind, considerate man who made friends wherever he went. They said he was a devoted husband and a loving father. That was affirmation for us, for we saw the virtues of this very humble and gentle man. Praise God for his life and his legacy.

Lenzo's first cousin Joyce "Joey Lee" Young was the only child of Cora Belle Gibbs. She was born in Eastman, Georgia and went to elementary school and high school there. She spent her whole life in Eastman. Her name was Joyce, but everyone called her Joey Lee. She married Morris Young and they had one child together, Joann Young. Joey Lee died at a very early age, leaving her mother, Aunt Belle, and her daughter, Joann, devastated.

Joey Lee's daughter, Joann was born on July 24, 1949, in Eastman. Joann was smart and energetic and was a fast learner. She enjoyed doing things, discovering things. She went to school in Eastman and graduated from Peabody High School in 1965. Joann attended Ft. Valley State College and absolutely loved it. She was later employed by the Dodge County School System as a Teacher's Aide in the Early Childhood Program. Joann married Douglas Coley in 1966 and they had three children together, Karen, Tawanna, and Kevin. Joann was a member of Mt. Zion C.M.E. Church, where she served so beautifully well, willing to do whatever she could to help everybody. She was elected to serve on the Board of Christian Education where she made a big difference in kids' lives. Joann died suddenly at 31 years, of a massive blood clot, leaving the family in shock and disbelief. Aunt Belle took over the care of Joann's children. It was October, 1980, and like I say all the time, "thank God for grandmothers." Karen, the oldest daughter came to Chicago to stay with us for a while. She did not like it at all. Karen soon returned to Eastman and her siblings where she was far more content. Tawanna went into education as a career after her college experience, following in her mother's footsteps. Kevin is working and building his family, also, in Eastman. The three of them are doing well with their families.

William Marion Edwards, Lenzo's first cousin, was born on February 26, 1929 to the union of Ernest Edwards and Marie Edwards in Lumber City, Georgia. William spent the early years of his life in Lumber City, but as soon as he could, he moved to Evansville, Indiana, where he completed his formal education. William became a Chrysler Corporation employee in 1952, after he served in the United States Army. He met Patricia Louise Garrett in Evansville and they married on September 21, 1957. They had one son, Tony, and he was the absolute center of both their lives. In 1959, he moved his family to St. Louis, Missouri where William later bought his beloved "Pat" a beautiful house. He continued to work for the Chrysler Corporation for some 40 years. William was the hardest working man who never missed work for any reason. He was totally committed to his job. He was disciplined and patient. He planned for saving money and for then buying what he wanted. He loved cars, but waited until he could get the very best. I admired him for the way he took care of his beloved family and the sacrifices he made to enjoy, not the moment, but the future moments. William accepted the Lord as his Savior when he was a young man in Evansville. He was baptized and united with the New Hope Baptist Church in Evansville.

William died suddenly of a heart attack on February 4, 1992 at the St. Anthony Medical Center in South County, Missouri. His legacy lives on in his son, Tony, who is a wonderful husband and father.

William's wife, Pat, and I were great friends during our young years. We were about the same age with Pat being born in 1934 and I was born in 1935. We were raising our children and building our families at about the same time. Her son, Tony, and my son, Kevin, were both born in March, 1960. Pat and I loved to "girl talk", and we both had a love of reading. I used to visit her at her home on Marick Dr. (and she visited me in Chicago) and she would read book after book. That was her joy. Pat died on November 7, 2010 and my son Kevin, my daughter-in-law, Twanda and I attended her funeral. It was held at the Bopp Chapel in Kirkwood, Missouri on November 12, 2010. I must mention that Pat called William, her husband, "Toots". I never heard her call him anything but "Toots".

William and Pat left a great legacy for their son, Antonio "Tony" Marion Edwards, their daughter-in-law, Kelly, and their grandchildren, La Toya, Alexis, Marissa, and Kristina. To God be the glory.

As I did the research on Lenzo's family history, it was so gratifying to see the resilience of the ancestors. How wonderful to see and experience the love and care of family members for each other. I remember him telling me that in his hometown of Eastman, no body messed with them because people said it was too many of them Edwards! If you fought one, you fought them all. His family, like mine, was large, diverse, and interesting. I was struck by the similarities, by the ironies, and also struck by the differences, as well.

We both came from families that started out in a small, southern town, and then migrated to northern cities looking for a better life. Another similarity is that there was always a strong family member that kept the family together, usually around food - eating and fellowshipping together.

One irony in our families is that Lenzo's mother's name was Dessie Mae; my paternal grandmother's name was Dessie. They both passed away in 1937. Lenzo's dad was born on March 16th, my dad was born on March 16th (different years).

My childhood experiences were full of discovery and anticipation each day. I enjoyed spending time with my cousins and my aunts. Lenzo's very early childhood memories were not pleasant. He remembers being unhappy, being hungry sometimes, but lovingly nurtured by his maternal grandmother.

We are who we are because of the legacy of our ancestors. We know how to raise families and we know how to survive; not only to survive, but to thrive with God's help. We have been together for over 60 years through much heartache, through much hardship, and through much sorrow, and we are still standing; still strong looking toward a bright future although we are in the twilight of our lives.

We now reside in South Holland, Illinois and love the village and its' community of churches. We have lived here since May, 1996 and have never regretted it. We enjoy the quiet and the beauty and the people.

Lenzo and I are quite different in our approach to living, on a daily basis at home:

I am animated, in constant motion, always in pursuit of the next task, and feeling great when the task is completed. I tend to be very retrospective and quiet, especially in the early morning hours. I do very little talking. And yet, with the children Le Shawn and Kyonna, I talk a lot. We interact constantly. I'm always chiding, always scolding, always encouraging, always exhorting them to be excellent in their thinking and in making choices. Also, when I'm speaking before a group, I tend to be thorough, long-winded, talking "a little bit about a lot of things." I look at very little T.V., only at certain times, and at certain shows. I like to write, or read, in silence. I enjoy my I Phone 5 C and using my I Pad. I use my laptop that Kevin and Twanda gave me sparingly, but I'm constantly on my personal computer, which Kevin rebuilt. He keeps the computer happy (and me) by cleaning up the viruses and fixing anything else that might happen with it. I love playing solitaire, spider solitaire, and free cell on the computer, sometimes for hours, seeking to keep my mind sharp and clear. It works as therapy for me when I'm stressed or frustrated.

Lenzo, on the other hand, is more of the "couch potato" kind. He loves T.V. and watches a variety of things, shows, and people. He enjoys watching sports, especially the Bulls and the Bears. He's a 24/7 television person. He's very knowledgeable and can speak intelligently on many topics. His favorite topic, I think, is politics. He talks constantly about the mayor and other politicians who he feels are exploiting and denigrating the black community. He deplores those politicians, Democrats and Republicans, who treat President Obama with disrespect and disregard.

Lenzo is adept at managing finances and could very well be an accountant if he had chosen to be one. He understands the "money game" and knows how to play it quite well. He takes a lot of time to make up his mind. No rash, quick decisions. When we were looking to buy a home back in the 90's, we stopped at our present house and my son, Lenard, and I were smitten. When I walked in the door, I knew I wanted this house with the earth tone colors and beautiful walls and 5 bedrooms and 3 bathrooms. Lenzo was not impressed and was not sure, at all. It took a lot of convincing from me and Lenard. We finally won him over.

But Lenzo has not always been a "couch potato" kind of person. In his younger days, he was very animated and quite the "man around town". He started early on to pursue his dream of becoming a prominent business man. He realized his goals, time and time again. He owned a restaurant, with his friend, Robert Davis for a few years. It was on 79th and Halsted. For years we owned a little corner grocery store back in the late 1960's and early 70's. Lenzo had a service station at 76th & Jeffrey for several years. His close friend, Willie Mims worked for him as the auto mechanic. Years later, when he got rid of it, he sold it to Mims. Lenzo was a partner with Jerry Butler in the Iceman Beverage Company for years. The offices were located on 64th & King Dr. Later, Jerry moved the office to 83rd St. As if that wasn't enough, he later worked in the Burger King Restaurant as a District Area Manager. He especially worked well with Garland C. Guice, who was the President of the organization which was called Inner City Foods, Inc. Mr. Guice was highly respected and he was one of the few business men Lenzo looked up to. Mr. Guice liked him and trusted him implicitly. As President of Inner City Foods, Inc., he was one of the country's more creative and innovative business men. His main thrust was heading a group of sixteen Burger King restaurants. He was listed in the Cosmopolitan Chamber of Commerce publication as one of the "Outstanding Men of America." Lenzo appears in the Chicago Defender Newspaper with Mr. Guice and others at one of their projects. Lenzo looked "spiffy" in one of his company sports jacket and a beautiful angled striped tie. The article and 2 pictures appeared on August 9, 1980. Unfortunately, Mr. Guice died suddenly on June 9, 1985. He was one of the great ones that Lenzo encountered over his long career. Another front page article about Lenzo and his work with Burger King appeared in the Chicago Defender on March 14, 1978 when he was promoted to Area Manager. The article told of Lenzo's rise from a little kid working in a grocery store in Eastman, Georgia to coming to Chicago and graduating from Wendell Phillips High School to majoring in business at Clarksville College in Tennessee to entering the fast food business to owning and operating his own small retail store.

Lenzo's path in life has led him to hob-nob with celebrities, rich and famous and otherwise. He brought me right along with him and I was only "star struck" once, and that was when I met Harry Belefonté. Lenzo's friend, Walter Turner, invited us to a party to honor Belafonté. He had performed here in Chicago and the party was on the top floor of one of the big, elegant hotels downtown. (I can't remember which one). Harry Belefonté was charming and breath-takingly handsome. He purposely took a sip out of a champagne glass that I was just holding. I took the glass with me when we left to go home and I kept that glass, without washing it for a long time. Lenzo made fun of me and told his friends about it later. Walter Turner, we called him "Turner", introduced Lenzo to many people of prominence, one being Muhammed Ali.

We attended several of Muhammad Ali's fights, made possible through Turner. It was an exciting time of our history. Ali won his fights, mostly; and I remember how everyone "dressed to the nines" to attend his fights. Excitement and anticipation were in the air; it was a kind of euphoria to be in the midst of that crowd. Usually, we went to Ali's dressing rooms after the fight. The men were with him and I stayed in the outer room with the other wives and women. I remember one "faux pas" moment at one of those fights. One of the buttons on my dress popped off, and I was in a panic. One of the ladies there just happened to have a safety pin and helped me get my dress back together. It's funny now, as I think about it, but it was serious, and I was embarrassed, although no one really paid much attention to it.

Lenzo and I were at the fight in New York City at the Madison Square Garden when Joe Frazier beat Muhammad Ali. It was March 8, 1971 and many dignitaries were there, including Frank Sinatra and Hubert Humphrey. I did not see them. Lenzo and I had seats that were not too close to the ring. We were stunned when Ali lost because he had won all his previous fights. Ali beat Frazier in their 2nd match in 1974, and again in 1975 in the Philippines. It was called the "Thrilla in Manilla", and some say it was the greatest fight of all times. We did not attend to any other fights after the one at Madison Square Garden. After that fight, the party of us went to the Copacabana. I still have the picture of us there, and later when we looked at the picture, we noticed that Adam Clayton Powell, Jr.

was there sitting at a table behind me. I always admired him for his fiery rhetoric, and his great service to, not only the city of New York, but the country.

Jerry Butler is a personal friend of Lenzo. He and his wife, Annette, have remained our friends over many years. Jerry Butler, the "Ice Man", was born in Sunflower, Mississippi. When he was 3 years old, the family moved north to Chicago, Illinois. In 1958, Jerry, then eighteen years old, wrote a song called "For Your Precious Love." It was destined to become the first gold record for him and the Impressions. This song can almost be considered the first "Soul Record".

Later that year Jerry left the Impressions to pursue a solo career, having his first million seller, as a solo artist in 1960 with another of his compositions, "He'll Break Your Heart". Of his association with the Impressions, Jerry said, "We were committed to the fact that we believed in our music and believed in ourselves, and when you believe in what you do, then what you do has a lasting quality."

During his long career, he has sold over thirty million records. He has earned seven gold records. Jerry has appeared on most of the major variety shows in the U.S. and Europe; in the 1990's, he appeared on the "Entertainment Tonight" Show. He has hosted six segments of the "Soul Show", shown for PBS television.

In 1977, Jerry was asked to be the featured performer at the National Black Caucus Convention. He has composed over 40 songs during his long career. He has produced and composed songs for Elvis Presley, Liberace, Oscar Brown, Jr., the Stylistics, Smokey Robinson, Isaac Hayes, and many others. He produced and composed commercials for Johnson Products Company, Coca Cola, McDonalds, and National Oats.

Jerry currently serves as Cook County Commissioner. I still have the article and picture from the Chicago Defender, dated Monday, November 11, 1985 when he was a candidate for the office. Lenzo was in that picture with Jerry and Annette and some of his supporters. He went from being the entertainer, the "Ice Man" to the political stage. He juggles the two careers, for he still performs, bringing joy to his fans and satisfaction to his constituents. One of Jerry's favorite sayings is, "a man's destiny usually finds him." This describes him, and his thinking as one of our most powerful celebrities.

Jerry Butler wrote a book entitled "Only The Strong Survive: Memoirs of a Soul Survivor" in 2001. He talks about the first group he was associated with, The Impressions, which included his friend, the late Curtis Mayfield. Jerry and Curtis were friends for almost 50 years before his death in December, 1999. Jerry recited the poem, "If" by Rudyard Kipling, from memory which he learned as a child from his mother at Curtis Mayfield's funeral. Jerry's book offers a rich first person account of African American musical history. It's a great "read" because it not only gives a bibliography and discography that allows you to gage timelines, but it gives an African-American cultural history.

Lenzo was in business with Jerry Butler in the early 1970's. It was called "Iceman Beverages" and served not only the south side of Chicago, but all over the city. With all of his fame and celebrity, Jerry remains a down to earth, regular guy. In his service as Cook County Commissioner, he works for the good of people and constantly looks for new ways to serve the black community.

Fred Cash, one of the original members of the Impressions' is Lenzo's longtime friend. The Impressions performed together until 1970 when Curtis Mayfield left to go solo. On his own Mayfield scored big with his monumental 1972 soundtrack "Superfly", which featured classics like the title track, "Freddie's Dead", and "Pusherman". It's associated with the civil rights movement. These weren't just songs, but were songs with a powerful message that meant something then as it still does today. Fred Cash and Sam Gooden were known for their lyrics of faith and inspiration. Their 1964 song, "Keep On Pushing" is widely regarded as the first R&B song to rally Blacks behind the Civil Rights' Movement. Some of the other songs were: "It's All Right", "People Get Ready", "Meeting Over Yonder", "Choice of Colors", "We're A Winner", and "Check Out Your Mind."

Fred Cash said of The Impressions: "We were young. The movement was happening. We had a lot of nerve. We still sing those songs. We didn't know it was going to be what it is today. Curtis was one of the great writers I've known in my lifetime." Sam Gooden said: "We told Curtis he was writing songs before his time. He was writing songs that still inspire people to keep on pushing. To sit and look at it now as they stand the test of time is fantastic."

Because of the strength of their vocal power, people were amazed that there were only three members. The whole sound of Chicago soul in the 60's is modeled on what these three guys developed with the song, "It's All Right." Fred said, "Back during that time, white artists would cover your songs. It would be much bigger than what you had. So we started singing way up so that people couldn't imitate us. If they did one of our songs, they had to put some work into it to make it happen."

Fred and Sam are still singing all over the world as they did in their early years. They have added a third member to their group to preserve that unique sound of the Impressions.

We have been with them through the 60's and 70's. Lenzo met many artists in the entertainment world through his friend Jerry Butler and his friend Fred Cash. We spent time with Fred and his first wife, Judy, when they lived in Chicago. Fred and Sam Gooden and his wife, Gloria now live in different states. We attended most of their shows, as their guests, when they came to Chicago. I loved their music and enjoyed seeing their shows over and over. Lenzo and Fred still talk several times a year on the phone.

Jamo Thomas, a friend of Lenzo's, as well, is from Eastman, Georgia. He is a musician and was with Jerry and Curtis and the Impressions all those years. Jamo seems an "enigma" to me, because he is one smooth character. He managed to be in the inner circle or "inner sanctum" of the most powerful of the entertainment world. He has a brilliant mind and very creative with an air of mystery and a secrecy about him that is very interesting to observe. He lives in Macon, Georgia now, but he and Lenzo keep up with each other several times a year. His son, Patrick Manual, runs his business operations. His friend, Cookie, is an excellent cook, preparing something delicious especially for us when we visited them in Macon.

Eddie Thomas has had a long and prosperous career in the music business. He managed the Impressions in the 1950's, and was instrumental in Curtis Mayfields' success. He recognized Curtis' talent and other groups like the Medallionaires. He started out managing these groups and then he eventually started his own promotions' business where he worked with other talents like Ray Charles, Chuck Berry, and Barry White. Over his career, Eddie has received many awards including in 1994 the George Foster Peabody (broadcasting's highest honor.) In 2000 he was inducted into "The History Makers" an association for outstanding achievements by African Americans in all categories of life. Additionally Eddie has received 61 gold and 11 platinum records. Eddie and his wife, Verlene, are still active in the music business. In 2006, they produced an inspirational jazz album titled "I Won't Be Lonely Anymore". In October, 2006 Eddie was inducted into the Wendell Phillips High School Hall of Fame.

Eddie and Verlene are friends of ours and when his first wife, Audrey, was living, we attended many of their lovely dinner parties where we saw and met celebrities in the music industry. Eddie and Audrey lived on the south side of Chicago where the "elite" resided, like Jesse Jackson and Gale Sayers, who were next door and across the street neighbors. Eddie and his second wife, Verlene live on the far north side in a beautiful, beautiful townhouse. Eddie and Lenzo keep in touch on a yearly basis. It is through our association with Eddie that we met Don Cornelius and was able to send my girls to dance on "Soul Train". The Soul Train was televised in Chicago at the Board of Trade Building at 141 W. Jackson. I have a picture of Curtis Mayfield, Don Cornelius, Tyrone Davis, and Eddie Thomas and George Williams kneeling in front. It was taken at the Soul Train studios downtown. These guys were the epitome of "cool".

Eddie and Verlene share a wonderful life together and they are thankful for the many blessings they receive each day.

Rev. Dr. Benjamin Garrett was a childhood friend of Lenzo. They were both kids in Eastman, Georgia. Later in life Ben moved to Chicago and met and married his wife, Ethel, and they built their family there. Ben got Lenzo a job at Maury Manufactoring Company during our early marriage. Ben worked hard and he became prominent as a result. He and Ethel also lived in Ida B. Wells Project at the same time we lived there, but they lived in a different high rise building. Ethel was bold and colorful, and I remember she wore high heeled mules every day, not just for dress up, but every single day. Ben realized his life's dream by becoming a pastor. He was the Pastor of the New Friendship Missionary Baptist Church in Robbins, Illinois which he loved. He was a dynamic preacher, and people flocked to his church in droves. He was friends with Rev. Dr. Clay Evans and Dr. Lou Della Evans Reid. I remember one of his sermons entitled "What can we render to God again for you?" The scripture verse was I Thessalonians 3:9. He said God is great and should be greatly praised. He mentioned "Presence, perpetuity, provision, protection, and perfection" of our God. It was a powerful message and I was inspired by it. Lenzo and I attended many of his sermons at his church in Robbins. He performed so many functions as a minister, not only in our family, but in other families also performing weddings and funerals and celebrations. Ben performed our renewing of our vows ceremony in 2002. He was respected and loved greatly by everyone who met him. Benjamin Garrett passed away a few years ago leaving a void in his family and friends which has not been filled by anyone else. Praise God for his life and the legacy he left to his children.

"Christianity does not exempt one from death; it only ensures triumph over death. All must die, there is no other way of entrance into our Heavenly Father's house." That saying appeared on the Obituary of Willie Mims, Lenzo's closest and best friend. We called him "Mims" and he and Lenzo were closer than brothers. Mims was born on July 19, 1935 in McCormick, South Carolina. He moved to Chicago in 1959 and married his beloved "Louise" in 1960. They had one son, Gregory, who I called "Gregs". I was the only one that called him that; everyone else called him "Greg." Mims accepted the Lord early in his life and joined the Southwestern M.B. Church on October 19, 1986. He was baptized on November 2, 1986. Mims was an important member of our family for he was an uncle to our children and of course, a brother to Lenzo. After the manner of Proverbs 18:24 – "a friend who sticketh closer than a brother." His son and our kids grew up together and our families shared big feasts and fried catfish together. Mims loved fried catfish. He enjoyed joking and laughing, although Mims was quiet and unassuming and sometimes very shy. He was witty and funny; always saying something that caught your attention; something worth repeating; and something worth remembering. Mims died of lung cancer on February 3, 1992, leaving a big void in our family.

Louise has kept up with us over all these years. When Lenzo and I renewed our vows on our 50th anniversary, in June, 2002, Louise and Gregs attended. Little did we know that 3 months later, Gregs would die suddenly in his sleep. Louise was devastated and has not gotten over it to this day. Recently, she told Lenzo that she misses both Mims and Gregs so much. The last time I saw Gregs was at our wedding anniversary, and I remember he was so glad to see me. He gave me that beautiful smile and I gave him a big, bear hug. Gregs lived a relatively short life, but during that time he developed into a warm, thoughtful person who laughed a lot and loved to smile. Gregory had accepted the Lord and joined the

Southwestern Baptist Church, the same church as his dad. He was a faithful member of the Sanctuary Choir, proving that he loved to sing and he loved to serve. To God be the glory for the life of Gregs, and to God be the glory for the life and legacy of Willie Mims.

Robert L. Davis was the very dear friend to Lenzo. He was a business partner in some of Lenzo's ventures. It was through Robert we acquired "the building" at 8201 So. Peoria. He was in real estate then. He and Lenzo went to Wendell Phillips High School together. They both got married and had somewhat parallel lives with having children. After high school, he went to Kentucky State University where he earned his undergraduate degree. He married Berlean Richmond Davis and they had six children together: Rosalynn, Rochelle, Rhonda, Robert, Jr., Regina, and Keith.

Robert proudly served in the United States Air Force for several years. When he returned to Chicago, he joined the Chicago Police Department and served for over 30 years. As a police officer, he was able to provide security for my school, Carver Middle School in the early 1990's, in Altgeld Gardens. He served there faithfully for 7 years.

Robert loved to talk (He was very knowledgable) and had strong opinions about issues. He was very positive and he loved helping people and he enjoyed interacting with the students at Carver Middle. He spent a lot of time with the basketball team, going to their games, and supporting their activities and working with their parents. He was a great role model for the boys at the school. Robert had confidence and strength and he believed in consistency, determination, and commitment to a goal. He loved computers and technology and "gadgets".

Robert and Lenzo were friends from high school and our two families have intertwined over the years. They went through good and bad business deals together. Also, they were part of a group of 6 or 7 guys including Roberts' brother-in-law, Larry. They hung out together and remained close friends into adulthood.

He had health issues of diabetes and high blood pressure for a number of years, and he developed prostate cancer and other complications. He died on a Wednesday morning, October 28, 1998, leaving a beautiful legacy to his six children, and his grandchildren. To God be the glory for His mercy and His grace.

Lenzo has had several "tried & true" friends over the years; long-time friends that are "there for you" when you need them. Some of them passed away some time ago, but they each have had a big impact on our family:

Walter "Pete" Driver, Jr. "Driver", as Lenzo called him, was a friend through Sam Gooden, one of the Impressions. Sam was married to Driver's sister, Gloria. Driver introduced Lenzo to the people at Burger King and the rest is history. Pete Driver retired from the Chicago Police Department Evidence and Recovery Property Section as a Technician after 20 years of service. He was married to Audrey and they had one son, Lloyd D'Angelo Driver. Pete Driver was a very, very nice guy with a smiling face, a quick wit, bear hugs, and a loving spirit. When he became ill, Lenzo and Lenard visited him several times, praying for his recovery. Driver died in January, 2006.

Milton Marion "Tim" Waters, III. "Tim", as we called him was a long time friend and the brother of Lenzo's buddy, Maurice Waters. Tim said he did not know his full name until he joined the U.S. Army where he served five years as a radio operator and projectionist. He had a deep, and loud voice that was unique and unmistakeable. You knew it was Tim when you heard that voice. Tim was our insurance guy for decades, when he worked for New York Life Insurance Company for some 30 years. He was absolutely devoted to his clients and he had a loving, caring heart. He loved to cook, especially his 7-Up cake. Tim loved his neighbors and devoted lots of time to organizing yearly block club parties and projects for his 100th and Eberhart block which his family called home since 1967. They loved him back and called him "Tim", and sometimes other "choice" names jokingly. He was a member of the Metropolitan Community Church where he served as a trustee and started a Boy Scout Troop. Milton Marion "Tim" Waters, III died suddenly of a heart attack on a Monday, December 5, 2005 leaving a rich legacy for his wife, Mildred, and his children, Timothy, Milton IV, and Michele. To God be the glory for Tim's life and his legacy.

Maurice Chevalier Waters. Maurice was Tim's older brother and he was Lenzo's "ace boon coon". They were lifelong friends and our families intertwined over many years. Maurice was one of the 6 or 7 guys that were friends. Maurice's dad, Mr. Waters, was a mentor for those guys. He provided a "safe haven" for them, always exhorting them and not only telling them but showing them how to be men. Mrs. Waters was just as wonderful for she always had food and warmth for the young people.

Maurice was one of eight children that Mr. and Mrs. Waters had, and ironically was born in Newport, Arkansas in 1932. Newport was close to my own birthplace, and was where we went "to town" on Saturday nights. Maurice, like Lenzo and their friends, attended Wendell Phillips grade school and the high school. He completed his last year of high school in the United States Air Force, where he served from 1951 to January, 1954. After his discharge from the service, Maurice worked as a Chicago Transit Authority bus driver. He later worked for the Belt Railroad for some twenty-five years.

I remember Maurice for his astute management of his finances. He "squeezed" each dollar as far as it would go, and he spent as little as possible. He was eccentric, being afraid of germs and different kinds of foods. He was absolutely "detailed" in every aspect of his life. He was attracted to my cousin, Irene, but she married Al Brown, and he married Lolita who understood him and loved him unconditionally. They had one daughter, Lorice, who was the apple of her dad's eye. Maurice absolutely adored his wife and daughter.

Maurice died suddenly of a heart attack on a Tuesday, November 8, 1983 at the young age of 51 years. His death was shocking and devastating. He left his mother and father, along with Lolita and Lorice to mourn his passing. He was the first to pass away of his siblings.

Samuel "Larry" Lewis was a long time friend of Lenzo's. He was born in January, 1932 in Birmingham, Alabama. His family later moved to Chicago, Illinois where Larry met and married Emma. Emma was Robert Davis' sister. She and Larry were so devoted to each other; in sync and with perfect chemistry, moving, in step, to the same drummer. They had seven children together; building that family in love and togetherness. Larry and Emma worked hard to provide for their family. They bought a two flat building, close to ours on Peoria, on 83rd and Morgan. Larry was a genuine, kind, smiling guy. He was tall and muscular, one that you would probably call a "gentle giant". I'm told he loved reading the bible. His favorite portion of scripture was Revelation 21:3-4.

Samuel Larry Lewis died on a Tuesday morning on August 4, 1987 at the age of 55, leaving his wife, Emma and their children to mourn his passing. Emma recently passed away after a long and productive life. I thank God for the life and legacy of our two friends, Larry and Emma, and pray that their surviving family members will keep God in their lives.

Prentis Pickens was another one of Lenzo's dear friends. Like Lenzo, "Prentis" prided himself on being an astute business man. Not only was he a manager at a Goodyear Tire Co., but he was the first black salesman at Goodyear, "back in the day," on 63rd & Lowe. Prentis owned and operated three dry cleaners, one of them located at 87th and Kimbark. He also owned and operated a liquor store on the south side of Chicago. My daughter, Sharon, played a part in the life of Prentis. Sharon met a guy named Jack Lynch who was affiliated with organ transplants' assignments. Sharon met him through another of our friends, Bill Thomas. Prentis fell ill and his kidneys started to fail. He needed an organ transplant, so Sharon introduced Prentis to Jack Lynch. Jack arranged for Prentis to receive a kidney transplant and Prentis lived many years after that transplant.

Prentis was a genuinely nice guy, always trying to help someone; always being a good friend; always giving support; and always having a shoulder for someone to cry on. Prentis was a personal friend of John Stroger. Prentis died several years ago, but Lenzo still has fond memories of his dear friend.

James L. Bullock was yet another friend to Lenzo. He was born on January 19, 1933 in Brownsville, Tennessee. He was a car salesman "extraordinaire". Lenzo met him when they both were in the Army and stationed at Fort Campbell, Kentucky. When we had the service station at 76th & Jeffrey, Mr. Bullock (I always called him "Mr. Bullock"; Lenzo called him "Bullock"), was a car salesman close to it. He worked for Mr. Ziloti, a car dealer, and he was serious about his job. He was the ultimate in selling cars. He was part of a prominent family with his uncle, Will Bullock, owning 3 liquor stores, with one being on east 71st St. James L. Bullock was Tina Turner's first cousin. His father and her father were brothers. Tina's real name was Anna Mae Bullock. They were from St. Louis, Missouri.

James Bullock had two sons, Ronald and Stanley. I'm told that he accepted the Lord early in his life at the Woodlawn Baptist Church in Brownsville, Tennessee. He died on a Tuesday morning on May 14, 1991. He left relatives in Detroit, Michigan and three uncles survived him – Leo Bullock of Elyria, Ohio, Will Bullock of Chicago, Illinois, and Robert

Bullock of Detroit, Michigan. Praise God for the life of James L. Bullock and for the positive effect he had on Lenzo's business career and experience.

Frank and Sylvia Waters have been our friends since childhood. Frank is the older brother to Maurice and Tim. Lenzo was best man to Frank at their wedding. He and Sylvia married on December 24, 1952. Lenzo and I had gotten married earlier that same year. Lenzo still talks to them by phone on every Christmas eve. Frank served in the U.S. Air Force for many years and when he had served his time, he joined the Chicago Police Department as a police officer. He served for decades until his retirement. Sylvia worked for the University of Chicago for about 30 years before she retired.

Frank was a jovial guy, always laughing and kidding around. He was serious (as a heart attack) about his love for his wife. He loves her with every "bone in his body". Sylvia is drop dead gorgeous, very outspoken and tells it like it is. When I thought of words to describe her when she was young, I thought that she resembled a more glamorous version of Katy Perry, the singer. Quincy Jones, who lived nearby, was enamored with Sylvia, but Frank wasn't having it! Sylvia and I always enjoyed talking girl talk, along with her BFF, Alsteen.

Frank and Sylvia had two children, a son and a daughter. The son, "Frankie" is now deceased. He was smart and articulate.

Mr. Waters was the dad of Frank, Maurice, and Tim. He was a wonderful mentor to his son's friends. He counseled them and talked to them constantly about how men behave. He left his door unlocked (it was a different world back then) so that the guys could come in and get a meal or just to talk. Mrs. Waters always had food for anyone who happened to drop by.

Frank and Sylvia lived two doors from my cousin, Irene, when she lived in London Town Homes. They continue to live their lives, enjoying their 64 year marriage, and giving God the glory for his blessings, that are new every morning.

Dave and Geraldine Henderson have been our close friends since high school. Dave was part of that group of guys that Lenzo hung out with as teens. Dave was always "closer than a brother" to Lenzo. He had a stuttering problem for years, but overcame it to pursue his dream of becoming a minister. He later achieved that goal, and spoke at several of our affairs and performed weddings, birthdays, etc. He is a genuinely nice guy, and a solid gold friend.

Lenzo acquired our store on 74th & Peoria from Dave and Geraldine. Geraldine and I were great friends, as well. She was brutally honest and outspoken. She did not "bite her tongue" about anything. Geraldine is now deceased but we spent a lot of time together back in the day. Lenzo has spoken to Dave over the years, but sometimes it is difficult to reach him because he lives in another state. His two sons are medical doctors and I've tried contacting Dave through one of them.

We still remember David and Geraldine with much fondness and admiration for their great friendship and brotherly love.

Our Children

Lenzo and I married as teenagers and did not know anything about how to successfully raise a family. By God's grace, we used our common sense and our "gut" feelings. As I look back on those days, I still marvel at how difficult some of those days were. I remember thinking "this too will pass", so I will keep going, taking each day's difficulty and dealing with it. I had "mountain top" days, as well, when I started having children because each one was a miracle, and I knew that, even back then.

My oldest child, and my first daughter is Sharon Marie Kilpatrick Tang, and I remember the day she was born, as if it was yesterday. She was born at Cook County Hospital, which was one of the few places I could go without insurance and without an income. During my pregnancy, I had regularly attended one of the many pre natal clinics in the city. They monitored my health monthly, checking on the growth of the baby. During the last month, they checked on me weekly. When I started having contractions that day, it was the most excruciating pain I had ever experienced. I remember thinking, "I'll never have another baby!" Two months later, I was pregnant with my second child, and second daughter, Linda. So much for my desperate wish. Sharon was born on September 4, 1952, and made us the happiest parents anyone could imagine. I watch them gush excitedly about their babies on television today and I completely identify with them, because that's how I felt when Sharon was born. She had the prettiest, big eyes, my complexion, and high cheekbones like her dad. She was a happy baby, giving everyone a smile.

Sharon grew steadily as a precious addition to our little family. She made everyone happy; nothing like a little baby to bring joy and happiness, and yes, wonder, to a family. As she went from new born to toddler and beyond, I was learning how to be a mom; learning how to juggle baby, husband, and household. All this as I struggled to carry my second baby, Linda, when Sharon was just 2 months old. Eleven months later, I was taking care of two babies. In spite of being a young mother, my babies thrived. They made us realize what love and sacrifice was all about. When we made plans, our babies came first. I dressed them as twins, and though we had meager resources, our two girls grew up having their needs met, and making us proud to see these two children grow into a reflection of us. We were a family and proud of it.

Even as a young girl, and into her teen years, Sharon was an over achiever. She was excellent in school, always doing special projects, and always earning good grades. I didn't have to remind her to do her homework, she did it on her own. She very seldom asked for help. She readily did her chores, and helped her sister do hers. I don't remember ever having to tell her what her responsibilities were. They did dishes for a week, then it was the other one's turn. Sharon kept her room neat and clean, feeling good about herself when she completed her chores.

Sharon attended the Doolittle Elementary School on 35th St. as a young student when we lived in the projects on 33rd St. She attended the Oglesby School on 72nd and Morgan when we moved to 7429 So. Sangamon and she went to the Bond Elementary School for 6th - 8th Grades where she graduated. She went on to attend her beloved Calumet High School where she and her classmates meet every year for a Class Reunion. Some of them remain her very dear friends, one being Sharon Jones Seals, Lou Della Evans' Reid niece. She and Sharon are close friends.

Sharon loved attending high school, involving herself in many extra curricular activities. She was good at everything she pursued. At Calumet is where she met her husband, Alex Tang, Jr. They carried on a torrid love affair, even to sometimes dressing alike for some special activities at the school. At graduation, Alex took Sharon to the prom. I had had Sharon's dress made and it was gorgeous. Linda's was made, also because, while

Sharon went to her senior prom, it was Linda's Junior prom. They were dressed to the nines, with flawless make-up and hair beautifully done. We lived on Sangamon, and on our block when the kids went to prom, everybody came out on their front porch to watch them take pictures and get in their parents' cars and drive away. Everybody was waiting to see the Kilpatrick girls come out. Sharon's date was Alex, and Bernard took Linda. We kept waiting for Alex to come, we were anxious because it got later and later. Finally, he arrived and came through the back because he didn't have socks on (unheard of at that time) and no car. Everything worked out because we got socks for him and Lenzo let them drive his car. Alex was teased about that for days. We remember it from time to time and really laugh about it at "Alex's expense." Sharon and Alex married that November, 1970, and began having a family when their first child, Shatese Latina Tang, was born on May 17, 1971. Shatese was born on our wedding anniversary, and our beloved Bro. Gall died a few days after she was born. Alexis Monique Tang, Sharon's second child, and second daughter was born on January 5, 1977, in Chicago, Illinois. Alex and I were in the waiting room when their third child, and first son, Sean Tang was born. It was at a Catholic hospital and we were so happy that it was a boy (and I was just happy that her hard labor pains were over): The staff at the hospital had to "shush" us because we shouted for joy. We forgot about the other patients there. Sean made all of us happy and proud. He is the spitting image of his dad and I'm told that's cause for "good luck".

As a young teenager, Sharon attended charm school, "Cari's Chateau", located on east 79th Street. I forget the name of the beautiful lady who ran the school, but it was a place for learning social skills such as etiquette, good posture, appropriate dress, etc. She taught the girls how to conduct themselves as ladies; and Sharon has carried over, even now, some of those "life lessons" like how to walk properly. Sharon has a "killer", model-like walk that is unmistakable and unique. She carries herself like a lady; head up, shoulders back, confident stride.

Sharon and Alex remained married for some 21 years, raising their children, and building a strong family unit. They are close-knit, spending time together almost daily as the children have since started their own families. Sharon calls her children every day, without fail. She knows what they are doing and they know what she is doing, daily. It is a unique relationship between mother and children, and is taken very seriously. When a need comes up, they are able to take care of it, because of the communication between them. It amuses me to watch my daughter with her children.

Alex, who is legally my ex son-in-law, will always be my son in law. He was/is a great father who put his kids first in his life. He spent time with them when they were growing up; doing things with them that fathers do. Even now, into their adulthood, Alex has remained true to his kids, being in their lives, and being "there for them" when needed. He is also a doting grandfather to his grandkids.

Sharon has been, and continues to be a great, "hands on" mom. She taught her daughters how to be strong women, and she permitted her son to develop into a strong, independent man.

Sharon has been successful, career-wise, as well. After getting married, and starting her family, she went back to school to earn her degrees. She received her Bachelor of Science in Business Education in December, 1982 from Chicago State University. In 1983, she was recommended by the Dean of Education for a position on the college level. She worked at the Richard J. Daley College, and National Louis University, Chicago, as an adjunct faculty member for five years. From 1990-1992, Sharon worked with the Carol Moseley Braun For U.S. Senate Campaign. She served as the Assistant to the Treasurer and she was the supervisor of the Data Entry Department. In addition to the skills she took into the Campaign, she came out equipped with more accounting skills that propelled her into the world of finances. She would go on to serve as treasurer and/or financial secretary in five organizations, including her church, Grace & Glory Gospel Chapel.

From 1992-1994, Sharon worked as a substitute teacher at my school, Carver Middle School, in Altgeld Gardens. I was proud to have her serve on the staff there, filling in, making sure the program continued, in spite of teacher shortage on a daily basis.

Sharon was introduced to the Assistant Principal, Ms. Lena Talley, of the Lake View High School, by Jetaun Jamerson. Sharon was hired as a teacher in the Accounting and Information Technology Department in September, 1994. She served there for 20 years, moving from teacher to Department Chair and then Administrative Team member. Over those years, in August, 2005, she earned her Type 75 State of Illinois

Administrative Certificate, General Administrative Endorsement from Northeastern Illinois University in Chicago. She retired from Lake View in 2012 and still holds a valid teaching and Administrative Certificate.

Sharon enjoyed her service at Lake View. She met life long friends there, still in contact, still in fellowship with many of them. She honed her skills there, making a big difference with the kids there; sometimes visiting them in their homes and meeting their parents. Her duties there included but were not limited to: coordinating school wide Choices Planner implementation; providing professional development for staff; identifying computer lab sites; and determining schedules for student classes. Sharon also served as Night School Supervisor upon need. During the summer, Sharon supervised the Mayor Daley's Summer Work Program which included: identifying students, staff, and work sites; overseeing payroll for students; developing programs like fine arts and "clean and green"; supervising staff; and serving as a liaison between the central office and the high school. Sharon coordinated junior and senior proms for many years during her tenure. Of course, Sharon did many more things over the course of 20 years. The Principal, Mr Scott Feaman, was impressed with her work ethic over the years. Sharon credits Mr. Scott Feaman, retired Principal of Lake View for her success there.

Sharon serves her community through five organizations:

- her church, Grace & Glory Gospel Chapel. She serves as one of the members of the Board of Trustees in the office of Treasurer/ Financial Secretary. In addition to watching and helping to manage the finances, she assumes other responsibilities, such as repairs and upkeep of the church building. The solvency of our assembly is partly due to her brilliant talent of watching the dollars; where they come from and where they go. She has demonstrated her integrity, her honesty, and her conscientiousness as an accountant and as a trustee. She enjoys a good relationship and fellowship with the saints at the church.
- Circle Y Ranch, the camp ministry of the brethren assemblies in Illinois, Michigan, and other states as well. Sharon has been a member of the Circle Y Women's Auxiliary for decades, and again serving as treasurer/financial secretary for all those years. As a member, she helps plan, each year, the fund raising activities; as

well as soliciting funds; writing letters; and making sure to write "Thank You" letters for participation and donations.

- CCWC – Chicagoland Christian Women's Conference. Sharon is a board member of the organization, and has served as its' treasurer/ financial secretary for decades. Beverly Yates invited her to become a member, and she has worked diligently and tirelessly since that time. She also doubles as the registrar, as well. Sharon watches the money "like a hawk", and is very frugal about the organization's spending. In that position, Sharon has served with dignity and respect; sometimes being criticized, but always managing to stay "above the fray" as she continued to do her responsibility and her commitment. She is loved and cherished by the other board members, and of course, she returns that same affection.

- Iota Phi Lambda Sorority, Inc., her sorority. Sharon belongs to the organization in the Alpha Tau Chapter, Chicago. The chapter is one of four chapters in the Chicagoland area. She currently serves as its' President, fulfilling the duties that office requires. She has been in the organization for some 25 years or more and has served locally, regionally, and nationally. In Alpha Tau, over the years, she has served in the office of treasurer, as well as, the office of financial secretary. On the regional level, she has continued to serve as treasurer and as financial secretary over many years. After doing 4 years in one office, she takes a year's break, and then she's asked to do 4 more years in the other office. She absolutely loves her sorority, so most of the times, she says "yes", but she has also said "no" a few times. The sorors simply adore Sharon, showing her deep love and great respect. And of course, she returns the sentiment, as well. Sharon was inspired by Yvette Barrett (CPA), a soror who was formerly in Alpha Tau Chapter.

- Lake View High School Social Committee Chairperson, Over her 20 years at Lake View, Sharon served on the social committee. As the chair, she was responsible for the social activities of the staff. She, along with the other members of the committee, planned and carried out the fun activities and social gatherings with the large staff at the school. She was solely responsible for managing the finances, and writing the checks. Like in the other organizations, Sharon has always been transparent and honest in her handling of everyone else's money.

Sharon has consistently been sensitive to the needs of others. After she and Alex married, Sharon developed a close bond with his family. She was friends with his sister, Ava Tang Williams, who was one year younger than Sharon, and they both attended Calumet High School together. Ava married James Williams after finishing high school and they had one son, Tyrone Williams. Ava was paralyzed on July 25, 1981 after being shot in a senseless and unfortunate incident. Sharon cared for her and took special care to meet her needs. I don't know of anyone who could have been a better care giver for Ava. She was Sharon's special sister-in-law, and she cared for her with the love and compassion of a sister. Although Ava suffered greatly, it did not dampen her spirit, nor her will to live. She remained fun-loving and jovial with a mischievous smile on her face. Ava had come to know the Lord as a member of Antioch Baptist Church when the Rev. W. N. Daniel was pastor. And during her long confinement, she realized the beauty of life and appreciated the simple things that are taken for granted daily. She felt that her life could be used as a deterrent to those who would seek to live life in the "fast lane".

A man who was studying to be a Muslim minister was later indicted on murder charges in the wounding of Ava and the murder of the man who was with her. The attacker shot George Gayles twice and shot Ava several times causing her to become a paraplegic. Ava survived because an off duty policeman intervened and arrested him. The man was charged with murder, attempted murder, aggravated battery and armed violence in shooting of Ava, and in the killing of her friend, who died on the scene.

Ava lived approximately 6½ years in that paralyzed state. She died at 12:52 A.M. on January 31, 1988. Her funeral was held on February 3, 1988, and Rev. Benjamin Garrett, Lenzo's dear friend, did the Eulogy. Rev. Wilbur Daniel, Pastor of Antioch Baptist Church brought Remarks. Bro. Willie Horton, Grace & Glory Gospel Chapel offered prayer; Elizabeth Reckley sang a solo, "He Looked Beyond My Faults"; and Valoree Harrington brought "Acknowledgements". My son, Kevin and Ava's brother, Aldolph served as Pallbearers. She left her father, and her step-mother, two brothers, and her three sisters to mourn her loss. Everyone is living and prosperous, with the exception of her father, Alex Tang, Sr., who passed away several years ago. It was a sad time for Sharon, who did everything she could to keep her alive.

Sharon's Friends

Sharon has three very close friends over many years that have impacted her life in a positive way. They remain her friends even unto today. Sharon, in turn, has been very helpful to all of them, as they pursued their career goals, and as they sought to dream bigger dreams, and climb the ladder of success one step at a time.

Sylvester E. Baker, Jr. was born in Chicago on August 18, 1953. He came from humble beginnings; the fifth of nine children. Baker's parents who both moved to Chicago from the south struggled to provide for their children. His parents provided a value system based on hard work and service to both church and community, which has shaped Baker's professional and political career path. His parents inspired him to further his education, start his own business, and mentor children in the Chicago Public School System (CPS). His religious upbringing inspired him to give back to the community, especially helping troubled youth.

Baker attended Chicago State University, earning a Bachelor's degree in psychology. He went to Governors State University and earned a Master's Degree in Public Administration. He is currently working on his Doctorate in Social Psychology at Walden University.

Dr. Martin Luther King, Jr. and Congresswoman Shirley Chisholm inspired Baker to get involved in politics. He learned the inner working of politics as a field worker for the late Congressman Ralph Metcalf, who ran as an independent in his 1972 re-election campaign. Baker saw those principles at work when he served in the 21st Ward Democratic Organization. He then learned community organizing under Alderman Niles Sherman. In 1982, Baker tested the political waters for the first time when he ran for State Representative of the 29th District and again in 1999 when he ran for Alderman of the sixth ward. In 2006, Baker ran for Sheriff of Cook County in the Democratic Party garnering more than 100,000 votes. In 2010, he attempted a second run for Sheriff, and again received 100,000 votes. Sharon managed both those campaigns, along with other supporters. And then again in 2013, he once again jumped into the fray of being a candidate for Sheriff of Cook County. There were several articles, citing his run, in the newspapers. I remember the one in the Chicago Independent Bulletin, June 13, 2013 spotlighting a southside community meeting at the Holy Trinity Missionary Baptist Church.

Baker was especially proud of his dad, Sylvester Baker, Sr. who died a few years ago. He talked of his accomplishments in glowing terms. His twenty-two year career in law enforcement was inspired by his father's military service. Baker has quite an impressive career in his own right. He started his career at the Sheriff's office in 1982 as a Corrections Officer assigned to the Cook County Jail. He worked through the ranks and in 1985 was selected for the Sheriff's Police Academy. He was assigned to the County's Swat Team in 1988. In 1990, Baker was assigned to the gang crimes/narcotics section, working in an undercover capacity on many occasions. In 1995, he was promoted to Sergeant. He supervised a team of investigators who targeted drug dealers, gang members, and conducted undercover operations to get drugs and guns off the streets in several communities including Evanston, Harvey, Ford Heights, Chicago Heights, Maywood, Palatine, and Robbins. In 1997, Baker and his squad received a citation from Evanston Mayor, Lorraine H. Morton for their outstanding undercover work. He had the pleasure of being assigned to the Illinois State Police for six months; the Drug Enforcement Agency for six months; and the FBI for 14 months. Baker retired in 2003, but continued to work for the community and took time to become the Assistant Director of Security for City Colleges of Chicago. He is a licensed Real Estate Broker manager operating his own business, Baker's Realty.

Baker remains a close friend to Sharon with our two families connected in a positive way. Sharon is godmother to his daughter, Kamilah. My grandson-in-law, Anthony and my grand daughter, Alexis are godparents to his grandson Kevin Jr.

Rev. Dr. Joseph "Joe" Rhoiney is another close friend of Sharon's. She met him years ago, and they became "fast friends." Joe is a prominent, dynamic, and influential man of God. He gave his testimony, leaving me amazed and thankful that God works so beautifully in each life to bring them unto Him. Joseph came to know the Lord as a teenager while attending a camp in Union, Michigan. He got involved in a parachurch youth group at the Chicago Gospel Youth Center. Some of the leaders there, many of whom were Moody students doing their Practical Christian Work (PCW) with Practical Christian Ministries' assignments, encouraged him to attend Moody Bible Institute. He attended Moody and was involved in and interested in many activities offered there. He remembers meeting and befriending people from around the world. His experiences at Moody Bible Institute prepared him for leadership in communications and world evangelism ministries. Joe felt led to begin a ministry that was targeted towards men and boys in the urban areas of America. He went on to found "Ministry One". The vision for the ministry was to minister to the world "one heart at a time". Through social media, he sought to teach biblical truths through radio, TV, and the internet. Through this ministry, he has gone to Ghana and West Africa taking the Word of God. Joe is passionate about spreading the good news also to South American countries beginning with Brazil, Chile, and Argentina.

Sharon and I had an opportunity to visit Joe's conference recently. The theme was "Coming Home – The Americas/Caribbeans Meet Africa – Our Family . . . Together Again." We were in awe of the beauty of the gathering. It was a church full of these three cultures and the presentations – sermons, videos, music – were breath-taking. It was emotional to see images of our "roots" from centuries past to President Barack Obama. It was a joyous occasion that I will always remember. Rev. Dr. Joseph Rhoiney has for several years, broadcast Global Media Ministries: TV: "The Jho Roni Show//Radio: Gospel Praise. He has great interpersonal skills, is multitalented and never content to accept the "status quo." Joe Rhoiney is forever seeking new challenges and new experiences as he explores the global community in the pursuit of making it a better place.

Sharon was on the interview team at Lake View when Marlon Conway was selected as a teacher/Dean of Students. Marlon was the only <u>male</u> African American faculty member of 105 in 2006! Marlon is an avid reader and never missed a day reading newspapers. He was a very present help to Sharon when students needed <u>severe </u>discipline. He was always there for our family in our time of bereavement. He is currently working on his Doctoral Degree in Education. He and Sharon are still good friends today.

Sharon has many close, dear friends that have been in her life for years, but time and space will not permit me to mention them in this publication, but I pray God will bless them all and meet them at the point of their need.

<u>Sharon's Children</u>

<u>Shatese Latina Tang Jenkins</u> was born to Sharon and Alex Tang in Chicago, Illinois on May 17, 1971. The date of her birth is seared on my memory because it was my 19th wedding anniversary, and our beloved Bro. Owbridge Fay Gall died a few days after she was born. Shatese was the

first child and first daughter. Sharon & Alex were deliriously happy and they became a "team" because every where they went, Shatese was right there with them. Shatese was the "perfect", little well-behaved, obedient baby. She laughed a lot. Then she became a teenager, and her mom "gave her a fit", trying to teach her how to buy her personal items like lotion, soap, cologne, etc. Sharon taught her how to handle her money and how to live a peaceful, drama free life. She taught her how to take care of her things and how to keep a neat house. Shatese learned her lessons well, always keeping her apartment and later, her house squeaky clean.

Shatese attended day care centers as a little girl. Sharon, getting her into Marjorie Stewart Joyner's excellent nursery school, at 5249 So. Wabash. She graduated in 1976. She went to Dixon Elementary School and then to Pirie. Statese went to Calumet High School where she graduated and began her adult career.

In July, 1992, Shatese had a son with Derek Rylon, Sr. His name is Derek Rylon, and he is her one and only child, only son. Derek attended elementary school in Chicago, in the city, but he went to Thornwood High School and received his diploma from there. He went on to aggressively seek the best possible job he could find; the one that paid good wages. He enjoyed the "work experience" and the independence and freedom it afforded him as a young man.

As before mentioned, Derek was born on July 18, 1992. His cousin, Tierra, was born on the same day, July 18th, one year earlier. Derek and Tierra were very close from babies unto now. When they were very young and for many years, they dressed alike on that one day a year, July 18th. They were like twins, one boy outfit, one girl outfit. They were close, but they had some loud disagreements and arguments. Derek and Tierra brought much joy to the family as we watched them grow into the teen years, and then into adulthood. Derek has a great job at Ford Motor Company, making a nice salary. He recently got his own apartment, a really nice studio apartment just right for him. He has made his mother very proud. I have a favorite picture of Shatese and Derek which shows the love between them; Derek was about three years old and they were dressed in identical outfits, yellow Nautica, sports 'tee shirts, the bluest jeans, and Nike gym shoes, and white sox. He had his hand around her shoulder and she had one hand around him; such a beautiful picture.

Shatese, over the years, has had many wonderful friends. Her special, close friend was Harry Dennis, III. Harry was a genuinely nice guy, a nice guy with a gentle manner, but a strong voice. He stood very tall and when he spoke, he demanded attention. He loved Shatese until he closed his eyes in death. He suffered greatly from diabetes, and sadly passed away on August 6, 2014. The funeral services were held here in Chicago at the A.R. Leak & Sons Funeral Parlor, on August 15, 2014. Harry is with the Lord, now. His death and the service was significant, and ironic to me because it happened on my daughter, Linda's birthday. My daughter, Trina, died on August 15th, exactly nine years ago. I will always remember Harry with fond thoughts and memories.

Shatese met her future husband, Steve Jenkins, in Chicago and they fell in love, "head over heels". He made sure that the verse, "He who finds a wife finds what is good and receives favor from the Lord: Proverbs 18:22 NIV", appeared on their wedding program. They got married on September 17, 2013 and had a big reception at the Dorchester Hotel on October 26, 2013. Both, Steve's family and our family was there en masse and it was a beautiful celebration. We enjoyed a delicious Buffet Luncheon and witnessed the Cutting of the Cake. Later, the guests danced to a D.J. and continued to "meet and greet." The program, fittingly, ended with another scripture verse:

"So they are no longer two, but one flesh. Therefore, what God hath joined together, let no man separate." Matthew 19:6 (NIV.)

Shatese and Steve relocated to Dallas, Texas after the wedding. They wanted to give their marriage a chance to succeed without the support (or interference) of family and friends. They wanted to do it alone, "willy nilly".

Shatese has one grandson, one grandchild that she calls her "grand monster." He's the cutest little guy in our family, and completely adorable. He's Derek's son with his high school sweetheart. His name is Macari and his mom is Marciara who takes beautiful care of Macari. Derek is in another relationship now with Keyanna who is like a "Barbie Doll" because she is so tiny. Keyanna has wonderful grandparents and ironically, her grandfather's name is James Jones, the same as my dad.

Shatese and Steve live, happily, in a little town outside Dallas, Texas where she joined T.D. Jakes' church, The Potter House. She speaks of his powerful message each Sunday morning, and is inspired to share them with her family and friends. On September 25, 2013, Shatese sent me, on Facebook, a picture and a scripture verse. The picture was a vivid, bright image that looked like a speeding earth headed toward a burst of light and colors. What I found wonderful and ironic about this message was that the scripture was:

"For the Lord God is a sun and shield; the Lord will give grace and glory. No good thing will he withhold from them that walk uprightly."

Sharing scripture verses shows what's in Shatese's heart and I couldn't be prouder of her and the choices she has made.

Alexis <u>Monique</u> <u>Tang</u> Jones was born in Chicago, Illinois on January 5, 1977. She was Sharon's and Alex's second child and second daughter. I think Lexie was "born smart", an old cliché, but true. She was bright and intelligent and eager to learn. She excelled, even in her little day care center. Lexie graduated from Church of God Day Care Center on June 27, 1982. She recited a poem: "Old Mother Hubbard" with her class. Sharon made sure that each one of her children got the best child care. She was determined to give them a good start, a good foundation from which to develop. It was not lost on Lexie; she excelled in elementary school and high school; developing great leadership skills. As an 8th grader, or high schooler – not sure which one – she was an "exchange student" with a family in Paris, France. This was a great trip taken through the school program with the students. Lexie took the trip and lo and behold, she developed the chicken pox while she was there. She had to be quarantined for a time, and Sharon was worried and concerned. Even though it was a trying time, Lexie completed the program and brought home fond memories, lasting friendships, and great pictures. It gave me "bragging rights" as a grandmother, and made me ever so thankful to the Lord for her safety and her protection and her joy.

Lexie's teen years were busy, fun, and exciting. She forged life-long friendships during those years at Simeon High School. Her friend, Amanda, has been her best friend since childhood. She and her grandmother, "Grannie," were neighbors so we were close with her family. Her friend, Lutrice, is a high school friend. Lexie and Amanda and Lutrice have gone through their lives with serving as bridesmaids at their weddings and being godmothers for their children. Lexie's friend, Kamilah, is also her friend from her teen years. Lexie served as Maid of Honor at Amanda's wedding to Fred Gaddy. Lexie's boyfriend in high school was Anthony <u>Darring.</u> He was a handsome guy and they were very much in love. They did everything together and went everywhere together. They were inseparable, and then tragedy suddenly changed all that. Anthony, who was my grandson, Bub's best friend, was shot and killed in a senseless, brutal murder. Bub was with him and witnessed the murder, and he has never gotten over that hurt and sadness. Lexie was inconsolable when she got the news; she literally hollered and screamed for hours. She couldn't believe it. She grieved for months and months, along with his parents. Lexie, to this day, has a close beautiful relationship with Anthony's parents. She visited them regularly after the tragedy. She remembers their birthdays and holidays and special occasions. She has prayed for them and checked on them during their illness and during hard times. They simply adore Lexie. They had a younger son, but no girls, so Lexie was like their own daughter that they never had.

After months of grieving for Anthony, Lexie moved on with her life. She continued to pursue her career goals and learning everything she could about the "world of work". She started to "feel" again, and sought to be happy again. In the interim, she met and fell for another "Anthony". This one was Anthony Jones, not only a nice guy, but a smart guy, and a "sports" guy. They fell in love and held a beautiful, beautiful wedding in Las Vegas, Nevada. Lexie's & Tony's family and friends flew to Las Vegas en masse to attend this highly anticipated wedding. The wedding was held on July 26, 2009 and we had a wonderful time celebrating with Lexie and Tony. Their son, Anthony Jones, Jr. was the Ring bearer. He was 8 years old and the pride and joy of his parents. Shatese was the Maid of Honor for her younger sister. Amanda was the Matron of Honor and Lutrice was one of the Bridesmaids. La Shundra, Lexie's cousin and Tierra, were bridesmaids. Karisha, Lexie's sister-in-law, and Kamilah and Ramona, her friends, also served as Bridesmaids. She had six bridesmaids and six groomsmen. Kyonna was the beautiful little Flower Girl in the wedding. Her colors were royal blue and black. After the wedding, a reception was held. The wedding party continued to party that night. Lenzo and I, of course, retired for the evening with the kids. We stayed 4 days in Vegas for the wedding and it is an experience that I will always cherish.

Lexie is not a teacher by trade, but she possesses those qualities of one. It is said that:

> "A teacher takes
> a <u>Hand</u>, opens
> a <u>Mind</u>, and
> touches a <u>Heart</u>."

She has done that, and is doing that with not only her son, but with Kyonna, and with the children she works with. Lexie is Administrator/Supervisor at the Ada S. McKinley Children and Family Services, and has held that position for several years.

My great grandson, Anthony, Jr. is super smart; not the typical "nerd" type, but more in the "being cool" mode. He has earned and maintained a straight "A" average from 1st grade. He is now a freshman at the very prestigious Lindbloom High School in an honors program. Anthony enjoys school because he has several friends and he excels in his classes.

Anthony was born on February 4, 2001, two months after Le Shawn.

Alexis Tang Jones is a beautiful grandchild as well as, a wonderful Mom. She has always been with me to help me lead a peaceful life; and she has helped me keep my sanity by involving herself in the lives of Le Shawn and Kyonna.

Lexie and her family currently live in a lovely home in Riverdale, a south suburb of Chicago, where they attend church every Sunday. Anthony serves as an usher and Lexie serves on the trustee board dealing with all finances of the church (like her mom). Anthony, Jr. attends the Sunday School class.

<u>Sean Tang</u>, was born in Chicago, Illinois on July 24, 1981 at St. Joseph Hospital. His dad, Alex and I were in the waiting room when he was born and we both were elated to welcome this new addition to our family. Sean is the third child of Sharon and Alex and the only son. Of course, he's the baby and simply loved and adored; not only by his parents, but also by his two older sisters. There is nobody like Sean in their eyesight.

Sean was blessed from the beginning. His mother named him after her favorite "cool" actor, Sean Connery of 007 fame. Like his siblings, he was smart and energetic, facing life "head on", with a vengeance. He was a happy kid, smiling and kidding around. He went to Stagg Elementary School where he was a fast learner. He and his friend, Marlon, enjoyed the neighborhood, as well. Marlon's grandparents were neighbors, and Marlon's sister, Ronnice was Latrina's close friend. Sean went on to high school and immediately started to dream big dreams. He always wanted to succeed and be somebody. He was not happy with the status quo of his existence; he wanted much, much more. As I look back on his life, he has achieved many of his goals already.

Sean met and fell in love with Annette Karisha Johnson. We all call her Karisha, and she is "drop dead" gorgeous; a beauty inside and outside. They dated for several months and then went to City Hall and got married. Seven years later, they renewed their vows with a beautiful, beautiful wedding and reception that was held at the Jesus Name Apostolic Church in Waukegan, Illinois. The music was romantic and apropo for the occasion: Ginuwine's "Differences"; Luther Van Dross' "So Amazing"; and Beyonce's "Love On Top". Sean's family and Karisha's family attended, en masse. Alex's (Sean's dad) step-mom, Lenora Tang, was part of the wedding party and was escorted down the aisle by Aldolph, Alex's brother. Sean and Karisha paid homage to their parents, their grandparents and the family members who had passed away. The Pastor of the Church, John I. Caples, performed the ceremony. Tyrone, Sean, Jr., and Jayden all participated in the wedding. During the Reception, Sean and Karisha danced to Babyface's "Everytime I Close My Eyes." The wedding was a beautiful affirmation of their marriage, which is steady and strong. They are both committed to each other and to their children.

Sean and Karisha had their children early in their marriage. Karisha had one son, Tyrone, from a previous relationship and then Sean, Jr. was born and then Jayden. They love their three boys with a passion and spend precious time raising them. All the boys participate in basketball. Sean, Jr. is a whiz. Tyrone plays football, as well. They all participate in a number of sports at their schools. Tyrone is now a freshman in his high school in Zion, Illinois and Sean and Jayden go to the local elementary school. The three boys are all "mama's boys." I'm told that when Jayden was in day care, he told a boy that was trying to bully him, "You better leave me alone or I'll tell my mama and she'll come up here and beat your a_ _!" I'm not surprised because Karisha is one strong woman. She's as tough as shoe leather.

Sean and Karisha have worked hard for their family ever since they met. She worked and Sean worked and he was going to training school as well. He was training to be a truck driver. They qualified to get a "Habitat for Living" home and they moved to this beautiful house in Waukegan, IL. It catapulted them into a lifestyle of prominence and success. They put their hard earned money back into their home to make it comfortable and beautiful and they put their money into investments for their kids. To put the icing on the cake, they found this bible teaching church and became active in community outreach and Sunday worship. One of their themes that appear on their tee shirts is: "God Is Good, all the time." I have three of the shirts, gifts from them.

Sean realized his goal of wanting to be a truck driver by finishing the training and has been driving one ever since. He now owns his own truck and does his own selected runs.

Sean and his beautiful family live prominently in Waukegan, IL where they, each day, thank the Lord for His mercy and His grace.

I'm proud of the way in which Sharon built her family over these many years. Her children and grandchildren have affirmed her in many ways; they have shown her by the way they are raising their families, that love and care and constant monitoring make a wonderful family unit. Her children had an opportunity to make their mom happy a few years ago, when they nominated her for a "Super Single Mama of the Year" Award.

Needless to say, Sharon won as one of those distinguished women who took home an Award. Thank the Lord for Sharon and her closely-knit family.

It is not a good idea to cruise through life, thinking that we are invincible and that everything is good and things are going to be just fine. We come to realize that we are far more fragile than we thought. Things that happen to us, remind us that life is extremely uncertain. None of us can be certain of another breath.

I learned that critical truth as I began to lose my children - one by one – Lenard on February 24, 2004; Katrina on August 15, 2005; and

Linda on January 31, 2008. The dates of their death is seared on my heart, causing me to never forget. I have to stop sometimes and remember their date of birth, but I have never forgotten those sad dates of their last day on this, God's earth.

Linda Susan Kilpatrick was born on August 15, 1953 in Great Lakes, Illinois on a military base. I named Linda after Shirley Temple's daughter, Linda Susan. Lenzo had just recently been inducted into the Army. My cousins Dorce and Sonny went with me because I was in labor and needed someone to give me support. It took a couple of hours to get there and by the time I arrived, the baby was ready to be born. She was a beautiful, little tyke and made me very happy. Lenzo, of course, was the proud dad. He was able to brag to his army buddies.

Linda was our second child and our second daughter, having been born exactly 11 months after Sharon. They were very close, almost like twins. I dressed them alike during those early years, so they were like "two peas in a pod". The two of them grew up happy kids, energetic and fast learners. Linda was somewhat low key, more thoughtful, and serious minded. She had a gentle manner and showed kindness, and great concern for others, even as a kid.

Linda went to Calumet High School where she made many friends. Like Trina, she was in one of those girls' group where they did a lot of things together. Some of them became her life long friends. Elois was one of those friends and Linda was very close friends with my cousin, Deborah. They shared many things in common.

Linda and my daughter, Trina and my future son-in-law Butch, used to dance on "Soul Train" in the early 70's. Soul Train came on television every weekend. Performers played the music that people listened to on the radio daily. On Soul Train, young people especially, learned how to dress, how to walk, how to talk, and of course, how to dance. It was where the Soul Train "line" was started, where you would be called on to dance your way between two lanes of dancers clapping and edging you on. Our friend, Eddie Thomas, introduced Lenzo to Don Cornelius and he invited my kids to come on the show. For a while, Linda & Trina & Butch danced every weekend. I didn't know at the time what a historical "moment" that was, and neither did my kids. We had a tape of Trina and Butch going down the "Soul Train" line, but it's been lost over the years. Don Cornelius died tragically on February 1, 2012. According to news reports, it was an apparent suicide. I will treasure the picture that Eddie Thomas gave me years ago; a picture of Eddie, Clinton Gent, and Don Cornelius and someone I don't recognize.

Linda had a kind heart and was always willing to help others in need. My dad, who lived in San Diego, California was having some health issues, so Linda went to stay with him to care for him. While there, she attended the Pivot Point Cosmotology Institute and received her training certificate to become a beautician. Linda loved "doing hair", specializing in hair design, hair care, and make up application. Her make up was always flawless and she did the same with her clients.

Linda met Willie Stevens in Chicago and they went every where together. They married by going to city hall and saying their vows there. They lived at the "building" for several years before separating and each going their separate ways. Willie was genuine and a classy guy. He was a beautician, as well. He did my hair for years. He was really close to my mother. They joked and kidded each other and just enjoyed being together. Willie was devastated upon hearing of Linda's passing.

Linda's special friend for over 20 years, Stewart, remained by her side, trying to meet her every need, as well as sticking like glue to her through "thick & thin"; through her many years of health issues, as well as, all her beautiful moments of bliss and good health. We are still close to Stewart, speaking often and seeing him from time to time.

Linda attended Grace & Glory Gospel Chapel from a baby in to adulthood. She accepted the Lord in her teens and participated in all the programs, e.g. Easter, Christmas, plays and special activities. Linda was deeply loved by others in the church for her kindness, gentle manner, and her concern for others. She prayed daily and never, ever took life for granted.

Linda loved her family with a passion, especially all the babies and children. She never had her own biological children, but she gave that natural mother's love to her many nieces and nephews. Linda was the "mother" to her great niece and nephew, Kyonna and Le Shawn. She devoted her life to them, providing for their every need. She nurtured and cared for them with a love that was truly remarkable. She was so proud of Le Shawn's brightness and his verbal skills. She was always amused at Kyonna for her little "grown up" antics of putting on make up and painting her nails. Linda was a good listener, serving as the "conscience" of the whole family. She wore bold red lipstick and was admired by our family for having beautiful eyes and a perfect figure.

Linda loved our family with an almost child-like affection and when she passed away on January 31, 2008 after a long bout with health issues, it left a void, a vast hole in our hearts that continues even to this day. She showed us how to gracefully accept physical challenges. During her years of difficulty, she kept a positive attitude, always <u>believing</u>, always <u>trusting</u>, always <u>hopeful</u>, always <u>prayerful</u>. Linda was 54 years old when she went to be with the Lord.

My Sorority sister, Carolyn Wortham, was President of Alpha Chapter, Iota Phi Lambda Sorority, Inc. when Linda died. She wrote a beautiful Resolution which was read at Linda's funeral as was other tibutes and resolutions.

When Linda was diagnosed with "Non-Hodgkins Lymphoma cancer, I gave her the following scripture, among others: "Commit thy way unto the Lord; trust also in him and he shall bring it to pass." She lived ten years with the cancer until her death in 2008.

My precious daughter, Linda, did not achieve the world's view of fame and fortune, but she lived her life in her own quiet way seeking to make others happy and continuing to pursue her own personal dreams. She is with the Lord now, and each day when I look up at the blue skies and white clouds, I think of her for she told me on the night before she died that she could see herself, on a cloud with Jesus.

To God be the glory for His mercy and His grace in the beautiful life of <u>Linda</u> <u>Susan</u> <u>Kilpatrick</u>.

<u>Katrina</u> <u>Rae</u> <u>Kilpatrick</u> was born on March 8, 1956 in Chicago, Illinois. She was the third child and the third daughter born to Lenzo and I. She was the most beautiful little baby, with a shock of silky black hair and dimples. As she grew, her hair grew longer and reminded me of black silk. "Trina" was known and admired for her hair, her stylish hats and sunglasses, and her "hatitude". She wore her hats slightly "off

center" . . . like a female Frank Sinatra. She dressed with a flair and loved to complement her outfits with her hats. Like Linda, she loved applying her makeup; she looked like a model after putting on her eye makeup and lipstick. She and Linda were truly professionals when it came to applying makeup.

Trina was very articulate and had great confidence. I thought she could have made an excellent teacher with the combination of that, plus her tough love to her four children. She didn't "cut any slack" with her kids. She whipped them for bad behavior and pretty much kept them in line. She and Butch married after La Shundra was born and stayed together many years trying to raise their kids. Their marriage failed after a while for they were on two different paths in the "pursuit of happiness." They never divorced, however and remained friends until her death.

Trina's childhood was good. She attended Stagg Elementary and Oglesby Elementary Schools. My friend, Annette's sister, Jacqueline M. Payne was one of Trina's teachers. She went to Calumet High School on Chicago's south side. She wasn't an "A" student, but she was ever learning, ever seeking knowledge, and honing her skills. She sought new things, new adventures, and yes, she experienced new challenges on a daily basis as she sought to reach her dreams, her career goals and aspirations.

As an adult, Trina worked at Harris Bank for quite a while and truly enjoyed it. She didn't want much, in terms of career; she was pretty well content to have a modest income.

Trina had met Charles Ray Levy, "Butch" as a teenager and they fell "head over heels" in love. They were inseparable and did everything they could to be together. They got married at Nanny's home on August 2, 1975 Butch's mom, and it was lovely with Trina's wedding dress having been especially made for her. Shundra and Shatese were her little flower girls. We all had such a great time. I still remember Trina saying, over and over, "this is my husss . . . band!" She held that first syllable and it was hilarious. They truly loved each other. The reception was held at our home at 7429 So. Sangamon. They lived in Chicago with their family for a while and then relocated to Huntsville, Alabama. Life was good for them until Butch lost his job. They then moved to Chattanooga, Tennessee where he got a very sought after job with the Tennessee Valley Authority. Butch was bright and smart with excellent math skills. They stayed there for a few years and then moved back to Chicago where they lived at the "building" for years. The "building", as we all called it was property that we owned and maintained. It had 3 apartments, with six rooms on the 1st and 2nd floors, and 3 rooms in the English basement which was really the first level. Each apartment had its own full bathroom. Kevin and Veleese and their family stayed on the 2nd floor; and Butch and Trina and their family were on the 1st floor; and Linda and her husband Willie Stevens stayed in the apartment of 3 rooms on the ground level.

Trina and Butch slowly drifted apart and they separated. Butch's sister, Finesse, and Nanny, moved to a small city in Pennsylvania named Harrisburg. Butch soon followed them, building a better life for himself and experiencing peace, and quiet, and a slower pace in every way. He hoped his children would do well in Chicago, and as he left, he was concerned for the safety of his sons. Later, his two sons Charles, Jr. and Tremaine moved to Harrisburg to be with their dad. They both started their families there, and later, his daughter, La Shundra, drove his youngest daughter, Latrina to Harrisburg where she got special help for her bipolar illness. The three of them reside in Harrisburg and the oldest daughter, La Shundra remains in Chicago, along with her daughter, Tierra.

Butch has never married again; he remains single some 11 years after Trina's death. He, like Alex, is my special person because he loves and cares for his kids, even to this day. As I mentioned earlier, we can't know the full measure of a man, but I look at the way Butch and Alex built their families and as a result, they have my love and my deep respect. Butch continues to support all of his children as he lives a peaceful life in Harrisburg where he is working on a prominent job. Life is good for him because he has found the Lord. Back in 2008, he gave his life to Christ, and immediately started attending meetings and bible studies. He says that Jesus is the answer for everyone. He has steadily, over the years, been involved in helping other people through community service and outreach programs.

Butch's mom, Frances Captory Levy Stanberry, passed away three years ago. She was 88 years old. I called her "Nanny" like her grandkids. We were close friends, but she and Mama were buddies. They had a lot of fun talking and gabbing about their grandkids (and kids). Nanny lived in Chicago most of her life, but in her later years, she went to live with her daughter and son in Harrisburg. While in Chicago, Nanny worked at the City of Chicago as the Assistant Treasurer of Cook County for many years.

She was admired and respected by her co-workers for her steadfastness and hard work on the job. She loved her job and went to work every day, without fail until she retired. She married Abrom Charles Levy in 1950 and they had two kids, Charles (Butch) and Finesse. She had 11 grandchildren. Finesse' two sons are: Mahlon Ranell Chase and Jelani NKosi Chase.

Nanny attended the Coppins A.M.E. Church of Chicago, after having accepted the Lord early on. She loved to travel, she loved to dance, and she loved playing bingo. She was actively involved in local and state politics serving as precinct captain and later ward committee person for the 16th Ward, Southside, City of Chicago. She was a woman of great compassion for all people, opening her doors to all who needed refuge, bed, meal or a prayer. She was instrumental in making sure all men and women who wanted to work had a job and a living wage to support a family. Nanny loved her family and her family adored her for her sparkling personality and her devotion to the well-being of everyone. Nanny will remain in my heart and I will remember her with fondness.

Trina was the youngest of my daughters and the third of my children for I had two sons after her. She grew up being a "mama's girl" and was pampered and loved by everyone. Trina had a flair about her. She was different in that she was "full of life", energetic, enthusiastic with a "zest for life". Her energy was contagious and her smile was bright and winning. She was lively and upbeat. Trina had a wonderful sense of humor making me laugh and making me "shake my head" with awe at this daughter of mind. I thought to myself, "The Lord broke the mold", when he made Trina.

She enjoyed her 2 year old grand daughter, Kyonna; Tierra, LeShawn, and little Tremaine, Jr. Her relationship with Linda and Sharon was as close as you could get as sisters. She and Linda talked several times a day; and she looked up to Sharon for support and understanding. She loved Kevin as her "big brother" although she was older than him. He was always there when she needed him. Trina & Lenard were buddies, spending time together "chewing the fat."

Her nieces and nephews called her "Trina", but treated her with dignity and respect. Shatese and Alexis helped her during her health issues over the last year of her life. Her Aunt Pearl took special care of Trina by checking on her daily and bringing her food and special treats. They had a special bond.

She was proud to talk about Tierra who had just started 9th grade and was a straight A student. She bragged about LeShawn's wonderful verbal skills; and she was delighted with Kyonna and her little antics. She loved little Tremaine, Jr. who was the spitting image of his Dad.

As I have intimated before, my daughter, Trina was "all the way live" with a bubbly personality. She loved to dance, starting out many years ago on the "Soul Train" T.V. program, along with Butch and Linda. They were "regulars" on the show during its infancy in Chicago. Her friends called her the "stepping Queen", and she was also admired for her singing, as well.

Trina accepted the Lord at Grace & Glory Gospel Chapel when she was a kid. She loved to recite scripture verses, even as a very little girl, and she could readily memorize sayings and parts for Easter Sunday plays and Christmas programs at the church. She was an easy learner and very bright. Trina had a nice sounding voice and perfect diction. It would have been great if she had wanted to go into education, but she told me that she was not interested in that career.

Ironically, when Trina was 5 or 6 years old, she was one of the little flower girls in Inez's wedding to her first husband, Joseph Washington. She wasn't happy to be in the wedding. And lo, and behold, Trina's youngest daughter Latrina "Tee", was a flower girl in Inez's second marriage, to Larry Clayton.

Trina did not achieve the world's view of fame and fortune, but she lived her life in her own way in the pursuit of her dreams. She told me, "Mama, I don't want to move. I want to stay right here in the 'hood". She cherished her friends, and her family, and her neighbors. Not only was she proud of her family's accomplishments, but she bragged about her friends and their many accomplishments. She spoke often of all the fun she had "Back in the day," and how tight she was with every body.

After a short, but full life, Trina passed quietly in her sleep on August 15, 2005, with her little granddaughter, Kyonna by her side. Her special friend, Thomas White, was devastated, and her friends were shocked and sad. It left a void in our hearts that will never be filled, but never the less, she transitioned from this life to the one prepared by her Lord.

La Shundra Rae Kilpatrick Levy was born to Katrina Rae Kilpatrick and Charles Ray Levy on February 12, 1973 in Chicago, Illinois. "Shundra", as she is affectionately called, was a beautiful baby, with her dad's complexion and her mom's pretty face. She went to Stagg Elementary School and was a fast learner. She was always very active, even to the point of breaking her arm at school, while playing.

Shundra and Shatese as children and teens were very close cousins; Shatese, my first grandchild, Shundra, my second. They sometimes dressed alike. I have a picture of them at Shatese's prom with identical dresses on. They both had beautiful hairdos, and escorted by their favorite guy at the time.

Shundra was the apple of her dad's eye, and her mom was so proud of her beautiful daughter. She has strong leadership skills, yet she has a quiet nature and sometimes painfully shy. Shundra is as smart as a whip, and very observant. She notices everything. She's social media savvy, happily keeping up with her friends and acquaintances on a daily basis.

She has several talents, one of them being able to "do hair". She often does my hair, always better than my regular beautician because of the love and special styling. Shundra helps a lot with Le Shawn and Kyonna. They are her sister's children and she has a special love for them. They call her "Auntie Shundra".

Shundra has an only child of her own, Tierra. Tierra was born on July 18, 1991 to her and Jenoit "Geno" Cameron. Tierra was a joy to everyone as a baby, but especially to my son, Lenard. He kind of took her as his own when she was just a baby, no matter that her mom had something to say about that, but he spent as much time as he could with Tierra. He primed her for success early on. And now, as an adult, we can appreciate and affirm his great influence in Tierra's development. Notwithstanding, Shundra raised her as a single mom, using tough love and discipline to assure her success. Tierra's dad has been in her life ever since her birth, as well. He's part of a beautiful family that includes his gorgeous mother, Chita, and his sister, Nene. They all adore Tierra, and she has the characteristics of both families. Tierra has been a strong member of our family, being an example for her cousins; being a positive role model for them and others in her generation. She was an excellent student in elementary school and high school, earning straight "A's" from 7th grade through 12th grade. She attended the University of Illinois at Urbana-Champaign and received her degree in June, 2013. We all attended her graduation. We drove down and spent the night. We were "off the chain" proud of her, and our thoughts turned to Lenard and how happy he would have been to see Tierra reach her academic goal. Shundra cried with the emotions of a proud mother who had done so much hard work to help her child finish college. It had not been easy, but it had been so worth it. Tierra had worked at Macy's and T.J. Maxx while at the University to help supplement the cost of books, food, and personal items.

I remember thinking about Tierra when she was a little independent three year old who posed for a picture with her little hands on her hips, with an expression of defiance on her face. I remember enrolling her and Kelley and Mia in ballet school, hoping they would become ballerinas. (None of them did) They took the classes and participated in the concerts at the end, but chose other activities to enjoy. Tierra was a cheerleader from 7th grade at McKinley Jr. High, and all through high school at Thornwood High School in South Holland. She loved being a cheerleader. At one point, she served as the captain of the team. Kelley chose the culinary arts, and Mia enjoyed the sales industry.

I remember Tierra at 9 years old doing about the best impression of Tina Turner I've seen. It was our family reunion here in Chicago, and Lenard and I got the entertainment part of the reunion together. He suggested having Tierra do "Tina" and having Derek do "Ike". Derek was 8 years old at the time. I went to the thrift shop on 112th and Western and found a Tina Turner wig and got a Ike Turner wig. I already had a pair of little heels that I had gotten from Walgreens in the toy department for Tierra. They were silver and the cutest little "Heels" for a little girl; just a slight heel, maybe 1½ inches. I found a pink, party dress that was glittery and shiny for a little girl; it was perfect and completed the outfit to look like Tina Turner. Lenard practiced with Tierra and Derek to get them ready to perform. It was done at the Banquet that Saturday night and it was hilarious. They performed "Proud Mary" and brought down the house. Derek had a play guitar and he and Tierra turned into Ike & Tina Turner. It was sheer joy to watch. That reunion is the most memorable one to me. Later that evening Shundra and Shatese and Latrice performed as the "Supremes" and it was absolutely fabulous. They had all the moves of the famous trio. Our family members from out of town complimented us on giving a wonderful family reunion. We, the Chi-Towners, were "off the chain" happy that we had done a successful event.

I thought about the years that I took Tierra and Kelley to my CCWC Annual Retreats. They were teenagers and needed to "know Christ and Make Him known". They enjoyed the conferences and learned a lot about, not only relationships with others, but how to trust the Lord to be successful in school. I was always proud of their participation at the Retreats.

Tierra has always been a positive force in our family, always willing to help wherever she was needed; and whenever she was needed. In June, 2012, I took Le Shawn and Kyonna to Harrisburg, Pennsylvania to visit their mother, my granddaughter, Latrina. I needed help with the kids, so I asked Tierra to go with me. She was delighted to go because it would give her a chance to not only see Tee, but to see her granddad, Butch, and her uncles Bub and Tremaine. She got a chance to see her great aunt, Finesse, and her great grandmother, Nanny, as well. Tierra helped with the kids as we went from activity to activity in Harrisburg. Everyone was so glad to see us. We visited Butch's apartment which was spotlessly clean and neat, everything in its rightful place. On one of those days there, we went to dinner at Red Lobster's and on one day, the kids got in the pool at the motel. We took one whole day to go to the facility to see Tee. I drove one car, and Butch drove the other car. It was a two hour trip, but seemed much longer than that. The kids really enjoyed the visit, and Tee was happy to see them.

I was proud of Tierra while she attended Thornwood High School for she was on the High Honor Roll and a member of the National Honor Society. Her name appeared in the Star Newspaper each year, highlighting her status as a student. The National Honor Society focused on those students who excel in academics. It helps to build student character and foster confidence. Tierra wrote on one of her papers: "I am driven, goal oriented, focused, and I have integrity." She said: "I was raised in a family that instilled strong moral values and who encouraged me to go to college." Also, she said: "I want to make my mom proud, because I know its hard being a single parent and putting me through school alone. If I go to college it will make me the first person out of my generation to complete school and get a good job. I want to be proud of all my accomplishments and represent my family in a good way. I don't want the easy way out, I'm in it for the long haul. It's not about the easy way out and getting a break it's about compassion, depth, energy, How you make it. I don't want to hold a position in the world to be noticed or standout. I want to be the person that changes it and makes it a better place for me and you. I want respect, because I earned it. I want to be known for me and not from anyone else. Those are my life's ambitions and goals."

Tierra went on to graduate from the University of Illinois at Urbana - Champaign with a fierce determination and commitment to finish with a great GPA. In spite of the many things young people do in college, what with the parties and other activities, Tierra kept her grades up, each year. She was successful because of her mom, Shundra, who used tough love and constant supervision to support her.

Tierra met her high school sweetheart, Jamal at Thornwood H.S. and after graduation, they attended different universities. Jamal remains my favorite for Tierra, even unto today.

Tierra recently got a job at the University of Chicago working in the Institute of Molecules Engineering (IME). She serves as the administrative support assistant in that department; and even though it is not what she quite wanted as a career, it is giving her the impetus, the financial support to pursue further academic goals.

Shundra is working each day, helping people in a service oriented facility and living contentedly in the home that Lenard got so many years ago in South Holland. Tierra stays with her, but has her eye on getting her own apartment in Hyde Park. Shundra, like my other granddaughters is very sweet to me.

When Trina died in 2005, Shundra was devastated. She had lost her mother, seemingly so quickly, and so unexpectedly. She's never quite gotten over her death, and I was so taken up with my own grief for my daughter, I didn't comfort her as I should've. I thought of it much later when I paid attention to Lenzo and Lexie and other members of the family. I had to acknowledge it before the Lord that I had been insensitive to my husband's feelings and the deep, hurt feelings of Trina's children – Shundra, Bub, Tremaine, and Tee.

I've talked to Shundra about Trina's death and she knows how I feel, so she's fine. I thank God for her and the way she has lived her life.

In December, 2013, I was writing and feeling so nostalgic about everything in my life. On December 1, 2013, I wrote this: "It is the beginning of the last month in the year 2013. It seems that "time flies" as the saying goes. The days and months "slip away" so quickly. Lenard has been gone for nine years; it will be ten years this coming February. Trina has been gone for eight years, and Linda has been gone five years; it will be six years this coming January. I miss them all so very much. Only the Lord knows what sadness and heartache I feel when I think of them. I try not to look back; I try not to live in the past, but it is sometimes a struggle." It is better now, for I have sought to look more to the future and whatever the future holds for Le Shawn and Kyonna. As I care for them each day, I'm content and satisfied, knowing that Trina would be so proud of them. Sometimes when I look at Kyonna, I remember that she was with Trina when she died, in her bed that night she slipped away. She was three years old and only the Lord knows what her thoughts were like to have gone through that trauma. Kyonna was a sad little girl for quite some time until she started day care/pre school at Ada S. McKinley. And now, she is bubbly and happy, with several close friends and doing well with her grades.

My grandson, Charles Ray "Bub" Levy was born on April 7, 1977 in Chicago, Illinois to the union of Katrina Rae Kilpatrick Levy and Charles Ray "Butch" Levy. When he was born, even then, he was the spitting image of his dad. Bub had a lot of energy and "quickness". Before long, he was crawling and then walking. He was bright, eager to see what life held for him as a kid. He went all over the neighborhood, checking out the neighbors, and finding every "nook and cranny" of the block. Everyone knew who Bub was, and whose he was.

He attended Stagg Elementary School, and enjoyed going because he had lots of friends. One teacher in particular, Mrs. Faris, took special interest in Bub (and the other Kilpatrick children) spending time exhorting him and encouraging him to do well as a young man. Lenzo, his granddad kept close tabs on him while he was at Stagg. Ms. Mary Kirby, a nun, was Principal of Stagg Elementary while Bub was there and she remembers that his grandfather kept him in line, kept him following the rules. Mary Kirby and I worked together as Retired Principals in the Bridge Summer Program at CPS.

Bub attended Simeon High School where he did well as a student and made many friends. Bub was well known and liked in the neighborhood around 82nd & Peoria. His closest friend was Anthony Darring; and he was Alexis' boyfriend. Bub witnessed Anthony being shot dead by a senseless killing. The "thug" was later (years later) apprehended, charged, and convicted for killing Anthony, but the loss of his friend in such a violent way, and right before his eyes left Bub devastated and traumatized. He never fully recovered, never really got over it. Not long after this tragedy happened, Bub and his younger brother, Tremaine, moved to Harrisburg, Pennsylvania to live near their dad.

Things started to get more and more dangerous in the neighborhood for our grandsons, so some decisions were made to try to ensure their safety. A couple of serious incidents happened with Bub that solidified our resolve to save our grandsons. They made that move to Harrisburg decades ago, and have no regrets. Things have been good for them there.

Bub got married some years ago to Tihiese and they have beautiful chemistry together as Bub continues to be the head of his household, taking his role as husband and father very seriously. Tihiese had a young daughter, Yasmine, when they got married and Bub has been an awesome step-father to her all these years. Yasmine was in elementary school moving on to high school with honors. Yasmine graduated from high school and went on to undergraduate school where she excelled, earning her degree. She is an adult now with an excellent job, which affords her the resources to be independent, as well as contributing to the family household. Their family, with Bub as the head, runs like a "well oiled machine." They are supportive of each other's needs and enjoy sharing their lives together.

Bub is a practicing barber, for a number of years. He cuts hair from his home, but is currently in school to get his license as a barber. Tihiese is loved by the family. She always, always has a smile on her face and a ready laugh. She is "all the way" live and that's why she is so admired, She finds a positive in everything. She absolutely loves coming to Chicago to visit. The younger generation enjoys partying with Tihiese. When they vacation, they meet up with Bub and Tihiese for a great time.

Their daughter, Yasmine, is a beautiful young adult who has never given her parents a moment of trouble. She finished her college degree and is currently pursuing her career goals, looking forward to a great future.

Tremaine Rayneal Levy was born in Chicago, Illinois on July 20, 1984 to the union of Katrina Rae Kilpatrick Levy and Charles Ray "Butch" Levy. Like his brother, he is the spitting image of his dad. He was a beautiful baby, and a "charmer" from the beginning. Tremaine was pleasant and easy going as a little kid. He attended the Garrett A. Morgan Elementary School and the teachers liked him, spending extra time and energy with him to make sure he understood the work. He readily made many friends and just seemed to enjoy being a kid.

He attended the Simeon High School and like Bub, he knew everybody, and enjoyed learning about the whole neighborhood. He, however, did encounter some trouble in the "hood" with some of the guys. We feared for him, and were determined to keep him from gang activity. Tremaine never got involved; he resisted pressure and intimidation. We sent him and Bub off to Harrisburg, Pennsylvania, and it wasn't a moment too soon. At Simeon, Tremaine was popular with the girls especially. He had grown into a "drop dead" handsome guy, so he had no trouble getting girlfriends.

In Harrisburg, Tremaine met the love of his life, Shavonne. He fell for her "like a ton of bricks." They remained together for about 6 years and had three beautiful kids together – Tremaine, Trina, and Trevon. When the baby, Tremaine, Jr. was a baby, Tremaine and Shavonne come to visit us. They stayed for about 2 weeks, so we got to spend a lot of quality time with them.

After Trina and Travon were born, we spent some time with them, as well. They were all babies when I last saw them. After Tremaine and Shavonne separated, her family kept the kids in Harrisburg. Bub visited them some time ago; they were still beautiful, looking just like Tremaine.

Tremaine has visited us several times over the years, and we cherish the time that he spends with us. He gets emotional at times, remembering his mother, and missing the rest of the family here in Chicago. He enjoys living in Harrisburg near his dad. They, along with Bub, are about as close as a father and sons can be. As they have grown into adults, they appreciate their dad more and more.

Latrina Shanae Kilpatrick Levy was born on December 23, 1985 in Chicago, Illinois at the University of Illinois Hospital to the union of Katrina Rae Kilpatrick Levy and Charles Ray "Butch" Levy. Tee was the second daughter and the fourth child. She was a beautiful baby with Trina's face and her complexion. From the time she was born and during her young years and teen years, people commented on how cute she was. Like Trina, she had a long, flowing head of black hair. Her hair was always difficult to comb because it tangled easily. Trina was good at managing Tee's hair.

Tee grew up at the building, and attended the Garrett A. Morgan Elementary School where Dr. Inez Walton was the Principal. Dr. Walton took a special interest in Latrina while she was at the school. I remember Dr. Walton for she did an excellent job in educating kids. After Tee left the school, Dr. Walton died suddenly of a massive heart attack. The school staff was devastated, and things were never quite the same. Morgan School has been closed for years now.

Latrina attended Calumet High School before having 2 beautiful children, Le Shawn Lemarr and Kyonna Rena. Their grandmother, Katrina, was happy to welcome these little babies to the family. Tee named Le Shawn after her sister, La Shundra Rae, and Katrina named Kyonna because she loved that name. Le Shawn was Linda's pride and joy. Even though he was her nephew, she loved him as her very own child.

It was discovered that Latrina "Tee" was suffering from an illness called bi-polar/schizophenia, so after the two children were born, they were cared for by Trina and Linda. Bi-polar disorder, as I understand it, is a condition in which a person has periods of depression and periods of being extremely happy, and sometimes being very "cross" or irritable.

When Trina passed away in 2005, Linda took on the care of both children. When she died in 2008, Lenzo and I then took them into our home, and we became parents again as we sought to raise Le Shawn who was 7 at the time, and Kyonna who was 5 years.

We have brought them up and cared for them in the best way possible for us. It is no easy task raising children, but we have continued to provide love, shelter, and support to meet their needs. My children and grandchildren accuse me of spoiling the kids, and I have to admit that my whole "milieu", my "modus operandi" is over compensation, over drive, more than enough mode; do over and beyond. I admit that I am overly protective, and sometimes obsessed with their progress. Oftentimes, it has worked against me, but I keep on pushing, trying to help them as they develop into "good people".

When they were younger, it seemed easier. Le Shawn and Kyonna wrote me little notes of love, (I kept them all), and little cards with pictures and little hearts drawn on them. One of the notes read: "Dear Mama you are sweet for saying that. we love to thank you for the note "agine" we love you from Kyonna & Le Shawn (with 3 people drawn on it)". And another one said: "from Le Shawn to moma I Love You," And: "I love you Mom - from Kyonna to Naomi" (with a picture drawn of her with her long hair). I have several like that and I cherish each one. For my birthday one year, they gave me a card that read at the bottom in their own manuscript writing: Happy Birthday, Love Le Shawn - you are my favorite Grandmother, Thanks for all you've done (no misspelled words). Kyonna wrote: Happy Birthday thank you for everything you have done from: Kyonna" (no misspelled words). In October, 2011 Le Shawn surprised me with a big dinner. He had asked my daughter, Sharon and my granddaughters to fix dinner for me so I wouldn't have to cook on Sunday. My daughter organized it and everyone brought a dish, (pot-luck) including me. I had made a macaroni & cheese cassarole for Sharon. We had a great time together and I couldn't hug Le Shawn enough for his "little kid" thoughtfulness.

As they continued to grow, the notes stopped, things became more difficult, and life became more complicated in our household. On February 22, 2013, I wrote: "It is about 5:55 AM. I got up at about 4:30 because I couldn't sleep. I'm concerned about Le Shawn, because he's not doing well in school. He's kind of a "quirky" little kid, kind of funny in a way. He's twelve years old and resistant to authority; reluctant to follow directions, and doesn't like to listen to what you have to say. "And yet, he's conscientious and very mannerable. He wants to succeed, but he doesn't want to follow through and search for the answer. When he hits a snag, he shuts down and doesn't complete the assignment.

Le Shawn is no stranger to discipline training. He attended the Spire Martial Arts Academy in 2008 when he was 7½ years old. He received a Certificate of completion for the course in the art of "Taekwondo", a yellow belt. It was presented to him by his instructor, Master Michael D. Adams, PHD. Le Shawn was trained: to have confidence, weight balance, stress relief, increased strength, discipline, poise, respect, self defense, and many other skills.

Le Shawn attended the Greenwood Elementary School in South Holland where Mr. William Kolloway is the Principal. Mr. Kolloway was instrumental in Le Shawn's success at that school. He took a special interest in Le Shawn's progress, providing a mentor to help develop his math and reading skills. When Le Shawn attended McKinley Elementary & Jr. High School, he was ready, starting at the 4th grade, to continue being an excellent student. He graduated from 8th grade in June, 2015 receiving his diploma from the school, and also receiving a Certificate from the State of Illinois, 99th General Assembly – House of Representatives in recognition of graduating from McKinley. When his peers described Le Shawn on the "Best" List as the "Math Whiz", he was surprised and elated. He also received a Certificate of Achievement for earning 40.3 Accelerated Reader Points in January, 2014.

Le Shawn's best friend is Kyran Smith, who lives down the street from our house. He and Kyran have been friends since 3rd grade. When Kyran turned 12 years old, he invited Le Shawn to his birthday "excursion". Kyran's aunt, Taffener "Taffy" Smith took them several places to celebrate Kyran's birthday: an arcade, a yogurt place, a place to eat pizza and hot dogs, and to a movie. It was an 8 hour "trek." Le Shawn got back home at about 9:20 P.M. He was exhausted and very happy. They had had a great time. I was appreciative of Taffy for including Le Shawn when taking Kyran places. They had gone to a "Legos" store and took a picture with a figure entirely made of legos. His colors were red, blue, white, and yellow, and a touch of black."

Kyran's grandmother was my neighbor, and we were good friends, being grandmothers together with the similar responsibility of raising our grandchildren as their parent. We shared many things about our experiences with these two boys. She died on December 16, 2012 and I was in total shock because I didn't see it coming. I knew she was ill and had some health issues, but I didn't know she was that ill. I attended her funeral and met some of her prominent family members. Mrs. Smith had 3 children that included twins, with Taffy being one of the twins. Kyran's dad was the single son. Mrs. Smith lived an interesting life from her birth on October 4, 1940 to her death. She loved reading and was an excellent student in school. As an adult, she was a primary school teacher with McCorkle School being one of those schools in the Chicago Public School System (CPS). She retired in 2000. Mrs. Smith loved riding her bike in South Holland, and she was an avid bridge player.

Kyonna Rena Kilpatrick was born March 19, 2003 in Chicago, Illinois to Latrina Shanae Kilpatrick. Kyonna is my great granddaughter; Katrina's granddaughter; and Latrina's daughter. She was 2½ years old and was the "apple of her eye." I don't know to what extent that experience of seeing her grandmother die had on Kyonna. I've often wondered about it and feel so sad that there was no warning to the family that Trina was so near death. I had seen her a few days before and she looked sick, but I was in denial and kept thinking she would get better. About a year before she died, Trina was told that she had to have dialysis, but she told me, "Mama, I'm not going on dialysis!" She refused, so her kidneys failed after a while and that's what took her life at 49 years old. Kyonna and Le Shawn were cared for by Linda, and remained with her until her death in January, 2008.

When we got the children in 2008, I had specific dreams for Kyonna. My dream was that she achieve excellence in every area of her life; e.g. academically, socially, physically, and spiritually. She will succeed because she is bright, energetic, and very, very observant. Like Shundra, she notices everything. As a little girl, she enjoyed "being a girl." She loved play makeup, high heels, and baby dolls. Kyonna was happy and curious, always looking for a challenge. Even now, Kyonna is trying to be a good student. Early on, she became an excellent reader by reading a lot of books. She absolutely loves writing in her journals, writing excellent sentences and paragraphs. She learned to count money by buying or paying for things and figuring out the change she should get, if any. She loved to draw, and kept her hands busy all the time, constantly trying to reach the next level.

Kyonna is friendly and gets along well with her peers. Her special friends are Ariel, Lauren, Rayah, and Kayla. She thinks well of her classmates and is learning to treat them and others with respect. My dream for her is being a model student who listens to her teachers, follows directions, and takes instruction with enthusiasm. Her social skills are meant to be used for succeeding academically, as well.

In her early years, Kyonna was in constant motion, moving from one activity to the next. That was then; now, with social media that has changed. Now there is an obsession with communication through the Iphone 6, Face time, instagram, etc. Then, Kyonna loved trying new things.

I wanted Kyonna to learn the value of family, and yes, I wanted her to realize just how precious and valuable she and Le Shawn are to the family. Knowing that you are loved, and cherished, and cared for has an impact upon the choices they make. After going to Sunday School and other church functions at Grace & Glory Gospel Chapel, she was taught the love of God and how she fits in this big, wide, wide world of ours, and getting smaller and smaller every day. Kyonna has learned, and is learning to treat others as she wants to be treated as she builds relationships.

It brings me great joy to watch Kyonna with her brother and cousins. She's the only girl among these six boys – Le Shawn, Anthony, Kevin, Tyrone, Sean, and Jayden – and she's tough. She can do whatever they do (except basketball) and sometimes better. Her experiences with them have helped her develop leadership skills that will usher her into the challenges of her life in the future.

Kyonna has a hearty "laugh out loud" laugh that brightens your day when you hear it. She laughs a lot with her friends and when she was younger, my sister in law, Pearl tickled her and teased her, making her laugh a lot.

Kevin Lamont Kilpatrick was born on March 3, 1960 in Chicago, Illinois to the union of Naomi Ruth Jones Kilpatrick and Lenzo H. Kilpatrick. He was the first son and fourth child, bringing happiness and joy to his parents. And even though he was loved and nurtured, like his sisters, his dad showed him "no slack." He was "working" at 6 years old in our little corner grocery store. There's a picture of him, around that age, in the store, with the loaves of bread in the background (at a ridiculous low price!), looking like he was the C.E.O. At nine years, he was helping his dad in the service station on 76th & Jeffrey. From a little kid, as you can see, he loved to work. At 16, he was doing summer work at the University of Chicago. Kevin also played softball with the team there. It was at the University that he got his first experience with computers, and thus began his vision.

Kevin attended the Stagg Elementary School where he was an outstanding student. He was the Valedictorian of his 8th grade graduating class. I was so proud of him, I went way overboard at the time, having most of his speech written for him, instead of letting him write his own.

He forgot the speech (Freudian slip) and ad-libbed his own words, which were far better.

As before mentioned, Kevin worked at the service station we owned at 76th & Jeffrey, under his dad's direction. Lenzo taught him certain things about running a business, and as an adult, Kevin reflected that training for he is very "business like" in dealing with people. What I mean by that is that he usually wears a suit & tie or otherwise in professional attire and he walks with confidence with excellent posture. He looks and acts professionally, usually carrying a brief case and his laptop to work.

As a kid, in the early 1960's, Kevin worked at our little grocery store at 74th & Peoria. Kevin, like his sisters, was taught to do things at the store, and was given duties that he had to perform. Junior (Fruitree) worked at the store, as well, at this time. Years later, when Lenzo gave up his businesses and worked as a district manager at Burger King Company, Kevin worked at one of the stores there, as well. Kevin worked at the one located at 79th & Paxton, where he was very well liked by the other employees.

Kevin's very first job, outside the family business, was a summer job at a Catholic School on Chicago's west side. Gwendolyn Stevenson Long's Mom gave him a position at her school, where she served as building principal. I'm not sure what his duties were, but it was probably a tutoring position during the summer school session.

Kevin grew up fast, falling in love and marrying at age 20. He married Veleese Smith in 1980; the wedding took place at our home at 7429 So. Sangamon, and the big reception was held immediately at a banqueting hall on 63rd & Jeffrey. They lived for several years at the building at 8201 So Peoria, before purchasing a home in Dolton, Illinois. They had 3 beautiful daughters, Keveesha Marie, Veleesha Mia, and Kelley. They were very proud of their kids and doted on them, trying to meet every need. They later moved their family to Crete, Illinois where they purchased a gorgeous house (I called it the "white house" because of the beautiful white walls. Kevin later had some of the walls painted with color, beginning with his living room wall which he painted a bold red. It was gorgeous, along with a fireplace and beautiful window dressings.

Veleese was a great mother to their girls, and they love her very much. She is part of a beautiful family with her mother, Lillia Bell Smith, at the head of that family. Mrs. Smith is now deceased, having passed away on November 10, 2013. She and my mother were great friends. Mrs. Smith was the ultimate mother and grandmother, loving her family with a passion. She loved to cook; one of her specialties was banana pudding. She baked it in the oven and no one has ever made banana pudding quite like hers. Her home was always filled with good food, love, and laughter. Mrs. Smith held a big birthday celebration/cookout every year, and all the neighbors looked forward to it. She was one classy lady.

Kevin and Veleese stayed together for 25 years and their marriage came unglued. They parted and each went their separate ways, seeking happiness on their own terms.

Kevin's best friend is Kimothy Lee, and in the early 1990's, they partnered in a business, a computer company. Kimothy had started the business in 1983, providing complete local and wide area networking solutions. Kimothy named his company, Bonsai Engineering Consultants, after the Bonsai tree which has strong roots. His thought was to build a family of employees who would gain strength from each other as they service their community. Kevin joined as a partnership in the 1990's. Kevin was described as the "constant thinker" behind Bonsai's strategic business tactics. It was a lucrative business venture for the two partners. They were in business for over 10 years. Their company was highlighted by the Voices of Cabrini newspaper, in the August/September, 1996 issue. It cited the friendly, warm greeting of the two receptionists – Linda Leigh and Beverly Prather – who happens to be Jesse Owens' daughter. The Data Entry Room was where data was entered into the computers for several companies, universities, etc. The newspaper reported that when they looked at Bonsai's ground work, – their format; their diversity; and their procedures – is not only run well, but is structured with the patience that families are made over time. The ties of unison had been planted – making the Bonsai "tree" ever more strong.

Kevin and Kimothy enjoyed much success at Bonsai. Kevin gave his brother Lenard a job, as well as his nieces a job while at Bonsai. It was also at this time, during those years that Kevin took his nephews to the Million Man March on October 16, 1995 in Washington, D.C. They rode a bus there with hundreds and hundreds of other African-American men. Minister Louis Farrakhan had called on men to "show up and stand up" at a March on Washington to highlight and address the growing gang problem, the devastating effects of the influx of crack cocaine during the 1980's and early 1990's, and unfair drug laws that criminalized addiction.

Kevin wanted his nephews to be exposed, personally, to what its' like to be a man and how important it is to stand for a worthy cause, and how to work for a solution for community problems. It was a rude awakening to see such a sea of men (although there were women present, as well) together focusing on helping others. They were exposed to the strength, the confidence, the commitment, and the comraderie of African-American men.

Minister Farrakhan, though controversial, called for all men of all faiths to attend to reflect on their roles in their households and beyond as they lined the National Mall for a day of peace, solidarity and recommitment to family and community. During the March, "gangbangers marched with fraternity men, police officers and firefighters joined clergy, entertainers walked alongside teachers to reframe America's narrative around Black manhood. This March happened just days after the polarizing not-guilty verdict in the trial of O.J. Simpson. The March was one of the most poignant moments in contemporary Black History.

After many successful years at Bonsai, Kevin left to form and build his own computer business. He remains close to Kimothy and they talk regularly on a weekly basis, keeping each other in the mix. They are typical best friends, having each other's back and a supporter, as well as, a critic when necessary. Of course, Kevin has several other close friends, as well: Randy, "Mr T", Gus, and Rudy.

Kevin met and fell in love with Twanda Taylor. She is drop dead gorgeous with a heart of pure gold and a winning smile. She laughs readily and has a pleasant personality. She loves kids and seeks to make their lives happy in any way that she can. She and Kevin married in August, 2008. They had a big wedding at one of those country clubs where he often played golf. The place was breath-takingly beautiful, which was the backdrop of their wedding. They had nine bridesmaids, nine groomsmen, two flower girls (Kyonna was one of them) and one ring bearer (Lil' Kevin) and our family friend, Lucius Farmer – an ordained minister – performed the ceremony. The wedding was held outside and the weather was beautiful, warm and pleasant. Twanda's colors were deep fuchsia pink and the men wore black. It was breathtaking and the bride was beautiful, like all brides. The reception was held inside and everyone had a complete "blast". Twanda's mom, Mary and I wore off-white dresses. My hair stylist, Val, swept my hair up into a chignon, and I wore the same dress I had worn for my 50th wedding anniversary in 2002. Mary and I were happy and proud Mothers of the Bride & Groom.

Twanda is part of a wonderful family. She raised three boys, Twan Taylor, Gerald Rowan, and Gordon Thornton who are all young adults now. All three guys are genuinely nice, smart, "cool" guys. No drugs, no cigarettes, no booze. They go to school (Gerald & Gordon) and they all have nice jobs. Gerald and Gordon work with their stepdad, Kevin. Twan, the oldest, has a baby, Melani Taylor, and she wraps everyone, especially Kevin, around her little finger. She calls him "Pa Pa". Twan, Gerald, and Gordon call Kevin "Pops". Kevin and Twanda also have a god daughter named Taliyah Bond, a pretty little girl with long braids, and extremely smart. She has been independent since she was 2 years old.

Twanda's sister, Kendra, is a great cook and shows her love to her family and others with delicious meals. Twanda's mom, Mary Johnson Taylor, is a beautiful woman who dotes on Twanda and took wonderful care of her own mother, Thelma L. Johnson, during her illness. Mrs. Johnson, "GG," as everyone called her, passed away last year on August 4, 2015, after a long illness. She leaves a great legacy for her grandchildren. GG was born in a small town called Cecil, Alabama in 1924. She learned the meaning of hard work during her childhood. At six years old, she began school and also began working in the family business of handmade mattresses. She accepted the Lord at the age of 10 and was baptized. The day after her baptism, her house burned down. The family kept on succeeding, however by growing sugar cane, peaches, plums, butter beans, and fig trees. It is said that people came from miles around to purchase their goods. They raised their own hogs and cows; they made their own lard and sausage and churned their own buttermilk, sharing it with their neighbors who were less fortunate. GG moved to Racine, Wisconsin where she married Mitchell Johnson and had her only child, Mary. She later moved to Chicago with her daughter where she worked for some great people who inspired her to continue pursuing her dream. GG was 90 years old when she passed away, leaving her family devastated at the loss, but proud of her rich legacy. GG left these words for her family: "Build your legacy and your own foundation. A house cannot stand unless the foundation is built well."

Twanda gets her beauty of character from her mom, Mary, who got it from her mom, GG. Kevin and Twanda are building their lives, building their family on a great foundation. It is what paves the way to continual success for both of them.

I love and admire Kevin, not just because he's my son, but because of the kind of person, the kind of adult he has become. He is a business man in a harsh business world of computers, yet when he speaks with me or addresses me as "Mom", it is with a softness and a tenderness and a love that could only come from a "God-sent" son. Kevin never leaves his dad out of the equation. He spends much time communicating with his dad, as well. Whenever I need anything that he can assist me with, he's right there, helping. He keeps me and my computer happy. He's always amazed at what I don't know about technology after all these years of having a computer. He tells me, "mom, its' common sense!" I said, "Yeh, Right!" I thought of Kevin when I read Micah 6:8 which states: "He has showed you, O man, what is good. And what does the Lord require of you? To act justly and to love mercy and to walk humbly with your God."

When I thought of words to describe him, these things come to mind: he is family oriented, loving, kind, super organized & together, and the ultimate "tech" guy. Kevin has all of our family members' birthdays on his calendar so that he can remember, and he is usually the first to call them on their special day.

Ironically, when I was writing one day about 2 years ago, Kevin walked in carrying a flat screen, 42 inch TV for our family room. It was a gift from him and Sharon and some of the grandkids. It was a sweet surprise. He set up the TV and put the old one that was in the family room, in our bedroom, so in one huge "swoop", he made our whole household happy.

Kevin has a lucritive business housed in Oak Brook, Illinois and his official title is Executive Director of Technical Support, but he is much more than that to his family and to me and his dad. He and Twanda live in a beautiful home in Hazel Crest surrounded by their 3 sons; their daughter; Kelley, their little granddaughter, Malani; her mom, Mary (often); and their goddaughter, Taliyah; a host of friends (always around) and a little dog that they call "a crazy little mutt"; A very happy family.

I don't want to give an impression of "bliss" all the time for Kevin; he's not living in a vacuum; so life for him is like everyone else's - ups & downs, good & bad, cloudy & sunshine, losses & births, - and so on. What is different is how he chooses to deal with difficulties; he likes to solve problems and then "keep it moving". He likes to keep things on an even keel.

Keveesha Marie Kilpatrick was born on May 2, 1980 in Chicago, Illinois to the union of Kevin Lamont Kilpatrick and Veleese Smith Kilpatrick. She is the first born child and the first daughter of her parents. "Veechie was a beautiful baby with just a few silk strands of hair. When I saw her, I knew her hair would grow to be long and pretty like her mom's; and it did. Although she had her mom's complexion, she favored her dad more. She had deep dimples in each cheek and the warmest smile. Even as a little girl, Veechie-Veech was a leader as she played with her sisters and her cousins who were younger. She oozed confidence, believing she could do just about anything.

As she grew into her teen years, Veechie made many life-long friends. When her family moved from the building on 82nd & Peoria and moved into their own home in Dolton, Illinois, Veechie knew all her neighbors and made great friends, developing relationships that have lasted until today.

I have such fond memories of Veechie at two of her proms. For one, she wore a gold, lame maxi dress that hugged her like a glove. Lenard helped her get dressed. The house was packed with family and best friends as they came over to see Veechie and her date go to the prom. The family had bought another home in Crete, Illinois, so we were there to see her off. Her hair was long and beautifully done and her makeup was flawless.

Veechie's second prom was just as lovely. We arrived early at their home in Crete to help her get dressed and to send her off with a "bang." I went to her room to check on her progress. Her room had bunk beds (white) with busy colored comforters and her white wall was covered with pictures of her favorite celebs – almost all guys, but a few girls, as well. Veechie had on red hose, so I figured she would be wearing a red dress. Red was the color of the dress and it was gorgeous. When she finished, she looked like she was headed to Hollywood's red carpet (pun intended). Her hair was swept up high, her makeup was flawless, lipstick the same color as her dress, which was sleeveless, bare shoulders, and a split on one side. Her earrings were white diamond, hanging slightly framing her beautiful face; and she wore a white, silk shawl; and her shoes were red. When her date arrived, he had on a black tuxedo with a red vest, white shirt, and red bow tie, and black shoes that were shining like new money. He slipped a red & white corsage on Veechie's wrist and they were ready to go and make their own history at the prom. Her parents and the rest of her family were bursting with pride.

We were there when Veechie graduated from elementary school in 1994, and when she graduated from high school in 1998. On a beautiful snapshot picture, she has her blue robe on with a bunch of flowers given to her by her dad. Her mom, Veleese and her dad, Kevin, her granddad, Lenzo (both in dark suits, white shirts, and dark ties) and her wonderful grandfather, Mr. Smith, was there towering over everyone and looking spiffy in a gray suit and a gray hat to match. I took the picture, and the smiles on their faces and their expressions were worth a thousand words. Her high school graduation was similar. The clothes were different with Veleese wearing a white dress, Kevin wore a dark brown suit with a nice tie and Lenzo wore a handsome beige suit, brown handkerchief in his jacket and a beige & gold tie, and brown shoes that were polished to perfection. Veechie's robe was again blue but with a white collar, and instead of a bouquet of flowers, she was given one yellow rose. Again, I took the picture and the smiles and expressions were the same-sheer pride.

Veechie, as an adult, has progressed and experienced many things; things that have taught her love and respect for her family. She is the one that sat for hours, every day, when her precious grandmother, Lillia Smith, was ill and in poor health. When her cousins or other family members need her, she's right there helping. She's very loyal, very seldom missing family gatherings; she loved the family reunions, continuing to communicate with her cousins on social media. (Veechie, even as a youngster, is very computer savvy. Kevin taught his three children how to use and enjoy computers. Veechie is just as adept with social media as well.).

She's very attentive to us, as her grandparents, calling and coming by often to check on us. She is very close to her two younger sisters, hovering over them, at times, like a mom. The three of them have their own unique communication with each other – joking, teasing, and competing – using their own special words.

One day after her 24th birthday, on May 3rd, 2004, Veechie gave birth to a baby boy, Kevin Lenard Kilpatrick. He was a beautiful baby with bright eyes, an olive complexion, and curly hair. Lil' Kevin was a happy baby, smiling and friendly, even to unfamiliar faces. Veechie doted on her baby. He was her pride and joy. Over the years, he has grown into a smart, bright, energetic kid. He earns good grades and has lots of friends. He goes to school in Alsip, Illinois. His dad, Jeff, keeps him through the week and takes him to school where he is excelling. He is currently the student council representative in his mixed classroom. He loves to swim and he loves sports, telling me recently, that he was playing football. He just made his 12th birthday and is well on his way to becoming a scholar like his granddad, Kevin. Lil' Kevin has a quirky, "funny" sense of humor. He notices everything and then teases his mom, his aunts, his cousins, and anyone else based on what he sees and hears. He did it as a little kid and we were all amazed at him. He never uses an unkind word, getting along well with his cousins, especially Kyonna. He and Kyonna are "jug buddies". He, like his granddad and his generation of kids, is computer savvy and knows how to navigate through the social media world.

Lil Kevin gave me a card one Mother's Day (he gives me a card <u>every</u> Mother's Day) that read: "Grandma . . . just a little "love ya" card on Mother's Day!" It was really cute!

Keveesha, like all my grandaughters, is exceptional. She is an outstanding mother to Lil Kevin, nursing him through his many times in the hospital (he's an asthmatic); meeting his needs, whatever they were – keeping him immaculately clean & neat; dressing him in the latest boy fashions; and finding the best schools for him to attend. She and his father work beautifully well together to make sure Kevin is well taken care of.

She is a workaholic; she loves to work and make things happen. She loves doing things to make others happy. She joined and was baptized at the New Faith Baptist Church, Matteson. It was at her baptism service that Lenzo had his life threatening experience. I thank God that Veechie realizes that it is important to have God in her life.

<u>Veleesha</u> <u>Mia</u> <u>Kilpatrick</u> was born on July 19, 1984 to the union of Kevin Lamont Kilpatrick and Veleese Smith Kilpatrick in Chicago, Illinois. She was born one day before her cousin, Tremaine, who was born on July 20, 1984. Katrina & Veleese had been happily pregnant at the same

time. The family calls her "Mia" fondly, sometimes even forgetting that her name is "Veleesha". Like her siblings, Mia was a beautiful baby, very light-complexioned like her mom, with deep dimples in each cheek. She was a happy, smiling baby and even today, as an adult, she still has that beautiful, coy smile, and a pleasant, positive personality. She's very easy to talk to and laughs after every sentence. It brings me joy just being around her. When I see her, I say "Mia, you're a sight for sore eyes!" She just laughs at me, and gives me a big hug.

Mia spent her childhood in Dolton at their first house where she made many, many friends. She met Serena Mix in that neighborhood, and they have remained best friends unto this day.

Mia attended the Crete/Monee High School and she did well in her classes. She quickly made a name for herself; e.g. she had one fight, with a guy, and she beat him up, to put it mildly. Although her parents frowned on her having had this fight, no one messed with her ever again during her four years at the school. There are beautiful pictures of Mia at several activities at the school:

- Homecoming, she went with her friend, Edward. She wore a classic, dark blue, denim jeans suit; hair long and beautifully coffed; she has a half smile on her face with her dimple enhancing her beauty.
- High School Prom, a picture of her and her mom before she dressed; a picture of her with (Lenzo & I); a picture of her (fully dressed) with her dad; a picture of her with her sister, Veechie; with her beloved grandmother, Lillia Smith; and my favorite picture of the event which shows Mia pinning the boutinier on her date after he presents her with a wrist corsage. Mia's dress was white with crystals and beads in the bodice and dripped down in layers to the bottom of the dress. It was silk and satin and off the shoulders; it had a train to the back of it and a split on one side. (Her parents paid a "fortune" for that dress) She wore a shawl of the same silk material as the dress. Her hair was brushed up and slightly to the side; her makeup was flawless; white hanging diamond earrings; a diamond choker around her neck; beautifully decorated nails; and a diamond bracelet, and see-through white shoes with diamonds; Her date was just as dramatic, he could have been a Mississippi Baptist Preacher for he was dressed to the tens.

He wore a white, long jacket tuxedo (Steve Harvey would have been jealous) with stripes on the pants, white shoes, white gloves, a white derby hat, white buttoned down shirt, and to complete his whole outfit – a white cane. They looked stunningly fabulous. It was typical for Mia's generation – they were serious about their high school prom, making sure they were dressed to draw "ooo's & ahs" from their friends.

As an adult, just like her teen years, Mia lives happily in her own world. Recently, she moved to a little place called Newton, Iowa with her friend, Will. I thought, what could have attracted her to this place? Newton is located about 30 miles east of Des Moines, Iowa and is known for Iowa Speedway, Maytag Dairy Farms, and the Dark Magician. Newton also is famous for its coal mines. The Maytag Washing Machine Company was prominent in the late 1930's until it became the Maytag Corporation around 2000. Whirlpool took over the Corporation in 2006 and by 2007, it closed the Newton Plant and corporate offices. The plant officially ended production in October, 2007, but community leaders and city Leaders worked together to develop a plan to diversify Newton's economy. As a result, several companies moved to Newton: Underwriters Laboratory, Trinity Structural Towers, TPI Composites, Caleris, Walter G. Anderson, the Iowa Speedway, Health Enterprises, Engineered Plastics Company, Pact Manufacturing, Advanced Wheel Sales, and Hawkeye Stages. The town attracted, recently, "green manufacturing". TPI Composites plans to open a plant to manufacture massive wind turbine blades. President Barack Obama visited the Trinity Structural Towers Plant on April 22, 2009, which was the year's Earth Day. While at the factory in Newton, the President said that he came to the factory in order to usher in "a new era of energy exploration in America." Newton was awarded the National Sustainable Community of the Year Award (Small City Category) by Seimens and the US Chamber of Commerce in 2010 for its successful, pro-active approach to recovery.

Although the economy has recovered, and Newton is considered a "boom town" by some, Mia loves it for another reason. She told me, "Mama, I like it for the peace and quiet, and the friendly people." She has a nice job there at Walmart's and enjoys making everyone happy when they visit the store. She gives them a smile which makes her dimples deeper in each cheek, and they leave the store, after purchases, with a nice pleasant feeling.

Kelley Kilpatrick, was born on April 11, 1992 to the union of Kevin Kilpatrick and Veleese Smith Kilpatrick in Chicago, Illinois. She is the third child and the last child born to this union, and the third daughter. She was a beautiful baby, with wispy, silk dark hair, dimples (like her sisters), and a very fair complexion. Growing up, her cousins thought Kelley was "white," because of her light skin. As a little kid, she one day asked her dad, "Daddy, are my grandparents (talking about Lenzo & me) from Africa?" Kevin said, "Yes", and so are you!" That took care of her questions from that point on. Kelley grew up with a healthy, positive, beautiful self awareness, understanding her place in our family and in the world.

Kelley attended the Homewood/Flossmoor high school and was an excellent student. She excelled in her academic classes and joined the dance classes and also, some drama classes. She is an excellent dancer, so she especially enjoyed participating with the other students as they prepared to put on the end of semester shows. I attended some of her shows, and was entertained and was amazed at what kids are able to do when guided and supported. Kelley made me very proud of her with her dancing talents and her leadership skills. She was in a "zone". She graduated with an excellent GPA and looked excitedly toward her bright future.

She attended Western Illinois University (WIU) and majored in business. It was quite an experience there and she made many friends. She learned life long lessons there and developed skills and talents that helped her decide her career path. She knew she wanted to start her own business, so she set her goals high and began to pursue them.

Kelley had always loved to cook, and she was good at it, especially bakery goods. So her concentration was on cakes, cup cakes. She would later start her little cup cake business on the internet with just beautiful, colorful, creative decorations of the cup cakes. I was impressed and proud when I saw her products. It's always a struggle to build a business, but Kelley is well on her way to success.

When she was growing up, we attended her graduations and her other events, as well. Her first graduation was from kindergarten, with Kelley being as "cute as a button" in her little white robe and cap. Veleese wore one of her favorite red pants suit and Kevin wore a spiffy beige suit, with a chocolate brown tie. They were dressed to the nines to see their daughter finish kindergarten!

She graduated from Homewood/Flossmoor High School in 2010 where she donned, again, a white cap & gown. She attended her prom wearing a beautiful dress that was a deep brown chocolate color with yellow and gold on one side, yellow sheer gloves and her date brought her a beautiful yellow wrist corsage. The dress was long, chiffon and silk, low in the front and sleeveless. Like her sisters before her, her makeup was flawless. Her hair was swept up in the back, but long on one side, almost covering her eye. Her earrings were hanging diamonds with a matching necklace. She looked absolutely stunning. She and her date had a wonderful time, making another great memory, never to be forgotten.

I have fond memories of my granddaughter, Kelley. After her 13th birthday, and every year after that for a few years, she and Tierra went with me to the CCWC Annual Retreat. I took them with me to the retreat for women and girls at the Hyatt Regency Hotel and later at other hotels. I took them to expose them to the Word of God; how to accept the Lord as Savior; and how to live a committed life as a young Christian. They were involved in the Youth Alive! teen girls group, pledging to keep God in their lives at the end of each conference. The conference was usually 3 days on the weekend, and the three of us had a beautiful, bonding time together.

L. Lenard Kilpatrick was born in Chicago, Illinois on a Friday, December 13, 1968 to the union of Lenzo H. Kilpatrick and Naomi R. Kilpatrick. It was a cold and snowy Friday the 13th outside, but it was a warm and beautiful feeling inside when his parents held him for the first time. Lenard was the fifth child, the second son, and the youngest child born to this union.

Lenard never liked his name, Lenzo Lenard Kilpatrick. I named him after his dad, but he disliked it altogether. I wanted to honor Lenzo and make Lenard happy as well. We all called him Lenard, by his middle name, but others outside of the family, called him "Leonard" (one syllable). Lenard is two syllables.

As my precious baby, he brought us so much joy. He was fast-moving, always animated. When I put him in his walker, he didn't just walk; after a while, he would run all over the house. He loved clinging to my skirt tails;

or just clinging to me, period. When he became school age, I sent him to a private school, Howalton. It was located on Chicago's south side, and it was the first African American private school in Chicago. It was founded in the summer of 1946 by three Chicago Public School teachers: June Howe, Doris Allen, and Charlotte Stratton. The three held an initial discussion, on a bus, of the deplorable educational facilities and instruction for children in the black community on Chicago's south side. These schools were overcrowded and inadequate, as well as, too old and no longer functional. Teaching skills were over borne by discipline problems in classrooms with 48 desks that were supposed to accommodate 50 or more children. In 1946, the teachers wrote to Mayor Edward Kelly complaining about the terrible conditions at Englewood High School, but Kelly did not respond. The three teachers then loaned the school the money to open, hoping to be repaid from tuition fees. Thus Howalton began as a "vacation school," a summer experiment for first and second graders needing additional work in reading and math. The teachers drew their students from the surrounding Forestville neighborhood and the Rosenwald Garden Apartments. In September, 1947 the school was chartered by the Illinois State Office of Public Instruction.

During the first 10 years of its operation, the school sharply expanded its enrollment and gained a reputation as a school where African American children could gain a top quality education, leading to successful work in high school and college.

Mildred Johnson served as principal of the school during the 1960's and was feted for her work as a poet, an author of children's books, and the director of SAY! Children's Theater. I have used her poetry for some of my speeches and for some of my letters, and sometimes just for reciting in group activities.

Historians suggest that Howalton Day School was one of the leading institutions to emerge from the Chicago Black Renaissance. (This information on Howalton was taken from Archives - 1946-1999 at the Chicago Public Library)

I enrolled Lenard in the Howalton Day School in 1974, and he attended for a year. He was very unhappy at the school. He was picked up for school and was dropped off at home (we were living at 7429 So. Sangamon). He told me he wanted to walk to school with his friends.

Also, he was only 5 years old and he did not want to leave his mom and siblings. Lenard had a very productive year at Howalton, however, with good grades, and a great experience, not withstanding against his will. So, after a year, I pulled him out of that school and enrolled him at Stagg Elementary School, one block from our house. He was very happy there and it affirmed that I had made a good decision. He loved his teachers (especially Ms. Farris) and did very well as a student at Stagg.

After Lenard graduated from Stagg Elementary School, he went on to Chicago Vocational High School (CVS). His experience at CVS was a "mixed bag" in that his grades were not A's & B's. He never failed a class, but it was "touch and go" for awhile. My friend, Willie Crittendon was the Assistant Principal at the time, at CVS, and she kept an eye on him and encouraged him in his studies. He graduated from CVS with the distinction of being the "Best Dressed" of the graduating class.

As an 8 year old kid, Lenard appeared on the cover of the Urban Ministries' Sunday School material, "Primary Street". The question on the cover was "How do you feel when you are sick?" The publication date was January 18, 1976. The lesson was "Jesus Helps Sick People", Matthew 9:35. On the back page, Lenard had drawn pictures of strong eyes, strong legs, and a smiling mouth. The editor at the time was Judith B. Hull, published by Urban Ministries, Inc. (It was such a sweet memory for me.)

After graduating from CVS, Lenard wasn't quite sure in what direction he wanted to go. He was interested in cosmetology and fashion design so he enrolled in Olive-Harvey Junior College on a scholarship. He received the scholarship because he got such a high score on his entrance exam. He received certification in Cosmetology from Pivot Point International School of Hair Design. He enjoyed the school experience and completed the course, but after working as a beautician in several salons, he discovered that that line of work was not what he really wanted to do.

Lenard, along with his sister, Sharon served as mentor/leader for several Lake View High School students during a four day college summit at Elmhurst College in July, 2001. The students were happy to be a part of Lenard's group because he shared his poetry and his life experiences with them.

Lenard worked with the Carol Moseley Braun's Campaign for U.S. Senate in 1992 with Kevin and Sharon. He enjoyed that experience and learned valuable lessons in the interim.

He worked at various restaurants, before working as a salesman at Neiman Marcus and Marshall Fields (now Macy's). After working in a couple of other departments at Marshall Fields, he ended up in the women's shoe department. He was in his element; he was the salesman "extraordinaire" at Fields. He was well liked by his co-workers. He made the customers happy by taking special interest in their purchases.

I have so many wonderful memories of my son, Lenard, but one shining moment is so vivid in my mind. My sorority sister, Clarice Brown, was the Chairman of the Top Ladies of Distinction, Inc. Annual Beautillion held in Chicago. She urged me to let Lenard become one of ten young gentlemen who would be presented to society at a big event. I consented and after spending big bucks and many months of practice for Lenard, the Beautillion was held at the American Congress Hotel in January, 1986. It was a big affair that included newspaper coverage and attendance by many high society people including: the Honorable John H. Johnson, President of Johnson Publishing Co., who was honored by TLOD; State Comptroller, Roland Burris who served as Master of Ceremonies; National TLOD President Lady Bobbie Moorehead; and honorary member Lady Jackie Vaughn, Chicago Teachers Union President. Everyone was dressed to the "tens" with the Beaux most elegant of all. There were ten of them with their "Belles", all dressed up in black tux's, white shirt and bow ties, white gloves, black top hats, and canes. Their dates, the ten Belles were dressed in identical, long, cranberry red dresses, with white, long gloves. Their pictures were featured in the Chicago Defender on Saturday, January 11, 1986. The parents were presented during the ceremony, so Lenzo and I proudly "stumbled" through a brief dance, (just kidding, we did fine!) and ritual. It was absolutely beautiful, an awesome experience for all of us. Our family & friends were part of the audience, so they were proud, as well. It was a moment that I will always remember and cherish.

Sadly, my beloved son passed away on February 24, 2004. It was a cold, dreary day, a Tuesday, one that I will never forget. I had gotten the call that they couldn't wake him up. His dad went over to his house; I couldn't look at him in death. I went to the house later and wailed in the car. I can't articulate my emotions except that it was the most painful thing I have ever experienced. Later that day, I called my dear friend, Beverly Yates, and she dropped everything that she was doing and she and Bro. Yates came over to comfort the family. My daughter's best friend, Juanita Stem and her husband, Tyrone, rushed over, as well. I don't know how I got through that day, or that week, or that month. Only by the grace of my Lord and Savior, Jesus Christ.

The funeral was held a week later on Tuesday, March 2, 2004 at the Harris Temple A.D.H. Church of God, Lenzo's nephew John L. Jackson's church. Jack, as we call him, gave the Eulogy as a packed audience mourned with us. Lenard's cousins came, en masse, from out of town and locally: Charles, Wayne, and Solomon Kilpatrick; Tony Edwards, Alonza Fruitree, David Jackson, David Kea, Derek Johnson, and Thurman Moore. His friends Kenny Baker, and Patrick Ward; and his mentor, Elder James Fair. Lenard's favorite aunt, Earselean "Ersé" West of St. Louis, Missouri.

Words of condolences, cards, phone calls, flowers, plants, and other comforts poured in at that time. My cousins, my sorors, and my friends brought food for my family, just blessings galore. This helped me – knowing that others care; knowing that others were feeling our pain; knowing that others were a "bridge over troubled waters" for us helped to comfort me at this, my darkest hour.

I was a part of the J G M J (Just Give Me Jesus) movement when Lenard died. This movement was sponsored by Moody Bible Institute and was on the scale of a Billy Graham Crusade. This J G M J movement was led by Anne Graham Lotz, Billy Graham's daughter. The women in that group were praying for my family.

Jennifer Salley Wallace created a beautiful piece of artwork with some of Lenard's words depicted on it. It has a dark frame with a green shadowed background of tall, slender trees. The words that are on the art work are:

> "Our family is a circle of strength and love . . . every
> joy shared adds more love. Smile when the trees bend with
> your kin, this night is beautiful so the faces of my family,
> the stars are beautiful, also, is the sun, beautiful also are
> the souls of my family."

It was a creative and wonderful thing to do for our family at such a sad time. I have treasured the art piece and Jennifer remains one of my most precious friends. Her art piece served as a permanent document of Lenard's words that he gave to his family on Thanksgiving, November 27, 2003; three months before his death.

Lenard, I think, was saying "goodbye" to us before he passed away. On Sunday, he came over and got a plate of food to take home. He gave me a big hug. I remember thinking that the jacket he had on that night wasn't warm enough, because it was a cold night. That Monday, he saw Sharon, and on Tuesday morning, he was gone. I had no idea that that Sunday would be the last time I would see my beloved son alive.

A month earlier, Lenard had written in Tierra's bible:

"To My Child": Tierra Kilpatrick, you are my hope for the future! Make me proud; stay in school until you've finished college. Most of all, Keep God First!!
Tierra called Lenard, "Lenar-red", from a little girl.

Lenard had a childhood friend, Lamarr, who grew up with him on Sangamon. We all called him by his nickname, "Butter". After Lenard's death, Butter wrote me a letter. It was beautiful. The words on the letter kind of summed up what his friends thought of Lenard. He wrote: "My friend, Lenard, my very first memory of us is that of children playing in snow with little plastic animals – we must have been six or seven and lived on 74th & Sangamon. We were the only kids outside on a Snowy winter morning, but we played outside as if it was June." Butter said that Lenard was his very first friend on the block. He remembers that Lenard was wearing a blue & brown parka, blue pants and brown boots. Lenard had some little plastic animals that they played with that day. Later on in their lives, they talked about that first day when they met. Butter remembers me taking him and Lenard to the library (now Woodson Library) at 95th St. & Halsted once a week. Butter then admits that he still has a book that he checked out. He smiles as he says "I wonder what the fee is on that book!" Butter says he remembers when my son, Lenard's brother Kevin made his own soda pop by mixing the flavors of banana, strawberry, and peach. He might have come up with a formula from school. Butter writes on: "I remember when Kevin took Lenard out to a very stylish/fancy restaurant for one of his birthdays and invited me to come along." He said that his sister, Ruthie always admired Lenard and thought he was such a "classy guy." Butter also remembers riding to St. Louis with Lenard and my mother, Cora, on some of her many trips from Chicago and back again. Kevin would go along, as well. He enjoyed spending time with the family and being such a special part of Lenard's family. He remembers talking to Sharon (Lenard's sister) about life, God, and moving on when you lose someone. It was a difficult time for her, but God's love will always take us through. Not long after, Butter fell in love with his "now" wife. Lenard was still alive when he talked about marrying her and he went ring shopping with Butter. Butter picked out two plain gold bands and Lenard gave him a "tongue lashing" and he actually picked out the wedding rings for him – Butter's with a hint of blue and hers with a hint of pink – that was Lenard's style and class. He was with Butter when he proposed to his wife and he now has two adult children. Lenard told Butter that he should not pass her up because she was such a cutie and so sweet.

Butter talked about Lenard's nieces and nephews and how they had grown since he last saw them. He says Lenard will always be his friend, he loves him and will never forget him. He said, "Time and distance means next to nothing; love means everything and I love you all . . . And oh yeah, little Miss Tierra always be good, your Uncle is watching. Make him very proud. God bless and keep you all." It was such a sweet letter; so many memories; such love & concern from Lenard's dear friend. To God be the glory.

And Tierra has made her uncle proud for she, on Saturday, May 11, 2013 graduated from the University of Illinois at Urbana - Champaign after 4 years of really good grades and a positive attitude and a supportive single mom, La Shundra. She earned a Bachelor of Arts degree from the College of Liberal Arts & Sciences. Her major was Communications/ Public Relations.

When Lenard died he left a museum of over 200 dolls from all over. The extensive doll collection was a display of beauty and style including many African American celebrities and Princess Diana. He left his doll collection to Tierra in his "Last Will & Testament".

The last two years of Lenard's life were filled with illness and health issues. I was "blindsided", not seeing his death coming, or maybe I was just in denial. Because he was so precious to us, I never dwelt on the possibility of losing him, of not having him in my life. And yet, on that bleak, cold Tuesday morning, he passed from this life to the bosom of our Lord Jesus Christ.

As I reflect on his life, I am reminded of how special he was and how he has added to the legacy of our family. He was the kindest, most warm-hearted person you could meet. He loved people, and he loved to talk and he loved to read. He was an avid reader, reading biographies, and history, and non-fiction books. I think he must have read every book written on the Kennedys. He was obsessed with Jacqueline Kennedy Onassis, and knew many trivia facts about her and her children.

In 1988, while Lenard was working at Rizzoli's book store, he purchased a rare publication of "JFK Remembered". It was one of only 50 published and was personally signed by the author, Arthur M. Schlessinger, Jr. I still have the tissue paper and the beautiful green & gold wrapping paper that he gave me when he presented the book to me. I have treasured it all these many years and cherish the message that he wrote inside.

He loved the "good life"; he loved really nice things. I told him he should have been born with a "silver spoon" in his mouth because his parents could not afford to live like royalty.

Lenard loved pets, owning 1 cat, Myles, and 2 dogs, Max and Murphy. We inherited Myles and he lived some 7 years after Lenard's death. Max was hit by a car while unleased. He died after suffering a painful death. Lenard was devastated and was sad over it for a long time. Murphy stayed with La Shundra after Lenard's death, living several years.

He was extremely knowledgeable about a lot of things. He watched the history channel and the discovery channel relentlessly. He loved watching old classic movies, on both T.V. and video. Those old movies that contained excellent "life lessons" were his favorite.

He was comfortable with the very rich, the very important, as well as, the poor, the meek, and the humble and anyone in between. He loved helping people and making others happy. The week before he died, he was trying to go to Detroit to see his cousin, Marvin, who was also ill. That was Lenard, my pride & joy, and not a day goes by without my thinking about him, and Trina, and Linda, and my mother.

As I close the pages on this chapter, this chapter that talks about my kids, I finish it knowing that we survived by the sheer grace of God. As I have relived these painful memories, I look in the mirror and see the effects of the losses in my eyes. I see sadness, but my spirit is strong and determined to not let my dear children's death be in vain. I'm committed to somehow make a difference, each day doing something to make this world a better place.

I am proud of this family that Lenzo and I have created. There is a thread of kindness and gentleness; a thread of care and concern for other people; a thread of "dire straights" – never give up; a thread of commitment and dedication; and a thread of a "thirst for knowledge; and a thread of peace and contentment; and a thread of love for family and friends which runs through our kids that came from both sides – Lenzo's & mine. This legacy came from our parents and we now pass it on to our kids and their kids and their kids. Through them, I honor the Brockman/Shockley family; the Kilpatrick/Edwards family; and the Jones/Thompson family.

May my children continue to be proud of who they are and where they came from. Not because they are better than other families, but because they are "like" other families, and are "akin" to other families; families that are striving to make this world a better place; families that are raising their children to follow rules and to be respectful; families that help their communities; families that have superior work ethics; and families that fear God.

From God's grace to God's glory!

Naomi, Lenzo, Sharon, Kevin

Chita Cameron, Son Jenoit, Grand daughter, Tierra, Naomi & Lenzo (seated)

Sharon with her Ex-husband, Alex, daughters, Shatese & Alexis, & Son, Sean

Lenzo & Sister, Pearl Harper

Friends & Family

Sharon & Her Friends

LaShundra with her Dad, "Butch", her aunt, "Finesse", her two brothers Bub & Tremaine & her friends, Wanda & LaShonda

The Kilpatrick Family

Lenzo & me in my favorite white dress (back then)

Bub and his grandmother, "Nannie"

CHAPTER NINE

Climbing the Ladder of Success

"He (Jacob) dreamed and behold a ladder set up on the earth, and the top of it reached to heaven: and behold the angels of the Lord ascending and descending it." Genesis 28:12

"Beloved, I wish above all things that thou mayest prosper and be in health, even as thy soul prospereth." III John 2

"For I know the thoughts that I think toward you, says the Lord, thoughts of peace and not of evil, to give you a future and a hope." Jeremiah 29:11

My academic career started early, when I was a kid. I remember, as a child, I wanted to "be" someone; something important in the world. My life seemed fine, but I wanted it to be more. When my cousins and I played, I was always the "mama", or the "teacher", or the one who told the others what to do. My elementary experience was very enjoyable; the teachers liked me because I was an eager and fast learner. I remember thinking, every day, I'm going to learn something new today! And I did. My love of reading must have come around that time, but I can't recall exactly when I started to read; don't remember the age, but I remember the "Dick & Jane" books with the big print. My grades were always "E's" (excellent) and "S's" (superior); very seldom did they fall below "G'" (good).

My early schooling was in St. Louis, Missouri where the family went after leaving Fitzhugh, Arkansas, my birth place. At eleven years old, we moved to Chicago and I attended Doolittle Elementary School for a short time. My 7th and 8th grades were spent at Douglas elementary where I graduated from 8th grade. My teacher there was Miss Brown who was fair-skinned, short, with short-cropped straight hair, and eye glasses.

She always wore a "smock" over her very neat clothes and she had this habit of pulling her sleeves up slightly when she was teaching her favorite subject, "English". Miss Brown was stern and strong willed. The students were not able to "pull the wool" over her eyes. She could "sting" with biting words, but she used so many words of encouragement, so many "words of wisdom." After graduation, I went to Wendell Phillips High School. My friend, Georgia Stewart Bolton, graduated and attended Phillips, as well. She married Ernest Bolton later on. Georgia and I, along with Susan Benson Anderson, remain friends after all these years; childhood friends. Our other 2 friends, Evelyn McGee and Yolanda Ellington, passed away some years ago. Evelyn's brother, Edward, and I were close friends, going to the movies together, holding hands, sitting on my front porch, and taking short walks around the block.

My high school years were pleasant, as well. I still have my first grades, a "course book" from my very first semester there. All Superior and one Excellent. I joined the National Honor Society while at Phillips until my junior year when I dropped out to get married and have a family. Dr. Virginia Lewis was principal at Phillips during that time and was well-loved and respected by the student body. She brought knowledge, confidence, and elegance to Phillips; and has over the years received many accolades, awards, citations, and other recognition for her great service to African American students and her contribution to the world of academia.

I got married in May, 1952 and began having my children: Sharon was my first-born, born in September, 1952; Linda was born 11 months later in August, 1953; Katrina "Trina" was born in March, 1956; and Kevin was born in March, 1960. I went back to school, Wilson Junior College, in 1962, and my youngest son, my last child, Lenard, was born after I started my teaching career in 1968, December.

My experience at the Junior College level was stimulating and rewarding. I had enrolled in a special program there because I had not finished high school. If I could maintain a "C" average for a year, I could enroll in the regular program. I did much better than C's; I excelled, especially in English, Literature, and Geography. I struggled with the math classes, but I studied hard and was able to pass every big test. I remember one instructor in particular, a white teacher, who showed no prejudice toward me, but encouraged me to major in Language Arts in pursuit of my teaching degree. After attending Wilson Junior College for 2 years, I enrolled in the 4 year college; Illinois Teachers College South. It was exciting to be pursuing my dream of being a teacher in such a positive way. I met my life long friends, Jackie Crook, Annette Campbell, Joan Redus, Lillie Clinton, and Gussie Rose. We formed a very close-knit study group to assure our success in the classes. We did not "fool around" nor do foolish, frivolous things. We were dead serious about getting our degrees. We had basically similar courses for we all wanted to be teachers. We studied hard and each was successful. Jackie taught for years before becoming a school librarian; Annette taught for years and brought in technology into her classroom (innovative at the time); Joanie, now deceased, got married and moved to another state where she taught for years; Lillie taught in Chicago for years, got married and moved to Detroit, Michigan where she continued to teach until her retirement – the 4 of us, Annette, Jackie, Lillie, and me had lunch just a few months ago when Lillie came to bury her beloved sister; Gussie, now deceased, taught at the high school level, at Chicago Vocational High School (CVS) until her retirement. Gussie brought me into the Iota Phi Lambda Sorority, Inc., Alpha Chapter back in 1974 and the rest is history. Nancy Mitchell was the only white girl of our group and there wasn't an ounce of prejudice in Nancy. We all supported and helped each other through personal losses, difficulties, hurt, and disappointments. We shared in marriage, the birth of our babies, and the tragic losses of our loved ones. I'm reminded of the poet, Edna Buchanan, who said, "True friends are those who really know you but love you anyway." And a famous educator once said, "A true friend knows your weaknesses but shows you your strengths; feels your fears but fortifies your faith; sees your anxiety but frees your spirit; recognizes your disabilities but emphasizes your possibilities." Everlasting friends go long periods of time without speaking and never question their friendship. We pick up our phones like we just spoke yesterday, regardless of how long it has been or how far away they live, and we don't hold grudges. They understand that life is busy; we know that we will always love each other as dear friends. We prayed for each other, in good times and bad times.

Jackie wrote the following about our friendship among the group of us from our college days:

"In the fall of 1964, a group of us (Annette, Lillie, Joanie, Nancy, Naomi, and Jackie) unaware of the other, enrolled as new undergraduate students at Chicago Teachers College. During the first few weeks of the trimester we met while engaging in several of our classes and began to meet for lunch. These dining dates led to the development of a study group that quickly emerged into a wonderful friendship where we laughed, chatted, shared class concerns, and simply enjoyed each other's company. Following graduation, as each of our lives and careers unfolded, we kept abreast of the important milestones, celebrated the big and small triumphs (marriages, birth of children and grandchildren) and offered love and support during times of sorrow. Almost fifty years have passed and we still meet occasionally for lunch where we share and give an update of the new experiences in our lives and reminisce and laugh about the old times.

"Our college experience can be defined as a time of growth, both academically and personally. On the academic level the classes varied greatly in their requirements and intensity. Some required considerable amounts of reading, writing and taking tests while others like math and science required memorizing and applying rules, formulas, and or theories. Whatever the courses entailed, we willingly accepted the challenge and with hard work and determination we went about fulfilling our course requirements. Again, our group was Jackie, Annette, Joanie, Nancy, Lillie, & Naomi.

On a personal level, we discovered attributes in ourselves that we didn't know we had. We came to the realization that we had the ability to quickly make important decisions, the ability to clearly understand what worked and what didn't work in our efforts to succeed, the ability to explore and clarify our academic interests, and the ability to develop personal skills that will be germane in our academic and professional endeavors.

Both the intellectual and personal growth developed not just through our course work and the teachers that challenged us in their courses, but also through interacting with fellow students as we participated in a study group and joined the Women's Glee Club. The study group provided a support network where we interacted by helping each other and not letting our pride get in the way. At times, we had to openly accept the fact that we needed help in some subject areas. At other times, we graciously assisted a fellow group member with interpreting an assignment or prepping for an exam. In addition to our study group, the Women's Glee Club offered an opportunity for connecting and bonding with fellow students while actively participating in an enjoyable experience. It was a pleasant break from the academic courses – one that was fun and full of school spirit. Overall, our formative years at Chicago Teachers College provided valuable experiences where we prepared ourselves for entering the professional world of educators on both the academic and personal levels."

Jackie spoke eloquently about our college experience, and we are proud of the training we received and the degrees we earned. Jackie continues to serve the CPS professionally and enthusiastically. She retired years ago, but she is working to help student teachers succeed. She is sharing her knowledge with others and as a result, she is "achieving immortality." Jackie celebrated her 70th birthday, a milestone, on June 15, 2013 at the Flossmoor Station Restaurant. Thank God for His mercy and His grace.

Annette Campbell

Annette spoke to her students some years later, when she began teaching in the Chicago Public Schools. Her message to the young people is just as apropo now as it was then. Here is an excerpt from that excellent speech:

" . . . there are obstacles that will seem bigger than you, but with God's help you can over come them. I do not suggest to anyone to tackle a task in this world without God. You need Him for guidance. In this world where there are so many choices to make how do I know which is best for me. The bible tells us that in all our ways acknowledge Him and He shall direct thy path. Do not make God someone that you need only when in trouble or old. This life is risky and uncertain, but our God is faithful and just in all of His dealings.

Our heritage is rich in victories because of our faith. When I think of how Harriet Tubman led over 300 people through enemy territory and did not lose a passenger and Frederick Douglass becoming a great orator and running a newspaper when we weren't supposed to know the English language. How can I not stay in the struggle? How can you not?"

Then Annette had a message for the Parents of her students as well:

"Parents, we too have a struggle. It's our responsibility to train our children in the way that they should go. They need our care and love and guidance at all stages of their growth. The teen years are confusing and difficult. It's our God given responsibility to see that our children are taught correctly. We need to study two things – the Bible and our African American past. The Bible because it's the only book that has been honest about man's plight in this world and man's promise of eternal life through belief in Jesus Christ. Our past because our children need to know that we come from a strong stock of overcomers and that the struggle of the mind has been fought for centuries and that there are scores of African Americans who have proven that it can be done.

Let's rekindle the flame of our struggle and know that you can stand tall in spite of the obstacles!"

Annette retired some years ago, but she continued, long after her retirement, to make a difference in the lives of families. From grace to glory!

In my early years education was very important to me. Now, as I look back on those years, it is more than a memory. My quest for knowledge was my own individual "movement". We, along with the others of my generation, were bold and brave as we sought to make the world a better place for our children, and their children, and other children. We were ordinary people, doing extraordinary things to create positive changes. That's how our legacies began, by seeking and pursuing our academic goals; leaving a path for our kids to follow. We did not know, back then, that we were "making history". I didn't have time to think about what my vision of the future would mean to my children; or that this would be my legacy. And now, in this moment of time, I'm proud to acknowledge the result of my quest for knowledge; the reward for my search for information; the evidence of many years of hard work; and the gratitude I feel and express to my Lord and Savior Jesus Christ for bringing me thus far.

Academic Journey

In early 1988, I was encouraged by my principal, at the time, Clara K. Holton, to take the "Principal's Exam". The exam was an 8 hour exam and rumored to be very difficult to pass. Unknown to me at the time, this would be the last exam given in this format. I did not have much confidence that I could pass this exam; some educators had taken it and didn't pass it. I was part of a study group and we met regularly to prepare ourselves to pass this exam. It was a two part exam, Part I was the 8 hour written exam, Part II was the oral exam. If you were successful on the written part, then you go on to take the oral part. You had to pass both parts to receive the coveted "Certificate of Principal". There were nine of us in the study group: Velma Wilson, Sandra Traback, Barbara Pulliam, Linda Layne, Naomi Kilpatrick, Mahalia A. Hines, Vinnie M. Hall, Mary Goosby, and Tam Boston Hill. Every one of us passed the written exam and the oral exam. Afterwards, we were given a "Certificate of Membership" for our group with "Congratulations" written on it and it had our names on it, as well. We were all estatic. It was dated June 21, 1988. I treasure that document. That month, June, 1988, I was awarded the "Certificate of Principal" in a "pomp & circumstance" ceremony by Manford Byrd, Superintendent of Schools. Hundreds had taken the exam, but only a few passed.

It was a happy time for me and my family. Lenard, my youngest son, got the letter from the mail, opened it and called me at work (M. Clark M.S.) with the result of the exam. He said, "Let's go to dinner, Mama!" We celebrated and celebrated. I thanked God for His grace and mercy; glory be to God for He brought me through that experience.

Reavis Elementary School

My very first experience with the Chicago Public School System (CPS) started in January, 1967. It was at the Reavis Elementary School located on Chicago's south side, right on the corner of 50ᵗʰ and Drexel. The school serviced students from kindergarten through eighth grade, as well as, special needs. My dear friend, Genevieve Carter, a member of Grace & Glory Gospel Chapel, was the Truant Officer at the Reavis School. Genevieve had watched me get my degree in teaching and she wanted me to come to Reavis. I had just graduated in December, 1966, from Illinois Teachers College and was ready to start my teaching career. I thought I was going to set the world on fire; every child was going to be anxious to learn, and everything was going to be rosy and bright. That thought didn't last long for after I started teaching children, reality set in.

Genevieve was responsible for my getting my first teaching position there at Reavis. She had told the principal, Mr. Raymond Hoffman, about me for there was a problem at the school with a particular second grade class. The students' teacher was ill with cancer and a different substitute teacher came to teach the class whenever she was ill, which became more frequent each week. The teacher passed away over the Christmas vacation, December, 1966. The children needed a stable educational environment, so in January, 1967, I took over the classroom. The students were unruly and out of control. It was very difficult for the first few days, but I was determined to get control of the classroom of 30+ children. I taught discipline and respect and routine. After the children realized I was going to be there, each and every day, they started to respond positively. At the end of the school year, the students were a different class. Mr. Hoffman was very pleased with my work with the class. The following year, he gave me a 6ᵗʰ grade class. The following year, he gave me a 4ᵗʰ grade class. In December, 1968, I left to go on maternity leave to have my second son, and last child, Lenard. I didn't have enough tenure in the system yet, so I lost my position at Reavis. After I had my baby on December 13, 1968, I began teaching, the following year, 1969, at the Fort Dearborn Elementary School.

When I started at Reavis, the staff was professionally supportive and accommodating of me as a brand new teacher. They taught me techniques and procedures that I was able to employ all during my career. The teachers that stand out in my memory were Mary Ella Smith, the future fiance of Mayor Harold Washington, Eunice Le Cesne, who "oozed" elegance and confidence, and Dr. Tena Roseman, teacher extraordinaire. Mrs. Le Cesne took a special liking to me and took me under her wing. She recently passed away, in her late nineties. Dr. Tena Roseman, served as a mentor and listening ear. I discovered much later that Dr. Roseman was quite an icon herself. She was born in 1909 and her family moved to Chicago, Illinois. She attended the Wendell Phillips High School and went on to graduate from Illinois Teachers College. She received her doctorate degree from Columbia University in New York. After serving the Chicago Public School System for 37 years, Dr. Roseman joined the staff at Du Sable Museum of African-American History. She established the Museum's Oratorical Contest seeking to increase knowledge and pride in black children. It was important to know their history and to take pride in their heritage. Dr. Tena Roseman died many years ago leaving a legacy of long life, love of life, world travel, and African pride.

It was at the Reavis School where the tragedy of Dr. Martin Luther King, Jr.'s death was shared with the staff and students there. We heard by radio, the lights were cut off at the school and staff and students were dismissed early. It was an eerie feeling and a deep, deep sadness with the teachers. On the way home, black people in cars drove with their headlights on in solidarity and acknowledgement of his death. And as history shows, that night people burned some neighborhoods on the west and south sides of Chicago. It was another one of those weekends where my family and I sat in front of a little black and white TV to watch the news of the assassination, the tributes and honors pouring in from all over the world in honor of Dr. King, and his funeral services which were conducted by Dr. Benjamin E. Mays and music rendered by Mahalia Jackson and others. It is seared in my memory as if it happened yesterday.

My experience at Reavis Elementary School lasted for 2 years and during that time, I "cut my teeth" as an educator, developing teaching style and attitude. I had begun my journey, taking my next step.

Fort Dearborn Elementary School

My experience at Fort Dearborn Elementary School was pleasant and fast moving. After returning from maternity leave in 1969, I got a teaching position at the school. It was a big school with a large student body.

Fort Dearborn Elementary School was an important part of my personal history because it is where I met my very dear friend, Betty Gene Wilson. As with everything else that she does, Betty gave excellent service to the students. When I left to go to Michele E. Clark Middle School, I persuaded Betty to come to the school. She was at Clark Middle for about a year, leaving to pursue her career goals at CPS. She worked herself up to the higher "echelons" of the Special Education Department. Betty became one of the most sought after counselors in the department; mostly because of her vast knowledge and her understanding of how the system works to benefit children. She cared deeply for children and their families and as a result of her work, children learned and excelled.

I persuaded Betty to join my sorority, Iota Phi Lambda, Alpha Chapter back in the 80's. She was outstanding in her service to the organization.

Betty is an ordained minister, taking the message of the gospel to the world. Evangelist Betty Wilson holds an Annual Breaking Bread Fellowship Ministry event where men and women give their testimonies of how the Lord has blessed them through financial difficulties, losses, illness, and other problems. In the interim, Betty is in their lives, helping them with their difficulties. There are 100 or more participants who attend each year. Betty attends the Apostolic Church of God where Dr. Byron T. Brazier serves as Pastor.

Betty lives in South Holland, IL where she serves as one of the spiritual leaders on the Board of Trustees. She often opens the meetings with prayer.

When I taught at the school, the enrollment was still high. In addition to the main building which housed hundreds of children, they had "demountables" on the school property. These demountables were called "Willis wagons" because Benjamin Willis was Superintendent of Chicago Public Schools at the time. They were little trailors that were just big enough to hold one class, one teacher. My 2^(nd) grade class was in one of these demountables. There was a kind of disconnect from the main building. When there were activities, assemblies, special classes, etc., I had to line my students up and take them to the main building. The children didn't mind and I was happy to have my own class so I carried on this way for three years until I transferred to Michele E. Clark Middle School.

Fort Dearborn had an excellent staff with their own culture of innovative reading programs, and many social activities. My close friend while there was a teacher named Felonese Cherry. She was very popular and had impeccable character. She took me under her wing and tried to give me information that was pertinent to becoming an excellent educator. She had no problem letting me know when I made mistakes, and then on the other hand, she was impressed with the way I responded to the needs of my students. Felonese was so devoted to her mother, and just devastated when her mom passed away. She did not want to continue to live in this world without her mother. A few years after her death, Felonese herself passed away. My demountable had been drab and unattractive when I took over my classroom. I quickly began changing the environment to cover all the walls with the children's work and their colorful art work, bulletins, pictures, and other things that reflected the progress of my students. It was transformed into an attractive learning environment, one that drew the children to pay attention to their work and one that elicited praise from the Assistant Principal, Maude Lightfoot.

Years later, those demountables were removed from, not only, Fort Dearborn, but from other schools as well. Jacquelyn Vaughn, CTU President, was instrumental in bringing about positive changes in the Chicago Public School System.

Michele E. Clark
Middle School

Michele E. Clark M. S. opened in August, 1972 as Austin Middle School, the only IGE (Individually Guided Education) School in Chicago.

Mrs. Clara K. Holton was the Principal of the school. She was bold and fearless as an administrator. She was my mentor and the reason my life took a drastic turn in 1972 and then again in 1988. I was teaching at Fort Dearborn Elementary School on Chicago's south side. My friend, Elizabeth Reckley, was moving to a brand new school, slated to open in August, 1972. She was a school guidance counselor and with Mrs. Laura Jolly's "urgings", Elizabeth decided to go to the new school to help the new principal, Mrs. Holton. Mrs. Jolly was a friend of Mrs. Holton's and was going to the new school as one of the assistant principals. Elizabeth persuaded me to apply to the new school as a teacher and I persuaded my friend Harriet to go with me to apply as well. Harriet was a primary teacher at one of the schools on the west side. Harriet and I went to the school, Austin Middle School I, which was also located on the west side of Chicago to try our luck with the new principal. It was later changed to Michele E. Clark Middle School. Neither one of us was adamant about going to a new school; we were content at our perspective schools, but there was a certain excitement, and a certain "buzz" about this school which was going to be a "Title I" school and one of its kind. When we arrived at the school and began the application process, Mrs. Holton assigned both Harriet and I as Team Leaders!

We would each lead a team of 6 teachers, 2 teacher aides, and 150 children. We had to prepare all the materials for the students. When we opened to the students in September, 1972, we had very little to work with as we sought to educate our students. We learned a lot and worked as a team for the success of the school. When I left Michele Clark in June, 1990 to accept my first principalship, I was prepared to go to any school, anywhere, and successfully "run" that school. It was a wonderful learning experience that resulted in skills that I was able to use for the rest of my career.

Mrs. Holton served as a role model of what a strong administrator, a strong leader, acts like. She encouraged, insisted, urged, and pushed me into taking the 1988 Principals' Exam in Chicago. It was to be the last exam offered to people seeking to become principals. I thought she must be out of her mind to think that I could pass an 8 hour exam on everthing from math to science, from social science to Analogies, and everything else in between! I didn't have much confidence at the time, but my friend, Velma Wilson and I joined a study group and started the process. It was a hectic time, but exciting. It seemed like the whole city was caught up in the excitement. It was early 1988, and hundreds applied and took the exam, but only about 300 passed. Amazingly, I was one of the lucky 300! Velma passed also, as well as, everyone of the nine women in our study group. My life took a different turn. I praise God, then and now for His mercy, and His grace.

Mrs. Laura Jolly, the Assistant Principal at Clark M. S. was "colorful" and unorthodox in her office. She was strong, uncompromising and "took no prisoners." Mrs. Jolly demanded excellence from her staff, and with her loud, articulate voice she kept reminding us. She was an outstanding administrator and as such, I wanted to highlight her accomplishments. In early 1979, my sorority published a book entitled "Alive Black Women".

I was on the committee, so I put Mrs. Jolly's name in as one of these outstanding women. Her bio and her many, many accomplishments were highlighted and celebrated in this publication. She was delighted to be included along side so many other beautiful women. Although I was not one of her favorite people, she appreciated the honor. Mrs. Jolly was close to Elizabeth Reckley, Regina McClellan, and Gwen Stevenson Long.

Alonza Leon Everage was an outstanding math teacher at Clark M. S. for many years before he retired. He at the same time, was an instructor at Roosevelt University. His passion was math and his students were the primary beneficiaries. Alonza died on August 28, 2013 at 67 years old having had a birthday right before he passed away. I was sad to see him go because I had talked to him a few months before and he told me he had inoperable cancer. The year before he had lost his beloved son, Khaldun, who took his own life. Alonza was devastated. Alonza's memorial service was held at the Broadview Baptist Church in Broadview, Illinois on September 6, 2013. Linda Edwards, Gloria Franchi, Petrina Patti, Renee Conley, Vivian Armstrong, Artyce Palmer and her husband were all at the memorial and we had a great time of reunion and fellowship. As an aside, Alonza was responsible for me serving at Roosevelt University, for approximately a year in the late 1990's, as an Adjunct Instructor. I monitored 6 student teachers at their schools and conducted weekly workshops, evaluating their portfolios. It was rewarding, I enjoyed working with the professors there, but it was overwhelming for I was involved in multiple projects. After a year, I left to continue other projects.

On January 12, 2014 at 9:23 A.M., my dear friend, Mary Ann Bridges passed away. She died at the Northwestern Hospital from a rare form of cancer. We met in 1972 at Michele E. Clark Middle School. She was one of my team teachers. She and Harriet Whitmore and I became BFF's and saw the children at the school grow academically each year. We became instant friends and were always together. The three of us worked with the children and were passionate about their learning. Mary Ann was bright, funny, witty, and "bubbly". She could "zing" you in a moment. She had a unique handwriting that was just as beautiful as script or calligraphy. She was super organized – wanting everything to be in place. Mary Ann loved fashion and dressed to the "10's", always developing her own style of dress. She had great leadership skills which she demonstrated, not only in the Chicago Public School System, but also at the Chicago Transit Authority. She worked as a trainer of new employees for several years after leaving

Michele E. Clark. She left the school and pursued her dreams in Florida for several years. She later returned to Chicago and her close knit family. She was passionate about her two daughters, Christa and Mary Ann, and her two precious grandchildren. She was so proud of their accomplishments. They gave her "bragging rights" to share with her friends and her extended family members. Mrs. Fook, Mary Ann's mother was equally beautiful, and beautifully attired from head to toe. I remember when she died; it took the "sails" out of her, but she recovered. Her dad, Mr. Fook, was a band leader, and a pretty cool gentleman. I can recall his death as well; and her brother, "Butch" who was a really nice, gentle guy. Butch died at a young age, leaving a wife and a beautiful daughter.

Mary Ann's death was shocking to me, having found out about a month before her death that she had a terminal illness. I didn't get a chance to visit her because she did not want anyone to see her during her illness. She was concerned about her appearance.

I know she knew the Lord. I will see her on the other side.

I spent 17 years at Michele E. Clark M. S., from August, 1972 to June, 1990. I left in 1990 to begin my principalship at Carver Middle School in the Altgeld Gardens Housing Projects. The years were filled with much of what defined my career. My time was consumed with the school. I involved my family, as well, with my daughter, Sharon, having been a substitute teacher there and my son, Lenard, having been a student tutor, and my granddaughters, Shatese and La Shundra worked as student tutors, as well. Gwen Long's mother was the Principal of a Catholic School at the time and she gave my son, Kevin, his very first job at her school. Gwen's mom was intelligent, and "bright" and very "classy". She liked Kevin and was delighted to share in his growth and development.

Michele Clark Middle School was a place of constant movement and advancement of, not only programs, but of ideas and hopes and dreams. My life was filled with service to the students at that school. I thought the school could not run unless I was there. Of course, I learned later that I was only one of many who felt the same way. All ten of the team leaders at the school ran their teams of 6 teachers, 2 teacher aides, and 150 children like a separate school. When each one left Clark M. S., they felt that they could be the administrator, the leader of any school, or organization for that matter. And they went on to do just that. They got principalships, assistant principalships, college professors, and CEO's of companies.

The two programs that I enjoyed the most were the Adopt-A-School Program and the Educational Leadership Institute – ELI – as we called it. JoAhn Brown-Nash was the President of ELI and her leadership left an imprint, positively, on my professional development. She died at an early age, but she was such a powerful influence on those around her. Jolean Washington Gray, who worked at Michele E. Clark and ELI, can attest to that fact. We were in Arizona with ELI when the U.S. dropped the first bombs during the Gulf War. We watched it on a huge, theater size screen and said a prayer for our country. Some time earlier, we had gone to San Francisco, California for a training session in leadership. It was a trip I will always remember. The sessions were challenging and sometimes stressful for me, but so stimulating and thought-provoking. Later, at the end of the program at Clark M.S., Jo Ahn presented a "Certificate of Excellence" to me for my participation.

The Adopt-A-School Program culminated, for my class, with a beautiful experiment that my students and two guys from Commonwealth Edison did together that ended up in "Time" Magazine back in April, 1982.

My students and I did a model of one street, on the west side of Chicago, near the school. It was a model on paper and a simulated model of each home on that block. This process took several weeks of working on this, with Com Ed. After setting up the model, my students were to calculate how much electricty each house used, calculate the whole block, and compare. It was a big "to do" and the students were lauded for their work. The 2 men from Com Ed were just great with the children. The project was so interesting, it generated a lot of "buzz" at the school. They came out from "Time" and took pictures of my students and the 2 Com Ed representatives. The project occurred over several weeks, but was completed in April, 1982. The article and one of the pictures with me leaning over, pointing to the project appeared in "Time" magazine on November 1, 1982. I was very proud of our accomplishment. I still have a copy of the original "Time" with De Lorean on the cover. I still have the note and the pictures that Mr. Steven M. Leonard sent me in January, 1983, informing me that the article had appeared in the November 1, 1982 issue.

Over all those years at Clark Middle School, my friend and fellow team leader, Peggy Maloblocki was with me. Peggy and I shared the same "house" at the school; I was House 2-team I and she was team leader of House 2-Team II. We worked very closely together; our teams of teachers worked together. We were in sinct together. Peggy and I attended workshops and seminars together. We went to the ELI seminar in San Francisco together. Any problems that occurred were handled together and I can't remember any unsolved or unresolved problems. Peggy was bright, smart, and intelligent and had an easy, but firm way with our kids. She was a true educator and administrator who helped the children at Clark M. S. grow and prosper.

The last thing about the "Time" magazine article: the Burston – Marsteller Public Relations firm produced a slide/tape presentation of the project for the Board of Education, CPS. Ms. Doris Cook wrote me a letter on April 21, 1982, thanking the class for their participation in the Adopt-A-School project.

And the "hits just kept on coming!" to use the words of Tom Cruise in "A Few Good Men". We were so engaged, so involved in trying to make things better at Clark M. S. In late April, again in 1982, we contacted Senator Charles H. Percy asking him about funding our education programs at the school. In December, 1979, the Chicago Public School System (CPS) "collapsed" with teachers, for the first time ever, not getting their paychecks. Michele Clark's school structure drastically changed. I was no longer "Team Leader". I had to go back into the classroom, 6th grade classroom. After we "settled in" after the shock of the shut-down, life at the school was again good, challenging, but good. I continued to work hard for Clark M.S.

Mrs. Clara K. Holton left Clark M. S. in July, 1989 to retire from the Chicago Public School System after many years of meritorious service. She was a "tried and true" educator who adopted many causes to make the school a true learning experience. She traveled extensively, going to foreign lands, lands that seemed so far away then but are now, so close. Mrs. Holton was always in search of "cures" for society, in search of solutions for women in crisis, and in distress. She was bold and strong in her voice, (along with her friend, Barbara Sizemore) against racism. I have this note from her, written so many years ago, where she writes:
" . . . Going to conference in South Africa on racism."

When Mrs. Holton announced to the staff that she was retiring, we gave her a big celebration that was sponsored by Mrs. Laura Jolly at her home. It was given on July 7, 1989 and the evening belonged to her because she was beloved and respected and admired by all of us. My tribute to her was long, but necessary.

The superlatives that I used back then to describe her were a little "over the top", I know, but it just goes to show my great admiration for Mrs. Holton. God sent her into my life for a reason and I thank Him. Ironically speaking, Beulah Bell, Mrs. Holton's sister was the Assistant Principal at Reavis, my first school. Beulah was a world traveler and she would come into each classroom and talk about her travel experiences. She was a great story teller so the children looked forward to her visit. Beulah was warm and personable and a great administrator, as well. It was a pleasant surprise when I got to Michele Clark and found out that Beulah Bell was Mrs. Holton's beloved sister, and only sister.

To my knowledge, Mrs. Holton wrote one book, "From A Broken Wing to a Sailboat". She attended Trinity Church where the Rev. Jeremiah Wright was Pastor, and she was part of the "writing ministry" there. She simply loved that ministry and might have published more, and might have written more works. Her writing was clear and precise. Mrs. Clara K. Holton passed away a few years ago from a brain tumor. She left a legacy of concern and love for others which is clearly articulated in her book. The last chapter is entitled "An Open Harbor". Listen to the sadness in her voice as she writes:

> "As we move through life we find that there are lots of pitfalls. The problem is that we don't know when these problems will become catastrophes. If we begin to drift because of inadequate moorings, then we may go too far and there will be no turning back. Without anchors, we have little energy sources within or without. There is nothing to hold on to. When you give up your anchors, memories of you fade, and you are forgotten. Your family and friends infrequently call your name. You become someone they once knew in the distant past. You have been forgotten. Time has passed and feelings they once had are long gone. There has been nothing during the intervening years to sustain a relationship.
>
> It is tragic to grow old and ill and no one cares about you, neither family nor friends. Sadder still if you are alone

in your final days. . . . The world is harsh and has little use for someone who has forsaken life."

Mrs. Holton ends her book on a sad note, but my memories of her are very different. May she rest in the arms of our Lord which is a far better place. I will remember her for all the good things she did for Michele E. Clark students and staff.

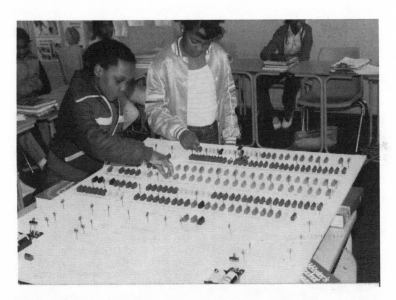

Carver Middle School

My first Principalship was at Carver Middle School, which is located right on the "tip" of the Altgeld Gardens' Projects, on the south end of the complex. The Carver Primary School and the Wheatley Child Parent Center jointly form the Carver/Wheatley Complex. The Carver Middle School is adjacent to the complex, a short walking distance away. Carver Middle School housed grades 5-8, and within walking distance is the Carver High School (now Carver Military Academy) servicing grades 9-12. The principal at Carver H.S. was Marcellus Stamps.

The Altgeld Gardens is a unique housing development with a rich history. The residents are 97% African American according to the 2000 U.S. Census. It was built in 1945 with 1,498 units, consisting primarily of two-story row houses spread over 190 acres. It was built by the federal government (Department of Housing and Urban Development) - to satisfy the need for improved housing for African American veterans returning from World War II. In 1956, the project was transferred to the Chicago Housing Authority. Located in an industrial area on Chicago's far South Side, Altgeld was named after John Peter Altgeld, an Illinois governor of the 1890's. As one of the first public housing developments ever built in the United States, it has been designated as a National Historic Landmark.

Over the last several years, 3,400 residents live in the Altgeld Gardens/ Murray Complex. When I was at Carver Middle, the residents mostly stayed within the complex for all their needs. Very few ventured out beyond its' borders. Now, of course, it is quite different; one factor being social media and a new generation of young people.

Altgeld Gardens' northern boundary is 130th Street, its southern boundary is 134th St, the eastern boundary is the campus of George Washington Carver Military Academy (formerly known as Carver Area H. S.), a public 4 year public high school and the Beaubien Woods Forest Preserve of Cook County. Numerous manufacturing plants, steel mills, landfills and waste dumps – once bordered the 190 acre site.

The residents still have a growing concern about the number of deaths annually from cancer and other diseases that may be related to environmental hazards of their industrial neighborhood. They had the same concerns back in the 90's when I was at Carver Middle School.

In addition, Altgeld Gardens was constructed at a time when asbestos was widely used in construction materials such as insulation, tile and other products. It has been found to be hazardous, and in 1980, residents organized a grassroots campaign in the project to advocate for its' removal from the complex flats.

Our President Barack Obama, then a local community organizer, participated in this campaign. He wrote about "The Gardens" in his book, "Dreams From My Father." Altgeld Gardens is located in one of the most dense concentrations of potentially hazardous pollution sources in North America. Many of the landfills that surround the project are unregulated, and some are still active. Since most of these landfills, as well as, many industrial plants are located along the waterways surrounding the area, 11 miles of the 18 miles of rivers and lakes surrounding Altgeld Gardens have been assessed as having water quality unfit for human consumption and recreation. Many local residents continue to fish in these waters, increasing their exposure to hazards by eating local fish.

Over the years, Altgeld Gardens has had various gang problems but the community is not considered to have the extreme sort of bloody rivalries endemic to the North Side's Cabrini - Green Community nor to the Robert Taylor Homes, near the historic Bronzeville neighborhood.

The early information about Altgeld Gardens was the backdrop to my experience there. I was cognizant of the school and the community before accepting the responsibility of Administrator. It was an experience that I cherish and feel proud to have been a part of that school. It, like all schools, had its' share of problems. The legislation that had been instituted by Mayor Harold Washington before his death, was in full force at Carver. The Local School Council (LSC) had the authority to hire and fire principals at that time. Many school LSC's were firing incumbents and hiring new principals, many of them women. At Carver Middle School, the staff was divided; many wanted the incumbent to remain, and others felt the need to have a brand new principal to meet the needs of the students. I applied to the District 10 Superintendent, Ms. Marjorie B. Branch for principalship of the school. Many hopefuls had applied, but I had met my friend, Carrie Clark, at a meeting and she was at Carver Middle School. She was very active with the LSC and the community. Carrie recognized me and said a word of support for me to the LSC. I got the interview with Marjorie Branch, the Superintendent, along with two other candidates on April

18, 1990. I was so excited to get the interview, which was not easy. I was interviewed, alone, by Dr. Richard Stephenson, Dist. 9 Superintendent and Ms. Marjorie B. Branch, Dist. 10, Superintendent. The other two candidates were interviewed as well. Ms. Branchs' office called to let me know I was to come for a 2nd interview. I was happy to know that I had a chance to be successful. The 2nd interview was held on May 9, 1990. The next day, May 10, 1990, Ms. Branch notified the chairperson of the LSC, Mrs. Eva Reid, of their decision. Mrs. Reid notified me and I was elated.

I began my Principalship on July 1, 1990 after a big "Going Away/ Celebration" at Michele E. Clark Middle School in June, 1990. I was determined to make a positive difference at the school. It was a daunting task and one I took seriously. I knew it would be a challenge, so I relied heavily on the Lord to "take me through". It was a "mixed bag" with some support, but mostly mistrust and uncertainly from the staff. Ms. Doris Loach was the Assistant Principal and the two of us "ran the school" with the help of Harriet Whitmore, who had joined me at Carver from M. Clark to be the Teacher Facilitator in charge of programs and curriculum. Mrs. Carrie Clark became my Assistant Principal after Ms. Loach retired. My administration accomplished much at the school: Some positive changes were:

- The staff was expected to teach children, managing discipline and instruction;
- The staff was rewarded for progress and success;
- Revamped the counseling program, by hiring an additional counselor;
- Developed the ancillary staff;
- Staff started a "Carver Middle Newsletter" to be used as a tool for communication between the school, parents, and community at large;
- Weekly inservices where staff was trained to work together cooperatively and cohesively to increase program effectiveness.
- Worked with parents providing workshops and programs to help them improve parenting and self-help skills;
- Purchased computer programs that allow parents to enhance their employability and life management skills, as well.
- Enhanced Career Day
- Extended Day Programs that also included Bible stories

- Enhanced the lunch program to include food that the children enjoy;
- Instituted the "Ribbon Pinning Ceremony" for graduates, a program we brought from Michele E. Clark Middle School. The parents simply loved it. It was "spiritual and meaningful".
- Along with the Local School Council (LSC), brought the Uniform Dress Code to Carver Middle, trying to bring uniformity to the school, in dress and attitude; and
- Students' academic achievement started to move closer to other high achieving schools.

These programs, projects, and activities were successful because of support from the staff and parents. We purchased a new library that included new tables, new chairs, and other furniture and new books and materials. New fold-up chairs were purchased to be used for the "Ribbon Pinning Ceremony" and other big events.

John Pate and Judith Booth Hunter coordinated the ESEA Program which was extremely successful. Carrie Clark and Harriet Whitmore wrote two winning grant proposals that brought big money to the school for students.

The first proposal for a grant entitled, "Carver Carves Character" focused on building students' and staff's self-esteem. As a result, an $11,500 planning grant was awarded to Carver Middle.

The second proposal was entitled, "Carver is Bullish on Milk", and generated over $800 in tickets for selected parents, students, and staff to attend a Chicago Bulls' Basketball Game. This proposal was written to heighten awareness of good nutrition and to foster a partnership effort between the school and the lunchroom.

The Student Council, which had been included in the School Improvement Plan, was sponsored by three staff members, Mrs. Jacqueline Sallamme, Mrs. Jeannine Jones, and Mrs. Judith Booth-Hunter. They guided the Council as they developed a student handbook, having students act as hall monitors, with parent patrol supporters, having students act as peer-tutors, and having a "make-it-take it" day.

One of the biggest highlights at Carver Middle School, and one of my proudest moments, was when Ms. Adrienne Le Dree, a teacher of the mentally handicapped, was selected as a recipient of the 1992 Kohl International Teaching Awards. It was in recognition of her innovative teaching skills.

Ms. Le Dree was one of the 10 Golden Apple winners and was honored on May 21, 1993 at a ceremony featuring former Chicagoan Mae Jemison, the first African American woman in space, and Illinois first lady, Brenda Edgar. It was broadcast at 9:00 P.M. on WTTW - Channel 11. It was a big, big event. My very dear friend, Jacquelyn Crook was also one of the 10 winners. Jacquelyn was a teacher/librarian at the Newberry Mathematics and Science Academy. It was an exciting night for both she and Ms. Le Dree. Each of the 10 winners received $2,500, an IBM computer, and a paid full-term leave for tuition-free study at Northwestern University.

It was a wonderful time at the school. It felt nice to see the fame and recognition come to the school where other teachers at Carver Middle were as excellent in their service to the students. The honor highlighted, not only Ms. Le Dree, but the other teachers as well.

The 8th Grade Graduation Ceremony was also a special time for me as the principal. The students were anxious to finish one phase of their academic career and to begin a higher level of learning. Commissioner Jerry Butler served as Guest Speaker at one of the Graduations. He gave thought-provoking remarks that encouraged children to never give up, and never let obstacles stop your climb to the top. Mrs. Marcella Morrison also served as Guest Speaker at one of my Graduations. She encouraged the graduates to set high goals, dream big dreams and pursue them with a vengeance.

Each year, the Graduation Ceremony followed the same format. The staff members worked diligently and tirelessly to put on a formal, excellent program. I always enjoyed Graduation, feeling that it appropriately culminated the school year, giving me a great "sigh of relief" on a great school year.

My experience at Carver Middle School was one of the most stimulating and most enjoyable of my long career. The relationship with the students and staff was a great "learning experience" for me personally, but I used it also as a "teachable moment" to further careers and to encourage service to our schools, to our community, to our nation, and to the world.

When I came to Carver Middle, I was part of a culture that talked about "failing schools", and the term "failing schools" is used as a reason for closing a school. The term is very demeaning and degrading to the students, to the teachers, and to the parents, because the school is a reflection of the people in the school, most notably the students. If these children come to school without the skills and incentives that facilitate learning and fail to achieve certain scores on a test, they do not deserve to be demeaned with the tag of "failure". Test scores were never meant to be used to create a caste system among schools and students and parents. Originally, test scores were meant to give the teacher a starting point for instruction based on the child's level of proficiency. Using test scores and graduation rates to label schools as good or bad is "out-moded" and needs to stop. A school has very little control over what the student brings to the school, but the school takes the responsibility to provide the necessary resources to deal with whatever deficiencies students show up with.

I still have faith in our school system in that they know to what extent they are harming students with these policies. If the students are put at the top of the totem pole, instead of at the bottom, the focus and thereby the results will be different.

The successful four (4) years at Carver M. S. were made possible by many, but I owe much to Carrie Clark, Doris Loach, and Robert L. Davis. Robert, a Chicago Police Officer and a childhood friend of my husband, served as the security officer at the school, keeping the staff safe, as well as the students. He was a strong force at the school. He is now deceased. Ms. Loach had a special concern and care for the students at Carver, which was her motivation until her retirement. She is now deceased. Carrie was the first supporter, and continued to support my programs, and shared my vision for the school. She was elected principal after I retired from the school. The most gratifying was the courage and excellence of the students who came to school, each day, challenging us, as adults, to make life better for them. I'm confident that happened, by His grace and His mercy.

Educational Specialties, Inc.

Elois Washington Steward was owner and CEO of Educational Specialties, Inc. in Chicago. Elois founded a school where she hired personnel to tutor students after school and during the day for day care. Her school had a big operation on Saturday, with several classes being taught concurrently. In addition to the school, Elois provided materials and supplies and furniture, at a reasonable price to CPS schools, as well as, private schools, and suburban schools.

During my principalship at Carver Middle School, I purchased furniture and supplies from Educational Specialties, Inc. with school funds exclusively for the school, by requisition and approval from the Region 6 Office for my school library and other school needs. Each school was given a budget for school needs, and approved suppliers were listed for our use. Educational Specialties, Inc. was on that list and many schools utilized her company.

In addition to her supply company and her tutoring program, Elois worked for CPS as a Consulting Firm. She hired several of us for her consulting workshops and computer training program. After I retired from Carver Middle School in 1994, I worked with Elois planning and conducting workshops and training sessions.

It was truly a challenge for me to prepare for the computer training sessions because I did not feel that I had the confidence to "pull it off", but Elois was so encouraging, so helpful, and totally confident that we would do an excellent job at each school. We consulted at several schools, providing training and support to staff and sometimes students at the schools, as well. It was a busy time that kept me going to a different school every day.

I admire Elois Washington Steward, and I recognize her as having been an icon. She was an African-American woman who loved educating children. She worked tirelessly to bring about change in her community. She was extremely bright, but so "down to earth"; She was smart and "savvy", knowing the system and how to work the system to benefit students. She was feisty and tough; not "backing down" when she felt she was right. I commend her for being an entrepreneur in every sense of the word.

Elois passed away a few years ago, but I have never forgotten her and the impact she had on my professional career. Her sister, Jolean Washington Gray, and I are still "in touch". Jolean is a Realtor/Broker. Jolean, Elois, and I were all at Michele E. Clark Middle School Together.

Esmond Elementary School

The Esmond Elementary School is located at 1865 W. Montvale Av., Chicago, Illinois. It is one of the oldest schools in Chicago. The school has grades PK-8, with an enrollment of about 340 students. The classrooms have 15 students to one teacher. Esmond is supported by a strong community and by a strong principal. The students show academic improvement each year which means that the programs are working for children.

I worked at the Esmond School in the late 1990's as Interim Principal. The assigned Principal was on sick leave and the school had been run for the last few months of her leave by a principal who was being removed. I was to serve until a permanent replacement could be made. I was there for about a year. The staff appreciated my being there as a stabilizing presence. They were supportive and helpful as I performed the daily duties of an Administrator. I was very seldom in the office, only for parent conferences. The schedule of the teachers was followed by me, also; being with the kids outside at recess and being in the lunchroom, and at dismissal time, and arrival time. It was so important to know what was happening with the students at all time. I was pleasantly surprised a few years ago when I encountered one of the teachers who had been at Esmond while I was there.

Ironically, she was my little great grandson's (Anthony) teacher. It was either kindergarten or first grade and Anthony had invited me to come to his school for "Grandmother's Day". Mrs. Stepancik and I saw each other at about the same time and embraced each other warmly. We talked about Anthony, who is a smart kid, straight A student from even the early grades – he's in 8th grade now. Mrs. Stepancic brought me up to date on Esmond staff and we had a nice visit for that morning.

My experience at Esmond was positive and challenging as I developed relationships with staff members, parents, and students. I remember making lemon bars for one of my classes. After they ate them, at lunchtime, the teacher had the children write "Thank you" notes, and they were to describe how they liked or did not like the bars. The teacher was delighted! I still have each note that the kids gave me that day.

I found the teachers to be hard-working and conscientious. They were anxious to bring success to the school by educating the students using innovative and interesting materials. Using computers in the classroom and in the library was still a relatively novel procedure. My friend, Annette Campbell, was one of the teachers who came in to help students learn computer skills at Esmond.

Prior to serving at the Esmond School, I worked for Schools and Regions (Central Office, CPS) as a Retired Principal in the "Summer Bridge Program". I was one of about 18 retired principals hired to help school principals set up their summer programs of reading and math. We were a very cohesive group that worked together for years. After the program ended, Joan Ferris, our Supervisor treated us to lunch, as a group, every year until her death a few years ago. Members of that group came to our 50th Wedding Anniversary where we renewed our vows in 2002. We were a pretty close-knit group.

I left the Esmond Elementary School to work at the newly built Barbara Vick Early Childhood and Family Center on Chicago's southwest side. I went there to stay 2 months, but stayed two years.

Barbara Vick Early Childhood & Family Center

Barbara Vick Early Childhood & Family Center is a model early childhood center housed in the former Sheldon School on the near west side of the 19th Ward in Region 6 of the Chicago Public School System. The Center is a collaborative effort between St. Xavier University and the Chicago Public Schools. The concept of the center grew out of a community need to service young children with disabilities. The Center receives both political and educational support from the community.

For years, the residents of the 19th Ward requested that a local school for their children with special needs be established. At the time, there was no special education school for preschool age children in the area. In response to this request, Alderman Ginger Rugai approached Dean

Beverly Gulley with the proposition that Saint Xavier University become a partner in this "unprecedented endeavor."

The first step was the formation of a unique coalition with Saint Xavier and the Public Schools. The goal of Saint Xavier University is to improve its relationship with the community. They wanted to expand its service to metropolitan Chicago, especially in the inner city and the southwest region. One way of expanding that service was to provide clinics and service programs for Chicago neighborhoods. The Barbara Vick Early Childhood & Family Center was one example of realizing that goal. Saint Xavier has, among the other services, teacher enhancement training programs, study programs for students who were struggling academically; and it offered high school students the opportunity to earn college credit. The University's School of Education provided management and staff development, while students in the education, speech pathology, and nursing departments can use the center as a clinical site to receive training. Thus began the partnership.

The official opening of Barbara Vick occurred in February 1999. It was a big event with then Mayor Richard Daley in attendance, as well as, St. Xavier University President Richard Yanikoski, then CEO of the Chicago Public Schools, Paul Vallas, 19th Ward Alderman Ginger Rugai, and Cathy Lawton, Director of the Center.

Barbara Vick Early Childhood & Family Center was named after, and in honor of Barbara Vick, community activist. She was prominent for being:

* A mother, wife, educator and community activist in the Morgan Park/Beverly Hills area who passed away in 1989.

I came to the Barbara Vick ECFC on the Monday after that grand opening, in February, 1999. I had been asked by the Office of Schools' & Regions, CPS, under Dr. Blondean Y. Davis' request to serve at the Center for approximately 2 months. I was to work as the Principal and partner to the Director, Cathy Lawton. My duty was to help her get the school "up and running" as a model school for pre kindergarten children with disabilities. Cathy and I worked together like a "fine-tuned" machine. We worked together, cooperatively, for two years which is the amount of time I spent there. It was also the beginning of a love relationship between me and the staff. The teachers absolutely loved the school building; it was beautiful, bright, and attractive when you walked through the doors. They simply adored those children, the little 3 to 5 years old "babies", who had special needs. I had not experienced, or seen, such loving care and nurturing of public school children. The staff cared for each other – they shared their personal info – families, siblings, husbands, sick loved ones, academic goals and pursuits, etc. And they saw the cooperation and teamwork between Cathy and I. We developed a relationship that was a "BFF" relationship. She (by my invitation) did a wonderful workshop presentation at my Sorority's regional conference a couple of years ago.

The staff had & set high goals and standards for Barbara Vick ECFC. It was an inclusive model of education, and provided multidisciplinary intervention and support. The teachers and staff members conducted screenings that involved a community-wide child find effort, and provided intervention services for 3-5 year old children. The school program enhanced and emphasized a close partnership between education, families, and the community on the behalf of the children served. The Center began with 170 children between the ages of three and five.

I performed my duties, enthusiastically, as principal. They included: observing teacher performance in the classroom; evaluating those teachers; having assemblies that included students, staff, and parents; conducting inservices and parent workshops; and conducting interviews for new staff; plus many other things that go along with being an administrator in a school. It was stimulating and challenging. When issues and concerns arose, we took care of it, and kept right on pushing. One of the big highlights at Barbara Vick was seeing our teacher, Marilyn Peterson, receive the 2000 Kohl/McCormick Early Childhood Teaching Award. She was one of five Outstanding Chicagoland Early Childhood Teachers that were honored with an award of $5,000 cash and a graduate-level course at Chicago's renowned Erikson Institute. The Kohl/McCormick Award was the only teacher recognition program exclusively designed to acknowledge the talents and contributions of early childhood educators working in schools, preschools, child care centers, Head Start programs, and licensed family child care homes, and has become a national model.

Cathy Lawton, the Director of the Center then (the Principal, now) was the ultimate professional, "just right" for Barbara Vick ECFC. I teased Cathy at times, telling her she was the "Esther" of the school. The Lord put her at that school for "such a time as this." Cathy and her husband Tom held very elegant dinner parties at their home, that Lenzo and I attended. We hobnobbed with VIP's from CPS and St. Xavier University, as well as Barbara Vick staff members. The administration and the staff at the school had a professional, as well as, a social relationship. In 2011, the Center expanded to include a second site. The vision is to grow Barbara Vick ECFC models all over the city.

I left the Barbara Vick ECFC in June, 2000, which accounted for my 2nd Retirement. Cathy Lawton and the staff of the Center and Beverly Gulley, Dean of St. Xavier University gave me a surprise dinner-elegant, honorable, huge, and extremely, unbelievably beautiful. The surprise Retirement Dinner included my children, my church family, my family, my friends, my colleagues, and many academic and political distinguished guests. Dr. Blondean Y. Davis was there, who was 2nd in command under Paul Vallas, Superintendent of Chicago Public Schools. It was a big, big event and it took days afterwards for me to come "back to earth"; I was on "cloud nine" over such a beautiful honor. I will never forget how the big surprise made me feel inside. First of all, I had been gone from the school since June – the party was held in November; I had been sick for days from one of my "colds" that always feel like the "flu"; the planning that went into this, must have been phenomenal. It was unbelievable, and totally unexpected. Lenzo & my family did a great job of diverting my attention.

My experience at Barbara Vick ECFC was one that I will always remember with pride and fondness. It taught me much about how great care and respect for each other in the school environment, benefits children and in general, ensures a quality education for local children with special needs.

Matteson S. D. 162

Matteson School District 162 is located in Richton Park, Illinois. The District serves the following communities: Richton Park, Matteson, Olympia Fields, and Park Forest. The District has 6 Elementary Schools, and 1 Middle School:

> Arcadia School – Olympic Fields
> Illinois School – Park Forest
> Indiana School – Park Forest

Richton Square School – Richton Park
Sauk School – Richton Park
Matteson School – Matteson
O.W. Huth Middle School – Matteson

District 162 is a district that pursues excellence and beyond for its students. The Superintendent is the brilliant, world-renowned Dr. Blondean Y. Davis.

I started in District 162 in 2003 at the Illinois School as a substitute administrator, sometimes serving as principal, sometimes as assistant principal. I served there for several months, getting to know the staff and the students. The teachers were serious about their responsibilities, working diligently to provide an excellent education to the students.

In February, 2004, my youngest son, Lenard, passed away. It was grievous and devastating, to me and to my family. It threw me into a deep depression, so much so, that I was having "pity parties" every day. It was difficult for me to "put one foot in front of the other". It was at this time, in March or April, 2004, that I received a call from Barbara Manning, Dr. Davis' secretary. The principal of the Indiana School was moving to New Orleans, LA leaving the office of principal vacant. There was no assistant principal at the time, so I was to fill in as Interim Principal until a permanent administrator could be appointed. I had to present my credentials of qualifications at the District 162 Office which included my Principals' Certificate, Type 75 Certificate, Teaching Certificate, Proof of training courses completed which qualified evaluation and observation of teachers, etc. At the Board Meeting, Dr. Davis presented me as Interim Principal at the Indiana School.

After giving my prepared response to the Board of Education of District 162, I stated: "I enthusiastically accept the responsibility of Interim Principal on an interim basis until such time as my services are no longer needed." I also said:
"I look forward to working in District 162 again. Thank you for the confidence you have placed in me for "what nobler employment, or more valuable to the district than that of the person who instructs the rising generation?"

Thus began my professional life at the Indiana School. I spent a wonderful, challenging 3 years at the school. Many good things happened, things that kept the school running daily, and things that were outstanding that took us to another level of expertise.

I Remember:

- My students participating in an honors program, debating an issue at the school in the gym
- A father reading to his child and four other students during Fathers' Recognition Day in the hallway at Indiana School
- Another father with his one child, outside a classroom
- Tracy Murray, my assistant principal during the 2006-2007 school year, working with some students in the gym, during the honors program; the students were dressed in shirts and ties, and girls wore nice blouses and skirts, and having their hair nicely styled
- A picture of Ms. Rajrani Chan and I with children who were participating in a special program. They also were dressed beautifully well with well shined shoes, suits and ties, skirts and blouses, and very nice smiles. It was taken in the hallway at Indiana School
- A newspaper article and picture in the "Star", dated December 1, 2005, with me taking my students to lunch to celebrate their academic achievements – they were all straight "A" students that had earned A's during the first quarter of the school year
- Another newspaper article and picture in the "Star" (a local newspaper dated May 4, 2006) reporting my students have formed long distance friendships with school children in Romania and quickly learned that 4th graders are very much alike all over the world. They had started the program by writing letters to students in a school in Pietra Neamt, Romania and established a flow of correspondence that has helped students learn about another country. Barbara Barr was the teacher at Indiana School who taught the cultural exchange.
- The staff for the 2005-2006 school year. It was my 2nd year at the school. At the time, there were 36 teachers, 14 para-personnel, and one assistant-principal, Frank Valderrama. Mr. Valderrama was good with the students at Indiana School, and for the year that he served, he was part of the success at the school.

- A picture of my students dressed up like Dr. Seuss as we celebrated reading. I'm standing in the midst of them in my office. It was ten students with big, tall red & white Dr. Seuss hats. They made a hat for me, as well.
- A picture of the 4th Grade teachers at Indiana School – Erin Carmichael, Amanda Godin, E. Stidham, P. Cogar, Bridgett Briody, J. Padalino, B. Barr, and Shelonda Porche – Box. These teachers worked together as a team; and as a team they encountered difficulties on a daily basis, making sacrifices for each precious child.
- A picture of me in my office at Indiana School doing my favorite thing, reading a book.
- A picture of the Principals in District 162 during the 2005-2006 school year. Dr. Davis gave us roses for having a really great year. I like this picture which reflects joy and pride and happiness on our faces. From left to right:

I left the Indiana School in 2007 after spending 3 years there. I went to Richton Square School, also in District 162, for a year. Time at Indiana School was stimulating and challenging. The teachers were awesome, going beyond the call of duty to provide a quality education to the students. Especially noteworthy were Linda Williams and Carolyn Cartman. Carolyn served as the Clerk/Secretary and Linda was the SSA, but worked along with Carolyn to do secretarial responsibilities, as well. They helped me tremendously with the technology part of the job. It was a team effort with office business and taking care of parent concerns. I enjoyed the experience and as I left to go to Richton Square, it was bittersweet. Indiana was "my" school and I loved it.

District 162 – Richton Square School

The Richton Square Kindergarten and Early Childhood Center is located at 22700 Richton Square Road in Richton Park, Illinois. It is a beautiful facility, all rooms on one level, spread out with a long, long hallway, beginning with the main office and the principal's office. In the front of the building, you notice the beautiful landscape and to the right side of the building, the nice playground is located. A very unusual, very beautiful garden stands in back of the school which adds to the attractive exterior of the school.

When I became Principal there, I arrived very early each morning, before teachers arrived, and walked each corner and each "nook & cranny" of the school. I checked inside and outside, making sure everything was ready for the students. I met the buses and received the children, touching each little hand as they came off and entered the school. At dismissal time, the process reversed as the kids boarded the buses on their ride home.

Jessica Washington, home-school coordinator; Janet Knol, librarian; and Leah Lacey, social worker, were three of my favorite people at Richton Square. I was very impressed with their work with individual students.

I was at Richton square on January 31, 2008, when my beloved daughter, Linda, passed away. The teachers were all there for me at that very dark time of my life; as well as Lorrie Clayton, secretary and Belinda Whittier, SSA. I left the school that dark morning to drive to the hospital where my family had already gathered. God's mercy helped me as I lost, yet another precious daughter.

I served District 162 for 4 years and in June, 2008, Dr. Davis gave me my third and final Retirement Celebration. It was held at the District Office with board members and all staff members of the district in attendance. It was a beautiful, beautiful event with my family there, as well. I will never forget the gracious words that were spoken and the many gifts and beautiful flowers that were presented to me. These precious memories make my service in the district worthwhile; an appropriate end to a stellar career.

Dr. Blondean Y. Davis over some 20+ years has been the most important person in my life, career wise, as I have gone from one job to another. She was there for me during the most grievous time of my life. She has, unconditionally, been a support and a mentor to me. Dr. Davis is very prominent, but she has always remembered me when the need arose. When I got the call from Barbara Manning, her secretary, in 2004, it was a "Godsend". It took me away from thinking only of myself in my grief, and made me focus on my responsibility to students. In addition to being the Superintendent of District 162, Dr. Blondean Y. Davis is the CEO of the Southland Charter College Preparatory High School in Richton Park, Illinois. In 2010, after less than a year of planning, in the belief that the area's students needed a choice and hope for their future, Dr. Davis spearheaded the launch of a new charter high school to serve at risk students in nine southwest Chicago suburban communities. Southland

Charter College Preparatory High School, which opened in temporary quarters in August of 2010, is the first charter public high school approved by the Illinois State Board of Education in Chicago suburbs. The charter high school moved into a newly renovated building in Richton Park in April, 2011.

I attended the first graduation of the students at Southland in 2014. It was the most spectacular, awesome high school graduation I have ever attended. Not surprisingly, it was elegant and classy, with classical music and a moving speech by Illinois Senator Dick Durbin. I sat mesmerized by the entire program, culminated by Dr. Davis personally shaking each graduate's hand and giving them a hug. Everything Dr. Davis touches "turns to gold."

I consider it an honor to have served in Matteson School District 162.

Naomi & her lifetime friends, Annette Campbell & Jackie Crook

CHAPTER TEN

My Groups

Iota Phi lambda Sorority, Inc.
Alpha Chapter

Iota Phi Lambda Sorority, Inc., like other organizations, has an unusual, rich, and fascinating history. A few sorors, years ago, decided to write their own history of Iota. They were: Ethel K. Green from Washington, D. C.; Doris General from Alpha Chapter; Irene Lane from Alpha Beta; and Alva Williams from Alpha Chapter. I have adapted the history with updates and inserts to give a more comprehensive view of our organization and specifically, Alpha Chapter, Chicago, Illinois.

Two great waves of migration of Blacks to northern cities took place between the periods 1916-1919 and 1921-1924, at which time a serious shortage of labor created opportunities for Blacks to seek employment in fields which had been previously closed to them. The problems of overcrowding, unwholesome sanitary conditions and later, poverty were common to most of the in-migrants. Migration to the north had quickened the hope among Blacks that they could achieve equality, but when they became disillusioned in consequence of the situation into which they were forced, a heightened sense of group consciousness developed.

Perhaps the idea of making Blacks economically independent was less spectacular than some manifestations of race consciousness; but the ideal was effective in stimulating the establishment of a large number of

416

enterprises which were either owned, operated, or controlled by Blacks. These included banks, insurance and real estate firms, wholesale businesses, retail stores, hotels, restaurants, cafes, and many beauty parlors. Then came the Depression of 1929 and the whole country had to contend with the problem of unemployment. Black men and women, but especially women, were among the millions trudging the streets and looking for work. Many of the Black businesses, recently established, failed. Black women, who had just become a part of these endeavors, were particularly hard hit; for they were doubly penalized by both race and sex. Rebuilding the economic structure would take time.

The greatest group - forming factor in society is the recognition by intelligent human beings that there are others like themselves in tradition, beliefs, aspirations, and ideals. It is such a social force that makes for fraternity. It is no spirit of exclusiveness; no lofty assumptions of superiority; it is simply a conviction that mental and moral likenesses are the basis for a pleasurable and profitable union.

Depressions are social problems. Since social problems are the product of social living, the best approach to the understanding and solution of these problems lies in social consideration and social action. Such was the concept of the Founder of Iota Phi Lambda Sorority.

Iota's history began with a small (in statue) "wisp" of a woman with a strong articulate voice, with a God-given vision, and a beautiful dream. Lola M. Parker saw that young, Black women, once they graduated from high school, weren't going anywhere. She decided to organize a sisterhood to do something about it. Mrs. Parker saw that there were problems facing Black women, many of them new to the business field, problems that were numerous and several of them seemed particularly vexing. One was the tendency of many in other fields of endeavor to deprecate or belittle young women who had chosen business as their careers. The implication was that this field required less innate ability and less formal preparation. Also, Black women were now in competition for employment, and there was great need to raise the level of efficiency among business women and girls throughout the country. There was also a need to increase the number of girls taking business courses beyond the high school level; therefore, girls should be encouraged to pursue these courses in college. Finally, there was a need to enhance the influence of the women engaged in business and to make it as effective as the influence wielded by women in the professions and the arts.

Mrs. Lola M. Parker believed that an organization of business women could solve some of these problems. She visualized the great possibilities of an organization that would serve to encourage specialization in definite phases of business; an organization that would stimulate, inspire, foster and give mutual assistance to those persons engaged in business.

Thus, In June, 1929, In Chicago, Illinois, Iota Phi Lambda Sorority had its' beginning. Lola Mercedes Parker called together six women who were her friends to share her dream. Prior to calling these six friends of hers – Ethel T. Edwards, Mildred G. Hardin, Harriet M. Robinson, Ophelia Harrison, Birdette Trigg, and Marjorie Tyndall – Mrs. Parker had consulted with Mrs. Irene McCoy Gainer, and Dr. L. K. Williams and the honorable Arthur W. Mitchell for their advice in making her dream a reality. Mrs. Parker's six friends were close friends, and they were quick to see the value of the planned undertaking. They were willing to become pioneers, along with Mrs. Parker, and meeting with her on the first day of June in 1929, formed the nucleus of Iota Phi Lambda Sorority. This group became the first chapter of the Sorority, Alpha Chapter.

Although designed to seek greater opportunities for the Black business woman, the organization was founded on the social principles of Jesus Christ – friendship, love, and loyalty. The Greek letters Iota Phi Lambda, were chosen because of their meaning – Ideals of friendship and love – which expressed best the Founder's hopes and aspirations, and the principles undergirding the plan. Just who was this woman with such lofty ideals and love for her fellowman?

Mrs. Lola Mercedes Parker, was born in Little Rock, Arkansas, where she received her elementary education at the W. M. Gibbs School. Later, she moved with her family to Kansas City, Missouri, and completed her high school training. In 1919 she became a resident of Chicago, Illinois. Here she pursued a course in business education at the Chicago Business College. At the time, Mrs. Parker conceived the idea of a sorority. She was employed as secretary to Dr. L. K. Williams, who for many years was president of the National Baptist Convention.

In keeping with her ambition for others, Mrs. Parker continued her education by taking courses in business administration, including business psychology, personnel management, and employer-employee relations. Subsequent to her employment with Dr. Williams she had held many other important positions, some of which were director of woman's activities, Chicago Negro Chamber of Commerce; department supervisor, Reuben H. Donnally Corporation; business manager, South Parkway YWCA; assistant to the administrator, Drexel House; and secretary-treasurer, Business and Professional Association Credit Union.

In addition to her affiliation as a Christian Woman with Olivet Baptist Church, Mrs. Parker served as National Vice-President to the Women's Army for National Defense and as secretary for the People's Welfare Organization. She had also been active with the NAACP and the YWCA. She was one of the founders and the first treasurer of the Chicago Chapter of the National Council of Negro Women.

Thus began the sorority and since its' inception Iota has continued to grow. Provision for annual scholarships were made. In 1936, the Lomepa Club, which is the pledge club, was recommended and adopted. In 1939, Future Iota Girls was organized and called FIGs. Since that time a boy's group has been organized, Future Intellectual Leaders, called FIL's. It was adopted in 1977.

Iota's national programs include: Founders' Day, Business Month, American Education Week, Black History Month, and National Correspondence Month.

The Auxillary groups are: the Lambds – husbands of the sorors, the Pelatis, and the Gems. Currently, changed:

MOI – Men of Iota – husbands of sorors;
Gems – now FIL's, the youth groups.

In the 70's, a restructuring of Iota Phi Lambda Sorority took place. Another historical milestone was reached in 1979 when the 50th Anniversary was observed in Chicago, its founding site.

In 1980, what had previously been two regions – the Northern Region and the Western Region merged to form what is now the Central Region.

The merger encompasses many states from Illinois to Kentucky, from Michigan to Nebraska, and from South Dakota to Wisconsin. The founding chapter, Alpha, my chapter is in this region. This region has added to its distinguished heritage of leadership with the following Past National Presidents after Lola Mercedes Parker who was President for several years:

> Mahala Evans, Alpha
> Bessie Coston, Alpha Nu
> Dr. Fredda Witherspoon, Alpha Zeta
> Clarice Brown, Alpha Beta and
> Marcella Morrison, Alpha Lambda.

Through the years, Iota Phi Lambda has conferred honorary membership on some of the country's outstanding African American women. These five women were National Honorary Members of Iota Phi Lambda Sorority, Inc:

- Mrs. Mary McLeod Bethune – Founder of Bethune Cookman College and The National Council of Negro Women; government official, international and interracial leader.
- Mrs. Mai Padmore – Wife of His Excellency, the Liberian Ambassador to the United States; expert in the field of business administration.
- Mrs. Irene McCoy Gaines – Former president, National Association of Colored Women, Inc.
- Mrs. M.I. Smith Morgan – Insurance woman, National Junior Counselor of the Supreme Camp of American Woodmen.
- Mrs. Edith S. Sampson – Noted lawyer, former U.S. Alternate Representative to the United Nations; guest lecturer and world traveler.

Over these many years, we have observed different periods of excitement and enthusiasm around our sisterhood. We called the 1930's-1960's, the Glory Years. During these years following the founding of Alpha Chapter in 1929, much growth in numbers occurred. Black women were proud to be a part of such a prestigious organization. Joining the sisterhood meant that you were also socially involved in your community. They were proud to help young women, not only succeed in business and higher learning, but also teaching them poise and manners and dress. The women in the early years wore elegant hats, and gloves, and beautiful, colorful dresses made of silk, chiffon, organza, and lace. Black young women often wore long gowns and also varying length dresses that had butterfly sleeves, and ruffles made of floral print. The shoes they wore were of modest heels, varying colors and usually very comfortable. They attended planning meetings dressed to the "nines".

The next period, we called the Prestigious 70's. The year 1975, was an excellent year for Helen Rush. She contributed much to Alpha Chapter, the Region, and the National. In 1975, she had the distinction of being the first Outstanding Soror of the Year from Alpha Chapter who went on to win at the Regional Level and finally won the National Soror of the Year. Soror Rush was the first SOTY at the National level awarded in Iota Phi Lambda Sorority.

On April 23-25, 1976, Alpha Chapter held the Western Regional Conference at the Conrad Hilton Hotel in Chicago, Illinois. Doris General was Alpha's President, and Theresa Faith Cummings was the Western Regional Director. Soror Parker, our Founder, did not attend, but sent a warm, welcome greetings' message to the Conference.

Before the merger of the Northern and Western Regions, much happened with Alpha Chapter. In anticipation of the merger, the Western Region conducted a contest to find the most productive and highest selling tickets, to win as "Ms. Iota" of the Western Region. Soror Naomi Kilpatrick was crowned "Ms. Iota" at the Conference in 1977. She was escorted by Lambd John Lassiter, Ethel's husband. Theresa Faith Cummings was Regional Director and Doris General was President of Alpha Chapter.

On June 1, 1979, the Western Regional Chapters published a book entitled "Alive Black Women." The book profiled Black Women as a salute to their involvement in the heritage and history of our country through their outstanding contributions to mankind in their respective communities and states. It was done in celebration of the 50th Anniversary. Copies of the book were placed in libraries and historical societies in each of the states where chapters are located so that young people may see the evidence of the good works of these women and receive inspiration to follow in their footsteps.

The Regional Sorors who coordinated the compiling of this book were:

Ms. Delores C. Brown, Alpha Beta
Mrs. Naomi Kilpatrick, Alpha
Ms. Valeska Hinton, Honorary Member, Alpha Beta

There were three Alpha Chapter Sorors honored in the book:

Madie Cannamoré, Willie Crittendon, and Helen Rush.

Soror Naomi Kilpatrick submitted two outstanding women for the book: Mrs. Laura Jolly and Mrs. Vernice Hatch. Their profiles are outlined in the book.

We held a huge celebration for Alpha Chapter's 50th year. It was held from August 10-16, 1979, in Chicago, Illinois with Alpha chapter serving as host. Fifty-Eight Alpha chapter sorors attended, as well as, a large contingent of Lambds and Pelatis. It was a wonderful National Convention with Doris General and Carnegia Gordon, Alpha, serving as Co-Chairpersons.

Soror Mahala S. Evans passed away that same year, 1979, before the Convention was held. Her loss was a deep blow to Alpha Chapter.

The next period of time we called "The Excitement of the 80's". In 1980, the Northern Region and the Western Region came together to form the Central Region. It was a cooperative merger with Soror Mary Louise Harris, Northern and Soror Dorothy Williams, Western serving as Co-Directors for the first Central Regional Conference that was held in 1981 in Chicago with Alpha Lambda serving as host chapter. Doris Murry, Alpha, was elected as National Recording Secretary.

The eighties were also one of great sorrow with the passing of several sorors including our founder, Soror Lola M. Parker. The services for Soror Parker were held on Monday, March 23, 1987 at the Taylor Funeral Home, 63 East 79th St; Chicago, Il. Rev. Albert Baker, Olivet Baptist Church, was the Officiant.

The "Fabulous 90's" saw much movement in Alpha Chapter. There were banquets, and bridge/whist card parties, theater parties, fashion shows, chapter meetings, regional conferences and national conventions.

In 1993, to celebrate American Education Week, Alpha Chapter, along with the other Chicago area chapters sponsored a program at Kennedy King Community college. The sorors honored leaders in the field of Education, presenting them with plaques to express their gratitude for their service to the schools. The theme was, "Better Schools Shape Better Tomorrows."

Alpha coordinated a joint affair at the Montgomery Place in Chicago, IL on November 18, 1995 in observance of American Education Week. Willie Crittendon, Alpha, served as speaker for the event.

Soror Agnes Hale, Alpha, passed away in December, 1995. Her transition service was held on January 2, 1996. The service was most reflective of her life's commitment to dedicated service. Scholarship Dinner

In July, 1997, Soror Dorothy White won the prestigious Lucille Watson Warfield Award for her attendance, her participation on committees, her participation in Founders' Day, her participation in selling raffle tickets, and her participation in the Card Party. The LWW Award is the highest award given to Alpha Chapter sorors who exhibit outstanding commitment to the chapter and its' programs and projects. From her days as a new soror, Soror White has demonstrated excellence in everything she does for the chapter. The sorors eagerly congratulated Soror White on her accomplishments.

In 1998 and 1999, we participated in the NCNW sponsored Collaborative Health Fair. In 1998, Alpha chapter served as "chair" of the event. The Health Fair was held at Olive Harvey Community College.

As the chapter closed out, and said, "So long," to the 90's and to the Sorors we lost, we were reminded of the words "running with the wolves", so to speak. Although we don't fit the "wild" part of the book ("Women Who Run with the Wolves"), Alpha Chapter sorors are "a powerful force, filled with good instincts, passionate creativity, and ageless knowing." It was a period where the sorors, as a group, reflected on the greatness of the legacy that permeated the chapter down through the years. We reflected on the bold dream of our founder, Lola Mercedes Parker, and the loyalty of her six friends; and how that changed the world for African American women; how the realization of that dream, gave them a future. We had an "Ahaaa" moment, as Oprah would say. We had to somehow, during this decade, and beyond, keep that excellence. Pass that torch! Raise that banner high! And yet, it had to be done with our skills, with our talents, with our dreams, and with our enthusiasm." Let the fun begin. And let it begin with Alpha Chapter . . ."

The years 2000-2010 were filled with much activity and great moments for Alpha Chapter. There was also tragedy and loss, too painful to elaborate on, and at times, disillusionment and discouragement. There were attempts to dampen our spirits by taking our eyes "off the prize". We were tempted to give up, to bow to the darkness, and to give in to despair. During those years, our Sorors "took a hit" that was devastating to our existence.

The entire nation was devastated by "911" and praise God we survived that tragedy. By 2010, we lost 9 Sorors. From 2004-2008, I lost 3 adult children and my beloved mother. We reeled from the losses, struggling to hold on to our dreams and aspirations.

Alpha Chapter hosted the 23rd Central Regional Conference from April 4-6, 2003 at the Radisson Hotel in Alsip, Il. Soror Corrine Compton was Central Regional Director, Lillian Parker was National President. The Business Luncheon was held on that Saturday, April 5, 2003. The Greetings were given by Conference Co-Chair, Sharon Kirby White and Invocation was given by Naomi R. Kilpatrick, Conference Co-Chair. The Guest Speaker was the Honorable Dorothy Brown, Clerk of the Circuit Court, Cook County. She exhorted the guests in attendance to be in control of your finances. We have the tools; we must put them to work. Her words resonated throughout the audience, giving rise to much hope for our students' future.

One of the biggest highlights in Alpha Chapter history occurred on June 12, 2004. It was Alpha's 75th Anniversary Scholarship Gala. Our theme was "Founder's Dream, Alpha's Vision." The event took place at the Radisson Hotel-Alsip, Illinois, starting at 6:00 p.m. Our National theme was so apropo for the affair: "Iota: Empowered Business and Professional Women Making a Notable Difference." Eight outstanding women and men well selected to receive a certificate and a plaque in honor of their dedicated service to their communities, including now President Barack

Obama who was Illinois Senator Barack Obama at the time, poised to run for the President of the United States of America. Of course, he won, to our delight! We recognized his greatness early on. The 8 honorees were:

- Dorothy Brown – Clerk of the Circuit Court of Cook County;
- Jerry Butler – Cook County Commissioner;
- Mary Flowers – State Representative, Illinois House;
- Dr. Alma Jones – Retired Principal, Chairman of the Local Board of Managers for Chicago Youth Centers;
- Barack Obama – Illinois 13th Senate District on Chicago's South Side;
- Richard Steele – Radio personality – both talk radio and music radio, WBEZ-FM;
- Elois Washington Steward PH.D – Founder of Educational Specialties, Member of the Board of the Business Enterprise Council for Minorities, Females, and Persons with Disabilities;
- Beverly Yates – Registered Nurse, Charter member and Past President, Chicagoland Christian Women's Conference (CCWC).

At the event, and as part of our entertainment, our new (and young) Sorors did a special performance of the music of "The Jeff Williams Project." They "wowed" the crowd, which was an excellent culmination of the beautiful event. Dorothy White was Alpha Chapter President; Tammy Gibson was Chairperson; Corrine Compton was Central Regional Director; and Charlotte M. Maull was National President. She honored Alpha Chapter by her presence at the Gala.

The year 2006 was a year of new opportunities for the chapter. Man of Iota (MOI) Thomas "Tommy" Wortham was stationed in Iraqi with the armed forces. He saw an opportunity to help the children in the area where he was stationed. He, through his mom, Soror Carolyn Wortham, elicited our help with the project. Alpha Chapter gladly participated in the Iraqi Children's Educational Project, donating books and school supplies to the children of the "AdDujayl" Province.

Business Month, 2009, was celebrated with a visit to Captain Hardtimes Restaurant owned by Mrs. Josephine Wade. Captain Hardtimes has been a vital part of the African American community for many years. It was the site of many political events. The walls feature pictures of the rich and famous in politics and the entertainment field. A certificate of appreciation was presented to Mrs. Wade.

The Sorors of Alpha Chapter were very involved in the Barack Obama presidential campaign. In the summer of 2008, we sponsored a backyard barbecue; participated in Camp Obama; and Soror Carolyn Wortham served as a member of Team Obama, representing the campaign as a speaker at several events held in Indiana and Illinois.

On Saturday, November 7, 2009, Alpha Chapter held its 80th Anniversary Luncheon/Fashion Show at the Hilton-Oak Lawn Hotel located at 9330 So. Cicero, Oak Lawn, Illinois. It was held from 12:30 p.m.-4:30 p.m. Minister Gloria Randolph was our special honoree. Gloria won the very prestigious Woman of the Year (WOTY) Award, and she won it locally (Alpha Chapter), regionally (Central Region), and nationally. Gloria brought excitement, dignity, beauty, and grace to our affair. She demonstrated her modeling skills as she served as "Guest Model", participating in four scenes: Sunday/Church Attire; Business Attire; Casual Wear; and Evening-Elegant Attire. It was a beautiful affair, but most importantly we raised money for the Scholarship Fund. The featured designer was Quintella. The audience was entertained by Lee England and his electric violin.

In 2010, Alpha continued to show its support for fellow Greek organizations and local business enterprises. During April, 2010, to celebrate Business Month, several Alpha Chapter sorors toured the "Little Black Pearl Art and Design Center." Little Black Pearl is a combination art gallery and art studio providing classes for neighborhood students and adults.

And then, in May, 2010, tragedy struck. "Tommy" Wortham, Soror Carolyn Wortham's son, was gunned down by a senseless act of violence. It happened in front of his parents' home (he had just visited them), and right in front of them. Mr. Wortham, his father, is also a policeman and was able to shoot two of the men, killing one and wounding the other one. Two other men escaped. They were all eventually apprehended, charged, tried and convicted. It was a trying, very painful process being in court with the men who killed your son. But by God's grace, they made it through the trial. The loss of Tommy left Carolyn and her family devastated; devastated and sad, but don't count them out. They did not sit at home having "pity parties" every day, Mr. Wortham, a retired Chicago policeman, had vowed that he would not let his son's death be in vain. He was determined to help young men avoid gun violence. He developed programs to work with young men and boys at his church – Trinity United Church of Christ where the Rev. Jeremiah Wright is Pastor Emeritus and a close friend - to mentor them and train them in community service. Much work had been done already by Tommy Wortham at the Nat King Cole Park on 82nd and King Dr. The Worthams have continued the work at that Park since his death. Sandra, Carolyn's daughter has just recently opened her first law firm. Carolyn and her family have traveled all over the country speaking out against gun violence and supporting families that have experienced a similar tragedy. They have also spoken before Congress in Washington, D.C.

The funeral that was held for Thomas Wortham IV was at the Trinity United Church of Christ, attended by thousands of friends, family, and mourners including Mayor Richard Daley, Police Superintendent, Jody Weiss and Rev. Jesse Jackson. They were there to pay their respects to this "good guy" that cared a lot about his community. He has always given to his country and to his city. The audience called Mr. Wortham, his dad, a hero for his actions to try and save his son. Hundreds had come out the night before for visitation in honor of Tommy.

Alpha Chapter Sorors were with Carolyn from the moment we found out which was about 6:00 a.m. that morning. And we went the "last mile" with her through her dark hour. I wrote and read the Resolution from Alpha Chapter in honor of Thomas Wortham, IV at the funeral. It was televised, so many people witnessed the solemn service. Our friend and regular speaker Evang. Makeda London, at CCWC conferences sent me an email about the Resolution. My nephew, Mitchell, called me that evening to let me know he had seen me on T.V. giving a Resolution tribute to Tommy. He lives in a small town in Georgia. I was "taken aback" by that, realizing that the funeral had been broadcast, nationwide.

Members of the Chicago Area chapters along with members of Alpha Chapter attended the renaming of Cole Park Playground for Man of Iota Thomas Wortham, IV, for work that he had done in the community and as President of the Cole Park Council. The dedication and ribbon cutting took place in October, 2011. Soror Stephanie Dilworth, Nat'l President-Elect of Iota Phi Lambda Sorority, Inc. was also in attendance.

Beginning in 2011, the chapter began to explore many avenues of attracting new members and becoming more visible in the city. Thus, began a partnership as a vendor with the city of Chicago Small Business & Entrepreneurship Expo. The chapter sponsored an informational booth displaying Iota memorabilia and membership information. We were able to create a "buzz" and participate in a citywide event. This led to several contacts and possible future members as we expand our focus to include more business activities. This was also carried over into the year 2012 as we helped to sponsor a combined informational session to attract potential new members.

Dr. Blondean Y. Davis was honored as Central Region's Outstanding Woman of the Year at the 82nd Anniversary National Convention on Saturday, July 16, 2011.

During the 2013 Central Regional Conference, Soror Tammy Gibson of Alpha Chapter was selected as Central Region's Outstanding Soror of the Year.

On Saturday, October 11, 2014, Alpha Chapter Sorors and Soror Sharon M. Tang (Naomi Kilpatrick's daughter) from Alpha Tau Chapter attended "Clear II, Inc., a Night of Enchantment", at 6:00 p.m. at the Flossmoor Country Club. Clear, II saluted cancer survivors and presented 2 powerful videos showing the effects of cancer on "real people". We shared a wonderful dinner together and received encouraging news to share with our communities. The program was hosted by Alpha Chapter's Outstanding Woman of the Year, Rev. Gloria Randolph.

Soror Corrine Compton's church, Chatham Fields Evangelical Lutheran Church showed the movie, "Selma" at their Chatham 14 Theater, Chicago, Illinois in 2014. The film was shown to highlight the importance of the march that was held some 50 years ago. Although the Civil Rights Act of 1964 legally desegregated the South, discrimination was still rampant in certain areas, making it very difficult for blacks to register to vote. In 1965, an Alabama city became the battleground in the fight for suffrage. Despite violent opposition, Dr. Martin Luther King, Jr. (David Oyelowo) and his followers pressed forward on an epic march from Selma to Montgomery, and their efforts culminated in President Lyndon Baines Johnson signing the Voting Rights Acts of 1965. Unfortunately, there are people who are trying to take us back 50 years. The struggle continues. Alpha Chapter Sorors supported the movie by their attendance and their donations.

The year, 2014, was by far the "shining moment" for Alpha chapter. It marked 85 years of exemplary service to our community; to young people; to young women; to women; and to families. The big event was the 85th Anniversary Gala. The date was June 1, Founders' Day.

The day began in early afternoon with Sorors, and visiting Sorors went to the gravesite of our Founder, Lola M. Parker. The National President, Mrs. Phyllis Shumate, was in attendance as was all Sorors, who gave honor to Soror Parker and her six friends who helped her found the organization. It was a solemn mood while Sorors performed the Memorial Service and the placing of the wreath and beautiful white roses. It was a special occasion to so many who had never visited the gravesite. For those of us who come to remember her each year, it was a time of reflection and rededication. Alpha Chapter's Gala was that evening, and several Sorors had come in from other states and other chapters to support our celebration.

That evening, at the Hilton Hotel, Oak Lawn, Illinois, the Sorors observed Founder's Day. At 6:00 p.m., the observance began, with the National President, Soror Phyllis Shumate there, Soror Doris Graham, Central Regional Director, was also in attendance. Soror Corrine Compton presided during the program.

The Reception for the 85th Anniversary Celebration began at 7:00 p.m. After 30 minutes of wine and music, Soror Naomi R. Kilpatrick invited the members of the Dais to be seated. Sandra Wortham, the daughter of Soror Carolyn Wortham and a former FIL of Iota, served as the Mistress of Ceremony.

Soror Jessica Brown, Alpha's President, introduced Mrs. Phyllis Shumate, National President, who was the keynote speaker for the evening. She presented the Founder's Day Message and gave a historical perspective of Iota Phi Lambda Sorority, Inc. She shared profound words that issued a challenge to the Sisterhood as well as encouragement to keep holding high the banner of excellence. Marcella Morrison, Past National President, gave an inspiring tribute to our Founder, Lola M. Parker. A presentation of song was given by "The Princess of Percussion", Taylor Moore & Friends.

Sandra Wortham and Jessica Edwards presented the 2014 Lola M. Parker Emerald Legacy Awards to the seven honorees for the evening. They were: Honorable Monique Davis, Dr. Jackie Taylor, Dr. Deena Marie Carr, Dr. Blondean Y. Davis, Rev. Gloria Randolph, Dr. Lisa Green, and Mrs. Carolyn Wortham.

These seven women were all outstanding in their field of work and their service to their community.

Alpha chapter, in partnership with the Worthams, instituted the Thomas Wortham IV Community Service Scholarship. The first winner was Jireh Martin. Jireh is a 2014 graduate of Urban Prep located in Englewood. Jirek plans to enroll in Indiana University and major in Mass Communications and Media Studies. He is a well-rounded student, participating in academic challenges, track and field, and the debate team. He also participated in S.T.E.M. Camp, After School Matters and Summer Leadership Business Institute. He thanks his mother for her guidance and influence in his life, helping him to believe and trust in God.

The 85th Anniversary Gala culminated the "shining moment" in the life of Alpha Chapter. We were so honored to have our illustrious National President, Phyllis Shumate share that "moment" with us, the first chapter. Soror Shumate is what I call a "southern belle". She has taken "elegance" to another whole level during her Presidency. I had the honor of serving as her assistant at the last National Convention, and I was impressed with her knowledge of Iota's Constitution & Bylaws and her "down to earth" manner, and her strong commitment and dedication to the Sisterhood. Her encouragement, her challenge to the Sorors was to keep climbing, keep shining, keep on moving "upward and onward."

Chicagoland Christian Women's Conference
CCWC

The Chicagoland Christian Women's Conference (CCWC) was born in the heart of Yvonne Rollerson Abatao and suggested to the ladies of Westlawn Gospel Chapel. Under her capable leadership and with the cooperation of the women of Westlawn and the Women of Grace & Glory Gospel Chapels, the first meeting of the conference was held in March, 1961.

The speaker that year was Frances Beerthis Norland. It was a blessed time at that meeting. Some led the very first discussion group and saw women come to Jesus Christ for salvation and dedication. The purpose of such a meeting was to promote the Gospel of Jesus Christ; to help other women to come to know Him and to stimulate spiritual fellowship among women regardless of religious background or church affiliation.

The goal was and is to encourage women to think, to study God's Word and to strive to reach their potential in Jesus Christ, to read good books and share this knowledge with others.

In 1969, the conference expanded its meeting to include a Friday night with overnight accommodations at the YMCA Hotel. Taking advantage of the overnight accommodations were fifteen women. From this conference the women were stirred to "Move Forward in Faith," a direction from self-concern and self-interest to the larger area of Christian women's involvement in their world. As a result, our first out-of-town retreat was held in March, 1971 at the Lake Geneva Conference Grounds in Lake Geneva, Wisconsin. A June Conference was held at the Great Hall of the Colonial House in Chicago. Adine Douglas was the Conference Chairman.

In 1973, the conference expanded its ministry again to include an Annual Day of Prayer and a Missionary Project, Camp Bethesda in Monrovia, Liberia. Millicent Lindo was chairman of the conference. The theme was "Jesus Calls Me To Follow Him", The Annual June Conference was held at Carter Temple each year through 1976. The Day of Prayer was being held in the Fall of the year at various churches in the city. The 1974 retreat speakers were Beverly Yates and Fannie McFerren.

By 1975, we'd outgrown the facilities at the Lake Geneva Conference Grounds and the retreat was moved to the George Williams College Facilities, Williams Bay, Wisconsin. In June, 1975, Cleo Sanders was elected as chairman. In 1976, the organization was chartered in the State of Illinois. A Constitution and By-laws governing the body was initiated with the official title "Chicagoland Christian Women's Conference". The 1977 Retreat theme was "God First, That The Generation To Come Might Know", speakers – Ruth Bentley and Millicent Lindo. For the June Conference held at the Conrad Hilton, Yvonne Abatso was our speaker.

The theme for the session was "Rebuilding the Family Structure (Women, What Is Our Part?)

By 1978, The Retreat reached its maximum at George Williams College; and the June Conference and Day of Prayer were growing, as well. Three additional missionary projects were included for support. They were: The Westside Holistic Family Center, Chicago, Illinois. Mrs. Millicent Lindo, Director; Circle Y Ranch Youth Camp, Bangor, Michigan, with Dr. Leroy Yates, Sr. serving as Director; and Camp Pioneer Youth Camp, Jackson, Mississippi; Dr. Maurice Bingham, serving as Director.

Three new members were added in 1978: Brenda Elmore, Barbara Ham Ying, and Rebecca Osaigbovo. The June Conference was again held at the Conrad Hilton. Our first hotel accommodations were held at the Red Carpet Inn in Milwaukee, Wisconsin for the Spring Retreat, 1979. Our prayer request was that God would send 400 women to share in the ministry. In answer to our request, God sent 425 women to take up residence in the hotel plus those who were already in the city commuted. Not only did He answer prayer in numbers, He answered prayer in that souls were saved. Women were coming to know Jesus Christ as Savior and Lord through the ministry of Aunt Hattie Johnson from Chattanooga, Tennessee. The Counselor Room overflowed. Among those who came to know Jesus Christ was the food manager of the hotel. It was an exciting time! Saturday evening, Pocahontas Jones blessed our heart at the Annual Banquet. This was her last time with us. The theme was, "The Joy of the Lord – My Strength." Sunday morning, during the sharing time, the Food Manager gave his testimony. We went away from that Retreat rejoicing and giving thanks for what the Lord had done.

The June Conference was held at Antioch Baptist Church and subsequently through 1982. Because of the large numbers attending the Retreat, we recognized that we were losing the closeness and the fellowship that once characterized us. The committee thought it wise to organize the Small Group Fellowship with hostesses assisting each leader. This group of caring ladies would meet during the year for training. At the Retreat, they serve as encouragers. They facilitate meetings after the general sessions to get acquainted with the newcomers, discuss topics of personal interest, pray, and give testimonies. Many needs are ministered to in these informal settings that could not be met in any other way. The on-going counseling class was organized to train counselors to meet the needs at the conferences and to keep in contact with those who came to know Christ and those needing special help. Included also is a session for older teens geared to their special needs and interests.

Through the seventies and then into the eighties, the Retreat was held at the Sheraton Oakbrook, Oakbrook, Illinois, with approximately 800 women attendees. The theme was "A Challenge to Wholeness" and Sis. Pearl Ayers Smith was the Speaker. It was almost a replica of the 1979 Retreat where many came to make commitments and for salvation.

In June, 1980, Beverly Yates was elected President. Again, we'd burst the seams and the 1981 Retreat was held at the Wagon Wheel, Rockton, Illinois. Over one thousand women were in attendance. Dr. Yvonne Abatso and Nadine Smith were the speakers. The year's theme was "Relating God's Truth to the 80's". Needless to say, the Wagon Wheel was too small for the 1981 Retreat and the 1982 Retreat. The Chicago Hyatt Regency O'Hare was the next place. Etta Latson was the speaker. The theme, "God First, That the Generation to Come Might Know," Psalm 78:4-6, was chosen for that signature year. In the Fall of 1981, a Leadership Conference was held in connection with the Day of Prayer at the Holiday Inn, 1 South Halsted. Reverend Brenda Piper Little was the speaker.

For 1983 and 1984, Chicago was the Retreat Headquarters with Inez Washington as the President. She was elected in June, 1983. Also in 1983, Adine Douglas and Brenda Piper Little were the speakers, with the theme being, "To Know Christ and to Make Him Known." That Retreat was held on March 25-27. The next year, the theme was "Christian Women's Response to a Nation in Crisis". Dr. Lillie White was the Retreat Speaker. Her focus was on the theme, "God's Women for Such a Time as This."

In June, 1985, Vernice Hatch was elected President. The Day of Prayer was held at the St. Stephens AME. Church. Aida Winfield was the speaker.

The 1986 Retreat was held at the Hyatt Regency O'Hare, and for many years after that because of our large number of attendees at the Conference. Hyatt Regency's facilities were adequate for us, and they could accommodate "break out rooms" for groups; they had spaces for venders; a special place for the Prayer Room; and a large ballroom for the general sessions. The Retreat theme for that year was, "The Joy of Intimacy with

God". The speakers were Pearl Ayers Smith, Hattie Johnson, and Alice Pittman.

CCWC Conferences and Retreats have always been characterized by spirited singing. Song time has always been a vital part of the retreat, the conference, and the day of prayer. The great hymns of the faith; spiritual songs, gospels both old and new are featured. "Sweet Holy Spirit" and "The Joy of the Lord is my Strength" continue to be the favorites.

In the early years of CCWC while yet at the YMCA Hotel, Virginia Marshall was Director of the First Conference Choir. The ladies met at Grace Conservative Baptist Church for rehearsals.

In 1973, a retreat choir was started at the Lake Geneva Youth Camp which continued under the direction of Destaleer Randolph and Inez Washington until 1981. This retreat choir was revised under the direction of Barbara Griffin in 1984 and Lou Della Reid in 1985 and 1986. This choir of volunteer attendees along with special soloists have added to the musical content of our retreats down through the years.

Mr. Lee Randolph designed our CCWC logo.

The Lord blessed our organization beyond our wildest dreams during those early years and expanding to the 90's and into the 21st century. We continued growing as an organization; continued serving, not knowing what plans God had for us in the future. The annual Retreats were held at the Hyatt Regency O'Hare in the 1990's. Beverly Yates was President in 1998 and 1999. Our Retreat in 1999 was really exciting and stimulating.

At the March 19-21, 1999 Retreat, Jannie Wilcoxson was the Guest Speaker and the theme was, "Word Up . . . God is Speaking". She articulated our theme with words from God that challenged and encouraged our hearts. We had five (5) workshops that were led by Minister Gloria Randolph, Michelle Yates, M.D., Evang. Carolyn Blunt, Sis. Victoria "Vickie" Johnson, and Sis. Louise Forshé. Delois Barrett Campbell and the Barrett Sisters provided the music, directed and accompanied by Lou Della Evans Reid and Barbara Griffin. Sheryl Stephens served as the Meeting Planner.

The Annual Retreat for 2002 was held again at the Hyatt Regency O'Hare Hotel with hundreds of ladies in attendance. We held the 2002 Annual Day of Prayer on November 2nd at Grace & Glory Gospel Chapel. Evang. Cheryl Dorsey served as Facilitator.

The next Annual Retreat was held on March 21-23, 2003 and marks a turning point in the Chicagoland Christian Women's Conference Retreats. It was the last one held at the Hyatt Regency O'Hare Hotel. The theme that year was "Run It Down to Jesus". Our Guest Speakers were Janie Wilcoxson and Lucille Badger.

It was a wonderful experience, enjoyed by not only the attendees, but by the Board of Directors, as well. However, we over anticipated our numbers, and ended up owing the Hotel more than we could pay. Even though the numbers were not there, because of our guarantee to the Hyatt, we owed that amount to the Hotel. We were devastated and perplexed for months. We didn't know how we were going to pay the debt, recognizing that the integrity of CCWC was at stake. Needless to say, after much prayer (from everyone) the Lord sent a miracle! The Hyatt Regency O'Hare Hotel dissolved the debt; we owed them nothing, zilch, zero – wonderful! We sent a letter of "Thanks" to the Managing Director of the hotel. Thus began a trek to a couple of other hotels for the annual retreat.

The First Progressive Church of Christ, the home church of CCWC Board Member, Cleo Sanders, held their Fifth Sunday Vesper Service on March 29, 2003 at 5:00 p.m. The Service was sponsored by the Senior Ministry of the Church. Naomi Kilpatrick was the Speaker at the Event and received the Women of Color Award for her service. The Reverend Derrias Colvin was the Minister-In-Charge, Bro. Columbus Bowens was the Deacon Board Chairman. "She Shall Be Called Woman" was the theme.

In the next year, the Annual Retreat was held at the Radisson Hotel – O'Hare in Rosemont, Illinois. It was held on March 26-28, 2004. It was a wonderful Conference with great numbers of women attending. It was a month after losing my son, Lenard, so it was a challenge for me to stay focused on the duties at hand. I did okay and things went beautifully well because we were a team, the Board of Directors. Everyone took their duty seriously and carried it out as unto the Lord. We had excellent speakers, workshop leaders, and musicians. The Guest Speakers were: Carolyn Blunt (now deceased), Alice Dise, Jamell Meeks, Gloria Randolph, and Rebecca Osaigbovo. They, each, in their own unique style addressed our theme and gave us a special blessing from the Lord. In addition to three of the speakers who served as workshop leaders: Diane Brandon Bonner, Delores Jones, and Bridgett Van Means involved each precious lady, in her group, to know Christ and to make Him known. Sandra Hudson and her sister, Vanessa Clark warmed our hearts with their praise as they served as the Soloists for the Conference; Lou Della Evans Reid and Barbara Griffin served as the musicians – the glue that held the whole music presentation together. The scripture we selected for the Retreat was Matthew 28:19-20:

The theme of the Retreat was: "Together . . . We Survive!" There is a picture on the brochure of all the Board Members at that time. There were 19 of us and we were all dressed in white outfits with matching white hats. I was President at the time, and I felt it "fitting", and oh so beautiful to wear white to take communion. Some younger Board members were not "happy campers" with this, but they acquiesced and as a result, it was a nice picture. The Lord looked down upon us and smiled His good pleasure. Some have gone to be with the Lord . . .

On Saturday, May 23, 2009, the Chicagoland Christian Women's Conference honored four outstanding women, chosen by the Board of Directors with a wonderful Luncheon held at the Crystal Sky Banquets in McCook, Illinois.

The four (4) women honored were:

Dr. Lillie White Shaffer is a Christian woman who loves God and His Word. She holds a Doctor of Education Degree from Nova Southeastern University and a Masters' Degree in English from Chicago State University. She was the Principal of Oglesby Elementary School from 1974-1992. She is currently the Academic Dean for the Chicago Baptist Institute. She was the State Director of Christian Education for the Baptist General State Convention of Illinois from 1997-2008. Dr. Shaffer holds many and varied certificates and awards in the area of Christian Education throughout the United States. She is the widow of the late Mr. Warren G. Shaffer, Sr., the mother of one son, John, grandmother of five and great-grandmother of eight. She is an active member of Lilydale First Baptist Church, under the pastorate of Rev. Alvin Love.

Mrs. Patricia McKinney resides in Brooklyn, New York with her husband of 30 years, Vaughn McKinney. She is the musical director of the East Flatbush Ecumenical Boys & Girls community choir. Patricia received her Bachelor of Music degree from the Berklee School of Music in Boston, Massachusetts. She is also the recipient of a Master of Science in Education and a Master of Science in Banking. Patricia is currently a Sunday School Teacher at Bethany. She enjoys the opportunity to teach her young students strong spiritual values and exercises these lessons through plays, and a church choir that she established and also directs. Patricia is also the President of the Bethany Women Sister Group. Patricia gives glory to God for His faithfulness and immeasurable blessings to her family. She has been attending the CCWC Retreat for many years bringing many New York ladies with her.

Mrs. Vertlee Williams is the First Lady of New Mt. Moriah M.B. Church. Sister Williams has been married to Pastor Marvell Williams for 49 years. They have three daughters; Mae, Rachel and Patricia; three grandchildren; Marvin, Ayesha, and Brittany and one great-grandchild; Aiden. Sister Williams has been the First Lady for 38 years. She is the President of the Gospel Choir, the leader for the Elderly Care and Sick Committee and she is the coordinator for the Women's Ministry. Sister Williams, for the last five years, has taken the highest group of attendees to the CCWC conference. You can see Sister Williams singing on Thursday mornings on WJYS, Channel 62 from 7:00 A.M. - 7:30 A.M. Sister Williams loves God and knows that her work is not in vain. Her favorite verses are: "Blessed are the pure in heart, for they shall see God. Blessed are the peacemakers for they shall be called the children of God." Matthew 5:8-9.

Dr. Lou Della Evans Reid has a national reputation as one of the most outstanding ministers of music this side of heaven. Her unique style of directing is majestic, as well as powerful, and has enhanced the services at her church for almost 35 years. Lou Della has played many pioneering roles during her lifetime. In 1950, she was the only woman among the five charter members of the Fellowship Missionary Baptist Church of Chicago, where her brother, the eminent Reverend Clay Evans, is the founder and Senior Pastor. Moreover, she gave birth to the church choir, served as its first pianist, and was appointed Minister of Music in 1963, during a time in which it was unusual for a woman to hold such a position. Lou Della's musical excellence has been showcased in many arenas, including over thirty musical releases of the Reverend Clay Evans and the Fellowship Missionary Baptist Church Choir, recordings of the National Baptist Convention, U.S.A., Inc., and numerous choral concerts across the country and throughout Europe. Musicians across the nation look to her for inspiration that seem to emanate from her whenever she directs. She has served as a workshop leader at many churches, staff musician and devotion leader for the Chicagoland Christian Women's Conference. Most recently, Lou Della was invited to be a guest director on the nationally known Bill Gaither Pioneer Gospel Hour. She is currently Minister of Music Emeritus at Fellowship Missionary Baptist Church and Music Advisor for the mass choirs of First Church of Deliverance.

Lou Della is respected and honored by many people for her many years of dedication to her Pastor and Church. Even the most reserved worshippers are affected by her powerful spirit and conviction. Many consider her a living legend and a dynamo that has exploded into the hearts of people all over the world.

We were so proud to present these ladies and honor them with the "Yvonne Abatso Award" and then to hear their beautiful responses to the honor. In addition to being one of the honorees, Dr. Lillie White Shaffer served as Guest Speaker, as well. Jennifer Salley, CCWC Board Member, gave the Invocation, and Mary Coultman was the "Ministry in Music" leader. We had a formal "Receiving Line" at the end of the program that was the culminating activity for the afternoon. The "Line" was called the "Ever Widening Circle of Love".

When Joyce Yates Austin was elected President of the CCWC Board of Directors, she brought a fresh, new dynamic to the office. She was full of ideas and she was enthusiastic about taking CCWC in another direction and excited about moving to the next level in the ministry. She wrote a letter to Board Members dated November 24, 2010. The letter was prefaced by the scripture, Psalm 100:1-5, which was apropo for encouragement in the ministry.

The Chicagoland Christian Women's Conference (CCWC) has seen a decline in attendees over the last several years. Women have been so blessed through this ministry, so much so, that they have formed their own groups, have formed their own organizations, and have formed their own ministries in their churches. By His grace, we have opened doors for others to "know the Lord and to make Him known." Our Retreats have changed, to a degree, and our programs have been affected, but we are still here, still praising God, and still carrying on the work of the Lord. We had a one day Retreat at the New Community Church, Dolton, Illinois on Saturday, March 17, 2012. And once again, our dynamic Speaker was Jannie Wilcoxson. Our workshop presenters were Rev. Alice Dise and Pastor Makeda London. Our friends, Patricia McKinney and her sister from New York attended. It was such sweet fellowship with them and the other attendees at the one day conference. It was a wonderful experience, showing us that we, as an organization, as a ministry, are "still here."

We are grateful to God for 50+ years. He has blessed us beyond our greatest dreams, and we are confident that, "He who has begun a good work in us will carry it on until it is finished on the Day of Christ Jesus." (Philippians 1:6)

Vineyard Partnership Investment Club

The Vineyard Partnership Investment Club was started on May 15, 1996 by a group of Christian ladies who wanted to be good shepherds over their finances. It was formed under the auspices of the laws of the State of Illinois. The purpose of the partnership was to invest the assets of the partnership solely in stocks, bonds, and securities for the education and benefit of the partners. It was decided that the group would meet once per month on the third Thursday of each month.

The members of the partnership were to share in the profits and losses of the club with the keeping of books of account that were open to inspection and examination by any member on the day of the meeting.

The Officers of the Vineyard Partnership Investment Club were the Senior Partner, the Junior Partner, Recording Partner, and Financial Partner and they are to be elected annually during the regular June meeting. The Senior Partner is to preside at meetings, appoint a parliamentarian; appoint committees, and oversee club activities. The Junior Partner will assume the duties of the Senior Partner when she is absent or temporarily unable to perform her duties. Additionally, the Junior Partner is responsible for the educational program of the club. The Recording Secretary keeps a record of the club's activities and reports on previous meetings. The Financial Partner has the distinction of ordering the selling and buying of stocks, with the partnership's instruction, collecting and disbursing funds, maintaining a set of books that cover the clubs financial operations, assets, and members' shares, and issuing receipts to partners for their deposits. She shall prepare an annual statement of liquidating value and shall prepare proper tax forms. Her records are audited each year by a committee within the group to inspect the club's records in conjunction with the Financial Partner.

The Partnership was agreed upon and declared that the parties had set their hands and seal that year on what had been written. Thus started the professional and legal organization entitled:

"Vineyard Partnership Investment Club."

These were all Christian ladies, committed to serve the Lord through their finances. There were spiritual lessons shared at every meeting and the focus was on doing those things that were well-pleasing to the Lord. They agreed upon the "Requirements For New Members:

1.) Must be Believers in Jesus Christ as their Personal Savior
2.) Must be compatible with present members.
3.) A. Should enter with $250.00 minimum down payment plus $35.00 monthly dues. Contribute $1000.00 within one year from the individual's date of entry into the club including NAIC fees. B. May elect to contribute money equal to the value of senior members' shares.
4.) Must attend an orientation meeting with officers of the club.
5.) The club will be open to 15 members.

Felecia Thompson and Sheryl Stephens invited me to join the club in late 1996. I was happy to join and then I invited Beverly Yates to join, and the "rest is history." Beverly invited her sisters, Sara Hennings and Olive Banks to join, Tanya Hicks came on board; Rosie Turner joined the club, and over the next several months, other members were added to the group. It never exceeded 15 members.

The years 1997 and 1998 were productive and stimulating. The meetings were filled with spiritual lessons, as well as financial information and wonderful fellowship among a group of Christian young (and older) women.

On May 21, 1998, the group set a big goal – take a cruise or go to Paris after 5 years. I don't remember if we were serious or just joking. At any rate, we did not take a trip to Paris or go on a cruise! Meetings were held from June, 1998 through December, 1998. Things seemed to kind of go downhill in the year 1999. The members were undergoing "trials and tribulations". Many prayers were being offered up to God and much encouragement was given, but some members were showing up at meetings intermittently; and some times paying dues and sometimes not. Some members felt that it was best to break up the club, but those of us who were totally committed to the Partnership "hung in there", determining to carry on with the club. However, those members that withdrew had to be given their share, so we made very hard decisions and made plans to do this without selling our stocks. We were able to accomplish this by the grace of God. We have been going, steady as you go, for some 15 years, and again by the grace of God we are still learning to be good stewards of the money that God gives us.

We, who were left in the Partnership after the others left, amended the Constitution/By laws and moved on from that point.

On June 21, 2001, the partnership met with 5 members present. The spiritual lesson was given on Eve, and pointed out that Eve used poor judgement by thinking that she could be independent of God, and how this is still a problem today. The next meeting was held on July 26, 2001. August 16, 2001 meeting was held and the members had an especially pleasant time of fellowship. The group admitted that there have been bumps in the road, but not to worry, at the time, the Partnership had 10 stocks in their portfolio, and had begun to use the stock selection guide to study stocks. Some of our strongest and staunchest members have left the Partnership over the years, but we have managed to pay off the individual valuation amount without having to sell stock. Just as many have left for various reasons, others have joined and continue to "stand by the stuff". Our stock portfolio has grown and we have sought to diversify, taking a risk on one stock which took us older ladies out of our "comfort zone".

The Vineyard Partnership has remained steady and strong as a group. We have recently acquired younger, new members and they have reenergized us to new ideas and innovative activities. A typical agenda contains the following items: A list of attendees at that meeting; a "Call to Order" usually means sharing scripture and offering a prayer to our God.

Beverly gives words of encouragement from the scriptures and then takes us to the throne of grace. The minutes are read from the last meeting to remind us and to keep us on track. Olive gives the financial statement, explanation of documents, and collects the dues. One of the keys to the success of the group is the payment of dues, each month by everyone. It seems, sometimes, a small thing just to pay $35 dues, but it is crucial, for it shows commitment and consistency. Current stock reports are given by the members, one or two per meeting, sometimes using the Stock Selection Guide, sometimes using the narrative from the company. We break for lunch; a lunch which usually looks more like a banquet feast with beautiful napkins, cloth napkins, silverware, fine glasses, and plates that are used with only special people. The table is so attractive, we know that whatever the food, it will taste delicious. Mildred Ferguson prepares the food and the ambiance, it's truly a gift of love and service. After lunch, sometimes during lunch, the Educational and spiritual lesson is presented by the Junior Partner. The date and place for the next meeting is announced and the meeting is Adjourned. At each meeting, the Psalms for that day and one chapter of Proverbs is presented: Example – if we meet on the nineteenth day of the month, we read Psalms 91, 92, 93, 94, and 95 and Proverbs, chapter 19.

Iota Phi Lambda Sorority, Inc. – Alpha & Alpha Tau Chapter
Standing: Pamela, Juanita, Safiyyah, Deborah, Sharon, Joyce, Doris, Sharon Kirby-White, Sarah, Loretta, Eugenia – Seated: Corrine, Naomi, Dorothy, Amy

Arlene Mays-Johnson,
Friend, Photographer

Vineyard Partnership Group – Investment Club Sara,
Marilyn, Beverly, Naomi, Olive, Tanya & Alicia

Chicagoland Christian Women's Conference (CCWC) LouDella, Jackie, Belle, Beverly, Naomi, Jennifer, Betty, Sara, Sharon, Olive

Chapter Eleven

My Favorite Things

You can tell much about a person by the books he owns, or reads, the magazines to which he subscribes, the movies he watches, the music he listens to, the friends he has, the jokes he tells, and the things that make him laugh. By looking at these things, you can tell whether or not a person is "a lover of what is good."

These are a few of my favorite things:

Ecclesiastes 3:1-8

To every thing there is a season,
and a time to every purpose under the heaven:
A time to be born, and a time to die;
a time to plant,
And a time to pluck up that which is planted;
A time to kill, and a time to heal;
a time to break down, and a time to build up;
A time to weep, and a time to laugh;
a time to mourn, and a time to dance;
A time to cast away stones, and a time to gather stones together;
a time to embrace, and a time to refrain from embracing;
A time to seek, and a time to lose;
a time to keep, and a time to cast away;
A time to read, and a time to sew;
a time to keep silence, and a time to speak;

A time to love, and a time to hate;
a time of war, and a time for peace.

Holy Bible, King James Version

<u>Scripture</u>

<u>"The Prayer of Jabez"</u>

"And Jabez called
on the God of Israel saying,
'Oh, that You would bless me indeed,
and enlarge my territory,
that Your hand would be with me,
and that You would keep me from evil,
that I may not cause pain!'
so God granted him what
he requested."
I Chronicles 4:10

Significant Others who have made a big difference in my life –

- <u>Ruth Davis Reed</u> –   led me to the Lord
- <u>Sis. Adine Douglas</u> –   a beautiful, enthusiastic, dynamic bible teacher
- <u>Inez Clayton</u> –   a true friend
- * <u>Bro. Owbridge Fay Gall</u> –   my spiritual mentor; I looked up to him as a dynamic preacher, and a great Christian man
- <u>Genevieve Carter</u> –   responsible for my very first teaching position at the Reavis School.
- <u>Elizabeth Reckley</u> –   who, in her quiet way, was a source of strength and encouragement.

- <u>Sharon Tang</u> – my daughter who has been one who honored me by following in my footsteps – letting me know that she admired my profession and the work that I was doing. She is not aware of how much I appreciate her.

- <u>Sis. Lucy Lewis</u> – who has been the epitome of what I wanted to be as a teacher. She was my example of what a teacher <u>should</u> be –

5 Power Principles

- P – prayer – our response to God is intimate and is driven by need
- O – obey – do not grieve the Holy Spirit.

  obey the urgings of the Holy Spirit

  confess disobedience – receive forgiveness
- W – word-filled – your word is a lamp to my feet and a light for my path to give direction to overcome the enemy God will not empower what is not His will
- E – endurance – "For you have need of endurance so that when you have done the will of God, you may receive what was promised." Heb. 10:36 Endurance involves effort.
- R – Resist Satan – "Submit therefore to God. Resist the devil and he will flee from you."

Ecclesiastes 12 – the chapter on aging

Proverbs 24 – chapter of the "old"

I Thessalonians 5 – Spiritual "CPR"

C – confession
P – petition verses 7-10
R – renewal verses 10-19
    restoration
    recommitment

- Three things in life that, once gone, never come back:

  1. Time
  2. Words
  3. Opportunity

- Three things in life that can destroy a person:

  1. Anger
  2. Pride
  3. Unforgiveness

- Three things in life that you should never lose:

  1. Hope
  2. Peace
  3. Honesty

- Three things in life that are most valuable:

  1. Love
  2. Family & Friends
  3. Kindness

- Three things in life that are never certain:

  1. Fortune
  2. Success
  3. Dreams

- Three things that make a person—

  1. Commitment
  2. Sincerity
  3. Hard work

- Three things that are truly constant - - -
  <u>Father</u>, <u>Son</u>, <u>Holy Spirit</u>

To be a Soul winner learn the

Roman Road

- Fact of Sin – Romans 3:23
- Penalty of Sin – Romans 6:23

- Penalty Must be Paid – Romans 14:12
- Penalty Has Been Paid – Romans 5:8

- Salvation is a Gift – Romans 6:23
- Gift Must Be Accepted – Romans 10:13
- Assurance of Salvation – Romans 10:9, 10

"The Guy In The Glass"

When you get what you want in your struggle for self
And the world makes you king for a day,
Just go to a mirror and look at yourself
And see what that man has to say.
For it isn't your father or mother or wife
Whose judgement upon you must pass,
The fellow whose verdict counts most in your life
Is the one staring back from the glass.
Some people might think you're a straight-shooting chum
And call you a wonderful guy.
But the man in the glass says you're only a bum
If you can't look him straight in the eye.
He's the fellow to please, never mind all the rest
For he's with you clear to the end,
And you've passed your most dangerous test
If the guy in the glass is your friend.
You may fool the whole world down the pathway of yours
And get pats on the back as you pass
But your final reward will be heartache and tears
If you've cheated the man in the glass.
By Peter Dale Wimbrow, Sr.
This poem was written in 1934 by Peter "Dale" Wimbrow, Sr. His children,
Sallydale Wimbrow and Peter Dale Wimbrough, Jr. give permission to use
this poem if proper credit is given to him. Mr. Wimbrow, Sr. wanted his
work to be a gift to the world.

<u>Some of My Favorite Things</u>

- fishnet stockings
- sexy shoes
- long skirts, long dresses
- beautiful broaches, pins
- elegant scarves
- clothes - black
- clothes - white

My Own Personal "Witticisms"

This too will pass.

My two little badnesses!

He's sitting there looking like a "whipper will"!

You are solid gold.

He doesn't know his behind from a whistle.

Thank you.

When someone does something nice for you,
<u>always</u> say "Thank you."

May God bless you and keep you in
His tender care.

If God closes a door, He opens a window.

"Luv you"

You must be outta your cotton-picking mind!

<u>Mary Mitchell</u>

Mary Mitchell's column dated June 16, 2002 really caught my eye. The article opened with words from Zora Neal Hurston's book, "<u>Their Eyes Were Watching God</u>" –

> "Ships at a distance have every man's wish on board. For some they come in with the tide. For others they sail forever on the horizon, never out of sight, never landing until the Watcher turns his eyes away in resignation, his dreams mocked to death by Time. That is the life of men. 'Now, women forget all those things they don't want to remember, and remember everything they don't want to forget. The dream is the truth. Then they act and do things accordingly."

Mary Mitchell, as a woman, and talking about getting older says: "Sure, I can now laugh about the foolish mistakes I've made and be grateful that I didn't 'land in a ditch'. (Using a metaphor, Mary continues) But the highway doesn't stretch out before me like it did in my youth . . . Faced with my dream, I was seized by a middle-aged impulse (to buy a SAAb-convertible) and my checkbook was in mortal danger." She bought a used SAAb and finished her column with these words: "I will never have my perfect life. But darn it, I can drive down the highway with the sun on my face. On a summer day, I can see blue skies and billowy clouds and watch the stars dance at night. Living means never arriving. <u>Now is my time to enjoy the ride</u>."

I love this!

- JOY   "O"   means nothing comes between my Lord & me!
  ↓ ↓
  Jesus you

- David – a man after God's own heart. I Sam. 13:14

- St. Luke is a good book to read on models of women:
  chapter 13:10-17; chapter 15;
  chapter 18; chapter 11:27

- The conversion of a soul is a miracle of a moment,
  But the growth of a saint is the task of a lifetime!

- 3 Waves that changed peoples' lives:
  1) Agricultural Wave (before 1600's)
  2) Industrial Revolution Wave (1600's)
  3) Computer – Electronics Wave (1960's)
                    (Space Wave)

- God made man without a woman or man
                    (Adam)
  God made man without a man
                    (Jesus Christ)
  God made man with a man & a woman

- There can be no <u>conquests</u>
  without <u>conflicts</u> – Bro. T. Michael Flowers

- God judgeth the righteous, and God is angry with the wicked every day. Psalm 7:11

- What kind of an influence do we have on people?

- 3 kinds of bones in the church

1) wishbones	20% of
2) jaw bones	the people
3) back bones – (workers)	do 80%
which "bones" are you?	of the work

- "3:16" verses in New Testament:

Matt 3:16 –   And Jesus when he was baptized, went up straightway out of the water;

Mark 3:16 –   And Simon he surnamed Peter;

Luke 3:16 –   John answered, saying unto them all, I indeed baptize you with water; but one mightier than I cometh, the latchet of whose shoes I am not worthy to unloose; he shall baptize you with the Holy Spirit and with fire.

John 3:16 –   For God so loved the world that he gave his only begotten Son, that whosoever believeth in him should not perish but have everlasting life.

Acts 3:16 –   And his name, through faith in his name, hath made this man strong, whom ye see and know; yea the faith . . . which is by him hath given him this perfect soundness in the presence of you all.

I Cor. 3:16 –   Know ye not that ye are the temple of God, and that the Spirit of God dwelleth in you?

Eph. 3:16 –   That he would grant you, according to the riches of his glory, to be strengthened with might by the Spirit in the inner man.

Col. 3:16 –   Let the word of Christ dwell in you richly, in all wisdom teaching and admonishing one another, in psalms and hymns and spiritual songs singing with grace in your hearts to the Lord.

II Tim. 3:16 –   All scripture is given by inspiration of God, and is profitable for doctrine, for reproof, for correction, for instruction in righteousness.

I Tim. 3:16 –   And without controversy great is the mystery of godliness: God was manifest in the flesh, justified in the Spirit, seen of angels, preached unto the nations, believed on in the world, received up into glory.

I Peter 3:16 –   Having a good conscience, that, whereas they speak evil of you, as of evil-doers, they may be ashamed that falsely accuse your good manner of life in Christ.

I John 3:16 –   By this perceive we the love of God, because he laid down his life for us; and we ought to lay down our lives for the brethren.

Mae West is included because I like her! Everyone knows who Mae West was, but I like her because she was sensitive to the disfranchised, the gay actors, and the African Americans at a time when it was extremely unpopular to do so. She patterned her first vaudeville act after a black entertainer. Her one line quotes are "laugh out loud" hilarious!

- You only live once, but if you do it right, once is enough.
- I generally avoid temptation unless I can't resist it.
- Between two evils, I always pick the one I never tried before.
- When I'm good, I've very good, but when I'm bad, I'm better.
- Ladies who play with fire must remember that smoke gets in their eyes.
- It's not the men in your life that matters, it's the life in your men.
- I'm single because I was born that way.
- Cultivate your curves – they may be dangerous but they won't be avoided.
- Too much of a good thing can be wonderful!
- Those who are easily shocked should be shocked more often.
- I never worry about diets. The only carrots that interest me are the number you get in a diamond.
- All discarded lovers should be given a second chance, but with someone else.
- I never said it would be easy, I only said it would be worth it.
- I used to be Snow White, but I drifted.
- If a little is great, and a lot is better, then way too much is just about right.
- Is that a gun in your pocket, or are you just happy to see me?
- You are never too old to become younger!

A little known fact about Mae West is she fought successfully for the inclusion of Duke Ellington's orchestra in her film, "Belle of the Nineties". Never before had a white singer shared the screen so democratically with black musicians. But she was ahead of her time in racial, as well as sexual matters – having written plays dealing with everything from interracial love to homosexuality. In one of her films, "Going to Town," Mae West was hilarious. In the film, a suitor vowed he would give up half of his life for just one kiss: She said, "See me tomorrow. I'll kiss you twice."

Water

I've read, years ago, that water is mentioned more often than any other natural resource in the bible. It was very important in the Near East because water was scarce. To deal with the problem, the Egyptians irrigated their lands from the annual Nile flooding, and the people of Israel depended upon seasonal rains, dew, and springs. They determined the location of their towns by the availability of a water supply. Deep wells were dug in arid areas, and both towns and individuals dug cisterns to conserve rain water. Scripture uses water as a symbol of salvation and its attendant blessings. Crossing the Red Sea symbolized Israel's initial deliverance from Egypt, the provision of water from the rock illustrated the daily refreshing supply for them in the desert. Jeremiah lamented that the people of his day had forsaken God, the "fountain of living waters," and had dug "broken cisterns" of their own devices that held "no water." Isaiah spoke often of water as spiritual refreshment. Jesus promised that He would provide an abundant supply of living water to those who believed in Him. In Revelation, water symbolizes blessings of the redeemed in the New Jerusalem. Isaiah said, "with joy shall ye draw water out of the wells of salvation." Water is actually plural, as is "wells", reminding us of the abundant supply. God's redeemed people can draw repeatedly from their salvation in Christ, and the wells will never run dry. This is a source of joy to all Christians.

What's On My Bookshelf – (Just a Few)

Our God Is Awesome – Tony Evans
Selected Poems – Gwendolyn Brooks.
Early Novels & Stories – James Baldwin
Collected Essays – James Baldwin
Faith Lift – Babbie Mason
Harold Washington – A Political Biography
All of John Steinbeck Books – Series of 6
Mark Twain's Books – Series of 6
Woman Thou Art Loosed! – T.D. Jakes
Ernest Hemingways' Books – Series of 6
The Great Thoughts – George Seldes
In His Own Words – Nelson Mandela
The Poetry of Robert Frost
Robert Coles – 5 Volumes of "Children In Crisis"
Wealth of Wisdom – Camille O. Cosby & Renee Poussaint
The Audacity of Hope – Barack Obama
The 21 Irrefutable Laws of Leadership – John Maxwell
J.R.R. Tolkien – Series of 3
Crowns, Jewels, Queens – Michael Cunningham

Heart of a Woman – Maya Angelou,
Maya Angelou – Series of 7 books
Lend Me Your Ears – Greatest Speeches in History – William Safire
The Collected Poems of Langston Hughes – Arnold Rampersad
The Knowledge of the Holy – A. W. Tozer
Wrapped In Rainbows – The Life of Zora Neale Hurston – by Valerie Boyd
Charles Stanley Series – 4 books
Gifted Hands – Ben Carson
The Classic Slave Narratives – Henry Louis Gates, Jr.
The Black 100 – Columbus Salley
Peace With God – Billy Graham
I Dream A World – Brian Lanker
20th Century Chicago – Adrienne Drell
My American Journey – Colin Powell
At Canaan's Edge – America in the King Years – 1965-68 by Taylor Branch
Black – A Celebration of a Culture – Deborah Willis
The Encyclopedia of African-American Heritage – Susan Altman
Just As I Am – The Autobiography of Billy Graham
The Century – Peter Jennings & Todd Brewster
A History of the World in the Twentieth Century – J.A.S. Grenville
The Best of Norman Rockwell – Tom Rockwell
Born to Rebel – Benjamin E. Mays
Roots – Alex Haley
Pride & Prejudice – Jane Austen

Women writers in the Early Years:

1) Phillis Wheatley (1753 - 1784)
   In her own words, "In every human breast, God has implanted a principle, which we call love of freedom; it is impatient of oppression and pants for deliverance. I will assert that same principle lives in us."
2) Sojourner Truth (1797-1883)
   Unlike Phillis Wheatley, most slaves faced endless days of labor and harsh treatment. Slaves who showed defiance or disobedience were subjected to severe beatings and other savage acts of punishment. Many risked their lives by running away. Among those who ran was the bold and brave woman who came to be known as Sojourner Truth. Sojourner Truth was born in 1797 and her name was "Isabella". In 1843, while working as a maid in New

York City, Sojourner became convinced that she had been called to go out into the world and "travel about the land spreading truth to the people." Changing her name to Sojourner Truth, she became a preacher.

The horrors of slavery are known today because slaves passed stories on through "oral tradition" of story telling. This helped preserve the history and culture until the day when someone could write them down. Writing is especially important.

The following women carried on the story-telling with the printed word during the Civil War Years and Reconstruction:

Civil War Women Writers.

1. Harriet Jacobs (1813-1897)
2. Frances E. W. Harper (1825-1911)
3. Ida B. Wells-Barnett (1862-1931)
4. Jessie Redmon Fauset (1884-1961)
5. Zora Neale Hurston (1891-1960)
6. Alice Moore Dunbar-Nelson (1875-1935)
7. Dorothy West (1907-1998)
8. Ann Petry (1911-1997)
9. Margaret Walker Alexander (1915-1998)

I admired these writers for their courage, dedication, and determination. They were vigilant as they sought to tell their stories. Their stories and ideas helped to make American literature great. These women of distinction by speeches, plays, and in novels and poetry spoke out against injustice, and told stories about the people and places they loved, and in turn, imagined the possibilities of a bright future.

Some of My Favorite Old Movie Stars & Their Movies

• Spencer Tracy – he made "Broken Arrow" and "Guess Who's Coming To Dinner"
• Henry Fonda – "My Darling Clementine"

In the 1940's, the movies were a big part of my young life. I saw them all and admired the actors that starred in them. Humphrey Bogart was the highest paid actor during that period. One of my favorites was "Casablanca (1943)", also starring Ingrid Bergman who was an outstanding actress. I saw every movie she made at that period in movie history. Cary Grant made "Notorious" in 1946, also with Ingrid Bergman. It was a captivating movie that I have watched dozens of times over the years. Bette Davis, my all time favorite movie star, made "Dark Victory" (1940's) and "All About Eve" (1950). James Cagney, who somehow reminded me of my dad, made "Yankee Doodle Dandy", 1942 and "White Heat", 1949. Gary Cooper made "High Noon" in 1952, with Grace Kelly. Ingrid Bergman, like Bette Davis, was fascinating to watch on the screen. I loved her in "Casablanca" and "For Whom The Bell Tolls", and of course, "Notorious". Elizabeth Taylor's "A Place in the Sun" in 1951 made a big impact on my physche; it stayed "in my head" long after the end of the movie. The movie was sad, but beautifully telling the tragic end to very bad choices.

Clint Eastwood, who I don't care for today, made excellent movies from the 1970's through the 1990's. Some of my favorites were: "Play Misty For Me" – a terrifying movie, very suspenseful telling of obsession with love and its' terrible consequences; "the "Dirty Harry" movies; "Unforgiven", and "In the Line of Fire."

<u>My Personal Favorites</u>

"Godfather I & II" – Marlon Brandon, Al Pacino
"Titanic" both versions – one with Barbara Stanwyck and Clifton Webb and Robert Wagner and of course the one with Kate Winslet and Leonardo Di Caprio.
"Steel Magnolias" – Shirley McClain, Julia Roberts, Sally Fields
"The Prince of Tides" – Barbra Streisand & Nick Nolte
"Ten Commandments" – Charlton Heston
"Samson & Delilah" – with Victor Mature & Hedy Lamarr"
"Gone With The Wind" – Clark Gable & Vivian Leigh & Hattie McDaniel
"To Kill a Mockingbird" – Gregory Peck
"The Way We Were" – Barbra Streisand, Robert Redford
"Funny Girl" – Barbra Streisand, Omar Sheriff
"The Razor's Edge" – Tyrone Power, Gene Tierney, Clifton Webb
"Legends of the Fall" – Brad Pitt, Anthony Hopkins, Julia Ormond
"The Sound of Music" – Julie Andrews, Christopher Plummer
"My Fair Lady" – Audrey Hepburn, Rex Harrison

The movies that were made in the 1930's, I saw later in my youth, maybe when I was about 10 or 11 years old. I went to the movies a lot as a kid, so I saw just about every movie made in the 30's. There are many movies I enjoyed in the 60's and 70's. It is too many to name. Many of them I watched over and over again.

<u>Favorite Black Movies</u>

1950 •	The Jackie Robinson Story:	Jackie Robinson, Ruby Dee, Minor Watson, Joel Fluellen, Richard Lane
1954 •	Carmen Jones:	Dorothy Dandridge, Harry Belafonte
1961 •	A Raisin in the Sun:	Sidney Poitier, Claudia McNeil, Ruby Dee, Diana Sands
1967 •	Guess Who's Coming to Dinner:	Sidney Poitier, Spencer Tracy, Katherine Hepburn, Katherine Houghton, Cecil Kellaway, Roy E. Glenn, Beah Richards, Virginia Christine, Isabell Sanford
1971 •	Shaft:	Richard Roundtree, Moses Gunn
1972 •	Buck & the Preacher:	Sidney Poitier, Harry Belafonte, Ruby Dee
1973 •	Coffy:	Pam Grier, Booker Bradshaw
1974 •	Claudine:	Diahann Carroll, James Earl Jones, Lawrence Hilton Jacobs
1975 •	Cooley High:	Glynn Turman, Lawrence Hilton-Jacobs, Jackie Taylor, Garrett Morris, Cynthia Davis
1985 •	The Color Purple:	Danny Glover, Whoopi Goldberg, Margaret Avery, Oprah Winfrey, Willard Pugh, Akosua Busia, Adolph Caesar, Rae Dawn Chong
1989 •	Lean on Me:	Morgan Freeman, Beverly Todd, Robert Guillaume, Robin Bartlett, Lynne Thigpen

1989 •	Glory:	Matthew Broderick, Denzel Washington, Morgan Freeman, Raymond St. Jacques
1991 •	Boyz' N the Hood:	Cuba Gooding, Jr., Ice Cube, Morris Chestnut, Larry Fishburne, Angela Bassett, Nia Long, Tyra Ferrell, Desi Arnez Hines, Regina King, Whitman Mayo.
1992 •	Bebe's Kids:	Voices – Faison Love, Vanessa Bell Calloway, Wayne Collins, Jonell Green, Marques Houston, Tone Loc, Nell Carter, Myra J.
1992 •	Malcolm X:	Denzel Washington, Angela Bessett, Albert Hines, Al Freeman, Jr., Delroy Lindo, Spike Lee, Theresa Randle, Kate Vernon, Lonette McKee,
1995 •	Waiting to Exhale:	Angela Bassett, Whitney Houston, Loretta Divine Lela Rochon, Gregory Hines, Dennis Haysbert, Mykelti Williamson, Michael Beach, LEON, Wendell Pierce, Donald Faison, Jeffrey D. Sams, Starletta Du Pois, Jazz Raycole
1997 •	Eve's Bayou:	Jurnee Smollett, Samuel L. Jackson, Lynn Whitfield, Meagan Good, Debbie Morgan, Jake Smollett, Ethel Ayler, Diahann Carroll, Vondi Curtis Hall, Roger Guenveur Smith, Lisa Nicole Carson, Branford Marsalis, Afonda Colbert, Tamara Tunie
1999 •	The Best Man:	Taye Diggs, Nia Long, Morris Chestnut, Harold Perrineau, Terrence Howard, Sanaa Lathan, Monica Calhoun, Melissa De Sousa, Victoria Dillard, Regina Hall

And three of Tyler Perry's films for their strong story line
and deep moral lessons:

2005 • Diary of a Mad Black Woman: Kimberly Elise, Steve Harris, Tyler
Perry, Shemar Moore, Lisa Marcos,
Cicely Tyson, Gary Anthony Sturgis

2007 • Why did I get married?:   Tyler Perry, Janet Jackson, Jill Scott,
Sharon Leal, Malik Yoba

2013 • Temptation: Jurnee Smollett Bell, Lance Gross,
Kim Kardashian, Vanessa Williams,
Robbie Jones, Renee Taylor, Brandy
Norwood.

Music

In <u>1993</u>, Janet Jackson was popular, Barbra Streisand's music was popular
and provided soundtracks for several movies. Whitney Houston sang "I'll
Always Love You" and the "Bodyguard" movie soundtrack "Baby face"
Edmonds was popular, as was Bobby Short.
My favorite musicians →(I love all of their music:)
Dinah Washington
Frank Sinatra
Sammy Davis, Jr.
Aretha Franklin
Kenny Rogers
Impressions

Gospel Music – Various Artists
Christmas Songs – Johnny Mathis
Old Negro Spirituals

<u>Absolute Favorites</u>
(All Old)

The Love I Lost – Harold Melvin & the Blue Notes
Inner City Blues – Marvin Gaye
What's Going On – Marvin Gaye
Having A Party – Sam Cooke

Oh Girl – The Chi Lites
Hold On I'm Coming – Sam & Dave
You Are Everything – The Stylistics
The Thrill Is Gone – B. B. King
Tell Me Something Good – Chaka Khan
Always & Forever – Heatwave
Kiss and Say Goodbye – The Manhattans
For Your Precious Love – Jerry Butler
Reunited – Peaches & Herb
You Make Me Feel Brand New – The Stylistics
That's what friends are for – Dionne Warwick
Rainy Night In Georgia – Brook Benton
I'll Be Around – The Spinners
A Change Is Gonna Come – Sam Cooke

Naomi

There are lyrics from a song in Grace & Glory's Believer's Hymn Book entitled "Naomi". I was attracted to it because of the title, but when I read the words, it is about "Prayer". I wanted to examine it more, so I looked at the author, James Montgomery. He lived from 1771-1854. He was born in Irvine, Ayrshire, Scotland where his father was a minister in the Moravian Church. When he was five years old, the family moved to the Moravian settlement at Gracehill. In 1783, his parents were sent off to the West Indies as missionaries leaving him at the Moravian settlement at Bracehill near Ballymena, County Antrim, Ireland where his education started. At the age of seven, he was sent off to begin his seminary training at Fulneck Seminary Yorkshire, and while there made a public profession of religion by uniting with the Moravian Church. Not long after they had gone, his parents died; his father is buried in Barbados, and his mother in Tobago. He supported himself until 1792 when he became assistant to the auctioneer and bookseller and printer of the Sheffield Register. In 1794, the auctioneer left England to avoid political prosecution. Montgomery took over the Sheffield Register and changed the name to Sheffield Iris, and continued to edit for 32 years. In 1797, he published a volume of poems, Prison Amusements, so named because some were written during his prison stay. In his youth, he had strayed from the church, but at his own request he was readmitted into the Moravian congregation at Fulneck when forty-three years of age. Thereafter he became an avid worker for missions and an active member of the Bible Society. About the same time, the English Church Missionary Society and the Baptist Mission Society had formed, evangelism in England had started in a big way, and it is apparent in Montgomery's hymns. Moreover the English Moravian church traces its' roots back to the Moravian Missionary Center in Hernnhut, Germany; it was the Moravian Society that sent Montgomery's parents to the West Indies.

He wrote 400 hymns in his career, approximately 100 are still in use; some are recognizable: "Hail to the Lord's Anointed", "Angels From the Realms of Glory," "Prayer is the Souls' Sincere Desire," "Lift Up Your Heads," and "For Ever with the Lord." Montgomery also wrote secular poetry, lecturing at the Royal Institution. He also published a volume of poems many of which denounced slavery. His poems brought him considerable popularity.

He never married and died quietly in his sleep, a day after he had written his last hymn, April 30, 1854 at age 83, at his home in Sheffield where his career and works accorded him the honor of a public funeral in that city.

In that hymn, "Prayer is the Soul's Sincere Desire" (Naomi), James Montgomery uses imagery of fire, sigh, tear; he contrasts "infant speech" and "sublimest strain." In an ironic twist, prayer is the "breath" of the dying one, by which he is ushered into the presence of God. It was so interesting to research the life of this very important man who gave us such beautiful hymns.

Oprah's "You in six words –

> Might as well eat that
> cookie.

> I have time to fix this.   Was hot.
>   Raised kids.
>   Lost cool.

Fat. Thin. Fat.   Every 20 years,
Thin. Fat. Thin.   I reinvent myself

Life gives lemons but
no juicer

Old too soon smart too
late

I live my best life now

Recipe for failure
changed my ingredients

I've made all the best
mistakes

Every problem has a
creative solution.

I refused to be a victim

Falling gracefully.
Hoping there's a
mattress.

The good child – until
I wasn't.

President Barack Obama

Barack Obama has been a hard-working, community minded, conscientious man. He moved from effecting change locally, in Chicago, to being a United States Senator from Illinois. Even before his fame, he had a sensitivity and a concern for people in need – black, white, latino, asian, whatever. He seemed to always be on the right side of history as he voted in the Senate. When he was elected President of the United States, first African-American to be so honored, he vowed to change the world. President Obama "hit the ground running" after his Inauguration in January, 2009, trying to help the country. He sought to keep his campaign promises and he sought to govern by working with the Senate and the House. He tried to appeal to the Republicans, as well as, to some in his own Democratic Party, to work together in a non-partisan way to move the country forward. He was rebuffed each time. Never the less, he accomplished much by using his intellectual skills, his compassion for people, and his presidential powers to get things done. From Day 1, the President worked tirelessly to end the war in Iraq, expand access to health care to all Americans, and implement an economic recovery program that has created nearly 3 million jobs.

President Obama's support among African American is as strong as ever, with 96% who voted for him in 2008. There are now 30 million new Americans in health care, 7 million are African American. We are all in this situation together. When the automotive industry was revived, blacks benefited, and whites and Latinos, as well. When President Obama raised Pell grants for students to help lower tuition costs, it helped all of us. When he came into office, banks collapsed. The automatic industry collapsed.

There was a lack of access to health care. The War in Iraq was expanding. President Obama's administration began to change the direction of these issues.

President Obama's support for gay marriage has alienated some African Americans, but no one can be a one-issue voter.

President Obama has succeeded against great odds since his first election in November, 2008. He has stood tall and remained steadfast throughout the years of his presidency. He and his beautiful, strong, smart first lady, Michelle Obama have made us proud and happy to be African American. We continue to pray for his family's safety, as well as, his own. I pray that "no weapon formed against him shall prosper." He has been blessed as he has sought to do what is best for the country. I don't always agree with him, but I know he has very big decisions to make that no one can really understand, so I continue to lift him up in prayer.

Some of these right wing Republicans call themselves "Christians," but according to the Word of God, we show that we are Christians by our love. I detect no love among this group, at all, not in the least. Some of them are prominent and have had a positive impact upon my spiritual growth down through the years. What has changed? The gift of millions of dollars to them and from them to "demonize" this black President. They have a hatred of him that is described (by me, only my opinion) as extreme, and un Christian-like. It reminds me of what I've read in Black History of how the white masters used the Bible to try and justify slavery and their utter disregard for black people and their families. Let me not condemn all for, I have beautiful friends and family who are white and/or Republican.

These "right-wingers" are men (and women) who know the Word of God and are responsible for leading others to salvation through faith in the Lord Jesus Christ. But, they have no monopoly on righteousness; they don't have a monopoly on the Gospel. God is no respecter of persons. He blesses us with His truth, also. He opens up the Word to us, also. He speaks to us through His Holy Spirit, also. God "lifted Pres. Obama up" to that position, and God will keep him by His might in that position.

I have searched the scriptures for some answers to my questions and for peace in my convictions. I feel that a proper respect for authority honors God. Romans 13 speaks to that point. As we let God's Spirit teach us, we can have a healthy attitude toward government. "It's for our good, the testimony of our faith, and most of all for God's honor."

President John F. Kennedy made the following quote about terrorism on September 25, 1961 at his Address to the United Nations:

"Terror is not a new weapon. Throughout history it has been used by those who could not prevail, either by persuasion or example. But inevitably they fail, either because men are not afraid to die for a life worth living, or because the terrorists themselves came to realize that free men cannot be frightened by threats, and that aggression would meet its own response. And it is in the light of that history that every nation today should know, be he friend or foe, that the United States has both the will and the weapons to join free men in standing up to their responsibilities."

A

    LITTLE

        BIT

           ABOUT

              A

                LOT

                  OF

                    THINGS

CHAPTER TWELVE

My Onslaught of "Nines"

Make the most of every sense; glory in all of the pleasures and
beauty which the world reveals to you . . . Helen Keller

The real things haven't changed. It is still best to be honest and truthful;
to make the most of what we have; to be happy with simple pleasures;
and have courage when things go wrong . . . Laura Ingalls Wilder

Be careful how you treat people on the way up, they
are the same people you meet on the way down.

Beauty is from the inside out.

If you keep doing what you're doing, you'll
keep getting what you're getting.

Leave no stone unturned.

There but for the grace of God go I.

I never knew a night so black
Light failed to follow on its track.
I never knew a storm so gray; It failed to have its clearing day.
I never knew such black despair, that there was not a rift somewhere.

I never knew an hour so drear
Love could not fill it full of cheer! . . . John Kendrick Bangs

The most solid comfort one can fall back upon is the thought
that the business of one's life is to help in some small way
to reduce the sum of ignorance, degradation and misery
on the face of this beautiful earth . . . George Elliot

Nine Friends Who Have Given Gifts of Love, Inclusion, and Books
Over Many Years

1.) Felecia Thompson
2.) Sheryl Stevens
3.) Linda Williams
4.) Loretta Gilbert
5.) Doris Murry
6.) Allie Thompson
7.) Dorothy White
8.) Sara Hennings
9.) Juanita Stem

Nine Movie Zingers

- "Frankly, my dear, I don't give a damn." – Clark Gable, Gone With the Wind, 1939
- "Here's looking at you, kid." Humphrey Bogart, Casablanca, 1942
- "I'm going to make him an offer he can't refuse." Marlon Brando, The Godfather, 1972
- "Fasten your seatbelts. It's going to be a bumpy night." Bette Davis, All About Eve, 1950
- "Go ahead, make my day." Clint Eastwood, Sudden Impact, 1983
- "May the Force be with you." Star Wars, 1977, Alex McCrindle
- "Made it, Ma!"
  "Top of the World!"
  James Cagney, White Heat, 1949
- "Love means never having to say you're sorry." Ali McGraw, Love Story, 1970
- "They call me Mister Tibbs!" Sidney Poitier, 1967
  In the Heat of the Night

Nine Scripture Verses ThatEveryone Should Know By Heart

1.	Genesis 1:1	In the beginning God created the heavens and the earth.
2.	John 1:1	In the beginning was the Word, and the Word was with God, and the Word was God.
3.	John 1:14	And the Word was made flesh, and dwelt among us (and we beheld his glory, the glory as of the only begotten of the Father) full of grace and truth.
4.	John 3:16	For God so loved the world that he gave his only begotten Son, that whosoever believeth in Him should not perish, but have everlasting life.
5.	Romans 6:23	For the wages of sin is death, but the gift of God is eternal life through Jesus Christ, our Lord.
6.	Hebrews 4:12	For the word of God is quick, and powerful, and sharper than any two edged sword, piercing even to the dividing asunder of soul and spirit, and of the joints and marrow, and is a discerner of the thoughts and intents of the heart.
7.	Romans 10:9	That if thou shalt confess with thy mouth the Lord Jesus, and shalt believe in thine heart that God hath raised him from the dead, thou shalt be saved.
8.	Romans 10:10	For with the heart man believeth unto righteousness; and with the mouth confession is made unto salvation.
9.	II Timothy 3:16	All scripture is given by inspiration of God, and is profitable for doctrine, for reproof, for correction, for instruction in righteousness . . .

Nine Favorite Jokes

1.) Why are people from the Windy City so bashful?

- Because it's Chi-town.

2.) What do you call a house between two other houses in the fields of Illinois?

- Middle House on the Prairie.

3.) Do you know what's strange about Chicago?

- Chicago Cubs Don't grow up to be Chicago Bears.

4.) . . . "But it's amazing the way people can get the wrong impression. One Russian official showed me a picture of the starving people in America. People without shoes and nothing to eat, absolutely desperate. And I couldn't argue with him . . . it was a picture of the bus station in Las Vegas. (Bob Hope)

5.) Truman could shake your hand and measure you for a suit at the same time. (Bob Hope)

6.) Budget Director David Stockton blabbed that Reagan's economic program was designed to help the rich. Well, if the Republicans won't help them, who will? (Bob Hope)

7.) Clinton loves to make long speeches. In fact, this will be the first inaugural address with an intermission. (Bob Hope)

8.) We came in here on a wing and a prayer. I had the wing. That's because all the girls on board told me I didn't have a prayer. (Bob Hope)

9.) I was in school the last time Halley's Comet appeared and I remember a test we had. It said, "A comet is a star with a tail. Name a famous one." I wrote down, "Rin Tin Tin." (Bob Hope)

Nine Examples of Faith

(1) • God used a man by the name of Paul, who hated the early church and persecuted Christians because of their faith. After his conversion, God used the apostle Paul to carry the message of the gospel, not only to the Jews but also to the Gentiles. Acts 9

(2) • God chose an unwed, teenage girl to be the mother of our Lord and Savior, Jesus Christ. Luke 1

(3) • A little boy named David slew a great big giant named Goliath with a sling and a stone. I Samuel 17

(4) • God greatly used Rahab, a known prostitute in the city of Jericho and one who was rejected by society. Rahab had two spies in her home. These men were on a mission from God. Joshua 2

(5) • God used Moses, a man with a speech impediment, to lead an entire nation of people to the promised land. Exodus 13

(6) • God defied the laws of nature to bless two older persons, the father of faith, Abraham, at one hundred years old, and his wife, Sarah, at ninety, to become first-time parents. Genesis 21

(7) • God caused Gideon and a mere three hundred fighting men to confuse and defeat thousands of Midianites without even drawing a weapon. Judges 7

(8) • The mark of a true Christian is not how good we look sitting in the pew in our church attire on Sunday. It is how well we serve others throughout the week."

(9) • "For I am persuaded, that neither death, nor life, nor angels, nor principalities, nor powers, nor things present, nor things to come, nor height, nor depth, nor any other creature, shall be able to separate us from the love of God, which is in Christ Jesus our Lord." Romans 8:38-39

Nine More Favorite Jokes

1.) Doctor, Doctor, I've been fighting and fighting this cold, and it won't go away.
"Never fight a cold. That only makes a cold sore."

2.) It's not the minutes spent at the table that put on weight – "it's the seconds."

3.) Nurse: – There is a man in the outer office with a wooden leg named Smith.
Doctor: "What is the name of his other leg?"

4.) I think it's great to be depressed. "You can behave as badly as you like."

5.) A man is walking along the street when he is brutally beaten and robbed. He lies unconscious, bleeding. While he is lying there, a police officer passes by, but he crosses to the other side of the road without trying to help.
A boy scout troop does the same – as do many pedestrians.
"Finally, a psychologist walks by and runs up to the man. He bends down and says, "Oh, no! Whoever did this needs help."

6.) You know you have bad breath when your dentist leaves the room and sends in a canary.

7.) George was having trouble with a toothache, so he decided to visit the dentist.

"What do you charge for extracting a tooth?"

"Thirty-five dollars," replied the dentist.

"Thirty-five dollars for only two minutes' work?"

"Well," replied the dentist, "if you wish, I can extract it very slowly."

8.) I've decided to stop worrying about what I eat. Why should I give up great food just to be able to spend three extra years in the geriatric ward.

9.) Patient: Doctor, I don't know what's wrong with me. Everything hurts. If I touch my shoulder just here, it hurts. If I touch my leg just here, it hurts. If I touch my leg here, it hurts. And if I touch my head here, it hurts.

Doctor: "It sounds like you've got a broken finger."

Nine More Jokes from Moms Mabley

1. If Elizabeth can run England, I can run America. What has she got that I didn't use to have and where can I get it again?

2. There ain't nothing an old man can do for me but to bring me a message from a young one… I'd rather pay a young mans' fare to California than tell an old man the distance.

3. Love is like playing checkers. You have to know which man to move.

4. Be careful children---don't speed on the highway. Play with your wife, not your life.

5. I don't want nothin' old but some old money. Buy me some young ideas, that's what I'm gonna do with it.

6. Quit it if you can't do nothing with it.

7. Never lose your head, not even for a minute---you need your head. Your brains' in it.

8. Help me make it through the night—if you can make it for half an hour, you're alright with me.

9. If you always do what you always did, you will always get what you always got.

<u>**Nine** References for Information</u>
(Without using the Internet)

1.) Almanac
- tables, charts, graphs, short descriptions, facts

2.) Atlas
- maps, locations, names of geographic land and water forms

3.) Biographical resources
- information about specific people or collection of people

4.) Chronology
- historical events arranged by date and/or year order

5.) Cookbooks
- specific information on food, recipes, and cooking

6.) Dictionary
- origins, pronunciations, and definitions of specific words.

7.) Encyclopedia
- facts on a general range of topics

8.) Indexes
- alphabetical information in periodicals and newspapers

9.) Quotations
- famous sayings from literature and history.

As you know, there are many more, but I love these nine.

Nine Significantly Important Dates That Left An Indelible Imprint On My Mind – And My Heart

1.) August 25, 1925 – A. Phillip Randolph organized the Sleeping Car Porters' Union. At the time, Pullman was the largest single employer of blacks in the country.
2.) April 9, 1939 – Soprano Marian Anderson sang before 75,000 people at the Lincoln Memorial after being refused permission to

perform at Constitution Hall by the Daughters of the American Revolution.

3.) May 31, 1955 – The U.S. Supreme Court ordered the end of school segregation "with all deliberate speed."

4.) February 1, 1960 – Four North Carolina A&T students staged a sit-in at a segregated lunch counter at Woolworth's in Greensboro, N.C.

5.) March 25, 1965 – Dr. Martin Luther King, Jr. led 25,000 people on a five-day march from Selma to Montgomery, Alabama to protest the denial of voting rights to African-Americans.

6.) November 5, 1968 – Shirley Chisholm becomes the first African American woman to be elected to Congress.

7.) December 16, 1976 – President Jimmy Carter appointed Andrew Young to be the first African American Ambassador to the United Nations.

8.) October 19, 1983 – The U.S. Senate, by a vote of 78-22, designated the third Monday in January of each year to be a federal holiday in honor of Dr. Martin Luther King, Jr.

9.) June 15, 1999 – President Bill Clinton presented the Congressional Gold Medal to Rosa Parks.

Nine Favorite Presidents

1. Barack Obama – first black president – smart, articulate, hard working

2. Jimmy Carter – great author, Christian who lives his life as such

3. John F. Kennedy – great orator, powerful words, popular

4. Lyndon Johnson – great civil rights president who stood up for black people

5. Harry Truman – "Give 'em hell, Harry", fearless, bold

6. James Knox Polk – only because my grandfather has his full name – James Knox Polk Jones

7. Abraham Lincoln – signed the Emancipation Proclamation

8. Bill Clinton – hired more black people in his cabinet and during his presidency than any other president

9. Franklin Delano Roosevelt – the very first president of my memory – I remember the excitement in the air when he was running for another term; instituted the social programs to help the poor – programs that still exist today – beloved president who showed concern for the poor and the disenfranchised.

Women's "Place" In Scripture

1.) I Timothy 2:17
2.) I Corinthians 14:33-40
3.) Proverbs 31
4.) II Timothy 2:7-15
5.) Acts 9:2-16
6.) Genesis 3:1-6
7.) Genesis 39
8.) Judges 16
9.) Revelation 2:18-23

Nine
Outstanding Women Who
Made A Difference In The World

These black American women have helped the United States develop into a world leader. Within themselves and in their own way, using their God-given talents, they believed they could change the way we look at the world. They took what they had to give and gave it with all their might. They did not let slavery, discrimination, racism, or indifference keep them from achieving and succeeding.

These nine women that I have selected represent a range of academic and social interests and they have overcome incredible odds to pursue their artistic goals while remaining true to themselves. Their lives provide a shining beacon of hope, determination, and compassion to others.

Woman #1

- Phillis Wheatley (1753-1784), although her life was tragically short, she left an indelible mark on American culture. As a child of seven, she was kidnapped in Senegal, in West Africa, and shipped across the Atlantic Ocean to slavery in the New World. From that "terrible" beginning Phillis emerged less than twenty years later as a poet of incredible grace and insight. By the time of her death, in her early thirties, she would hold the distinction of being the first published African-American poet.
  When one reads her works today, you are struck by their poignant expression of religious faith and her belief in the goodness of

mankind. Writing in heroic couplets, Phillis Wheatley transformed her newfound Christian religious beliefs into poems of redemption and salvation. More than two hundred years after her death, she remains an inspiration to millions of American writers - and especially to the long line of black women who have sought to live up to her literary legacy. She wrote a poem especially for some students at Harvard University in New England. The students were awestruck as she read it to them.

Phillis Wheatley continues today to embody the artistic contribution of black American women. She left a legacy that will survive throughout the ages.

Woman #2

* Mary McLeod Bethune, (1875-1955)
  By the time Mary McLeod Bethune died in 1955. The college she founded in 1904 had educated thousands of young black women; the National Association for the Advancement of Colored People (NAACP), where she once served as vice-president, had become the leading civil rights organization in America. And her work in the highest levels of the U.S. government – during several administrations, including the long Franklin Delano Roosevelt presidency - had sown the seeds for educational and economic gains that black Americans would reap during the rest of the twentieth century.

Mary McLeod Bethune's version of the classic story spans the Reconstruction era and our modern era, from the official end of slavery in America to the dawn of integration and black nationalism.

With a hefty sense of personal dignity, a sharp intellect, and a legendary ego. Mary McLeod Bethune rose from the streets of a tiny South Carolina village to the place of national leaders and international heads of state. She served as key advisor to presidents on matters of race and women and helped the world community devise the United Nations charter during a historic week in San Francisco in 1945. She helped set an agenda for the educational and economic advancements of generations of African Americans to come.

She was sent in 1945 by President Harry S. Truman, to San Francisco, where she consulted with organizers of the United Nations. Along with the educator and sociologist W.E.B. Du Bois, she represented the concerns of black Americans in the coalition of world leaders who included people of color from Europe, Africa, and the Caribbean. While their agenda was received coolly by white members of the United Nations, Mary stood firm. At the end of the conference, she declared that the gathering in San Francisco "is not building the promised land of brotherhood and security and opportunity and peace . . . We still have a long way to go."

The whole nation mourned when Mary McLeod Bethune died unexpectedly of a heart attack in 1955. Her years of service did not go unnoticed, and private and government organizations pitched in to help keep the college and the Mary McLeod Bethune Foundation alive. In 1975, the two story home where she had launced her long career of public service was declared a National Historic Landmark.

Woman #3

• Mahalia Jackson, (1911-1972) earned the title of "the Queen of Gospel Song" during a life of singing and performing spirituals. She grew up in the Deep South, in a strict household headed by her father, a Baptist minister. With the onslaught of the civil rights movement in the late 1950's, Mahalia became a vital part of the demonstrations and activism that brought about revolutionary social changes in America. As a valued friend to notable civil rights figures, like Dr. Martin Luther King, Jr., Jesse Jackson, Sr., Andrew Young, and Medgar Evers, she lent her heavenly voice and strong sense of justice to the historic movement. Her strong voice and deep religious faith required her to contribute to the uplifting of millions of exploited black Americans.

From her base in Chicago, Mahalia could bring together an array of black citizens, politicians, and activists in support of justice and dignity. After the bombing of a Birmingham Church in which four little black girls died, there were several showdowns between police and black Birmingham residents. Mahalia decided to host a concert and rally in the Windy City.

Sure enough, within days of the horrific police actions in Birmingham, Mahalia had gotten together one of the most important rallies of the movement. After a huge gathering at Chicago's Wrigley Field and a motorcade ride to the shores of Lake Michigan, Dr. Martin Luther King, Jr. arrived at a concert planned by Mahalia.

Between Mahalia's performances "around the globe", she contributed her unique talent to the growing civil rights movement. Along with such singers and actors as Lena Horne, Paul Newman, Marlon Brando, and Sammy Davis, Jr., Mahalia entered the fight to end racial discrimination in America. In 1963, she participated in the legendary "March on Washington". She joined thousands of civil rights activists on the Mall in Washington, where Dr. Martin Luther King, Jr. made his historic "I have a Dream" speech. For the years afterward, Mahalia sang for worthy causes. She died in 1972, leaving a void in the "elusive place where entertainment meets social activism." Yet, thanks to recordings of dozens of her concerts, Mahalia's voice and spirit remain a vital part of our cultural history.

Woman #4

- Susan Taylor —rose from an entry-level job as part time beauty editor of a new and unknown magazine to one of the best-known and most influential black women in America. Under her skilled eye, Essence magazine grew into a power house publication with a loyal readership of more than five million black women. It was a long climb, but Susan accomplished it with vigor, dignity, and integrity. Susan Taylor was born on January 23, 1946 to parents, Lawrence and Violet Weekes Taylor. They were Caribbean immigrants who owned a clothing store in Harlem. She excelled at the Catholic Schools she attended, and was also popular among her fellow students and teachers.

At age twenty-four, she discovered that becoming an adult would involve challenges and sacrifices above and beyond anything she had ever experienced. She mustered her resources and set out to find more meaningful work. Her doctor told her that she must immediately reduce the stress in her life. She was stunned.

Walking home from that medical appointment, she thought: "I have no money to ride the bus, let alone take a cab," but she came upon an unexpected source of inspiration. A local church was having an afternoon service, and she decided to attend. At that instant, Susan realized that she could in fact seize control over her life. Sure enough, in a matter of weeks following that eventful day, she had landed a second job.

After seeing a copy of a little-known magazine, Essence, in a local store, Susan went to the publication's offices and applied for a job as a part-time beauty editor. The small publication was just beginning when she was hired, and she began to help turn it into a successful addition to the world of women's magazines.

A lack of a college degree didn't hinder Susan, as her warm and outgoing personality and stylish flair quickly endeared her to her co-workers and the magazine's budding readership. Susan was devoted to the idea that black American women needed to feel that they could accomplish their dreams on their own terms.

Named publisher of Essence shortly thereafter, Susan is one of the few African-American women in United States history to head a successful monthly publication.

As she wrote in her popular column, "In the Spirit", Susan believed in the value of the individual and in the level of commitment, intelligence, and compassion that black women have contributed to the United States.

Woman #5

- Dr. Yvonne Rollerson Abatso was born in Chicago, Illinois and now resides in Dallas, Texas. Formerly she was a faculty counselor and Director of the Women's Center at North Lake College in Dallas. Yvonne graduated from Wheaton College in Wheaton, Illinois and received her PH.D. from the University of Chicago. She has traveled extensively to various parts of the world serving as professor, psychologist and speaker.

Yvonne came to know the Lord Jesus Christ as her savior at a young age and has been active ever since in proclaiming the meaning of that relationship to her contemporaries. She is married to Dr. George Abatso, a surgeon, and has three children.

Yvonne founded an organization of women back in 1961 in Chicago, Illinois. During that year and the following years of the "sixties", much history was being made. It was the year that social, legal, and political movement was taking place with the intent of ending discrimination against African Americans across the United States. The years 1960 and 1961 were the years of the "Freedom Riders" and the "Sit-In movement". Tactics ranged from legal and judicial action to picketing, marches, demonstration, voter registration, and various forms of civil disobedience. One reason for the success of the civil rights' movement was the presence of television cameras that captured the readiness of police to ignore and/or indulge in criminal behavior in order to suppress peaceful civil rights demonstrations. The televised brutality infuriated millions of Americans, who put tremendous pressure on Congress and the White House to pass civil rights legislation.

Although the movement's emphasis on non-violent action drew on the sentiments of Mohandas Gandhi and Henry David Thoreau, the idea of non-violent, passive sacrifice, even to the point of martyrdom, is basic to Christian tradition and was readily accepted by movement leaders, most of whom were Christian ministers. This interweaving of civil rights strategy and Christian religious thought attracted the support of thousands of churches, white as well as black. The nonviolent tactics used by civil rights demonstrators not only attracted widespread religious support but also allowed television cameras to cast them in a heroic light and permitted a minority group (blacks were approximately 10% of the U.S. population) with little economic and political leverage to gain the moral high ground.

Other factors in the movement's success included a strong belief in the integrity of the civil rights leadership and the ability of the leadership to put forth precise, obtainable demands that could be readily met through legal and/or political action. While thousands of whites supported civil rights, the movement grew out of, and was solidly anchored in, "black institutions and organizations, particularly the black churches, the black colleges, and the black civil rights organizations."

Then, with this "backdrop" of history, comes on the scene, Yvonne Rollerson Abatso. She witnessed these happenings across America and was moved to actions of her own. She felt the need to help black women. After much prayer and meditation, Yvonne sought to provide leadership development and outreach for Christian women. It was her concern that women have a forum in which they could apply biblical truths to issues relevant to women and that they could expand beyond their local congregations as they fellowshipped with other Christians. The conference format provided an opportunity for women to share their many diverse gifts with other women. Equally as important was a desire to share Christ with unsaved women and to have an impact on the City of Chicago. Thus was born the "Chicagoland Christian Women's Conference" (CCWC) in 1961 at the Westlawn Gospel Chapel, Chicago, Illinois.

Yvonne believed firmly that growth and maturity develop as believers experience the often painful process of relationship building within the context of agape love. Women needed to be initiators of that process while working together to know Christ more fully and to make Him known more accurately to a needy world. Hence the theme of the conference was/is - "To Know Christ and To Make Him Known". She envisioned that the group process of a small band of women working through their differences, overcoming barriers of personality and that emphasis could demonstrate the love that identifies us as God's people and attract others to become His disciples.

Woman #6

• Mrs. Adine E. Douglas (1920-2005(?) stood beside Yvonne Abatso to help make sure the dream came true. Adine saw that the challenge of the early 1960's that confronted a group of Christian women, was the need to reach out, beyond the boundaries of their local gathering. Sis. Douglas was constrained by the Savior's love and felt compassion for Christian women who were hurting. They were a group of approximately 10 fervent, praying ladies no longer satisfied to be complacent and unconcerned about the other side of the walls. So, with a zeal to share Christ, assist each other in a fellowship based upon God's infallible Word, they began. They met initially in various homes praying and planning for the day when Christian women would join strengths, spiritual gifts and resources in order to pursue the course which would 'keep the unity of the Spirit in the bond of peace.'

It was not easy for Adine and Yvonne. There were areas of indecisions, some disappointments and some dedicated ladies felt that the type of meetings requiring hotel accommodations for conferences and retreats might not yield the desired results. Nevertheless, they obeyed the guidance of the Holy Spirit and because of consistent, faithful 'sowing and watering', the "Chicagoland Christian Women's Conference" (CCWC) realized that God had given the increase.

The Chicagoland Christian Women's Conference provided the impetus for women to gain success in their families, in their churches, and on their jobs.

Woman #7

- Mrs. Beverly Pannell Yates helped to found the Chicagoland Christian Women's Conference in 1961. She was a board member from it's inception and served as president many times – from 1968-1970, from 1979-1982, and from 1986-1990. Beverly helped develop programs for "CCWC" that included seminars, Bible studies, workshops and retreats for some 2000 women. The organization quickly grew from a small group of dedicated, Christian women into a large group that included hundreds of women. It was a new concept in 1961 to bring women together, women of different religions and cultures. The Chicagoland Christian Women's Conference was one of the first, if not the first, to bring these women together in a conference format. It was founded with the Lord Jesus Christ as the "center". His name was "lifted up" during the planning and execution of each conference activity. God blessed the organization and "ordered the steps" of its' leaders. The numbers are smaller now, but the organization is still flourishing, still making a difference in the lives of women as it lives up to its' theme: "To Know Christ and To Make Him Known."

Beverly Pannell Yates was born in Sturgis, Michigan to the union of William and Olive Gertrude Pannell. She had one brother, William; and six half brothers and sisters by her mother's second marriage. She married Leroy L. Yates, Sr. in December, 1951 and they produced three girls and two boys. Beverly came to know the Lord at age 16 and has continued to follow Him to this very day, not only to follow Him, but has followed Him "in the beauty of holiness". She graduated from high school in Sturgis, Michigan. To prepare for her career, Beverly attended the University of Illinois Hospital, Cook County School of Nursing from 1950-1953. She attended Moody Bible Institute's Evening classes in the 1980's.

Beverly Pannell Yates has been a frequent speaker and teacher at Christian conferences and workshops in the Chicago area. She is the author of several magazine articles, including "Heart Health for Black Women: A Natural Approach to Healing and Preventing Heart Disease (2000); and contributed to "Women's Ministry Handbook, ed. Carol Porter (1992). Beverly wrote a compelling article entitled, "Sarah: Is Anything Too Hard For God?" in the "Women of Color Study Bible, 1999. In the article, Beverly noted that Sarah was a beautiful woman armed with God's promises. We all know the story of how Abraham put Sarah in a compromising position to save his own life. Abraham had forgotten God's promises.

Beverly Pannell Yates is a mother, a grandmother, and a great-grandmother, and a Pastor's wife-extraordinaire. Her ministry with the Chicagoland Christian Women's Conference (CCWC) is well known to everyone. She is synonymous with the organization, she's part of the fabric that is CCWC. She is also a professional bible study teacher, and active in her church's (Westlawn Gospel Chapel) Senior Ministry. Beverly serves as the President of the Vineyard Partnership Investment Club, but I am moved by some other things in her life: she went through the hardship of illness, having heart surgery and then surviving cancer surgery. She nursed her husband back to good health, never seeming to "skip a beat"! She is constantly helping others as they go through trials and tribulations, and through grief and heartache. Down through the years, she has ministered to hundreds of women through CCWC and to the Board Members as well. During one of our Retreats, held on Saturday, April 1, 1978, Beverly presented a workshop. The workshop was entitled, "Stategy For Coping With Family Conflicts".

A few years ago, Beverly Pannell Yates served as Guest Speaker at a local church in Chicago, Emmanuel Baptist Church. It was a Women's Day Celebration with men and women in attendance. I don't remember the theme, but I do remember Beverly giving them the unadulterated, plain and simple, gospel of Jesus Christ our Lord, several times during her message. As usual, I was struck by her love of God and her love and devotion to people.

In 2004, my sorority, Iota Phi Lambda Sorority, honored Beverly Pannell Yates as one of its' Eight Outstanding Americans; both men and women were honored, among them – then Senator Barack Obama and Jerry Butler, Cook County Commissioner. Beverly had recently undergone surgery and could not attend. Her daughter, Joyce Austin Yates, (current President of CCWC) accepted the award in her place.

Beverly Pannell Yates has made a big impact on her family, her friends, her community, and her church. She has slowly and systematically changed the course of the world.

Woman #8

- Lorraine Hansberry: (1930-1965)
  Although Lorraine Hansberry lived a relatively short life, she none the less produced powerful, and excellent work. In her first published play, "A Raisin in the Sun", Lorraine successfully dramatized important social issues in a "piquant" family setting that engaged and enlightened critics and the public alike when it opened on Broadway in 1959.

As the daughter of a prominent Chicago businessman, Lorraine had lived a fairly comfortable life, albeit one that was defined by the poverty and lack of opportunity that many thousands of other black Chicagoans faced. Lorraine's parents could have sent her to a private school, but they wanted her to know the reality of life for most African Americans in Chicago in the thirties and forties. The twelve years that she spent in poorly funded, primarily black public schools forever shaped her political outlook.

Carl Hansberry, her father was a former political candidate, and the owner of a successful real estate management business. He wanted his family to experience the American Dream: a nice life in a nice house in a nice neighborhood So while Lorraine was in the primary grades in Chicago's predominantly black public schools, Carl Hansberry sued a white landowner and the city of Chicago, charging that the unstated, "separate-but-equal" housing politics were exclusionary and unfair. And shortly after Lorraine's tenth birthday, following a 1940 Supreme Court decision in Hansberry's favor, the family moved into an all-white suburb.

Lorraine was thrust into a new world. On the good side, her inquisitive nature had plenty of new questions to ponder: Why were human beings cruel to each other? How could blacks and whites hate each other if they did not even know each other? On the downside, she found herself in a sea of unfriendly faces, and the sensitive young girl endured taunts and threats from many of the white children in her new neighborhood.

In "A Raisin in the Sun", the story of the Younger family is a study in modern relationships as well as a depiction of the lingering impact of slavery and racism in America. She took the title from a Langston Hughes poem, "Harlem", about hopes dashed, that asks what happens to a dream deferred, and Lorraine chose it for its lyricism and poignant sadness. Over the years many notable actors, among them Sidney Poitier, Danny Glover, Louis Gossett Jr., Ossie Davis, and Ruby Dee, have starred in productions of "A Raisin in the Sun."

While Lorraine did not think of herself as a prodigy, her first play was widely considered a flawless achievement. When the young director Lloyd Richards agreed to direct it, Lorraine was flattered and anxious. As the play went into readings, she struggled with tying together all the important points she hoped to make: that men and women must work harder at understanding each other, and that black Americans must continue finding the moral high ground in the midst of seemingly insurmountable opposition.

On the night of March 11, 1959, the play opened at the Ethel Barrymore Theatre on Broadway. Hailed by critics as an impressive debut and a thoughtful treatment of race relations in America, "A Raisin in the Sun" went on to win the coveted New York Drama Critics-Circle Award for best dramatic play of 1959. Moreover, the play drew thousands of black Americans to the Barrymore, a venue that did not often offer mainstream productions with themes of direct concern to African-American theatergoers. When the prestigious New York Drama Critics Circle Awards were announced, Lorraine's name and image were broadcast worldwide. At age twenty-nine, she had successfully bridged her two worlds, finding a remarkable union between her political and social beliefs and her artistic vision.

By the end of 1964, as her second play was about to enter previews, Lorraine began experiencing severe headaches. On January 12, 1965, Lorraine Hansberry died from a brain tumor. "The Sign in Sidney Brustein's Window" opened that same night, and the entire theater district seemed to register sadness over her death.

Lorraine's seminal work still stands as a shining example of how black women have shaped the nation's understanding of the intricacies of personal relationships. Although "The Sign in Sidney Brustein's Window" did not fare well on Broadway, other works met critical acclaim upon their posthumous publication, including the unfinished play Les Blancs; a short story, "The Drinking Gourd"; and her autobiography, "To Be Young, Gifted and Black".

Woman #9

• <u>Gwendolyn Brooks</u> (June 7, 1917 - December 3, 2000)

As a young black girl growing up in Chicago, Gwendolyn Brooks realized early on that reading provided a means of travel out of the tenements of the segregated inner city and into the wide adventurous world. After Gwendolyn first discovered her love of books, she shared with the world "her unique vision and hopes for a better America.

Born on June 7, 1917, in Topeka, Kansas, in her grandmother's home, Gwendolyn Brooks was raised in Chicago. By the time she had completed elementary school, she displayed a remarkable knack for reciting classic poetry and for writing her own rhymes.

Gwendolyn excelled in school. By the time she was thirteen, Gwendolyn had her first poem published in a local newspaper. Her hard work began to pay off early when she became a regular contributor to the foremost black newspaper in the nation at that time, the "Chicago Defender".

Her teachers, impressed by her determination, encouraged her to go to college. While attending Wilson Junior College in Chicago, Gwendolyn became a popular student, admired for her friendly nature and serious devotion to literature. I felt a kinship to her because I also attended Wilson Junior College in Chicago (in the 1960's). She graduated from college in 1937, and by that time, her poetry had appeared in two anthologies of contemporary writers. It was an impressive beginning, soon developing the writing style and work habits that would distinguish her work for the rest of her life.

An astute observer of human nature, she began to focus on the community of black professionals, newly arrived Southerners, and struggling artists in her Chicago neighborhood. As she began to seek work, she was shocked to find that the only jobs available to a young, black, college-educated woman in Chicago in the early forties was that of a maid. She still continued to look for work that suited her artistic vision, and eventually landed work at a monthly publication called the "Women's National Magazine". In the interim, Gwendolyn quietly wrote deeply personal poems.

In 1950, she learned that she had received one of the highest honors any writer could hope for: a Pulitzer Prize. Along with a sizable cash award, the Pulitzer enabled Gwendolyn to continue her special style of socially conscious poetry.

During much of the turbulent sixties, Gwen presided over a dynamic community of black artists and activists in Chicago. She taught poetry to gang members in Chicago, opening her own home to the troubled teens when public schools had rejected them. Beginning in 1963, she also taught writing at local universities and organized poetry workshops for many disadvantaged children.

Gwendolyn Brooks received more than fifty honorary doctorates over many years, and while the literary and academic worlds showered her with awards, she kept her eyes focused on the real world around her and remained true to her personal beliefs and vision.

After the death of her husband, Henry, in the mid-nineties, she continued writing. She still relied on the wise words of her mother to help her stay strong as she entered her ninth decade.

Gwendolyn Brooks died on December 3, 2000 after having lived a long fulfilling life.

Nine Laws That Changed America

- Brown vs. Board of Education, 1954
  The unanimous Supreme Court decision ended segregation in public education

- Civil Rights, 1964 and Voting Rights Acts, 1965
  Without these laws, African-Americans would still be living in an Apartheid America.

- Medicare and Medicaid Acts, 1965
  The core pillars of America's social safety net provided essential access to health care for the elderly and poor.

- Headstart, 1965
  It was one of the most successful programs in our history. It still provides free preschool to millions of low-income African-American children.

- Affirmative Action, 1965-1973
  Without it, the corridors of power and privilege would still be all white and all male.

- Fair Housing Act, 1968
  Block-busting real estate agents and redlining banks no longer can police the boundaries of white neighborhoods.

- Omnibus Crime Bill, 1994
  Mass incarceration under this law decimated Black communities.

- Personal Responsibility And Work Opportunity Reconciliation Act, 1996
Welfare-to-work pushed people off government assistance after five years but has never addressed the underlying racial disparity in employment and opportunity.

- Patient Protection And Affordable Care Act, 2010
President Obama's health reform provides coverage to more than 30 million formerly uninsured Americans.

On May 10, 2012, Elder Willie Horton presented scripture verses that are "Non-Lost" Verses
They are:

1.) John 15:6
2.) Ezekiel 3:20, 21
3.) II Peter 2:20-22
4.) Hebrews 10:26-29
5.) Matthew 12:43-45
6.) Galatians 5:4
7.) Exodus 32:31-33
8.) Revelation 22:19
9.) I Corinthians 9:27

Nine Ministers of God Who Are Not of the Brethren Assemblies. They have changed the world through their ministries.

"The law of the Lord is perfect, converting the soul; the testimony of the Lord is sure, making wise the simple." Psalm 19:7

Rev. Billy Graham: I was saved in 1956 and soon afterwards, I began listening to Moody Bible Institute. Moody was a radio station in Chicago that broadcasts Christian programs from sun-up to sun-down. (They didn't have the frequency to broadcast after dark). I was a young mother, trying to raise three little girls, so I was home during the day and listened to the radio station all day long. Various speakers, teachers, evangelists, and musicians taught and shared the word of God non-stop. Rev. Billy Graham's name was revered and mentioned almost daily on Moody Bible School Radio. He had been ordained as a Southern Baptist Minister and rose to celebrity status in 1949 with the national media backing of William

Randolph Hearst and Henry Luce. His sermons were broadcast on radio and television and some are still being re-broadcast today.

During this time in the late 1950's and as I began to learn more and more about the Lord Jesus Christ, Dr. Billy Graham's name was prominent. It was during the civil rights movement and Dr. Graham began to support integrated seating for his revivals and crusades. In 1957, he invited Rev. Dr. Martin Luther King, Jr. to preach jointly at a huge revival in New York City. They appeared together at Madison Square Garden, and Dr. Graham bailed Dr. King out of jail in the 1960's when he was arrested in demonstrations.

I deeply respected Billy Graham and felt that he was a compassionate, Godly man seeking to evangelize the world, sharing the gospel as only he could. He had a commanding voice that made you want to accept the Lord over and over again. He was converted in 1934 at age 16 and eventually graduated from Wheaton College in Wheaton, Illinois with a degree in anthropology in 1943. It was during that year, that Dr. Gaham decided to accept the Bible as the infallible word of God. He launched a new radio program on January 2, 1944 and recruited George Beverly Shea as his director of radio ministry. Graham scheduled a series of revival meetings in Los Angeles in 1949, for which he erected circus tents in a parking lot. During the Los Angeles crusade and within five days, Graham gained national coverage. Since his ministry began, he has conducted more than 400 crusades in 185 countries and territories on six continents. The first Billy Graham Crusade was attended by 6,000 people. He was 29 years old. He called them "crusades," after the medieval Christian forces who tried to conquer Jerusalem. He would rent a large venue, such as a stadium or park. As the sessions got larger, he arranged a group of up to 5,000 people to sing in a choir. He would preach the gospel and invite people to come forward. Such people were called inquirers and were given a chance to speak one-on-one with a counselor, to clarify questions and pray together. The inquirers were often given a copy of the Gospel of John or a Bible study booklet.

• Reverend Dr. Clay Evans is the founder of the Fellowship Missionary Baptist Church where he served as pastor and shepherd for fifty years. He became known as the pastor of pastors around Chicago and vicinity, and today is affectionately referred to as "The Godfather." Dr. Evans was born June 23, 1925 to the late Henry Clay and Estanauly Evans in

Brownsville, Tennessee. He has been married to Lutha Mae Hollingshead for sixty-four years. They are the proud parents of five children, one of whom preceded them in death in December, 1996. He was ordained a Baptist Minister in 1950, but matriculated through various institutions of higher learning including Chicago Baptist Institute, Northern Baptist Theological Seminary, Trinity College and International Bible Institute & Seminary, and the University of Chicago Divinity School. He also received an Honorary Doctor of Divinity Degree from Arkansas Baptist College.

Rev. Evans has been responsible for launching the ministerial careers of ninety-three persons. He has been a leader in the Civil Rights Movement since 1965.

He is the Founding Chairman of Operation PUSH and Chairman Emeritus of Rainbow PUSH. He is the Founding National Chairman of the African American Religious Connection (AARC), the Founding President of Broadcast Ministers Alliance (BMA), and the Founder of the Clay Evans Scholarship Fund, Inc. (CESF). He has served as advisor and board member of numerous civic and religious organizations, including the National Baptist Convention, USA, Inc.

He has been the featured soloist on more than thirty albums recorded with both his 250 voice choir and the AARC Mass Choir. He also recorded several albums featuring his powerful sermons, including "Job's Greatest Problems" and "Every Kind in the Net."

Rev. Evans retired as pastor of the Fellowship Missionary Baptist Church on December 8, 2000 (Le Shawn's birthday) (the actual day he was born), but he continues to minister at churches all over the United States, preaching those same powerful sermons. He is someone that everyone should get to know.

Pastor Don Cole

Pastor Don Cole and his wife, Naomi, along with their three children were missionaries in Angola, Africa for 18 years. Not able to return due to a change of government, they stayed in the United States in 1966 and he later joined the faculty of Emmaus Bible College in Oak Park, Il.

Looking for someone to communicate the foundational truths of God's Word in a personable, understandable way, Moody Radio invited Pastor Don to step in as Moody Radio Pastor for Robert J. Little who was retiring after 17 years of service. Pastor Cole's gentle, honest manner during "Open Line", a Bible question and answer broadcast that he hosted from 1982-2008, proved to be a source of hope for many listeners. In addition to "Open Line" which Pastor Cole stopped in April, 2008, he was also involved with the "Christian Perspectives on the News" broadcast, verse-by-verse Bible studies in "The Living Word" and insightful commentaries toward the end of his career. He received the William Ward Ayer Distinguished Service Award and was inducted in the National Religious Broadcasters Hall of Fame in 2006. He wrote several books including "How to Know You're Saved," "Thirsting for God," "Basic Christian Faith", and many more. I used to listen to Pastor Cole and his wife, Naomi on Moody. His answers to questions were always based upon the Word of God and he was always confident, knowledgeable, and always gentle and non-judgemental. It was a pleasure to listen to him. He also, in his early years, visited Grace & Glory Gospel Chapel a couple of times, along with his wife. The way he served his community and the humble, unselfish way he dealt with people earned respect and admiration with me. I was a young Christian trying to learn as much as I could about the Lord. He and Naomi helped me in my growth as a Christian wife, mother, and Sunday School teacher.

Pastor Cole died on Saturday, August 4, 2012 and his wife, Naomi went to be with the Lord two weeks later on Saturday, August 18, 2012. They were memorialized at Wheaton Bible Church on August 31, 2012.

Bishop Arthur M. Brazier

Bishop Arthur M. Brazier was a dynamic preacher and an activist in the civil rights movement, and the pastor emeritus of Apostolic Church of God in Chicago. I enjoyed looking at his church service every Sunday morning at 8:00 A.M. He was from the "old school" of preachers who took each scripture verse of the Word of God and made it real to me with his historical reference and personal application. He demanded respect and earned my admiration. He also founded the Woodlawn Organization, an organization that served as a beacon of hope for so many disenfranchised people, people in the "hood."

It was Bishop Brazier's church where then candidate Barack Obama came to deliver his Father's Day speech in 2008, after the whole Rev. Wright controversy.

In the 1960's, Bishop Brazier marched through the streets of Chicago alongside the Rev. Martin Luther King, Jr. in the struggle against segregation in housing and schools. Bishop Brazier was a Penecostal pastor of the Apostolic Church of God in Woodlawn for more than 48 years, building a congregation of 20,000 members before handing church leadership over to his son, the Rev. Dr. Byron Brazier, in 2008. For decades, Bishop Brazier fought gangs and crime and pushed for more affordable homes and better schools. As the founding president of the Woodlawn Organization, he opposed plans by the nearby University of Chicago to expand, which would have displaced residents and would have used land he hoped to develop for low-income housing.

While he refused to preach politics from the pulpit, his wide influence made the Apostolic Church of God an obligatory campaign stop for politicians. Barack Obama visited the church during his presidential campaign on Father's Day, 2008, and emphasized the significance of family and the need for men to become responsible, reliable dads to their children.

Bishop Arthur M. Brazier, 89 years old, died on Friday, October 22, 2010.

J. Vernon McGee

I remember as a young Christian, I listened to Moody Bible Institute, everyday, all day, without fail. J. Vernon McGee was one of the "staples" on the radio. I was struck by his command of the scriptures, his passion, and his wisdom. I loved hearing his verse by verse exposition. He shared so many, sometimes hidden treasures from the Word of God. His teaching added much to my growth as a Christian. His program was called "Thru the Bible Radio Network".

Dr. McGee was born in Hillsboro, Texas. He graduated with his B.D. from Columbia Theological Seminary and his Th.M. and Th.D. from Dallas Theological Seminary in Dallas. He served many Presbyterian churches before he moved with his wife to Pasadena, California, where he accepted a position at the Lincoln Avenue Presbyterian Church. He moved from Pasadena to Los Angeles and became the pastor of the Church of the Open Door in 1949, where he continued as pastor until 1970. Dr. McGee also served as chairman of the Bible department at the Bible Institute of Los Angeles and as a visiting lecturer at Dallas Theological Seminary.

In 1967, he began the "Thru the Bible Radio Network" program. In a systemic study of each book of the Bible, Dr. McGee took us, his listeners, from Genesis to Revelation in a two and one-half year "Bible bus trip"... as he called it. After he retired from the pastorate in Juanuary, 1970, he realized that two and a half years was not enough time to teach the Bible, he completed another study of the entire Bible in a five year period. He was slowed down by getting cancer, but he refused to give in to his illness. I remember him saying that he was going to continue his study; he was not ready to die yet. He fully recovered from that bout of cancer. However, a heart problem surgically corrected in 1965 resurfaced, and he died in his sleep in 1988 at the age of 84. After his death, the five year program of "Thru the Bible" still continued to air on over 400 radio stations in North America, and was heard in more than 100 languages and was broadcast worldwide via radio, shortwave, and the internet.

Rev. Otis Moss, Jr.

Rev. Otis Moss, Jr. is a pastor, theologian, speaker, author, and activist. I am so impressed with his involvement in the Civil Rights movement and his friendship with Dr. Martin Luther King, Jr. and his friendship with Dr. King's father, Martin Luther King, Sr.

Rev. Moss's son, Otis Moss, III is the pastor of the very "high-profile" Trinity United Church of Christ in Chicago, Illinois.

Rev. Moss was born on February 26, 1935 in La Grange, Georgia 20 days after I was born. That makes him a "kindred spirit" with me.

Dr. Otis Moss, Jr. was preacher at the Washington National Cathedral on the day that newly elected President Barack Obama, First Lady Michelle Obama, and their family went to worship.

Rev. Moss earned his B. A. at Morehouse College in 1956, before earning his Master of Divinity from the Morehouse School of Religion in 1959. While there, he was taught and mentored by Benjamin Mays, who was also a mentor to Dr. Martin Luther King, Jr. At Morehouse, Dr. Moss helped lead sit-ins and other activities to protest segregation. He finished his graduate coursework at the Interdenominational Theological Center from 1960 to 1961. He earned a Doctor of Ministry from United Theological Seminary in 1990, where he was taught by Samuel De Witt Proctor and became friends with Jeremiah Wright, who was pastor of the Trinity United Church of Christ in Chicago and pastor of President Barack Obama. Moss' son, Otis Moss, III, would later take over as senior pastor for Rev. Wright after the controversy during the 2008 presidential election over the content of sermons he gave during the time in which Barack Obama attended the church.

Rev. Moss, Jr. became the pastor of Mount Olive Baptist Church in La Grange in 1954 to 1961. From 1956 to 1959, he served as senior pastor at Mount Olive also, and at the same time, at the Providence Baptist Church in Atlanta. Next, he pastored Mount Zion Baptist Church in Lockland, Ohio from 1961 to 1975. During this time he was the regional director of Martin Luther King, Jr.'s Southern Christian Leadership Conference, leading several campaigns to fight various forms of segregation and discrimination. He participated in the Selma, Alabama civil rights march with Dr. King. Dr. King also performed the marriage ceremony of Rev. Moss and his wife, Edwina. In 1971, he spent one year away from the church to co-pastor Ebenezer Baptist Church in Atlanta with Dr. Martin Luther King, Sr. – Dr. King's father.

After leaving Mount Zion Baptist Church in 1975, he left to pastor the Olivet Institutional Baptist Church in Cleveland, which was then the largest black church in the state of Ohio. He led the church for 33 years before retiring in 2008. "During his time at the church, besides continuing to be a sought-after speaker and influential figure in social justice movements, he was an advisor to President Jimmy Carter and also befriended such figures as Bill Clinton, President Barack Obama, Oprah

Winfrey, and Jesse Jackson". In 1997, Rev. Moss partnered with University Hospitals to create the Otis Moss Jr. Medical Center.

Rev. Moss has lectured at hundreds of colleges and churches throughout the world, including at the Oxford Roundtable at Oxford University and in the Lyman Beecher Lecture Series at Yale University, and the National Cathedral in Washington, D.C. He has also spoken in Hong Kong, Taiwan, Japan, Jordan, Israel, and South Africa. I attended a lecture at Trinity United Church on February 19, 2011 to observe Black History Month. The lecture was given by Rev. Moss, Jr. and he talked about his involvement in the Civil Rights Movement in the 1960's.

Rev. Moss talked about "Creation, Liberation, and Salvation" as it relates to the Civil Rights' Movement. There was economics, politics, and theology involved. The white establishment found that it was economically profitable, politically protective, and they used theology for permission, to "ease their conscience" as they violated the rights of African-Americans. It was a powerful presentation that stirred my pride in and affirmed my belief in the strength and dignity of the human spirit.

Dr. Charles Frazier Stanley

I have been listening to Dr. Charles Stanley for decades now. I've also read his books. I have in my possession his "In Touch" Study Series, so I have experienced the joy of his wisdom. He seems, on the T.V. screen, an humble, sincere Christian. He has a great love for the lost. He sees his mission as sharing the good news of the Gospel with the world. His series includes "Listening to God"; "Relying on the Holy Spirit"; "Experiencing Forgiveness"; and "Advancing Through Adversity".

Dr. Charles Frazier Stanley is the senior pastor of the First Baptist Church of Atlanta and the founder of "In Touch Ministries". His popular radio and television broadcast," In Touch with Dr. Charles Stanley," can be heard around the world in every nation and in more than 50 languages.

In the mid 1980's, Dr. Stanley also served two terms as president of the Southern Baptist Convention. Dr. Stanley is best known for providing solid biblical truth through the practical teaching style that can be applied to everyday life.

Charles Stanley was born on September 25, 1932 in Dry Fork, Virginia. His childhood was marked by the tragic death of his father, Charley at a very early age. He recalls feeling the support of God during that difficult time, chiefly through the strong example of his young, widowed mother,

Rebecca Stanley, and his godly grandfather, who instilled in him a desire to trust and obey God's Word.

By the age of 14, Charles Stanley had begun to sense a call to follow God in full-time Christian ministry. First, he earned a bachelor of arts degree from the University of Richmond in Virginia and later a bachelor of divinity degree at Southwestern Theological Seminary in Texas. He obtained his master of theology and doctor of theology degrees at Luther Rice Seminary in Georgia.

I've always been impressed with the many hours of service that Dr. Stanley puts into his ministry. He is constantly proclaiming the Word of God.

Everyday, In Touch Ministries broadcasts proclaim the Gospel in 60 languages, helping millions take steps toward Christ, and utimately helping their own nations experience the blessings America has enjoyed for so long. God is continuing to bless this ministry.

Dr. Tony Evans

Dr. Tony Evans, Th.D, is a Christian pastor, speaker, author, and a widely - syndicated radio and television broadcaster in the United States. He was the first African-American to earn a doctorate in Theology from Dallas Theological Seminary. He taught evangelism, homilectics and black church studies at DTS, and serves on its Board of Incorporate Members.

Dr. Evans serves as Senior Pastor to the over 9,500 member Oak Cliff Bible Fellowship in Dallas, Texas, which was founded in 1976 with 10 members meeting at his home. He is also founder and president of The Urban Alternative, a national organization that seeks to bring about spiritual renewal in urban America through the church. "The Alternative with Dr. Tony Evans" can be heard over 1,000 outlets daily throughout the U.S. and in over 100 countries worldwide. The broadcast can also be viewed on several television stations. He is a speaker on the Promise Keepers' platform, as well as speaking regularly in crusades and Bible conferences in the United States and abroad.

Dr. Evans is married to Lois Evans, and they have four children: Chrystal, Priscilla, Anthony, Jr., and Jonathan. His oldest child, Chrystal Hurst, is a worship leader and writer. She recently co-authored the book, Kingdom Woman, with her father.

His daughter, Patricia Shirer is a New York Times Best-Selling Author, Christian speaker and founder of "Going Beyond Ministries". We, in my CCWC organization, participated in the study material from her ministry. It was a powerful presentation geared toward the spiritual growth of the CCWC Board of Directors.

His son, Anthony Evans, Jr. is a Christian musical artist with multiple CD's including "Home", "Letting Go", and "Even More". He has collaborated with Grammy Award winning singer Kirk Franklin. He was also a contestant on Season Two of the Voice.

His son Jonathan, was a professional football player in the National Football League. He played fullback for the Buffalo Bills, Washington Redskins, and the Dallas Cowboys.

Through his local church and national ministry, Dr. Evans has set in motion a Kingdom Agenda philosophy of ministry that teaches God's comprehensive rule over every area of life as demonstrated through the individual, family, church, and society.

I have enjoyed Dr. Tony Evans' (radio) messages over Moody Bible Institute for decades. He is fearless in his pursuit of building onto God's Kingdom; and telling it the "way it is."

Rev. Jeremiah Wright

Rev. Jeremiah Wright, who was President Barack Obama's former pastor, gained national attention in March 2008 when ABC News, after reviewing dozens of Wright's sermons, excerpted parts which were subject to intense media scrutiny. Obama denounced the statements in question, but after critics continued to press the issue of his relationship with Wright, he gave a speech titled "A More Perfect Union", in which he denounced Wright's remarks, but did not disown him as a person. The controversy began to fade, but was renewed when Rev. Wright made a series of media appearances, including an interview on Bill Moyers Journal, a speech at the NAACP and a speech at the National Press Club. After the last of these, Pres. Obama spoke more forcefully against his former pastor and resigned his membership in the church.

Although Rev. Wright surprised me with some of his comments, I sought to remember him in his earlier ministry. I found him to be dynamic and electrifying in his sermons. I attended an ordination ceremony that he conducted for Sis. Nola Hicks son-in-law decades ago. I have never forgotten that experience.

I have attended his sermons over the years, and he preached the Word of God beautifully. He was your typical "fire & brimstone" preacher. I was impressed, also, with his military service and his community activism.

Jeremiah Alvesta Wright, Jr. was born on September 22, 1941 in Philadelphia, Pennsylvania. He was born and raised in a racially mixed section of Philadelphia called Germantown. His father was Jeremiah Wright, Sr., a Baptist minister who pastored Grace Baptist Church in Germantown, Pennsylvania from 1938 to 1980. His mother, Dr. Mary Elizabeth Henderson Wright, was a school teacher who was the first black person to teach an academic subject at Roosevelt Junior High. She went on to be the first black person to teach at Germantown High and Girls High, where she became the school's first black vice-principal.

Rev. Wright graduated from the Central High School of Philadelphia in 1959, among the best schools in the area at the time. At that time, the school was around 90% white.

From 1959 to 1961, Rev. Wright attended Virginia Union University, in Richmond and is a member of Omega Psi Phi fraternity, Zeta Chapter. In 1961, Wright left college and joined the United States Marine Corps and became part of the 2nd Marine Division attaining the rank of private first class. In 1963, after two years of service, Wright joined the United States Navy and entered the Corpsman School at the Great Lakes Naval Training Center. Wright was then trained as a cardio-pulmonary technician at the National Naval Medical Center in Bethesda, Maryland. He was assigned as part of the medical team charged with care of President Lyndon B. Johnson after his 1966 surgery. Before leaving the position in 1967, the White House Physician, Vice Admiral Burkley, personally wrote Rev. Wright a letter of thanks on behalf of the United States President.

In 1967, Rev. Wright enrolled at Howard University in Washington, D.C., where he earned a bachelor's degree in 1968 and a master's degree in English in 1969.

Rev. Jeremiah Wright became pastor of the Trinity United Church of Christ, Chicago, on March 1, 1972; it had some 250 members on its rolls, but only about 90 or so were actually attending worship by that time. By

March 2008, Trinity United Church of Christ had become the largest church in the mostly white United Church of Christ denomination.

Rev. Wright attended a lecture by Dr. Federick G. Sampson in Richmond, Virginia, in the late 1980's, on the G. F. Watts painting "Hope", which inspired him to give a sermon in 1990 based on the subject of the painting – "with her clothes in rags, her body scarred and bruised and bleeding, her harp all but destroyed and with only one string left, she had the audacity to make music and praise God . . . To take the one string you have left and to have the audacity to hope . . . that's the real word God will have us hear from this passage and from Watt's painting." Having attended Wright's sermon, Barack Obama later adapted Wright's phrase "audacity to hope" to "audacity of hope" which became the title for his 2004 Democratic National Convention keynote address, and the title of his second book.

I viewed Watt's painting and it is truly awe inspiring. I was moved to connect with the message that Rev. Wright brought and I could see and understand the passion with which then Senator Barack Obama delivered his speech on "Hope" for America.

Rev. Wright received the Rockefeller Fellowship and seven honorary doctorate degrees. He was also awarded the first Carver Medal by Simpson College in January, 2008, to recognize Wright as "an outstanding individual whose life exemplifies the commitment and vision of the service of George Washington Carver.

Rev. Jeremiah A. Wright, Jr.'s wife is Ramah Reed Wright, and he has four daughters, Janet Marie Moore, Jeri Lynne Wright, Nikol D. Reed and Jamila Nandi Wright, and one son, Nathan D. Reed.

Nine favorite scripture verses on "Love"

I have searched the scriptures for God's word to me on "love". What does it mean in terms of my relationship to the Lord, to my family, and to others?

1.) II Sam. 1:26 "I am distressed for thee, my brother Jonathan; very pleasant hast thou been unto me. Thy love to me was wonderful, passing the love of women."

2.) Proverbs 10:12 "Hatred stirreth up strifes, but love covereth all sins."

3.) Prov. 15:17 "Better is a dinner of herbs where love is, than a stalled ox and hatred therewith."

4.) Song of Solomon 2:4 "He brought me to the banqueting house, and his banner over me was love."

5.) Song of Solomon 8:6 "Set me as a seal upon thine heart, as a seal upon thine arm; for love is strong as death, jealousy is cruel as the grave; its coals are coals of fire, which hath a most vehement flame."

6.) Jeremiah 31:3 "The Lord hath appeared of old unto me, saying, Yea, I have loved thee with an everlasting love; therefore, with loving-kindness have I drawn thee."

7.) Hosea 11:4 "I drew them with cords of a man, with bands of love; and I was to them as they that take off the yoke on their jaws, and I laid food before them."

8.) Matthew 24:12 " . . . And because iniquity shall abound, the love of many shall grow cold."

9.) John 13:34 "A new commandment I give unto you, that ye love one another; as I have loved you, that ye also love one another."

All nine scripture verses were taken from the King James Version of my personal bible.

CHAPTER THIRTEEN

Cultural Pride and Celebration

History is made up of significant events that shape our future and outstanding leaders who influence our destiny. These events and these leaders create for African Americans a cultural pride and an ongoing, never ending celebration. The <u>Reverend Dr. Martin Luther King, Jr.</u> was one of those outstanding leaders. The events that took place in and around his life were "earth shattering", for they represented an America that was hostile and indifferent to the inequalities and injustices suffered by Black Americans. Dr. King relentlessly sought to jolt the conscience of white America; he tried to stir their concern by his speeches and dialogues. He led campaign after campaign in the streets of America from 1955 to 1968, when he was brutally assassinated on April 4, 1968.

Dr. King was a big factor in the cultural pride that African Americans feel. However, history records events that led up to Dr. Martin Luther King's service and others who followed him.

According to Cameron McWhirter, in 1919, Chicago was changing demographically as a steady flow of African Americans, mostly from Southern states, invaded the city. Because of ingrained racial prejudices and harsh economic circumstances, many white Chicagoans did not welcome them. Chicago did not turn out to be the "promised land" that migrants hoped to find. Instead many found themselves locked in a fierce ethnic competition for jobs, housing and political power. The result of these conditions was violence, leading to injuries and deaths. White mobs and

Black mobs clashed, fighting along the Lake Michigan beaches, then spreading west and south and north. African-Americans were undeterred as they proudly served their country during World War I. It was not acknowledged, but they have always faithfully, and courageously served in every war fought by the United States of America. The violence between whites and blacks in 1919 was usually instigated by whites who called themselves Christians, but they "acted like godless barbarians" (similar to some of them today). Lynchings of black men and burning them alive by throwing them into bonfires was commonplace. Most of the black men had done nothing illegal or wrong. Mr. McWhirter feels that the happenings in the year 1919, was a turning point in the lives of blacks. Many think about death and destruction in Watts, 1964; in Newark and Detroit, 1967; Dr. King's assassination, 1968; and Los Angeles, 1992 but Mr. McWhirter puts more emphasis on 1919.

Long before 1919 in Chicago, a man named Jean-Baptiste Points Du Sable was settling in a place that is now called Chicago. It was 1773 and he began by purchasing 30 acres of land, upon which he built a large house. After involvement in the Revolutionary War and as a liaison officer between Indians of the Port Huron region and white officials, Du Sable returned to Chicago in 1782, where he became a fur trapper and trading post owner.

DuSable left behind a rich and impressive legacy. He left behind a wealth of accolades in his honor, including: a plaque on a building at the corner of Pine and Kinzie Streets in Chicago, indicating the site of the first house erected in the city. Also in his honor is the Du Sable High School located at 49th and State Streets in Chicago, and the Du Sable Museum of African American History, one of the largest museums of African-American culture in the United States, also in Chicago.

Harold Washington was the first Black mayor of Chicago. He was born in Chicago on April 15, 1922. He succeeded his father, Roy Washington, as a Democratic Party precinct captain in the 3rd Ward in 1954. On February 22, 1983, Washington won the Democratic Primary, narrowly beating Jane Byrne and Richard M. Daley. On April 29, 1983, after beating Republican challenger Bernard Epton in March, Harold Washington gave his Inauguration Speech.

From April 30, 1983-May, 1986, Washington waged a hard, bitter three year battle between him and his supporters in the City Council and the Vrdolyak 29" – the bloc of alderman led by Alderman Edward Vrdolyak. It dominated most of Harold Washington's first term.

On April 7, 1987, after defeating Jane Byrne for the Democratic Nomination, Washington beat City Council foe Edward Vrdolyak 53.8% to 42% and is re-elected as mayor. He was the only Chicago mayor at the time, not named "Daley" to be reelected to two terms as Chicago mayor since the elder Daley was first elected in 1955.

Harold Washington had a style all his own. There has never been an African American politician in the city to capture a moment in a phrase or feeling the way Washington could. He had personality, bigger than life. He was brilliant. That is his greatest legacy, in my opinion.

He paved the way for Carol Moseley Braun for Senate. He helped create the image of Barack Obama. That's his legacy. He was the first.

When Mayor Washington died suddenly in November, 1987, the city was in shock and I was totally devastated. He was a hero, not only to me, but to others as well. He had accomplished a great thing when he won as mayor of Chicago – a racist, segregated city. I was working at Michele E. Clark Middle School at the time of his untimely death and we paid tribute to him.

Recognitions and remembrances and tributes came in from all over the world. He was a great leader.

Chicago's Other Heroes

- Marla Gibbs graduated from Wendell Phillips H.S. in Bronzeville. She started acting at 44 years old and shortly afterwards, she landed a job on "The Jeffersons" as a maid in 1975. She starred on the sitcom "227" which was originally a play.
- Lou Rawls was raised by his grandmother in the Ida B. Wells projects. He graduated from Dunbar Vocational H.S. Lou developed his singing talents as a member of the Greater Mount Olive Baptist Church Choir.
- Curtis Mayfield – grew up in the Cabrini Green Projects. He was a self-taught guitarist and pianist. He was considered the leading

musician of the Civil Rights movement in the 60's and 70's with songs like "People Get Ready", and "It's Alright".

- Bessie Coleman – At the age of 23 in 1929, Bessie Coleman moved to Chicago. Working as a manicurist, she would hear stories about flying from pilots that were returning home from World War I. This sparked an interest in Bessie for flying and she began to explore the option of obtaining a pilot license. But in 1922, during a time of both extreme gender and racial discrimination, Coleman was denied entry into U.S. pilot schools and shunned by Black male pilots. Determined to succeed, she sought out help and gained encouragement from Robert Abbot, founder of the Chicago Defender and financial backing from banker, Jesse Binga. With their support Bessie taught herself French and moved to France, earning her license in just seven months. She specialized in stunt flying and parachuting, earning a living performing aerial tricks. Coleman would not live long enough to live out her dream of establishing a school for Black aviators but her pioneering achievements served as an inspiration for generations of African American men and women.

- Samuel B. Fuller "Self Made Millionaire" – inspired future leaders such as John H. Johnson of Johnson Publishing and George Ellis Johnson, founder of Johnson Products. S.B. Fuller has been called the greatest salesmen of the 20th Century. Born on June 4, 1905 in Monroe, Louisiana, Fuller began selling door to door as a means to support his family. After moving to Chicago in 1929, Fuller was determined to succeed and borrowed $25, using his car as collateral, to invest in a load of soap supplies to sell from Boyer International Laboratory. He went on to become a top salesman at the company. For four years he continued to work for someone else as he built his own business by hiring salesman and building his product line. In 4 years Fuller was able to offer 30 products. The additional growth was enough for the company to open its own factory in 1939 and by 1947 he secretly purchased his old company, but for fear of being shut down, had to keep his ownership a secret. He then began to manufacture his own line from deodorant to hair care to clothing, the first African American during this time. Fuller also purchased several newspapers including the New York Age and Pittsburg Carrier, and also went on to own the South Center Department Store and the Regal Theater in Chicago. During his brief heading of the South Side NAACP, he tried to organize a purchase of the Segregated Bus Company during the Montgomery Bus Boycott. During the 1950's, Fuller was one of the richest African Americans in the United States. His cosmetic company alone had $18 million in sales. His philosophy of business was simply "you've got to have something to sell." Samuel B. Fuller died on October 24, 1988 at 83 years old.

- Jesse Binga was the first African American to own a bank in the city of Chicago. After migrating from Detroit, Binga opened his first business where he paid $10 per month in office rent and bought a battered old desk for $1.50. His first profitable project was renting an apartment in the same building where he had his office, fixing it up and subletting it at a premium. After seeing the value in real estate, Binga began to take advantage of the Great Migration to Chicago by buying property from whites who wanted to move, fixing it up, and then reselling it to blacks who needed a place to live. From real estate he moved into banking. In 1908, he took over a failed bank at State and 35th Streets and reopened it as Binga Bank, the city's first black-owned financial institution. Binga moved to 5922 South Parkway (now known as King Drive) in 1917. The Washington Park Neighborhood was then all-white. He received death threats and the house was repeatedly bombed. He had to hire 24-hour security guards. Binga defiantly refused to move. Binga was a true trail brazer and visionary of his time. He died in June, 1950 at 85 years old.

- The Rev. Jesse L. Jackson, Baptist Minister, presidential candidate and civil rights leader – is a Chicagoan that we can be proud of; he is a cultural icon. A friend and supporter of the late Dr. Martin Luther King, Jr., Jesse Jackson became involved in the civil rights' movement while in college. In 1971, he founded "People United to Save Humanity" (PUSH), an organization devoted to gaining economic power for African Americans. It was in this organization that he gained support from the Black community to run for the 1984 Democratic presidential nomination. He was also an unsuccessful candidate for the 1988 Democratic presidential nomination, but his strong campaign fostered a new respect for him and his family.

- Oscar Stanton De Priest was the child of ex-slave parents, born in Florence, AL in 1871. His father was a teamster and farmer, his mother a part-time laundress. But his humble beginnings didn't stop him from being ambitious and persistent in obtaining his goals. In 1889, De Priest moved to Chicago, and worked as a painter, decorator, and eventually became an independent contractor and real estate broker. He affiliated himself with the Republican Party, and his service with them attracted the attention of some influential party leaders. After years of participating in the political life of Chicago, De Priest was elected as an Illinois Republican to the U.S. House of Representatives in 1928. His election was historic, because De Priest was the first African American congressman to be elected from a northern state. De Priest's greatest legislative achievement came in 1933 when passage of his amendment to prohibit discrimination in the Civilian Conservation Corps due to race, color, or creed was approved.

He retired from politics in 1947, and died in 1951, after being struck by a bus and suffering a kidney ailment.

A school on Chicago's west side is named after Oscar De Priest, in his honor. When I was at Michele Clark Middle School, De Priest School was one of our "feeder" schools. After reading his story, to honor him seems only fitting.

Dr. Margaret Burroughs was a teacher for almost forty years in the Chicago Public Schools' System (CPS). She was a founder of the South Side Community Art Center, the Lake Meadows Art Fair, the Chatham Art Fair, the National Conference of Artists and the Du Sable Museum of African American History. She is an author and poet of several books and winner of many awards including a citation by President Jimmy Carter. She is the author of the world famous poem, "What Shall I Tell My Children Who Are Black?" I used that powerful, significant, apropo poem with my students at Michele E. Clark Middle School, back in the day.

Other Famous Chicagoans

Melvin E. Banks, Sr. Litt. D.
Melvin Banks is the founder and president of Urban Ministries, Inc. (UMI), the nation's only independent publisher of Afrocentric Christian education curriculum. Under his direction UMI has become one of the

leading publishers of Christian education resources for churches in the African American community. The company serves several thousand churches directly, plus several denominations indirectly.

Melvin Banks was born on October 15, 1934, in Birmingham, Alabama. He accepted Christ at the tender age of nine. Three years later, an old, white-haired Black man heard Melvin's testimony, on one of the back roads of Birmingham, and quoted this verse to him: "My people are destroyed for lack of knowledge" (Hosea 4:6). This verse made a great impression on Melvin, and he determined to yield himself to God so that he could be used to help bring the knowledge of His Word to Black people.

He graduated from Moody Bible Institute in 1955. Shortly thereafter, he enrolled in Wheaton Bible College where he earned two Bachelor of Art degrees, one in theology and the other in archeology. He also earned a Master's in Biblical Studies. After graduation, Melvin was employed by Scripture Press Publications. Among other things, his responsibilities included leadership development and literature distribution. His experiences during this period led to the founding of Urban Ministries, Inc.

During the turbulent sixties many Black churches were hesitant to purchase Christian education materials that were not Black oriented. In 1970, Melvin invited several friends to form the Board of Directors of a new company called Urban Ministries, Inc. During its first 12 years UMI operated out of the basement of the Banks' family home. My daughter, Sharon, as well as many others, helped with typing the lessons before moving to the new headquarters. In the spring of 1996, UMI completed construction and took occupancy of a new headquarters facility in the Chicagoland area.

UMI now produces more than 50 different products, all of which are designed for the unique needs of the Black church. The UMI product line includes: Sunday School curriculum for six different age groups; Vacation Bible School materials for various age levels; Adult leadership training books, and more recently, Christian videos, all of which depict or speak to people of color in the context of their culture.

Dr. Banks, along with Leroy Yates and Harvey Rollerson, co-founded the Westlawn Gospel Chapel back in the year, 1956. The church is located on Chicago's West Side.

He is also a co-founder of Circle Y Ranch, a camp geared toward African American children. Circle Y accommodates as many as 500 children per summer. He has authored a book, <u>Winning</u> <u>and</u> <u>Keeping Teens</u> <u>in</u> <u>Church</u>. In 1993, Melvin was awarded an Honorary Doctorate Degree by his alma mater.

Melvin Banks resides in South Holland, Illinois with his wife, Olive. They have three adult children, Melvin, Jr., Patrice, and Reginald.

<u>Timuel</u> <u>D</u>. <u>Black</u>

When Timuel D. Black, historian, donated boxes of Memorabilia to the Chicago Public Library, it was received with amazement and appreciation. It marked a "turning over" of his legacy to be shared by future generations.

He was born on December 7, 1918, in Birmingham, Alabama, but was raised in Chicago's then Black Belt, graduating from an integrated Burke Elementary School, then an all-black Du Sable High School in 1935, where classmates included Johnson Publishing Company founder John H. Johnson, and the soon to be famous jazz musician Nat King Cole.

It was during the Depression, and Timuel would work various jobs after high school, until Pearl Harbor launched America's entry into World War II and he was drafted into a segregated U.S. Army in 1943.

He returned from the war to civilian life with militant political views. An organizer in the labor and social justice movements of the 1940's and 1950's, he worked with such activists as Paul Roberson and W.E.B. DuBois.

Mr. Black helped to establish the Congress of Racial Equality and United Packinghouse Workers of America, among more than 100 organizations he was to be active in over seven decades.

While attending Roosevelt University, Black met classmate Harold Washington – who some 30 years later was elected the city's first black mayor, aided by an independent, progressive black political movement pioneered by Timuel Black, who coined the phrase "plantation politics". Black got his master's degree from the University of Chicago in 1954.

He worked alongside Dr. Martin Luther King, Jr. in the 1960's, helping to organize Chicagoan's participation in the 1963 March on Washington.

Timuel's teaching career began in the Chicago Public Schools at the Du Sable, Farragut, and Hyde Park high schools. He entered the City Colleges of Chicago system in 1969 as a dean at Wright College; vice president at Olive Harvey from 1971-1973; head of communications systemwide from 1973-1979; then taught at Loop College until his retirement as professor emeritus in 1989. In the wake of the 2000 presidential election, he was the lead plaintiff in the ACLU's Black vs. McGuffage lawsuit, which charged the Illinois voting system discriminated against minorities. The suit led to the ban of punch card ballots and a new uniform voting system in Illinois. His two - volume book, "Bridges of Memory: Chicago's First Wave of Great Migration, chronicles black Chicago history from the 1920's to the present, through interviews of great and small who were among the Great Migration.

This information was taken from an article in the Chicago Sun Times on Wednesday, February 1, 2012 in honor of Black History Month. The excellent article was written by Maudlyne Ihejirika, Staff Reporter

Sam Cooke, singer, composer

Sam Cooke, a handsome man with a voice to match, was unquestionably one of the most important bridges between black music and the lucrative realms of mainstream pop. According to some, Cooke was the most important soul singer in history; he was also the inventor of soul music, and is its most popular and beloved performer in both the black and white communities. He was a veteran of the gospel circuit, and as such he took on an ultrasmooth stage persona calculated to drive the ladies well past the limits of decorum. Sam successfully took his act from R&B hot spots like the Apollo Theater straight into the heart of white show business with SRO stands at places like the Copacabana.

He also was among the first modern black performers and composers to attend to the business side of the music business, and founded both a record label and a publishing company as an extension of his careers as a singer and composer. Yet, those business interests didn't prevent him from being engaged in topical issues, including the struggle over civil rights. Cooke appealed to all groups and the parents of white teenagers as well – yet he never lost his credibility with his core black audience. As a gospel singer, he originally recorded secular material under the pseudonym Dale Cooke to avoid alienating his church following. As a pop star of major proportions, he tailored his act to the color of the crowd. His impressive string of hits tells the story: 1957's "You Send Me," reached number one in both pop and R&B categories and was followed by a succession of double-barreled "chart burners" that included: "Everybody Loves to Cha Cha Cha", "Wonderful World", "Chain Gang", and "Having a Party". Before his untimely and sordid death in 1964 at age 29, Cooke had achieved a match of black style with white sensibilities that would rarely be equaled in the annals of American music.

He was born Sam Cook in Clarksdale, Mississippi on January 22, 1931, one of eight children of a Baptist minister and his wife. Even as a young boy he showed an extraordinary voice and frequently sang in the choir in his father's church. During the middle 1930's, the Cook family moved to Chicago's South Side, where the Reverend Charles Cook quickly established himself as a major figure in the religious community.

As a teenager, he was a member of the Teen Highway QC's, a gospel group that performed in churches and at religious gatherings. His membership in that group led to his introduction to the Soul Stirrers, one of the top gospel groups in the country, and in 1950 he joined them. Over the next six years, his role within the group and his prominence within the black community rose to the point where he was already a star, with his own fiercely admiring and devoted audience, through his performances on songs like "Touch the Hem of His Garment," "Nearer to Thee", and "That's Heaven to Me." His biggest selling single of the 1950's, was "You Send Me", which sold over two million copies on the tiny Keen Records' label, and hit number one on both the pop and R&B charts. Although it seems like a tame record today, "You Send Me" was a pioneering soul record in its time, melding elements of R&B, gospel, and pop into a sound that was new and still coalescing at the time.

During that time, however, Cooke did achieve the financial and creative independence that he'd wanted, including more money than any black performer had ever been advanced before, and the eventual ownership of his recordings beginning in November of 1963 – he had achieved creative control of his recordings as well, and seemed poised for a breakthrough. It came when he resumed making records, amid the musical ferment of the early 1960's. He was keenly aware of the music around him, and was particularly entranced by <u>Bob Dylan's</u> song, "<u>Blowing in the Wind</u>", its treatment of the plight of black Americans and other politically oppressed minorities, and its success in the hands of <u>Peter,</u> <u>Paul</u> & <u>Mary</u> – all of these factors convinced him that the time was right for songs that dealt with more than "twisting the night away." The result was "A Change Is Gonna Come," perhaps the greatest song to come out of the civil rights struggle, and one that seemed to close and seal the gap between the two directions of Cooke's career, from gospel to pop.

This heralded a new era for him and a new phase of his career, with seemingly the whole world open to him. None of it was to be. Early in the day on December 11, 1964, while in Los Angeles, Cooke became involved in an altercation at a seedy motel, with a woman guest and the night manager, and was shot to death while allegedly trying to attack the manager. The case is still shrouded in doubt and mystery, and was never investigated the way the murder of a star of his statue would be today. His death shocked the black community and reverberated throughout the country. I remember his death well, and like everyone else, I was shocked and sad for his family. They were very close. I remember Sam as a teenager; he was not very friendly, mostly, even then, carried himself like a celebrity. His girlfriend was Barbara Campbell – she was a twin to Beverly. They were really pretty girls. Sam was older, but I went to high school with his brother, L. C. Cook. L. C. and I were close friends (I almost married him). Later, after high school, I worked at Alden's Mail Order Company with his sister Agnes. Sam, L. C., and Agnes all had "perfect" diction and a "smoothness" to their voices. It was part of their family, maybe a family "trait". The whole family were singers, like the Evans family – Rev. Clay Evans and Lou Della Evans Reid.

Mr. Truman K. Gibson, Jr. was a friend of Lenzo's and was our attorney and legal advisor until his death at 93 years old in 2005. Mr. Gibson, a Chicago lawyer, was the last surviving member of the Roosevelt - Truman "black Cabinet", a group of prominent African Americans picked to represent the interests of black America in government during the Depression and World War II. Mr. Gibson served in the War Department. His work was dedicated to abolition of racial segregation. As a result of Mr. Gibson's work, the Army for the first time began to agree on practical if not policy changes. He reported for duty in the War Department in Washington, D. C. in December, 1940. The things that he came face to face with, about the realities of race in America, disturbed and angered him. He was even more alarmed that the Army had abandoned black men who had been called to the service of their country, had been ruled, abused, assaulted and even murdered by white civilians in the South of the Jim Crow era.

After about one year on the job, Mr. Gibson organized a conference of black editors and publishers. Among the 14 notables who turned out were Bill Nunn of the Pittsburgh Courier and John Sengstacke of the Chicago Defender. As it happened, this meeting in Washington came in Dec., 1941, the day before the country was staggered by the Japanese attack on Pearl Harbor. The conference convened with anxieties and emotions running high. The newspaper men, like all Americans, knew their country faced years of war, sacrifice and unknown danger in the struggle against fascism. The editors and publishers were, to say the least, disappointed in what they heard. It only confirmed the stories of segregation and exclusion at Army posts that they had published in their own newspapers. In the end, the service of 800,000 black men in the military during World War II and the thousands more who served in the post war years and the Korean conflict swelled into the irresistable force that ultimately desegregated the Army. But that was to come later.

The more immediate consequences of the enlistment of black men into the war effort were tragic. Virtually, all the basic training camps were in the South. The Army, bowing as its policy dictated to the norms of civilian life, directed that its military bases would have to follow the mores, social code and laws of the communities in which they existed. That dictated that Jim Crow ruled on Army posts large and small. Segregated units meant separate barracks and mess halls. Black soldiers rode at the back of buses. Black servicemen spent off duty hours at inferior theaters and post exchanges, or PX's as the Army stores were called.

The stage was set at Army posts across the South for ugly confrontations that all too often erupted into fights and even riots and ended with African Americans facing court martial, being beaten up and being killed. During the 1940's, so many black soldiers were bludgeoned or shot to death by white police, deputies and civilians in the South that it might be only a slight exaggeration to say more black Americans were murdered by white Americans during the course of World War II than were killed by Germans. Enraged and dispirited young men wrote of their plight to their families, their churches, civil rights organizations, politicians and newspapers. They, in turn, wrote to the War Department. The complaints eventually landed on the desk of Mr. Gibson.

No black serviceman was secure from bigotry. Perhaps the most famous recruit who rebelled against this blatant racism was Jackie Robinson, who after the war would break the color barrier to become the first black player in Major League baseball. But he already was a famous athlete when the war began; he had excelled in four sports and won an all-American rating in football at UCLA. But to the racist officers of the Army, he was just "another one of them." After induction into the Army, Robinson was assigned to Fort Riley, the basic training post for cavalry soldiers. Robinson had almost completed his Cavalry Officer Candidate School training when one day he heard a white captain call an African American soldier a bad name. The captain called Jackie one, too.

Never a man to suffer an insult, Robinson had an explosive temper, and he packed a powerful punch. He slugged the officer, knocking out his front teeth. Robinson faced court martial, prison, and, who knows, given the lawless nature of race relations in those days, possibly even death.

Also at Fort Riley then completing enlisted man's basic training was Mr. Gibson's friend, Joe Louis, the world boxing champion. Louis immediately called about Robinson's predicament. Mr. Gibson flew down to the post and they met the officer in charge. Mr. Gibson, a lawyer, laid out Robinson's case. Then Louis began talking. He said that he was finishing his basic training and wanted to give the general a memento. The champ pulled out an expensive Piaget watch and presented it to the officer. Robinson was then able to finish his course. Robinson had another confrontation with a white driver. The bus driver drew a revolver, but his draw wasn't as fast as Robinson, who wrestled the pistol away and massaged the driver's mouth with it, depriving him of many teeth. Joe Louis called Mr. Gibson again and he flew to Texas. But, as matters turned out, he didn't have to make any arguments on Robinson's behalf. The brass at Camp Swift knew who Robinson was, apparently understood the injustice of the situation, in all likelihood reached the logical conclusion that Robinson would not put up with this kind of raw bigotry, and realized only more trouble lay ahead. Robinson was honorably discharged for the good of the service, with no court martial.

Mr. Truman Gibson was an unsung hero. He was very instrumental in getting President Harry Truman to consider desegregating the armed services. And all through his life, he sought to help people. He had a compassion to help those who were incarcerated in prisons and jails. Mr.

Gibson was a friend of my husband, Lenzo. We attended several of his receptions and office parties. He, along with his partner, <u>Wanemond Smith</u>, helped when we needed power of attorney documents, and with other legal problems as they occurred.

Mr. Gibson died on December 23, 2005. He was 93 years old. His wife, Isabelle, died in 2001. He leaves a daughter, Karen Kelley, and some grandchildren, great grandchildren, and great, great grandchildren.

<u>Dr</u>. <u>Marjorie</u> <u>Stewart</u> <u>Joyner</u>, was a woman who fully deserves the title by which she was known in Chicago: "a living legend." That she was also known as the "Grande Dame of Black Beauty Culture," the "Godmother of Bethune-Cookman College," and the "Matriarch of the Bud Billiken Parade" underscores the diversity and richness of her legacy. She was born on October 24, 1896, high up in the Blue Ridge Mountains of Virginia where her early life was marked by poverty and the dissolution of her parents' marriage. Her father, George Stewart, an itinerant schoolteacher, and her mother, Annie Doughty Stewart, divorced soon after the couple moved to Dayton, Ohio. By 1912, Marjorie was sent to live with her mother in Chicago. She married Dr. Robert S. Joyner, a noted Podiatrist, in 1916 and after a brief beauty school education, she opened her first beauty shop at 5448 South State Street. Convinced by her mother-in-law that she needed further education to properly care for black hair, Marjorie enrolled in a course taught by Madame C. J. Walker. Their intense association in the three years before Walker's death led to Dr. Joyner becoming National Supervisor of the more than two hundred Walker Beauty Colleges. She ceaselessly sought improvements in cosmetology, inventing a "permanent wave machine" which was patented in 1928, as well as such products as "Satin Tress". In 1945, disgusted with the racism of the white beauty associations, she founded the United Beauty School Owners and Teachers Association and the Alpha Chi Pi Omega Sorority and Fraternity.

Dr. Joyner infused her organizations with a universal consciousness and led one hundred and ninety-five black cosmetologists on a 1954 trip to Paris to learn the latest methods, thus circumventing the color line.

She began working with Dr. Mary McLeod Bethune during World War I, and went on to become one of Bethune-Cookman College's most successful fund-raisers and advocates. She helped Bethune organize the National Council of Negro Women in 1935, and worked with Eleanor

Roosevelt on black and women's issues during World War II. Dr. Joyner's political activities led her to close association with every Chicago mayor since Edward Kelly, as she organized service men's centers and charity fundraisers. Among all her Chicago civic endeavors, she is perhaps best known for her association with the Bud Billiken Parade from its' inception in 1929 and for her work as Chairwoman of Chicago Defender Charities.

Marjorie Stewart Joyner was honored in 1987 by an exhibit on black migration at the Smithsonian Institute in Washington, D.C. Her achievements were also noted in exhibits at the University of Illinois at Chicago, Illinois, the Du Sable Museum of African American History, the University of Chicago Hospitals, and the Carter G. Woodson Library.

Dr. Joyner was widowed in April, 1973, and she was devastated when she lost her daughter, Ann Fook in June, 1976. Ann Fook was the mother of my friend, Mary Ann Younger-Bridges. Mary Ann recently passed away, as well. Marjorie Stewart Joyner passed away on December 27, 1994 at the ripe old age of 98 years. I knew Dr. Joyner as Mary Ann's grandmother. We called her "Ma Mu". Ma Mu was the director of the Day Care center where my granddaughter, Shatese, went to school. I admired Dr. Joyner's strength and determination as she pursued her many goals and aspirations.

Dr. Lou Della Evans Reid has a national reputation as being one of the most outstanding Minister's of Music in our country. Her unique style of directing has been described as powerful, and has enhanced the services at her church for 50 years. Lou Della has played many pioneering roles during her lifetime. In 1950, she was the only woman among the five charter members in the organizing of the Fellowship Missionary Baptist Church of Chicago, Illinois where her brother, the Rev. Clay Evans, is the founder and Pastor. Moreover, she gave birth to the church choir, served as its first pianist, and was appointed Minister of Music in 1963, during a time in which it was unusual for a woman to hold such a position.

Lou Della studied music during her childhood under the late Kate Evans of Brownsville, Tennessee. She then began to use her musical ability by playing the piano for her church in Tennessee, and eventually at the Fellowship Missionary Baptist Church. She also studied music under Rev. Charles Walker who was also a musician of Fellowship. Her musical excellence has been showcased in many arenas, including the over thirty musical releases of the Rev. Clay Evans and the Fellowship Missionary

Baptist Church choir, recordings of the National Baptist Convention, USA Inc., and numerous choral concerts across the country and throughout Europe. Musicians across the nation look to her for inspiration that seem to emanate from her whenever she directs. She has served as a workshop leader at many churches, staff musician and devotion leader for the Chicagoland Christian Women's Conference, and guest Director for the National Baptist Convention, USA, Inc. Most recently, Lou Della was invited to be a guest director on the nationally known Bill Gaither Pioneer Gospel Hour.

Lou Della is respected and honored by many people for her many years of dedication to her Pastor and her church. Even the most reserved worshippers are affected by her powerful spirit and conviction. She is considered by many a living legend, a dynamo that has exploded into the hearts of people all over the world. She loves the Lord and has dedicated her life in glorifying Him in everything she does.

Lou Della was married to the late Mr. Robert L. Reid. She is the mother of the late Eldred Louis Reid and Minister Tonia Johnson. She is also the grandmother to Moneca, Rajni, and Shakira. She is the great-grandmother of five.

Over the years, Lou Della has received numerous awards. Because of her dedication and her love for her work and her God, on May 12, 2000 at Arkansas Baptist College in Little Rock, Arkansas, Lou Della was conferred with a Honorary Degree of Doctor of Humane Letters.

Lou Della is a beloved member of the Chicagoland Christian Women's Conference (CCWC). She has served the organization as musician, director, teacher, workshop leader, and speaker, for over 30 years. Dr. Lou Della Evans Reid is revered by CCWC Board of Directors, as well as, the ladies of the conference. Her unique way of directing and engaging congregations is known worldwide and appreciated by everyone who is blessed to meet her. Lou Della, along with the Honorable Reverend Clay Evans, her brother, are part of a family of musicians and ministers. God and music is their whole life experience, which they readily share with people in Chicago, in Illinois, in the nation, and in other parts of this world that we live in. To God Be The Glory!

Dr. Samuel Stephens, RPH – was a trail-blazer and drum major in the field of pharmacy. He was among the last of the old-time druggists who delivered prescriptions to the ailing and gave credit to customers who were short of cash. Dr. Stephens was one of the first blacks in the nation to found and operate a pharmaceutical manufacturing business. From 1941 to 1996, he headed Stephens Prescription Pharmacy and Stephens Pharmaceutical Co. at 505 E. 61st St.

Dr. Stephens, along with his brother James, opened a drug store on the corner of 47th and Langley Ave. in Chicago in September, 1927. In 1933, The Great Depression closed the door of their dreams. From 1933 to 1941, Samuel was employed with the Illinois Department of Public Aid.

He then opened the Stephens Prescription Pharmacy at 505 E. 61st St. in Chicago, just three months prior to the bombing of Pearl Harbor and the outbreak of World War II. His store hours were from early morning until late evening, with delivery of prescriptions until, very often, 1:00 AM in the morning on the South and West sides of Chicago. His reputation for superior service dictated the need for 19 phone lines and a large staff of pharmacists to fill the hundreds of daily orders. He remained at that location for fifty-five years until July, 1996 when he fully retired.

Immediately following his graduation, he became a teacher of pharmacy at MeHarry Medical School in Nashville, Tennessee for one year. Dr. Stephens attended the University of Chicago Divinity School, Moody Bible Institute and Emmaus Bible College. After being ordained into the ministry, he co-founded the Southside Gospel Church in 1947, at 863 E. 64th St. and remained an elder in the church and was affectionately called "Bishop." Through his academic training and continual study of the scriptures, he became a known bible expositor. Over the years he traveled all over the U.S. on speaking engagements at various churches.

Through the years Dr. Stephens mentored many young men in the church and the ministry. He was also instrumental in helping to found other forms of Christian outreach. Some of them were: Business men for Christ; Door of Hope Mission; Evangelical Christian School; the South Side Youth For Christ; Circle Y Camp. He was also in the origin of the Unshackled radio program.

His influence was both felt and demonstated in the fall of 1968 when he was instrumental in introducing the idea of training registered pharmacists as PARAMEDICS to serve and act in emergencies to get the sick and injured from their point of origin to the hospital where they could be both examined and admitted and relay their vital signs en-route. This would eliminate a doctor first having to examine them at the point of origin before the police or fire department ambulance would be allowed to take them to the hospital. This idea by Dr. Stephens was read in the subscription magazine "Pharmacy Magazine."

After meeting with the Chicago Fire Department Fire Chief, and convincing him of the idea, Fire Chief Edwards was asked to get the support of the Fire Commissioner in order for it to become a reality. Almost immediately the idea was sanctioned and implemented with the approval of the Mayor. This was the beginning of the term PARAMEDIC. This procedure is still in use to this day.

Dr. Samuel Stephens died on July 6, 1998 leaving a rich legacy of accomplishments. He was a man ahead of his time with a zeal and love for mankind which he expressed through giving of himself and his ideas to better the circumstances of those around him. He was truly a Drum Major for economic parity for his enhanced pharmaceutical arena, his community and the entire City of Chicago.

This article about Dr. Samuel Stephens was taken from the Chicago newspaper "Black Pages" dated 1999.

I remember seeing Dr. Stephens on a regular basis, years ago, at Southside Gospel Church during anniversaries and other church functions. He was usually accompanied by his wife, <u>Alvai</u>. His daughter is Jeanne Stephens Cooper, a sorority sister of mine in the Iota Phi Lambda Sorority, Inc.

There were other famous African Americans over the many years starting with the 1700's, the 1800's, the 1900's, and into the new millennium – 2000 and beyond. They were and are trail blazers who without "fear or favor" made the world smaller and better by their sheer determination and "gall"; by their commitment and boldness; by their dedication and stamina; and by their never, ever giving up on their dream, their vision for black America and ultimately the world.

<u>Paul Robeson</u> was an academic genius, scholar, famous athlete, actor, singer, lawyer, linguist and undaunted champion of his people. He was born in Princeton, N.J. on April 9, 1898, the son of a runaway slave and a free

black woman. At an early age, he became committed to the self-generated basics of what it takes to bring closer one's vision of a better world.

Robeson went on to become the nation's first black all-American football star; the star of the plays "Othello" and "Show Boat"; and one of the first blacks to play professional football. He could speak and write in 20 languages; starred on Broadway and at England's Savoy Theatre and Drury Lane; and was acclaimed as a singer/activist in Africa, Asia, England, and Eastern and Western Europe.

His enemies blacklisted him and stifled his professional career, but his words and examples live on. Paul Robeson died in Philadelphia on January 23, 1976.

Note: I got that information from a column written by Vernon Jarrett in the Chicago Sun-Times, dated April 6, 1993.

George Washington Carver was called a "Black Leonardo", but he may be best known for his research and promotion of alternative crops to cotton, such as peanuts and sweet potatoes. However, equally as important are his accomplishments in the area of improving racial relations, mentoring children, poetry, and painting. In 1941, Time Magazine named Carver a "Black Leonardo". The analogy was made because Leonardo da Vinci has been described as a renaissance man whose "unquenchable curiosity was equalled only by his powers of invention.

George Washington Carver was born in 1865 to parents, Mary and Giles, who were slaves. They had been purchased 10 years earlier by a German immigrant, Moses Carver, for $700. George, his mother and his sister were kidnapped and sold in Kentucky. He was later rescued, though his mother and sister had died, and returned to Moses Carver.

After slavery was abolished, Moses and his wife, Susan, adopted George and his brother and raised them as their own, encouraging George to continue his educational pursuits. George took Carver's last name. Later, in an effort to avoid confusion with another George Carver in his classes, he began to use the name George Washington Carver.

After earning his high school diploma, he spent years applying to colleges, and was finally accepted at Highland College in Highland,

Kansas. Carver traveled to the college to start school, only to be rejected when they discovered he was black. He went on to attend Iowa State Agricultural College as the first black student and later became the first black faculty member.

In 1896, Carver was invited by Booker T. Washington, founder of Tuskegee University, to lead the Agriculture Department. He accepted the position and remained there for 47 years, during which time he had the opportunity to teach former slaves farming techniques for self-sufficiency.

Carver reportedly discovered more than 300 uses for peanuts and hundreds more for soybeans, pecans and sweet potatoes. His reported list of discoveries included: adhesives, axle grease, bleach, ink, linoleum, meat tenderizer, metal polish, shaving cream, shoe polish, talcum powder and wood stain. Of all of his discoveries, he applied for and obtained only three patents, none of which were commercially successful in the end.

Carver died on January 5, 1943. A summary on his life written on his tombstone reads: "He could have added fortune to fame, but caring for neither, he found happiness and honor in being helpful to the world." Sun-Times Article written by Sandy Mather, Tuesday, February 17, 2009.

George Washington Carver was one of my heroes from childhood. My first principalship was at the George Washington Carver Middle School in Altgeld Gardens' Housing Projects. I was proud to serve at a school bearing his name.

Dorothy Height, one of the leading female voices of the 1960's civil rights movement, often took part in historic marches with the Rev. Martin Luther King, Jr. and others.

Ms. Height, whose activism on behalf of women and minorities dated to the New Deal, led the "National Council of Negro Women" for 40 years. She continued speaking out into her 90's, often getting rousing ovations at events around Washington, where she was recognized by the bright, colorful hats she wore.

She died at 98 years old, at Howard University Hospital, where she had been in serious condition for weeks. In a statement, President Obama called her "the godmother of the civil rights movement" and a hero to Americans.

As a teenager, Dr. Height marched in New York's Times Square shouting, "Stop the lynching." In the 1950's and 1960's, she was the leading woman helping King and other activists orchestrate the civil rights movement, often reminding the men heading the movement not to underestimate their female counter parts. One of her sayings was, "If the time is not ripe, we have to ripen the time." She liked to quote 19th century abolitionist Frederick Douglass, who said the three effective ways to fight for justice are to "agitate, agitate, agitate."

Dr. Height was on the platform at the Lincoln Memorial, sitting only a few feet from King, when he gave his famous "I Have a Dream" speech at the March on Washington in 1963.

She felt that the feeling of unity created by the 1963 march had faded, and that the civil rights movement of the 1990's was on the defensive and many black families still were not economically secure.

Thurgood Marshall was such a huge figure, a bigger than life icon, and a relentlessly "just" man, that almost everyone knows his story. He was born on July 2, 1908 and he died on January 24, 1993. When he died at 84 years old, comments and accolades came from near and far. I especially appreciate Vernon Jarrett's tribute that appeared on Monday, January 25, 1993 – an article in the Chicago Sun-Times.

It was a young Thurgood Marshall who in 1936 began to form in his mind a long, tortuous legal road leading to the Brown vs. Board of Education decision. That's when, as a recent graduate of the Howard University School of Law, he went to a Maryland appeals court and defeated a state law barring the enrollment of blacks at the Maryland University Law School. Henceforth, he chartered the strategy of four major graduate school victories, culminating in the Brown decision.

In 1950, he led the successful assault on an attempt by the state of Texas to hastily build a Jim Crow graduate school for blacks in order to bar Heman Marion Sweatt from attending the University of Texas law school. That same year, the NAACP under Marshall's brilliant guidance ended the University of Oklahoma's practice of segregating G. W. McLourin, a black student, in its classrooms, library and dining room.

Meanwhile, in 1948, he was the leader of a legal team that scored another landmark victory in Shelley vs. Kraemar, a case partially emanating from Chicago. In that decision the Supreme Court voided the covenants design to keep blacks from renting or owning property in all-white communities.

Fayard Nicholas, who with his brother, Harold, wowed the tap dancing world with their astonishing athleticism and inspired generations of dancers, from Fred Astaire to Savior Glover, died at 91 years old on Jan. 24, 2006. He died from pneumonia and other complications of a stroke.

The Nicholas brothers were still boys when they were featured at New York's Cotton Club in 1932. Though young, they were billed as "The Show Stoppers"! And despite the racial hurdles facing black performers, they went on to Broadway, then Hollywood. Astaire once told the brothers that the acrobatic elegance and synchronicity of their "Jumping Jive" dance sequence in "Stormy Weather" (1943) made it the greatest movie musical number he had ever seen. In the number, the brothers tap across music stands in an orchestra with the fearless exuberance of children stone-hopping across a pond. In the finale, they leapfrog seamlessly down a sweeping staircase.

I loved the movie "Stormy Weather" with Lena Horne and Bill "Bojangles" Robinson. The Nicholas brothers performed that unbelievable dance number in that movie. It was amazing to watch. I watched the movie over and over. It is my favorite musical, hands down.

Mr. Nicholas had a unique style that changed the face of tap dance. He and his brother Harold didn't just use their feet to dance, they used their whole bodies. And it had an electrifying quality. They used ballet, they used jazz, they used acrobatics; they combined it all. The two brothers were vaudeville brats who toured with their musician parents, learning the "tricks of the trade" in the meantime. Fayard Nicholas, stealing dance steps as they went along, taught them to his brother, who was seven years younger. Their dancing betrayed, not only creative genius, but the athletic marvel of what no one else would dare attempt. Their trademark no hands splits - in which they not only went down but sprang back up again without using their hands for balance – left film audiences wide-eyed.

Gospel singer, Inez Andrews passed away on December 19, 2012. She was 83 years old. Inez was part of the Caravans gospel group between 1957 and 1962. One of her hits was "The Battle Is Not Yours" and in 1970, she recorded the hit "Lord, Don't Move the Mountain." Her son, Richard Gibbs is the pianist for Aretha Franklin.

Mrs. Andrews was the last great female vocalist of gospel's golden age, according to her admirers. She ranked among the likes of Mahalia Jackson, Marion Williams, Sister Rosetta Tharpe and Clara Ward. From a seductive, bluesy sound - often singing behind the beat – Ms. Andrews could burst into an impassioned, raspy cry.

She was born in Birmingham, Alabama on April 14, 1929, to Theodore and Pauline McConico. Her mother died when she was 2. Her father, a coal miner, was often out of work during the Depression. Inez was a teenager when she married Robert Andrews. By the time they divorced, when she was 18, she was the mother of two daughters. Working at menial jobs, including cleaning the steps of the Birmingham courthouse, she earned $18 a week. Still she sang at church and came to the attention of the Harmonettes.

Ms. Andrews' second husband, Richard Gibbs, Sr. died in 1964; her third husband, Wendell Edinburg, died in 2006.

In 1972, Aretha Franklin recorded what became the biggest selling gospel album of her career, "Amazing Grace." It's biggest hit was a reprise of Ms. Andrew's version of "Mary Don't You Weep." In 1962, Ms. Andrews left the Caravans, and by 1967, she was touring as a soloist, and in 1973 she recorded her biggest hit, "Lord Don't Move the Mountain/Give me the strength to climb."

In 2002, Ms. Andrews was inducted into the Gospel Music Hall of Fame. For her, the message was about God, according to the Chicago Tribune in 1994. In one of her best-known solos, "Just for Me," which she wrote and recorded in 1983, she sang, "Just for me, just for me/ When you start out blessing, Lord, have one just for me."

The Du Sable Museum of African American History was founded in the 1960's in three small rooms of an old South Side Michigan Avenue home of its founder, Dr. Margaret Burroughs. In 1973, the Chicago Park District allowed the museum to use its building in Washington Park if the museum would raise funds and remodel it. More than a million and a half dollars were raised. Then in 1984, a capital fund drive was held which added much more space to its' quarters. In 2013, plans were made to build a new addition to the museum.

The Du Sable Museum is the only major independent institution in Chicago established to preserve and interpret the historical experiences and achievements of African Americans. The museum is proud of its diverse holdings that number more than 15,000 pieces and include paintings, sculpture, print works, and historical memorabilia. Special exhibitions, workshops and lectures are featured to highlight works by specific artists, historic events or collections on loan from individuals or institutions.

The museum is very special to me for early on, I took my children on several visits to Du Sable Museum. It had very few exhibits, at first. Over the years, I have watched proudly as it has grown into a famous, beautiful institution that is a "must" for all people, all children.

Carter G. Woodson and his founding of the Association for the Study of African American Life and History was known as the Father of Black History, Woodson (1875-1950) was the son of former slaves, and understood how important gaining a proper education is when striving to secure and make the most out of one's divine right of freedom. Although he did not begin his formal education until he was 20 years old, his dedication to study enabled him to earn a high school diploma in West Virginia and bachelor and master's degrees from the University of Chicago in just a few years.

In 1912, Woodson became the second African American to earn a PH.D at Harvard University.

Recognizing the dearth of information on the accomplishments of blacks in 1915, Dr. Woodson founded the Association for the Study of Negro Life and History, now called the Association for the Study of African American Life and History (ASALH).

Under Woodson's pioneering leadership, the Association created research and publication outlets for black scholars with the establishment of the Journal of Negro History (1916) and the Negro History Bulletin (1937), which garners a popular public appeal.

In 1926, Dr. Woodson initiated the celebration of Negro History Week, which corresponded with the birthdays of Frederick Douglass and Abraham Lincoln. In 1976, this celebration was expanded to include the entire month of February, and today Black History Month garners support throughout the country as people of all ethnic and social backgrounds discuss the black experience. ASALH views the promotion of Black History Month as one of the most important components of advancing Dr. Woodson's legacy. In honor of all the work that Dr. Carter G. Woodson has done to promote the study of African American History, an ornament of Woodson hangs on the White House's Christmas tree each year.

The Vivian G. Harsh Research Collection of Afro-American History and Literature, housed in the wing of the Carter G. Woodson Regional Library (9525 So. Halsted) is recognized by scholars as the premier collection of rare documents about the black experience in the Midwest. The collection is named for Vivian Harsh, the first black librarian in the Chicago public library system. In 1932 Harsh began gathering documents for a "Special Negro Collection," and in 1975 the collection was moved to the newly opened Carter G. Woodson Regional Library.

In February, 2004, portions of Harsh's collection examined the legal history of the civil rights movement entitled, "Celebrating the 50th Anniversary of Brown vs. Board of Education:" Looking Back and Moving Forward." The display examined the landmark decision issued by the U.S. Supreme Court on May 17, 1954 in the case of Oliver Brown et al v. Board of Education of Topeka Kansas.

Some of the original documents on display include slave insurance policies, posters advertising rewards for the return of runaway slaves and letters from slave owners attempting to track runaway slaves.

Provident Hospital – I asked my friend Jacquelyn Crook to describe Provident Hospital. She was President of its' auxiliary for years. She said: "During the seventies an umbrella of auxiliaries pledged to give financial assistance and/or volunteer service to Provident Hospital, one of the historically Black hospitals in the United States. The Professional Women's Auxiliary – PWA (later changed to Provident Women's Auxiliary) and the Horseshoe Derby were two of the fundraising arms. Each planned and brought to fruition an annual event . . . PWA – a dance and the Horseshoe Derby a night at the race track. PWA and the Horseshoe Derby contributed more than a half million dollars to the hospital, as well as logged countless hours of volunteer service. Provident Hospital as we knew it closed in 1987, but reopened in 1992 as Provident Hospital of Cook County. Both Provident Women's Auxiliary and the Horseshoe Derby were proud to have been affiliated with this historic institution whose mission focused on providing health services for a community greatly in need."

Jackie belonged to Provident Women's Auxiliary and served as President several times over the years. I belonged to the Horseshoe Derby for years. I enjoyed being a part of that elite group, and even though I was not into the actual races, I was happy to help raise money for Provident Hospital.

The Guild 1963

My friend Annette, who I met in Undergrad school and we've been friends ever since, was a member of a group called, "The Guild". She was one of 18 ladies who annually planned a big fashion show for the purpose of donating to charitable causes/organizations. The Guild began in May, 1963 at the Ebenezer M.B. Church as the Young Women's Service Guild of Ebenezer. Under the guidance of Addie M. Brooks, Electa Jackson, and Estella Reid, fifteen young women were assembled and Connie Williams was elected president. In the fall of that year, they sponsored a hat show and made $50. They turned it over to the church. They did nothing in 1966, but in 1967, Theresa J. Williams recalled all members and was elected President. Guild members modeled clothes and hats and tried to sell 150 tickets to the affair. They had these shows in succeeding years, and as the membership grew to twenty, the attendance grew as well. The Guild became incorporated in 1972 and simultaneously recognized the needs of many charitable organizations.

The success of the Guild rested on a Christian background, informal meetings, and respect for each other. In addition to supporting worthy organizations, they provided clothing designers, furriers, clothing and shoe store owners and aspiring models, opportunities to "strut their stuff" before appreciative audiences.

(Taken from the 1985 "Heritage Calendar" honoring black women and their organizations.)

Silver Horseshoe Derby

The Silver Horseshoe Derby Committee was formed in 1976 by an enthusiastic group of young women who were anxious to lend their support to Provident Hospital. The 4 women were 1) Alice Manney 2) Rosita Materra 3) Nancy McKeever 4) Virgie J. Smith. They made a decision to provide this support through profits made from "A Night at the Races" which would be held annually at Maywood Park Race Track. This track, because the Black Horseman's Association was affiliated with it, became the permanent track for their affair. Through the cooperation of Lester McKeever and William Moore, members of the Black Horseman's Association, the Silver Horseshoe Derby Committee hosted many successful "Night at the Races" affairs.

Through the support of friends and business people, the group gave enough money to Provident to furnish the cafeteria which serviced employees and visitors to the impressive edifice located in the heart of the community that it served. A plaque hung in the hospital cafeteria recognizing the Horseshoe Derby Committee for it's generous contribution. In the year 1984, proceeds from the 8th Annual Horseshoe Derby Night At The Races went towards the purchase of a Cat Scan Machine which would enable the doctors to provide even more efficient services to their patients.

At that time, the Silver Horseshoe Derby Committee was made up of thirty-two active members and the numbers kept growing.

Our motto was to think big . . . reach for the stars. Our membership consisted of Black women from all walks of life, all ages, all professions, all occupations, all economic groups, and from all areas of the city and suburbs . . . working harmoniously together for Provident Hospital. We were dedicated to raising funds and we sought the community's support to help us each year to reach our goal.

I was invited to be a member of the Silver Horseshoe Derby by my sorority sister, Delores Brown. She was in Alpha Beta Chapter, Iota Phi Lambda Sorority, Inc. and I was in Alpha Chapter. Our two chapters shared many fun activities as we carried out the duties of our Sisterhood. Delores is now deceased, but she was a hardworking soror who contributed much to the growth of Iota, and to the community.

Rev. Al Sharpton is the founder and President of the National Action Network (NAN), a not-for-profit civil rights organization headquartered in Harlem, New York, with over 47 chapters nationwide. Born on October 3, 1954 in Brooklyn, New York, Rev. Sharpton began his ministry at the tender age of four, preaching his first sermon at Washington Temple Church of God in Christ in Brooklyn. Just five years later, the Washington Temple Church's legendary Bishop F.D. Washington licensed Al Sharpton, his protégé, to be a Penecostal minister. Rev. Sharpton was educated in New York public schools and attended Brooklyn College. He has an Honorary Doctorate of Divinity from Bethune-Cookman University and an honorary degree from A.P. Bible College.

Rev. Sharpton's civil rights career began almost as early as his ministry. At thirteen, Rev. Jesse Jackson and Rev. William Jones appointed Sharpton as youth director of New York's SCLC Operation Bread Basket, an organization founded by Dr. Martin Luther King, Jr. in 1971.

At the age of sixteen, Sharpton founded the National Youth Movement, Inc. which organized young people around the country to push for increased voter registration, cultural awareness, and job training programs. It was at that time that he forged a friendship with Teddy Brown, the son of the "Godfather of Soul" James Brown. Tragically, Teddy was killed in a car accident and, in the months that followed his passing, James Brown took Rev. Sharpton in as though he was his own and they developed an inexplicable bond.

Rev. Sharpton is the host of "Politics Nation" on MSNBC that analyzes the top political and social news of the day featuring the country's leading newsmakers. He also hosts a nationally syndicated radio show "Keepin it Real" that is heard daily all over the country, and two local New York radio shows. Rev. Sharpton delivers live remarks at NAN's weekly Saturday Rally at its' Harlem headquarters – the "House of Justice" which is broadcast live on NAN's website.

Rev. Sharpton says his religious convictions are the basis for his life and on most Sundays he preaches to congregations across the nation. Rev. Sharpton has two daughters from his marriage to Kathy Jordan Sharpton, Dominique and Ashley.

(NAACP) Clarence Mitchell, Jr.

Clarence M. Mitchell Jr. worked tirelessly for the NAACP, as well as Benjamin Todd Jealous. Although his name seems to disappear from the pages of history, still we are standing on his bold shoulders.

Nicknamed the 101st senator by colleagues on Capitol Hill, Mitchell led the fight for justice and equality as a lobbyist for the NAACP. As chief of the Washington Bureau from 1950 to 1978, his work in building relationships on both sides of the aisle led to the passage of the Civil Rights

Acts of 1957, 1960, and 1964, as well as the 1965 Voting Rights Act and the 1968 Fair Housing Act. In 1980, President Jimmy Carter awarded Mitchell the Presidential Medal of Freedom, the highest civilian honor in the country.

Mitchell registered to vote as an independent so as not to appear biased toward either party. At the time he took the job, most blacks in the U.S. identified with the Republican Party and notorious segregationists Strom Thurmond and Jesse Helms were Dixiecrats.

Mitchell's relative obscurity is the reason two native Baltimoreans took it upon themselves to make sure that the man, his work and his legacy were acknowledged on what would have been his 100th birthday. It was collaborated to not only recognize, but also to educate people about the work of native son, Mitchell.

During the writing of "Cultural Pride & Celebration," I found that I was completely in awe of the survival of our people, our ancestors; but I celebrate the legacy – the skills and talents and creativity and boldness and wisdom – that added to, contributed to the greatness of this country. In spite of great odds; in spite of Jim Crow laws; in spite of discrimination; in spite of brutal killings and lynchings; in spite of hatred and bigotry; in spite of financial struggles, God brought them through the valleys up to the mountain tops; through the rain into the bright sunshine; and through the storms into the peaceful calm. Our heroes have been brought, over many years, to places of prominence and eras of success which includes strong families and strong careers. Even until now, they are continuing to make a big difference in the country. Even until now, they have rich histories to share. There are many more stories to tell and I would love to hear them.

CHAPTER FOURTEEN

An Appropriate Ending

Isaiah 45: 2-3

> "I will go before thee, and make the crooked places straight: I will break in pieces the gates of brass, and cut in sunder the bars of iron: and I will give thee the treasures of darkness, and hidden riches of secret places, that thou mayest know that I, the Lord, which call thee by thy name, am the God of Israel."

The journey back into my history has been a 30 year vision and a five year pen to paper experience. God took me through those years and made the "crooked places straight." My confidence was lacking, but my enthusiasm was strong. My goal was lofty, but my aim sometimes fell short. The knowledge that other people were writing their stories caused me to doubt and wonder about the necessity of such a task. I knew my children would read it, but would others even be interested in that journey?

God used "people, places, things," as well as sayings, poetry and so much scripture to "give me the treasures of darkness, and hidden riches of secret places" to encourage and to keep me on the path to victory; the victory of the achievement of this goal; a goal not only for me, but a goal to glorify God, my Heavenly Father and His Son, the Lord Jesus Christ.

I'm reminded of a beautiful poem by Joyce Kilmer, entitled "Apology" that reflects my feelings about reaching my goal. I was drawn to this piece because Joyce Kilmer also wrote the poem "Trees" which is one of my favorite poems. He says:

> "For blows on the fort of evil
> That never shows a breach,
> For terrible life-long races
> To a goal no foot can reach,
> For reckless leaps into darkness
> With hands outstretched to a star,
> There is jubilation in Heaven
> Where the great dead poets are."

The writing of this manuscript is the fruition of a dream. Thank God it didn't "dry up like a raisin in the sun." My doubts over the years have been many, doubts about "things", but I am reminded of others who have had challenges and yet succeeded.

My dream is similar to Dr. Martin Luther King, Jr's. He did not see his dream to fruition, but millions now have benefitted from his dream. My dream of writing this book will not reach millions, but like Dr. King, I did not give up on my dream. I thought "never give up on my hopes and aspirations, just keep on pushing."

My dream is similar to James McBride's determination to tell his personal story. It took 10 years for completion of his book. He told the story of his Jewish mother and his Black father and his siblings and the very difficult, very traumatic years of growing up and then becoming prominent (his siblings as well) and productive. He was blessed throughout and continued to praise the Lord. He never thought his life was interesting, and yet his book, "The Color of Water" sold millions, and mostly to Jewish readers. I appreciate his story, not only because it was interesting, but because it took him a number of years to write it.

I admire, so much, Diana Nyad who became the first person to swim successfully from Cuba to Florida at the "tender age" of 64 years. She had tried unsuccessfully to swim the Florida Strait four times over some 30 years. After completing the swim, she said, "This is a lifetime dream of mine and I'm very, very glad to be with you." The newspaper article called it "historic" and "marvelous". More than the athletic feat, she wants to send a message of peace, love, friendship, and happiness . . . between the people of the United States and Cuba.

In each life, and in each pursuit, and in achieving each dream, I see the hand of our great God at work. He sends great examples into our lives daily; examples of dedication, commitment, hard work, and never giving up on a dream.

Somewhere in my past, I read that if you adopt a "beautiful vision" and if your heart has a "lofty" ideal, you can one day achieve it. I have internalized this saying.

The writing of this book has been stimulating and wonderful. Some have celebrated with me while others have questioned the necessity for a "memoir", laying bare my family history. I have used some big words, but I was more interested in big ideas expressed in a simple way. Like Alex Haley, "In my writing, as much as I could, I tried to find the good, and praise it."

Howard Thurman put it best when he said:
"Waiting is a window opening on many landscapes . . . To continue one's journey in the darkness with one's footsteps guided by the illumination of remembered radiance is to know courage of a peculiar kind – the courage to demand that light continue to be light even in the surrounding darkness. To walk in the light while darkness invades, envelopes, and surrounds is to wait on the Lord. This is to know the renewal of strength. This is to walk and faint not."

So, as I continued to write, I continued to grow. As I continued to put down words, I continued to wonder and imagine. As I continued to think thoughts, I continued to explore possibilities. And at the "end of the day", the goal has been reached; the vision has come to fruition; and the dream has been realized. I took a backward glance at history, my history, and found that history making is perhaps the most valuable asset we have as human beings. By stepping back and looking at the big picture of the past, I was able to see God's hand in what I thought was chaos, and His blessing in what looked like doom. What's even more amazing is that the Bible, God's Word, is continually changing the way history plays out.

Scripture has inspired some of history's greatest people to change the future by enacting God's Word in their lives. Martin Luther could not have known how far his commitment to God's Word or his writings would outlive him and how greatly they would affect the church today. Or Corrie ten Boom (one of my most favorite persons), who obeyed God at all costs, probably never understood the extent that her faith would impress upon lives even in the 21st Century. They believed in God's Word completely, and that changed everything.

During the process of writing this book, there were "light", comical moments that sometimes made me smile, and other times made me laugh out loud. I would smile every time I missed my deadline, because I asked myself, "Do you really know what you are doing?" On November 27, 2010, I wrote, "I have committed to try and write <u>something</u> each and every day. My deadline for finishing the book is November 1, 2011." On December 24, 2011, I wrote, "This is the day before Christmas and it is around 8:00 A.M. I am planning to start preparing my Christmas dinner today. We are meeting at Sharon's house for dinner after we attend service at Grace & Glory Gospel Chapel." I smiled after reflecting, for I missed deadline after deadline; "life" got in the way. I wrote again these words:

> "Today is February 10, 2012. I got up at 4:50 A.M, took a shower, fed my cat, Myles, and made a cup of green tea. It was stimulating. I had neglected to do devotions all week, but today I read James 1:12-27. I was especially moved by verses 12 and 17. James 1:12 says:
> "Blessed is the man that endureth temptation; for when he is tried, he shall receive the crown of life, which the Lord hath promised to them that love Him." When I read that verse, I was struck by the sheer fact and truth of scripture. I was in awe of how God blesses us when we seek to do things that are right; things that are disciplined and thought through; things that are reasonable. Sometimes I am so impulsive; sometimes I am so self-centered; sometimes I do things that don't make sense; sometimes I say things that don't make sense; sometimes I say things that are mean-spirited and unkind. But when I think carefully, when I pause a minute, when I think beyond the desire of the moment, I make the right decision, the

right choice. Then I behold the blessings of God. I thank
Him, over and over for His blessings."

My "laugh out loud" moments came when I wrote chapter 12, "My
Onslaught of Nines". I had searched through books, articles, magazines,
sayings, etc. looking for jokes and funny stories. The jokes by Bob Hope
were the funniest, maybe because I remember him being on television
(back in the day) and delivering these hilarious stories and jaw-dropping
one liners. He made everyone "laugh out loud". He seemed "unflappable";
the consumate entertainer who I admired for his great service to men and
women in the military over seas. Milton Berle was another favorite, along
with Dean Martin and his "Dean Martin Roasts". Richard Pryor was the
funniest of all, but so risque it was difficult to watch and listen to.

My family and friends who know me, know that I love poetry and
sayings. Other writers and poets are able to express, sometimes profoundly,
my thoughts and feelings when I can not articulate them or can not find
the right words. Interspersed, throughout my book, you will find poetry
and sayings and, of course, many scripture verses. It gave me the greatest
of pleasure to research sources for my book.

For example: Gloria Randolph, minister and evangelist, but most
importantly, friend, presented this poem to me as we shared together the
loss of our sons. The words are powerful and served as an encouragement
to me on this journey. The title of the poem is: "<u>The</u> <u>Oak</u> <u>Tree</u>"

"A mighty wind
blew night and day.
It stole the oak tree's leaves away.
Then snapped its boughs
and pulled its bark
Until the oak was tired and stark.
But still the oak tree held its ground
While other trees fell all around."…

The author goes on to say that the strong wind was
not able to bring the tree down; it stood its ground and
triumphed in the end.

Chapter one was my church's history. Someone asked me why did I start with the history of the church instead of starting with my family history. My life is entertwined with the church from the time of my youth until this day. I seek spiritual growth, on a daily basis, as the service continues.

As I wrote Chapter two, "The Challenge of the Times", I was filled with nostalgia, some sadness, but with gratitude that I was privileged to have lived through that period of time.

The superlatives that I used in Chapter three, were words, my words to describe my feelings and my thoughts about the people of Grace & Glory. The intent was not to "flatter" them, but to look at the bright side, the positive side, the good in people. When I have seen it in others, I have sought to express it. I don't portend to know the "measure of a man" for we are "fearfully and wonderfully" made (Psalm 139:14). I sought to, in a small way, open up the window of my perception and admiration.

Chapter four, "Events & Happenings" is a "little bit about a lot of things"; a few of the activities at the church that are enjoyed and activities that give Grace & Glory it's unique "flavor".

As I wrote Chapter five, "The Early Years", I was happy to look <u>back</u> on those times in my youth. Of course, the experiences back then helped shape the person I have become today, but I remember being "awkward" and sometimes feeling "out of place." I tended to second guess myself in social situations; I tended to over think my interactions with others; and I tended to feel insecure about how I was perceived by others. However, this awkwardness never got in the way of my pursuing my goals. No matter what my issues in life were, no matter what my limitations were, God brought me through them, sometimes with a vengeance.

Writing Chapter six was challenging and, at times, very sad as I remembered my dad and his siblings. It is a long chapter which includes, not only my aunts and uncles, but my cousins, as well. I have precious memories of my cousins, when we were kids and into our adult years and beyond. As kids, my cousins and I lived our lives, daily, without thinking of segregation, or racism, or discrimination. We knew it was there, but we didn't talk about it. Our lives revolved around doing our chores, going to school, and spending a lot of time in church. We were totally immersed in family, e.g. family events, holidays, birthdays, weddings, and yes, funerals as well. I don't remember being discriminated against, personally, at school. Nothing really stands out that I can point to as blatant racism. I remember being a relatively happy child, living the life of the "times" I was blessed to be in. In chapter six, I tried to paint a picture of my dad and his struggles as a black man in America, but I wanted to show his other side, his humor and his fun-loving side. I think of him every day, thanking the Lord that I had a father who cared for me with a special love – a love that only dads can give their daughters. Daddy and so many of his siblings are gone now which is why I was sad, but they leave such a beautiful legacy for me and my cousins to follow. It is a privilege and an honor to walk in their shadow.

The "Fine as wine in the Summertime" chapter is about my mother and her family. I enjoyed writing about my mother; she was some kind of a woman! My children quote her witticisms all the time, which brings me great joy. She left an impression on her grandkids, and especially with me. To God be the glory for my mother.

Chapter eight, "Marriage, Children, Family" was the most difficult to write because of my children. I relived their deaths over and over again. Could I, . . . as their mother, could I have done more to help them survive longer? I thought about that phrase "survival of the fittest" and although it might be a true statement in some cases, as it relates to my children it was more of "choices," choices in what you eat or don't eat; choices of life style – healthy living like exercising, visiting the doctor regularly and the dentist regularly; choices of positive thinking and being satisfied in the "state you are in"; and then choices of spiritual living, being in fellowship with God, having accepted Him into your heart and making Him the center of your life. I think that has affected our family more than anything else. And as I completed the chapter, I prayed especially for my family that they will:

- eat healthy and drink plenty of water
- stay active, stay busy, stay productive
- check on their health regularly
- set high goals for their family
- plan something that they can look forward to doing every day
- develop a financial plan to save some of their money, spend some of their money
- And lastly, but most importantly, keep the Lord at the center of their life, always.

Chapter nine includes some of the degrees and awards that hang on my "ego wall" at home. It was written especially for my great grand children who think I "don't know anything". Because of my lack of knowledge in technology and social media and sometimes I can't answer a math problem (I always looked it up) or do a math equation (I was excellent in algebra in undergrad school and loved working those long equations to the end), they got the impression that I "don't know anything". My point for including this information about my academics was to show them that with an average intelligence coupled with enthusiasm and a lot of hard work, one could accomplish "impossible dreams."

I enjoyed sharing information about my "Groups." I feel blessed and especially honored to be among such prestigious and dignified women whether they are my sorority sisters in "IOTA"; or my board members in "CCWC"; or partners in the "Vineyard Partnership" investment club. That was chapter 10.

Chapter eleven brought laughter and amusement and pride as I shared some of "My Favorite Things." My favorite books are "all over the place", meaning, I read all kinds of books. I love them all. As a child, I lived for movies. It was an escape for me.

The music of my younger years were the most loved. I loved singing along and "dreaming" at the same time. It was a wonderful time in my life, but I didn't know it at the time. To remember all those wonderful songs and the artists who sang them was nostalgic and beautiful.

Another favorite of mine and millions of other people is President Barack Obama. He has been and continues to be one of the strongest presidents on record. He continues to stand tall as he is bombarded from all sides, especially the Republican Party, and many times from his own party. With God's help, he has been able to "stand" and get many things accomplished for the good of the country, for the good of all American citizens. Some of those things are listed in Chapter eleven. He is one of my favorites, along with Franklin Delano Roosevelt, Jimmy Carter, John F. Kennedy, and Bill Clinton. That makes President Barack Obama a member of a very elite club, in my opinion. To God be the glory for He "sets up one, and brings another down."

When I started writing chapter thirteen, I had no idea of the scope of things, events, and people; the range is from the "great" to the "greater" and the "greatest" in their respective fields of endeavor. It's one of the longest chapters, and another of my "a little bit about a lot of things." I researched and finally chose a few of the icons of our lifetime. I was in awe of their great contributions to our country; and yet, they are like our own families, your own families — grandparents, parents, aunts, uncles, sisters and brothers, husbands and wives, and other loved ones. They were ordinary people who did extra ordinary and wonderful things.

The cultural icons in the chapter are well known and celebrated, but the fascinating thing about it is, during my research, I discovered things that I did not know. I did not know the extent of Howard Thurmond's writings. He is awesome. I learned more about the city of Chicago and the fighting black citizens who fought along the Lake Michigan beaches during World War I, in 1919. I relived the days following Mayor Harold Washington's death. I had forgotten that Samuel B. Fuller, a self-made millionaire, influenced the great John H. Johnson, founder of Johnson Publishing and also George Ellis Johnson, founder of Johnson Products.

Also, in Chapter Thirteen, I wrote about cultural icons who were personal friends or acquaintances. Some of them are: Dr. Melvin E. Banks, Sam Cooke, Truman K. Gibson, and Dr. Marjorie Stewart Joyner.

Many more "cultural icons" could have been mentioned in that chapter. I didn't mention Dudley Randall, who wrote the poem "Ballad of Birmingham" on the occasion of the bombing of a church in Birmingham, Alabama in 1963 when four beautiful young girls were killed.

I did not include a quote from the 1961 commencement address of Jonathan Daniels who was the valedictorian of Virginia Military Institute. He was a theology student at the Episcopal Divinity School when, in the summer of 1965, he stepped in front of a sheriff who aimed a gun at two black girls to prevent them from entering a convenience store. The bullet Daniels took was fatal. Here is an excerpt of that 1961 commencement address, his words, which were poetic and poignant and predictable:

> "I wish you the joy of a purposeful life. I wish you new
> worlds and the vision to see them. I wish you the decency
> and the nobility of which you are capable."

I did not write about <u>Bob</u> <u>Dylan</u> in Chapter thirteen. <u>Bob</u> <u>Dylan</u> wrote a poem about James Meredith when he desegregated the University of Mississippi (Ole Miss') in Oxford, Mississippi. The title of the poem is "Oxford Town".

I've mentioned Dr. Martin Luther King, Jr. on several pages throughout this book, but what Howard Thurman wrote about him is awe-inspiring, and stunning. In "The Search for Common Ground," he wrote these words:

> "As a result of a series of fortuitous circumstances there appeared on the horizon of the common life a young man who for a swift, staggering, and startling moment met the demands of the hero. He was young. He was well-educated with the full credentials of academic excellence in accordance with ideals found in white society. He was a son of the South. He was steeped in and nurtured by familiar religious tradition. He had charisma, that intangible quality of personality that gathers up in the magic the power to lift people out of themselves without diminishing them. In him the "outsider" and the "insider" came together in a triumphant synthesis. Here at last was a man who affirmed the oneness of black and white under a transcendent unity, for whom community meant the profoundest sharing in the common life. And his name was Martin Luther King, Jr."

Dr. Martin Luther King, Jr. was assassinated on April 4, 1968. He was memorialized at Morehouse Campus. Howard Thurman died on April 10, 1981 in San Francisco at the age of eighty. Benjamin Mays died just short of his eighty-ninth birthday on March 28, 1984. He is interred in a marble memorial on the Morehouse Campus. On the campus, the spacing of the memorials to Howard Thurman, Benjamin Mays, and Martin Luther King, Jr. forms a triangle.

So many things, over the years, affected us culturally as a people, as a nation, and worldwide. Like I can remember when African Americans could not yet sit at the lunch counter at the Woolworth's store. None the less, we bought food there and some of the prices in the 1950's were:

Bacon & Tomato Sandwich – 50¢
Baked Ham & Cheese Sandwich – 60¢
Chicken Salad Sandwich – 65¢
Egg Salad Sandwich – 30¢
American Cheese Sandwich – 30¢
Deluxe Sundae – 25¢
Banana Split – 39¢
Extra Rich Ice Cream Soda – 25¢
Milk Shake – 25¢
Apple Pie – per cut – 15¢
King Size – Coca Cola – 10¢

There was "Pop Culture" Projects that have helped define the African American experience over the last several decades: This is another one of my "a little bit about a lot of things." In the 1970's, "The Wiz" movie brought pride and joy and entertainment. The brilliance of the cast – including Michael Jackson, Nipsey Russell, Diana Ross, and Ted Ross – was enough to put this 1978 musical over the top. But it was Quincy Jones' "funked-out" soundtrack music that proved that soul music was also pop music. The "Roots" miniseries was based on a novel by Alex Haley that came out in 1977 and showed the horrors of slavery for many American viewers and it inspired pride in the African-American community showing the perseverance of our ancestors.

The album "Thriller" came out in 1982, and with one glittering white glove in the air, the incredible, brilliant Michael Jackson broke all the music records. It was his sixth solo album and is still the best selling album of all time – revolutionizing the sound of pop music in the process.

On TV, the "Cosby Show" and its spinoff, "A Different World", becomes a hilarious, iconic sitcom in 1987. It debunked stereotypes of Black Americans, and spurred interest in the Historically Black Colleges & Universities (HBCU's), and introduced jazz to a younger audience.

Hip Hop was mainly considered a Black American phenomenon until MTV debuted a landmark series in 1988 entitled "Yo! MTV Raps." It brought rap not only to suburbia, but also spreading the culture worldwide.

John Singleton's movie, "Boyz N the Hood" gave an explosive take on the Los Angeles gang scene in 1991. It started an important conversation about the number of Black youth losing their lives to violence in the streets.

In 1995, the movie "Waiting to Exhale" was on the "heels of the national crack epidemic. The film starred Angela Bassett, Loretta Divine, Lela Rochon, and Whitney Houston. It proved that Black women had another story to tell – and it could be profitable. It was mentioned in Chapter 13, but it was one of my favorite movies to watch.

After the new millennium, and by 2003, "The Oprah Winfrey Show" on TV became a staple in many American households. The talk show had debuted in the 1980's, and was Oprah's formidable media empire for decades. By 2003, she had become the nation's first Black billionaire.

And in 2012, executive producer Shonda Rhimes created the first major network drama featuring an African-American female lead in 38 years. Starring Kerry Washington, the super successful series became the catalyst for renewed talks about diversity in Hollywood.

And so, I finished with my "Cultural Pride and Celebration" chapter on a "high note", being thankful for a "partial victory," an "almost there" to an "R We There Yet"? I had written and completed 13 chapters of a journey that started decades ago. I looked up and thanked the Lord for bringing me thus far along the way. I knew I had to keep going to the very end, but it was euphoric to see the light, bright and clear, "at the end of the tunnel".

And so, this is the last chapter of the sharing of my life story. Within these chapters are found the very essence of what my life has been. Through it all, as you can see, God's grace is immeasurable; His mercy is inexhaustible; His peace is inexpressible; and His love is inexplicable.

In writing this book, I wanted it to be more than just a history; I wanted it to be an interesting "read"; I wanted it to be, in places, an "aha" moment as someone shares a same experience; and I wanted it to be a work of "art". In keeping with that process, I have hand-written the complete manuscript; using yellow legal pads and Pilot P-700 (fine) pens. I was anxious for my family and friends to examine each page of my book to discover surprises and little known facts.

I have sought to share the memories of my life; memories of joy; memories of hurts and pain; and memories of great losses and unspeakable grief. There have been secrets, deep in my heart and soul that have been shared with the Lord only. These were words that were too painful to dwell on, too painful to put "pen to paper" so I have hidden them away. I feel like Joni Mitchell who said, "There are things to confess that enrich the world, and things that need not be said." Amen.

We love to share with others, through media, or social network, and with our family and friends. We freely give our thoughts and our ideas and sometimes this is a good thing; but Christ tells us to keep some things – holy things – separate and unshared. I cherish those things that are just between me and God.

The things that happened to me, from childhood up to these 80 plus years, have made me who I am. I have admired so many people over the years; my mentors who I listened to and learned from have been my mother and my aunts and others, yet I would not change places with any of them. I have learned from the mistakes and I have been rewarded for the things I have gotten "right." There have been wonderful and blissful moments in my life that I have sought to share with anyone who would listen or with anyone who was interested. God has been good to me, whereas I am glad. I have been blessed beyond measure. O' for a thousand tongues to sing His praises.

I have used poetry and sayings throughout my manuscript; poetry, in some instances, affirmed my feelings, my thoughts; poets are able to articulate and "maneuver" words that elicit a range of emotions, from happiness to joy; from gladness to sorrow; and from frustration to despair.

I have used much scripture to show my love for God, His Word, and His Son, Jesus Christ. I am in awe of the scriptures and continue to learn new things, new truths from the Word of God each day. God encouraged me, God inspired me, God exhorted me, and God has been merciful to me over these many years.

This book is dedicated to the Believers at Grace & Glory Gospel Chapel for their love of God and His Son, Jesus Christ, and for their love and support of each other. I commend them for "standing by the stuff" though very few in number. They have remained "steadfast and unmovable" in their Christian walk. They have exhibited great faith over the years; faith that is like a "bridge over troubled waters". I honor them for their love of children. Over these years, through the morning service; and Sunday School classes; and special events; the Saints have sought to tell our young people to continue to demonstrate integrity. They were encouraged to have a strong sense of character; a uniqueness of spirit; a pride of blackness; a pride of self; and a moral of character. The youth were exhorted to "stand tall" as they go out into the world in pursuit of their dreams. And as a church family, we encouraged them to be bold and courageous, for with the Lord's help, they could overcome the world.

I honor Grace & Glory because of the wonderful, exciting, and interesting people who have passed through and in and out of its' doors. Some have gone on to be with the Lord, which is far better. Others have left and gone to other assemblies, other churches. And as they go, they take a part of Grace & Glory with them to share with the world. They spread the "good news" to all parts of the country and ultimately to the whole world. I think of Ceolia Henry and James Fair who left and founded their own churches. I think of Harvey Rollerson who went on to become Elder and Pastor at Westlawn Gospel Chapel. Inez Douglas Washington Clayton, Agnes Williams, and Agnes Wilson left and went to other churches where they used their talents and God-given gifts to serve others. Emily Donahue left to go to another church where she developed bible studies and classes to teach others. Ramona Susberry and Henrietta Broussard left and spread the news of the gospel taught at Grace & Glory. They both did home visits and witnessed to the poor and disenfranchised. Ramona's sons went on to become ministers in their own church. These are just a few reminders of the far reaching ministry of Grace & Glory Gospel Chapel.

I honor Grace & Glory because it has been an important spiritual and moral support for not only me, but for people from the 1950's to the present. In general, black churches, traditionally, have provided comfort to our people since slavery. So, I hold high the record of Grace & Glory Gospel Chapel; and I devote this book to the continued work and inspiration offered by this ministry, by its' elders and by its congregation.

544

This is the end of the "whole matter" which is the history of my life, my existence. It has been a "fabulous ride". And as the Lord continues to teach me, to guide me, and to bless me, I say like Nick Nolte at the end of the movie, "Prince of Tides", it is "more than enough". To God be the glory.

Enough said. Amen.

BIBLIOGRAPHY

BOOKS

- Alice Dise, "A Church With A Purpose, Vernon Park Church of God, 55 Years Of History"
- "Change We Can Believe In, Barack Obama's Plan To Renew America's Promise", 2008 by Barack Obama, Three Rivers Press
- Benjamin E. Mays, "Born to Rebel", Charles Scribner & Sons, New York, 1971
- "Black Women Writers at Work", Claudia Tate, Editor
- Caroline Kennedy, "A Family of Poems," Hyperion, NY
- Cynthia Reid Wills, "Content of Character"
- David H. Sorenson, "Touch Not The Unclean Thing, The Text Issue and Separation"
- Delaney Sisters, "Having Our Say"
- Edward P. Jones, "The Known World," Harper-Collins, NY., 2003
- Gwen Ifill, "The Break Through," Politics & Race in the Age of Obama, Doubleday, 2009
- H. G. MaCray, "Assembly Distinctives," Everyday Publ., 1981
- Inez Clayton, "The Christian Brethren Movement," 1985
- H.A. Ironside, "A Historical Sketch of the Brethren Movement"
- Jill Abramson, "The New York Times, Obama, The Historical Journey," 2009
- James McBride, "The Color of Water", Riverhead Books, NY., 1996
- Kenneth C. Davis, "Don't Know Much About Geography," William Morrow Co., 1992

- Lawrence Perkins, "Transcending Greatness," Heart Thoughts Publ., 2011
- Lean'tin Bracks, "African-American Almanac, 400 Years of Triumph, Courage, and Excellence," Visible Ink Press, 2012
- Lewis V. Baldwin, "Thou, Dear God", Prayers That Open Hearts and Spirits," Beacon Press, 2012
- Lerone Bennett, Jr., "Before The Mayflower"-A History of Black America"
- Leonides A. Johnson, "The African American Church"
- Mariano Gonzalez, "Ministry and The Christian Woman"
- Marlo Thomas, "The Right Words at the Right Time," Volume 2
- Melanie Fonder & Mary Shaffrey, "American Government," The Complete Idiots Guide," 2002
- Michael Eric Dyson, "I May Not Get There With You, The True Martin Luther King, Jr." The Free Press, 2000
- Parrish Smith, "The Scroll"
- Patrice Turner, "Muslim to Minister"
- Peter Jennings, & Todd Brewster, "The Century", Doubleday, 1998
- R.P. Amos, "The Church-A Discipleship Manual for the Body of Christ"
- Sharon Harley, "The Times Tables of African American History," 1995
- T.D. Jakes, "Let It Go," Forgive So You Can Be Forgiven," Atris Books, 2012
- Truman K. Gibson, Jr., "Knocking Down Barriers- My Fight For Black America, A Memoir"
- Velma J. Benson-Wilson, "What's In The Water? – Fannie, A Legacy of Love," Xlibris Pub., 2011
- "The Encyclopedia of American Religion" – A Comprehensive Study of the Major Religious Groups in the United States and Canada. Volume III, J. Gordon Melton, Editor, 1991., Copyright, 1989 by Gale Research, New York, NY
- "The Roosevelts-The American Family That Changed the World," Time Books
- The Words of African American Heroes," Edited by Clara Villerosa, Newmarket Press, New York, 2011

MAGAZINE ARTICLES

- American Legacy-The Magazine of African American History & Culture, page 61
- Ebony, December, 2007, A Johnson Publication
- Ebony, June, 1995
- Ebony, 50 Years of JPC, Special Edition, November, 1992
- "Famous Black Quotations", Edited by Janet Cheatham Bell, 1986, 1991, 1995, Warner Bros., Inc.
- JET, November 7, 2011
- JET, December 26, 2011/January 2, 2012
- People Tribute, May/June 1998-
- Precious Seed Magazine
- Vanity Fair-Africa, July, 2007

NEWSPAPER ARTICLES

- April, 1975, Springfield, Illinois, "Miss IOTA", Crowned, Submitted by Theresa Faith Cummings
- Sun-Times, Chicago, November 15, 1981(Classroom at Michele E. Clark School)
- TIME Magazine- November 1, 1982, picture and article explaining the Clark/Commonwealth Edison Collaboration, Adopt-A-School Science Project
- Article, The BULLETIN, Chicago, June, 2004- Alpha Chapter's 75th Anniversary
- Article, The CRUSADER, June, 2004- Alpha Chapter's 75th Anniversary
- Publication, Spring, 1999, Saint Xavier, Opening of the Barbara Vick ECFC., Article, picture.

Thanks & Acknowledgements

To my husband, Lenzo, for his support and his patience, and his understanding of my "pursuit of this dream";

To my two children, Sharon and Kevin, for their unconditional love;

To my daughter in law, Twanda, for her "tips and taps";

To my sister in law, Pearl, who has been the sister I never had for over 60 years;

To my 13 grand children and their spouses;

To my 16 great grandchildren and one great, great grand child;

To my last precious aunts, Deborah Lyons and Earselean West and my last loving uncle, Theodore Roosevelt "Sonny" Jones for their ever present optimism;

To my aunt in law, Shirley Jones, for encouraging me in my pursuit, and promising to write her own history;

To my 5 maternal cousins, Dorce, Irene, Mildred, Maxine, and Bobbie, for their encouraging words;

To my 36 paternal cousins – who were so patient over the years as I kept telling them, "I'm writing a book . . .";

To my nephews, especially De Juan and David, for their intelligent conversations and unrelenting faith in me;

To my dear friend, Clara Hampton, for her support;

To the Henry Family for their warmth and anticipation;

To Dorothy and Gwen, my cousins, who were there from the beginning;

To Dr. Blondean Y. Davis, Earnestine Foster, and Yvonne Williams for their help and support at a very difficult period in my life;

To my dear friend, Jackie, for her beautiful words of constant (time after time) encouragement; and to Annette, for her belief in me; and to Lillie, my friend, for being there from the beginning;

To my granddaughters, Shundra, Lexie, and Tierra for helping me "keep my sanity";

To my Vineyard Partnership Group for sharing my enthusiasm;

To Fonzie Richmond, CPS technology person in the 1990's, for being inspired to write his church's history;

To Tracey Murray and Leah Lacey of SD 162 for giving me beautiful, unusual journals to encourage my writing project;

To Linda Williams and Carolyn Cartman for believing in me;

To Gloria Randolph for her joy in the Lord and her eternal optimism;

To Alice Dise who encouraged and inspired me to keep on writing;

To my CCWC Sisters, Joyce, Beverly, Mary, Belle, Cora, Helen, Deborah, Charlotte, and to the beautiful Eilleen and Jennifer, and Millicent, and Brenda, and my daughter, Sharon for lifting me up to the throne of grace as I continued to write;

To my Sorority Sisters – Dorothy, Carolyn, Loretta, Deborah, Eugenia, Allie, Doris Murry and Doris Smith, Corrine, Sharon, Jessica, Tammy, Safiyyah, Sarah, Dr. Keenan, Joyce, Amy, and Ruth for their dignity and grace;

To the believers and friends in the other Brethren churches for suggestions, tips, scripture verses, humor, and prayers;

To Sis. Peak for her words of wisdom and for her happiness at the prospect of reading my book;

To Joyce Bolt Digby and her family for their story;

To Harvey Rollerson, Tanya Hicks, Emily Donahue, and Mildred Ferguson for giving me pieces of Grace & Glory's history;

Although they are with the Lord now, I am indebted to Inez Clayton, Nola Hicks, and Allison McClean (Bro. Gall's daughter) for giving me information – information that was sometimes pleasant, and sometimes not so pleasant – about the church;

To my two cousins, Thurman Moore and Floyd Boykin for digging deeply into our family history, looking for an always expanding legacy;

To my cousin, Alfred Moore, for sending me my daddy's favorite music, which was mostly the "blues", and for sending me "goo gobs" of pictures;

To my cousin, Herbert Boykin and his beautiful wife, Helen, for making me feel "10 feet tall";

To my cousin, Delores, for pictures and for sharing Aunt Thelma's beautiful jewelry;

To Mildred, Pamela, and Karen for being an example for mothers and daughters everywhere;

And to my church family for their love; for their prayers; for their support; and for their patience.

Thank you.

Editors – Jacquelyn Crook, Willie Horton, Sharon Tang
Picture Coordinator/Typist – Sharon Marie Kilpatrick Tang
Photo Credits: Arlene Mays Johnson
                Suzette Watkins
                Tyrone & Juanita Stem
                Valoree Harrington
                Mildred Ferguson
                The Bolt Family
                Willie Horton

Photo Shoot: Arlene Mays Johnson

Back Cover Photo: Arlene Mays Johnson

Book Cover Design: Charles "Chuckie" Harrington